The Aliens

A History of Ethnic Minorities in America

edited by

Leonard Dinnerstein

University of Arizona, Tucson

Frederic Cople Jaher

University of Illinois, Champaign

APPLETON-CENTURY-CROFTS

Educational Division

New York   MEREDITH CORPORATION

For
Andrew and Julie
and
Diane and David

Preface

Today the American people regards the plight of its deprived minorities with conflicting attitudes. These mixed feelings arise from traditional attachments to equality and justice which conflict with a long history of racial repression and hostility. Unprecedented amounts of public and private assistance are now offered to ease the dispossessed into the middle-class world. Yet a growing number of Americans feel that too much is being done too soon for the minorities. The persistence of the minority problem prevents national unity from emerging out of ethnic diversity. By exploring the history of minority groups from colonial beginnings to the present day we seek to comprehend and communicate a vital aspect of the national existence—the experience of America's ethnic groups.

In varying degrees, depending upon approximation to the Anglo-Saxon ideal, ethnic minorities have been considered foreign even when native born. Accordingly we categorize as ethnic minorities all groups of non-English origin. Included in our working definition are peoples of different national backgrounds such as the Scotch, the Irish, and the Germans; of different racial origins such as the Negroes, the Indians, and the Orientals; and religious minorities such as the Jews.

We emphasize the harsher aspects of minority group experiences in the United States, for we feel that the conflicts and frustrations of minority life in America have often been minimized or overlooked. Students of American history are too frequently ignorant of the humiliating conditions that these people have endured. Although most minorities achieved, with varying degrees of difficulty, middle-class homogenized American goals, we feel that it is more instructive and accurate to emphasize the struggle and cost of this process and to indicate where the outcome has been exclusion and failure rather than acceptance and accomplishment. Although we have included articles that represent various phases of minority group life our emphasis on struggle and ordeal reveals our concern about past and present group conflicts in American society.

A number of people have helped us prepare this book. Mrs. Shirley Lerman, Mrs. Helen Cermak, Miss Connie Nosbisch, and Mrs. Betty Hampel have typed the manuscript skillfully. Mrs. Jocelyn Ghent has been an uncomplaining and painstaking researcher and proofreader. Michael Ebner made some bibliographical suggestions. Professors Oscar Handlin, Moses Rischin, and Clyde Griffen evaluated our original outline and suggested ways of improving it. We would particularly like to thank Professor J. Joseph Huthmacher and Miss

Sydney Diamond for their superb critical suggestions, and our editor, Walter J. Green, for his insightful commentary. Myra Dinnerstein and Susan Jaher receive special gratitude for combining wifely devotion with honest evaluation.

University of Arizona   L. D.
Tucson

University of Illinois   F. C. J.
Champaign-Urbana

Contents

The Industrial Transformation   173

Ethnic Minorities in Contemporary America   285

Coda

The Aliens

Introduction

America was created and shaped by successive waves of migrants. First a recently discovered outpost of the great age of European exploration and colonization, inhabited primarily by tribes of Indians, the new land quickly attracted people from Europe. They later brought shiploads of chained Africans. When the series of great migrations ended in the 1920s over thirty-five million foreigners had come to the United States. Democracy and capitalism, the core of the American social system, were implanted, sustained, and expanded largely through the migrants' strong backs, quick minds, and grim determination.

Yet newcomers have rarely received a warm reception. The inscription on the Statue of Liberty in the harbor of New York City begins:

> Give me your tired, your poor,
> Your huddled masses yearning to breathe free

but many Americans throughout history have rejected people with alien cultures. At one time French Huguenots, Scotch-Irish, and Germans received the scorn and maltreatment that are visited upon Negroes, Indians, and Spanish-speaking Americans today.

Because of a predominantly English heritage in the colonial period, the United States, a country of many peoples, often has evaluated its varied citizenry by a single standard: white, Anglo-Saxon, middle-class Protestantism. Although popular rhetoric glorified the country as a melting pot of different peoples, in actuality this has meant melting diversity into conformity with Anglo-Saxon characteristics. Those unable or unwilling to accomplish the transformation have suffered varying degrees of abuse and ostracism because middle-class America demands conformity before it gives acceptance.

Despite confidence in their Anglo-Saxon superiority, the British adopted liberal immigration policies for their New World colonies because mercantilism, the prevailing economic system which shaped English policy in the seventeenth and eighteenth centuries, identified national power with imperial domain. Colonies were thought necessary to relieve the mother country of overpopulation and to create a favorable balance of trade by providing a source of cheap raw materials and a market for domestic exports. Britain encouraged European emigration to North America. English policy, aimed at increasing permanent agricultural settlement, differed from the strategy of France and Spain, which used colonies as trading posts rather than large permanent markets. Uninterested

3

in agricultural settlement, France and Spain restricted entry to those Catholics who would accept centralized direction from the throne.

Revolution and restoration of the monarchy in England left the colonies to their own devices until the 1660s. Although intervention thereafter increased, the policy of salutory neglect persisted until 1763. Consequently, immigration policy emanated from provincial needs rather than from specifically English interests or the global considerations of empire. Settlers were needed to populate the hinterland, subdue the frontier, resist Indians or French and Spanish competitors, and further the growth of trade and agriculture. Through a large part of the seventeenth century it seemed that the demand for newcomers could be satisfied by English immigrants alone. Widespread unemployment, religious persecution, and political unrest brought a considerable number of Englishmen to these shores. After 1660 internal tranquility and improved living conditions curbed emigration from England, but religious, political, and economic grievances continued to draw other nationalities, chiefly Scotch-Irish, Germans, French Huguenots, Scandinavians, and Dutch. They found few obstacles to settlement in English provinces because the need for manpower outpaced the labor supply. The labor scarcity resulted in enforced importation of blacks and encouraged the development of slave labor.

Despite the need for new settlers English colonials had mixed feelings about foreign arrivals. Anglo-Saxon mobs attacked Huguenots in Frenchtown, Rhode Island, and destroyed a Scotch-Irish frontier settlement in Worcester, Massachusetts. Virginia in 1699 instituted a fifteen shilling tax on servants coming from anywhere except England and Wales; Pennsylvania in 1729 imposed a forty shilling tax on foreigners (Irishmen paid only twenty shillings), but dropped it the next year after protests from Germans in the colony; and Rhode Island in 1729 required ship captains to post bonds for all persons who had not embarked from the British Isles.

Germans and Scotch-Irish, with Indians and blacks the largest ethnic minorities in colonial times, suffered many of the abuses historically associated with American minority groups. Southern planters contemptuously stereotyped the German farmer as a "boorish peasant, close-fisted, ignorant, rude in his manners, outlandish in his dress." Germans attempted to maintain their own language and customs in Pennsylvania and the South but social pressures forced second- and third-generation settlers to anglicize. In one tale a self-conscious German addressed a compatriot who had spoken German, "O, gay vay mit your Deutsch; you know I besser English." Striving for acceptance, many Germans claimed English, French, or Scotch heritage to elevate their social status. The Scotch-Irish endured similar criticism from colonials of English extraction. They were considered "clannish, contentious, and hard to get along with." Ethnic conflict was not restricted to difficulties between those of English stock and other races and nationalities. Quarrels over land and juxtaposition of groups with different cultures led to disputes between recently arrived minorities, as in the case of the Germans and Scotch-Irish on Pennsylvania's frontier in the eighteenth century.

Non-English immigrants suffered mild and temporary difficulties compared to those of Indians and blacks. Within three generations Germans and Scotch-Irish dropped their "foreign" characteristics, assimilated to the dominant culture, and disappeared (except for a few German settlements in Pennsylvania) as distinct ethnic groups. Red men and black men were not as readily incorporated into the larger community. By the 1670s the English provinces, now expanding beyond the eastern seaboard, confronted Indians resentful of repeated encroachments upon their land. A number of wars ensued. King Philip's War (1675–76) between five Indian tribes and the New England Federation was the bloodiest of these early conflicts. By the end of the struggle one out of every sixteen settlers of military age in New England had been killed, twelve towns totally destroyed, and half the towns suffered damage. More historically noteworthy than the casualties, the conflict ended attempts to Christianize the Indians.

The pattern of black slavery became fixed until emancipation in 1865. The process of bondage for blacks was worked out early in American history: seizure in native Africa; brutal passage to the western hemisphere; enslavement in America perpetuated by total control over individual and family life. By the 1640s and '50s scattered Virginia records show marked differences in treatment between black and white servants: blacks received severer penalties for running away, miscegenation became a criminal act, black bondsmen could not bear firearms and were listed as tithables. Court cases of these years indicated that life servitude already existed for Afro-Americans. During the 1660s Virginia formulated the first slave code. The process of enslavement evolved similarly in Maryland. South Carolina, settled later, skipped the preliminaries by providing for slavery in its fundamental constitution of 1669.

In the North, where slavery was not rooted in the economic system, most bondsmen acted as household servants or coworkers. Under these conditions black servitude was on a smaller, less formal scale. But slave revolts in New York City in 1712 and 1741 indicate that blacks also found the system humiliating and oppressive in the North. New England, except for Rhode Island, had fewer slaves than any other region. In 1700, blacks numbered 1,000 out of a population of approximately 90,000 in Massachusetts, Connecticut, Rhode Island, and New Hampshire. Economically independent of slave labor and inhabited by relatively few bondsmen, this region enacted the mildest servitude regulations. But even these restrictions were confining and humiliating: slaves could not strike white men or appear on the streets after 9 P.M.; they could not buy liquor; and they could be bought or sold at the owner's wish. Unlike southern slaves, however, northern slaves frequently owned property, testified against whites, and learned to read and write.

America's growth in wealth, territory, and power resulted in disaster for Indians and blacks. After the colonies separated from Great Britain, land-hungry Americans encroached upon Indian territory once protected by the British to foster imperial harmony and enhance the fur trade. When Indians resisted the white men's expansion or sought to reoccupy their old hunting grounds, they were beaten back. From 1790–96 five-sixths of the federal government expenditure went into the Indian war in the Northwest territory as northern tribes vainly attempted to halt white pioneers at the Ohio River. Under the leadership of the Shawnee chief Tecumseh the Indians organized their most determined resistance against the advance of white settlers into the Old Northwest. But General William Henry Harrison's army destroyed the tribal confederacy at the battle of Tippecanoe, Indiana, in 1811. As white Americans relentlessly moved westward conflicts with Indians continually recurred. Some Indians unsuccessfully fought while others yielded to the inevitable and moved westward peacefully; eventually all of those tribes not completely destroyed moved northward to Canada or else accepted a restricted life on reservations.

Hopes for blacks improved after America emerged victorious from the Revolutionary War with Great Britain. The widespread belief in the Enlightenment philosophy of the rights of man and natural equality inspired emancipation legislation in the 1780s in Massachusetts, Rhode Island, New York, and New Jersey. In the Upper South, a number of Virginians and North Carolinians also spoke out boldly for manumission but the state legislatures rejected the necessary statutes. A few years later the growth of the textile industry in the United States and Great Britain created a large demand for raw cotton and advocates of emancipation diminished in number. Eli Whitney's cotton gin by facilitating the gathering of short staple upland cotton revitalized the plantation system. Northern merchants and manufacturers who profited from cotton raw materials and exports said little about what southerners called the "peculiar institution."

Between 1800 and the Civil War, blacks, whether in the North or South, slave or free, steadily lost civil and human rights. Through conquest and legislative compromise, slavery expanded into new areas. In many of the new slave states, for example, Louisiana and Mississippi, climate and the rawness of frontier capitalism made bondage more onerous. In the Upper South being sold "down the river" to the recently settled cotton lands was a form of control used to threaten or eliminate troublesome bondsmen. But even in the mellower regions, slavery's profitability and expansion worsened the conditions of bondage. States passed laws making it virtually impossible to free slaves, prohibited or curtailed bondsmen's movements, and forced free blacks to leave or accept a constrained existence.

In the "free North" blacks' status also deteriorated. By 1860 only Massachusetts, New Hampshire, Vermont, and Maine allowed them to vote on an equal footing with whites. The Old Northwest, Ohio, Indiana, and Illinois, influenced by large numbers of southern settlers, constitutionally restricted black immigration. In the Far West California prohibited them from testifying against white men and Oregon forbade them from holding real estate, making contracts, or initiating lawsuits. In northern cities, for example Boston and New York, custom and law segregated neighborhoods, schools, and transportation. Competition between the older black enclaves and newly arrived ethnic groups for low-paying manual labor jobs and marginal housing resulted in racial conflict in northern cities. During the 1830s and '40s race riots broke out in Philadelphia, New York, Pittsburgh, Cincinnati, and other areas where black men were excluded from the more remunerative skilled trades.

Slaves were the chief source of manual labor for southern planter-capitalists. In the North and the Far West by the 1830s large numbers of migrants from Europe and Asia provided mercantile and industrial capitalists with fresh sources of labor. Irish Catholics on the East Coast and Chinese on the West worked in construction and railroad gangs. In New England textile towns Irish immigrants replaced native-born farm girls in cotton cloth factories. When

not directly employed in the industrial system the Irish sought
as coachmen or maids. Nativist bigotry and lack of urban ind\
restricted the Irish and the Chinese to those odd jobs whi\
backs rather than sophisticated skills.

Impoverished Irish and Chinese immigrants remained \
barkation like Boston, New York, and San Francisco, but \
central and north central European newcomers moved out in\
Communities of Norwegian pioneers tilled the soil in Iowa, Wisconsin, ...
sota, and the Dakotas. German farmers bought land in Ohio, Michigan, and
Illinois. Many Germans settled in Chicago, Cincinnati, and St. Louis. These
cities, points of exchange between east and west, grew with the settlement of
their back country and with developing interregional commerce. The Germans,
too, prospered as skilled tailors, carpenters, mechanics, brewers, and bankers or
small shopkeepers.

Americans stereotyped the foreign born. Swedes and Finns, for example,
were deemed stolid, honorable sons of the soil. Germans had a mixed reputation. Although respected for enterprise, industry, and commercial success, they
were criticized as boorish beer swillers who clung to their native language and
violated the American sabbath by drinking, gaming, and other forms of un-
Christian carousal. Social views, as well as personal habits, drew hostility from
native Americans. The revolution-tainted "1848ers" were attacked for abolitionism and atheism. Opposition toward Germans reached such a peak in the
state of New York in the 1850s that the legislature refused to charter a Turnverein Association for fear that the social club was an anarchist nest.

On the West Coast, California, which repressed Chinese, Indians, blacks,
Hawaiians, South Americans, Mexicans, and Frenchmen, stands out as the
archetypal nativist state. Frontier violence, land hunger, squabbles over mineral rights, and the presence of a large number of southerners (nearly a third of
the population in the middle of the nineteenth century) contributed to California's hostility toward minority groups. Chinese, along with Indians and
blacks, were barred from voting by the 1848 state constitution, denied legal
protection when driven from gold stakes, forbidden to testify in state courts,
and plundered with impunity. The 150,000 "Digger" Indians, a peaceful, pastoral people, if picked up as vagrants (white law enforcers defined vagrancy
arbitrarily), were fined and/or sold for a maximum term of four months' slave
labor (minors could be sentenced to terms of servitude lasting until they were
30 years of age) and driven from their homes or murdered by gold rush
miners. The San Francisco *Californian* epitomized the region's ethnic bigotry
in a March 15, 1848, statement: "We desire only a white population in California."

Californians were not the only Americans who viewed the United States
as a white man's country. The attitude that the West Coasters expressed so
bluntly eventually led to repressive and exclusive national legislation. Unlike
Indians and blacks, the Chinese could very easily be kept out. In 1882 the
United States Congress suspended Chinese immigration for ten years and forbade the naturalization of Orientals already in the country. Repeated resistance
to Chinese entry culminated in 1924 when Congress excluded all Orientals. A

eneration later this policy was repudiated; the Immigration Act of 1965 eliminated ethnic origins as a qualifying factor for newcomers.

Regulating the presence of Indians and blacks presented different problems. The former were the true natives and could not be barred. But they could be slaughtered and put in reservations. The period between the Civil War and the battle of Wounded Knee in 1892 marked the most ferocious Indian wars. White Americans continually pushed westward. The government in Washington tore up and renegotiated peace treaties which guaranteed Indians the right to land in what subsequently became Nebraska, the Dakotas, Montana, Wyoming, Oklahoma, and other western states.

Some white Americans were concerned with the "Indian problem" and sought ways to solve it. Unfortunately their efforts were directed by misguided notions of reform which, as in other reform activities of the period, meant enforcing white middle-class standards. The United States government set up an Indian Bureau, ostensibly to supervise and train Indians for useful work in American society, and Congress appropriated the necessary sums for mechanical and agricultural education. The "good" intentions of some Congressmen, however, rarely affected the insipid or brutal policies of the Indian agents, who too often were ill-fitted for their supervisory positions. Even if the personnel had been humane, the disruption of tribal culture caused by the new policy added to the Indians' already anguished existence. The Dawes Severalty Act of 1887 provided for the dissolution of the Indian tribes as legal entities and the distribution of tribal lands among individual members. It also stipulated that Indians should become American citizens by 1906. Congress, however, did not grant the Indians citizenship until 1924.

While native-born ethnic minorities struggled to acculturate themselves, the arrival of new groups of European, Asian, and Latin-American immigrants intensified national tensions. The industrial revolution spawned the growth of cities and created millions of unskilled jobs. Into this gap flowed Italians, eastern Europeans, Jews, Hungarians, Greeks, Japanese, Mexicans, and Caribbean blacks. Like earlier arrivals they sought economic opportunities and peaceful communities.

Heretofore northern and western Europeans with fair skin, blond hair, and blue eyes had provided the bulk of America's foreign born. Except for the Irish, they were mainly Protestants searching for farmland. Beginning in the 1880s, however, swarthy types from more alien cultures predominated among the newcomers. Southern and eastern Europeans, frequently Jews and Roman or Greek Catholics, lacked the capital that many German and Scandinavian migrants had possessed and remained in the coastal cities upon arrival. Others, either helped by relatives or recruited at the dock by scouts for large employers, flocked to the mining and manufacturing communities in Illinois, Pennsylvania, Ohio, and Indiana, where work could be found that required neither skills nor knowledge of English. They toiled at the most menial, backbreaking tasks for abominably low wages and lived in crowded, unhealthy tenements or shanties.

The prospects of "alien hordes" overrunning the United States upset many Americans of older lineage. A Progressive journalist, Burton J. Hendrick, began an article in 1913 with the prediction that in less than 100 years "the

I

10

United States will be peopled chiefly by Slavs, negroes [sic], years earlier a writer in the *Popular Science Monthly* had w: many Jews entered the United States, "We shall lose our inheri ideals, and instead of a perfect amalgamation, we shall confro a complete racial substitution."

Renowned members of the American intelligentsia twist theories to support concepts of racial inferiority. The historian Cabot Lodge supported legislation in Congress which would have effectively barred most of the "new immigrants" from entering this country. Political scientist John W. Burgess wrote treatises glorifying Anglo-Saxons and debasing blacks and Orientals. And University of Wisconsin sociologist E. A. Ross devoted reams of paper to glorifying the "innate ethical endowment" of northern Europeans while castigating Slavs for being "noisome and repulsive" and Italians for being unable "to take rational care of themselves."

Anxieties about foreigners supplanting "real" Americans stimulated the establishment of organizations like the Immigration Restriction League whose views were advertised by their names. Beginning in the 1890s various groups of patriotic societies, laborers, and politicians from the South and the West who did not have to worry about any ethnic voters agitated for a more restrictive policy. The culmination of these efforts came in 1924 when Congress severely limited further immigration from Europe and all but excluded Africans and Orientals. Latin Americans were exempt from this statute.

The barring of further large-scale immigration from Europe and Asia hastened the process of assimilating European immigrants. But animosity continued toward those whose skin pigmentations were darker than the Europeans'. Blacks, Indians, Orientals, and many Spanish-speaking citizens bore and still bear incomparably different burdens from American Caucasians. The difference lies in the crucial distinction between race and nationality. Americans of European extraction have always considered darker complexioned minorities genetically inferior to themselves.* For Caucasians, at least legally, until the late nineteenth century America had lived up to its ideal as a refuge for the oppressed from other lands. But from their first associations with settlers of Anglo-Saxon or other European origins, yellow men, red men, brown men, and black men were treated as servants, slaves, and savages, and aroused hostility, fear, and contempt in the dominant culture. While others have suffered similar humiliations and deprivations, they have not endured such prolonged and severe hardships.

Since World War II discrimination against Amercans of Oriental extraction has subsided. Chiefly confined to the West Coast, repression of the Chinese and Japanese persisted despite a favorable image of Orientals as industrious, courteous, and cultured. In the 1930 s, for example, "Charlie Chan" (Chinese) and "Mr. Moto" (Japanese) appeared as highly honorable and sophisticated movie detective heroes. With victory over Japan in the Second World War and a deepening sensitivity to and rejection of bigotry, these positive stereotypes encouraged the acceptance of Chinese- and Japanese-Americans.

* See chapters 1 and 2 in Winthrop Jordan, *White Over Black* (Chapel Hill: University of North Carolina Press, 1968); see also Louis Ruchames, "The Sources of Racial Thought in Colonial America," *Journal of Negro History*, LII (1967), 251–77.

Another group victimized by white Americans is the Spanish-speaking minority in Colorado, Texas, New Mexico, Arizona, and California. Characterized in 1950 as "the least known, the least sponsored, and the least vocal large minority group in the nation," the Spanish-speaking Americans are, in a sense, both the oldest and newest of minorities. As long ago as 1598 they founded villages in what is now the state of New Mexico. After the Mexican-American War ended in 1848 about 75,000 residents of the Southwest and Far West found that their lands had been ceded to the United States. Some of these people returned to Mexico but most remained in their homes. Few were prosperous; most were downtrodden and their descendants have remained so. Another group of Mexican-Americans in the Southwest crossed the Texas-Mexico border as itinerant laborers (those who waded across the Rio Grande illegally were known as "wetbacks"). Some of the newcomers have remained in the United States. The recent settlers are considered inferior by most white Americans (or "Anglos" as they are referred to in the Southwest) because of their mixed black, Indian, and Spanish ancestry. Reinforcing Anglo prejudices are the poverty-ridden communities in which unskilled Mexican-Americans live. A Texas farmer described conventional Anglo attitudes when he said: "You can't mix with a Mexican and hold his respect. It's like the nigger; as long as you keep him in his place he is all right."

On the East Coast the Puerto Ricans, another Latin American minority, began to arrive on the mainland after World War I but their presence in large numbers did not arouse concern until after World War II. They have also suffered racial slurs and an impoverished existence. Like many before them they came primarily for the job opportunities available to them. In 1959 more than 95 percent of the Puerto Ricans lived in New York City (there are now colonies in Bridgeport, Connecticut; Newark, New Jersey; Philadelphia; Rochester, New York; and Chicago). An overwhelming number replaced Jews and Italians at unskilled and semiskilled occupations in the garment industry.

Although Mexican-Americans and Puerto Ricans now demand equal rights, they are primarily regional minorities and outside of the Southwest, Far West, and major cities few Americans are aware of their circumstances. The same may also be said of the Indians in the Rocky Mountain area and the Eskimos in Alaska.

One minority, however, is indeed a national concern today and "minority problems" are frequently no more than a euphemism for black problems. No other ethnic group in the United States has ever been subjected to prolonged enslavement or to the frustrations, disappointments, and humiliations that the black man has borne for more than three centuries. The Civil War formally freed the slave but white America kept his descendants in a subordinate position. Consequently the nineteenth-century black man had little opportunity for education or advancement. In 1895 Booker T. Washington advised his race to become self-dependent and prove to whites that they were worthy of equality. To foster this responsibility Washington advocated industrial education. If blacks would learn skilled trades they would be able to care for themselves, he reasoned, even though manual training would keep them out of the middle class and in continued subordination to whites.

After 1900 persisting repression and poverty convinced a younger generation of blacks that accommodation had failed. The Niagara Movement, founded by William E. B. Du Bois in 1905, demanded "the abolition of all caste distinctions based simply on race and color." Its members opposed school segregation in Philadelphia and Chicago and brought suits against railroad segregation. In 1909 most of the members of the Niagara Movement, along with liberal whites, established the National Association for the Advancement of Colored People (NAACP), an organization dedicated to securing racial equality. In 1915 the NAACP brought suit in the Supreme Court against southern disfranchisement of blacks, thus beginning the long legal struggle for civil rights.

The high point in the drive for equality was reached in the 1950s and early 1960s when a series of legislative and judicial actions apparently guaranteed equal civil rights and heralded the end of segregation in education, housing, and jobs. These victories were largely the result of a combination of tactics by different black organizations. The NAACP fought for civil rights through the courts and by encouraging influential white liberals to bring political pressure on all levels of government. The Congress of Racial Equality (CORE), the Southern Christian Leadership Conference (SCLC), and the Student Nonviolent Coordinating Committee (SNCC), composed of the younger, postwar generation of whites and blacks and inspired by Martin Luther King's successful boycott of the segregated Montgomery, Alabama, bus system in 1955–56, turned to direct action through sit-ins and voter registration.

Not all blacks believed that integration would solve America's race dilemma, however. Marcus Garvey, founder in 1914 of the Universal Negro Improvement Association (UNIA), contended that whites would remain bigoted; consequently the black must develop "a distinct racial type of civilization of his own and . . . work out his salvation in his motherland, all to be accomplished under the stimulus and influence of the slogan, 'Africa for the Africans', at home and abroad." To implement this vision, Garvey urged blacks to support business and the UNIA organized groceries, restaurants, laundries, and a printing plant. Garvey emphasized the African part and declared that God and Christ were black.

A generation later the Black Muslims under the leadership of Elijah Muhammad and Malcolm X emerged as the leading black nationalist movement. Through appealing to middle-class Puritanism and race pride, the Muslims rehabilitated a number of black addicts and criminals. At first their message of white hatred and talk of violence aided the civil rights movement by making integration a desirable alternative to whites. However, black nationalism gained adherents as black family income failed to keep pace with that of whites. When black unemployment continued to rise and de facto segregation in schools and neighborhoods increased despite legislation to the contrary additional followers hopped on the bandwagon. CORE and SNCC rejected the integrationism of the early 1960s to demand black control over black communities and over the civil rights movement. New leaders like Stokely Carmichael and H. Rap Brown challenged the older, leading integrationists, Bayard Rustin, A. Philip Randolph, and even Martin Luther King, Jr. Rifts opened between the new militants and traditional civil rights organizations like the NAACP and the National Urban League.

The growth of militant separatism, the ghetto riots in the 1960s, and the recent tendency, manifested by the Black Panthers and others, for elements of the black community to become involved in violent confrontations with the white establishment occur at a time of unprecedented emphasis on civil rights and improvement in political, vocational, and educational opportunities. Although most blacks still desire to become accepted as full-fledged Americans and the majority regard the late Martin Luther King, Jr., as their most beloved leader, the confrontation between white and black grows more intense. Initial advancement raised blacks' expectations and the slow pace of their fulfillment aggravates frustration. Conversely, most whites think the blacks are "moving too fast" and are obtaining too much help in their recent social and economic progress. Black resentment combined with white anxiety and mutual hostility have created the present impasse.

Although American attention focuses primarily upon the black minority today this may be a temporary phenomenon. Just as minority groups in the past have settled into comfortable anonymity, so too, hopefully, may the blacks. If in the future civilized societies make minority group adjustment a central concern, racial antipathies, riots, and tensions might be minimized or avoided.

Selected Bibliography

After each sectional introduction are a number of items which should be of interest to those who want to know more about minorities in the United States. We have made no attempt to be exhaustive in our coverage; we are merely listing one or two titles which broadly cover the different groups. Most of our suggestions contain significant bibliographical essays which might be pursued with profit by the interested student.

There are no adequate histories of minority groups as a whole. J. Joseph Huthmacher's A Nation of Newcomers* *(New York: Dell Publishing Co., 1967) is a brief survey of the more important immigrant groups and is obviously intended for high school students. Carl Wittke's* We Who Built America *(rev. ed.; Cleveland: The Press of Western Reserve University, 1964) is a summary of the experiences and contributions of all American minorities except the blacks with little attempt at analysis. Carey McWilliams'* Brothers Under the Skin* *(rev. ed.; Boston: Little Brown, 1964) contains sympathetic essays on the most victimized of America's minorities. John Higham's* Strangers in the Land* *(New York: Atheneum, 1965) is a superb study of American nativism for the period from the 1870s through the 1920s while Oscar Handlin's* The Uprooted* *(Boston: Little Brown, 1951) is a profound, provocative, and moving evocation of the immigrant experience during the mass migration from Europe to the United States.*

Two groups that are covered in all of our sections are the Indians and the blacks. It would be impossible to list even the most prominent of the works on each group but a good beginning on the Indians might be made with Peter Farb's Man's Rise to Civilization as Shown by the Indians of North America, From Primeval Times to the Coming of the Industrial State *(New York: Dutton, 1968); William T. Hagan,* American Indians* *(Chicago: University of Chicago Press, 1961); John Collier,* The Indians of the Americas* *(New York: New*

* Asterisked titles are available in paperback.

American Library, 1947); and two worthwhile collections of essays: Wilcomb E. Washburn, ed., The Indian and the White Man* *(Garden City, N. Y.: Doubleday and Co., 1964), and Jack D. Forbes, ed.,* The Indian in America's Past* *(Englewood Cliffs, N. J.: Prentice-Hall, 1964). The best book to start with on the blacks is Arnold Rose's abridged version of Gunnar Myrdal's* An American Dilemma *entitled* The Negro in America* *(New York: Harper & Row, 1964). Also of value is John Hope Franklin's* From Slavery to Freedom* *(rev. ed.; New York: Alfred A. Knopf, 1968). Gilbert Osofsky's* The Burden of Race: A Documentary History of Negro-White Relations in America* *(New York: Harper & Row, 1967) has an excellent collection of items from colonial times through the 1960s.*

The Colonial Era

Ethnic conflict in America began well before the first white settlements of the sixteenth century; Indian tribes with conflicting cultures and interests battled each other repeatedly. With the arrival of Spanish, French, British, Dutch, and Swedish immigrants came additional struggles. Missionaries tried to convert Indians, Congregationalists banished Quakers from Massachusetts Bay, and territorial squabbles among the French, Spanish, and British occurred over land, the fur trade, and ultimately the destiny of the continent.

For most of the seventeenth-century English-speaking groups concentrated in New England and Virginia; Dutch and Swedes settled along the Hudson and Delaware Rivers; Germans established themselves in Pennsylvania; and French Huguenots made their homes in the infant cities of Charleston, Philadelphia, New York, and environs. The British settlers came in greater numbers and they came to stay. Except for the relatively small numbers of Huguenots and German Pietists, there were no intense religious controversies in other European countries that would impel, as it did the Pilgrims, Puritans, and Quakers in England, great numbers toward permanent emigration. Immigrants from other nations either accepted British rule or were too weak to challenge British sovereignty. When large numbers of Germans emigrated to the New World in the eighteenth century, they settled in areas already governed by the English. While Pennsylvania, Plymouth, Massachusetts Bay, Virginia, and the Carolinas became sites of permanent settlement, the Dutch, Spanish, and French enclaves were mostly armed trading posts intended for quick profit through commerce. By the eighteenth century, when colonization replaced trade as the primary reason for New World establishments, the English were far ahead of their rivals, the French, in the strength and sophistication of their settlements.

During the first seventy-five years of the eighteenth century the Scotch-Irish constituted the largest immigrant group from the British Isles. They had been driven out of Ulster and Scotland by depression in the linen industry and by enclosure of farming and grazing acreage which made small farmers landless. (Large landowners would consolidate smaller properties in order to gain profits and efficiency of large-scale farming.) Most migrants, too poor to pay their own way, came as indentured servants, selling their labor for a number of years in return for free transportation to the colonies. The majority of these, after working out their passage, drifted into the cities where they became un-

skilled laborers. But many exservants and the larger proportion of those wealthy enough not to have to mortgage their first years in the new country sought the frontier where land was most easily and cheaply acquired, or became (with little training) physicians, lawyers, and merchants in Boston, New York, and other colonial cities. The Scotch-Irish were most in evidence on the frontiers of Pennsylvania, New York, Virginia, Georgia, and the Carolinas. Their un-polished manners, evangelical religion, lack of education, demands for protec-tion against the French and Indians, and opposition to the Eastern religious, political, and social establishment raised hackles in Tidewater Virginia, Charles-ton, New York City, and Philadelphia. Pennsylvania Quakers labelled them a "pernicious and pugnacious people." "Poverty, wretchedness, misery, and want are become almost universal among them," commented a writer in The Penn-sylvania Gazette *in 1729. At the same time that they received such condemna-tion Scotch-Irish were welcomed for expanding settlement and acting as a buffer against hostile Indians, French, and Spanish.*

Another large outpouring of immigrants came from the German states in central Europe. They included Moravian Pietists, who came primarily be-cause of religious persecution, as well as Lutherans and members of the Ger-man Reformed Church who sought greater economic opportunities in the New World. Unlike the Scotch-Irish they usually settled behind the edge of the frontiers. The reputedly thrifty and diligent Germans made more efficient and prosperous farmers than the Ulsterites on the frontiers. By 1766 enclaves of German farmers dotted Pennsylvania as well as the Cumberland and Shenan-doah Valleys of Maryland and Virginia.

African slaves, the third largest migrant group, first made their appearance in sixteenth-century Spanish colonies. For economic and philosophical reasons colonists preferred black bondsmen to captive Indian labor. The image of the noble red man, God's innocent child of nature, generated a certain reluctance to enslave the native population. Moreover, the Indians, remaining in their native habitat, were considerably more intractable than Africans, cut off from their culture. Or perhaps more importantly the Indian population, decimated by its contact with European civilization, proved insufficient to fulfill the expanding labor demands of the colonial settlements.

After 1697, with the end of the Royal African Company's monopoly on the slave trade, the importation of blacks increased tremendously. During the eighteenth century approximately 200,000 arrived in America. Ninety percent of them went to the South, a region more suited to slavery than the North because of its larger land holdings. Slave labor, the existence of few cities, and preemption of the best land by large planters discouraged other types of im-migration as white newcomers found better opportunities for land and labor in the North. The South's failure to attract the white foreign born, a disability partly attributable to the slave system, continued into the twentieth century and left the section dependent upon bondsmen for its labor supply and more com-pletely committed to a plantation economy.

Although there were relatively few white immigrants, the existence of large numbers of blacks (two-fifths of the population of Virginia, one-third that of North Carolina and Maryland, more than one-third that of Georgia, and nearly two-thirds that of South Carolina) made the colonial South less ethnically homogeneous than New England. New England, partly due to the greater economic opportunities in the Middle Colonies, and partly due to the aloofness of the first-generation Puritans, who wished to prevent "contaminaton" of Massachusetts Bay Colony by alien sects, remained the most ethnically uniform region. In the Middle Colonies, however, settlers of English extraction comprised only about one-half the total population. New York City, with its polyglot citizenry, and Pennsylvania, with its large English, German, and Scotch-Irish settlements, are the most notable examples of the ethnic mixture in the region.

Labor shortages, the need for frontier defense against the French, Spanish, and Indians, availability of land, and the desire of colonies to advance settlement and develop resources guaranteed a generally favorable reception for Protestant newcomers. Colonists used a variety of strategies to attract European emigrants: Virginia and Maryland gave land to those who brought over settlers (the "head right" system, in which a man had the right to claim an additional 50 acres for each person or head that he brought over); some legislatures exempted immigrants from taxes or debt action for specified periods of time; others provided new arrivals with free land or tools; most enacted easy naturalization laws. William Penn undertook a vigorous advertising campaign to entice migrants while Massachusetts employed immigration agents and offered bounties to defray the costs of ocean passage.

Despite these lures ethnic conflicts that would someday reverse the generally proimmigration attitudes of colonial times are revealed in the restrictions and hostility directed toward some of the newcomers. Most colonies levied head taxes on Roman Catholics, paupers, and felons; New Englanders shunned Quakers and Scotch-Irish; hostility flared between the Germans and Scotch-Irish settled near each other; Pennsylvania English manifested contempt for Pennsylvania Germans (Benjamin Franklin called them "Palatine Boors"); and prejudice against blacks and Indians pervaded all of the colonies.

Ethnic groups in the few cities assimilated more rapidly into the dominant English culture than those in the more isolated rural settlements. In New York City, by the beginning of the eighteenth century, the Dutch families remaining from New Netherland days succumbed completely to anglicizing while their upstate cousins still worshipped in the ritual and spoke in the tongue of the old country.

Well before independence fundamental aspects of the American creed appeared. On the eve of revolution the colonies established themselves as a land of refuge and opportunity for Europeans and as a place of oppression for blacks and Indians. The need for labor overcame prejudices against the admission of prisoners, blacks, Catholics, and non-English Europeans and ethnic conflict did not then seriously disturb the development of white America. The European born established their own communities or assimilated into the dominant culture. America would change greatly in the century after independence but the pattern of ethnic friction and assimilation fixed in colonial times remained remarkably constant.

Selected Bibliography

The white man's justification for his treatment of the Indians is described best by Wilcomb E. Washburn, "The Moral and Legal Justifications For Dispossessing the Indians," in James M. Smith, ed., 17th Century America* *(Chapel Hill: University of North Carolina Press, 1959). Alden Vaughan's* New England Frontier* *(Boston: Little, Brown, 1965) is a revaluation of the Puritans' relationship with the Indians. He finds much to praise in Puritan thoughts and actions. An unpublished doctoral dissertation by Maurice M. Wasserman, "The American Indian as Seen by the 17th Century Chroniclers" (University of Pennsylvania, 1954), details contemporary attitudes.*

Winthrop D. Jordan's magnificent White Over Black: American Attitudes Toward the Negro, 1550–1812* *(Chapel Hill: University of North Carolina Press, 1968) supersedes all previous studies on the subject. Jordan's bibliographical essay provides all the additional readings necessary for the curious reader.*

Little has been written about colonial Germans in recent times but Albert B. Faust's The German Element in the United States *(2 vols.; Boston: Houghton Mifflin, 1909) and Lucey Forney Bittinger's* The Germans in Colonial Times *(Philadelphia: J. B. Lippincott, 1901) are still useful.*

On the Scotch-Irish see Henry Jones Ford's The Scotch-Irish in America *(3rd ed.; Hamdon, Conn.: Archon Books, 1966) and James G. Leyburn's* The Scotch-Irish *(Chapel Hill: University of North Carolina Press, 1962), which also contains a superb bibliography.*

The enterprising student will find an almost unexplored area if he surveys the history of Huguenots in colonial America. Arthur H. Hirsch's The Huguenots of Colonial South Carolina *(2nd ed.; Hamdon, Conn.: Archon Books, 1962); James L. Bugg Jr.'s "The French Huguenot Frontier Settlement of Manakin Town,"* Virginia Magazine of History and Biography, *61 (1953), 359–394; and Esther Bernon Carpenter's "The Huguenot Influence in Rhode Island,"* Rhode Island Historical Society Proceedings, *1885–1886, pp. 46–74, are among the few items extant.*

Indians

DAVID BUSHNELL

The Treatment of the Indians in Plymouth Colony

The first group in American history to be treated as a minority was already here when the European settlers arrived. The Indians, while romanticized as "nature's noblemen," were never recognized as the white men's equal by the overwhelming majority of newcomers. Nor, in fact, did the migrants acknowledge the Indians' legal rights to the land upon which they dwelled. The English colonists never doubted that the New World claimed by the Crown belonged to the King and that he alone had the right to bestow his possessions upon whomever he favored.

In the article below Professor David Bushnell shows how the Pilgrims attempted, in their own way, to be just with the red men. Nevertheless the cultural gap between the two groups precluded harmonious relations. The colonists were convinced the white man was better than the red man and Christianity was superior to paganism.

The initial experience between the Indians and the Pilgrims set the stage for future relations between the two races. Since colonial times American attitudes and policies toward the Indians have been at best paternalistic and at worst brutal.

In the popular tradition concerning Plymouth Colony, the Indian Squanto has acquired a place almost as honorable as the Mayflower Compact and the first Thanksgiving, and it can fairly be said that Massasoit does not lag far behind. This is as it should be, for the Compact could easily have remained a dead letter and Thanksgiving might never have become a holiday if the Indians of southeastern Massachusetts had chosen to pounce upon the Pilgrim settlement in the dreary winter of 1621. Despite the obvious importance of Indian relations, however, it does not appear that the Pilgrim Fathers carried with them a preconceived Indian policy when they set out from Holland. We know from Bradford that the lurid tales of Indian savagery then circulating through Europe had prepared them to expect the worst,[1] but they seem to have trusted in Cap-

Reprinted by permission of the publishers from *The New England Quarterly,* 26 (1953), 193–218.
[1] William Bradford, *History of Plymouth Plantation* (Boston, 1898), 33–34.

tain Miles Standish to improvise a system of defense after their arrival in America. For their other relations with the natives, they trusted in the Ten Commandments. They would attempt to behave with Christian charity toward the Indian, and they intended to be treated with similar decency in return.

Thus the Pilgrims did not doubt for a moment that they should ultimately pay the Indians for the corn and utensils which they found abandoned on Cape Cod and at New Plymouth, nor did they hesitate to demand the promptest restitution whenever the natives stole property of their own. When Squanto was found guilty of petty intrigues inimical to Massasoit they agreed in principle to hand him over to justice, although they were naturally delighted to see the Wampanoag envoys return home before extradition of the interpreter was finally decreed.[2] On the other hand, the Pilgrims insisted that all Indian grievances should be pressed through proper channels. They did not deny the Massachusetts Indians' grievances against Weston's men, but the red men were fully justified in their fear that Plymouth would not permit the Wessagusset settlement to be wiped out by force. And when the natives therefore determined to wipe out the Pilgrims as well, Captain Standish hurried off to stage a preventive massacre at Massachusetts Bay. No further punishment was inflicted, however, and no action whatever was taken against the Cape sachems who had been implicated in the Massachusetts' conspiracy.[3] The natives were given to understand that treachery would not be tolerated, and the English settlers were consequently spared much future trouble. But it was also made clear that the Pilgrims bore the Indians no ill will, and that the aborigines had nothing to fear so long as they behaved themselves.

From the battle of Wessagusset to the outbreak of King Philip's War few spectacular events mark the history of Plymouth Colony, and fewer still concern the Pilgrims' relations with the Indians. During these fifty years of peace both peoples were learning little by little to know each other better. The Indians had much to teach about New England geography, while the superior technical knowledge of the English soon worked great changes in the natives' way of living. It must be admitted, however, that this intercourse was rather one-sided. Squanto deserves full credit for his first lessons in corn cultivation, but the Pilgrims more than repaid the favor by instructing the Indians how to use metal farm instruments.[4] It is certain that for a time the settlers were very glad to buy Indian basketwork.[5] Other than this, however, the Indians had nothing to offer save their labor, their land, and a few furs. Their labor, moreover, was never economical. It was occasionally used for cutting firewood and even for ordinary farm work, but the Town of Plymouth expressly forbade the employment of Indians in the former occupation because of their wasteful methods.[6]

The Indians' land was a different matter. In the strictest legal sense no

[2] Alexander Young, editor, *Chronicles of the Pilgrim Fathers* (Boston, 1841), 285–292.

[3] Bradford, *History of Plymouth Plantation,* 155–159; Young, *Chronicles of the Pilgrim Fathers,* 298–302, 309–312, 327–345.

[4] Bradford, *History of Plymouth Plantation,* 123.

[5] Charles C. Willoughby, *Antiquities of the New England Indians* (Cambridge, 1935), 252.

[6] *Records of the Colony of New Plymouth* (Boston, 1855–1861), IV, 183; VII, 161 (henceforth referred to as P.C.R.); *Records of the Town of Plymouth* (Plymouth, 1889), I, 172–173.

"land question" ever existed, for the Pilgrims recognized that in English and also in Divine law the sole title to landed estate in New England belonged to the English crown. Even on a practical level, Indian claims to the greater part of Plymouth Colony were extremely weak, since most of their territory was used only intermittently as a game preserve. Along the western shore of Cape Cod Bay, furthermore, the native inhabitants had been almost entirely wiped out by the recent plague, so that the Pilgrims scarcely needed Massasoit's gracious permission to take all the land they could use.[7]

Nevertheless, the Pilgrims were scrupulously careful to extinguish Indian rights of "occupancy" whenever they pressed beyond the vacant tract on which they raised their first settlements. This was done by means of hoes, cloth, fencing, wampum, or a day's ploughing; and since the Indians commonly recognized a joint title to lands, the settlers often attempted to have as many Indians as possible affix their marks to the deed of transfer.[8] There was, however, no strict rule. At times the sachem and his son sealed the transaction alone; often both the sachem and the Indians who had enjoyed immediate use of the purchased tract would sign the deed; and occasionally individual Indians were reputed to have full power to sell the land they occupied. At the eastern end of Cape Cod there even lived a certain "Paumpmunitt alias Charles" who seems to have made a business of buying land from his fellow Indians in order to resell it to the Plymouth planters.[9] On still other occasions lands were granted outright by the Indians. The gift of Massasoit to the original settlers is the most notable example, but later donations were also made in recognition of "kindness, respect, and love" shown an Indian's parents, or perhaps to win the favor of an influential politician.[10] But if, at the other extreme, the Indians resolutely refused to part with their lands, the colonial government simply instructed prospective purchasers to look elsewhere. Under Plymouth law it was apparently necessary to pay for totally unoccupied lands if an Indian claimant presented himself, and at least one Indian was able to make his claim good twenty-two years after the English established themselves on his property.[11]

Since these transactions seem to have been almost invariably open and aboveboard it would be unnecessary to discuss the process of purchasing land at any length if it were not for the common opinion that land was a permanent bone of contention between colonists and Indians, and a direct cause of King Philip's War. For one thing, it has often been claimed that the English cheated the Indians unmercifully by paying far less than their lands were actually worth, and at first glance this charge appears to have some basis in fact. Since early colonial deeds were often vague in setting down the boundaries of the tracts purchased, and since the money value of corn, shoes, kettles, and other legal tender varied with both time and place, it is impossible to construct a

[7] Young, *Chronicles of the Pilgrim Fathers,* 245.
[8] P.C.R., II, 131; III, 145; Donald G. Trayser, *Barnstable* (Hyannis, 1939), 29; Ronald Oliver MacFarlane, "Indian Relations in New England 1620–1760" (MS. thesis, Harvard University, 1933), 21.
[9] P.C.R., V, 152; XII, 227–228, 235–236, 238–242; Alice Austin Ryder, *Lands of Sippican* (New Bedford, 1934), 21.
[10] Cf. Josiah Paine, *A History of Harwich* (Rutland, Vermont, 1937), 40, 64 note, 82–83.
[11] P.C.R., II, 164; IV, 109; Francis Baylies, *An Historical Memoir of the Colony of New Plymouth* (Boston, 1866), II, 219–220.

table showing the average price per acre of land bought from the Indians. Even if a precise scale in pounds, shillings, and iron hoes were available, it would not greatly clarify the problem, for just as land was less valuable to the Indians than to the Pilgrims, all metal artifacts were more highly prized by the natives than by the English settlers. Nevertheless, the Indians can hardly have failed to grasp the fact that a Pilgrim syndicate could buy native lands at Freetown and resell them within a few years at a five hundred per cent profit,[12] and it is likely that even sharper rises in land values were not uncommon.

In defense of the Pilgrims it can fairly be said that they were no more to blame than the Indians themselves for what was a natural consequence of economic laws. Lands effectively brought within the range of world-wide economic forces by the expansion of English settlement were obviously worth more than a native hunting reservation, and the profit was not necessarily speculative when lands were improved before being resold. King Philip himself, who cited land "injuries" as one motive for his hostilities against Plymouth Colony, did not hesitate to continue his sales of tribal land almost up to the outbreak of war, the better to enjoy luxuries brought by the English.[13] As a matter of fact, the sums paid by the English were often far from insignificant; in 1672 Philip sold sixteen square miles to Taunton for £190,[14] and similarly high prices were not infrequent after the early years of settlement.

Still another line of attack on the Pilgrims' land purchases has to do with the mental reservations which the Indians are supposed to have made when transferring their lands to the English. In particular it has been charged that whereas the Indians imagined they were transferring a mere right of usufruct, the English were no less convinced that they were acquiring absolute ownership. Although it is impossible to reconstruct exactly what went on in the Indians' minds, their notions of property were so indefinite that some such confusion may easily have existed both in Plymouth and elsewhere in New England. However, it seems unreasonable to suppose that the Pilgrims' interpreters were never able to find an intelligible rendering of the word "forever" which constantly appeared in the deeds of purchase, and when the Indians actually did attempt to reassert a right of ownership over land they had already sold, the English were generous in buying off their pretensions. A long list could be made of the so-called "quit-claim" or "confirmatory" deeds which a new sachem would issue, for a slight compensation, for the purpose of renouncing any rights in tracts of land that had been formally alienated by his predecessors. The Pilgrims were equally reasonable with regard to lands claimed by more than one tribe or band of Indians.[15] Multiple purchases of one sort or another became so frequent that in 1659 the Colony saw fit to issue firm orders against the practice, on the plausible grounds that such transactions cast doubt on the legality of the original purchase.[16]

[12] Richard LeBaron Bowen, *Early Rehoboth* (Rehoboth, 1945–1946), I, 80.
[13] John Easton, "A Relacion of the Indyan Warre," in *Narratives of the Indian Wars* (Charles H. Lincoln, editor, New York, 1913), 9–11; Samuel G. Drake, *The Old Indian Chronicle* (Boston, 1867), 58–62.
[14] Samuel H. Emery, *History of Taunton* (Syracuse, New York, 1893), 114–120.
[15] Baylies, *New Plymouth*, II, 225; IV, 90–91.
[16] P.C.R., XI, 124.

Whatever the Indians may have thought regarding the length of tenure accorded to English purchasers, there is no doubt that they frequently intended to continue hunting or fishing or gathering rushes on their former lands after the English had moved in. Certain Cape Indians likewise desired the right to continue taking blubber from whales washed up on the shore.[17] Indeed, the fact that such conditions were carefully written into the terms of purchase is one reason to doubt that the Indians were entirely unaware of what they were doing in parting with their lands. The specific recognition of Indian rights, moreover, must have spared the Pilgrims much controversy in later years. The records of Plymouth Colony contain numerous instances of Indians prosecuted for "trespass" on English property, and at times a township felt compelled to issue special orders for the purpose of excluding unwelcome Indians from its land.[18] But it would be rash to assume that such misdemeanors resulted simply from the natives' theory of property, for Englishmen were frequently charged with exactly the same offense.

Unfortunately land prices and terms of occupancy were not the only questions capable of causing friction between Pilgrims and Indians. The vague boundaries established in the first land deeds inevitably led to occasional difficulties, although it seems that an amicable settlement was usually reached. While there may well have been instances of obtaining an Indian's "signature" to a deed while he was drunk or other cases of swindling the "poore Indians," the Plymouth authorities were more zealous than most colonial governments to prevent such abuses. From the very start of the settlement a legal permit from the Colony was required before land could be purchased from the natives,[19] and this rule protected the Indians quite as much as it furthered the cause of an orderly English settlement. The law was not always enforced with equal severity, but at least one Pilgrim was actually disfranchised for the offense.[20]

Even more significant is Plymouth's readiness to guarantee the Indians a full legal title to their lands. At times an Indian would request the government to register his property among the records of the Colony; in such cases the required document was promptly drawn up and the Indian's possession was secured on the same terms as English lands.[21] The official registration of Indian wills, which became increasingly frequent as the natives learned the ways of judicial procedure, and which often amounted to a virtual entail, had exactly the same effect.[22] In the case of Mount Hope, Pocasset, and other leading sites of Indian settlement it seems that the Pilgrims anticipated the natives' wishes, for it was ordered that such lands might not be purchased even if the Indians agreed to sell.[23] The colonists did not necessarily object even if the Indians desired to live and farm alongside the English. They acquiesced when the Indians

---

[17] Cf. P.C.R., II, 131; Paine, *Harwich*, 84; Enoch Pratt, *A Comprehensive History Ecclesiastical and Civil of Eastham, Wellfleet, and Orleans* (Yarmouth, 1844), 11.
[18] *Records of the Town of Plymouth*, I, 94; Leonard Bliss, *History of Rehoboth* (Boston, 1836), 49.
[19] P.C.R., XI, 41, 183.
[20] P.C.R., III, 101.
[21] See, for instance, P.C.R., XII, 225, 242.
[22] P.C.R., XII, 228, 231, 233–234; Paine, *Harwich*, 393.
[23] William Hubbard, *A Narrative of the Troubles with the Indians* (Boston, 1677), 13.

insisted on retaining a reservation for their own use within the bounds of a township that had otherwise extinguished the native titles; and the records of the Town of Plymouth contain more than one instance of land rented or granted outright to individual Indians.[24]

For the main body of Pilgrim settlers trade was far less important than land. Indian corn was found necessary for the survival of the colonists during their first years in New England, and it was the fur trade that allowed the struggling colony to win its financial independence from the London adventurers. But as soon as the Colony became agriculturally self-sufficient it did not need Wampanoag corn. The fur resources of the Pilgrims' immediate neighbors were always limited, so that Plymouth fur traders were soon compelled to look farther afield, in Maine and Connecticut. The local trade nevertheless throws considerable light on the Pilgrims' relations with the Indians. Official policy was to organize it as a monopoly on somewhat the same lines as the fur trade on the Kennebec. To make matters more certain, the colonists were strictly forbidden to do any trading whatever that involved paying the Indians in money, arms, or liquor.[25] But the monopoly system does not seem to have been rigorously enforced, and the holders of the concession were not always very active. In 1640, therefore, it was decided that any colonist might "trade for corne, beades, venison, or some tymes for a beaver skine" without violating Plymouth laws.[26]

A more effective limitation on the local trade was the continuing prohibition of giving the Indians money, liquor, or arms. The first of these prohibitions was finally lifted in 1669, only to be restored eight years later on the plea that the Indians might use their money for liquor.[27] And this excuse is not at all improbable, for the Pilgrims felt very strongly indeed on the subject of "drinking Indians." "They drinke themselves drunke," it was observed, "and in their drunkenes committ much horred wickednes, as murthering theire nearest relations, &c, as by sadd and woefull experience is made manifest."[28] Even for medical purposes a permit was required before liquor could be given to a native,[29] and a few crimes appear so often in the Plymouth court records as the sale of liquor to the Indians.

The colonists felt almost equally strongly on the subject of arming the natives. It is well known that their strongest objection to Thomas Morton of Merrymount was the fact that he supplied his Indian friends with arms and ammunition.[30] This concern is understandable. Whereas the liquor traffic was frowned upon as much because it endangered the Indians' souls as because it threatened to disturb public order, the sale of guns to the Indians was deemed to strike at the very basis of the colonists' security. It is thus remarkable that throughout the 1660's and up to the eve of King Philip's War the prohibition was repeatedly suspended as regards powder and shot and then put back in full force;[31] but on the whole it was strictly enforced, and precautions were taken

[24] *Records of the Town of Plymouth,* I, 41, 97, 172.
[25] P.C.R., I, 54; XI, 33, 184.
[26] Cf. P.C.R., I, 50–51, 130; II, 4; MacFarlane, *Indian Relations,* 377–379.
[27] P.C.R., XI, 184, 244.
[28] P.C.R., III, 60.
[29] P.C.R., XI, 184.
[30] Bradford, *History of Plymouth Plantation,* 287–291.
[31] P.C.R., XI, 184–185, 215, 219, 237.

to prevent the transfer of arms to the natives under the pretense of lending them guns to hunt game in English employment.[32]

Despite the list of prohibited articles, the Indians remained eager to trade with the Pilgrims. They were gradually replacing their traditional clothing, tools, and household utensils with the English products,[33] and their sudden awakening to the benefits of civilization is strikingly illustrated by the growing use of wampum as a medium of exchange. Before the coming of the Pilgrims, the Wampanoags and their satellites had felt little need for either commerce or a form of money. But soon after the Dutch instructed the Pilgrims in the potential value of shell beads, this situation changed abruptly. Even so, wampum did little more than facilitate the act of trading; it did not provide the Indians with a favorable trade balance. The Indians of Plymouth Colony could satisfy some of their needs by turning to the manufacture of wampum themselves, but in this industry they never attained the proficiency of the Narragansetts and Pequots.[34]

To obtain English manufactures, therefore, the Wampanoags and Nausets had to supplement their meagre stocks of furs and wampum with the one thing which they had in abundance and which the English ardently desired: their lands. It is thus easy to understand why the relative values of land and iron kettles were very different among the Indians from what they were among the Pilgrims, and one consequence of this relation was that the trade and land questions tended to merge together. The best examples of the process are to be found among the sachems themselves, who combined the greatest ambition for personal improvement with the greatest territorial resources. Massasoit's son Alexander, for instance, sold land to redeem a debt which he owed to a Plymouth tavern-keeper who was later convicted of repeatedly selling liquor to the natives; another of Alexander's deeds could not be recognized as valid in later years until it was established by witnesses that he had been fully sober when affixing his mark to the paper.[35] There is no evidence, however, that the liquor traffic was a major factor in the land problem. A better example of the connection between trade and land sales is offered by Alexander's brother and successor, King Philip, who is said to have been exceedingly fond of elegant apparel. As a result of this weakness, Philip surpassed all other Indians in the number of his ill-considered land sales.[36]

The problems of land tenure and trade with the Indians, strictly speaking, could not be separated from the broader question of English authority over the native tribes of New England. The territorial claims of the King of England were more modest in extent than those of the Crown of Castile, and they were based on the sighting of new lands by Cabot and his successors rather than on discovery and a Papal bull. From the point of view of the native inhabitants, however, there could be little difference. The entire process of acquiring land

[32] P.C.R., XI, 185. On the enforcement of these regulations, see the index to the first six volumes of the P.C.R.; during King Philip's War giving arms to the Indians became a capital offense (P.C.R., V, 173).

[33] Daniel Gookin, *Historical Collections of the Indians in New England,* 1 *Coll. Mass. Hist. Soc.,* I, 152–153.

[34] Bradford, *History of Plymouth Plantation,* 282; Willoughby, *Antiquities,* 265–266.

[35] Bowen, *Early Rehoboth,* I, 79–83.

[36] Drake, *Old Indian Chronicle,* 58–62.

from the natives was based on the assumption that all property rights in New England resided ultimately in the English crown. Similarly the granting of fur monopolies and the careful regulation of all Indian trade reflected a firm belief that the only legitimate government in New England was that of the English king and the colonial authorities acting in his behalf. In his first treaty with the Pilgrims, to be sure, Massasoit obtained the anomalous status of "friend and ally" to his ultimate sovereign, James I, but such glaring inconsistencies do not appear in subsequent treaties.[37] The mere fact of agreeing to become His Majesty's subjects did not, however, place the Indians in the same category as his English vassals. On one occasion, the town of Rehoboth asked Plymouth Court to approve the admission of "Sam, the Indian that keeps the cows," as an inhabitant, but the absence of any further reference to Sam suggests that the petition was not granted.[38] Nor did any Indian ever obtain political rights in Plymouth Colony.

The status of the Indians was further differentiated by the existence of a distinct system for their immediate government. Though willing to assert their jurisdiction over the entire native population of the Colony, the Plymouth authorities were not equally willing to accept the responsibilities and the nuisance of regulating all the Indians' affairs. As a result, the Pilgrims were extremely slow to part with the services of the sachems. When a group of Sandwich Indians asked the Colony Court in 1665 for permission to organize "some orderly way of government," apparently under the supervision of the missionary Richard Bourne, the Colony agreed only on condition that the new arrangement in no way interfere with the prerogatives of their "superior sachem."[39] Respect for the sachems was not, however, an invariable rule. As the Indians grew more familiar with English judicial procedure and brought their own disputes into Plymouth courts, the authorities sometimes bluntly told them to refer them to their sachems.[40] But the colonial government increasingly saw fit to intervene in such cases, and this was particularly true whenever English interests were indirectly involved. It is not surprising that Plymouth Court agreed to hear a case in which an Indian sued squaw sachem Awashunks of Saconet for illegally retaining lands which he desired to sell to the English settlers, nor that the Court found in favor of the plaintiff.[41] Neither was there ever any doubt regarding jurisdiction in disputes between Englishmen and Indians. The procedure in such cases was not clearly formulated before 1670, when Plymouth enacted that all ordinary disputes between the two races should be heard in first instance by the selectmen of the towns, but the principle had never been questioned. Indeed, the Colony Court seems to have taken a hand directly in many instances, despite the order of 1670, and it reserved the right to treat all cases involving land titles or capital crimes.[42]

[37] Young, *Chronicles of the Pilgrim Fathers,* 193; Nathaniel Morton, *New Englands Memoriall* (New York, 1937), 29; P.C.R., I, 133; IV, 25–26.
[38] Bliss, *Rehoboth,* 60.
[39] P.C.R., IV, 80.
[40] P.C.R., V, 102.
[41] P.C.R., VII, 191. The details of this case are not entirely clear. See also Thomas (Benjamin) Church, *Entertaining Passages Relating to Philip's War* (S. G. Drake, editor, Boston, 1875), 6, note 12; Samuel G. Drake, *The Aboriginal Races of North America* (New York, 1880), 251; Baylies, *New Plymouth,* IV, 63–67.
[42] P.C.R., XI, 227–228.

The separate status of the Indian population was also emphasized by the existence of a special legislation which affected the native but not his white neighbor. The best-known examples of such laws are those already mentioned regarding the sale of arms and liquor, but many more restrictions were imposed upon the Indians. The Indian could not buy a horse without a permit from the Colony, nor could he acquire any boat except his own primitive canoe.[43] He could not be trusted with sales on credit,[44] nor could he shoot his gun or make other unpleasant commotion on the Sabbath day or at night. Indeed, the pagan Indian was arbitrarily required to keep the Sabbath as quietly as the Christian settler.[45] Since the conglomeration of Indians in the capital during court sessions was distasteful to the Pilgrims, the natives were forbidden to draw near on such occasions.[46]

Even regulations that held good for members of both races were not always equally applied. Thieves of either race could be compelled to make amends by labor; but in the case of at least five Indian thieves this servitude was made perpetual, and they were sold as slaves.[47] However, even though the penalties against Indians were often different from those decreed for English criminals, they were not necessarily harsher. It was suggested to one group of Indians that they might pay for killing an English mare by destroying wolves on the Colony's account.[48] Moreover, an "ingenuous" confession sufficed more than once to win easy terms for an Indian culprit. A striking case is that of an Indian who had readily confessed to raping a white woman. The statutory penalty was death, but the Indian was let off with a whipping and an order to leave the Colony "considering hee was but an Indian, and therefore in an incapacity to know the horiblenes of the wickednes of this abominable act, with other cercomstances considered."[49]

Similar reasonableness is shown in the law of 1674 which held that Indians should not be bound by English rules of sworn testimony in court, but instead should testify as in a court of chancery; the Plymouth judges were to use their own discretion in assessing the value of their declarations.[50] Likewise, Indian jurors were occasionally empanelled in cases involving their fellows,[51] although this was not a frequent occurrence. But the Pilgrims' interest in fair treatment of the natives is shown best of all by the willingness of Plymouth courts to grant the Indians redress whenever they were wronged by their white neighbors. The most common offense of the English was negligence in pasturing their cattle, pigs, and horses, with the result that the Pilgrims' animals repeatedly trampled down the Indians' corn fields. The frontier settlement of Rehoboth was the most "unsufferable" offender. Year after year Indian complaints reached the Plymouth court, which ordered the townspeople to build fences around Indian fields at their own expense, and to construct a pound where the Indians might keep delinquent animals until proper compensation was paid. The chief exception

[43] P.C.R., XI, 65, 184.
[44] P.C.R., XI, 259.
[45] P.C.R., XI, 60–61, 66.
[46] P.C.R., VI, 113; XI, 243.
[47] P.C.R., V, 151–152, 270; VI, 108, 153.
[48] P.C.R., IV, 17.
[49] P.C.R., VI, 98.
[50] P.C.R., XI, 236.
[51] P.C.R., V, 167–168; Paine, *Harwich,* 435.

was made in the case of Rhode Island horses, which were to be seized outright.[52] In 1671 the Colony went so far as to name officers in each town to view the damage done to Indian fields, and only in the case of Indians living within an English township did the responsibility for fencing rest entirely with the natives.[53]

The same protection was accorded Indians who suffered burglary, false witness, and abuse at the hands of the English, or even those who found that their kettles had been penetrated by a hunter's stray bullet.[54] Recourse was had to intercolonial diplomacy when a Boston man failed to pay a Cape Indian for his services in catching fish.[55] The most spectacular instance of Pilgrim justice, however, was the execution of three English servants for the murder of an Indian bearing wampum. Bradford relates that "some of the rude and ignorant sort murmured" in protest, but exemplary justice was inflicted.[56]

The Plymouth authorities were not content with mere protection of the Indian against English settlers; they were no less eager to save him from the Devil. With the friendly Massasoit, surprisingly enough, the Christian Gospel found no acceptance. The Wampanoag sachem was primarily interested in the material advantages which a new religion had to offer,[57] and it would seem that he never received a satisfactory answer in this respect. Shortly before his death, Massasoit unsuccessfully attempted to write a clause against further missionary efforts into the terms of a sale of land.[58] With the Indians of Cape Cod, however, the Pilgrims had better luck. The Cape Indians, like Mayhew's charges on Martha's Vineyard, were relatively isolated from their fellow heathen, and the Cape was the scene of the earliest and most vigorous missionary activity. It appears that Richard Bourne, a wealthy merchant of Sandwich, and Captain Thomas Tupper, a Pilgrim soldier, began their work among the natives even before John Eliot's first visits to the Indians of Massachusetts Bay,[59] but Eliot himself turned his attention to the Cape as early as 1648. In that year he was sent by the United Colonies to end dissension within the English Church at Yarmouth; and Eliot did not miss the opportunity to preach to the local Indians. One deceitful sachem promised to bring his subjects to hear the Apostle's lesson and then sent them off on a fishing expedition instead. Other Indians, however, were more amenable, and Eliot was happy to learn of a vague local tradition that the natives had once known the true God but had somehow lost contact with Him in the course of time.[60]

The most intensive missionary work, on the other hand, had to await the formation of the Corporation for the Propagation of the Gospel in New Eng-

---

[52] P.C.R., III, 21, 106, 167, 192, 222. The Indians were likewise instructed to build pounds, possibly because the frontiersmen were slow to carry out the Colony's orders.

[53] P.C.R., V, 62; XI, 143.

[54] P.C.R., II, 20, 89; V, 152; VI, 24, *passim*.

[55] John A. Goodwin, *The Pilgrim Republic* (Boston, 1888), 545.

[56] Bradford, *History of Plymouth Plantation,* 432–435; John Winthrop, *History of New England* (Boston, 1853), I, 321–323.

[57] Henry Whitfield, "The Light Appearing More and More Towards the Perfect Day," 3 *Coll. Mass. Hist. Soc.,* IV, 117.

[58] Hubbard, *Narrative,* 8.

[59] Nathaniel Morton, *New England's Memorial* (Boston, 1855), 379, 382, 384.

[60] Thomas Shephard, "The Clear Sun-shine of the Gospel Breaking Forth upon the Indians in New-England," 3 *Coll. Mass. Hist. Soc.,* IV, 42–44.

land by act of Parliament in 1649.[61] It is possible that Plymouth received less than its due share of the Corporation's remittances, but Bourne and his associates obtained regular grants for the hiring of interpreters and miscellaneous expenses, while the Plymouth authorities were generally assigned a few pounds a year to distribute among "well deserving Indians."[62] Richard Bourne continued to lead the way; in 1670 he was formally ordained over the Colony's first Indian church, and to assure the permanence of his efforts, he obtained a grant of land for his converts at Mashpee. Similar reservations of "Praying Indians" were established elsewhere.[63] On the eastern side of the Cape the Reverend Samuel Treat rivalled Bourne in the number of his conversions, becoming especially popular with the natives through the visits that he made to their wigwams.[64] By the outbreak of King Philip's War, progress had even been made in the center of the Colony, in the vicinity of Middleboro; here John Sassamon, a Harvard alumnus and protégé of Eliot, was established as the first regularly settled Indian minister in New Plymouth.[65]

As a result of these combined efforts, Plymouth contained well over a thousand Indian converts in 1674; in addition, 142 of these had learned to read their own language, and nine had been taught to read English.[66] By 1685 the total was approaching 1,500. Naturally a small proportion of these Indians were fully accredited members of a Christian Church; the lists merely included "such as do, before some of their magistrates or civil rulers, renounce their former heathenish manners, and give up themselves to be Praying Indians. . . ."[67] But neither could all the English settlers be enrolled as Visible Saints. The fact remains that the Indian population of Plymouth Colony was almost as thoroughly Christianized in 1685 as the Pilgrims themselves, for there were little more than two thousand Indians living in the Colony when the English arrived,[68] and the most obstinate had meanwhile been eliminated by King Philip's War.

The extent of the missionaries' success is further shown by the fact that the natives had come to shoulder the greater part of their own spiritual guidance. From the very start, the missionaries had been assisted by Indian "teachers" and interpreters, and by 1686 a friend of the natives could complain that Indian teachers received three or four pounds a year for constant work, whereas English missionaries were paid up to £20 for preaching to the Indians only three or four times.[69] Equally significant was the loyalty of the Praying Indians to Plymouth Colony during King Philip's War.

The long years of peace with the Indians that had distinguished Plymouth

[61] George Parker Winship, editor, *The New England Company of 1649 and John Eliot* (Boston, 1920), xiv–xxii.
[62] P.C.R., X, 183, 205, 219, 246, 263, 277, 296, 317, 331, 356, 367.
[63] Plymouth Church Records 1620–1859 (*Coll. Colonial Soc. of Mass.*, XXII–XXIII), XXII, 146; Baylies, *New Plymouth*, II, 283; Gookin, *Historical Collections of the Indians in New England*, 198.
[64] "A Description and History of Eastham," 1 *Coll. Mass. Hist. Soc.*, VIII, 170, 174.
[65] Goodwin, *Pilgrim Republic*, 536–538.
[66] Gookin, *Historical Collections of the Indians in New England*, 197–198; Morton, *New England's Memorial* (1855 ed.), 390–391.
[67] The Hinckley Papers, 4 *Coll. Mass. Hist. Soc.*, V, 133–134.
[68] James Mooney, *The Aboriginal Population of North America North of Mexico* (Smithsonian Miscellaneous Collections, LXXX, no. 7, Washington, 1928), 4.
[69] *The Hinckley Papers*, 131–132.

Colony came to an abrupt end in the reign of Philip, the third Wampanoag
sachem known to the Plymouth settlers. In view of the generally fair treatment
which had been accorded to the Plymouth Indians, it is surprising that an Indian war should begin in New Plymouth; and it is more so that the Indians
should attribute the entire guilt to the Pilgrim Fathers. Yet Philip himself did
not hesitate to remind the people of Massachusetts Bay that they were shedding
the blood of their sons merely to pull Plymouth chestnuts out of the fire.[70]
Moreover, the bitter controversy between Philip and Plymouth Colony has given
rise to a strong tradition that pictures Philip as a veritable Indian statesman
who saw the impending doom of his race at the hands of his grasping neighbors
and staked the redress of countless legitimate grievances on a carefully laid
conspiracy against English rule in New England. If the war was well planned,
however, the evidence does not seem to support it. Philip appears to have begun
the struggle with a wholly inadequate store of arms, and despite both threats
and entreaties many of his immediate neighbors had not yet decided which side
to support when war broke out.[71]

Philip's unpreparedness can probably be explained by the hypothesis that
he had only begun his scheming when his hand was forced by premature revela-
tion of the plot. The necessity for his supreme effort is less easily established.
Philip laid greatest stress on the unfair absorption of the Indians' "planting
lands," both by unjust arbitration of land disputes and by such practices as
getting an Indian drunk in order to purchase his lands for a fraction of their
worth,[72] but the general land policy of Plymouth Colony would suggest that he
can have had no very serious grievances in this respect. In particular there is
no specific mention in Plymouth records or in contemporary narratives of major
land disputes with Philip; and though the English settlers would hardly leave a
fair statement of Philip's complaints, one could at least expect a passing reference. Likewise it has never been shown that the Wampanoags lacked sufficient
farm land; by the time of Philip's War, in fact, they could get along with much
less than before, thanks to new methods learned from the English. Nor could
the reduction of their hunting lands have disastrous effects for a primarily agricultural people. Philip further complained of the damages done to Indian corn
by English cattle and of the sale of liquor to the natives.[73] In both cases, however, the Plymouth government was quite as anxious as he was to correct the
abuse. The frontier settlements found some difficulty in enforcing the Colony's
orders, yet probably neither abuse was so serious as to explain a recourse to
arms.

Thus it is not impossible that Palfrey was right in regarding the war as a
wholly wanton and even irrational attack by the Indians upon Plymouth Colony; such an hypothesis is indirectly supported by the legends that Philip
himself opposed war but that his policy was influenced by young braves chafing
under an unwelcome peace.[74] A wild venture of this sort would naturally be

[70] John Gorham Palfrey, *History of New England During the Stuart Dynasty*
(Boston, 1876), III, 188, note 2; Goodwin, *Pilgrim Republic*, 551.

[71] Church, *Entertaining Passages*, 5–14; Thomas Hutchinson, *History of Massachusetts* (Salem, 1795), I, 267.

[72] Easton, *Narratives of the Indian Wars*, 9–11.

[73] Easton, *Narratives of the Indian Wars*, 10–11.

[74] Palfrey, *New England*, III, 222–229; John Callendar, *An Historical Discourse
on . . . Rhode Island* (Providence, 1838), 126–128.

encouraged by the various petty irritations which arose along the frontier, and for which both Englishmen and Indians were to blame. In fairness to Philip, however, it must be said that the trampling of cornfields and the sale of liquor were not the only irritations. There were also political grievances that the sachem for some reason failed to emphasize. It has already been seen that the Indians' normal acceptance of Plymouth authority became increasingly real as the English settlements were consolidated; and even though one cannot unreservedly state the rights and wrongs of the matter, it appears that the Plymouth authorities tended to be somewhat tactless in their dealings with the later Wampanoag rulers.

Only once was there any serious doubt of the loyalty of Massasoit; it was cast by Squanto, and the white man's good friend nearly lost his life when his falseness was discovered. In return for the chief's friendship the English more than once came to his support against Indian rivals.[75] On the accession of Massasoit's son Alexander in 1662, however, rumors of treachery at once began to gain credence, and the sachem was ordered to come to Plymouth to explain his conduct. After a probably justifiable delay he appeared at the Pilgrim capital, satisfied the authorities of his loyalty, and was immediately dismissed. Despite the romantic tale that Alexander died of chagrin soon afterwards, there is no real evidence that he was mistreated by the English settlers during this episode.[76] Yet no sooner had he been succeeded by his younger brother than exactly the same process was repeated with Philip. Again it seems that there was no basis for Plymouth's suspicions, and the incident was closed with a renewal of the treaty between the English and the Wampanoags. New suspicions arose in 1667. Once more the authorities recognized in the end that they possessed no concrete evidence and let the matter drop, although they compelled Philip to pay the cost of the proceedings.[77] Nevertheless relations with Philip were, on the whole, friendly during the first part of his rule. On one occasion, he apparently vowed to suspend land sales for a seven-year period, but the exact circumstances of this decision are by no means clear.[78] He did not keep his pledge, and it is probable that his need for English money to live in royal state was as much responsible for his change of heart as pressure from the Plymouth authorities.

In 1671, however, more serious trouble occurred. The usual rumors had arisen, in part because of a murder near Boston in which Philip was rumored to have had a hand;[79] but it is quite possible that the English had more important grounds for their suspicions, since they viewed the matter in a much more serious light than any of the preceding "conspiracies." Philip ultimately agreed to meet Plymouth envoys at Taunton on April 10, provided a Massachusetts delegation went along to ensure fair play, but far from showing remorse over his recent activities, he countered by accusing Plymouth of certain unspecified injuries to his "planting land." According to the colonists, it was then

[75] P.C.R., IX, 15; Frank G. Speck, *Territorial Subdivisions and Boundaries of the Wampanoag, Massachusetts, and Nauset Indians* (*Indian Notes and Monographs*, no. 44, New York, 1928), 33–35.
[76] Drake, *Old Indian Chronicle*, 32–42; Hubbard, *Narrative*, 9–10; Goodwin, *Pilgrim Republic*, 542–543.
[77] P.C.R., IV, 25–26, 151, 164–166.
[78] Drake, *Aboriginal Races*, 198–199.
[79] Drake, *Old Indian Chronicle*, 65–66.

shown that his charges were absurd, whereupon Philip admitted his military preparations but claimed they were directed against the Narragansetts. This, too, is said to have been disproved, and Philip finally admitted that he had been conspiring against the English "from his own naughty heart." He reaffirmed his allegiance to the English crown and to New Plymouth, and agreed to deposit his arms as security for future good behavior.[80]

Peace now seemed to have returned, and at this juncture the Praying Indians of Cape Cod came loyally to the government's support with a spate of treaties couched in the most picturesque phrases:

> . . . forasmuch as the English, and wee, the poor Indians, are as of one blood, as Acts 17th, 26, for wee doe confess wee poor Indians in our lives were as captives under Sathan, and our sachems, doeing theire wills whose breath perisheth, as Psalmes 146, 3, 4; Exodus 15, 1, 2, &c; but now wee know by the word of God, that it is better to trust in the great God and his strength. Psalm 118, 8, 9; and besides, wee were like unto wolves and lyons, to destroy one another; but wee hope and believe in God; therefore wee desire to enter into covenant with the English respecting our fidelitie, as Isai: 11, 6. . . .[81]

Not all Indians, however, showed this humility. Since the alarm had been general, Plymouth also attempted to disarm many of Philip's friends and subjects, and in this endeavor the authorities met with some resistance. Awashunks of Saconet, for instance, was bullied into accepting the English demands, but she could induce only forty-two of her subjects—not including her two sons—to obey the order for surrender of arms.[82] Nor was this truly surprising, since even a largely sedentary people such as the Indians of Plymouth Colony still derived at least part of their livelihood from hunting, and it would seem that the bow and arrow had long gone out of fashion. Philip himself, moreover, bluntly refused to meet the full demands of the colonial government. He insisted, probably with some justification, that the treaty of Taunton referred only to arms that he and his men had left outside when they entered to confer with the English, and he refused to hand over any more. Moreover, he appealed to the government of Massachusetts Bay which strangely informed Plymouth that the Taunton agreements did not make Philip a subject of the Colony, but merely a friend. Nevertheless Philip was finally brought to terms in much the same manner as before. A general conference was arranged, although this time Connecticut, too, sent a delegation; a full confession was obtained; and Philip agreed to pay a fine of £100 and to kill a yearly quota of five wolves in payment for the trouble he had caused.[83]

The fine which was thus levied against Philip was clearly unreasonable, even for an Indian chief; indeed it may well be connected with the fact that one year later Philip was compelled to mortgage a small tract of land in view of his inability to pay certain monies that he owed to the Colony.[84] This time, however, peace really did return to New Plymouth, and it lasted until early in 1675. The

[80] P.C.R., V, 63; Drake, *Old Indian Chronicle,* 64–72; Hubbard, *Narrative,* 11–12.
[81] P.C.R., V, 66–67.
[82] P.C.R., V, Drake, *Old Indian Chronicle,* 74–75, 81–82.
[83] P.C.R., V, 76–79.
[84] P.C.R., V, 101.

English chroniclers, to be sure, were convinced that Philip began plotting a general war immediately after the humiliation at Taunton, but conditions were outwardly so calm that the embargo on giving arms and ammunition to the Indians was partially lifted in 1674.[85] Then in February of the following year new reports of Philip's impending treachery were carried to Plymouth by John Sassamon, the Indian preacher at Middleboro. Following the traditional procedure, Philip came to Court, but no conclusive evidence was found against him, and he was allowed to return home with a mere admonition.[86] Yet the problem was not so easily solved, for, a week after his own visit to Plymouth, Sassamon had been found dead beneath the ice of Assowamsett Pond. There were at once some suspicions of foul play, and later in the spring of 1675 "by a strange Providence, an Indian was found, that by Accident was standing unseen upon a Hill [and had seen three of Philip's men] murder the said Sassamon."[87]

The tardy appearance of such a witness seems somewhat suspicious, and the Indians had a story that the informer was merely trying to avoid payment of a gambling debt by having his creditors executed for murder. Still another version implied that Sassamon was murdered because of his missionary activities.[88] On the other hand, it is not impossible that the Indian was telling the truth. There is nothing inherently implausible in the explanation that he had refained from doing his duty sooner for fear that the same thing would happen to him that had happened to Sassamon, and that the truth was finally divulged when he shared his knowledge with a Praying Indian.[89] Be that as it may, the three Indian culprits were haled before Plymouth Court, tried by a jury to which certain of the "most indifferent, gravest, and sage Indians" had been added, and duly executed.[90]

Nothing was done, however, about Philip himself, for Plymouth showed a laudable dislike of proceeding on mere suspicion. Plymouth hoped that as soon as the Wampanoag sachem observed that no action was intended against him for lack of evidence he would desist from his warlike intentions; around the middle of June a conciliatory message was sent off in which he was merely requested to disband his forces.[91] But, unfortunately, the authorities were too optimistic. Whether Sassamon had been correct in February or not, by June there was no doubt that Philip was engaged in a general conspiracy. The hostile nature of his activities was amply confirmed by so trustworthy a witness as Benjamin Church, who obtained his information directly from meetings with his good friend Awashunks and with other Indians, including the very envoys sent out by Philip to win support for his cause.[92] After the middle of the month, border incidents became frequent, and after an English settler had been goaded into firing the first shot, the Indians launched their war with the Swanzey massacre of June 24.[93]

[85] Hubbard, *Narrative*, 13; P.C.R., XI, 237.
[86] P.C.R., X, 362–363.
[87] Hubbard, *Narrative*, 15; Increase Mather, *History of King Philip's War* (Boston, 1862), 47–48.
[88] Easton, *Narratives of the Indian Wars*, 7–8; "The Present State of New England with Respect to the Indian War," in Drake, *Old Indian Chronicle*, 122.
[89] Hubbard, *Narrative*, 15; Increase Mather, *King Philip's War*, 47–48.
[90] P.C.R., V, 167–168; Drake, *Old Indian Chronicle*, 96.
[91] P.C.R., X, 363–364; Hubbard, *Narrative*, 16–17.
[92] Church, *Entertaining Passages*, 5–14.
[93] "The Present State of New England," in Drake, *Old Indian Chronicle*, 123–127.

The military history of King Philip's War is too well known to require retelling, and the most important engagements took place outside Plymouth Colony. The struggle, nevertheless, had a profound effect upon the condition of Plymouth's Indian inhabitants. The Praying Indians, to begin with, were subjected to considerable suspicion despite their unwavering loyalty to the English. This distrust was unfounded, but it is easily understandable in view of the aroused feeling of the English settlers and the common report that an Indian's chief delight was to "rob, kill and roast, lead captive, slay . . . blaspheme.[94]" It was some time before the Pilgrims could realize that such things were not going to happen on Cape Cod; and hence it was only in the face of a rapidly deteriorating military situation that the Colony finally agreed to a general enlistment of loyal Indians.[95] But such slights as this were nothing compared with the lot of the hostile Indian. An indeterminate number perished as casualties of war or fled from the Colony never to return; a relatively small number, including Church's friends from Saconet, were permitted to make a timely submission and resettle in Plymouth Colony on much the same terms as before. The rest of Philip's followers, however, were classed as prisoners of war and formally enslaved. It would seem that many Indians who had been encouraged to surrender in the hope of kinder treatment met exactly the same fate.[96]

The General Court of November, 1676, determined that all adult male captives must be sold out of the Colony,[97] but the rule did not apply in every case. Ringleaders of the revolt and any Indians who had taken part in major atrocities were summarily tried and executed; nor did the authorities spare certain war criminals who had been given quarter by Captain Church, for his commission did not authorize an indiscriminate show of mercy.[98] Likewise Philip's young son, though scarcely an adult male Indian, was condemned to be sold as a slave to Bermuda; but this might almost be termed an act of generosity, since several Plymouth clergymen, citing Scriptural precedents, had advised that he be put to death for the future security of the state.[99] Women and children, on the other hand, were allowed to remain in the Colony, where they were employed as domestic servants or perhaps taught some useful craft. Indeed, a few male prisoners were similarly favored; Captain Church, for instance, was allowed to retain some of his own captives on the interesting condition that they should perform military service under his command if need arose.[100]

Although the fate of the hostile Indians thus varied rather widely, they were all eliminated as an independent factor in the life of Plymouth Colony. The problem of Indian relations, therefore, was decidedly eased in many respects. Military preparedness could be comfortably forgotten as far as any in-

[94] From "Upon the Elaborate Survey," by B. H. in Hubbard, *Narrative;* no page number in original, page 24 in Drake edition (Roxbury, 1865).
[95] P.C.R., V, 186–187; Church, *Entertaining Passages,* 67–69. It is not true, however, that Plymouth used no Indian troops until the spring of 1676; acting apparently on his own authority, Church had made use of them at the very start of the war.
[96] P.C.R., V, 173–174, 210, 215; Church, *Entertaining Passages,* 45–47, 79–92; Easton, *Narratives of the Indian Wars,* 13.
[97] P.C.R., XI, 242.
[98] P.C.R., V, 204–206; Hubbard, *Narrative,* 98, 109; Church, *Entertaining Passages,* 100, 101, 178–179.
[99] Baylies, *New Plymouth,* III, 190–191.
[100] P.C.R., V, 207, 225; MacFarlane, *Indian Relations,* 631.

ternal danger was concerned. Similarly the land question was greatly simplified by the confiscation of rebel lands, and, in fact, one group of loyal Indians was asked to accommodate a few English settlers on their lands in payment for the Colony's services in defending them against King Philip.[101] The decline of the pagan population, moreover, brought the first phase of missionary activity to its close.

The elimination of the stronger sachems, however, finally compelled the Colony to devise a regular system of Indian government. This was done by a law of July, 1682, which ordered that every ten adult Indians should unite to elect one of their numbers as a "tithingman" for the general supervision of their affairs. All the Indian "tithingmen" of a given township, in turn, were to gather together to hold courts among the natives, to name Indian constables, and to assess the Indians' taxes. In these functions they were to be assisted by a specially appointed English overseer, who was instructed to collect his charges and once each year read aloud the laws of Plymouth Colony.[102]

Otherwise there was no major change in the treatment of the Indians; they were about as well cared for in Plymouth courts as before, and they continued to be protected against guns and liquor. Instead it was the Indians who had changed, for Plymouth was now truly a Christian commonwealth, and in the fight for survival the lowly Praying Indians had shown themselves fitter than King Philip. Their descendants, in fact, are still living in the Old Colony today. They are, of course, much fewer in number, but this results in part from a natural process of race mixture. In any case, it would be unfair to blame the Pilgrim Fathers for the extinction of the Indian population. The most that can be said against them is that they introduced a new system of diseases and of society to which the Indians could not fully adjust themselves for several generations. Certainly the battle casualties of the Wampanoags cannot be blamed solely upon the English. It is true that the Pilgrims generally treated the natives as a race apart, but there is no evidence that, on the whole, they dealt more harshly with the Indians than with one another.

[101] P.C.R., V, 224–225; VI, 63; X, 407–408.
[102] P.C.R., XI, 252–253.

Blacks

STANLEY M. ELKINS
The Dynamics of Unopposed Capitalism

*A number of American historians have explored the origins of slavery in the
British colonies and, not surprisingly, have failed to reach a unanimous ver-
dict. Oscar and Mary Handlin, in their essay "Origins of the Southern Labor
System" (William and Mary Quarterly,* Third Series, VII, April, 1950, 199–
222), *concluded that there was essentially little difference between the treatment of black and white servants in the South between the time the first boat-
load of Africans landed at Jamestown in 1619 and the enactment of the Navigation Acts (which regulated trade between Great Britain and her colonies) in
the 1660s. Only after tobacco cultivation had expanded, and unit costs of production had to be lowered for increased profitability, did slavery emerge as
a clearly defined institution and then, primarily, because the blacks provided
the "cheapest, most available, most exploitable labor supply." Carl Degler* (Out
of Our Past, *New York: Harper & Row, 1959), on the other hand, argued that
"discrimination preceded slavery and thereby conditioned it," by showing examples of differential treatment between black and white servants during the
forty-year period, 1619 through 1660. He concluded that slavery was in vogue
earlier than the Handlins suggested. In the most recent historical analysis of
blacks in colonial America,* White Over Black *(Chapel Hill: University of
North Carolina Press, 1968), Winthrop D. Jordan takes a midway approach.
He acknowledges the existence of slavery before 1660 but refuses to generalize
about the conditions of the blacks in the colonies before that time. Jordan
points out that too little is known about colonial policies between 1620 and
1640 to make any intelligent evaluation; that between 1640 and 1660 slavery
existed but available evidence is too scanty to suggest its extent; and that only
after 1660 did the institution crystallize.*

*The reasons for the varieties of opinion are easy to fathom. Relatively few
social records of the times are available; the status of the slave was not clearly
spelled out in colonial statutes until after 1660; and there were too few African
servants to warrant significant attention. Perhaps 2 percent, or about 300, of
Virginia's 15,000 people in 1649 were black; in 1671 the Governor estimated
5 percent. These figures contrast sharply with the totals of 24 percent in 1715
and 40 percent in 1756.*

In the article below Stanley Elkins, whose book Slavery *provides one of the
most provocative and original analyses of the subject, gives his explanation of
the development of slavery after the 1660s.*

Reprinted from *Slavery* by Stanley M. Elkins by permission of The University
of Chicago Press and the author. © 1959 by the University of Chicago.

How had Negro slavery in the United States come into being? There was nothing "natural" about it; it had no necessary connection with either tropical climate or tropical crops: in Virginia and Maryland, where the institution first appeared and flourished, the climate was hardly tropical, and the staple crop— tobacco—might have been grown as far north as Canada. It had nothing to do with characteristics which might have made the Negro peculiarly suited either to slavery or to the labor of tobacco culture. Slavery in past ages had been limited to no particular race, and the earliest planters of colonial Virginia appear to have preferred a laboring force of white servants from England, Scotland, and Ireland, rather than of blacks from Africa. Nor was it a matter of common-law precedent, for the British colonists who settled the areas eventually to be included in the United States brought with them no legal categories comparable to that of "slave," as the term would be understood by the end of the seventeenth century. "Slavery," considered in the abstract as servile bondage, had existed elsewhere for centuries; indeed, the natives of Africa had known it intimately. Yet nothing was inherent, even in the fact of *Negro* slavery, which should compel it to take the form that it took in North America. Negro slavery flourished in Latin America at that same period, but there the system was strikingly different. In certain altogether crucial respects slavery as we know it was not imported from elsewhere but was created in America— fashioned on the spot by Englishmen in whose traditions such an institution had no part. American slavery was unique, in the sense that, for symmetry and precision of outline, nothing like it had ever previously been seen.

An important essay by Oscar and Mary Handlin has focused new attention upon these facts.[1] Although the first shipload of twenty Negroes had arrived in Virginia in 1619, it was not until the 1660's that the key item in the definition of their status—term of servitude—was clearly fixed in law. It was apparently possible for the earliest Negroes to fall into the various servant categories long familiar to the common law of England, none of which in a practical sense included perpetual and inherited chattel bondage.[2] The bulk of agricultural laborers coming into the colonies at this period were white servants whose terms, as time went on, were to become more and more definitely fixed by indenture, and the Negroes, so far as the law was concerned, could be regarded as "servants" like the rest; there was no articulated legal structure in the colonies to impede their becoming free after a term of service and entering society as artisans and holders of property. Indeed, it was still assumed that the profession of Christianity should itself make a difference in status.[3] Manumis-

[1] See Oscar and Mary F. Handlin, "Origins of the Southern Labor System," *William and Mary Quarterly,* 3d Series, VII (April, 1950), 199–222.
[2] The state of villeinage, which had once flourished in England during the Middle Ages, had many of the attributes which later characterized plantation slavery. Yet one crucial aspect of slavery—the legal suppression of the personality—was never present in villeinage. The status of villein, moreover, had by the seventeenth century become virtually extinct in England.
[3] This assumption, having its roots in tradition, was still persistent enough throughout most of the seventeenth century that, as late as the 1690's, colonial assemblies felt the necessity to declare, in legal enactments, that baptism did not confer on the slave the right to be manumitted. See John Codman Hurd, *The Law of Freedom and Bondage in the United States* (Boston: Little, Brown, 1858), I, 232, 250, 297, 300–301.

sion, moreover, for whatever reason, was a practice common enough to be taken for granted and was attended by no special legal restrictions.[4]

Yet all this began changing drastically with the 1660's. The very need for new colonists to people the country, and the very preference of planters for English-speaking whites rather than African savages as laborers, had already set into motion a trend to define in law the rights of white servants. To encourage the immigration of such servants and to counteract homeward-drifting rumors of indefinite servitude under desperate conditions, it was becoming more and more the practice to fix definite and limited terms of indenture—five or six years—as a guaranty that a clear future awaited the white man who would cast his lot with the colonies. The Negro, as the Handlins put it, "never profited from these enactments. Farthest removed from the English, least desired, he communicated with no friends who might be deterred from following. Since his coming was involuntary, nothing that happened to him would increase or decrease his numbers."[5] In short, every improvement in the status of the white servant, in widening the gulf between his condition and that of the Negro, served to dramatize the deepening significance of color and in effect to depress the black ever closer to a state of perpetual slavery. This tendency was ultimately recognized by the legislatures of Maryland and Virginia, and they were led to embody in law

[4] The implications of the Handlin thesis are sufficient for the limited purposes for which it is being used here. To the extent that the Handlins appear to argue that an indentured status was automatically assumed in this period, in the absence of automatic legal guaranties of slavery, to that extent is their essay quite misleading. Insofar as they point, on the other hand, to a condition legally indeterminate—with practice still sufficiently blurred as to allow a number of exceptions, unthinkable a generation later, to automatic slavery—they do no violence to what is known about the period.

This very indeterminancy has sustained a minor debate going back more than fifty years. James C. Ballagh in 1902 first challenged the accepted notion that slavery in Virginia dated from 1619. The parcel of twenty Negroes sold in that year to the Virginians from a Dutch ship were not held as slaves, Ballagh insisted, but rather as servants, and Virginia law did not recognize out-and-out slavery until more than forty years later. John H. Russell, writing in 1913, accepted Ballagh's position. While admitting that lifetime servitude in Virginia existed long before it was given statutory recognition, he agreed that without a prior system of slavery or a slave code it was "plausible that the Africans became servants who, after a term of service varying from two to eight years, were entitled to freedom." Russell cited examples of Negroes who sued for their freedom or who became independent landowners. The Ballagh-Russell thesis—accepted by Ulrich Phillips—was not questioned until Susie Ames's *Studies of the Virginia Eastern Shore* appeared in 1940. Miss Ames held that there was not enough evidence to support Ballagh and Russell, and that Russell's examples may simply have been of manumitted slaves (in other words, if Negroes were not automatically considered as indentured servants—which she thought doubtful—then they must have been automatically considered as slaves: it had to be one thing or the other). Wesley Frank Craven in 1949 gave further support to Miss Ames's position; in his opinion it was likely that "the trend from the first was toward a sharp distinction between . . . [the Negro] and the white servant." The Handlins, taking issue with Miss Ames, in effect brought the argument back to Ballagh and Russell—not asserting flatly (for Miss Ames and Mr. Craven were at least right about the scarcity of evidence) but calling it "much more logical to assume with Russell that these were servants who had completed their terms." And there the argument rests. See James C. Ballagh, *History of Slavery in Virginia* (Baltimore: Johns Hopkins, 1902), pp. 9–10, 27–31; John H. Russell, *The Free Negro in Virginia, 1619–1865* (Baltimore: Johns Hopkins, 1913), pp. 23–31; Ulrich B. Phillips, *American Negro Slavery* (New York: D. Appleton & Co., 1918), p. 75; Susie M. Ames, *Studies of the Virginia Eastern Shore in the Seventeenth Century* (Richmond, Va.: Dietz, 1940), pp. 100–106; Wesley Frank Craven, *The Southern Colonies in the Seventeenth Century, 1607–1689* (Baton Rouge: Louisiana State University, 1949), pp. 218–19. See also n. 7 below.

[5] Handlin and Handlin, "Origins of the Southern Labor System," p. 211.

what had already become fact. "All negroes or other slaves within the province [according to a Maryland law of 1663], and all negroes and other slaves to be hereafter imported into the province, shall serve *durante vita;* and all children born of any negro or other slave, shall be slaves as their fathers were for the term of their lives."[6] Such was the first legal step whereby a black skin would itself ultimately be equatable with "slave."

Now there is not much doubt that in actual practice the Negro in Virginia and Maryland had become a slave long before this time. There were precedents in English colonial practice—if not quite in law—that might have been drawn from Barbados any time after the 1630's.[7] In all likelihood the delay in defining Negro status may be ascribed to the fact that their numbers prior to the 1660's were never very great and hardly warranted special legislation.[8] But there is much significance simply in the fact that a state of legal indeterminacy existed for some forty years. During that period there are just enough examples of Negro suits for freedom, Negro ownership of property (with the legal incidents thereof), and so on, to convince one that even so small a margin between automatic lifetime slavery and something else made all the difference—considering what plantation slavery, both in law and in fact, would be a generation later.[9] It meant a precious margin of space, not to be discounted, for the conservation of traditional human rights. However, once the initial step had been taken, and once Negroes began arriving in appreciable numbers—as they did in the years following the Restoration—there was, as it turned out, little to impede the restless inclination of the law to remove ambiguities. A further course of legislation in the colonies—to which by then had been added the Carolinas—was inaugurated in the period roughly centering upon the turn of the seventeenth century; this

[6] Quoted in Hurd, *Law of Freedom and Bondage,* I, 249. A Virginia act of the year before had assumed and implied lifetime slavery. It provided special punishments for servants who ran away in the company of "negroes who are incapable of making satisfaction by addition of a time." Helen T. Catterall, *Judicial Cases concerning American Slavery and the Negro* (Washington: Carnegie Institution, 1926 ff.), I, 59. The matter was made explicit when in 1670 it was enacted that "all servants not being Christians, imported into this colony by shipping, shall be slaves for their lives. . . ." Hurd, *Law of Freedom and Bondage,* I, 233.

[7] It should be noted that the Handlins do rule out rather too hastily the possibility of the Virginians' adapting the status of slavery from the West Indies, claiming as they do that Negroes there were still regarded as "servants" as late as 1663. Their assertion is not entirely correct. There were, indeed, few Negroes in the West Indies prior to the 1630's, and there was no slave code there until 1663. But by 1636, Negroes were already coming into Barbados in great enough numbers that the governor's council felt it necessary in that year, law or no law, to issue a regulation declaring that all Negroes or Indians landed on the island would be considered as slaves, bound to work there for the rest of their lives. See Sir Harry Johnston, *The Negro in the New World* (London: Methuen & Co., 1910), p. 211; Vincent Harlow, *A History of Barbados* (Oxford: Clarendon, 1926), pp. 309–10. Even in the Spanish colonies, lifetime servitude had been familiar for nearly a century.

Some kind of statutory recognition of slavery in the American colonies occurred as follows: Massachusetts, 1641; Connecticut, 1650; Virginia, 1661; Maryland, 1663; New York and New Jersey, 1664; South Carolina, 1684; and Rhode Island, 1700. The apparent significance of this chronology diminishes, however, when it is noted that although enactments in the Northern colonies recognized the legality of lifetime servitude, no effort was made to require all Negroes to be placed in that condition. The number of Negroes, moreover, was so small that in Massachusetts it was not until 1698 that any effort was made to consider the important problem of slave children's status. See Ballagh, *Slavery in Virginia,* pp. 35, 39.

[8] See n. 14 below.

[9] Russell, *Free Negro in Virginia,* pp. 24–39.

legislation began suppressing, with a certain methodical insistence, whatever rights of personality still remained to the Negro slave. It was thus that most of the features marking the system of American slavery, as the nineteenth century knew it, had been stamped upon it by about the middle of the eighteenth.

Yet before reviewing in greater detail the legal aspects of this servitude, we should note that the most vital facts about its inception remain quite unaccounted for. The reasons for its delay have been satisfactorily explained—but why did it occur at all? Why should the drive to establish such a status have got under way when it did? What was the force behind it, especially in view of the prior absence of any sort of laws defining slavery? We may on the one hand point out the lack of any legal structure automatically compelling the Negro to become a slave, but it is only fair, on the other, to note that there was equally little in the form of such a structure to prevent him from becoming one. It is not enough to indicate the simple process whereby the interests of white servants and black were systematically driven apart: what was its dynamic? Why should the status of "slave" have been elaborated, in little more than two generations following its initial definition, with such utter logic and completeness to make American slavery unique among all such systems known to civilization?[10]

Was it the "motive of gain"? Yes, but with a difference. The motive of gain, as a psychic "fact," can tell us little about what makes men behave as they do; the medieval peasant himself, with his virtually marketless economy, was hardly free from it. But in the emergent agricultural capitalism of colonial Virginia we may already make out a mode of economic organization which was taking on a purity of form never yet seen, and the difference lay in the fact that here a growing system of large-scale staple production for profit was free to develop in a society where no prior traditional institutions, with competing claims of their own, might interpose at any of a dozen points with sufficient power to retard or modify its progress. What happens when such energy meets no limits?[11]

Here, even in its embryonic stages, it is possible to see the process whereby capitalism would emerge as the principal dynamic force in American society. The New World had been discovered and exploited by a European civilization which had always, in contrast with other world cultures, placed a particularly

[10] The common-law tradition actually worked in more than one direction to help perfect the legal arrangements of slavery. Not only was there little in the common law, simply as law, to prevent the Negro from being compelled into a state of slavery, but the very philosophy of the common law would encourage the colonial courts to develop whatever laws appeared necessary to deal with unprecedented conditions.

[11] Ever since the time of Marx and Engels (and indeed, before), the idea of "Capitalism" has been a standard tool in the analysis of social behavior. Up to a point this tool is useful; it can throw light on changes in behavior patterns at the point where capitalistic methods and habits in a society begin to supersede feudal ones. In Europe it made some sense. Here is how Engels argued: "According to this conception," he wrote in *Anti-Dühring,* "the ultimate causes of all social changes and political revolutions are to be sought, not in the minds of men, in their increasing insight into eternal truth and justice, but in changes in the mode of production and exchange; they are to be sought not in the *philosophy* but in the *economics* of the epoch concerned." But then this idea cannot tell us much about the differences between two societies, *both* capitalist, but in one of which the "means of production" have changed into capitalistic ones and in the other of which the means of production were never anything *but* capitalistic and in which no other forces were present to resist their development.

high premium on personal achievement, and it was to be the special genius of Englishmen, from Elizabeth's time onward, to transform this career concept from its earlier chivalric form into one of economic fulfilment—from "glory" to "success." Virginia was settled during the very key period in which the English middle class forcibly reduced, by revolution, the power of those standing institutions—the church and the crown—which most directly symbolized society's traditional limitations upon personal success and mobility. What the return of the crown betokened in 1660 was not so much "reaction" as the fact that all society had by then somehow made terms with the Puritan Revolution. Virginia had proven a uniquely appropriate theater for the acting-out of this narrower, essentially modern ideal of personal, of *economic,* success. Land in the early days was cheap and plentiful; a ready market for tobacco existed; even the yeoman farmer could rise rapidly if he could make the transition to staple production; and above all there was a quick recognition of accomplishment, by a standard which was not available in England but which was the only one available in Virginia: success in creating a plantation.[12]

The decade of the 1660's, inaugurated by the restoration of the Stuart monarchy, marked something of a turning point in the fortunes of the colony not unrelated to the movement there and in Maryland to fix irrevocably upon the Negro a lifetime of slavery. It was during this decade that certain factors bearing upon the colony's economic future were precipitated. One such factor was a serious drop in tobacco prices, brought on not only by overproduction but also by the Navigation Acts of 1660 and 1661,[13] and the market was not to be fully restored for another twenty years. This meant, with rising costs and a disappearing margin of profit, that commercial production on a small-scale basis was placed under serious disabilities. Another factor was the rise in the slave population. Whereas there had been only about 300 in 1650, by 1670 there were, according to Governor Berkeley, 2,000 slaves in a servant population of 8,000. This was already 25 percent of the servants, and the figure was even more significant for the future, since the total white servant population in any given period could never be counted on to exceed their average

[12] Despite the relative mobility of English society since Tudor times, personal achievement and status still inhered in any number of preferable alternatives to trade and production. But the openness of Virginia lay in the fact that purely capitalistic incentives were being used to get people to come there. No nobles, with their retinues of peasants, migrated to the colony; indeed, there was little reason why the ideal of "making good" should in itself hold many attractions for an aristocracy already established. But for others there were rewards for risk-taking which were simply not available in England. True, Virginia did develop its own aristocracy, but it had to be a created one, based on terms peculiar to the new country, and—at least as a basis for aspirations—theoretically open to everyone. At any rate, the standards for joining it were not primarily chivalric: to be a "gentleman" one must first have been a successful planter.

[13] These acts embodied the Puritan mercantilist policy which Cromwell had never been able to enforce but which had been taken over by the Restoration government. Their general purpose was that of redirecting colonial trade (much of which had been engrossed by the Dutch during the Civil War) through the hands of English merchants. Their immediate effects on tobacco, before the market could readjust itself, was, from the viewpoint of colonial planters, most unfavorable. By limiting the sale of Virginia tobacco to England and requiring that it be transported in English ships, the Navigation Acts cut off Virginia's profitable trade with the Dutch and temporarily crippled its profitable foreign markets. This, according to Thomas J. Wertenbaker, was the basic cause for the serious drop in tobacco prices. See *Planters of Colonial Virginia* (Princeton: Princeton University Press, 1922), pp. 85–87, 90.

annual immigration multiplied by five or six (the usual term in years, of their
indenture), while the increase of slaves over the same period would be cumu-
lative.[14] Such a development would by now be quite enough to stimulate the
leaders of the colony—virtually all planters—to clarify in law once and for all
the status of lifetime Negro servitude. The formation in 1662 of a Royal Company of Adventurers for the importation of Negroes symbolized the crown's
expectation that a labor force of slaves would be the coming thing in the colonies.[15]

It was thus in a period of relatively hard times that it became clear, if the
colony of Virginia were to prosper, that capitalism would be the dynamic force
in its economic life. "Success" could no longer be visualized as a rise from small
beginnings, as it once could, but must now be conceived as a matter of substantial initial investments in land, equipment, and labor, plus the ability to
undertake large annual commitments on credit. With the fall in tobacco prices,
and with the tiny margin of profit that remained, the yeoman farmer found it
difficult enough to eke out a bare living, let alone think of competing with the
large planter or of purchasing slaves' or servants' indentures.[16] Success was still

[14] "40,000 persons, men, women, and children, of which 2,000 are black slaves,
6,000 Christian servants for a short time. Gov. Berkeley." Evarts B. Greene and Virginia D. Harrington, *American Population before the Federal Census of 1790* (New
York: Columbia University Press, 1932), p. 36. This figure may be looked at two
ways. From the standpoint of *later* populations, one may call attention to its small-
ness. But consider how it must have appeared to the man looking back to a time only
two decades before, when the number of Negroes was negligible. Now, in 1670, with
Negroes constituting a full quarter of the servant population (a proportion which gave
every promise of increasing), they become a force to be dealt with. By now, men
would take them into account as a basis for future calculations in a way which previously they had never needed to do. The very laws demonstrate this. Moreover, Negroes had accumulated in large enough parcels in the hands of the colony's most powerful men to develop in these men deep vested interests in the Negroes' presence and
a strong concern with the legal aspects of their future. Among the land patents of the
sixties, for example, may already be seen Richard Lee with eighty Negroes, Carter of
Corotoman with twenty, the Scarboroughs with thirty-nine, and numerous patents listing fifteen or more. Philip Alexander Bruce, *Economic History of Virginia in the
Seventeenth Century* (New York: Macmillan, 1907), II, 78.
[15] The subsequent increase of slaves in Virginia was not largely the work of this
company. But its formation under royal protection, coming at the time it did, appears
to form part of a general pattern of expectations regarding the future state of labor
in the plantation colonies. This, taken together with the drop in tobacco prices and
coincident with the Navigation Acts and the first general laws on perpetual servitude,
all coming at once, seem to add up to something: profitable enterprise, when possible
at all, would henceforth as never before have to be conceived in terms of heavily capitalized investment, and more and more men were recognizing this.
[16] This had not always been so; the aspirations of a farmer in, say, 1649, with
prices at 3 pence a pound, could include a wide range of possibilities. But now, with
the price at one-fourth of that figure and costs proportionately much greater than formerly, he could hardly think of the future realistically in terms of becoming a planter.
See Lewis Cecil Gray, *History of Agriculture in the Southern States to 1860* (Washington: Carnegie Institution, 1933), I, 263. Now this does not mean that after 1660
the yeoman farmer invariably faced destitution. A great deal depended on how such
a farmer conceived his future. The man who made his living from diversified subsistence farming and who planted tobacco as an extra-money crop would undoubtedly
suffer less from a drop in prices than the heavily capitalized planter. However if this
same farmer hoped to emulate "his predecessors of the earlier period in saving money,
purchasing land . . . and becoming a substantial citizen, the task was well nigh impossible of accomplishment." Wertenbaker, *Planters of Colonial Virginia*, p. 97. See
also *ibid.*, pp. 96–100, for an extended discussion of the effects of this depression on
the yeomanry as a class.

possible, but now its terms were clearer, and those who achieved it would be fewer in numbers. The man who managed it would be the man with the large holdings—the man who could command a substantial force of laborers, white or black—who could afford a sizable yearly investment in the handling of his crop: in short, the capitalist planter.

The period beginning in the 1680's and ending about 1710 marked still a new phase. It saw, now under conditions of comparative prosperity, the full emergence of the plantation as the basic unit of capitalist agriculture. By about 1680 the market for Virginia and Maryland tobacco had been restored, though it is important to note that this was accompanied by no great rise in prices. It was rather a matter of having recaptured the European market by flooding it with cheap tobacco and underselling competitors. Returning prosperity, therefore, meant something far more concrete to the man with resources, who could produce tobacco in large enough amounts to make a slim profit margin worthwhile, than to the one whose productivity was limited by the acreage which he and his family could work. These years also witnessed the initial exploitation of the Carolinas, a process which moved much more directly toward large agricultural units than had been the case in Virginia.[17] The acceleration of this development toward clarifying the terms of commercial production—large plantations and substantial investments—had a direct connection with the widening of the market for slaves during this same period. Hand in hand with large holdings went slaves—an assumption which was now being taken more or less for granted. "A rational man," wrote a South Carolina colonist in 1682, "will certainly inquire, 'when I have Land, what shall I doe with it? What commoditys shall I be able to produce, that will yield me money in other countrys, that I may be inabled to buy Negro-slaves, (without which a planter can never doe any great matter)?'"[18] The point had clearly passed when white servants could realistically, on any long-term appraisal, be considered preferable to Negro slaves. Such appraisals were now being made in terms of capitalized earning power, a concept appropriate to large operations rather than small, to long-term rather than short-term planning.

It was, of course, only the man of means who could afford to think in this way. But then he is the one who most concerns us—the man responsible for Negro slavery. Determined in the sixties and seventies to make money despite hard times and low prices, and willing to undertake the investments which that

[17] The Carolina proprietors had a far clearer notion of the terms on which money was to be made from their colony than had been true of the London Company of sixty years before with regard to Virginia. They appear at the very outset to have fostered the establishment of large estates, and a number of such estates set up in the 1670's and 1680's were organized by Barbados men with first-hand plantation experience. See Gray, *History of Agriculture,* I, 324–25; also J. P. Thomas, "Barbadians in Early South Carolina," *South Carolina Historical Magazine,* XXXI (April, 1930), 89. Although a dominant staple was not to emerge until some time later, with rice and indigo, it seems to have been conceived in terms of large units to a degree never envisaged at a comparable stage in the development of Virginia. One index of this is quickly seen in the composition of the laboring population there; a little over a generation after the first settlements the ratio of Negro slaves to whites in the total population could be safely estimated at about one to one, whereas the same ratio would not be attained in Virginia until late in the eighteenth century. Greene and Harrington, *American Population,* pp. 124, 137.

[18] Quoted in Gray, *History of Agriculture,* I, 352.

required, he could now in the eighties reap the fruits of his foresight. His slaves were more valuable than ever—a monument to his patience and planning. What had made them so? For one thing he, unlike the yeoman farmer, had a large establishment for training them and was not pressed by the need, as he would have been with white servants on limited indenture, to exploit their *immediate* labor. The labor was his permanently. And for another thing, the system was by now just old enough to make clear for the first time the full meaning of a second generation of native-born American Negroes. These were the dividends: slaves born to the work and using English as their native tongue.[19] By the 1690's the demand for slaves in the British colonies had become so great, and the Royal African Company so inefficient in supplying them, that in 1698 Parliament revoked the company's monopoly on the African coast and threw open the traffic to independent merchants and traders. The stream of incoming slaves, already of some consequence, now became enormous, and at the same time the annual flow of white servants to Virginia and the Carolinas dropped sharply. By 1710 it had become virtually negligible.[20]

What meaning might all this have had for the legal status of the Negro? The connection was intimate and direct; with the full development of the plantation there was nothing, so far as his interests were concerned, to prevent unmitigated capitalism from becoming unmitigated slavery. The planter was now engaged in capitalistic agriculture with a labor force entirely under his control. The personal relationship between master and slave—in any case less likely to exist on large agricultural units than on smaller ones—now became far less important than the economic necessities which had forced the slave into this "unnatural" organization in the first place. For the plantation to operate efficiently and profitably, and with a force of laborers not all of whom may have been fully broken to plantation discipline, the necessity of training them to work long hours and to give unquestioning obedience to their masters and overseers superseded every other consideration. The master must have absolute power over the slave's body, and the law was developing in such a way as to give it to him at every crucial point. Physical discipline was made virtually unlimited[21]

[19] This is another point of view from which to consider the 1671 figure (cited in n. 13 above) on the Virginia slave population. The difference between the 300 Negroes of 1650 and the 2,000 of 1670 is substantial—nearly a sevenfold increase. According to Berkeley's testimony the importations over the previous seven years had not been more than two or three cargoes. If this were true, it would be safe to estimate that a significant number of that 2,000 must already have been native-born American Negroes. As for the period to which the above paragraph has reference—fifteen or twenty years later—the number of native-born must by then have increased considerably.

[20] Greene and Harrington, *American Population,* pp. 136–37; Gray, *History of Agriculture,* I, 349–50.

[21] As early as 1669 a Virginia law had declared it no felony if a master or overseer killed a slave who resisted punishment. According to the South Carolina code of 1712, the punishment for offering "any violence to any christian or white person, by striking, or the like" was a severe whipping for the first offense, branding for the second, and death for the third. Should the white man attacked be injured or maimed, the punishment was automatically death. The same act provided that a runaway slave be severely whipped for his first offense, branded for his second, his ears cut off for the third, and castrated for the fourth. It is doubtful whether such punishments were often used, but their very existence served to symbolize the relationship of absolute power over the slave's body. Hurd, *Law of Freedom and Bondage,* I, 232; Thomas Cooper and D. J. McCord (eds.), *Statutes at Large of South Carolina* (Columbia, S.C., 1836–41), VII, 357–59.

and the slave's chattel status unalterably fixed.[22] It was in such a setting that those rights of personality traditionally regarded between men as private and inherent, quite apart from the matter of lifetime servitude, were left virtually without defense. The integrity of the family was ignored, and slave marriage was deprived of any legal or moral standing.[23] The condition of a bondsman's soul—a matter of much concern to church and civil authority in the Spanish colonies—was here very quickly dropped from consideration. A series of laws enacted between 1667 and 1671 had systematically removed any lingering doubts whether conversion to Christianity should make a difference in status: henceforth it made none.[24] The balance, therefore, involved on the one side the constant pressure of costs, prices, and the problems of management, and on the other the personal interests of the slave. Here, there were no counterweights: those interests were unsupported by any social pressures from the outside; they were cherished by no customary feudal immunities; they were no concern of the government (the king's main interest was in tobacco revenue); they could not be sustained by the church, for the church had little enough power and influence among its own white constituencies, to say nothing of the suspicion its ministers aroused at every proposal to enlarge the church's work among the blacks.[25]

[22] Slaves in seventeenth-century Virginia had become, as a matter of actual practice, classed on the same footing as household goods and other personal property. The code of 1705 made them a qualified form of real estate, but that law was in 1726 amended by another which declared that slaves were "to pass as chattels." Bruce, *Economic History,* II, 99; Hurd, *Law of Freedom and Bondage,* I, 242. The South Carolina code of 1740 made them "chattels personal, in the hands of their owners and possessors and their executors, administrators and assigns, to all intents, constructions and purposes whatsoever. . . ." *Ibid.,* I, 303.

[23] Bruce (*Economic History,* II, 108) describes a will, written about 1680, in which a woman "bequeathed to one daughter, . . . a negress and the third child to be born of her; to a second daughter, . . . the first and second child to be born of the same woman."

[24] See Handlin and Handlin, "Origins of the Southern Labor System," p. 212. The Maryland law of 1671 could leave no possible doubt in this matter, declaring that any Christianized slave "is, are and shall att all tymes hereafter be adjudged Reputed deemed and taken to be and Remayne in Servitude and Bondage and subject to the same Servitude and Bondage to all intents and purposes as if hee shee they every or any of them was or were in and Subject vnto before such his her or their Becomeing Christian or Christians or Receiving of the Sacrament of Baptizme any opinion or other matter or thing to the Contrary in any wise Notwithstanding." William Hand Browne (ed.), *Archives of Maryland* (Baltimore, 1884), II, 272. See also n. 3 above.

[25] What this meant to the Negro is admirably reflected in a book by Morgan Godwyn, an Anglican minister who served in the 1670's both in Barbados and in Virginia. Godwyn's book, *The Negro's and Indian's Advocate,* was a plea for the care of the Negro's soul. He attacked the planters for keeping religion from the slaves, for "not allowing their children *Baptism;* nor suffering them upon better terms than direct *Fornication,* to live with their Women, (for Wives, I may not call them, being never married). And accounting it Foppish, when Dead, to think of giving them *Christian,* or even decent Burial; that so their pretence for Brutifying them, might find no Contradiction" (p. 37). In Godwyn's eyes the planters were men "who for the most part do know no other God but money, nor Religion but Profit" (Preface). He quotes one Barbadian who "openly maintained . . . that Negroes were beasts, and had no more souls than beasts, and that religion did not concern them. Adding that they [his fellow Barbadians] went *not* to those parts to save souls, or propagate religion, but to get Money" (p. 39). Even the care of white souls in the colonies appears to have occupied a rather low order of concern. The Attorney-General of England in 1693 objected strenuously to the erection of a college in Virginia, though he was reminded of the need to educate young men for the ministry and was begged to consider the souls of the colonists. "Souls! Damn your souls," he replied, "make tobacco." Quoted in Wertenbaker, *Planters of Colonial Virginia,* p. 138. It is doubtful

The local planter class controlled all those public concerns which most affected the daily life of the colony, and it was thus only in matters of the broadest and most general policy that this planter domination was in any way touched by bureaucratic decisions made in London. The emergent institution of slavery was in effect unchallenged by any other institutions.[26]

The result was that the slave, utterly powerless, would at every critical point see his interests further depressed. At those very points the drive of the law—unembarrassed by the perplexities of competing interests—was to clarify beyond all question, to rationalize, to simplify, and to make more logical and symmetrical the slave's status in society. So little impeded was this pressure to define and clarify that all the major categories in law which bore upon status were very early established with great thoroughness and completeness. The unthinking aggressions upon the slave's personality which such a situation made possible becomes apparent upon an examination, in greater detail, of these legal categories.

---

that the planters of Virginia were quite so brutal as the Barbadians in their attitude toward the Negro or in the management of their plantations, but even in Virginia Godwyn found that the idea of teaching religion to the Negro slave was thought "so idle and ridiculous, so utterly needless and unnecessary, that no Man can forfeit his Judgement more, than by any proposal looking or tending that way" (p. 172). That such an attitude had not changed by the eighteenth century is suggested by a piece in the *Athenian Oracle* of Boston in 1707 in which the writer declared, "Talk to a *Planter* of the *Soul* of a *Negro,* and he'll be apt to tell ye (or at least his actions speak it loudly) that the Body of one of them may be worth twenty pounds; but the Souls of an Hundred of them would not yield him one Farthing." Quoted in Marcus W. Jernegan, "Slavery and Conversion in the American Colonies," *American Historical Review,* XXI (April, 1916), 516.

[26] For the control exercised over colonial institutional life by this planter elite, see Craven, *Southern Colonies,* pp. 153, 159, 170–72, 274–78; Philip A. Bruce, *Institutional History of Virginia in the Seventeenth Century* (New York: Putnam, 1910), I, 468; and George M. Brydon, *Virginia's Mother Church, and the Political Conditions under Which It Grew* (Richmond: Virginia Historical Society, 1947), I, 94–96, 232.

Germans

GLENN WEAVER

Benjamin Franklin and the Pennsylvania Germans

The Germans were the most important non-English-speaking immigrants in the colonial era. Originally attracted to Pennsylvania, where William Penn had promised them religious freedom, large numbers of Germans also settled in the South and in New York. They formed tightly knit enclaves, preferring to live apart from the rest of the community.

The colonists feared the Germans would refuse to learn the English language or teach their children "American" ways, and the Germans initially resisted outside interference in their culture. Benjamin Franklin became the spokesman for the English-speaking majority in Pennsylvania. He castigated the Germans for clinging to supposedly inferior, non-English customs that might eventually dominate Pennsylvania and "Germanize us instead of Anglifying them."

In the following article Professor Glenn Weaver discusses the controversies between the Germans and English in Pennsylvania and their eventual resolution.

On March 10, 1787, an act of assembly chartered Pennsylvania's third institution of higher learning, Franklin College in the borough of Lancaster. That the institution was named in honor of one of Pennsylvania's leading citizens is, in itself, not remarkable, for the founders of Dickinson College had already set the precedent. The ironic significance was that Franklin College—conceived by German-speaking Pennsylvanians of Lutheran and Reformed religious persuasions for the training of both civil and ecclesiastical leaders—was to be named for a Deist who had seldom spared words in pointing out the political immaturity and social incivility of the Germans of his state.

From the beginning of his business and public career Benjamin Franklin had been suspicious of German business honesty and political loyalty. Although his feelings toward the "sect" Germans were doubtless determined by the pacifism of such groups as the Mennonites, Amish, and Dunkers, his estimate of the "church" (or Lutheran and Reformed) Germans was little better than his views of the pacifists. Franklin knew the Germans well. In his day Germantown was regarded as the "German capital,"[1] and in Philadelphia, the place of Frank-

Reprinted from *William and Mary Quarterly*, 3rd series, 14 (1957), 536–59. By permission of the author and the publisher.
[1] Earl F. Robacker, *Pennsylvania German Literature* (Philadelphia, 1943), p. 16.

lin's residence and business establishment, there were numerous German inhabitants. According to Franklin's own observations in 1753, Pennsylvania had several German printing houses, German signs had appeared on the streets, and the magistrates had even recognized the use of the language in drawing up legal instruments.[2]

As a young man, Franklin had catered to the German-reading public by issuing several volumes in their language—the most significant of which were two books published in 1731 for the Ephrata Brethren. In 1732 he attempted a German edition of his newspaper,[3] but only a few numbers appeared, partly because Franklin lacked competent German printers and partly because of his failure to secure subscribers. In the first trial issue of the *Philadelphische Zeitung* on May 6, Franklin's German editor stated that the paper would appear weekly if three hundred subscribers could be found. A second issue, June 24, reported that not more than fifty persons had subscribed and that, in view of the poor support, the *Zeitung* would be published fortnightly. Apparently this was the last number.[4]

Although the Germans continued to give some of their job printing to Franklin,[5] after 1738 they had their own "official" printer in the person of Christopher Sower.[6] He and his son, Christopher, Jr., were to print at least 150 books, an annual almanac, a newspaper, and innumerable pamphlets and broadsides.[7] In that same year, the Ephrata Brethren also established their own printery and entered into an agreement with Sower whereby the Brethren were to assist in typesetting and proofreading while Sower would provide the ink and type. Thus the Germans had little need to look to Franklin to supply their literary wants. Franklin, however, decided to nip this competition in the bud, and for a while it seemed that he was in a position to do so. As he controlled the entire stock of printing paper in Pennsylvania, he was able to demand cash which neither the Brethren nor Sower possessed. Conrad Weiser, who was later to hold the same position of leadership among the church Germans as Sower was to hold among the sect Germans, foiled Franklin's plans by traveling from his home in Tulpehocken to Philadelphia to pledge his credit in behalf of the German printers.[8] Weiser's credit, which was said to be good anywhere in the

---

[2] Franklin to Peter Collinson (and Richard Jackson?), Philadelphia, May 9, 1753, in *Letters and Papers of Benjamin Franklin and Richard Jackson,* ed. Carl Van Doren (Philadelphia, 1947), pp. 38–39. Hereafter cited as *Franklin-Jackson Correspondence.* One writer says that in the mid-eighteenth century the population of Philadelphia was chiefly Quaker and German. Nathan G. Goodman, *Benjamin Rush, Physician and Citizen, 1746–1813* (Philadelphia, 1934), p. 1.

[3] This was merely a translation of his English paper.

[4] Edward W. Hocker, *The Sower Printing House of Colonial Times* [Pennsylvania-German Society, *Proceedings and Addresses,* LIII] (Norristown, 1948), pp. 13–14; Robacker, *Pennsylvania German Literature,* pp. 29–30; Clarence S. Brigham, *History and Bibliography of American Newspapers, 1690–1820* (Worcester, Mass., 1947), II, 963.

[5] E.g., Franklin published in 1742 the *Authentische Relation . . . ,* which was the report of the Minutes of the Congregation of God in the Spirit in which Count Zinzendorf, the Moravian leader, attempted to unite the German sects of Pennsylvania into a single body. The "Congregation" is discussed in detail in Jacob John Sessler, *Communal Pietism among Early American Moravians* (New York, [1933]), pp. 20–71.

[6] Robacker, *Pennsylvania German Literature,* pp. 30 ff.; Albert Bernhardt Faust, *The German Element in the United States* (New York, c. 1909), I, 143–146.

[7] Hocker, *The Sower Printing House,* pp. 1–2.

[8] Paul A. W. Wallace, *Conrad Weiser, 1696–1760* (Philadelphia, 1945), p. 103.

province, was something which Franklin could not easily refuse, and Sower and the Ephrata Brethren received their needed paper. Both Sower and Franklin soon came to realize that "business was business," for when Sower announced his plans for the publication of a German Bible in 1742, Franklin was designated as one of the Philadelphia agents for its sale. Franklin reciprocated and appointed Sower one of the first agents for the sale of the Franklin stove.[9]

In the affairs of the colony Franklin had always played a leading part. Likewise, Franklin was one of Philadelphia's most ardent "boosters" and even in his own day he was regarded by the citizenry as one of the city's principal benefactors. Pennsylvania's more than one hundred thousand Germans were of peasant stock and took little interest in the social life of the city so dear to Franklin's heart. Needless to say, their language served as an additional barrier between them and their neighbors. As representatives of an alien culture, the Germans were, to say the least, somewhat skeptical of English institutions. The English interpreted this skepticism as a stubborn conservatism resulting from gross ignorance. Certainly few English-speaking Pennsylvanians thought that the Germans could ever be assimilated. Many thought that they would always retain their language and customs and would thus forever stand in the way of the colonies' achieving an effective union of colonial thought and action against the French.[10] In 1747, when it was apparent that the Quaker assembly of Pennsylvania would not enact legislation to provide for the colony's official participation in King George's War, Franklin, with the encouragement of Governor Thomas, organized an extralegal militia known as the Associators. In his recruiting tract, *Plain Truth,* Franklin appealed to the Germans to enlist, referring to the *"obstinate* courage" of the *"brave* and *steady* GERMANS."[11]

There was, however, no response by the Germans to the appeal of *Plain Truth.* Instead of joining the Associators, the pacifist Germans came to feel that their political allegiance, slight though it may have been, was to be with the Quakers rather than with the proprietary party with which Franklin was identified.[12] Although the Germans continued to go their own way, actually showing no real sympathy for either side, Franklin could see them only as a disruptive element. In a letter of March 20, 1750, to James Parker, he wrote that because of the "disagreeableness of [the] disonant Manners" of the Germans, their English-speaking neighbors would have preferred to move away.[13] Franklin may have been speaking only for himself, but there is little doubt that

[9] Hocker, *The Sower Printing House,* p. 39; Horace W. Smith, *Life and Correspondence of the Rev. William Smith* (Philadelphia, 1880), I, 48n. Franklin, it would seem, had a regular German clientele in his bookshop. Conrad Weiser, for example, was a regular customer for a number of years. Wallace, *Conrad Weiser,* pp. 105, 171, 250.

[10] Estimates range from 110,000 to 150,000. Arthur D. Graeff, *The Relations between the Pennsylvania Germans and the British Authorities (1750–1776)* [Pennsylvania-German Society, *Proceedings,* XLVII] (Norristown, 1939), pp. 16–24; J. Thomas Scharf, *History of Western Maryland* (Philadelphia, 1822), I, 63, 367; William Smith, *A Brief State of the Province of Pennsylvania,* Sabine Reprints (New York, 1865), p. 10; Faust, *The German Element,* I, 285.

[11] *The Writings of Benjamin Franklin,* ed. Albert Henry Smyth (New York, 1905–07), II, 352.

[12] Whitfield J. Bell, Jr., "Benjamin Franklin and the German Charity Schools," American Philosophical Society, *Proceedings,* XCIX (Dec. 1955), 381.

[13] Franklin to James Parker, Mar. 20, 1750, in *Writings of Franklin,* ed. Smyth, III, 44.

many prominent colonials regarded German-speaking cultural enclaves in the colonies as potentially dangerous. Three years later Franklin wrote: "Those who come hither are generally the most stupid of their own nation. . . . Not being used to liberty, they know not how to make a modest use of it. And as Kolben says of the young Hottentots, they are not esteemed men until they have shown their manhood by *beating their mothers,* so these seem not to think themselves free, till they can feel their liberty in abusing and insulting their teachers."[14]

Franklin's accusations were extreme, for the Germans of Pennsylvania had been largely indifferent to the comings and goings of the English. Despite liberal naturalization laws, few Germans before the middle of the eighteenth century had become citizens,[15] much less had secured public office where they could abuse and insult their "teachers." Nevertheless, when in the spring of 1753 war in the Ohio Valley was regarded as imminent, Franklin's distrust of the Germans was at high tide. He wrote: "The French, who watch all advantages, are now themselves making a German settlement, back of us in the Illinois country, and by means of these Germans they may in time come to an understanding with ours; and, indeed, in the last [King George's] war, our Germans showed a general disposition that seemed to bode us no good . . . [declaring that] the French, should they take the country, would not molest them."[16]

It would be indeed difficult to determine the basis of this statement. Even though the Germans had separated themselves both socially and politically, there is little reason to believe that they would have considered changing their allegiance—nominal though it may have been—from the English, whose lands they had accepted as a haven of refuge, to the French, whose armies in their devastation of the Rhineland were in part responsible for the German migration to Pennsylvania.[17] To the contrary it may be pointed out that, except for the few thousands inhabiting either Philadelphia or Germantown, most of the Germans lived in remote and more or less isolated districts and were quite unaware of developments either in Philadelphia or along the Ohio.

The peaceable intentions of the *Pennsylvania* Germans notwithstanding, elsewhere in the British New World some of their compatriots soon behaved in such a fashion as to give at least a measure of substance to Franklin's fears. In December of 1753 a French emissary convinced the Germans at Lunenburg, Nova Scotia, that they were being exploited by the colonial officers and persuaded them to attack the barracks and storehouses in the village.[18]

The Reverend William Smith, in a letter to the secretary of the Society for

[14] Franklin to Collinson (and Jackson?), Philadelphia, May 9, 1753, *Franklin-Jackson Correspondence,* ed. Van Doren, p. 38.

[15] Lawrence Henry Gipson, *The British Empire before the American Revolution* (Caldwell, Idaho, and New York, 1936—in progress), III, 174.

[16] Franklin to Collinson (and Jackson?), Philadelphia, May 9, 1753, *Franklin-Jackson Correspondence,* ed. Van Doren, p. 39. Professor Gipson notes that Franklin is probably in error regarding a German settlement in the Illinois Country. *The British Empire before the American Revolution,* IV, 142n.

[17] Walter Allen Knittle, in *Early Eighteenth Century Palatine Emigration* (Philadelphia, c. 1937), pp. 1–3, regards this devastation of the Palatinate as one of the major motives in the German migration.

[18] Duncan Campbell, *Nova Scotia, in its Historical, Mercantile and Industrial Relations* (Montreal, 1873), p. 113; D. Luther Roth, *Acadie and the Acadians* (Philadelphia, 1890), pp. 187–203.

the Propagation of the Gospel, echoed Franklin's fear that the Germans could hardly be trusted in the event of conflict between the English and the French. Smith, however, offered a practical solution to Franklin's vexing problem— namely, the establishment of a school system, the purpose of which would be to force the Germans to adopt the English language and customs.[19]

Smith's efforts bore fruit when a "Society for the Propagating of Christian Knowledge among the Germans" was organized in England for the purpose of establishing English schools among the Germans of Pennsylvania. This system of "charity schools"[20] was placed under the supervision of the Reverend Michael Schlatter, a German Reformed clergyman. As one of the school trustees, Franklin, as well as most of his colleagues on the board, hoped that the twenty-five schools which were to comprise the system (only about half that number were actually opened) would "Anglicize" the Germans and lead them away from any pro-French sympathies. Contrary to Franklin's hopes—but precisely as he might have expected—the schools were not supported by the Germans and were even openly opposed, so that by 1763 the last had gone out of existence. Short-lived as they were, the "charity schools" were the occasion of a pamphlet war between Franklin and Sower. Franklin was soon forced to withdraw from the fray because he was again unable to find competent German editors and printers. Sower attacked the "charity school" system in his paper and in his personal correspondence. He wrote to Conrad Weiser, who was also a trustee, that such prominent colonials as Franklin, Richard Peters, and William Allen "care little about religion; nor do they care for the cultivation of the minds of the Germans, except that they should form the militia and defend their properties."[21] Sower, in his indignation, had perhaps expressed greater truth than he realized, for Franklin and the others were indeed interested in forming a Pennsylvania militia.

With their great numbers, the Germans—if they had so wished—could have gained control of the Pennsylvania assembly. Instead, because of their indifferent attitude, those few who voted had allowed themselves to become the tools of the Quakers, who in 1754 controlled the colonial legislative body.[22] When the assembly on August 15, 1754, rejected Franklin's Albany "plan of union"[23] the Germans doubtless gave sighs of relief, for a measure which provided for both taxation and conscription must have been odious to their thrifty and peace-loving natures. In the election in the fall of that year the "Governor's party," led by Franklin, made a bid for the German vote, but again—because of the influence of Sower's editorials warning that to become a "Governor's man" would mean a betrayal of the freedom which the Germans had long enjoyed— Franklin had little appeal for the Germans. Arguing that unless the Quakers

[19] In H. W. Smith, *Life and Correspondence of the Rev. William Smith,* I, 29–38; see also Franklin to Cadwallader Colden, Aug. 30, 1754, in *Writings of Franklin,* ed. Smyth, III, 228.

[20] A good short treatment of the "charity schools" is S. E. Weber, "The Germans and the Charity-School Movement," *Pennsylvania-German,* VIII (July 1907), 305–312. For an account of Franklin's part in the establishment of the charity schools, see Bell, "Benjamin Franklin and the German Charity Schools," Am. Phil. Soc., *Proceedings,* XCIX, 381–387.

[21] Hocker, *The Sower Printing House,* pp. 59–60.

[22] Gipson, *The British Empire before the American Revolution,* III, 174.

[23] *Pennsylvania Archives* (Philadelphia, 1852–56; Harrisburg, 1874–1919), 8th Ser., V, 3732–33.

were returned to office the Germans would face the possibility of being reduced to slavery,[24] Sower "got out the German vote." Even the Mennonites of Lancaster County, who seldom exercised their voting rights, turned out at the polls en masse[25] to help defeat Franklin's party.[26]

The new assembly was indifferent to pushing a campaign against the French on the Ohio, and the German inhabitants of the Pennsylvania hinterland were thought to be disloyal, or at best the political allies of the pacifist Quakers. Therefore, when General Braddock marched toward the Ohio he avoided Pennsylvania and chose a more southern route through western Virginia and Maryland. Although the Germans themselves were doubtless a major factor in the change of route, Sir John St. Clair, quartermaster general of Braddock's army, suggested that wagons and trains be secured from the German settlers at the foot of the Blue Ridge.[27] When called upon to supply this military transportation, the Germans refused, and when the quartermaster general's threats to impress teams failed, Franklin was asked to obtain the needed equipment from the farmers of his colony. He promised good pay to the teamsters and held out the threat of dire punishment for those who refused.[28] Although he achieved his immediate purpose, the German drivers cut loose their horses and fled homeward when Braddock's defeat seemed imminent.[29] They were not slow, however, in making claim to the pay which was due them. Urged on by Sower, who had chided them for having been intimidated by Franklin's threats,[30] they continued to press the issue until late in February 1756, when a commissioner for the King brought money from England to pay the claimants.[31] Nor did the Germans hesitate to present their claims for damages done to their crops by the troops who had retreated to Philadelphia after the defeat on the Monongahela.[32]

Braddock's defeat and the uncovered retreat of the British left the French and their Indian allies in control of western Pennsylvania. Cumberland County, then a large expanse of territory west of the Susquehanna, was the first to feel the full effect of Indian warfare,[33] and both German and Scotch-Irish residents —the latter having been the dominant element in the region—fled eastward almost to a man. Having crossed the Susquehanna about thirty miles north of Harris' Ferry (Harrisburg), the Indians attacked the settlements to the south and east and passed through the gaps in the Blue Mountains into the territory populated

[24] Graeff, *Relations between the Pennsylvania Germans and the British Authorities,* pp. 55–56.
[25] Wilbur J. Bender, "Pacifism among the Mennonites . . . ," *Mennonite Quarterly Review,* I (July 1927), 32.
[26] This must not be interpreted as a German victory but rather as a Quaker victory, for the Germans were of political use to the Quakers rather than the Quakers to the Germans.
[27] Graeff, *Relations between the Pennsylvania Germans and the British Authorities,* p. 81, quoting Robert Orme, "Orme's Journal" (1755) in Pennsylvania Historical Society, *Memoirs,* V (1868).
[28] *Pennsylvania Archives,* 1st Ser., II, 294–295.
[29] Franklin, *Autobiography,* in *Benjamin Franklin's Own Story,* ed. Nathan G. Goodman (Philadelphia, 1937), pp. 151–152, hereafter cited as Franklin, *Autobiography;* Albert S. Bolles, *Pennsylvania, Province and State* (Philadelphia, 1899), p. 326.
[30] Graeff, *Relations between the Pennsylvania Germans and the British Authorities,* p. 87.
[31] *Ibid.,* p. 93.
[32] *Pennsylvania Archives,* 8th Ser., V, 4014 ff.
[33] *Ibid.,* 1st Ser., II, 385–386.

almost solidly by Germans. In this Blue Mountain region as early as 1741, Conrad Weiser, almost alone and certainly without avail, had urged the Germans to oppose any candidate who should seek election on an antimilitia platform. Weiser's appeal had fallen upon deaf ears, for the Germans had been persuaded by the Quakers that the peace which William Penn had made with the Indians would not be broken.[34] Consequently no preparations had been taken against Indian attack. When the attacks came, however, the frontier Germans realized their folly, and in response to a "call to arms" issued by Weiser seven hundred volunteers appeared at the Weiser homestead at Tulpehocken, some from points as distant as Reading and Lancaster.[35]

Weiser's small and untrained "army" accomplished little,[36] and their marchings hither and yon only added to the confusion of the settlers. Rumors of approaching French armies[37] caused a virtual exodus from even the Tulpehocken region. Easton, Nazareth, and Bethlehem became crowded with refugees, and appeals were sent to the authorities at Philadelphia for guns, ammunition, provisions, and troops.[38] Although these urgent appeals met with no response from the Quaker assembly, which the Germans had helped to elect, the Germans weakened their own cause by once more helping to re-elect a Quaker majority in 1755. Even though by this time the Germans of the Blue Mountain region wanted a change, Sower—again playing his hand against Franklin—exerted his influence upon the "peace sects," who were relatively safe at the periphery of the Philadelphia area, and warned that a change would bring about the passing of a militia act placing the German sectarians under arms.[39] Sower was again successful, and the Quakers were returned to the assembly. Again petitions and appeals for assistance and protection were sent to the assembly by the leading citizens (German and English) of Berks, Cumberland, Lancaster, and York counties,[40] but again the appeals met with no response. This time the Germans from the hinterland, six hundred strong, marched to Philadelphia where they "called upon" the governor, showing him the scalped corpses which they had brought along in wagons. After having the governor's assurance that a militia act had been made possible through a gift of £5,000 from the Proprietors, the Germans proceeded to the Statehouse. Fortunately for the intentions of the Germans, the assembly was in session, and when the mob arrived at the Statehouse they were addressed by none other than Benjamin Franklin.[41]

With the promise of Governor Morris and the reassurance of Franklin that something would be done for their protection, the Germans returned to their homes without further threats or disturbance. After their departure, the Statehouse became the scene of much wrangling between the assembly and the gov-

[34] Weiser to Governor Morris, July 21, 1755, in Clement Z. Weiser, *The Life of (John) Conrad Weiser* (Reading, 1876), pp. 106–107.
[35] Weiser to Governor Morris, Oct. 30, 1755, in *ibid.,* pp. 207–211.
[36] *Ibid.*
[37] Weiser to William Allen, Oct. 30, 1755, in *ibid.,* p. 312.
[38] Weiser to Governor Morris, Nov. 19, 1755, in *ibid.,* pp. 217–218; A. D. Chidsey, Jr., "Easton before the French and Indian War," *Pennsylvania History,* II (July 1935), p. 165.
[39] Graeff, *Relations between the Pennsylvania Germans and the British Authorities,* p. 125.
[40] *Colonial Records of Pennsylvania, 1683–1790* (Harrisburg, 1851–53), II, 448, 450; VI, 647–649, 667.
[41] J. Bennett Nolan, *General Benjamin Franklin* (Philadelphia, 1936), p. 14.

ernor. Again it seemed that the Germans were to have no effective protection. Perhaps the assembly and governor would have remained deadlocked indefinitely had not the massacre at the Moravian settlement at Gnadenhutten (Weissport), Pennsylvania, occurred.

To the English-speaking Pennsylvanians the Moravians—concentrated in the lower Lehigh Valley—were something of an enigma, since they could hardly be clearly identified with either the "Church People" or the "Sect People."[42] Although the total number of Moravians in the New World at that time did not exceed nine hundred,[43] their elaborate and efficient Indian missionary organization operated in various places from the West Indies to New York and Massachusetts.[44]

In 1749 the Moravians had secured a parliamentary indemnity from bearing arms and taking oaths.[45] The Brethren had asked for this indemnity because a decade earlier they had made themselves unwelcome in Georgia for their refusal to bear arms. Elsewhere, too, the Moravians had encountered difficulties. In 1747 they had been roundly denounced by Governor Gooch of Virginia,[46] and in 1744 the government of New York had ordered the dissolution of a Moravian mission in Dutchess County because it was believed that the missionaries were attempting to induce the Indians to support the French.[47] Apart from their pacifist inclinations there were other factors which aroused official suspicions of the Moravians. Semiannually the Brethren made missionary journeys through the Indian country of Virginia, western Pennsylvania, New York, New England, and even into Canada.[48] The suspicions that the Moravians were French agents were accentuated by the fact that when the Brethren went on their missionary journeys they wore black robes and prominently displayed crucifixes.[49] The Moravian representative on the board of trustees for the lecture hall built in Philadelphia to accommodate George Whitefield and other visiting preachers became so unpopular that, despite the custom of having each religious denomination represented, his successor was selected from another communion.[50]

These popular suspicions notwithstanding, the Moravians were totally ignorant of any hostile disposition of the Indians toward the English, and only after fourteen Moravians had been killed in the Indian raid upon Shamokin did the Brethren realize that their own faith in the red men had been unwarranted.[51]

---

[42] A good summary of Moravian doctrines of the eighteenth century is to be found in Sessler, *Communal Pietism among Early American Moravians,* passim.
[43] *Ibid.,* p. 74.
[44] John Heckewelder, *A Narrative of the Mission of the United Brethren among the Delaware and Mohegan Indians, from its Commencement . . .* (Philadelphia, 1820), pp. 17 ff.
[45] A. Gertrude Ward, "John Ettwein and the Moravians in the Revolution," *Pennsylvania History,* I (Jan. 1934), 198.
[46] Faust, *The German Element,* I, 204; John Walter Wayland, *The German Element of the Shenandoah Valley of Virginia* (Charlottesville, 1907), p. 109.
[47] *The Documentary History of the State of New York,* ed. E. B. O'Callaghan (Albany, 1849–51), III, 1012–27.
[48] Heckewelder, *Narrative,* pp. 41–44; Faust, *The German Element,* I, 203; Oscar Kuhns, *The German and Swiss Settlements of Colonial Pennsylvania* (New York, 1901), p. 203.
[49] Graeff, *Relations between the Pennsylvania Germans and the British Authorities,* p. 70.
[50] Franklin, *Autobiography,* p. 128.
[51] Heckewelder, *Narrative,* p. 41.

It was, similarly, only after the night of November 24, 1755, when the Indian mission at Gnadenhutten was attacked and all but four whites in the settlement were put to death, that the colonial government was made aware that the Moravians were not in league with the French.[52]

On November 25, 1755, the assembly quickly passed an act providing for a militia of which the governor was to act as commander in chief.[53] Shortly after passing this act, the assembly voted to erect a chain of forts which was to extend along the Blue Mountains in a southwesterly direction from the Delaware River to the Maryland boundary.[54]

Franklin, by virtue of his office as head of the colony's committee of defense, journeyed northward early in January 1756 to superintend the construction of the first of the forts, Fort Allen, which was to occupy the site of the Indian mission at Gnadenhutten. On January 7, when Franklin stopped at Bethlehem en route, he found, much to his surprise, the supposedly pacifist Moravians armed to the teeth. Between the time of the destruction of Gnadenhutten and Franklin's arrival in Bethlehem, the Brethren had thrown a stockade around the principal buildings and had brought a sizable quantity of arms and ammunition from New York. The upper stories of the women's quarters had been supplied with small stones which the occupants could hurl at invaders.[55]

Franklin was cordially received by Bishop Spangenberg[56] who, perhaps with some embarrassment and probably without justification, explained that nonresistance was not one of the essential Moravian tenets but that in order to guarantee liberty of conscience for certain individuals among their number, the entire body had obtained exemption from compulsory military service.[57] Franklin saw much of the Moravian community life during his short stay in Bethlehem. He attended worship at the Moravian Church, and at his meals he was serenaded by the skilled musicians of the town.[58] When Franklin and his party resumed the journey to Gnadenhutten, the Brethren supplied teams and wagons to transport tools and supplies.[59]

In April 1757 Franklin went to London as agent of the Colony of Pennsylvania, not to return until 1762. Despite his absence from the colony, he could hardly have been ignorant of the part which the church Germans of Pennsylvania—and of the other colonies as well—took in the war. From their first attitude of caution, and even indifference, the church Germans had changed to one of unreserved support of the British cause. From Maine to Georgia the Germans had erected forts and had enlisted in the militia.[60] Indeed, the German

---

[52] *Ibid.*, pp. 44–46.

[53] *Pennsylvania Archives,* 1st Ser., II, 516–619.

[54] For Franklin's description of the plan see Franklin to William Parsons, Dec. 5, 1755, in *Writings of Franklin,* ed. Smyth, III, 304–305.

[55] Franklin, *Autobiography,* p. 156.

[56] "Franklin in the Valley of the Lehigh, 1756" [Extracts from the Diary of the Moravian Congregation at Bethlehem], *Pennsylvania Magazine of History and Biography,* XVIII (1894), 377.

[57] Franklin, *Autobiography,* p. 156.

[58] "Franklin in the Valley of the Lehigh," *Pa. Mag. of Hist. and Biog.,* XVIII, 378.

[59] Franklin, *Autobiography,* p. 157.

[60] M. R. Ludwig, *Ludwig Genealogy: Sketch of Joseph Ludwig* (Augusta, 1866), pp. 24, 29–30, 39; Cyrus Eaton, *Annals of the Town of Warren* (Hallowell, 1851), p. 89; *Documentary History of New York,* ed. O'Callaghan, I, 333–339; George von

American Regiment with a "paper strength" of four thousand men (which saw service at Louisburg, Fort Hunter, Fort Stanwix, Crown Point, Ticonderoga, Fort Duquesne, Fort Niagara, and Quebec) had been recruited largely from the German population of the colonies.[61] Of these developments Franklin could hardly have been ignorant. Nor would it likely have escaped his attention that German Lutheran and Reformed clergy had done much to encourage the Germans in their support of the war effort by preaching "recruiting sermons" and by serving as chaplains to the militia companies and the Royal American Regiment.[62] Likewise, Franklin, who missed few details of the news from Pennsylvania, must certainly have known that toward the end of the conflict even the "peace sects" (in addition to the Moravians) had compromised their pacifist principles to a considerable extent. The Mennonites generously contributed food and clothing for the use of the refugees fleeing eastward from the frontier,[63] and the Schwenkfelders, while they could not bring themselves to bear arms personally, sent substitutes to the militia, donated money to the Pennsylvania assembly, and assisted with the recruiting.[64]

Upon his return to Pennsylvania, Franklin used his good offices at least once in behalf of the Germans. In May 1764 he wrote a letter of introduction for Reverend Rothenbuler, pastor of the "new Calvinist German Church" of Philadelphia, who was on his way to Boston to seek donations for the completion of his church. On this occasion Franklin wrote, "they are an industrious, sober people"—one of his few kind remarks about them.[65]

Although he had been identified with the so-called proprietary party, Franklin had always been, at best, lukewarm toward the proprietors of Pennsylvania. During his stay in England he fell in with a movement to oust the Penns and to make Pennsylvania a royal colony.[66] It was incidental to his antiproprietary activity upon his return to Pennsylvania that Franklin found the Germans a force to be reckoned with. While in England, Franklin had been re-elected annually to his seat in the assembly as a matter of course. In the election of

---

Skal, *History of German Immigration in the United States* ([New York], 1908), p. 18; Faust, *The German Element,* I, 153; Charles Albro Barker, *The Background of the Revolution in Maryland* (New Haven, 1940), p. 207; John Walter Wayland, *A History of Rockingham County, Virginia* (Dayton, Va., 1912), pp. 51–54; *Records of the Moravians in North Carolina,* ed. Adelaide L. Fries (Raleigh, 1922–54), I, 159 and passim; Chapman J. Milling, *Red Carolinians* (Chapel Hill, 1940), p. 121; Amos Aschbach Ettinger, *James Edward Ogelthorpe: Imperial Idealist* (Oxford, 1936), p. 219.

[61] J. G. Rosengarten, *The German Soldier in the Wars of the United States,* 2d ed. (Philadelphia, 1890), pp. 19–20.

[62] Conrad Weiser to Governor Morris, Oct. 30, 1755, in C. Z. Weiser, *Conrad Weiser,* p. 208; *The Journals of Henry Melchior Muhlenberg,* trans. Theodore G. Tappert and John W. Doberstein (Philadelphia, 1942), I, 386; William J. Mann, *Life and Times of Henry Melchior Muhlenberg* (Philadelphia, 1888), 314–320; Faust, *The German Element,* I, 124.

[63] Graeff, *The Relations between the Pennsylvania Germans and the British Authorities,* p. 122 and passim.

[64] Howard Wiegner Kriebel, *The Schwenkfelders in Pennsylvania* (Lancaster, 1904), pp. 140–146; see also my *The Schwenkfelders during the French and Indian War* (Pennsburg, 1955), pp. 10–17.

[65] Franklin to Jonathan Willis, May 24, 1764, in *Writings of Franklin,* ed. Smyth, IV, 247.

[66] This subject is admirably treated by Carl Van Doren in *Franklin-Jackson Correspondence,* Introduction, pp. 7 ff. and in *Benjamin Franklin* (New York, 1938), pp. 283 ff.

1764, however, he and his friend Joseph Galloway ran on an antiproprietary platform as the "Old Ticket." The campaign was a most spirited one. Franklin and Galloway, to be sure, were advocating what was doubtless regarded as a radical measure, but there were plausible arguments both for and against the revocation of the proprietary patent, and it would seem that opinion in the colony was about evenly divided at the outset of the campaign. At this point, however, one of Franklin's earlier scientific writings, perhaps more than any other factor, turned the vote away from the "Old Ticket."

In 1751 Franklin had written a treatise entitled "Observations Concerning the Increase of Mankind, Peopling of Countries, Etc." in which he both anticipated the Malthusian theory of population growth and quite accurately predicted the rate of American population increase for the following century and a half. As the subject was addressed to an English audience, the "Observations" were first published in the *Gentleman's Magazine,* in November 1755. In 1760 the essay was again printed in England, this time appended to Franklin's pamphlet, "The Interest of Great Britain considered, with Regard to her Colonies."[67]

It would seem that neither edition of the "Observations" was extensively read in Pennsylvania, and certainly not by the Germans of the colony. In the last paragraph but one, Franklin had written, "why should the *Palatine Boors* be suffered to swarm into our Settlements and, by herding together, establish their Language and Manners, to the Exclusion of ours? Why should *Pennsylvania,* founded by the *English,* become a Colony of *Aliens,* who will shortly be so numerous as to Germanize us instead of our Anglifying them . . . ?"[68] In an appeal to the German vote, the proprietary party used the "Observations" as a campaign document and even, according to Franklin, garbled the author's reference to *"Palatine Boors* herding together" so that it read "a *Herd of Hogs."*[69] The use of the document had its intended effect: out of a total vote of about four thousand, one thousand ballots were cast by the Germans from Philadelphia and Germantown, and Franklin was defeated by twenty-five or twenty-six votes.[70]

Franklin naturally smarted under this defeat, but some of the bitterness must have been offset by the fact that, although the antiproprietary party lost the seats from Philadelphia, the "Old Ticket" still had a majority in the assembly. Late in October the assembly again appointed Franklin agent to England and this must have gone a long way toward salving the wound.[71]

While in England, Franklin made no retaliation against the Germans even though the opportunity soon presented itself. When being questioned by a committee of the House of Commons regarding the Stamp Act, specific reference was made by one of the questioners to alleged dissatisfaction of the Pennsylvania Germans with the act. Franklin's reply was in general terms. Regarding those who had been so instrumental in his recent defeat, he made but two ob-

[67] Printed in *Writings of Franklin,* ed. Smyth, III, 63–73. For the history of the "Observations" see *ibid.,* III, 63, n. 1 and *Franklin-Jackson Correspondence,* ed. Van Doren, editor's note, p. 188.
[68] *Writings of Franklin,* ed. Smyth, III, 72.
[69] Franklin to Jackson, Oct. 11, 1764, in *Franklin-Jackson Correspondence,* ed. Van Doren, pp. 188–189.
[70] *Ibid.;* Van Doren, *Benjamin Franklin,* p. 316.
[71] Van Doren, *Benjamin Franklin,* p. 316.

servations: 1) that the Germans seemed to be more dissatisfied than the English, and 2) that many of the Germans had seen service during the recent war.[72]

Subsequently Franklin's interests in the British New World were broadened by his successive appointments as agent for Georgia in 1768, for New Jersey in 1769, and for Massachusetts in 1770. It would not be incorrect to describe Franklin as "agent-general" or even "ambassador" for the colonies, for as the time of the American Revolution approached he came to be regarded more and more as the spokesman for the colonies.[73] Although the German population of Pennsylvania at the time of his first mission comprised roughly one third of the white inhabitants, the German element in the three other colonies was much smaller, and in the total population of the seaboard from Maine to Georgia the Germans probably did not exceed 10 per cent.[74] Thus it would be reasonable to believe that as Franklin's interests and responsibilities widened the Germans came to be of less importance in his thinking.

From the early years of the French and Indian War the Germans, too, had undergone a change. The death of Sower in 1758 and the subsequent banishment from Pennsylvania of his son and successor—for criticism of the Pennsylvania and British authorities—put an end to the aggressively pro-German propaganda there. The removal of this irritant probably had a calming effect on the Germans, and on Franklin too.[75] At any rate, so pronounced was the transformation that it may well be regarded as the first step toward the Americanization of the Germans.[76] In their ecclesiastical affiliation the Germans remained apart from the English colonists,[77] but otherwise the gap was slowly narrowing. Except for the Sect People, who still refused to become a part of the main stream of American life, the Germans were gradually beginning to use the English language as, at least, a poor alternate to their "Pennsylvania-Dutch"; they began to adopt English-style clothes; an occasional German youth found his way to one of the colonial colleges;[78] the scientific world was enriched by

[72] The Examination of Doctor Benjamin Franklin &c., in the British House of Commons, Relative to the Repeal of the American Stamp Act, in 1765, in *Writings of Franklin*, ed. Smyth, IV, 416.

[73] Van Doren, *Benjamin Franklin*, pp. 359–360, 495 ff.

[74] See my article, "German Settlements in British North America before the French and Indian War," *Social Studies*, XLIV (Dec. 1953), 287; cf. Faust, *The German Element*, I, 285.

[75] James Owen Knauss, Jr., *Social Conditions among the Pennsylvania Germans in the Eighteenth Century, as Revealed in the German Newspapers Published in America* (Lancaster, 1922), pp. 3–4; Martin G. Brumbaugh, "Christopher Sower, Jr.," *Pennsylvania German*, II (Apr. 1901), 54; Lucey Forney Bittinger, *The Germans in Colonial Times* (Philadelphia, 1901), pp. 160–162.

[76] I have discussed this process in "The Lutheran Church in the French and Indian Wars," *Lutheran Quarterly*, VI (Aug. 1954), 248–256.

[77] If the testimony of one contemporary can be believed, however, the Lutherans were drawing closer to the Anglicans and were eager to accept the oversight of the Bishop of London, provided the Anglicans would not raise the question of the validity of Lutheran ordination. William Smith to the Bishop of London, Dec. 18, 1766, in H. W. Smith, *Life and Correspondence of the Rev. William Smith*, I, 403–504.

[78] Adam Kuhn, son of a German immigrant of Germantown, studied medicine in Germany and Sweden, was graduated M.D. from the University of Edinburgh in 1767, and received his A.B. from the College of Philadelphia in 1768. In the latter year he became a member of the Medical Faculty at the college; *ibid.*, I, 419. For instances of German youths attending the college of New Jersey (Princeton College) see *Minutes and Letters of the Coetus of the German Reformed Congregations in Pennsylvania, 1747–1792* (Philadelphia, 1903), p. 269.

discoveries made by these supposedly backward people;[79] and certainly of no small significance was the fact that several Germans had risen to positions of public trust.

During Franklin's stay in England, Pennsylvania had experienced something of an internal political revolution. At the close of the French and Indian War the colonial assembly had gradually drifted back into the hands of the Quakers, who, once restored to power, were unwilling to see the political affairs of the colony again pass from their control. Political domination could be enjoyed by the party which controlled the three southeastern counties of Philadelphia, Chester, and Bucks which, with only one third of the colony's population, sent twenty-six of the thirty-six representatives to the assembly. The allocation of representatives had been made at a time when the other five counties were sparsely populated and when the outlying counties' inhabitants cared little about participation in government. Traditionally the Quakers had been of the proprietary party but their loyalty had gradually weakened. As property holders, they came to resent the exemption of the estates of the proprietaries from taxation. As the group in political control of the colony, the Quakers objected to the Penns' secret instructions to the deputy governors. When the sons of William Penn became Anglicans, the Quakers shifted to a definitely antiproprietary position. The Anglicans, traditionally of the antiproprietary party, while not making as complete an "about face" as the Quakers, at least formed the nucleus of an anti-Quaker party and began to look for allies. The common experience of hardship on the frontier brought the western Germans into alliance with the Scotch-Irish, and, of course, both groups wanted a more equitable share in the government than the Quakers had allowed them. As the political sides lined up in 1774, the Quakers and the Philadelphia merchant princes were for a while ranged against the Anglicans of the east and the Scotch-Irish and Germans of the back country.[80]

Within a year this temporary political alliance had given way to still another. When hostilities began at Lexington and Concord, the citizens of Pennsylvania, as in most of the colonies, quickly realigned themselves, largely on the question of the British policy of coercing the colonists. Although there was no clear-cut ethnic or religious division, the Anglicans generally opposed action on the part of the colonies against the British; the Scotch-Irish and church Germans (still going along with the Scotch-Irish) favored resistance, and the Quakers and sect Germans took a neutralist position. Thus Franklin, one of the most ardent supporters of firm action against the British, found himself on the same side of the political fence as the church Germans. Of course, the dissatisfaction of the Scotch-Irish and church Germans with the Quaker assembly was capitalized upon by such militant and opportunist Whigs as Franklin, Joseph Reed, and Thomas McKean.

As the extralegal governmental machinery of the Revolution was put into operation, the frontiersmen placed their trust in it and found it to be much

[79] Franklin to Peter Collinson, Sept. 24, 1764, in *Writings of Franklin,* IV, 261. While in England, Franklin had some correspondence of a scientific nature with Michael Hillegas, a German merchant of Philadelphia. Franklin to Hillegas, Mar. 17, 1770, in *ibid.,* V, 250–251.

[80] Wayland F. Dunaway, *A History of Pennsylvania,* 2d ed. (New York, 1948), pp. 121–124, 170–171.

more representative and considerably more to their liking than the Quaker-controlled provincial government. In the committee of correspondence, the committee of safety, and in the provincial conventions the Germans found opportunity for political expression if not for political leadership. Franklin and the other Whig radicals found the Germans useful, and not unwilling, tools. As a measure of desperation, the old assembly in February 1776 voted to reapportion the representation, but the reform came too late. In July a provincial convention met in Philadelphia, assumed control of the machinery of government just as though the old legislative body had never existed, and drew up a constitution which rendered Penn's charter obsolete and made Pennsylvania an independent commonwealth.[81]

Throughout the conflict, the Sect People stood by the Quakers in their opposition to taking radical measures against the British. This was certainly to be expected, but what was of utmost significance was that by 1776 the Church People—who had no scruples about bearing arms—constituted 90 per cent of the German population of Pennsylvania. As indication of the changed feelings of the Germans, no Christopher Sower came forth to denounce the political leaders and to turn German thought from that of the majority. Surely Franklin could have found little of which to complain.

The Lutheran and Reformed clergy were virtually unanimous in their support of the movement for American independence.[82] In the army, Generals Nicholas Herkimer and Peter Muhlenberg appeared in the field. Michael Hillegas served as treasurer for the Continental Congress and continued in office when the Treasury Department was created by the Congress of the United States in 1789. Another German, Augustus Conrad Muhlenberg, was a delegate to the Continental Congress. Franklin again noted that the Moravians were willing to compromise their pacifist principles. On June 2, 1775, he wrote to the Right Reverend Nathaniel Seidel, a Moravian bishop of Bethlehem, praising the Moravians for their good work in the French and Indian War and expressing the hope that the Continental Congress would not press into service any Moravians who had scruples about bearing arms. At the same time, he commended the Moravians for not restraining the young men who had chosen "to learn the military discipline."[83]

Hardly had the overthrow of the Quakers been effected and the new government established when Franklin again left Pennsylvania—this time for France, where he was to secure a treaty of friendship and alliance for the Continental Congress with the French government and have a leading part in drawing up the Peace of Paris of 1783. When Franklin returned to Philadelphia in September 1785, he was almost immediately elected to the council (or plural executive) of Pennsylvania, and the council, in turn, chose Franklin as its president.

[81] *Ibid.,* pp. 174–181. That the Germans had become a powerful political force is attested to by Benjamin Rush; Rush to Elias Boudinot, Aug. 2, 1783, in Benjamin Rush, *Letters,* ed. L. H. Butterfield (Princeton, 1951), I, 308.

[82] It would seem that they took particular delight in preaching berating sermons to captive Hessian prisoners. H. M. J. Klein, *The History of the Eastern Synod of the Reformed Church in the United States* ([Lancaster], 1943), pp. 68–69.

[83] Franklin to Seidel, June 2, 1775, in *Writings of Franklin,* ed. Smyth, VI, 403–404.

When the general assembly met, he was elected president of the commonwealth with but two dissenting votes and one of these his own.

Franklin's first major move as president of Pennsylvania was to take a firm stand against the "test act," which had been passed by the assembly while Franklin was in France. The act stipulated that no person could vote or hold public office who would not take an oath of allegiance to the Pennsylvania constitution of 1776. Franklin objected to the act not only on constitutional principles, but also because, by requiring an oath, it excluded both the Quakers and the sect Germans from any participation in the government. The act was modified by the assembly to require merely an oath or an affirmation (which would have accommodated both the Quakers and the Sect People) that the individual had renounced allegiance to the King of England, that he was loyal to the commonwealth, and that he had not since the Declaration of Independence given aid to the British.[84]

It may well be argued that Franklin cared little about the scruples of the Quakers and the sect Germans on oath-taking and that he used them again (and this time the peculiar religious beliefs of some of them) for his own political advantage. While it is true that Franklin was anticonstitutionalist (in reference to the constitution of 1776 with which he had so much to do), the aged philosopher doubtless realized that since the outbreak of the Revolution the Germans—at least the Church People—had evidenced a genuine desire for intelligent participation in public affairs and that, with some encouragement, the Sect People might ultimately have the same aspirations. By this time Franklin had sound reason to believe that most of the Germans were taking a long second step toward complete Americanization.

Actually the Germans had begun this long second step with a new interest in higher education. The Germans had always been careful to provide elementary education for their children,[85] and Franklin's early quarrel with Sower had not been over whether German children should be educated or not, but largely over whether their education should be in the English or in the German language. Two wars had virtually cut off the supply of missionary clergy, and the church Germans began giving serious thought to training their own clergy in America. As a first step, when the College of Philadelphia was reorganized in 1779 as the University of the State of Pennsylvania, the Germans succeeded in having a German School established as one of the departments of the University. The purpose of this school was to prepare Germans—particularly those intending to study for the church—for admission to the college classes. Although the school flourished (there were as many as sixty students enrolled at one time),[86] the matriculation lists of the college suggest that few Germans continued their studies on the college level at the university.[87] Even though the school had been established to meet the German demands, the German people had misgivings

---

[84] Franklin's part in the "test act" controversy is described in Van Doren, *Benjamin Franklin*, p. 735.

[85] See my "German Settlements," *Social Studies,* XLIV, 288.

[86] Joseph Henry Dubbs, *History of Franklin and Marshall College* (Lancaster, 1903), pp. 8–10.

[87] *University of Pennsylvania: Biographical Catalogue of the Matriculates of the College* (Philadelphia, 1894).

regarding the institution. There were always the old fears that the use of the English language in the classroom would completely Anglicize the students. Furthermore, as a mere "annex" to the university, the German School enjoyed little real prestige, and certainly both Germans and English realized the futility of a bilingual institution.[88] Although Franklin himself had no part in the creation of the German School, the institution was an appendage to the college which he had helped to found.

The German School was certainly not serving the purpose for which it had been begun. The only real solution to the problem of higher education for the Germans was a German college, and as early as 1784 plans for the creation of one had gotten under way.[89] The chief promoters were, of course, Lutheran and Reformed clergymen: Justis Heinrich Christian Helmuth, Lutheran pastor of Philadelphia; G. H. C. Muhlenberg, Lutheran of Lancaster; Caspar Dietrich Weyberg, Reformed of Philadelphia; and Johann Wilhelm Hendel, Reformed of Lancaster.[90] Apparently the attempt to begin the new institution was well timed, for the promoters immediately won the endorsement of the Lutheran and Reformed governing bodies. Although the original purpose was to prepare German clergy,[91] the thoughts of the promoters soon turned to the broader purpose of having "German youth instructed in such languages and sciences as to qualify them in the future to fill public offices in the Republic."[92]

With such a purpose, it was certain that the proposed institution should come to the attention of leading Pennsylvanians. One of the first was Benjamin Rush, physician of Philadelphia and close associate of Franklin.[93] Though he had long cultivated the friendship—or at least the medical practice—of the Pennsylvania Germans,[94] Rush had little more regard for their intellectual achievements than Franklin had, but he had more respect for their potentialities.[95] Sometimes about 1785 Rush learned of the proposal for a German college and became intensely interested in the project.[96] He had been one of the principal promoters of Dickinson College, which had just been opened. Dickinson College was begun under Presbyterian auspices, and Rush's interest there was chiefly because of his religious affiliation. In the German college, however, political considerations were doubtless paramount.[97] Rush, like Franklin, favored abandoning the Pennsylvania constitution of 1776: the Germans had had no little part in its adoption and, according to Rush, about half of them still favored

[88] Dubbs, *History of Franklin and Marshall College*, pp. 11–13.
[89] Coetal Letter of 1784 in *Minutes and Letters of the Coetus*, p. 392.
[90] Dubbs, *History of Franklin and Marshall College*, pp. 15–16.
[91] Coetal Letter of 1784 in *Minutes and Letters of the Coetus*, p. 392; Coetal Letter of 1786 in *ibid.*, pp. 409–410.
[92] Coetal Letter of 1790 in *ibid.*, p. 441.
[93] Goodman, *Benjamin Rush*, p. 343.
[94] When Rush began his medical practice he even attempted to learn the Pennsylvania dialect. Rush to Ebenezer Hazard, May 21, 1765, in Rush, *Letters*, ed. Butterfield, I, 14; see also editor's note, p. 16.
[95] *Ibid.*, I, 368, editor's note.
[96] Rush to John Montgomery, Aug. 21, 1785, in *ibid.*, I, 362.
[97] See L. H. Butterfield's editorial note in *A Letter by Dr. Benjamin Rush, Describing the Consecration of the German College at Lancaster in June, 1787* (Lancaster, 1945). This is Rush's letter to Annis Boudinot Stockton, June 19, 1787, in Rush, *Letters*, ed. Butterfield, I, 420–427.

its retention.[98] Also like Franklin, Rush favored a more complete union of the states and the improvement of the Articles of Confederation toward that end.[99] It was noted that the opposition to granting increased powers to the central government came chiefly from the outlying counties, including those inhabited principally by Germans. Rush seized the opportunity to turn the German college to political ends and, perhaps encouraged to do so by the German promoters of the College of Philadelphia,[100] he published in the *Pennsylvania Gazette* of August 31, 1785, an address "To the Citizens of Pennsylvania of German Birth and Extraction: Proposal of a German College,"[101] in which he appealed to the political ambitions of the Germans by pointing out how higher education would qualify them for officeholding. Although he made much of their political naïveté, he flattered the Germans by declaring them to be "a temperate, patient, and industrious people; . . . [and] therefore the best subjects for learning as well as the best members of republican governments."

As Rush was probably the "first wholehearted friend the Germans gained among the front-rank leaders of non-German stock in the state,"[102] there can be no doubt that the prospects of the college were enhanced by the address. Rush was soon joined in his support of the college by such other prominent non-Germans as Robert Morris, George Clymer, Thomas Mifflin, and, of course, Franklin—all leaders in the anticonstitutional party (or, as it was soon to be called, the Federalist party).[103]

On March 10, 1787, the German college came into existence by legislative act as Franklin College. The choice of name was doubtless that of the English-speaking members of the original board of trustees even though they comprised only twelve from a total of forty-five.[104] Although the English-speaking trustees —of whom Franklin was himself one—selected the name of a member of their own political party, it should be noted that Franklin was president of the State of Pennsylvania, as John Dickinson had been when Dickinson College was created. It would seem that no particular political significance was attached to the naming of the college, nor is it known whether any Germans recalled Franklin's words of a third of a century earlier.

Franklin headed the subscription list with a donation of £200 in specie,[105]

---

[98] Rush to Charles Nisbet, Aug. 27, 1784, in Rush, *Letters,* ed. Butterfield, I, 336–337.

[99] Rush to Nathanael Greene, Apr. 15, 1782, in *ibid.,* I, 268.

[100] *Ibid.,* I, 368*n.*

[101] *Ibid.,* I, 364–368.

[102] *Ibid.,* I, 368*n.*

[103] To what extent English-speaking support to Franklin College endeared the Federalists to the Germans would be purely a matter of conjecture. In 1788 Benjamin Rush thought that they were active in support of the Federal Constitution, but there is some reason to believe that the Germans were more inclined to support the anti-Federalists. Rush to G. H. E. Muhlenberg, Feb. 15, 1788, in *ibid.,* I, 452; Glenn Weaver, "The German Reformed Church and the Civil Government," *Pennsylvania History,* XVI (Oct. 1949), 319.

[104] Dubbs, *History of Franklin and Marshall College,* pp. 25–26. Of the thirty-three Germans sixteen were clergymen—the only clergy represented on the board, seven Lutheran, seven Reformed, one Moravian, and one Roman Catholic. *Ibid.,* p. 27.

[105] Rush to John Montgomery, Jan. 21, 1787, in Rush, *Letters,* ed. Butterfield, I, 410.

but during the remainder of his life he evidenced little interest in the college.[106] He was unable to attend the formal consecration on June 13, 1787,[107] and the assembled dignitaries—both English and German—drank a toast to the venerable gentleman.[108] Franklin had only three more years to live. As these few years passed he gave less time to public affairs. In the summer of 1788 he made his will, and the following year he added a lengthy codicil in which, contrary to popular opinion,[109] he left no bequest to the college which bore his name.

On April 17, 1790, he died at his home in Philadelphia. His funeral attracted a crowd of twenty thousand people, the largest seen in Philadelphia up to that time. In the funeral procession, before the corpse, marched all of the clergy of the city—including the German clergy. On March 1 of the following year, the American Philosophical Society honored its founder at a memorial service. Franklin's old enemy, the Reverend William Smith, former provost of the College of Philadelphia, paid glowing tribute to Franklin in an address prepared jointly by himself and Thomas Jefferson, Benjamin Rush, David Rittenhouse, and Jonathan Williams. The service was held in the German Lutheran Church at Fourth and Arch Streets in Philadelphia.[110]

During the eighty-four years of Franklin's lifetime the Pennsylvania Germans had undergone a long process which had made "Americans" of them. From a timid, misunderstood, and misunderstanding national minority they had become accepted by English-speaking Americans, and although they succeeded in preserving much of what was good in their own culture, they came to accept the dominance of the English element in what is "American." The Germans and Franklin, in the course of long association, had come to stand on the common ground of American nationality.

[106] The college was never a subject of his correspondence.
[107] J. H. Dubbs has gone to great lengths to prove that Franklin was present at the laying of the cornerstone. *History of Franklin and Marshall College,* pp. 40–58. It is now commonly accepted that Franklin was not present. Van Doren, *Benjamin Franklin,* p. 741.
[108] Rush to Annis Boudinot Stockton, June 19, 1787, in Rush, *Letters,* ed. Butterfield, I, 424.
[109] Van Doren, *Benjamin Franklin,* pp. 761–762; *Writings of Franklin,* ed. Smyth, I, 210; Smyth has reproduced the will and codicil in *Writings of Franklin,* X, 493–510.
[110] Van Doren, *Benjamin Franklin,* p. 781. The text of the address is in H. W. Smith, *Life and Correspondence of the Rev. William Smith,* II, 329–344.

Scotch-Irish

JAMES G. LEYBURN
Frontier Society

In the following selection, taken from what has been called the best book on the Scotch-Irish, sociologist James G. Leyburn gives renewed vitality to the controversial and oft-discussed frontier thesis of Frederick Jackson Turner. In 1893, Turner, one of the most imaginative historians the United States has ever produced, enunciated what was then considered a revolutionary interpretation of America's growth: "The existence of an area of free land, its continuous recession, and the advance of American settlement westward, explain American development." He credited the strength and well-being of the American people to this continually receding frontier where men had to build society out of wilderness and individuals through persevering labor could earn their status. The desolate conditions of frontier, according to Turner, fostered democracy, individualism, and cooperation. Where all men operated under the same conditions hereditary gradations in position or selfish aloofness could not survive.

The Scotch-Irish (known simply as the "Irish" in colonial parlance), one of the first immigrant groups to pass through the settled areas and make homes on the western borders of established communities in New England, Pennsylvania, and the southern colonies, emigrated from Ulster, Ireland, in the early part of the eighteenth century. About 100 years earlier their ancestors had left Scotland in the hope of finding a better life in Northern Ireland. By the beginning of the 1700s, however, the British navigation acts and other restrictive policies had severely affected Ulster woolen and linen manufacturers, shipbuilders, and cattle grazers. Absentee landlords charged prohibitive rents, taxes had to be paid to support the Anglican Church regardless of religious affiliation (most of the Scotch-Irish were Presbyterian), and the Scotch-Irish could neither vote, hold office, nor maintain their own schools. These disabilities proving too burdensome, between 1717 and 1776 about 250,000 left Ulster for the New World. As described by Leyburn, the Scotch-Irish experiences in British North America conform almost exactly to the Turner thesis.

For many Americans there exists a mental image of a "typical pioneer," living with his large family in a log cabin set in a space he had cleared in the forest.

Reprinted from James G. Leyburn, *The Scotch-Irish* (Chapel Hill: University of North Carolina Press, 1962), pp. 256–72; by permission of the author and publisher.

There he led a rough but simple life, hunting and trapping, farming with crude implements and wasteful methods, and occasionally having to fight Indians. He drank a great deal of corn whisky, scorned refinement, loved practical jokes, danced vigorous reels and hoedowns to a scraping fiddle, and enjoyed such rough sports as fights with his bare fists. Yet at bottom his character was sound and his impulses were right. He and his kind, according to this image of pioneer life, conquered the wilderness and laid the foundations of democratic faith and practice.

Frederick Jackson Turner and his successors suggested that each time the pioneers moved another stage farther west one more layer of civilization was stripped off, one more tie that bound men to European standards and institutions was loosed.[1] They believed that the unique experiences of frontier life called into being qualities of character and, more significantly, democratic ideas, which together have made later generations Americans rather than transplanted Europeans.

In both the image of the typical pioneer and in the Turner thesis the Scotch-Irishman plays a significant role. He is regarded as America's first true backwoodsman, showing the way to the winning of the west, leading the vanguard of those who cross the Alleghenies to open up for settlement that great valley in the heart of continental United States. It must therefore be asked whether the Scotch-Irish pioneers actually lived in the rough, hardy, but upright manner regarded as typical; and whether, in addition, they were among the shapers of an almost anarchic democracy, anti-intellectual and equalitarian in its results.

It is curious to observe that most histories of the American frontier begin with the movement into the Ohio Valley, after the American Revolution, as if the preceding 150 years of settlement in the wilderness from Maine to Georgia had had no such effects as making the pioneers strip off European habiliments, while leaving them crude in manners and democratic in outlook.[2] The almost mystical influence of frontier life could apparently begin to exert its force only when the colonists had gained their independence and had moved away from the Atlantic seaboard. Yet here is a confusion. Since the Scotch-Irish migration had occurred before the Revolution, it should logically show the social characteristics, say, of New England or New Jersey rather than those of Kentucky and Ohio. On the other hand, because Scotch-Irish settlement was always in the back-country, far away from the seaboard and its European connections, it should produce the typical pioneer characteristics of manners and outlook. The Frontier School of historians do not resolve this dilemma. They seem only occasionally to regard the Scotch-Irish in colonial times, while east of the mountains, as representative of the new type of American character; yet after 1783, when many moved west, the wild frontier began, according to the theory, to exert its mysterious influence.

---

[1] Frederick Jackson Turner, *The Frontier in American History* (New York, 1920), especially the influential essay on "The Significance of the Frontier in American History," appearing as the first chapter in this book of Turner's essays.

[2] See, for example, Frederic L. Paxson's *History of the American Frontier* (Boston and New York, 1924); E. D. Branch's *Westward: The Romance of the American Frontier* (New York, 1930); Robert E. Riegel's *America Moves West* (New York, 1930); and many others.

It would seem wise to consider the social life of the Scotch-Irish as it actually was, rather than to view it as either confirming or refuting a thesis.

Ulster itself had constituted something of a frontier environment in 1610, for there were homes to make and wild natives to subdue; but by 1717 Ulster was "civilized," even in the eyes of the English Parliament. Ulstermen believed in orderly government and courts; they knew and respected standards of morality and propriety with the same degree of rigidity and laxity apparent in any society; they accepted without challenge the existence of monarchy as the proper form of government and of social classes as the right ordering of society. They came to America to escape none of these, but because times were hard in Ireland whereas America seemed to be a land of endless opportunity. As has been noted, they objected to certain governmental policies, bitterly resenting the restrictions on trade and on Presbyterian magistrates; but it would be a serious distortion of history to claim that the exodus from Ulster was a crusading search for freedom. On the contrary, all of the evidence shows that the people hoped to find social institutions in America very much like the ones they were leaving.

These they did find, in the settled areas around their ports of debarkation. When they took farms in the wilderness they set to work forthwith to establish familiar institutions.

Their immediate task was, of course, to build a home and plant a crop as soon as possible. In these first days and months every family in the community lived under conditions roughly similar to those of their neighbors. The life of newly arrived frontiersmen was the same practically everywhere, north or south, and whether the people had come straight from Europe or had moved from a community along the American seaboard. Crude and makeshift arrangements did not first begin on the western side of the Alleghenies. The important question seems to be how long these arrangements were tolerated— how strong the impulse was to change them into something resembling settled life. In the following account, which happens to be a description of pioneering in New Hampshire, one has the details of the early days of people on a frontier; it might have been an account of pioneers in Virginia or Pennsylvania, in Scotch-Irish settlements or in English ones, in early colonial regions or in the much later settlements around the Ohio country.

"They frequently lie out in the woods several days or weeks together in all seasons of the year. A hut composed of poles and bark, suffice them for shelter; and on the open side of it, a large fire secures them from the severity of the weather. Wrapt in a blanket with their feet near the fire, they pass the longest and coldest nights, and awake vigorous for labour the succeeding day. Their food . . . is salted pork or beef, with potatoes and bread of Indian corn; and their drink is water mixed with ginger; though many of them are fond of distilled spirits. . . . Those who begin a new settlement, live at first in a style not less simple. They erect a square building of poles [that is, a log cabin], notched at the ends to keep them fast together. The crevices are plaistered with clay or the stiffest earth which can be had, mixed with moss or straw. The roof is either bark or split boards. The chimney a pile of stones; within which a fire is made on the ground, and a hole is left in the roof for the smoke to pass out. Another hole is made in the side of the house for a window, which is occasionally closed with a wooden shutter. In winter, a constant fire is kept, by night as well as by day; and in summer it is necessary to have a continual smoke on account of the musquetos and other insects with which the woods abound. The same defence is used for the cattle; smokes of leaves and brush are made in the pastures where they feed by day, and in the pens where they are folded by night. Ovens are built at a small distance from the houses, of the best stones which can be found, cemented and plaistered with clay or stiff earth. Many of these first essays in housekeeping, are to be met with in the new plantations, which serve to lodge whole families, till their industry can furnish them with materials, for a more regular and comfortable house; and till their land is so well cleared as that a proper situation for it can be chosen. By these methods of living, the people are familiarised to hardships; their children are early used to coarse food and hard lodgings; and to be without shoes in all seasons of the year is scarcely accounted a want. By such hard fare, and the labour which accompanies it, many young men have raised up families, and in a few years have acquired property sufficient to render themselves independent freeholders; and they feel all the pride and importance which arise from a consciousness of having well earned their estates.[3]"

Characteristic (and practical) frontier actions occurred among the Scotch-Irish as elsewhere: neighborly help was expected and given in log-rolling, house-raising, tree-felling. No doubt one cabin so much resembled every other that a visitor would have supposed that no social distinctions could exist. Coming with few household goods or implements, each family must camp out until the cabin could be built. With the preliminary preparations made, erection of a house usually required but a day, with a rough division of labor among the helpers. With the walls up, a man could at his own leisure construct his furniture, shape his wooden dishes and buckets, build a stone chimney, and make a floor to cover the bare earth. The indispensable equipment of every pioneer consisted of rifle, pouches, powder horn, axe, and hoe; beyond these a man's acquisitions marked his economic progress.

Many Scotch-Irish have left memoirs of these earliest days, with all the earthy details still vivid in their memories. It is actually the testimony of these accounts that has led to the impression of the rough crudity of all true pioneer society. What is sometimes forgotten is that the people regarded such conditions as a temporary, if necessary, makeshift, to be endured until a better life could replace it—and "better" meant having the institutions and established order of civilized Ulster. Progress to that order could be marked in almost precise stages: first, the building of a church and securing a minister—and if a school could be managed, so much the better; second, the appearance of a store and possibly a tavern, as links with settled communities in older parts of the country and with the outside world; and third, bringing the neighborhood under the jurisdiction of a court, near enough to assure effective law and order.

The American pioneer, whether Scotch-Irish or any other, must begin as a jack-of-all-trades. Almost the only professions represented among the early Ulstermen were the ministry and teaching, usually performed by the same individual. In the later settlement of the south, surveyors and then lawyers were especially useful: squatting, verbal agreements, and guesswork as to boundary lines resulted in conflicting claims, and the Scotch-Irish were often regarded as "a very litigious people." Farming, of course, was the major concern of every-

[3] Jeremy Belknap, *The History of New-Hampshire* (Boston, 1792), III, 257–59.

one, often even of the minister. Individual farmers who developed particular skills were called upon by neighbors who needed specialized work done; the obligation would be repaid by return service in another specialty, by extra help on farm chores, or (rarely) by money payments. Some of these specialists might choose to set up shop in a village or town, when settlement increased. The most usual and necessary of crafts were those of the blacksmith, wheelwright, wagon-maker, joiner, cooper, weaver, fuller, tailor, hatter, rope-maker, and wine-maker.

More significant for American life than the familiar details of pioneering is the gradual modification of concepts of social distinctions. What occurred among the Scotch-Irish between 1717 and the end of the century was an augury, almost a pattern, of things to come in the United States.

When the Great Migration began in 1717 no one in his right mind, either in the British Isles or in the colonies, questioned the fact of social superiority and inferiority. Some families were wellborn, some were "middling," and most belonged to the "lower orders,"—and so it had been since the beginning of time. Such distinctions seemed clearly to be in the natural order of things. The stability of society derived from this order: people always knew where to look for leadership, and the training in responsibility was assumed in families of property, education, and background. The system of social classes was not immutably rigid, for men might occasionally rise, and persons of "family" often shirked their duties; but in the main the system worked.

Coming to America meant for Ulstermen months of primitive living, yet it would not be long before the social distinctions of the old country would manifest themselves, not only in the leadership assumed by "substantial" men but by the rapid material progress they made. They had started with the advantage of more money than the average immigrant had to spend on implements and livestock. They could not, at the outset in the wilderness, be above the hard manual labor required for making a farm; but they were intent upon having homes equal, even superior, to the ones they had left. Why else had they come to the New World? Such men were not so enamored of adventure that they wished to live as on a permanent camping trip. If they could afford to buy the labor of indentured servants or to hire young helpers, they could clear more ground than their neighbors, extend their homes, and improve their grounds.

Within months the old social distinctions were visible to all. Substantial men were not called aristocrats; the Old World vocabulary changed in America, and the ancient word "peasant" disappeared altogether; but the social order remained. Any community could name its good families, its middle group of respectable people, and the lower orders who ranged toward the shiftless. It was observed that in colonies where frontier counties were organized, the Scotch-Irish invariably chose gentlemen from the good families to represent them in the Assembly. If a church were organized, these men were made elders. It was they who pressed for civil institutions and economic betterment of the community.

Social status in a Scotch-Irish community was revealed by objective criteria, such as the size and condition of the dwelling, care of the farm, work done by women in the family, personal character and morality, or even diversions engaged in.

The quality of a family's home quickly revealed status. On arrival at the site chosen for the farm, the first shelter could be only a hastily constructed lean-to; this soon was replaced by an "open Logg Cabbin," consisting of a roofed structure closed on side and back, but open on the front to the elements. If a man endured such an arrangement for many months, the neighborhood knew instantly where to place him in the social order—as it did the man whose permanent cabin was most ambitiously laid out and most neatly constructed.

A glance round a farm after two or three years would reveal the man's social standing. Good, respectable families had their fields unencumbered with stumps, more land cleared each year, clean crops and careful farming. The cow was the most valuable domestic animal, and the observer could see whether enough cattle were being raised to sent east to market for cash or goods.[4] Other animals in variety were further clues to the standard of living in the family. Pigs were certain to be found on every farm, for the Scotch-Irish quickly lost their ancient prejudice against pork, the preferred meat on most American frontiers.[5] Sheep, so plentiful in Ulster, were rare on frontier farms, for they required either shepherds or fences, and labor was not available for either; but the presence of even a few sheep bespoke the quality of clothes the family would wear. As for food, no pioneer need ever want, even before his first crop was harvested. Forests teemed with game, wild fruits, nuts, and berries, and the streams with fish. It marked the quality of the family, however, if it long depended chiefly on what nature offered, instead of cultivating a garden that contained not only the staples of the Old World, but the attractive vegetables of the New—corn, sweet potatoes, new varieties of beans, squash, and pumpkins.

An almost absolute clue to status was afforded by the women in a family. Were the wife and grown daughters permitted to work in the fields? If so, that family belonged to the lowest class. All women worked, and worked hard; but the proper place for a woman of good family or of respectability was in the home. Marriage was early, for a bachelor could hardly survive in a frontier community without a wife, unless he left home to become a perpetual explorer, hunter, trapper, or Indian trader. Domestic economy depended upon the women: cooking, baking, the making of clothes, washing, milking cows, making butter, spinning, weaving, pickling, all the other manifold duties of a housewife, in addition to being mother to eight or ten children, nursing them, caring for them through illness without a doctor, and teaching them if a school were not available. How efficiently and successfully a wife and mother accomplished her endless tasks was, justly or unjustly, considered a mark of status. Not even in the most trying days of early settlement, however, would a man who valued his social position permit field labor for his wife and daughters.[6]

[4] For well over a hundred years—indeed, until the 1890's—it was a familiar sight to see droves of cattle on their way to markets in Philadelphia, Baltimore, Charleston, and other ports and markets. The drover, generally a younger son, would arrange to reach the farm of an acquaintance by nightfall, and there find water and pasture for his cattle and hospitality for himself and his helpers.

[5] Scots had for centuries surprised the English by their aversion to pork. Highlanders apparently did not conquer their prejudice until after 1746. Scott's novels contain many references to this dietary peculiarity. See, for example, *The Fortunes of Nigel*, II, 161, 347; and *Waverley*, I, 362, from Sir Walter Scott, *Novels* (Boston: Houghton Mifflin, 1923).

[6] Almost every historian who comments upon domestic life on the frontier includes a well-deserved eulogy upon the courage, fortitude, and even heroism of the frontier wife. Wayland F. Dunaway (*The Scotch-Irish of Colonial Pennsylvania,* Chapel Hill, 1944, p. 189) justly says: "On some towering mountain peak of Pennsylvania, the Commonwealth should erect to [the Scotch-Irish woman] a monument as a worthy memorial of her character and deeds."

It could well be reasoned that the informal, but very real, social class system of the Scotch-Irish was based upon character. One of the strongest checks on laxity of behavior had been removed upon the American scene: the farm village. In Ulster, as almost everywhere else in the British Isles, tenants on an estate lived in houses close by each other along a village street, each tenant going thence every day to work on his own plot of land. This close proximity had the inevitable result of making every man aware of his neighbors and their opinion, for each person was in truth his brother's keeper. In the New World, however, the farm village was characteristic only of New England. Among the Scotch-Irish, and thereafter across the frontier to the end of the Great Plains, it seemed more practical for each farmer to live near the center of his own land. Until the prairies were reached, a man's land had to be cleared out of the forest, and with his hunting grounds might include three hundred acres or more. A village could come into being only when specialists—a store-keeper, lawyers, a smith, a tavernkeeper, the minister—were present, or when a courthouse marked the final arrival of civilization. For families living alone on an isolated farm, it would be easy to fall into compromises, to let standards deteriorate, in short, to become shiftless in the absence of daily surveillance by close neighbors. Families who, removed from watchful eyes, still upheld the best standards they knew, had proved their worth.

More than this, life in the wilderness offered special temptations to laxity. Long accustomed to the use of whisky in Scotland and Ireland, the pioneers quickly learned how to turn their new crop, corn, into whisky. Stills abounded, for in whisky the Scotch-Irish found their first product easily marketable and easily conveyed in compact form to trading centers. With no voice yet raised against drinking, with plentiful supplies of whisky in every home (even the homes of ministers), and with corn liquor the one social drink expected at every social gathering, many people became hard drinkers. Here again, character and self-control revealed the man: sobriety (not abstention) distinguished itself from occasional drunkenness, and this in turn from "drinking too much."

Diversions afforded still another criterion of social class. Pioneer remi-niscences devote many pages to the vigorous athleticism of most frontier sports, all of them ones that brought people together—for the men, wrestling, com-petitive shooting for a mark, racing; for the women, quilting parties and co-operative work at the men's house-raisings, corn-huskings, and harvest-times. Strenuous dancing marked most festival occasions. Imperceptibly, as pioneers moved farther away from settled communities, many of their diversions de-generated into crudity. Travelers in Kentucky and the Ohio Valley were often shocked at the wrestling matches in which men gouged out each other's eyes, at brutal fist fights, at such sports as "gander-pulling," in which a live fowl was suspended by its legs from a limb, while men on horseback galloped by and tried to twist the head off the creature's greased neck. From every part of the frontier came stories of wedding celebrations, to which the whole community had been orally invited: the occasion generally began with the young men racing for a bottle of whisky, the winner having the right to be the first to kiss the bride; and it ended with the "bedding" of the couple, accompanied by ribald good wishes for the beginning of a large family and finally by a "shivaree" (charivari)—a raucous serenade on pots and pans.

This widespread crudity was explained and justified by comments on the boisterousness of high animal spirits, the youth of the pioneer, the need for uproarious relaxation after a day's or a week's steady and monotonous labor on an isolated farm. Out of such occasions seem to have grown many traits commented upon with distaste by European travelers: the American addiction to practical jokes, the tall tale, the preference for exaggeration rather than understatement in humor.[7]

In this realm of amusements there was also an opportunity for social distinctions, for what was congenial to ordinary folk was often not "proper" for their betters. An elder's family might well participate in many of the amusements, however vigorous; but a subtle line was drawn where behavior seemed to be in bad taste. The appearance of village life—the goal, it may be repeated, of all ambitious Scotch-Irish pioneers—provided a steady pull away from the excesses of folk hilarity. Indeed, the two poles are clearly seen: at one extreme the wild frontier, always moving beyond the reach of established institutions and their restraints; at the other extreme the settled village, drawing people toward refinement of manners.

These contrary influences no doubt occasioned a serious tension for many individuals, especially the younger ones. On the one hand, there was the desire to become respected and substantial citizens by the traditional standards of education and community responsibility. The church, as the dominant social institution, with all of the prestige of authority and continuity and with its customary surveillance of one's personal life, abetted parental influence in drawing youth to the high standards expected of the best families and the respectable. On the other hand, the challenge of launching out for oneself, of making one's own way by conquering his own difficulties, combined with the pressure of population on the supply of attractive land in the East to lure one away to the new frontier. There the restraining hand of church and community watchfulness would be removed; one need not be actually rebellious to understand the appeal of deciding for himself and the appeal of good-natured, if crude, practices.

Excitement and adventure as contrasted with routine were also aspects of the tension. Hunting and tracking game, which had been necessities for survival at the beginning, soon became favorite pastimes. Scotch-Irishmen learned Indian methods of forest-craft as quickly as they had learned Indian methods of fighting, and many of the men became expert hunters, even addicts, who preferred life in the woods to the tameness of life in a village. Moving west to unknown country, with a possibility of danger from wild beast and Indian, was preferable for many young men to safe security.

Life in Scotch-Irish communities, therefore, though it differed in detail from life in Ulster, continued to reflect for many years the familiar social distinctions between families. Gradually, however, especially as people moved beyond Pennsylvania and Virginia into the Carolinas, class lines became blurred and criteria for distinguishing them vague. By the end of the eighteenth century there were even those who expressed resentment against emphasis on family and what it implied of social superiority. The Scotch-Irish did not cause this social transformation; many deeply regretted it; but it was among them that the old

[7] See Allan Nevins, *American Social History as Recorded by British Travellers* (New York, 1923), especially chapters 4 and 6.

standards of social class began to be eroded. No democratic theory attacked the old system. It was weakened by the fact that people by the thousands were constantly on the move.

Stable social classes flourish only when residence is continuous in a community, so that men agree upon what brings prestige and position; when upper classes are fairly exclusive in their marriages; when sons are indoctrinated with the idea that they have not only rights but also obligations of leadership and responsibility; and when tradition guides institutions into conservative channels. The mobility of the Scotch-Irish simply swept away all of these foundation stones of the class system for thousands of the people. However much the first settlers expected to reproduce the standards of the Old World, there was always a drift of the restless and a pull of the young and ambitious to a new settlement, and beyond that to a still newer one. Every fresh move meant that life had, at least momentarily, to be primitive again—chopping trees, making first crops, living in camp. Maturing youths married their available neighbors and could not wait for persons of good family to appear. In a new frontier region there is no school for children, no church for anyone. Weddings, baptisms, and funerals, if they can be performed by anyone, must depend upon the arrival of an itinerant preacher, who might be illiterate and wholly unlike a Presbyterian divine. If not even an itinerant is at hand, then at least the baptisms and funerals can wait. Where, under such frontier conditions, are class distinctions, especially if the young folk and the restless move off to repeat a process so corrosive to tradition?

There was, indeed, a certain tug in the direction of preserving the old system. The age of a settlement, nearness to economic markets, the presence of an organized Presbyterian Church, established courts and civil institutions, the growth of villages and towns—all of these were conserving influences. Yet they could not exert their steadying force upon the thousands who came in each year from Ulster looking for cheap lands, nor upon the ambitious young people of the prolific Scotch-Irish who felt that they must strike out for themselves. At any given moment in the latter half of the century, settlements could be found in every stage of "civilization," with each newest stage suspending and modifying old standards. In 1765, for example, communities in Pennsylvania and Virginia had become stable, orderly, accustomed to social and economic amenities; here class distinctions were visible. In the Carolinas, however, the social order was still in the making, with Regulation movements in both provinces a political indication of unstable institutions. The observer here would find not the amenities of orderly life but various degrees of pioneering crudities.[8]

[8] The most graphic account of the shocking effect upon a conventional mind of this primitive life is that given in the Journal of the Reverend Charles Woodmason. This Anglican itinerant traveled constantly among settlers of the South Carolina upcountry from 1766 to 1768. Discounting to the fullest Woodmason's belligerent attitude toward dissenters, his naïveté, bias, and prejudices, one can still perceive the almost elemental nature of much of the life in the region at that time.

Population increase had far outstripped institutions. There were families, of course; but many couples lived together and had children without being married—for who was there to perform the ceremony? No courts were present to secure justice nor were there schools or churches. Lawlessness, vile manners, ignorance, and slovenliness were commonplace, with people unaware of how far they had sunk from "civilized" life. To Woodmason it seemed not a hopeful sign that Presbyterians and Baptists were at work among these people, but rather as an evidence of Satan's presence to pervert

The half century during which Scotch-Irish immigration and settlement occurred, therefore, sounded the knell of social classes based upon family background. It was the constant movement of people into new territory that caused the erosion of traditional distinctions, and it was among the Scotch-Irish that it first occurred on a large scale. Among the older settlements in the East—in Boston, Philadelphia, the Tidewater, Charleston, for example—the respected distinctions not only persisted but continued to be regarded as part of the natural order; but henceforward the class system, so calmly accepted in 1700, was bound to disintegrate under the steady movement of swelling numbers to new lands of the West.

The experience of the Scotch-Irish in this matter of classes was doubly interesting. It was true that, with them, the old order faded away; but it was also with them that a new order appeared and one that came to be fairly representative of American life. People always make social distinctions. They are always conscious of prestige, even though the attainments that bring prestige change over the years and change radically. What disappeared among the Scotch-Irish and among most Americans thereafter was the idea of *permanence* of social distinctions, the belief that families must be given deference simply because they have always had it. What was retained among the Scotch-Irish and later Americans was acceptance of social distinction, even social class, based upon whether an individual family, in this generation and for this generation alone, achieved the qualities that were admired, respected, and honored at the time and place.

A shift had been subtly and imperceptibly made from the criterion of family heritage to that of individual achievement. One's own strength of will, self-control, inward determination, were now the primary factors determining status in a community. The goals worth achieving were to change in the nineteenth century from those of the eighteenth: wealth meant more in the later period than living like a "gentleman," for example. Yet an unbiased examination of any predominantly Scotch-Irish community from Pennsylvania to Georgia in 1800 would reveal the reality of class distinctions. These would simply not have been the same ones men's grandfathers would have honored in the same community fifty years before.[9]

Scotch-Irish settlements east of the Appalachians marked, in effect, a turning point in American life. They were a field, as the Tidewater was not,

---

men from the true (that is, the Anglican) faith. Yet it was simple tragedy that so many of the people had moved so far, and so often, from civilized society that thousands had never even heard of God, religion, or church. Often where religious institutions had made their start, bigotry and denominational animosities were so rampant that one sect would try to drive another from the region. (See Charles Woodmason, *The Carolina Backcountry on the Eve of the Revolution. The Journals and other writings of Charles Woodmason, Anglican Itinerant,* ed. Richard J. Hooker, [Chapel Hill, 1953].)

[9] In such a characteristic Scotch-Irish town or village of 1800, the upper class would almost certainly consist of those who were educated, members of the Presbyterian Church, financially capable of having servants, engaged either in gentleman-farming or in an enterprise in which manual labor was not involved, with leisure for riding and visiting and reading, opposed to enthusiasms whether in religion or politics, and moral with a puritanical rigidity. Memoirs preserved in county historical societies throughout the whole area of Scotch-Irish predominance attest the validity of this picture.

in which opposing values found full play, with those who chose one set remaining in the settled communities and those who chose the other set going on farther west. Those who stayed showed their belief in stability, viable institutions, community control of morality, amenities of social intercourse, decency and order, the worth of tradition. Those who moved away preferred instead the values of individualism, adventure, independence of action, making their own way in the world, taking risks. The region of Scotch-Irish settlement, simply by its geographical location, was both the last bastion of traditional standards and the threshold across which Americans could pass to more egalitarian ways of life.

As the Frontier School of historians have noted, each new move to the West strengthened the democratic impulse as it weakened traditional distinctions. It has become commonplace to remark that in the wilds the judgment of a man was not made on the basis of his antecedents but upon his virility, courage, and ingenuity. Book learning and intellectuality were no longer the criteria for respect, but rather physical qualities. Neighborliness was essential for survival in a wilderness; no family could hold itself apart; marriage was necessary, and one's choice was more and more likely to be made on the practical basis of availability and personal characteristics, not upon who one's family might have been in the East. Where people share comradeship in protecting themselves against Indians, and neighborliness in house-raisings, where all join to find diversion, where neither church nor sedate older people are present to emphasize tradition, a rough equality is bound to exist.

Children and grandchildren of the original Scotch-Irish settlers in America were always among the leaders in the move to the new West; but they were no longer Scotch-Irish in their social characteristics and outlook. Just as they were likely to become Methodists and Baptists instead of remaining Presbyterians, so they were likely to marry persons whose background may have been English or German. The memory of Ulster and its respectabilities and distinctions meant little or nothing to these constant pioneers. They were Americans.[10]

One problem that beset the lives of immigrants to America in the nineteenth century was spared to most of the Scotch-Irish: except in New England, and rarely elsewhere, they never felt themselves to be a "minority group." Beginning in 1846, with the first mighty influx of Irishmen escaping from the potato famine, and continuing until 1921 when Congress effectively closed the door to mass immigration in this country, newcomers poured into the United States. The first years for these immigrants after 1846 were, in the majority of cases, spent in the cities and settled regions of the East, where American culture

[10] The temptation to ascribe social characteristics to a specific cause is difficult to resist. It is here that the Frontier School of historians has been most at fault, for these scholars have attributed many American national characteristics to the influence of frontier life, as if this alone were the explanation. In the same fashion, certain social scientists have named the Industrial Revolution as the cause of "mass society," supposedly an American characteristic. They name as trends within this mass society a decline of kinship ties, the growth of specialization, of secularism and rationality, of associations formed for specific purposes rather than of communities, of mobility. (See, for example, Leonard Broom and Philip Selznick, *Sociology* [2d ed.; Evanston, 1958], pp. 35-39). Frontier life was essentially individualistic and thus diametrically different from a mass society; yet it, too, stimulated mobility and a decline of kinship ties, two of the supposed results of the Industrial Revolution.

had long since taken shape. Immediately the immigrant was confronted with standards, values, and mores unlike his own—often radically different from his own. An individual's mind is free only when he does not have constantly to make personal judgments of right and wrong, only when he accepts, as second nature, the standards of his culture. These later immigrants, however, were "marginal men," caught between two cultures in conflict for their loyalty: the familiar culture of their childhood, deeply ingrained in their souls, and that of the country to which they had come with high hopes. If the immigrant conscientiously retained the old standards, he saw his children accept the new, so that the conflict was sudden, sharp, and centered in his very home. His life was, in effect, a battleground on which he must be perpetually on guard—and worse, he must decide both tactics and strategy for himself, for he was not now fully a member of any society whose culture he could wholly accept. He was on the margin of two cultures and two societies, pulled sentimentally and by his conscience toward one and by his hope and commitment of life toward another.

Durkheim calls this state of mind *anomie*—normlessness, an absence of clear standards to follow.[11] Anomie was an experience unknown to the Scotch-Irishman, for he moved immediately upon arrival to a region where there was neither a settlement nor an established culture. He held land, knew independence, had manifold responsibilities from the very outset. He spoke the language of his neighbors to the East through whose communities he had passed on his way to the frontier. Their institutions and standards differed at only minor points from his own. The Scotch-Irish were not, in short, a "minority group" and needed no Immigrant Aid society to tide them over a period of maladjustment so that they might become assimilated in the American melting pot. Like all people, whether immigrants or stay-at-homes, they must have known individual discouragement and disappointment; some may even have had a heightened feeling of inner loneliness, a quality of mind Weber attributes to most Calvinists who reflect upon the implications of the doctrine of predestination.[12] But to the extent that their neighbors shared similar experiences and attitudes, without pressure from other Americans to be different, the Scotch-Irish were not anomic, were not marginal men. They were, on the contrary, full Americans almost from the moment they took up their farms in the back-country.[13]

[11] *Le Suicide* (Paris, 1897), ch. 1. (Translated by George Simpson, *Suicide* [Glencoe, 1951].)

[12] Max Weber, *The Protestant Ethic and the Spirit of Capitalism,* trans. Talcott Parsons (London, 1930), pp. 111 ff.

[13] For a discussion of the mental problems of later immigrants, see Everett V. Stonequist, *The Marginal Man* (New York, 1937), throughout.

The Young Republic

Between the end of the American Revolution and the start of the Civil War 5,250,000 immigrants came to the United States. The vast majority, approximately 5,000,000, arrived between 1815 and 1860, that is, after the defeat of Napoleon again opened the sea lanes across the Atlantic and before the Civil War temporarily halted the influx from abroad. After 1808, when the official closing of the slave trade led to the smuggling in of African blacks, recorded newcomers came almost exclusively from northern and western Europe. The tremendous increase of migration during the post-1815 period, and particularly after the 1820s, can be attributed chiefly to a population explosion in Europe beginning around 1750, which created a surplus of manpower on the farms and in the cities; to the development of the factory system, which dislocated many artisans; and to the emergence of large-scale, market-oriented, scientific agriculture, which displaced millions of peasant farmers and agricultural laborers. This last factor operated with the greatest severity during the enclosure movements, which consolidated estates in Britain, Ireland, Scandinavia, and southwestern Germany. Political frustrations played a less important role in stimulating emigration but brought over many defeated revolutionaries or counter-revolutionaries from France during the 1790s and refugees from the abortive republican and nationalist uprisings of the 1840s in Germany, Italy, Austria, Hungary, and Ireland. Religious persecutions of Norwegian Quakers and Prussian Lutherans, for example, accounted for a minor part of the great ethnic migrations in this era. The mass movement from the Old World to the New was further facilitated when England, Scandinavia, and Germany dropped their emigration restrictions during the years between 1820 and 1860, by the spread of information about America, and by the establishment of regular, faster, safer, and more inexpensive transportation across the Atlantic.

Relatively few newcomers entered before the 1820s despite the arrival of a few individuals who achieved enormous fame and success in America. These were most notably the Swiss aristocrat Albert Gallatin, Thomas Jefferson's Secretary of the Treasury; the English artisan Samuel Slater, who established the first American cotton factory in Pawtucket, Rhode Island; and John Jacob Astor, the German butcher's son, whose achievements in the fur trade and in New York real estate made him the richest American of his time.

Mass migrations of Europeans began in the 1830s when almost 600,000 people entered the United States. The major nationalities involved in this ti-

*tanic movement—1,713,000 came in the 1840s and 2,314,000 in the 1850s—
were the Irish, Germans, English, and Scandinavians.*

More than two million Irish emigrants embarked for America in the thirty
years preceeding the start of the Civil War. In Europe they suffered the greatest
population density and endured an iniquitous agricultural system of absentee
landlords (mostly British), rural poverty, high rents, and insecure land tenure.
Overpopulation in Ireland had led to intense competition for land that was subdivided because of the system of land inheritance into tiny plots barely suf-
ficent to provide enough food for survival. The collapse of Irish grain exports
after the Napoleonic Wars, the opening of the British market to Irish farm
produce in 1826, the enclosure of small units into more efficient larger holdings,
and the potato blight of 1845–49 drove millions of starving peasants from
Ireland.

Similar but less harsh circumstances accounted for the German immigration.
The exodus, chiefly from Wurtemburg, Baden, and Bavaria, peaked in the decade from 1846 to 1855 when revolution and crop failures combined with land
consolidation by wealthy farmers or nobles to bring 1,000,000 Germans to the
United States. The movement then diminished because the conversion of south-
western German agriculture into a modern process had been completed. German immigrants as a whole were better off than the Irish because they had been
more prosperous in their home country, and because they numbered a greater
proportion of middle-class revolutionaries, wealthy farmers who feared for the
future, and artisans, merchants, and professionals.

The 750,000 Englishmen who arrived during these decades were chiefly
artisans and skilled workers displaced by the introduction of machinery into
the textile and mining industries and by unemployment during the depression
of the 1840s, and agricultural laborers whom the enclosure movement rendered
landless and who feared disastrous agricultural competition after repeal of the
protective tariffs on grains after 1846. Since their ranks included skilled workers and some prosperous farmers, and since English agriculture was not as impoverished as Irish, they, too, brought more wealth with them than Ireland's
peasants.

Scandinavian immigration began in large numbers in the 1820s and gained
momentum in the 1840s. Conflicts between Pietists and the established church
in Norway influenced some to leave, but the fundamental cause, agricultural
displacement as a consequence of modern farming technique and organization,
was similar to the situation which spurred emigration from England and Germany.

Out of the total American population of 31,500,000 in 1860, 4,136,000
were foreign born. With the exception of 500,000 recorded in the slave states
the newcomers lived north of the Mason-Dixon line and east of the Mississippi.
New York, Pennsylvania, Ohio, Illinois, Wisconsin, and Massachusetts, in
descending order, contained the most numerous foreign born. Among these were
the states with the highest levels of urbanization and industrialization and with the
most accessible fertile land. By 1860 it was already apparent that the destinies
of the city and the immigrant were intertwined. The heaviest concentration
of the foreign born lay in urban centers. Nearly 50 percent of the populations
of New York, Chicago, Milwaukee, Detroit, and San Francisco consisted of

European immigrants; 60 percent of the residents of St. Louis and one-third of those in New Orleans, Baltimore, and Boston came from abroad.

Poverty, enduring bitterness over their agrarian experience at home, and need for immediate employment confined the Irish, more than any other ethnic minority, to the city. In 1860 two-thirds of the 1,611,000 Irish Americans lived in New York, Pennsylvania, New Jersey, and New England, the vast majority dwelling in the cities of these states. Germans, wealthier and more determined to resume farming, were more likely to leave the cities. About one-half of the 1,301,000 Germans who had come to this country by 1860 resided on fertile farms in the Upper Mississippi and Ohio Valleys, particularly in Illinois, Wisconsin, and Missouri. Lacking capital and also skill with the axe and rifle, Germans and other immigrants, such as the Scandinavians, who settled mainly in Minnesota, Iowa, and Illinois, avoided the frontier and sought land that had already been cleared. More than 50 percent of the nearly 600,000 Americans of British birth could be found immediately south of the Great Lakes, in New York, Michigan, Wisconsin, and Illinois, while most of the rest concentrated themselves in New England. As with other nationalities their place of settlement was determined by port of disembarkation, financial resources, occupational skills, and available jobs. Many of the British, along with great numbers of other immigrants, followed the course of ocean commerce from Liverpool to New York or Boston. Upon arrival, Welsh coal miners made their way to western Pennsylvania's coal fields, Cornish miners to the lead, copper, and iron mines in Wisconsin, Illinois, and Michigan, and textile workers to the cotton manufacturing centers in Massachusetts and New York. Smaller ethnic groups also gravitated toward certain localities and vocations: Dutch settled on farms in Michigan, New York, Wisconsin, and Iowa; and Jewish petty tradesmen or professionals appeared in cities and small towns or scoured the country as peddlers. Chinese, attracted by menial labor jobs in Gold Rush mining camps, immigrated to California in the 1840s and '50s.

No ethnic group in this period, except for the Indian and the blacks, endured greater deprivation than the Irish. In 1855 one-half of the Irish working population in New York City were laborers, carters, porters, waiters, or domestic servants; in Boston during the same years, two-thirds occupied menial positions. In contrast, during the 1850s New York City's Germans made up only 5 percent of its laborers, carters, and waiters. The immigrants, again particularly the Irish, were also overrepresented in proportion to their percentage of the population in crime and poverty statistics. Over one-half the paupers recorded in mid-nineteenth-century New York and Boston were foreign born; over half of those arrested for crime in Boston in 1859 came from abroad. In most cases drunkenness, petty thievery, and disorderly conduct rather than serious dereliction accounted for the arrests. Nonetheless the brushes with the law indicate friction between the newcomers and those who received them and reveal difficulties in adjustment to the new environment.

Flurries of resentment on the part of the native born added to the problems of the new arrivals. Typically, the Irish and the Chinese experienced the greatest difficulties. The mass migrations between 1830 and 1860 roughly coincided with the gradual disintegration of the union and many uneasy native-born Americans discerned in the newcomers another threat to national unity. Some suspicions existed that German immigrants in the west were tainted with atheistic radicalism, but hostility was primarily directed against the Irish because of anxiety over so-called papal intrigue. America had always been a predominantly Protestant country and a large share of the new arrivals were Catholics. The first massive Catholic influx raised fears among those who associated freedom with Anglo-Saxon Protestantism that the country's liberty would be destroyed. Dramatic manifestations of negative feelings started in the 1830s with the burning of the Ursuline Convent in Charlestown, Massachusetts, and the publication of a false but sensational account of sex and sadism in a Catholic convent, Maria Monk's Awful Disclosures of the Hotel Dieu Nunnery of Montreal. *In the 1840s the public school controversy over use of the King James Bible and anti-Catholic riots in Philadelphia and New York intensified the xenophobia. During the next decade the agitation reached its height, culminating in 1855 when the nativist Know-Nothing or American Party elected six governors, dominated several state legislatures, and sent many congressmen to Washington.*

On the West Coast the Chinese suffered even more oppression than the Irish did in the East. Xenophobia in California kept Orientals in low-paying, backbreaking menial labor and denied the immigrants fundamental civil rights. They could not testify in state courts until 1870 and therefore were unable to defend property claims against Caucasian interlopers; they also were subject to discriminatory taxes and barred from public schools.

The trials of the nation's older ethnic minorities, the blacks and Indians, dwarfed the problems of the immigrants. The Indians continued in a dreary round of broken treaties, forced removals, and futile resistance. Fifty thousand Cherokees, Creeks, Choctaws, Chicasaws, and Seminoles found themselves gradually surrounded by the expansion of white settlements into the South and Southwest. In the North, the Sacs, Foxes, Kickappos, Pottawatomies, and other tribes were forced ever westward by the oncoming settlers. Georgia refused to observe treaties contracted between the United States and the Cherokees and evicted the tribe in the 1830s. In the same decade the Choctaws migrated in midwinter from Mississippi to the Red River country, the Creeks resisting expulsion from Alabama left in chains, and the Seminoles were tricked and terrorized into leaving Florida. When the Indians resorted to battle in order to resist these encroachments, as in the cases of the Black Hawk War in Illinois in 1832 and the Seminole War of 1835, they were invariably defeated with heavy loss of life.

For the nation's largest ethnic minority, the blacks, the Revolutionary era had given promise of terminating bondage. Even Southern slave owners apologized for the institution and there were hopes for eventual manumission. Optimistic views faded, however, by the 1830s. With the discovery of the cotton gin in 1793, the growing demand for raw cotton, and the spread of slavery into Texas, Alabama, Mississippi, and Louisiana, the position of the blacks, liberated or slave, significantly deteriorated. Abolitionist tirades combined with so-called slave revolts—notably Gabriel's Revolt (1800), Denmark Vesey's Plot (1822), which may only have been a figment of the slaveholders' imaginations, and Nat Turner's insurrection (1831)—led guilty and harried whites to pass more restrictive legislation resulting in the exclusion of free blacks from most southern states. The legislation made bondage more onerous by restricting movement, by making emancipation extremely rare and quite difficult, and by prohibiting the education of blacks and unsupervised religious activities on the plantation. After the 1820s the South, increasingly dependent on and isolated by the slave system, became more rigid in its desire to preserve the "peculiar institution."

Between 1830 and 1850 America experienced the first of a series of mass migrations from the Old World and the first significant influx of Orientals to the West Coast. Those most alien to the national culture, the Chinese and Irish, were the most poorly received. Conversely the Germans and English, considered contributors to America's cultural and commercial growth, were welcomed more eagerly. Massive waves of post-Civil War newcomers would experience similar treatment. Those, like the Irish, who came with minimal skills and capital and who aroused hostility from other Americans would suffer most under the burdens of poverty and bigotry. For the Indians and blacks the era between Independence and the Civil War resulted in tragic massacre, displacement, and heightened repression. Later immigrant groups would repeat the cycle of poverty and alienation but most managed to assimilate into the dominant majority. Generations of Indians and blacks, however, were doomed to genocide or suppression.

Selected Bibliography

Reginald Horsman's Expansion and American Indian Policy, 1783–1812 *(East Lansing: Michigan State University Press, 1967) is a good summary.*

On the blacks the literature is voluminous. The four most stimulating treatments of slavery are: Eugene D. Genovese's The Political Economy of Slavery* *(New York: Vintage Books, 1967) and* The World the Slaveholders Made *(New York: Pantheon, 1969); Kenneth Stampp's* The Peculiar Institution* *(New York: Vintage Books, 1956); and Stanley M. Elkins'* Slavery* *(New York: The Universal Library, 1963). Allen Weinstein and Frank Otto Gatell have gathered excerpts from the most significant writing in* American Negro Slavery* *(New York: Oxford University Press, 1968). The book has a superb bibliography and must be regarded as the basic work for all students interested in pursuing the subject. An interesting and readable collection of essays emphasizing the life of the slave in the antebellum South is Irwin Unger and David Reimers, eds.,* The Slave Experience in the United States* *(New York: Holt, Rhinehart & Winston, 1970). Leon Litwack's* North of Slavery* *(Chicago: University of Chicago Press, 1961) is a fine survey of black experience above the Mason-Dixon line before the Civil War. John Hope Franklin's* The Free Negro in North Carolina, 1790–1860 *(Chapel Hill: University of North Carolina Press, 1943) is an important volume on an often-neglected topic. Other essays on the subject worth looking at are Ralph B. Flanders, "The Free Negro in Ante-Bellum Georgia,"* North Carolina Historical Review, *9 (1932), 250–72; J. Merton England, "The Free Negro in Ante-Bellum Tennessee,"* Journal of Southern History, *9 (1943), 37–58; and Charles S. Sydnor, "The Free Negro In Mississippi Before the Civil War,"* American Historical Review, *32 (1927), 769–88.*

Americans of Norwegian descent are fortunate to have had their expe-

riences chronicled by outstanding historians. Among the most scholarly and informative are Theodore C. Blegen, Norwegian Migration to America, 1825–1860 *(Northfield, Minn.: Norwegian-American Historical Society, 1931); Carlton C. Qualey, "The Fox River Norwegian Settlement,"* Illinois State Historical Association Journal, *27 (1934), 133–57; and "The Norwegian Element in the Northwest," in Laurence Larson,* The Changing West *(Northfield, Minn.: Norwegian-American Historical Society, 1937). Also of interest is Theodore C. Blegen, ed.,* Land of Their Choice *(Minneapolis: University of Minnesota Press, 1955), a collection of letters written to relatives and friends in Norway by pioneers in the United States.*

For the Swedes see George M. Stephenson, "The Stormy Years of the Swedish Colony in Chicago Before the Great Fire," Transactions of the Illinois State Historical Society, *36 (1929), 166–84, and George T. Flom, "The Early Swedish Immigrants to Iowa,"* Iowa Journal of History and Politics, *3 (1905), 583–615.*

John A. Hawgood's The Tragedy of German America *(New York: G. P. Putnam's Sons, 1940) is a telling analysis of nineteenth-century Germans in the United States. Richard O'Connor,* The German-Americans *(Boston: Little, Brown, 1968), is a more popular and readable survey of their experiences in the United States from colonial times to the present. Two recent monographs worth looking into are F. C. Luebke,* Immigrants and Politics: The Germans of Nebraska, 1880–1900 *(Lincoln: University of Nebraska Press, 1969), and Klaus Wust,* The Virginia Germans *(Charlottesville: University of Virginia Press, 1969).*

Oscar Handlin's Boston's Immigrants* *(Cambridge, Mass.: Harvard University Press, 1941) is the classic study of the Irish in America. George W. Potter,* To the Golden Door *(Boston: Little, Brown, 1960), devotes a good deal of attention to conditions in Ireland before the migrants left and traces Irish experiences in the United States to the Civil War. William Shannon,* The American Irish *(New York: Macmillan, 1963), is a well-written survey laden with interesting anecdotes. Max Berger, "The Irish Emigrant and American Nativism as Seen by British Visitors, 1836–1860,"* Pennsylvania Magazine of History and Biography, *70 (1946), 146–60, is excellent. Thomas N. Brown,* Irish-American Nationalism, 1870–1890 *(Philadelphia: Lippincott, 1966), is also worth going through.*

Mary Coolidge, Chinese Immigration *(New York: H. Holt and Company, 1909), is still the classic work on the Chinese in the United States. Gunther Barth,* Bitter Strength: A History of the Chinese in the United States, 1850–1870 *(Cambridge, Mass.: Harvard University Press, 1964), and Elmer C. Sandmeyer,* The Anti-Chinese Movement in California *(University of Illinois Press, 1939), are both useful and important monographs. See also Rose Hum Lee,* The Chinese in the United States of America *(Hong Kong: Hong Kong University Press, 1960).*

Indians

MARY E. YOUNG

Indian Removal and Land Allotment:
The Civilized Tribes and Jacksonian Justice

Colonial society attempted to find a place for the Indian in the white man's world. By the early national period, however, Americans had an apparently insatiable desire for land and an increasing obsession with the vision of continental empire. Indians forced into the interior during the seventeenth and eighteenth centuries had little desire to move again but most Americans believed that the red man had to be pushed still further west. What territory could be purchased was purchased, what had to be fought for was fought for, and what could be obtained by mutual agreement was obtained by mutual agreement. Indians who moved willingly were lauded. Regardless of obstacles, and willing to adopt any means necessary to acquire land, Americans pressed ever westward. In the following essay Mary Young details the methods Americans used to obtain desired tracts from 60,000 Cherokees, Creeks, Choctaws, and Chickasaws in the southeastern United States.

By the year 1830, the vanguard of the southern frontier had crossed the Mississippi and was pressing through Louisiana, Arkansas, and Missouri. But the line of settlement was by no means as solid as frontier lines were classically supposed to be. East of the Mississippi, white occupancy was limited by Indian tenure of northeastern Georgia, enclaves in western North Carolina and southern Tennessee, eastern Alabama, and the northern two thirds of Mississippi. In this twenty-five-million-acre domain lived nearly 60,000 Cherokees, Creeks, Choctaws, and Chickasaws.[1]

The Jackson administration sought to correct this anomaly by removing the tribes beyond the reach of white settlements, west of the Mississippi. As the President demanded of Congress in December, 1830: "What good man

Reprinted by permission of the author from the *American Historical Review*, 64 (1958), 31–45. This article, in slightly different form, was delivered as a paper at the joint meeting of the Southern Historical Association and the American Historical Association in New York City, December 29, 1957.
[1] Ellen C. Semple, *American History and Its Geographic Conditions* (Boston, Mass., 1933), p. 160; Charles C. Royce, "Indian Land Cessions in the United States," Bureau of American Ethnology, *Eighteenth Annual Report, 1896–1897* (2 vols., Washington, D.C., 1899), II, Plates 1, 2, 15, 48, 54–56.

would prefer a country covered with forests and ranged by a few thousand savages to our extensive Republic, studded with cities, towns, and prosperous farms, embellished with all the improvements which art can devise or industry execute, occupied by more than 12,000,000 happy people, and filled with all the blessings of liberty, civilization, and religion?"[2]

The President's justification of Indian removal was the one usually applied to the displacement of the Indians by newer Americans—the superiority of a farming to a hunting culture, and of Anglo-American "liberty, civilization, and religion" to the strange and barbarous way of the red man. The superior capacity of the farmer to exploit the gifts of nature and of nature's God was one of the principal warranties of the triumph of westward-moving "civilization."[3]

Such a rationalization had one serious weakness as an instrument of policy. The farmer's right of eminent domain over the lands of the savage could be asserted consistently only so long as the tribes involved were "savage." The southeastern tribes, however, were agriculturists as well as hunters. For two or three generations prior to 1830, farmers among them fenced their plantations and "mixed their labor with the soil," making it their private property according to accepted definitions of natural law. White traders who settled among the Indians in the mid-eighteenth century gave original impetus to this imitation of Anglo-American agricultural methods. Later, agents of the United States encouraged the traders and mechanics, their half-breed descendants, and their full-blood imitators who settled out from the tribal villages, fenced their farms, used the plow, and cultivated cotton and corn for the market. In the decade following the War of 1812, missionaries of various Protestant denominations worked among the Cherokees, Choctaws, and Chickasaws, training hundreds of Indian children in the agricultural, mechanical, and household arts and introducing both children and parents to the further blessings of literacy and Christianity.[4]

The "civilization" of a portion of these tribes embarrassed United States

---

[2] James Richardson, *A Compilation of the Messages and Papers of the Presidents of the United States* (New York, 1897), III, 1084.

[3] Roy H. Pearce, *The Savages of America: A Study of the Indian and the Idea of Civilization* (Baltimore, Md., 1953), p. 70; *House Report* 227, 21 Cong., 1 sess., pp. 4–5.

[4] Moravian missionaries were in contact with the Cherokees as early as the 1750's. Henry T. Malone, *Cherokees of the Old South: A People in Transition* (Athens, Ga., 1956), p. 92. There is a voluminous literature on the "civilization" of the civilized tribes. Among secondary sources, the following contain especially useful information: Malone, *Cherokees;* Marion Starkey, *The Cherokee Nation* (New York, 1946); Angie Debo, *The Rise and Fall of the Choctaw Republic* (Norman, Okla., 1934) and *The Road to Disappearance* (Norman, Okla., 1941); Grant Foreman, *Indian Removal: The Emigration of the Five Civilized Tribes of Indians* (2d ed., Norman, Okla., 1953); Robert S. Cotterill, *The Southern Indians: The Story of the Civilized Tribes before Removal* (Norman, Okla., 1954); Merrit B. Pound, *Benjamin Hawkins, Indian Agent* (Athens, Ga., 1951). Among the richest source material for tracing the agricultural development of the tribes are the published writings of the Creek agent, Benjamin Hawkins: *Letters of Benjamin Hawkins, 1796–1806* in Georgia Historical Society *Collections,* IX (Savannah, 1916), and *Sketch of the Creek Country in the Years 1798 and 1799* in Georgia Historical Society *Publications,* III (Americus, 1938). For the Choctaws and Cherokees, there is much information in the incoming correspondence of the American Board of Commissioners for Foreign Missions, Houghton Library, Harvard University. On the Chickasaws, see James Hull, "A Brief History of the Mississippi Territory," Mississippi Historical Society *Publications,* IX (Jackson, 1906).

policy in more ways than one. Long-term contact between the southeastern
tribes and white traders, missionaries, and government officials created and
trained numerous half-breeds. The half-breed men acted as intermediaries between the less sophisticated Indians and the white Americans. Acquiring direct
or indirect control of tribal politics, they often determined the outcome of
treaty negotiations. Since they proved to be skillful bargainers, it became common practice to win their assistance by thinly veiled bribery. The rise of the
half-breeds to power, the rewards they received, and their efforts on behalf of
tribal reform gave rise to bitter opposition. By the mid-1820's this opposition
made it dangerous for them to sell tribal lands. Furthermore, many of the new
leaders had valuable plantations, mills, and trading establishments on these lands.
Particularly among the Cherokees and Choctaws, they took pride in their
achievements and those of their people in assimilating the trappings of civilization. As "founding Fathers," they prized the political and territorial integrity of
the newly organized Indian "nations." These interests and convictions gave birth
to a fixed determination, embodied in tribal laws and intertribal agreements, that
no more cessions of land should be made. The tribes must be permitted to develop their new way of life in what was left of their ancient domain.[5]

Today it is a commonplace of studies in culture contact that the assimilation of alien habits affects different individuals and social strata in different
ways and that their levels of acculturation vary considerably. Among the American Indian tribes, it is most often the families with white or half-breed models
who most readily adopt the Anglo-American way of life. It is not surprising
that half-breeds and whites living among the Indians should use their position
as go-betweens to improve their status and power among the natives. Their
access to influence and their efforts toward reform combine with pressures from
outside to disturb old life ways, old securities, and established prerogatives. Resistance to their leadership and to the cultural alternatives they espouse is a
fertile source of intratribal factions.[6]

To Jacksonian officials, however, the tactics of the half-breeds and the
struggles among tribal factions seemed to reflect a diabolical plot. Treaty negotiators saw the poverty and "depravity" of the common Indian, who suffered
from the scarcity of game, the missionary attacks on his accustomed habits and
ceremonies, and the ravages of "demon rum" and who failed to find solace in
the values of Christian and commercial civilization. Not unreasonably, they
concluded that it was to the interest of the tribesman to remove west of the
Mississippi. There, sheltered from the intruder and the whisky merchant, he
could lose his savagery while improving his nobility. Since this seemed so ob-

[5] Paul W. Gates, "Introduction," *The John Tipton Papers* (3 vols., Indianapolis, Ind., 1942), I, 3–53; A. L. Kroeber, *Cultural and Natural Areas of Native North America* (Berkeley, Calif., 1939), pp. 62–63; John Terrell to General John Coffee, Sept. 15, 1829, Coffee Papers, Alabama Dept. of Archives and History; Campbell and Merriwether to Creek Chiefs, Dec. 9, 1824, *American State Papers: Indian Affairs*, II, 570; Clark, Hinds, and Coffee to James Barbour, Nov. 19, 1826, *ibid.*, p. 709.

[6] See for example, Edward M. Bruner, "Primary Group Experience and the Proc-
esses of Acculturation," *American Anthropologist*, LVIII (Aug., 1956), 605–23; SSRC Summer Seminar on Acculturation, "Acculturation: An Exploratory Formulation," *American Anthropologist*, LVI (Dec., 1954), esp. pp. 980–86; Alexander Spoehr, "Changing Kinship Systems: A Study in the Acculturation of the Creeks, Cherokee, and Choctaw," Field Museum of Natural History, *Anthropological Series*, XXXIII, no. 4, esp. pp. 216–26.

viously to the Indian's interest, the negotiators conveniently concluded that it was also his desire. What, then, deterred emigration? Only the rapacity of the half-breeds, who were unwilling to give up their extensive properties and their exalted position.[7]

These observers recognized that the government's difficulties were in part of its own making. The United States had pursued an essentially contradictory policy toward the Indians, encouraging both segregation and assimilation. Since Jefferson's administration, the government had tried periodically to secure the emigration of the eastern tribes across the Mississippi. At the same time, it had paid agents and subsidized missionaries who encouraged the Indian to follow the white man's way. Thus it had helped create the class of tribesmen skilled in agriculture, pecuniary accumulation, and political leadership. Furthermore, by encouraging the southeastern Indians to become cultivators and Christians, the government had undermined its own moral claim to eminent domain over tribal lands. The people it now hoped to displace could by no stretch of dialectic be classed as mere wandering savages.[8]

By the time Jackson became President, then, the situation of the United States vis-à-vis the southeastern tribes was superficially that of irresistible force and immovable object. But the President, together with such close advisers as Secretary of War John H. Eaton and General John Coffee, viewed the problem in a more encouraging perspective. They believed that the government faced not the intent of whole tribes to remain near the bones of their ancestors but the selfish determination of a few quasi Indian leaders to retain their riches and their ill-used power. Besides, the moral right of the civilized tribes to their lands was a claim not on their whole domain but rather on the part cultivated by individuals. Both the Indian's natural right to his land and his political capacity for keeping it were products of his imitation of white "civilization." Both might be eliminated by a rigorous application of the principle that to treat an Indian fairly was to treat him like a white man. Treaty negotiations by the tried methods of purchase and selective bribery had failed. The use of naked force without the form of voluntary agreement was forbidden by custom, by conscience, and by fear that the administration's opponents would exploit religious sentiment which cherished the rights of the red man. But within the confines of legality and the formulas of voluntarism it was still possible to acquire the much coveted domain of the civilized tribes.

The technique used to effect this object was simple: the entire population of the tribes was forced to deal with white men on terms familiar only to the most acculturated portion of them. If the Indian is civilized, he can behave like a white man. Then let him take for his own as much land as he can cultivate, become a citizen of the state where he lives, and accept the burdens which

---

[7] Wilson Lumpkin, *The Removal of the Cherokee Indians from Georgia* (2 vols., New York, 1907), I, 61–77; Thomas L. McKenney to James Barbour, Dec. 27, 1826, *House Doc.* 28, 19 Cong., 2 sess., pp. 5–13; Andrew Jackson to Colonel Robert Butler, June 21, 1817, *Correspondence of Andrew Jackson,* ed. John Spencer Bassett (6 vols., Washington, D.C., 1926–28), II, 299.

[8] For brief analyses of government policy, see Annie H. Abel, "The History of Events Resulting in Indian Consolidation West of the Mississippi," *Annual Report of the American Historical Association for the Year 1907* (2 vols., Washington, D.C., 1908), I, 233–450; George D. Harmon, *Sixty Years of Indian Affairs, 1789–1850* (Chapel Hill, N. C., 1941).

citizenship entails. If he is not capable of living like this, he should be liberated from the tyranny of his chiefs and allowed to follow his own best interest by emigrating beyond the farthest frontiers of white settlement. By the restriction of the civilized to the lands they cultivate and by the emigration of the savages millions of acres will be opened to white settlement.

The first step dictated by this line of reasoning was the extension of state laws over the Indian tribes. Beginning soon after Jackson's election, Georgia, Alabama, Mississippi, and Tennessee gradually brought the Indians inside their borders under their jurisdiction. Thus an Indian could be sued for trespass or debt, though only in Mississippi and Tennessee was his testimony invariably acceptable in a court of law. In Mississippi, the tribesmen were further harassed by subjection—or the threat of subjection—to such duties as mustering with the militia, working on roads, and paying taxes. State laws establishing county governments within the tribal domains and, in some cases, giving legal protection to purchasers of Indian improvements encouraged the intrusion of white settlers on Indian lands. The laws nullified the legal force of Indian customs, except those relating to marriage. They provided heavy penalties for anyone who might enact or enforce tribal law. Finally, they threatened punishment to any person who might attempt to deter another from signing a removal treaty or enrolling for emigration. The object of these laws was to destroy the tribal governments and to thrust upon individual Indians the uncongenial alternative of adjusting to the burdens of citizenship or removing beyond state jurisdiction.[9]

The alternative was not offered on the unenlightened supposition that the Indians generally were capable of managing their affairs unaided in a white man's world. Governor Gayle of Alabama, addressing the "former chiefs and headmen of the Creek Indians" in June of 1834 urged them to remove from the state on the grounds that

> you speak a different language from ours. You do not understand our laws and from your habits, cannot be brought to understand them. You are ignorant of the arts of civilized life. You have not like your white neighbors been raised in habits of industry and economy, the only means by which anyone can live, in settled countries, in even tolerable comfort. You know nothing of the skill of the white man in trading and making bargains, and cannot be guarded against the artful contrivances which dishonest men will resort to, to obtain your property under forms of contracts. In all these respects you are unequal to the white men, and if your people remain where they are, you will soon behold them in a miserable, degraded, and destitute condition.[10]

The intentions of federal officials who favored the extension of state laws are revealed in a letter written to Jackson by General Coffee. Referring to the Cherokees, Coffee remarked:

[9] Georgia, *Acts,* Dec. 12, 1828; Dec. 19, 1829; Alabama, *Acts,* Jan. 27, 1829; Dec. 31, 1831; Jan. 16, 1832; Dec. 18, 1832; Mississippi, *Acts,* Feb. 4, 1829; Jan. 19, 1830; Feb. 12, 1830; Dec. 9, 1831; Oct. 26, 1832; Tennessee, *Acts,* Nov. 8, 1833; George R. Gilmer to Augustus S. Clayton, June 7, 1830, Governor's Letterbook, 1829–31, p. 36, Georgia Dept. of Archives and History.

[10] Governor John Gayle to former chiefs and headmen of the Creek Indians, June 16, 1834, Miscellaneous Letters to and from Governor Gayle, Alabama Dept. of Archives and History.

88   *The Young Republic*

Deprive the chiefs of the power they now possess, take from them their own code of laws, and reduce them to plain citizenship . . . and they will soon determine to move, and then there will be no difficulty in getting the poor Indians to give their consent. All this will be done by the State of Georgia if the U. States do not interfere with her law— . . . This will of course silence those in our country who constantly seek for causes to complain—It may indeed turn them loose upon Georgia, but that matters not, it is Georgia who clamors for the Indian lands, and she alone is entitled to the blame if any there be.[11]

Even before the laws were extended, the threat of state jurisdiction was used in confidential "talks" to the chiefs. After the states had acted, the secretary of war instructed each Indian agent to explain to his charges the meaning of state jurisdiction and to inform them that the President could not protect them against the enforcement of the laws.[12] Although the Supreme Court, in *Worcester* vs. *Georgia,* decided that the state had no right to extend its laws over the Cherokee nation, the Indian tribes being "domestic dependent nations" with limits defined by treaty, the President refused to enforce this decision.[13] There was only one means by which the government might have made "John Marshall's decision" effective—directing federal troops to exclude state officials and other intruders from the Indian domain. In January, 1832, the President informed an Alabama congressman that the United States government no longer assumed the right to remove citizens of Alabama from the Indian country. By this time, the soldiers who had protected the territory of the southeastern tribes against intruders had been withdrawn. In their unwearying efforts to pressure the Indians into ceding their lands, federal negotiators emphasized the terrors of state jurisdiction.[14]

Congress in May, 1830, complemented the efforts of the states by appropriating $500,000 and authorizing the President to negotiate removal treaties with all the tribes east of the Mississippi.[15] The vote on this bill was close in both houses. By skillful use of pamphlets, petitions, and lobbyists, missionary organizations had enlisted leading congressmen in their campaign against the administration's attempt to force the tribes to emigrate.[16] In the congressional debates, opponents of the bill agreed that savage tribes were duty-bound to

[11] Feb. 3, 1830, Jackson Papers, Library of Congress.
[12] John H. Eaton to John Crowell, Mar. 27, 1829, Office of Indian Affairs, Letters Sent. V, 372–73, Records of the Bureau of Indians Affairs, National Archives; Middleton Mackey to John H. Eaton, Nov. 27, 1829, Choctaw Emigration File 111, ibid.; Andrew Jackson to Major David Haley, Oct. 10, 1829, Jackson Papers.
[13] 6 *Peters,* 515–97.
[14] Wiley Thompson to Messrs. Drew and Reese, Jan. 18, 1832, Indian Letters, 1782–1839, pp. 173–74, Georgia Dept. of Archives and History; John H. Eaton to Jackson, Feb. 21, 1831, *Sen. Doc.* 65, 21 Cong., 2 sess., p. 6; Cyrus Kingsburg to Jeremiah Evarts, Aug. 11, 1830, American Board of Commissioners for Foreign Missions Manuscripts; Tuskeneha to the President, May 21, 1831, Creek File 176, Records of the Bureau of Indian Affairs; Journal of the Commissioners for the Treaty of Dancing Rabbit Creek, *Sen. Doc.* 512, 23 Cong., 1 sess., p. 257.
[15] 4 *Statutes-at-Large,* 411–12.
[16] J. Orin Oliphant, ed., *Through the South and West with Jeremiah Evarts in 1826* (Lewisburg, Pa., 1956), pp. 47–61; Jeremiah Evarts to Rev. William Weisner, Nov. 27, 1829, American Board of Commissioners for Foreign Missions Manuscripts; *Sen. Docs.* 56, 59, 66, 73, 74, 76, 77, 92, 96, 21 Cong., 1 sess.

relinquish their hunting grounds to the agriculturist, but they argued that the southeastern tribes were no longer savage. In any case, such relinquishment must be made in a freely contracted treaty. The extension of state laws over the Indian country was coercion; this made the negotiation of a free contract impossible. Both supporters and opponents of the bill agreed on one cardinal point —the Indian's moral right to keep his land depended on his actual cultivation of it.[17]

A logical corollary of vesting rights in land in proportion to cultivation was the reservation to individuals of as much land as they had improved at the time a treaty was signed. In 1816, Secretary of War William H. Crawford had proposed such reservations, or allotments, as a means of accommodating the removal policy to the program of assimiliation. According to Crawford's plan, individual Indians who had demonstrated their capacity for civilization by establishing farms and who were willing to become citizens should be given the option of keeping their cultivated lands, by fee simple title, rather than emigrating. This offer was expected to reconcile the property-loving half-breeds to the policy of emigration. It also recognized their superior claim, as cultivators, on the regard and generosity of the government. The proposal was based on the assumption that few of the Indians were sufficiently civilized to want to become full-time farmers or state citizens.[18]

The Crawford policy was applied in the Cherokee treaties of 1817 and 1819 and the Choctaw treaty of 1820. These agreements offered fee simple allotments to heads of Indian families having improved lands within the areas ceded to the government. Only 311 Cherokees and eight Choctaws took advantage of the offer. This seemed to bear out the assumption that only a minority of the tribesmen would care to take allotments. Actually, these experiments were not reliable. In both cases, the tribes ceded only a fraction of their holdings. Comparatively few took allotments; but on the other hand, few emigrated. The majority simply remained within the diminished tribal territories east of the Mississippi.[19]

The offer of fee simple allotments was an important feature of the negotiations with the tribes in the 1820s. When the extension of state laws made removal of the tribes imperative, it was to be expected that allotments would comprise part of the consideration offered for the ceded lands. Both the ideology which rationalized the removal policy and the conclusions erroneously drawn from experience with the earlier allotment treaties led government negotiators to assume that a few hundred allotments at most would be required.

The Choctaws were the first to cede their eastern lands. The treaty of Dancing Rabbit Creek, signed in September, 1830, provided for several types of allotments. Special reservations were given to the chiefs and their numerous family connections; a possible 1,600 allotments of 80 to 480 acres, in propor-

[17] Gales and Seaton, *Register of Debates in Congress,* VI, 311, 312, 320, 357, 361, 1022, 1024, 1039, 1061, 1110, 1135.
[18] *American State Papers: Indian Affairs,* II, 27. A general history of the allotment policy is Jay P. Kinney, *A Continent Lost—A Civilization Won: Indian Land Tenure in America* (Baltimore, Md., 1937).
[19] 7 *Statutes-at-Large,* 156–60, 195–200, 210–14; Cherokee Reservation Book, Records of the Bureau of Indian Affairs; Special Reserve Book A, *ibid.;* James Barbour to the Speaker of the House, Jan. 23, 1828, *American State Papers: Public Lands,* V, 396–97.

tion to the size of the beneficiary's farm, were offered others who intended to emigrate. These were intended for sale to private persons or to the government, so that the Indian might get the maximum price for his improvements. The fourteenth article of the treaty offered any head of an Indian family who did not plan to emigrate the right to take up a quantity of land proportional to the number of his dependents. At the end of five years' residence those who received these allotments were to have fee simple title to their lands and become citizens. It was expected that approximately two hundred persons would take land under this article.[20]

The Creeks refused to sign any agreements promising to emigrate, but their chiefs were persuaded that the only way to put an end to intrusions on their lands was to sign an allotment treaty.[21] In March, 1832, a Creek delegation in Washington signed a treaty calling for the allotment of 320 acres to each head of a family, the granting of certain supplementary lands to the chiefs and to orphans, and the cession of the remaining territory to the United States. If the Indian owners remained on their allotments for five years, they were to receive fee simple titles and become citizens.[22] Returning to Alabama, the chiefs informed their people that they had not actually sold the tribal lands but "had only made each individual their own guardian, that they might take care of their own possessions, and act as agents for themselves."[23]

Unlike the Creeks, the Chickasaws were willing to admit the inevitability of removal. But they needed land east of the Mississippi on which they might live until they acquired a home in the west. The Chickasaw treaty of May, 1832, therefore, provided generous allotments for heads of families, ranging from 640 to 3,200 acres, depending on the size of the family and the number of its slaves. These allotments were to be auctioned publicly when the tribe emigrated and the owners compensated for their improvements out of the proceeds.[24] Although the fullblood Chickasaws apparently approved of the plan for a collective sale of the allotments, the half-breeds, abetted by white traders and planters, persuaded the government to allow those who held allotments to sell them individually.[25] An amended treaty of 1834 complied with the half-breeds' proposals. It further stipulated that leading half-breeds and the old chiefs of the tribe comprise a committee to determine the competence of individual Chickasaws to manage their property. Since the committee itself disposed of the lands of the "incompetents," this gave both protection to the unsophisticated and additional advantage to the half-breeds.[26]

[20] 7 *Statutes-at-Large,* 334–41; manuscript records of negotiations are in Choctaw File 112, Records of the Bureau of Indian Affairs.
[21] John Crowell to Lewis Cass, Jan. 25, 1832, Creek File 178, Records of the Bureau of Indian Affairs.
[22] 7 *Statutes-at-Large,* 366–68.
[23] John Scott to Lewis Cass, Nov. 12, 1835, Creek File 193, Records of the Bureau of Indian Affairs.
[24] 7 *Statutes-at-Large,* 381–89.
[25] John Terrell to Henry Cook, Oct. 29, 1832 (copy), John D. Terrell Papers, Alabama Dept. of Archives and History; Benjamin Reynolds to John Coffee, Dec. 12, 1832, Chickasaw File 83, Records of the Bureau of Indian Affairs; Terrell to John Tyler, Feb. 26, 1841 (draft), Terrell Papers; G. W. Long to John Coffee, Dec. 15, 1832, Coffee Papers; Rev. T. C. Stuart to Daniel Green, Oct. 14, 1833, American Board of Commissioners for Foreign Missions Manuscripts.
[26] 7 *Statutes-at-Large,* 450–57.

Widespread intrusion on Indian lands began with the extension of state laws over the tribal domains. In the treaties of cession, the government promised to remove intruders, but its policy in this respect was vacillating and ineffective. Indians whose allotments covered valuable plantations proved anxious to promote the sale of their property by allowing buyers to enter the ceded territory as soon as possible. Once this group of whites was admitted, it became difficult to discriminate against others. Thus a large number of intruders settled among the Indians with the passive connivance of the War Department and the tribal leaders. The task of removing them was so formidable that after making a few gestures the government generally evaded its obligation. The misery of the common Indians, surrounded by intruders and confused by the disruption of tribal authority, was so acute that any method for securing their removal seemed worth trying. Furthermore, their emigration would serve the interest of white settlers, land speculators, and their representatives in Washington. The government therefore chose to facilitate the sale of allotments even before the Indians received fee simple title to them.[27]

The right to sell his allotment was useful to the sophisticated tribesman with a large plantation. Such men were accustomed to selling their crops and hiring labor. Through their experience in treaty negotiations, they had learned to bargain over the price of lands. Many of them received handsome payment for their allotments. Some kept part of their holdings and remained in Alabama and Mississippi as planters—like other planters, practicing as land speculators on the side.[28] Nearly all the Indians had some experience in trade, but to most of them the conception of land as a salable commodity was foreign. They had little notion of the exact meaning of an "acre" or the probable value of their allotments.[29] The government confused them still further by parceling out the lands according to Anglo-American, rather than aboriginal notions of family structure and land ownership. Officials insisted, for example, that the "father" rather than the "mother" must be defined as head of the family and righteously

[27] William Ward to Secretary of War, Oct. 22, 1831, Choctaw Reserve File 133; Mushulatubbee to Lewis Cass, Feb. 9, 1832, Choctaw File 113; W. S. Colquhoun to General George S. Gibson, Apr. 20, 1832, Choctaw Emigration File 121; A. Campbell to Secretary of War, Aug. 5, 1832, Choctaw File 113; John Kurtz to Benjamin Reynolds, Aug. 9, 1833, Office of Indian Affairs, Letters Sent, XI, 74; S. C. Barton to Elbert Herring, Nov. 11, 1833, Choctaw File 113; William M. Gwin to Lewis Cass, Apr. 8, 1834, Choctaw File 84, Records of the Bureau of Indian Affairs; Mary E. Young, "The Creek Frauds: A Study in Conscience and Corruption," *Mississippi Valley Historical Review*, XLVII (Dec., 1955), 415–19.

[28] Benjamin Reynolds to Lewis Cass, Dec. 9, 1832, Apr. 29, 1835, Chicasaw File 83, 85, Records of the Bureau of Indian Affairs; David Haley to Jackson, Apr. 15, 1831, *Sen. Doc.* 512, 23 Cong., 1 sess., p. 426; Elbert Herring to George W. Elliott, Jan. 23, 1833, Office of Indian Affairs, Letters Sent, IX, 516, Records of the Bureau of Indian Affairs; J. J. Abert to J. R. Poinsett, July 19, 1839, Creek File 220, *ibid.* See Special Reserve Books and Special Reserve Files A and C, and William Carroll's List of Certified Contracts for the Sale of Chickasaw Reservations, Special File, Chickasaw, Records of the Bureau of Indian Affairs, and compare Chickasaw Location Book, Records of the Bureau of Land Management, National Archives.

[29] George S. Snyderman, "Concepts of Land Ownership among the Iroquois and their Neighbors," in *Symposium on Local Variations in Iroquois Culture,* ed. William N. Fenton, Bureau of American Ethnology *Bulletin 149* (Washington, D.C., 1951), pp. 16–26; Petition of Choctaw Chiefs and Headmen, Mar. 2, 1832, Choctaw Reserve File 133; James Colbert to Lewis Cass, June 5, 1835, Chickasaw File 84; Benjamin Reynolds to Elbert Herring, Mar. 11, 1835, Chickasaw File 85, Records of the Bureau of Indian Affairs.

refused to take cognizance of the fact that many of the "fathers" had "a plu-
rality of wives."[30]

Under these conditions, it is not surprising that the common Indian's legal
freedom of contract in selling his allotment did not necessarily lead him to make
the best bargain possible in terms of his pecuniary interests. Nor did the proceeds of the sales transform each seller into an emigrant of large independent
means. A right of property and freedom to contract for its sale did not automatically invest the Indian owner with the habits, values, and skills of a sober
land speculator. His acquisition of property and freedom actually increased his
dependence on those who traditionally mediated for him in contractual relations
with white Americans.

Prominent among these mediators were white men with Indian wives who
made their living as planters and traders in the Indian nations, men from nearby
settlements who traded with the leading Indians or performed legal services for
them, and interpreters. In the past, such individuals had been appropriately
compensated for using their influence in favor of land cessions. It is likely that
their speculative foresight was in part responsible for the allotment features in
the treaties of the 1830's. When the process of allotting lands to individuals
began, these speculative gentlemen made loans of whisky, muslin, horses, slaves,
and other useful commodities to the new property-owner. They received in return the Indian's written promise to sell his allotment to them as soon as its
boundaries were defined. Generally they were on hand to help him locate it on
"desirable" lands. They, in turn, sold their "interest" in the lands to men of
capital. Government agents encouraged the enterprising investor, since it was in
the Indian's interest and the government's policy that the lands be sold and the
tribes emigrate.[31] Unfortunately, the community of interest among the government, the speculator, and the Indian proved largely fictitious. The speculator's
interest in Indian lands led to frauds which impoverished the Indians, soiled
the reputation of the government, and retarded the emigration of the tribes.

An important factor in this series of complications was the government's
fallacious assumption that most of the "real Indians" were anxious to emigrate.
Under the Choctaw treaty, for example, registration for fee simple allotments
was optional, the government expecting no more than two hundred registrants.

[30] Memorial of Chickasaw Chiefs to the President, Nov. 25, 1835, Chickasaw File
84; Thomas J. Abbott and E. Parsons, Sept. 7, 1832, *Sen. Doc.* 512, 23 Cong., 1 sess.,
pp. 443–44; Elbert Herring to E. Parsons, B. S. Parsons, and John Crowell, Oct. 10,
1832, *ibid.,* p. 524; Leonard Tarrant to E. Herring, May 15, 1833, Creek File 202,
Records of the Bureau of Indian Affairs; Alexander Spoehr, "Kinship Systems," pp.
201–31; John R. Swanton, *Indians of the Southeastern United States,* Bureau of American Ethnology *Bulletin 137* (Washington, D.C., 1946).

[31] John Coffee to Andrew Jackson, July 10, 1830, Creek File 192, Records of the
Bureau of Indian Affairs; John Crowell to John H. Eaton, Aug. 8, 1830, Creek File
175, *ibid.;* John H. Brodnax to Lewis Cass, Mar. 12, 1832, *Sen. Doc.* 512, 23 Cong.,
1 sess., III, 258–59; John Terrell to General John Coffee, Sept. 15, 1829, Coffee
Papers; J. J. Albert to [Lewis Cass], June 13, 1833, Creek File 202, Records of the
Bureau of Indian Affairs; contract between Daniel Wright and Mingo Mushulatubbee,
Oct. 7, 1830, *American State Papers: Public Lands,* VII, 19; W. S. Colquhoun to
Lewis Cass, Sept. 20, 1833, *ibid.,* p. 13; Chapman Levy to Joel R. Poinsett, June 19,
1837, Choctaw Reserve File 139, Records of the Bureau of Indian Affairs; James Col-
bert to Lewis Cass, June 5, 1835, Chickasaw File 84, *ibid.;* Chancery Court, Northern
District of Mississippi, Final Record A, 111, M, 235–37, Courthouse, Holly Springs,
Mississippi.

When several hundred full-bloods applied for lands, the Choctaw agent assumed that they were being led astray by "designing men" and told them they must emigrate. Attorneys took up the Choctaw claims, located thousands of allotments in hopes that Congress would confirm them, and supported their clients in Mississippi for twelve to fifteen years while the government debated and acted on the validity of the claims. There was good reason for this delay. Settlers and rival speculators, opposing confirmation of the claims, advanced numerous depositions asserting that the attorneys, in their enterprising search for clients, had materially increased the number of claimants.[32] Among the Creeks, the Upper Towns, traditionally the conservative faction of the tribe, refused to sell their allotments. Since the Lower Towns proved more compliant, speculators hired willing Indians from the Lower Towns to impersonate the unwilling owners. They then bought the land from the impersonators. The government judiciously conducted several investigations of these frauds, but in the end the speculators outmaneuvered the investigators. Meanwhile, the speculators kept the Indians from emigrating until their contracts were approved. Only the outbreak of fighting between starving Creeks and their settler neighbors enabled the government, under pretext of a pacification, to remove the tribe.[33]

Besides embarrassing the government, the speculators contributed to the demoralization of the Indians. Universal complaint held that after paying the tribesman for his land they often borrowed back the money without serious intent of repaying it, or recovered it in return for overpriced goods, of which a popular article was whisky. Apprised of this situation, Secretary of War Lewis Cass replied that once the Indian had been paid for his land, the War Department had no authority to circumscribe his freedom to do what he wished with the proceeds.[34]

Nevertheless, within their conception of the proper role of government, officials who dealt with the tribes tried to be helpful. Although the Indian must be left free to contract for the sale of his lands, the United States sent agents to determine the validity of the contracts. These agents sometimes refused to approve a contract that did not specify a fair price for the land in question. They also refused official sanction when it could not be shown that the Indian owner had at some time been in possession of the sum stipulated.[35] This protective action on the part of the government, together with its several investigations into frauds in the sale of Indian lands, apparently did secure the payment of more money than the tribesmen might otherwise have had. But the effort was seriously hampered by the near impossibility of obtaining disinterested testimony.

[32] Mary E. Young, "Indian Land Allotments in Alabama and Mississippi, 1830–1860" (manuscript doctoral dissertation, Cornell University, 1955), pp. 70–82; Franklin L. Riley, "The Choctaw Land Claims," Mississippi Historical Society *Publications,* VIII (1904), 370–82; Harmon, *Indian Affairs,* pp. 226–59.
[33] Young, "Creek Frauds," pp. 411–37.
[34] Lewis Cass to Return J. Meigs, Oct. 31, 1834, *Sen. Doc.* 428, 24 Cong., 1 sess., p. 23.
[35] Lewis Cass, "Regulations," for certifying Creek contracts, Nov. 28, 1833, *Sen. Doc.* 276, 24 Cong., 1 sess., pp. 88–89; *id.,* "Regulations," Feb. 8, 1836, Chickasaw Letterbook A, 76–78, Records of the Bureau of Indian Affairs; Secretary of War to the President, June 27, 1836, Choctaw Reserve File 136, *ibid.* For adjudications based on the above regulations, see Special Reserve Files A and C and Choctaw, Creek, and Chickasaw Reserve Files, Records of the Bureau of Indian Affairs, *passim.*

In dealing with the Chickasaws, the government managed to avoid most of the vexing problems which had arisen in executing the allotment program among their southeastern neighbors. This was due in part to the improvement of administrative procedures, in part to the methods adopted by speculators in Chickasaw allotments, and probably most of all to the inflated value of cotton lands during the period in which the Chickasaw territory was sold. Both the government and the Chickasaws recognized that the lands granted individuals under the treaty were generally to be sold, not settled. They therefore concentrated on provisions for supervising sales and safeguarding the proceeds.[36] Speculators in Chickasaw lands, having abundant resources, paid an average price of $1.70 per acre. The Chickasaws thereby received a better return than the government did at its own auctions. The buyers' generosity may be attributed to their belief that the Chickasaw lands represented the last first-rate cotton country within what were then the boundaries of the public domain. In their pursuit of a secure title, untainted by fraud, the capitalists operating in the Chickasaw cession established a speculators' claim association which settled disputes among rival purchasers. Thus they avoided the plots, counterplots, and mutual recriminations which had hampered both speculators and government in their dealings with the Creeks and Choctaws.[37]

A superficially ironic consequence of the allotment policy as a method of acquiring land for white settlers was the fact that it facilitated the engrossment of land by speculators. With their superior command of capital and the influence it would buy, speculators acquired 80 to 90 per cent of the lands alloted to the southeastern tribesmen.[38]

For most of the Indian beneficiaries of the policy, its most important consequence was to leave them landless. After selling their allotment, or a claim to it, they might take to the swamp, live for a while on the bounty of a still hopeful speculator, or scavenge on their settler neighbors. But ultimately most of them faced the alternative of emigration or destitution, and chose to emigrate. The machinations of the speculators and the hopes they nurtured that the Indians might somehow be able to keep a part of their allotted lands made the timing of removals less predictable than it might otherwise have been. This unpredictability compounded the evils inherent in a mass migration managed by a government committed to economy and unversed in the arts of economic planning. The result was the "Trail of Tears."[39]

The spectacular frauds committed among the Choctaws and Creeks, the

[36] "Memorial of the Creek Nation . . . ," Jan. 29, 1883, *House Misc. Doc.* 18, 47 Cong., 2 sess.

[37] Average price paid for Chickasaw lands computed from William Carroll's List of Certified Contracts, Special Reserve File, Chickasaw, Records of the Bureau of Indian Affairs; Young, "Indian Allotments," 154–67.

[38] See calculations in Young, "Indian Allotments," 141–42, 163–64. No system of estimating percentages of land purchased for speculation from figures of sales is foolproof. The assumption used in this estimate was that all those who bought 2,000 acres or more might be defined as speculators. Compare James W. Silver, "Land Speculation Profits in the Chickasaw Cession," *Journal of Southern History,* X (Feb., 1944), 84–92.

[39] For the story of emigration, see Foreman, *Indian Removal;* Debo, *Road to Disappearance,* pp. 103–107 and *Choctaw Republic,* pp. 55–57. Relations between speculation and emigration can be traced in the Creek, Choctaw, and Chickasaw Emigration and Reserve Files, Records of the Bureau of Indian Affairs.

administrative complications they created and the impression they gave that certain self-styled champions of the people were consorting with the avaricious speculator gave the allotment policy a bad reputation. The administration rejected it in dealing with the Cherokees,[40] and the policy was not revived on any considerable scale until 1854, when it was applied, with similar consequences, to the Indians of Kansas.[41] In the 1880's, when allotment in severalty became a basic feature of American Indian policy, the "civilized tribes," then in Oklahoma, strenuously resisted its application to them. They cited their memories of the 1830's as an important reason for their intransigence.[42]

The allotment treaties of the 1830's represent an attempt to apply Anglo-American notions of justice, which enshrined private property in land and freedom of contract as virtually absolute values, to Indian tribes whose tastes and traditions were otherwise. Their history illustrates the limitations of intercultural application of the Golden Rule. In a more practical sense, the treaties typified an effort to force on the Indians the alternative of complete assimilation or complete segregation by placing individuals of varying levels of sophistication in situations where they must use the skills of businessmen or lose their means of livelihood. This policy secured tribal lands while preserving the forms of respect for property rights and freedom of contract, but it proved costly to both the government and the Indians.

How lightly that cost was reckoned, and how enduring the motives and rationalizations that gave rise to it, may be gathered from the subsequent experience of the southeastern tribes in Oklahoma. There, early in the twentieth century, the allotment policy was again enforced, with safeguards hardly more helpful to the unsophisticated than those of the 1830's. Once more, tribal land changed owners for the greater glory of liberty, civilization, and profit.[43]

[40] Hon. R. Chapman to Lewis Cass, Jan. 25, 1835, Cherokee File 7, Records of the Bureau of Indian Affairs; Lewis Cass to Commissioners Carroll and Schermerhorn, Apr. 2, 1835, Office of Indian Affairs, Letters Sent, XV, 261, *ibid.;* "Journal of the Proceedings at the Council held at New Echota . . . ," Cherokee File 7, *ibid.;* "Joint Memorial of the Legislature of the State of Alabama . . . ," Jan. 9, 1836, *ibid.;* William Gilmer to Andrew Jackson, Feb. 9, 1835, Jackson Papers; 7 *Statutes-at-Large,* 483–84, 488–89.
[41] Paul W. Gates, *Fifty Million Acres: Conflicts over Kansas Land Policy, 1854–1890* (Ithaca, N.Y., 1954), pp. 11–48.
[42] "Memorial of the Creek Nation on the Subject of Lands in Severalty Among the Several Indian Tribes," Jan. 29, 1883, *House Misc. Doc.* 18, 47 Cong., 2 sess.
[43] Compare Angie Debo, *The Five Civilized Tribes of Oklahoma: Report on Social and Economic Conditions* (Philadelphia, Pa., 1951) and Kinney, *Indian Land Tenure,* pp. 243–44.

Blacks

W. E. B. DU BOIS
The Black Worker

Slavery in America was defended as an agency for civilizing and Christianizing black savages, as paternalistic protection for a childlike race, and as a necessary mudsill for the flowering of southern culture. Although many southerners sincerely believed these explanations, in retrospect they seem justifications rather than reasons for the slave system. Servitude was fundamentally designed to obtain, organize, and exploit cheap labor.

In this selection W. E. B. Du Bois analyzes the role that black labor played in the antebellum American economy. He focuses on the conditions of labor and bondage, the reaction of the blacks, the tension between the assertions of democracy and the reality of race repression, the relationship between poor whites and black bondsmen; and he compares the circumstances of northern free blacks with the plight of southern slaves. Du Bois concludes that the black worker was the "founding stone of a new economic system in the nineteenth century and for the modern world" and that slavery was the "underlying cause" of the Civil War.

Du Bois, one of America's greatest historians, is a tragic example of the agony and deprivation that has been the black man's burden in a racist society. Black Reconstruction, published in 1935, anticipated modern scholarship by twenty years. Only recently have students of Reconstruction begun to share Du Bois's conclusion that the post-Civil War alliance of blacks, northerners, and cooperative southerners held great promise for the South as a section and for blacks as a race. Despite Du Bois's brilliance his race excluded him from professional recognition. His bitter experience with bigotry in the academy began at Harvard University, where segregation isolated him from the other undergraduates. Du Bois led the opposition against Booker T. Washington's accommodationism and in 1909 helped found the National Association for the Advancement of Colored People. By the 1930s, disgusted with the lack of progress in civil rights, Du Bois forsook the NAACP and the cause of integration for Marxism and black nationalism. In a final act of defiance against the bigotry and political persecution he endured, the historian left the United States to spend his last years (1961–63) as a citizen of Ghana, an African nation whose black government and Communist sympathies were the antithesis of the society which had rejected him.

How black men, coming to America in the sixteenth, seventeenth, eighteenth and nineteenth centuries, became a central thread in the history
of the United States, at once a challenge to its democracy and always an
important part of its economic history and social development.

Easily the most dramatic episode in American history was the sudden move
to free four million black slaves in an effort to stop a great civil war, to end
forty years of bitter controversy, and to appease the moral sense of civilization.

From the day of its birth, the anomaly of slavery plagued a nation which
asserted the equality of all men, and sought to derive powers of government
from the consent of the governed. Within sound of the voices of those who said
this lived more than half a million black slaves, forming nearly one-fifth of the
population of a new nation.

The black population at the time of the first census had risen to three-
quarters of a million, and there were over a million at the beginning of the
nineteenth century. Before 1830, the blacks had passed the two million mark,
helped by the increased importations just before 1808, and the illicit smuggling
up until 1820. By their own reproduction, the Negroes reached 3,638,808 in
1850, and before the Civil War, stood at 4,441,830. They were 10% of the
whole population of the nation in 1700, 22% in 1750, 18.9% in 1800 and
11.6% in 1900.

These workers were not all black and not all Africans and not all slaves.
In 1860, at least 90% were born in the United States, 13% were visibly of
white as well as Negro descent and actually more than one-fourth were probably of white, Indian and Negro blood. In 1860, 11% of these dark folk were
free workers.

In origin, the slaves represented everything African, although most of them
originated on or near the West Coast. Yet among them appeared the great Bantu
tribes from Sierra Leone to South Africa; the Sudanese, straight across the center of the continent, from the Atlantic to the Valley of the Nile; the Nilotic
Negroes and the black and brown Hamites, allied with Egypt; the tribes of the
great lakes; the Pygmies and the Hottentots; and in addition to these, distinct
traces of both Berber and Arab blood. There is no doubt of the presence of all
these various elements in the mass of 10,000,000 or more Negroes transported
from Africa to the various Americas, from the fifteenth to the nineteenth centuries.

Most of them that came to the continent went through West Indian tutelage, and thus finally appeared in the United States. They brought with them
their religion and rhythmic song, and some traces of their art and tribal customs.
And after a lapse of two and one-half centuries, the Negroes became a settled
working population, speaking English or French, professing Christianity, and
used principally in agricultural toil. Moreover, they so mingled their blood
with white and red America that today less than 25% of the Negro Americans
are of unmixed African descent.

So long as slavery was a matter of race and color, it made the conscience
of the nation uneasy and continually affronted its ideals. The men who wrote
the Constitution sought by every evasion, and almost by subterfuge, to keep
recognition of slavery out of the basic form of the new government. They

founded their hopes on the prohibition of the slave trade, being sure that without continual additions from abroad, this tropical people would not long survive, and thus the problem of slavery would disappear in death. They miscalculated, or did not foresee the changing economic world. It might be more profitable in the West Indies to kill the slaves by overwork and import cheap Africans; but in America without a slave trade, it paid to conserve the slave and let him multiply. When, therefore, manifestly the Negroes were not dying out, there came quite naturally new excuses and explanations. It was a matter of social condition. Gradually these people would be free; but freedom could only come to the bulk as the freed were transplanted to their own land and country, since the living together of black and white in America was unthinkable. So again the nation waited, and its conscience sank to sleep.

But in a rich and eager land, wealth and work multiplied. They twisted new and intricate patterns around the earth. Slowly but mightily these black workers were integrated into modern industry. On free and fertile land Americans raised, not simply sugar as a cheap sweetening, rice for food and tobacco as a new and tickling luxury; but they began to grow a fiber that clothed the masses of a ragged world. Cotton grew so swiftly that the 9,000 bales of cotton which the new nation scarcely noticed in 1791 became 79,000 in 1800; and with this increase, walked economic revolution in a dozen different lines. The cotton crop reached one-half million bales in 1822, a million bales in 1831, two million in 1840, three million in 1852, and in the year of secession, stood at the then enormous total of five million bales.

Such facts and others, coupled with the increase of the slaves to which they were related as both cause and effect, meant a new world; and all the more so because with increase in American cotton and Negro slaves, came both by chance and ingenuity new miracles for manufacturing, and particularly for the spinning and weaving of cloth.

The giant forces of water and of steam were harnessed to do the world's work, and the black workers of America bent at the bottom of a growing pyramid of commerce and industry; and they not only could not be spared, if this new economic organization was to expand, but rather they became the cause of new political demands and alignments, of new dreams of power and visions of empire.

First of all, their work called for widening stretches of new, rich, black soil—in Florida, in Louisiana, in Mexico; even in Kansas. This land, added to cheap labor, and labor easily regulated and distributed, made profits so high that a whole system of culture arose in the South, with a new leisure and social philosophy. Black labor became the foundation stone not only of the Southern social structure, but of Northern manufacture and commerce, of the English factory system, of European commerce, of buying and selling on a world-wide scale; new cities were built on the results of black labor, and a new labor problem, involving all white labor, arose both in Europe and America.

Thus, the old difficulties and paradoxes appeared in new dress. It became easy to say and easier to prove that these black men were not men in the sense that white men were, and could never be, in the same sense, free. Their slavery was a matter of both race and social condition, but the condition was limited and determined by race. They were congenital wards and children, to be well-treated and cared for, but far happier and safer here than in their own land. As the Richmond, Virginia, *Examiner* put it in 1854:

"Let us not bother our brains about what *Providence* intends to do with our Negroes in the distant future, but glory in and profit to the utmost by what He has done for them in transplanting them here, and setting them to work on our plantations. . . . True philanthropy to the Negro, begins, like charity, at home; and if Southern men would act as if the canopy of heaven were inscribed with a convenant, in letters of fire, that *the Negro is here, and here forever; is our property, and ours forever;* . . . they would accomplish more good for the race in five years than they boast the institution itself to have accomplished in two centuries. . . ."

On the other hand, the growing exploitation of white labor in Europe, the rise of the factory system, the increased monopoly of land, and the problem of the distribution of political power, began to send wave after wave of immigrants to America, looking for new freedom, new opportunity and new democracy.

The opportunity for real and new democracy in America was broad. Political power at first was, as usual, confined to property holders and an aristocracy of birth and learning. But it was never securely based on land. Land was free and both land and property were possible to nearly every thrifty worker. Schools began early to multiply and open their doors even to the poor laborer. Birth began to count for less and less and America became to the world a land of economic opportunity. So the world came to America, even before the Revolution, and afterwards during the nineteenth century, nineteen million immigrants entered the United States.

When we compare these figures with the cotton crop and the increase of black workers, we see how the economic problem increased in intricacy. This intricacy is shown by the persons in the drama and their differing and opposing interests. There were the native-born Americans, largely of English descent, who were the property holders and employers; and even so far as they were poor, they looked forward to the time when they would accumulate capital and become, as they put it, economically "independent." Then there were the new immigrants, torn with a certain violence from their older social and economic surroundings; strangers in a new land, with visions of rising in the social and economic world by means of labor. They differed in language and social status, varying from the half-starved Irish peasant to the educated German and English artisan. There were the free Negroes: those of the North free in some cases for many generations, and voters; and in other cases, fugitives, new come from the South, with little skill and small knowledge of life and labor in their new environment. There were the free Negroes of the South, an unstable, harried class, living on sufferance of the law, and the good will of white patrons, and yet rising to be workers and sometimes owners of property and even of slaves, and cultured citizens. There was the great mass of poor whites, disinherited of their economic portion by competition with the slave system, and land monopoly.

In the earlier history of the South, free Negroes had the right to vote. Indeed, so far as the letter of the law was concerned, there was not a single Southern colony in which a black man who owned the requisite amount of property, and complied with other conditions, did not at some period have the legal right to vote.

Negroes voted in Virginia as late as 1723, when the assembly enacted that no free Negro, mulatto or Indian "shall hereafter have any vote at the elections of burgesses or any election whatsoever." In North Carolina, by the Act of 1734, a former discrimination against Negro voters was laid aside and not re-enacted until 1835.

A complaint in South Carolina, in 1701, said:

"Several free Negroes were receiv'd, & taken for as good Electors as the best Freeholders in the Province. So that we leave it with Your Lordships to judge whether admitting Aliens, Strangers, Servants, Negroes, &c, as good and qualified Voters, can be thought any ways agreeable to King Charles' Patent to Your Lordships, or the English Constitution of Government." Again in 1716, Jews and Negroes, who had been voting, were expressly excluded. In Georgia, there was at first no color discrimination, although only owners of fifty acres of land could vote. In 1761, voting was expressly confined to white men.[1]

In the states carved out of the Southwest, they were disfranchised as soon as the state came into the Union, although in Kentucky they voted between 1792 and 1799, and Tennessee allowed free Negroes to vote in her constitution of 1796.

In North Carolina, where even disfranchisement, in 1835, did not apply to Negroes who already had the right to vote, it was said that the several hundred Negroes who had been voting before then usually voted prudently and ju-diciously.

In Delaware and Maryland they voted in the latter part of the eighteenth century. In Louisiana, Negroes who had had the right to vote during territorial status were not disfranchised.

To sum up, in colonial times, the free Negro was excluded from the suf-frage only in Georgia, South Carolina and Virginia. In the Border States, Dela-ware disfranchised the Negro in 1792; Maryland in 1783 and 1810.

In the Southeast, Florida disfranchised Negroes in 1845; and in the South-west, Louisiana disfranchised them in 1812; Mississippi in 1817; Alabama in 1819; Missouri, 1821; Arkansas in 1836; Texas, 1845. Georgia in her consti-tution of 1777 confined voters to white males; but this was omitted in the constitutions of 1789 and 1798.

As slavery grew to a system and the Cotton Kingdom began to expand into imperial white domination, a free Negro was a contradiction, a threat and a menace. As a thief and a vagabond, he threatened society; but as an educated property holder, a successful mechanic or even professional man, he more than threatened slavery. He contradicted and undermined it. He must not be. He must be suppressed, enslaved, colonized. And nothing so bad could be said about him that did not easily appear as true to slaveholders.

In the North, Negroes, for the most part, received political enfranchise-ment with the white laboring classes. In 1778, the Congress of the Confederation twice refused to insert the word "white" in the Articles of Confederation in asserting that free inhabitants in each state should be entitled to all the priv-ileges and immunities of free citizens of the several states. In the law of 1783, free Negroes were recognized as a basis of taxation, and in 1784, they were

[1] Albert Edward McKinley, *The Suffrage Franchise in the Thirteen English Colo-nies in America* (Boston: Ginn & Co., Agents, 1905), p. 137.

recognized as voters in the territories. In the Northwest Ordinance of 1787, "free male inhabitants of full age" were recognized as voters.

The few Negroes that were in Maine, New Hampshire and Vermont could vote if they had the property qualifications. In Connecticut they were disfranchised in 1814; in 1865 this restriction was retained, and Negroes did not regain the right until after the Civil War. In New Jersey, they were disfranchised in 1807, but regained the right in 1820 and lost it again in 1847. Negroes voted in New York in the eighteenth century, then were disfranchised, but in 1821 were permitted to vote with a discriminatory property qualification of $250. No property qualification was required of whites. Attempts were made at various times to remove this qualification but it was not removed until 1870. In Rhode Island they were disfranchised in the constitution which followed Dorr's Rebellion, but finally allowed to vote in 1842. In Pennsylvania, they were allowed to vote until 1838 when the "reform" convention restricted the suffrage to whites.

The Western States as territories did not usually restrict the suffrage, but as they were admitted to the Union they disfranchised the Negroes: Ohio in 1803; Indiana in 1816; Illinois in 1818; Michigan in 1837; Iowa in 1846; Wisconsin in 1848; Minnesota in 1858; and Kansas in 1861.

The Northwest Ordinance and even the Louisiana Purchase had made no color discrimination in legal and political rights. But the states admitted from this territory, specifically and from the first, denied free black men the right to vote and passed codes of black laws in Ohio, Indiana and elsewhere, instigated largely by the attitude and fears of the immigrant poor whites from the South. Thus, at first, in Kansas and the West, the problem of the black worker was narrow and specific. Neither the North nor the West asked that black labor in the United States be free and enfranchised. On the contrary, they accepted slave labor as a fact but they were determined that it should be territorially restricted, and should not compete with free white labor.

What was this industrial system for which the South fought and risked life, reputation and wealth and which a growing element in the North viewed first with hesitating tolerance, then with distaste and finally with economic fear and moral horror? What did it mean to be a slave? It is hard to imagine it today. We think of oppression beyond all conception: cruelty, degradation, whipping and starvation, the absolute negation of human rights; or on the contrary, we may think of the ordinary worker the world over today, slaving ten, twelve, or fourteen hours a day, with not enough to eat, compelled by his physical necessities to do this and not to do that, curtailed in his movements and his possibilities; and we say, here, too, is a slave called a "free worker," and slavery is merely a matter of name.

But there was in 1863 a real meaning to slavery different from that we may apply to the laborer today. It was in part psychological, the enforced personal feeling of inferiority, the calling of another Master; the standing with hat in hand. It was the helplessness. It was the defenselessness of family life. It was the submergence below the arbitrary will of any sort of individual. It was without doubt worse in these vital respects than that which exists today in Europe or America. Its analogue today is the yellow, brown and black laborer in China and India, in Africa, in the forests of the Amazon; and it was this slavery that fell in America.

The slavery of Negroes in the South was not usually a deliberately cruel and oppressive system. It did not mean systematic starvation or murder. On the other hand, it is just as difficult to conceive as quite true the idyllic picture of a patriarchal state with cultured and humane masters under whom slaves were as children, guided and trained in work and play, given even such mental training as was for their good, and for the well-being of the surrounding world.

The victims of Southern slavery were often happy; had usually adequate food for their health, and shelter sufficient for a mild climate. The Southerners could say with some justification that when the mass of their field hands were compared with the worst class of laborers in the slums of New York and Philadelphia, and the factory towns of New England, the black slaves were as well off and in some particulars better off. Slaves lived largely in the country where health conditions were better; they worked in the open air, and their hours were about the current hours for peasants throughout Europe. They received no formal education, and neither did the Irish peasant, the English factory-laborer, nor the German *Bauer;* and in contrast with these free white laborers, the Negroes were protected by a certain primitive sort of old-age pension, job insurance, and sickness insurance; that is, they must be supported in some fashion, when they were too old to work; they must have attention in sickness, for they represented invested capital; and they could never be among the unemployed.

On the other hand, it is just as true that Negro slaves in America represented the worst and lowest conditions among modern laborers. One estimate is that the maintenance of a slave in the South cost the master about $19 a year, which means that they were among the poorest paid laborers in the modern world. They represented in a very real sense the ultimate degradation of man. Indeed, the system was so reactionary, so utterly inconsistent with modern progress, that we simply cannot grasp it today. No matter how degraded the factory hand, he is not real estate. The tragedy of the black slave's position was precisely this; his absolute subjection to the individual will of an owner and to "the cruelty and injustice which are the invariable consequences of the exercises of irresponsible power, especially where authority must be sometimes delegated by the planter to agents of inferior education and coarser feelings."

The proof of this lies clearly written in the slave codes. Slaves were not considered men. They had no right of petition. They were "devisable like any other chattel." They could own nothing; they could make no contracts; they could hold no property, nor traffic in property; they could not hire out; they could not legally marry nor constitute families; they could not control their children; they could not appeal from their master; they could be punished at will. They could not testify in court; they could be imprisoned by their owners, and the criminal offense of assault and battery could not be committed on the person of a slave. The "willful, malicious and deliberate murder" of a slave was punishable by death, but such a crime was practically impossible of proof. The slave owed to his master and all his family a respect "without bounds, and an absolute obedience." This authority could be transmitted to others. A slave could not sue his master; had no right of redemption; no right to education or religion; a promise made to a slave by his master had no force nor validity. Children followed the condition of the slave mother. The slave could have no access to the judiciary. A slave might be condemned to death for striking any white person.

Looking at these accounts, "it is safe to say that the law regards a Negro slave, so far as his civil status is concerned, purely and absolutely property, to be bought and sold and pass and descend as a tract of land, a horse, or an ox."[2]

The whole legal status of slavery was enunciated in the extraordinary statement of a Chief Justice of the United States that Negroes had always been regarded in America "as having no rights which a white man was bound to respect."

It may be said with truth that the law was often harsher than the practice. Nevertheless, these laws and decisions represent the legally permissible possibilities, and the only curb upon the power of the master was his sense of humanity and decency, on the one hand, and the conserving of his investment on the other. Of the humanity of large numbers of Southern masters there can be no doubt. In some cases, they gave their slaves a fatherly care. And yet even in such cases the strain upon their ability to care for large numbers of people and the necessity of entrusting the care of the slaves to other hands than their own, led to much suffering and cruelty.

The matter of his investment in land and slaves greatly curtailed the owner's freedom of action. Under the competition of growing industrial organization, the slave system was indeed the source of immense profits. But for the slave owner and landlord to keep a large or even reasonable share of these profits was increasingly difficult. The price of the slave produce in the open market could be hammered down by merchants and traders acting with knowledge and collusion. And the slave owner was, therefore, continually forced to find his profit not in the high price of cotton and sugar, but in beating even further down the cost of his slave labor. This made the slave owners in early days kill the slave by overwork and renew their working stock; it led to the widely organized interstate slave trade between the Border States and the Cotton Kingdom of the Southern South; it led to neglect and the breaking up of families, and it could not protect the slave against the cruelty, lust and neglect of certain owners.

Thus human slavery in the South pointed and led in two singularly contradictory and paradoxical directions—toward the deliberate commercial breeding and sale of human labor for profit and toward the intermingling of black and white blood. The slaveholders shrank from acknowledging either set of facts but they were clear and undeniable.

In this vital respect, the slave laborer differed from all others of his day: he could be sold; he could, at the will of a single individual, be transferred for life a thousand miles or more. His family, wife and children could be legally and absolutely taken from him. Free laborers today are compelled to wander in search for work and food; their families are deserted for want of wages; but in all this there is no such direct barter in human flesh. It was a sharp accentuation of control over men beyond the modern labor reserve or the contract coolie system.

Negroes could be sold—actually sold as we sell cattle with no reference to

[2] *A Picture of Slavery Drawn from the Decisions of Southern Courts* (Philadelphia: Crissy & Markley, 1863), p. 5.

calves or bulls, or recognition of family. It was a nasty business. The white South was properly ashamed of it and continually belittled and almost denied it. But it was a stark and bitter fact. Southern papers of the Border States were filled with advertisements:—"I wish to purchase fifty Negroes of both sexes from 6 to 30 years of age for which I will give the highest cash prices."

"Wanted to purchase—Negroes of every description, age and sex."

The consequent disruption of families is proven beyond doubt:

"Fifty Dollars reward.—Ran away from the subscriber, a Negro girl, named Maria. She is of a copper color, between 13 and 14 years of age—bareheaded and barefooted. She is small for her age—very sprightly and very likely. She stated she was *going to see her mother* at Maysville. Sanford Tomson."

"Committed to jail of Madison County, a Negro woman, who calls her name Fanny, and says she belongs to William Miller, of Mobile. She formerly belonged to John Givins, of this county, who now owns *several of her children.* David Shropshire, Jailer."

"Fifty Dollar reward.—Ran away from the subscriber, his Negro man Pauladore, commonly called Paul. I understand Gen. R. Y. Hayne *has purchased his wife and children* from H. L. Pinckney, Esq., and has them on his plantation at Goosecreek, where, no doubt, the fellow is frequently *lurking.* T. Davis." One can see Pauladore "lurking" about his wife and children.[3]

The system of slavery demanded a special police force and such a force was made possible and unusually effective by the presence of the poor whites. This explains the difference between the slave revolts in the West Indies, and the lack of effective revolt in the Southern United States. In the West Indies, the power over the slave was held by the whites and carried out by them and such Negroes as they could trust. In the South, on the other hand, the great planters formed proportionately quite as small a class but they had singularly enough at their command some five million poor whites; that is, there were actually more white people to police the slaves than there were slaves. Considering the economic rivalry of the black and white worker in the North, it would have seemed natural that the poor white would have refused to police the slaves. But two considerations led him in the opposite direction. First of all, it gave him work and some authority as overseer, slave driver, and member of the patrol system. But above and beyond this, it fed his vanity because it associated him with the masters. Slavery bred in the poor white a dislike of Negro toil of all sorts. He never regarded himself as a laborer, or as part of any labor movement. If he had any ambition at all it was to become a planter and to own "niggers." To these Negroes he transferred all the dislike and hatred which he had for the whole slave system. The result was that the system was held stable and intact by the poor white. Even with the late ruin of Haiti before their eyes, the planters, stirred as they were, were nevertheless able to stamp out slave revolt. The dozen revolts of the eighteenth century had dwindled to the plot of Gabriel in 1800, Vesey in 1822, of Nat Turner in 1831 and crews of the *Amistad* and *Creole* in 1839 and 1841. Gradually the whole white South became an armed and commissioned camp to keep Negroes in slavery and to kill the black rebel.

[3] Compare Frederic Baucroft, *Slave-Trading in the Old South* (Baltimore: J. H. Furst Company, 1931); Theodore Dwight Weld, *American Slavery As It Is* (New York: American Anti-Slavery Society, 1839).

But even the poor white, led by the planter, would not have kept the black slave in nearly so complete control had it not been for what may be called the Safety Valve of Slavery; and that was the chance which a vigorous and determined slave had to run away to freedom.

Under the situation as it developed between 1830 and 1860 there were grave losses to the capital invested in black workers. Encouraged by the idealism of those Northern thinkers who insisted that Negroes were human, the black worker sought freedom by running away from slavery. The physical geography of America with its paths north, by swamp, river and mountain range; the daring of black revolutionists like Henson and Tubman; and the extra-legal efforts of abolitionists made this more and more easy.

One cannot know the real facts concerning the number of fugitives, but despite the fear of advertising the losses, the emphasis put upon fugitive slaves by the South shows that it was an important economic item. It is certain from the bitter effort to increase the efficiency of the fugitive slave law that the losses from runaways were widespread and continuous; and the increase in the interstate slave trade from Border States to the deep South, together with the increase in the price of slaves, showed a growing pressure. At the beginning of the nineteenth century, one bought an average slave for $200; while in 1860 the price ranged from $1,400 to $2,000.

Not only was the fugitive slave important because of the actual loss involved, but for potentialities in the future. These free Negroes were furnishing a leadership for the mass of the black workers, and especially they were furnishing a text for the abolition idealists. Fugitive slaves, like Frederick Douglass and others humbler and less gifted, increased the number of abolitionists by thousands and spelled the doom of slavery.

The true significance of slavery in the United States to the whole social development of America lay in the ultimate relation of slaves to democracy. What were to be the limits of democratic control in the United States? If all labor, black as well as white, became free—were given schools and the right to vote—what control could or should be set to the power and action of these laborers? Was the rule of the mass of Americans to be unlimited, and the right to rule extended to all men regardless of race and color, or if not, what power of dictatorship and control; and how would property and privilege be protected? This was the great and primary question which was in the minds of the men who wrote the Constitution of the United States and continued in the minds of thinkers down through the slavery controversy. It still remains with the world as the problem of democracy expands and touches all races and nations.

And of all human development, ancient and modern, not the least singular and significant is the philosophy of life and action which slavery bred in the souls of black folk. In most respects its expression was stilted and confused; the rolling periods of Hebrew prophecy and biblical legend furnished inaccurate but splendid words. The subtle folk-lore of Africa, with whimsy and parable, veiled wish and wisdom; and above all fell the anointing chrism of the slave music, the only gift of pure art in America.

Beneath the Veil lay right and wrong, vengeance and love, and sometimes throwing aside the veil, a soul of sweet Beauty and Truth stood revealed. Nothing else of art or religion did the slave South give to the world, except the Negro song and story. And even after slavery, down to our day, it has added but little to this gift. One has but to remember as symbol of it all, still unspoiled by petty artisans, the legend of John Henry, the mighty black, who broke his heart working against the machine, and died "with his Hammer in His Hand."

Up from this slavery gradually climbed the Free Negro with clearer, modern expression and more definite aim long before the emancipation of 1863. His greatest effort lay in his coöperation with the Abolition movement. He knew he was not free until all Negroes were free. Individual Negroes became exhibits of the possibilities of the Negro race, if once it was raised above the status of slavery. Even when, as so often, the Negro became Court Jester to the ignorant American mob, he made his plea in his songs and antics.

Thus spoke "the noblest slave that ever God set free," Frederick Douglass in 1852, in his 4th of July oration at Rochester, voicing the frank and fearless criticism of the black worker:

"What, to the American slave, is your 4th of July? I answer: a day that reveals to him, more than all other days in the year, the gross injustice and cruelty to which he is the constant victim. To him your celebration is a sham; your boasted liberty, an unholy license; your national greatness, swelling vanity, your sounds of rejoicing are empty and heartless; your denunciation of tyrants, brass-fronted impudence; your shouts of liberty and equality, hollow mockery; your prayers and hymns, your sermons and thanksgivings, with all your religious parade and solemnity, are, to him, mere bombast, fraud, deception, impiety and hypocrisy—a thin veil to cover up crimes which would disgrace a nation of savages. . . .

"You boast of your love of liberty, your superior civilization, and your pure Christianity, while the whole political power of the nation (as embodied in the two great political parties) is solemnly pledged to support and perpetuate the enslavement of three millions of your countrymen. You hurl your anathemas at the crown-headed tyrants of Russia and Austria and pride yourselves on your democratic institutions, while you yourselves consent to be the mere *tools* and *bodyguards* of the tyrants of Virginia and Carolina. You invite to your shores fugitives of oppression from aboard, honor them with banquets, greet them with ovations, cheer them, toast them, salute them, protect them, and pour out your money to them like water; but the fugitives from your own land you advertise, hunt, arrest, shoot, and kill. You glory in your refinement and your universal education; yet you maintain a system as barbarous and dreadful as ever stained the character of a nation—a system begun in avarice, supported in pride, and perpetuated in cruelty. You shed tears over fallen Hungary, and make the sad story of her wrongs the theme of your poets, statesmen, and orators, till your gallant sons are ready to fly to arms to vindicate her cause against the oppressor; but, in regard to the ten thousand wrongs of the American slave, you would enforce the strictest silence, and would hail him as an enemy of the nation who dares to make those wrongs the subject of public discourse!"[4]

Above all, we must remember the black worker was the ultimate exploited; that he formed that mass of labor which had neither wish nor power to escape from the labor status, in order to directly exploit other laborers, or indirectly,

---

[4] Carter G. Woodson, *Negro Orators and Their Orations.* (Washington, D.C.: The Associated Publishers Inc., 1925), pp. 218–19.

by alliance with capital, to share in their exploitation. To be sure, the black mass, developed again and again, here and there, capitalistic groups in New Orleans, in Charleston and in Philadelphia; groups willing to join white capital in exploiting labor; but they were driven back into the mass by racial prejudice before they had reached a permanent foothold; and thus became all the more bitter against all organization which by means of race prejudice, or the monopoly of wealth, sought to exclude men from making a living.

It was thus the black worker, as founding stone of a new economic system in the nineteenth century and for the modern world, who brought civil war in America. He was its underlying cause, in spite of every effort to base the strife upon union and national power.

That dark and vast sea of human labor in China and India, the South Seas and all Africa; in the West Indies and Central America and in the United States—that great majority of mankind, on whose bent and broken backs rest today the founding stones of modern industry—shares a common destiny; it is despised and rejected by race and color; paid a wage below the level of decent living; driven, beaten, prisoned and enslaved in all but name; spawning the world's raw material and luxury—cotton, wool, coffee, tea, cocoa, palm oil, fibers, spices, rubber, silks, lumber, copper, gold, diamonds, leather—how shall we end the list and where?All these are gathered up at prices lowest of the low, manufactured, transformed and transported at fabulous gain; and the resultant wealth is distributed and displayed and made the basis of world power and universal dominion and armed arrogance in London and Paris, Berlin and Rome, New York and Rio de Janeiro.

Here is the real modern labor problem. Here is the kernel of the problem of Religion and Democracy, of Humanity. Words and futile gestures avail nothing. Out of the exploitation of the dark proletariat comes the Surplus Value filched from human beasts which, in cultured lands, the Machine and harnessed Power veil and conceal. The emancipation of man is the emancipation of labor and the emancipation of labor is the freeing of that basic majority of workers who are yellow, brown and black.

> Dark, shackled knights of labor, clinging still
> Amidst a universal wreck of faith
> To cheerfulness, and foreigners to hate.
> These know ye not, these have ye not received,
> But these shall speak to you Beatitudes.
> Around them surge the tides of all your strife,
> Above them rise the august monuments
> Of all your outward splendor, but they stand
> Unenvious in thought, and bide their time.
>   LESLIE P. HILL

Scandinavians

GEORGE M. STEPHENSON

When America Was the Land of Canaan

Although the bulk of the Scandinavians reached American shores between the Civil War and the end of the nineteenth century, immigration from Norway, Sweden, and Denmark had already reached significant proportions during the Jacksonian era. The Scandinavians tended to settle in the midwestern plains states (Illinois, Wisconsin, Minnesota, Iowa) and unlike most minority groups had relatively little difficulty with "native" Americans. In fact, they were more quickly accepted by the majority than either the Germans or the Irish, the other two major European minorities of the mid-nineteenth century. One Norwegian traveler expressed the existing feeling in a letter to his compatriots at home. "Never," one of the native Americans had told him, "have I known people to become civilized so rapidly as your countrymen; they come here in motley crowds, dressed up with all kinds of dingle-dangle just like the Indians. But just look at them a year later: they speak English perfectly, and, as far as dress, manners, and ability are concerned, they are quite above reproach."

No minority group enthused more over its initial American experiences. Letters to the old country rhapsodized over equality and freedom found in the United States: employees and employers wore similar clothing, wages were higher, and abundant quantities of land were available for those willing to work hard. Food was so plentiful that America seemed "the land of Canaan." "Just think what an impression it would make on a poor highlander's imagination," a Norwegian wrote home, "to be told that some day he might eat wheat bread every day and pork at least three times a week!"

The Scandinavians did encounter some of the difficulties that plagued recent arrivals of other ethnic origins. Land was not always as fertile as had been anticipated and some found turning wilderness into farms too strenuous. Homesickness, however, created the greatest difficulty. Regardless of abundant economic opportunities and relative equality of treatment by other whites, many of the newcomers had not anticipated the strength of attachments to family and friends in the old country.

In the following selection, George Stephenson captures the feelings of those Swedish emigrants who pioneered in the New World. His remarks are applicable to the experiences of other Scandinavian groups in the United States.

Minnesota History, 10 (1929), 237–60. Reprinted with permission from MINNESOTA HISTORY, the quarterly magazine of the Minnesota Historical Society.

Volumes have been written on the causes of emigration from the various countries of Europe to the United States, and it may appear superfluous to add to the numerous articles that have appeared in print.[1] A plethora of emigration statistics is available; monographs have appeared by the score; and it would seem that the subject has been attacked from every conceivable angle. But the historical profession still awaits the man with the magic touch, who by a process known only to the master can convert this tremendous mass of material into a masterpiece of historical synthesis. This master must sound the depths of the human soul and he must analyze the noblest as well as the basest emotions that play on the human heart. He will not concern himself with the people on whom fortune has smiled graciously, nor will he relate the exploits of the battlefield and portray the lives of kings and nobles; he will study the documents that betray the spirit, hopes, and aspirations of the humble folk who tilled the soil, felled the forest, and tended the loom—in short, who followed the occupations that fall to the lot of the less favored majority in every land.

Emigration from Sweden was a class movement that spread from the rural districts to the cities and towns. The fever sought its victims among those who were not inoculated with the virus of social distinction and economic prosperity; and when the epidemic was transported three thousand miles across the water, it took a more virulent form. In fact, it was transmitted most effectively by the thousands of letters that found their way from America to the small red cottages hidden among the pine-clad, rocky hills of Sweden.

It has become a commonplace that emigration from Sweden began in earnest after the close of the American Civil War, when, according to a newspaper account published in 1869, "the emigrants, as if by agreement, gathered from the various communities on certain days, like migratory swallows, to leave, without apparent regret, the homes and associations of their native land, in order to begin a new life on another continent."[2] Statistically this statement is accurate enough, but historically it is entirely misleading. Emigration from Sweden began in earnest in the decade of the forties, when the first "American letters" found their way back to the old country. These letters made a tremendous impression on certain persons at a time when a new world—a new and ideal world—was dawning in literature and in the press.[3] Into this realm of the idealist the "America letters" fell like leaves from the land of Canaan. They were not only read and pondered by the simple and credulous individuals to whom they were addressed, and discussed in larger groups in homes and at markets and fairs and in crowds assembled at parish churches, but they were also broadcast through the newspapers, which, unwittingly or not, infected parish after parish with the "America fever." The contents of these documents from another world were so thrilling and fabulous that many editors were as

[1] This paper, read on June 14, 1929, at the first Hutchinson session of the eighth state historical convention, is based mainly upon documentary materials discovered in Sweden by the author as a fellow in 1927–1928 of the John Simon Guggenheim Foundation of New York. *Ed.*

[2] *Nya Wexjö-Bladet* (Växjö), May 22, 1869.

[3] Papers like *Aftonbladet* (Stockholm), *Östgötha Correspondenten* (Linköping), *Norrlands-Posten* (Gävle), and *Jönköpings-Bladet* and writers like Karl J. L. Almqvist and Pehr Thomasson foreshadowed a new day in religion, politics, society, and economics.

glad to publish them as were the recipients to have them published. The result was that the most fanciful stories were circulated about the wonderful country across the Atlantic—a land of milk and honey.

A correspondent from Linköping wrote to a Jönköping paper in May, 1846, as follows:

> The desire to emigrate to America in the country around Kisa is increasing and is said to have spread to neighboring communities. A beggar girl from Kisa, who has gone up into the more level country to ply her trade, is said to have painted America in far more attractive colors than Joshua's returned spies portrayed the promised land to the children of Israel. "In America," the girl is reported to have said, "the hogs eat their fill of raisins and dates that everywhere grow wild, and when they are thirsty, they drink from ditches flowing with wine." Naturally the gullible *bondfolk* draw the conclusion from such stories that it is far better to be a hog in America than to be a human being in Sweden. The emigration fever seizes upon them, and the officials are so busy making out emigration permits that they cannot even get a night's rest.[4]

One cannot escape the suspicion that this beggar girl from Kisa had read or had heard discussed a letter written at Jefferson County, Iowa, on February 9, 1846, by Peter Cassel, who the previous year had led a party of twenty-one emigrants—men, women, and children—from this parish. The departure of this man in his fifty-sixth year at the head of a large company of emigrants—large for that time—created a sensation in his parish and in neighboring parishes; and information about his adventure was eagerly awaited by his large circle of friends and relatives. And they were not disappointed. In describing the wonders of America, Cassel's pen vied with Marco Polo's. Iowa's corn, pumpkins, and hogs, seen through the medium of his letters, appeared as monstrous to the peasants of Sweden as Gulliver to the inhabitants of Lilliputia; and in contrast with the earnings of the American farmer the income of the Swedish husbandman shrank to insignificance. Even the thunder in Sweden sounded like the report of a toy pistol, compared with the heavy artillery of the heavens in America.[5] In his first letter Cassel wrote thus:

> The ease of making a living here and the increasing prosperity of the farmers . . . exceeds anything we anticipated. If only half of the work expended on the soil in the fatherland were utilized here, the yield would reach the wildest imagination. . . . Barns and cattle sheds are seldom, if ever, seen in this vicinity; livestock is allowed to roam the year around, and since pasturage is common property, extending from one end of the land to the other, a person can own as much livestock as he desires or can take care of, without the least trouble or expense. . . . One of our neighbors . . . has one hundred head of hogs. . . . Their food consists largely of acorns, a product that is so

[4] *Jönköpings-Bladet,* May 26, 1846.
[5] For a sketch of Cassel and a reprint of his letters, see George M. Stephenson, "Documents Relating to Peter Cassel and the Settlement at New Sweden, Iowa," in the *Swedish-American Historical Bulletin,* 2:1–82 (February, 1929).

abundant that as late as February the ground is covered in places. . . .
Corn fields are more like woods than grain fields.

This *bonde* (land-owning farmer) not only was impressed with America's rich
soil, its forests, its abundance of coal and metals, its rivers and lakes swarming
with fish, but also wanted his friends at home to know that in other respects he
had found a better world:

> Freedom and equality are the fundamental principles of the constitu-
> tion of the United States. There is no such thing as class distinction
> here, no counts, barons, lords or lordly estates. . . .[6] Everyone lives in
> the unrestricted enjoyment of personal liberty. A Swedish *bonde*, raised
> under oppression and accustomed to poverty and want, here finds him-
> self elevated to a new world, as it were, where all his former hazy ideas
> of a society conforming more closely to nature's laws are suddenly
> made real and he enjoys a satisfaction in life that he has never before
> experienced. There are no beggars here and there never can be so long
> as the people are ruled by the spirit that prevails now. I have yet to see
> a lock on a door in this neighborhood. . . . I have never heard of
> theft. . . . At this time of the year the sap of the sugar maple is run-
> ning and we have made much sugar and syrup.[7]

If the beggar girl from Kisa had heard this letter read and discussed by
simple-minded folk, little wonder that her imagination ran away with her.
Surely Joshua's spies could not have found a more ideal land if they had gone
to the ends of the earth. And this girl was not the only purveyor of "information" about America. In many parishes stories were current that in Gothenburg there was a bureau that provided emigrants with all the necessities for the
journey—free of charge; that several vessels were waiting to transport emigrants
to the promised land—also free of charge; that in two days enough money could
be earned to buy a cow that gave fabulous quantities of milk; that all pastures
were common property; that the grass grew so tall that only the horns of the
grazing cattle were visible; that there were no taxes in that fortunate land; that
rivers ran with syrup; that cows roamed at large and could be milked by anyone.[8]

There may have been occasional "America letters" published in the news-

[6] "There is peace and prosperity here. I have come in contact with millions of
people of all sorts and conditions, but I have never heard of dissension, and we have
never been snubbed. There are black and brown people, but all are friendly and
agreeable." Letter from Samuel Jönsson, Buffalo, New York, November 22, 1846, in
Östgötha Correspondenten, May 26, 1847.
[7] This letter, dated February 9, 1846, was published in *Östgötha Correspondenten*
on May 16, 1846. It is reprinted, with English translation, in the *Swedish-American
Historical Bulletin*, 2:22–28, 55–62 (February, 1929). The abundance of fish and
game was mentioned frequently in letters to the old country. See, for example, a
letter from A. M. D——m, Taylor's Falls, Minnesota, in *Östgötha Correspondenten*,
July 27, 30, 1853.
[8] Correspondence from Döderhultsvik to *Kalmar-Posten*, April 23, 1852;
Landskrona Nya Tidning, cited in *Borås Tidning*, June 13, 1854; *Hwad Nytt?*
(Eksjö), February 18, 1869; *Wäktaren*, cited in *Dalpilen* (Falun), July 17, 1869;
Aron Edström, "Blad ur svensk-amerikanska banbrytarelifvets historia," in *Svensk-
amerikanska kalendern*, 61–64 (Worcester, Massachusetts, 1882).

papers of Sweden prior to 1840, but they were rare, chiefly because the few Swedes in America were usually adventurers or deserters from vessels, who did not find it expedient to let their whereabouts be known. The interest of the press in these letters began with the publication of *Aftonbladet,* in January, 1842, of a long letter from Gustaf Unonius, a young man who had received some notice as the author of a volume of poems before emigrating with his bride and a few of the "better folk" in the early autumn of 1841. He used the columns of this widely read Stockholm daily to inform his friends and acquaintances, especially in and around Upsala, where he had been a student, about his experiences in the new world. Unonius was essentially a student and his letters were carefully phrased, with the advantages and disadvantages of America weighed in the balance; but he could write after a residence of one month in Wisconsin that it was unlikely that he would ever return to his native land, because he found his youthful dream of a republican form of government and a democratic society realized. He found no epithets of degradation applied to men of humble toil; only those whose conduct merited it were looked down upon. "Liberty still is stronger in my affections than the bright silver dollar that bears her image," he wrote. Three months later he could write: "I look to the future with assurance. The soil that gives me sustenance has become my home; and the land that has opened opportunities and has given me a home and feeling of security has become my new fatherland." The readers of his letters learned that the young idealist seeking to escape from the trammels of an older society had found something that approached a Utopia on the American frontier, although his writings about it resembled more the reflections of a man chastened by unaccustomed toil and hardships than the song of a pilgrim who had crossed the river Jordan.[9]

Within a few weeks an emigrant who preceded Unonius to Wisconsin by three years was heard from through the same journalistic medium, the man to whom the letters were addressed having been prompted to publish them by reading the Unonius document. The writer was John Friman, a member of a party consisting of a father and three sons, who settled at Salem, Wisconsin Territory, in 1838. The serious illness of the youngest son necessitated the return to Sweden of father and son, but the eldest son remained to carry on the correspondence with the "folks back home."[10] In a later letter the young pioneer told about his first meeting with Unonius in the latter's home at New Upsala:

> We are healthier and more vigorous than we ever were in Sweden.
> Many people from England and Ireland have already come here. Last
> fall, in October, a few Swedes from Upsala came here from Milwau-
> kee, Mr. Gustaf Unonius and wife, married only six weeks when they
> left Sweden. A relative, Inspector Groth, and a Doctor Pålman have
> settled on a beautiful lake near a projected canal, twenty-eight miles
> west of Milwaukee, Milwaukee County. They have named the settle-

[9] His first letter was dated at Milwaukee, Wisconsin Territory, October 15, 1841, and published in *Aftonbladet,* January 4, 5, 1842; his second letter was dated at New Upsala, Wisconsin, January 23, 1842, and published in *Aftonbladet,* May 28, 30, 31, June 3, 7, 9, 1842.

[10] Letters dated January 18, 1841, and July 4, 1842, in *Aftonbladet,* April 6, October 6, 13, 1842.

ment New Upsala *and the capital of New Sweden in Wisconsin.* They are expecting several families and students from Upsala this summer. . . . I visited New Upsala last fall. They wanted me to sell out and move there. Father has probably heard of them. Last fall Unonius wrote to *Aftonbladet.* I hope his letter will awaken the desire to emigrate among the Swedes. . . . Altogether we own two hundred acres of land, and when we have our farm fenced and eighty acres broken . . . I wouldn't trade it for a whole estate in Sweden, with all its ceremonies. Out here in the woods we know nothing of such. . . . Give our love to Herman and say to him that we hope his health will be better than it was the first time he was here.[11]

Herman's health was restored sufficiently to enable him, in company with a young man from another city, to undertake the journey to the "states" a few weeks later. Imagine the sorrow of the father when he received a letter informing him that Herman had entirely disappeared, his companion, who had arrived at the Friman farm in due time, being unable to give a satisfactory explanation of the mystery.[12] The public in Sweden was informed of the misfortune through the publication of the letter in the papers, and interest was even more quickened by the letter from the father of the companion, answering *seriatim* the charges of the elder Friman brother that Herman was the victim of misplaced confidence in his fellow traveler;[13] for weeks thousands eagerly searched the columns of the papers for the latest word about "brother Herman." The wonderful adventures the prodigal son related when he finally accounted for himself at the Friman farm not only cleared the name of his companion and relieved the anxiety of both fathers, but it gave to the "America letters" a halo of romance that made them, in a very real sense, news letters from the rich, mighty, and romantic land out there in the West.[14] The muse of history suffers no violence by the assertion that one of the most interesting and widely read features of the Swedish papers were the "America letters."

In that unique and valuable work that emerged from the survey of a commission appointed by the Swedish government, some twenty years ago, to seek out the causes of emigration, appears a volume entitled "The Emigrants' Own Reasons," comprising letters written at the request of the commission by Swedish immigrants who had lived a longer or shorter period in the United States and Canada.[15] These letters have their value, but it must be recognized that the writers unconsciously injected into them the retrospections of several months or years. There is, therefore, a vast difference between these letters and the "America letters"—naïve accounts of experiences written for relatives and friends, who were as simple and naïve as the writers themselves, and before retrospection had wrought its havoc. It is just this "unconscious" and naïve quality of the "Amer-

[11] Letter dated February 10, 1843, in *Skara Tidning,* May 18, 1843. Unonius mentions the meeting with Friman in his *Minnen från en sjuttonårig vistelse i nordvestra Amerika,* I:182 (Upsala, 1861).

[12] Letter dated February 10, 1843, in *Skara Tidning,* May 18, 1843.

[13] Letter from J. C. Melander, Eksjö, June 27, 1843, in *Skara Tidning,* July 13, 1843.

[14] Extracts from several letters in *Skara Tidning,* November 2, 1843.

[15] *Emigrationsutredningen,* 7:131–263 (Stockholm, 1908).

ica letters" that opens for the historian windows through which he can look into the cottages in Sweden and into the log cabins in the adopted country. The student of emigration who is satisfied with poring over statistics, government reports, and "social surveys" will never sound the depths of one of the most human phenomena in history. The much-abused psychologist in this instance is an indispensable co-laborer with the historian, for the theme of the historian of emigration is the human soul. The emigrant was a product of his environment, but he was not held in bondage by it; his soul could not be shackled, even though his body was the slave of harsh taskmasters.

In the large the contents of the "America letters" written in the years from 1840 to 1860 may be divided into two categories: (1) impressions of and experiences in America; and (2) comments on conditions in Sweden. With the exception of a few letters written by men of the type of Gustaf Unonius, the great mass of them were the products of men who had only a meager education and who grew to manhood before the generation that enjoyed the advantages provided under the act of 1842, by which every parish was required to provide a public school. The spelling is faulty, to say the least, and the punctuation is atrocious. New York becomes "Nefyork" and "Nevyork"; Chicago, "Sikago" and "Cicaga"; Illinois, "Elinojs"; Iowa, "Adiova" and "Jova"; Pennsylvania, "Pensarvenien"; Galesburg, "Gillsborg" and "Galesbury"; Albany, "Albano" and "Albanes"; Troy, "Troij"; Princeton, "Princeldin"; Rock Island, "Rockislan" and "Räckarlan"; Peru, "Pebra" and "Perru"; and Henry County, "Hendi counti." Not only were liberties taken with American place names but even many innocent Swedish words were mutilated beyond recognition. But the person who has the patience to spell his way through a mass of these documents cannot fail to acquire a profound respect for the ability of the writers to express themselves and for their sound and wholesome instincts. They reveal that in their native land they had thought seriously, and evenly deeply, about their own problems and those of their communities—probably more than they or their neighbors at the time realized; but it was during the first weeks and months in America that they gave vent to their feelings and emotions and tried the powers of expression that had previously lain dormant. America gave them a basis for comparison and contrast: church, government, society, and officials at home appeared in an entirely different light; and the contrast was such that the emigrant had no desire to return in order to relate to his countrymen his strange experiences; on the contrary, he did all in his power to urge them to follow his example—to emigrate. The emigrant became an evangelist, preaching the gospel of America to the heavy-laden. For him the year of jubilee had come.

There are, of course, among the "America letters" that have been preserved a number that express regret that the transatlantic adventure was undertaken and reveal a feeling of bitterness towards those who had painted America in such attractive colors and in that way had lured the writers into poverty and misery; but the overwhelming number of them are almost ecstatic in praise of the adopted country and bitterly hostile to the land that gave them birth. Some writers even went to the length of ridiculing or deriding those to whom their letters were addressed for remaining in a land unworthy of the man and woman of honest toil and legitimate ambition. Extracts from two letters written before 1850 are illuminating in this regard:

I doubt that any one will take the notion of returning to Sweden, because the journey is too long and expensive; and even if these considerations were minor with certain individuals, I doubt that they would go, for the reason that nothing would be gained. . . . Not until this year have I fully realized how grateful we ought to be to God, who by His grace has brought us away from both spiritual and material misery. How shall we show our appreciation for all the goodness the Lord has bestowed upon us! In like manner does He bid you, my relatives and friends, to receive the same grace and goodness, but you will not heed His voice. What will the Lord render unto you now? He will allow you to be deprived of all this during your entire lives and in the future to repent bitterly of your negligence. We have the word of prophecy . . . and you will do well to heed it. . . . Ought not a place of refuge and solace be acceptable to you? . . . Now I have said what my conscience prompts me to say and on you rests the responsibility for yourselves and your children.[16]

The other letter contains the following admonition:

Tell Johannes . . . and others not to condemn me for failing to return home at the appointed time, as I promised and intended when I left Sweden, because at that time I was as ignorant as the other stay-at-homes about what a voyage to a foreign land entails. When a person is abroad in the world, there may be many changes in health and disposition, but if God grants me health I will come when it pleases me. If it were not for the sake of my good mother and my relatives, I would never return to Sweden. No one need worry about my circumstances in America, because I am living on God's noble and free soil, neither am I a slave under others. On the contrary, I am my own master, like the other creatures of God. I have now been on American soil for two and a half years and I have not been compelled to pay a penny for the privilege of living. Neither is my cap worn out from lifting it in the presence of gentlemen. There is no class distinction here between high and low, rich and poor, no make-believe, no "title sickness," or artificial ceremonies, but everything is quiet and peaceful and everybody lives in peace and prosperity. Nobody goes from door to door begging crumbs. . . . The Americans do not have to scrape their effects together and sell them in order to pay heavy taxes to the crown and to pay the salaries of officials. There are no large estates, whose owners can take the last sheaf from their dependents and then turn them out to beg. Neither is a drink of *brännvin* forced on the workingman in return for a day's work. . . . I sincerely hope that nobody in Sweden will foolishly dissuade anyone from coming to this land of Canaan.[17]

[16] Peter Cassel to relatives and friends, December 13, 1848, in the *Swedish-American Historical Bulletin*, 2:78 (February, 1929).
[17] Letter from Johan Johansson, Burlington, Iowa, November 12, 1849, in *Östgötha Correspondenten*, April 5, 1850. Compare the following statement in a letter from Stephan Stephanson, May 17, 1854: "There is no class distinction here, but all are equals, and not as in Sweden, where the working people are looked down upon and are called 'the rabble,' whereas the lazy gentlemen are called 'better folk.'" This manuscript is in the author's possession.

This letter may be said to be a prototype of the "America letters." It contains a mass of details, and almost every sentence breathes a deep-seated dissatisfaction with government, institutions, and society in Sweden and at the same time a remarkable satisfaction with everything American. This tone is characteristic even of letters written by persons whose first experiences in the new country were anything but pleasant. An emigrant from Småland, who emigrated with his wife and eight children in 1849,—one of the "cholera years"— buried one of his daughters on the banks of an inland canal, suffered several weeks with malaria, and just escaped being cheated out of his hard-earned savings, was happy over his decision to emigrate and looked to the future with high hopes for a better existence in spiritual as well as material matters.[18] Another enthusiast, who had been exposed to dangers of various kinds, wrote: "We see things here that we could never describe, and you would never believe them if we did. I would not go back to Sweden if the whole country were presented to me."[19]

It is obvious that statements like these were topics of lively discussion in the cottages of Sweden. The astonished people naturally hungered for more information and some of them inquired of their "American" friends how the morals of this marvelous country compared with those of their own communities. Where everything was so great and rich and free, and the population was recruited from all parts of the world, how could the Americans be so honest, sympathetic, and kind as the letters pictured them? A correspondent in 1852 gave his explanation of the miracle. The country was large, he said, and the rascals were not concentrated in any one place; and if such persons did come to a community, they found no evil companions to add fuel to their baser instincts. Moreover, if they did not mend their ways, a volunteer committee of citizens would wait upon them and serve notice that they had the choice of leaving the community or submitting to arrest. The Americans would not brook violations of law and therefore drunkenness, profanity, theft, begging, and dissension were so rare as to be almost entirely absent. This letter of recommendation did not stop here. It praised the observance of the Sabbath and asserted that the young people did not dance, drink, or play cards, as was the case in Sweden.[20]

Unlike the earlier travelers in America, who usually belonged to the upper classes in Europe, the emigrants found the moral standards on a much higher plane than in Sweden. During a residence of nine months in the new Utopia one emigrant had not heard of a single illegitimate child—yes, one case had actually come to his knowledge, and then a Swede was the offender. He found whiskey-drinking very unusual and the advancement of temperance almost unbelievable. In a midwestern town of about two thousand inhabitants (the seat of a college with seven professors and three hundred and thirty-nine students) one had to be well acquainted in order to purchase whiskey or strong wine. "From this incident you may judge of the state of temperance in American

[18] Steffan Steffanson to relatives and friends, October 9, 1849, in Swedish Historical Society of America, *Yearbooks,* 11:86–100 (St. Paul, 1926).

[19] Unsigned letters from New York in *Norrlands-Posten,* December 29, 1856; and from Chicago, September 9, 1853, in *Nya Wexjö-Bladet,* October 7, 1853.

[20] Unsigned letter, dated January 23, 1852, in *Bibel-Wännen* (Lund), September, 1852.

cities," he confided. After a residence of four years in southeastern Iowa, Peter Cassel testified that he had "dined in hundreds of homes," and had "yet to see a whiskey bottle on the table. This country suits me as a friend of temperance, but it is not suitable for the whiskey drinker."[21]

It is hardly conceivable that the Swedish immigrants were unanimously enthusiastic about temperance, whether voluntary or imposed by law, and the student of American social history would dot the map of mid-nineteenth-century America with thousands of oases; but it is nevertheless a fact that the Middle West, to which most of the immigrants gravitated, was in striking contrast to Sweden, where every land-owning farmer operated a still and where the fiery *brännvin* at that time was as much a household necessity as coffee is today. Men, women, and children partook of its supposed health-giving properties in quantities appropriate to the occasion. To many immigrants who had heard the speeches or had read the tracts of the great apostles of temperance in Sweden, George Scott and Peter Wieselgren, and had patterned their lives after their precepts, the rural communities of Iowa, Illinois, Wisconsin, and Minnesota must have approached their ideal.

We must not be deluded into thinking that all the earlier Swedish immigrants were saints or models of virtue, but many of their letters bear testimony to the fact that there was profound dissatisfaction with the state of religion in Sweden. The writers had listened attentively to pietistic pastors and Baptist and lay preachers with sufficient courage to violate the conventicle act or to incur the displeasure of the church authorities, many of whom made merry over the flowing bowl and served Mammon rather than God. One cannot escape the conclusion that religion played a greater role in stimulating the desire to emigrate than writers have hitherto suspected; and if the student of immigration wishes to understand why the Swedes in America have turned away in such numbers from the church of the fathers in favor of other denominations or have held aloof from all church connections, he will find a study of religious conditions in the homeland a profitable one. It is by no means purely accidental that the beginnings of emigration coincide with the confluence of various forms of dissatisfaction with the state church.

The immigrants quickly sensed the difference between the pastors in America and Sweden. In 1849 a writer put it thus:

> There are also Swedish preachers here who are so well versed in the Bible and in the correct interpretation that they seek the lost sheep and receive them again into their embrace and do not conduct themselves after the manner of Sweden, where the sheep must seek the shepherd and address him with high-sounding titles.

Another requested his brother to send hymn books and catechisms, because the old copies were almost worn out with use.

> We have a Swedish pastor. He . . . is a disciple of the esteemed Pastor Sellergren [*Peter Lorenz Sellergren, a prominent evangelistic pastor*

---

[21] L. P. Esbjörn to Peter Wieselgren, Andover, Illinois, May 23, 1850, a manuscript in the *Stadsbibliotek* of Gothenburg; Cassel to relatives and friends, December 13, 1848, in the *Swedish-American Historical Bulletin*, 2:81 (February, 1929).

in Sweden]. . . . During the past eleven months he has preached every Sunday and holiday; on week days he works the same as the rest of us, because his remarkable preaching ability makes it unnecessary for him to write his sermons. One Sunday I heard him preach for over two hours, and he was as fluent the second hour as the first.[22]

A faithful disciple of the prophet Eric Janson drew an even sharper contrast between the two countries:

> I take pen in hand, moved by the Holy Ghost, to bear witness to the things I have seen, heard, and experienced. We had a pleasant voyage . . . and I was not affected in the least with seasickness. . . . My words are inadequate to describe with what joy we are permitted daily to draw water from the well of life and how we have come to the land of Canaan, flowing with milk and honey, . . . which the Scriptures tell us the Lord has prepared for his people. He has brought us out of the devilish bondage of the ecclesiastical authorities, which still holds you in captivity. . . . Here we are relieved of hearing and seeing Sweden's satellites of the devil, whose tongues are inspired by the minions of hell and who murdered the prophets and Jesus himself and snatched the Bible from Eric Janson's hands and came against us with staves, guns, and torches, together with ropes and chains, to take away the freedom we have in Christ. But praised be God through all eternity that we are freed from them and are now God's peculiar people. . . . This is the land of liberty, where everybody can worship God in his own way and can choose pastors who are full of the Spirit, light, and perfection. . . . Therefore, make ready and let nothing hinder you . . . and depart from Babel, that is, Sweden, fettered body and soul by the law.[23]

The legal prohibition of conventicles and its consequences were fresh not only in the memory of fanatical Eric-Jansonists but also in the mind of a former master shoemaker from Stockholm, who wrote:

> The American does not bother about the religious beliefs of his fellow men. It is the individual's own affair to worship God according to the dictates of his conscience, without interference from prelates clothed with power to prescribe what one must believe in order to obtain salvation. Here it is only a question of being a respectable and useful member of society.[24]

[22] Steffan Steffanson to relatives and friends, October 9, 1849, in Swedish Historical Society of America, *Yearbooks,* 11:97 (St. Paul, 1926); Peter Cassel to relatives and friends, December 13, 1848, in the *Swedish-American Historical Bulletin,* 2:75 (February, 1929).
[23] Letter from Anders Jonsson, Bishop Hill, Illinois, February 9, 1847, in *Hudikswalls-Weckoblad,* July 17, 1847.
[24] Letter from Erik Hedström, Southport, Wisconsin, in *Aftonbladet,* September 20, 1843.

Another letter describes the situation in America as follows:

> It is not unusual for men of meager education to witness for the truth with much greater blessing than the most learned preacher who has no religious experience. There are no statutes contrary to the plain teaching of the Word of God which prohibit believing souls from meeting for edification in the sacred truth of our Lord Jesus Christ.[25]

The sum and substance of the religious situation in America and Sweden is graphically stated in the words of an emigrant:

> America is a great light in Christendom; there is a ceaseless striving to spread the healing salvation of the Gospel. The pastors are not lords in their profession, neither are they rich in the goods of this world. They strive to walk in the way God has commanded. They minister unceasingly to the spiritual and material welfare of men. There is as great difference between the pastors here and in Sweden as there is between night and day.[26]

One of the highly prized advantages America offered to the immigrant was the opportunity to rise from the lowest to the highest stratum of society. He found a land where the man whose hands were calloused by toil was looked upon as just as useful to society as the man in the white collar. The man who chafed under the cramped social conventions of Europe could not conceal his joy at finding a country where custom and tradition counted for little and where manual labor did not carry with it a social stigma. He had probably heard that the American people had elevated to the highest position of honor and trust such men of the people as Andrew Jackson and William Henry Harrison, but the actuality of the democracy in the "saga land" proved to be greater than the rumors that had kindled his imagination back home. And so he sat down to write about it to his countrymen, who read with astonishment that knew no bounds such statements as the following:

> The hired man, maid, and governess eat at the husbandman's table. "Yes, sir," says the master to the hand; "yes, sir," says the hand to the master. "If you please, mam," says the lady of the house to the maid; "yes, madam," replies the maid. On the street the maid is dressed exactly as the housewife. Today is Sunday, and at this very moment what do I see but a housemaid dressed in a black silk hat, green veil, green coat, and black dress, carrying a bucket of coal! This is not an unusual sight—and it is as it should be. All porters and coachmen are dressed like gentlemen. Pastor, judge, and banker carry market baskets.[27]

[25] Letter from Jon Andersson in *Norrlands-Posten,* January 12, 1852.
[26] Letter from Åke Olsson, Andover, Illinois, February 20, 1850, in *Norrlands-Posten,* June 3, 1850.
[27] Letter from New York in *Aftonbladet,* reprinted in *Barometern* (Kalmar), June 5, 1852.

And read what a boon it was to live in a land where there were no laws minutely regulating trades and occupations and binding workers to terms of service:

> This is a free country and nobody has a great deal of authority over another. There is no pride, and nobody needs to hold his hat in his hand for any one else. Servants are not bound for a fixed time. This is not Sweden, where the higher classes and employers have the law on their side so that they can treat their subordinates as though they were not human beings.[28]

The writer of this letter had probably felt the hard fist of his employer, because at that time physical chastisement was by no means unusual. If it was a great surprise to learn that a fine pedigree was not a requirement for admission to respectable society and to all classes of employment, no less sensational was the fact that the inhabitant of the western Canaan was not required to appear before an officer of the state to apply for a permit to visit another parish or to change his place of residence. In Sweden, of course, this official red tape was taken for granted, or its absence in America would not have called forth the following comment:

> I am glad that I migrated to this land of liberty, in order to spare my children the slavish drudgery that was my lot; in this country if a laborer cannot get along with his employer, he can leave his job at any time, and the latter is obliged to pay him for the time he has put in at the same wage that was agreed upon for the month or year. We are free to move at any time and to any place without a certificate from the employer or from the pastor, because neither passports nor certificates are in use here.[29]

This newly won freedom was, in some cases, too rich for Swedish blood. One of the first pastors among the immigrants was rather disturbed about the conduct of some of his countrymen:

> This political, religious, and economic freedom is novel and astonishing to the immigrant, who sees the spectacle of twenty-two millions of people ruling themselves in all orderliness. As a rule, the Swedes make use of this liberty in moderation, but a number act like calves that have been turned out to pasture. In most cases their cavorting is harmless, but sometimes they run amuck. They seem to think that a "free country" gives them license to indulge in those things that are not in harmony with respect, uprightness, reliability, and veneration for the Word of God. . . . A rather characteristic incident illustrates this. A small boy, upon being reproved by his mother for appropriating a piece of cake replied: "Why, mother, aren't we in a free country now?"[30]

[28] Letter from Åke Olsson, Andover, Illinois, February 20, 1850, in *Norrlands-Posten,* June 3, 1850.

[29] Letter from Stephan Stephanson, May 17, 1854, in the authors' possession.

[30] Letter from L. P. Esbjörn, Andover, Illinois, May 6, 1850, in *Norrlands-Posten,* June 20, 1850.

Making due allowance for the orthodox pessimism of a minister of the Gospel in every generation, historical research applied to certain Swedish settlements confirms the observations of this shepherd.

To a Swede, whose tongue was trained to flavor with cumbersome titles every sentence addressed to superiors and carefully to avoid any personal pronoun, the temptation to overwork the second person singular pronoun in America was irresistible. The Swedish passion for high-sounding names and titles gave to the humbler members of society designations that magnified by contrast the grandeur of those applied to the elect. In his own country the Swede was shaved by Barber Johansson, was driven to his office by Coachman Petersson, conversed with Building Contractor Lundström, ordered Jeweler Andersson to make a selection of rings for his wife, and *skåled* with Herr First Lieutenant Silfversparre. There were even fine gradations of "titles" for the members of the rural population. Every door to the use of *du* was closed except in the most familiar conversation. The youngest member of the so-called better classes, however, might *dua* the man of toil, upon whose head rested the snows of many long Swedish winters. Can the sons of those humble folk in America be blamed for abusing the American privilege of using *du?* What a privilege to go into a store, the owner of which might be a millionaire, and allow one's hat to rest undisturbed! How much easier it was to greet the village banker with the salutation "Hello, Pete!" than to say "Good morning, Mr. Banker Gyllensvans!" "When I meet any one on the street, be he rich or poor, pastor or official, I never tip my hat when I speak," wrote an emigrant from Skåne in 1854. "I merely say 'Good day, sir, how are you?' "[31] On the other hand, what a thrill it was for the immigrant to be addressed as "mister"—the same title that adorned the American banker and lawyer and the first title he had ever had! "Mister" was much more dignified than "Jöns," "Lars," or "Per."

The equality that the law gives is not the equality of custom. The lack of political rights is comparatively easy to remedy, but social customs are harder to deal with because they are not grounded in law. From his birth the Swede was hampered by restrictive conventions which, though not always seen by the eye, were always felt by the emotions. The walls between the classes of society and various occupations were practically insurmountable. A person could not pass from a higher social class to an inferior one, even though the latter better became his nature or economic status, because that would be an everlasting disgrace. If a *bonde* had come into financial straits, the step down to the condition of a *torpare*[32] would have wrecked his spirit. Class distinctions in America did not assert themselves in the same way; very often the foreman and laborer were neighbors, sat in the same pew, and belonged to the same lodge. One immigrant wrote of this in 1854 as follows:

> Titles and decorations are not valued and esteemed here. On the other hand, efficiency and industry are, and the American sets a higher value

---

[31] *Carlshamns Allehanda,* August 3, 1854. Anders Andersson, who for some time after his emigration corresponded with a crown official in Norrland, soon changed his style of address from *ni* to *du.* See his letters edited by Anna Söderblom, "Läsare och Amerikafarare på 1840-talet," in *Julhelg,* 80–93 (Stockholm, 1925).

[32] "Renter" suggests the meaning.

on an intelligent workingman than on all the titles, bands, and stars that fall from Stockholm during an entire year. It will not do to be haughty and idle, *for that is not the fashion in this country, for it is to use the axe, the spade, and the saw and some other things to get money and not to be a lazy body.*[33]

If the men appreciated the equality in dress and speech, the women were even more enthusiastic. In the old country married as well as unmarried women were labeled with titles of varying quality and their work was more masculine, judged by the American standard. In the "promised land" they were all classified simply as "Mrs." or "Miss," and the heavy, clumsy shoes and coarse clothing gave way to an attire more in keeping with the tastes and occupations of the "weaker sex." In Sweden the maid slept in the kitchen, shined shoes, and worked long hours; in America she had her own room, limited working hours, regular times for meals, and time to take a buggy ride with Ole Olson, who hailed from the same parish. If she had learned to speak English, she might even have a ride by the side of John Smith—and that was the height of ambition! And for all this she was paid five or six times as much as she had earned in Sweden. In letter after letter one finds expressions of astonishment and enthusiasm over this equality in conversation and dress. One writer relates that the similarity in dress between matron and maid was such that he could not distinguish between them until the latter's peasant speech betrayed her. It is easy to imagine the thorn of envy in the hearts of the women in Sweden when they learned how fortunate their American sisters were. Another letter contains the information that the duties of the maid were confined to indoor work in the country as well as in the city and that even milking was done by the men, an amusing sight to a Swede.

It is rather strange that there was not more serious complaint about the hard work that fell to the lot of the immigrants. It is true that more than one confessed that they did not know what hard work was until they came to America, but there was a certain pride in the admission. It was probably the American optimism that sustained their spirits. They saw everything in the light of a future, where their "own farm" plus a bank account was the ultimate goal. This feeling of independence and self-confidence was also heightened by the vast distances of the Middle West, its large farms, billowing prairies, and cities springing up like magic.[34] In contrast with the small-scale agriculture and the tiny hamlets of his native parish, the immigrant felt that he was a part of something great, rich, and mighty, the possibilities of which were just beginning to be exploited. Said a Swedish farmer in 1849:

> Here in Illinois is room for the entire population of Sweden. During the present winter I am certain that more grass has been burned than there is hay in the entire kingdom of Sweden. . . . The grass now is just half grown, and the fields give the appearance of an ocean, with a house here and there, separated by great distances.[35]

[33] Unsigned letter from Chicago, August 3, 1854, in *Skånska Posten,* reprinted in *Carlshamns Allenhanda,* October 4, 1854.
[34] Letter to *Götheborgs Handels-och Sjöfarts-Tidning,* April , 23, 1852.
[35] Letter of O. Bäck, Victoria, Illinois, in *Norrlands-Posten,* April 3, 1849.

The Swede who came to the Mississippi Valley found a frontier society, with many institutions in advance of those of an older society and without the multitude of officials that strutted and blustered in Sweden. In fact, as one immigrant wrote, he was hardly conscious of living under a government, and the system of taxation fooled him into thinking that there were no taxes at all. The salary of the president of the United States was a mere pittance compared with the income of the royal family—a fact not omitted in the letters.[36]

Not a few of the "America letters" go to extremes in setting forth contrasts between "poverty-ridden Sweden" and the rich and mighty republic. Here is an example:

> We hope and pray that the Lord may open the eyes of Svea's people that they might see their misery: how the poor workingman is despised and compelled to slave, while the so-called better classes fritter away their time and live in luxury, all of which comes out of the pockets of the miserable workingman. . . . We believe that all the workers had better depart and leave the lords and parasites to their fate. There is room here for all of Svea's inhabitants.[37]

Quotations from the "America letters" could be multiplied to show the reaction of the Swedish immigrants to the American environment, but a sufficient number have been presented to demonstrate that they were unusually responsive to the impressions that rushed upon them soon after they had cast their lot with their brothers and sisters from Great Britain, Ireland, Germany, Norway, and Holland. And not only that, but their letters remain to record the fact that in America they found a society that nearly approached their conception of an ideal state. This explains why students of immigration agree almost unanimously that the Swedes assimilated more rapidly and thoroughly than any other immigrant stock. After all, why should anyone be hesitant about taking out naturalization papers in the land of Canaan? Some letters written by men who had had scarcely time enough to unpack their trunks read like the Fourth of July orations:

> As a son of the great republic which extends from ocean to ocean, I will strive to honor my new fatherland. A limitless field is opened for the development of Swedish culture and activity. Destiny seems to have showered its blessings on the people of the United States beyond those of any other nation in the world.[38]

The Sweden of 1840–1860 is no more and the America of Abraham Lincoln belongs to the ages; but for hundreds of thousands of people in the land of the midnight sun America, in spite of the geographical distance, lies closer to them than the neighboring province. In some parts of Sweden the "America

---

[36] *Götheborgs Handels-och Sjöfarts-Tidning,* April 22, 23, 1852.
[37] Letter from Åke Olsson, Andover, Illinois, February 20, 1850, in *Norrlands-Posten,* June 3, 1850.
[38] Letter from C. P. Agrelius, New York, April 14, 1849, in *Östgötha Correspondenten,* July 4, 1849.

letters" from near relatives brought Chicago closer to them than Stockholm. They knew more about the doings of their relatives in Center City, Minnesota, than about Uncle John in Jönköping.

In deciphering an "America letter" the historian is prone to forget the anxious mother who for months—perhaps years—had longed for it, and the letter that never came is entirely missing from the archives and newspaper columns. But if he turns the musty pages of the Swedish-American newspapers, his eyes will fall on many advertisements similar to the following:

> Our dear son Johan Anton Petersson went to America last spring. We have not heard a line from him. If he sees this advertisement, will he please write to his people in Sweden? We implore him not to forget his aged parents and, above all, not to forget the Lord.[39]

If many letters were stained with tears in the little red cottages in Sweden, there were not a few written by trembling hands in the log cabins of Minnesota and later in the sod houses of Nebraska. And sometimes the heart was too full to allow the unsteady hand to be the only evidence of longing for parents and brothers and sisters, as the following quotation reveals: "I will not write at length this time. Nothing of importance has happened, and if you come, we can converse. God alone knows whether that day will ever dawn—my eyes are dimmed with tears as I write about it. What a happy day it would be if, contrary to all expectations, we children could see our parents."[40] Miraculous things happened in the land of Canaan; it could transform a conservative Swedish *bonde* into a "hundred per cent American" in spirit, but it could not so easily sever the ties of blood. Neither could the storm-tossed Atlantic prevent sisters, cousins, uncles, and aunts from accepting invitations embalmed in "America letters" to attend family reunions in the land of Canaan.

[39] *Chicago-Bladet,* January 13, 1885.
[40] Mary H. Stephenson to her relatives, November 3, 1867, in Swedish Historical Society of America, *Yearbooks,* 7:90 (St. Paul, 1922).

JOHN A. HAWGOOD

The Attempt to Found
a New Germany in Missouri

During the colonial era Germans settled primarily in Pennsylvania and the interior regions to the South. After the American Revolution German immigration subsided, but between 1830 and 1890 more than three million Germans came to the United States, attracted by cheap lands, low taxes, and an absence of government conscription. They settled mainly in the Middle Atlantic and midwestern states, the largest numbers in New York, Pennsylvania, Illinois, Wisconsin, and Ohio. Some ventured further west and south into Texas and Missouri, but Germans generally shunned the Old South because they opposed slavery. Many of the newcomers hoped to form enclaves where German customs and language could survive; except for a few scattered settlements their efforts failed.

The nineteenth-century German arrivals aroused the anger of puritanical Americans who resented their pleasure-loving ways and careless observance of the sabbath. In the 1850s American nativists castigated the "Godless Germans" and assaulted Rhinelanders in Cincinnati, Ohio, Covington, Kentucky, and Baltimore, Maryland. After a brawl between Germans and other Americans in Columbus, Ohio, on July 4, 1854, police, spurred on by mobs shouting epithets like "Hang the damned Hessians," arbitrarily arrested American citizens of German descent.

After two or three generations German-Americans assimilated into the mainstream of life in the United States and except for isolated groups like the Amish in Pennsylvania a distinguishable German minority no longer exists.

In the following essay John Hawgood describes the attempts of a German minority to replant the ways of old Germany in the New World in the nineteenth century.

Missouri became a state in 1821 when its population was already around 70,000, but very few German immigrants settled there until after 1824, when the writings of Gottfried Duden began to exert their influence. Even then, there is no evidence of any German having found his way to the state, or persuaded others

Reprinted from *The Tragedy of German-America* (New York: G. P. Putnam's Sons, 1940), pp. 109–36.

to do so, with the intention of founding a New Germany, until the arrival of the members of the *Giessener Gesellschaft* in 1834. Certainly Duden was innocent of any such intention, though his influence is generally claimed as having been the chief factor in attracting his fellow countrymen to Missouri during the decade following his own settlement there.

Even the Giessen emigrants did not originally intend to settle in Missouri, but decided upon that state only after having reached America. Their original plan, as expressed in the pamphlet they published in Germany before they set out, was rather vague concerning their intended location. They talked of "The foundation of a German state, which would naturally become a member of the American Union, but which would maintain a form of government that would guarantee the permanence of German civilization and the German language, and provide for a free and democratic existence," and of "a free German state, a rejuvenated Germany in North America." Their first idea appears to have been not to go to an existing state, but to a territory not yet organized.

When they landed at New Orleans their intention still seems to have been to settle in the territory of Arkansas, but at that point they changed their minds and went to St. Louis with the new object of conducting their experiment in the state of Missouri. Again Duden seems to have been the inspiration of this choice. The society knew little or nothing about Missouri apart from what they had read in Duden; it was not even understood that it was a slave state. Gustav Koerner, who made a tour of the German settlements in Missouri in the region between St. Louis and Jefferson City in 1834, and who visited Duden's own farm (Duden himself had returned to Germany a few years before) criticises Duden for having misled the *Giessener* and other immigrants. Apart from the question of slavery, he points out that by the thirties there was no good public land still left available in the Missouri river bottoms east of Boone and Howard counties, in which counties frontier conditions (for which the Germans were not suited) still obtained. The German farmer, who refused to own slaves (and Koerner declares that no German in Missouri did own any) was greatly handicapped, because slaves presented the only way out of the labour problem, and his American neighbours had no scruples about owning them. In Ohio, Indiana and Illinois, where slavery did not exist, the German was not at this disadvantage. In addition, says Koerner, the scarcity of timber west of the Mississippi river adds to the difficulty of the farmer. Missouri, he thought, was even less attractive to the immigrant wishing to follow his old-world profession than to one intending to take up farming. There were already by 1833, too many doctors in St. Louis, where over 60 administered the needs of under 10,000 inhabitants, while the German lawyer (he spoke from personal experience) had a hard time before him while mastering a new procedure and a new language. Duden, he thought, had painted the attractions of his settlement too vividly and omitted to refer to the drawbacks of life in remoter parts of Missouri. "He who leaves Europe permanently," warns Koerner (Duden had returned after only three years in America), "must bid farewell to all museums, galleries, gothic monuments, gardens and theatres, which have perhaps given him so much many-sided enjoyment, and must console himself with the thought, that he must for ever content himself, as substitutes for these, with the green of the thick forests and the flowering of the wide prairies."

The leaders of the Giessen society, Paul Follen and Friedrich Münch persisted in their intention of attempting to found a New Germany in Missouri, and both settled in Warren County, north of the Missouri river, and very near to Duden's original farm. But they did not take all the members of the society with them, for the project as a mass migration may be said to have ended when the party arrived in St. Louis. Some members stayed in the city, some settled in Illinois, and only a few followed Münch and Follen. What is more, the Giesseners who did settle in Missouri do not appear to have made any concerted attempt in their new home to set up a New Germany. The sincerity of Münch and Follen themselves is not to be doubted, and indeed, it is asserted by Koerner, who knew them both, that Münch, a true German patriot, had only been persuaded to emigrate and to desert his Fatherland by the prospect of "creating for German civilization a worthy home across the Atlantic Ocean" placed before him by Follen; but unaided by others they were helpless. Follen and Münch did little directly toward attaining their ideal after they had settled in Missouri, but their inspiration popularized the idea among others, and their indirect influence was considerable.

The failure of the Giessen society itself cannot be ascribed simply to an ignorance of conditions in America and to a consequent unwise choice of location. To begin with, the practicability of their whole grandiose scheme is very questionable, and in addition they were hardly suited to carry such a scheme out. Koerner has fruitfully contrasted the Giessen migration to Missouri with the Mormon migration to Utah. The Giesseners, he concludes, had too many outstanding personalities among them, all of whom would have ideas of their own. They lacked the singleness of purpose of a group following a religious leader, attributing to him almost divine powers and obeying him blindly. Without such a prophet and such conditions the odds were against them. It should perhaps be added that the Mormons too, failed to establish their ideal in the Middle West, and were forced to move on to an entirely unsettled and isolated region before they could do so, but there is undoubtedly a good deal in Koerner's comparison.

Neither were the Giesseners of the type that would tend to succeed as farmers. The group had been hand-picked by Follen, but he appears to have chosen them more for their uprightness, idealism and public-spirit than for their practical knowledge of farming and rural conditions. "They had wielded the pen, but had never handled the hoe, they had stood in the pulpit but never behind a plow; they had lectured from the cathedra and pleaded in court, but had never driven an ox-team. They were but little prepared for the hardships that were in store for them."

As farmers they were not particularly successful, and those trained in some profession tended soon to drift into the cities. Follen himself left his farm for journalism in St. Louis, and died in 1840. David Goebel, another member of the society who had settled near him, became geometer in the United States Land Survey Office at St. Louis, leaving his son to carry on the farm. Münch was rather more successful in his settlement, but gradually concentrated his energies upon other things—journalism, politics and the stimulation of immigration. Münch's younger brother, Georg, on the other hand, who followed him in 1837, made a great success of the culture of the vine at Augusta, Missouri.

The German settlers who had preceded the Giesseners to Missouri, and who were their neighbours, were not very suitable material for conversion to the New Germany cult. In 1824 Duden and Eversmann had settled in Mont-gomery (later Warren) County and Duden's influence had brought other im-migrants from Germany. Like the Giesseners, many of these were not very well suited to the life they had chosen. "Unfortunately the first settlers were not practical farmers, but were mostly noblemen, officers, traders and scholars." There was no organized immigration, but a group of German families was set-tled near Duden's original dwelling, and another founded the neighbouring community of Dutzow. Others settled in the Bonhomme Bottom in Franklin County, south of the river. Friedrich Münch, who with Paul Follen, settled near Marthasville, in Warren County, just north of the river, and 56 miles west of St. Louis, almost on the site of Duden's farm, recounts that "We found already living here a party of Westphalian labourers, who had made the neces-sary preparations, and a mixed aristocracy of Germany counts, barons, schol-ars, preachers, economists, officers, traders, students and others, and many more arrived during the following years." These early settlers appeared to him to be settling down on the land and accepting conditions as they found them; they had been brought there by the "Dudenic Idyll" and preferred country-life to the attractions of civilization; they had cut themselves adrift completely from Germany and from Europe and "Niemals ihren Blick rückwärs richteten." As the years passed Münch too seems to have fallen under the same spell as his neighbours and to have quietly abandoned his earlier ideals, and he states that certainly by 1848 he and his fellow immigrants were firmly wedded to America. In that year, he says, "We almost repented of having given up our Fatherland as hopeless, and would willingly have thrown ourselves into the struggles there, but already we and our families had taken deep root in the life of the new world."

Münch did not entirely abandon his Germanism, but he shifted his ground from the idea of a New Germany to the more modest aim of giving a German flavour to American life and of building up the influence of the German pop-ulation in American affairs. He himself gives most of the credit to Duden, say-ing, "In the course of many editions and reprints Duden's works were spread far and wide, and to his influence is mainly to be ascribed the fact that after 1830 thousands of our countrymen settled in Ohio, Missouri, Illinois, Indiana, Wisconsin, Iowa and elsewhere, and thus laid the foundations of the German-ism (*Deutschtum*) which since then has become so strong and so influential," but others credit Münch himself with a very considerable influence upon Ger-man immigration. "F. Münch," it is stated, "wrote several books on Missouri, setting forth its resources, and which (*sic*) were largely distributed all over Germany. . . . His writings brought thousands of immigrants across the sea and to Missouri."

The extent of his influence is difficult to assess (there is rather less evi-dence for it than for earlier writers such as Duden and Sealsfield) but perhaps these efforts on the part of Friedrich Münch may be regarded as a form of sublimation of the idea of founding a New Germany in America which had animated his own emigration. Certainly, though what came to pass was very different from what had been set out as their ideal by the Giesseners, and though no "New Germany" in Follen's sense of the word can ever be said to have come into anything more than a most transitory existence, Münch seems to have persuaded himself in his later years that the Germans in America had actually created what could be recognised, in this sublimated sense, as a New Germany. Writing in 1870, he is of the opinion that "The once faint hope of the first German pioneers who settled in the western prairies and forest lands, of seeing the creation here of a 'New Germany,' is being fulfilled more quickly and more completely as time goes on."

In the settlements of the Giesseners themselves and in those of the Germans who were directly inspired by their example to settle near them in Missouri, there was little then and there is even less now to support this opinion, but one attempt to found a New Germany in Missouri a few years after the Giesseners arrived there, an attempt which without doubt was indirectly inspired by them and received inspiration from their ideas, did attain some measure of success, though on a far smaller scale and in a rather different way from that planned by its originators and patrons. This was the settlement planted by the Philadelphia German Settlement Society at Hermann, in Gasconade County, on the southern banks of the Missouri river and a few miles to the west of the settlements of Duden, Follen and Münch on the opposite bank.

The influence of the Giessener society, which had originated in Germany, upon this Philadelphia society originating in America three years later was undoubtedly considerable, but the latter started with the advantage of understanding American conditions better, and of being better able to explore the ground in advance. J. G. Wesselhöft, owner and publisher of a German newspaper in Philadelphia, the *Alte und Neue Welt,* was prominent in the founding of the society, and his paper became as it were its official organ. Herein can be followed not only the ideas of the members of the society, some of which have been already quoted, concerning the nature of the projected new Germany, but also the careful investigations of possible locations for the experiment. The first proposal (in June 1836) was Texas, but Texas had only just won her independence from Mexico and was rejected as politically too unsettled. As a preliminary to more ambitious schemes it was then suggested that a "Deutschheim" should be established in Western Pennsylvania, not only as a separate settlement but also as a centre for promoting German cultural interests, by setting up schools, libraries, and societies among the "Pennsylvania Dutch" who were rapidly becoming, if they had not already become, completely American. No definite decision concerning the larger scheme was reached in 1836, except that the idea of asking for a direct grant of land from Congress at Washington was abandoned. The province of Tamulipas in Mexico was then proposed, but the society decided to confine its experiment to the territories of the United States. After the choice had been cut down to Pennsylvania, Ohio, Arkansas, Missouri, Illinois, Wisconsin, Indiana, Eastern Michigan and Western New York, representatives were sent to explore likely places and to choose a state and location for the main settlement. They reported in July 1837 in favour of Missouri.

It cannot be said of the Philadelphia Society that it did not make this choice with its eyes open, and it is hardly credible that some of the "disadvantages" of Missouri listed by Koerner would all have escaped the notice of the society. Therefore it must be concluded that these did not weigh heavily or were outweighed by what were considered to be much greater advantages. At that time the state of Missouri was very much in the public eye, owing to the recent "Missouri Compromise," the entry of the territory into the Union as a fully-fledged state, the Mormon troubles within its boundaries, the other things. To Germans the writings of Duden and the arrival of the Giessen *Gesellschaft* added to the interest of Missouri, while in 1835, a book by a German named Bromme had been published in Baltimore, describing Missouri and providing an immigrant guide to the state. Bromme had particularly praised Montgomery County as a place for German settlement, pointing out that Duden had lived there, that the remnants of the Giessen Society were located there and that other German groups, such as the "Berliner Gesellschaft" were not far away.

Though counting Missouri's advantages as greater than its disadvantages, and regarding the presence of a large navigable river as more than counterbalancing the fact that Missouri was a slave state, the delegates of the Philadelphia society chose land south and not north of the river (where most of the German immigrants had hitherto settled) and having bought between eleven and twelve thousand acres of land in Gasconade County, selected a town-site to serve as centre of the settlement, on the south bank of the Missouri river about seven miles east of its confluence with the Gasconade river.

The delegates were both thorough and ambitious, for in anticipation of the future development and needs of this New Germany they planned a large city on the selected site, and streets were laid out on paper and named on a grand scale. The society then proceeded to offer its land to German settlers at a very cheap rate, and advertised the project extensively among the Germans in the eastern states and in Europe. Branches of the society had been established in Albany, Baltimore, Pittsburgh, and agencies were also active in New Orleans, Montreal, Cleveland and Cincinnati, while propaganda leaflets were issued for enclosure with private letters to relatives and friends in Germany. A very large response to this widespread appeal was undoubtedly expected.

An advance party of seventeen spent a precarious winter of 1837-1838 on the chosen land, and were joined from the spring of 1838 onward by a steadily growing stream of German settlers. During 1838 two hundred and thirty arrived, and in May 1839 the *Alte und Neue Welt* reports 450 inhabitants, 90 houses, 5 stores, 2 inns and a post-office. A school was being built and both Catholic and Lutheran churches were projected. A musical society had already come into existence. The future was bright.

Further to encourage the settlement of Germans on its land the Philadelphia society next established bureaux of information concerning the project in St. Louis, Pittsburgh, Cincinnati and Louisville, for the benefit of immigrants already on their way to settle in the Middle West, and of Germans settled in or near these cities who might be attracted to move once more. Propaganda in the eastern states and in Germany was continued at full strength, but the society rather sharply refused to co-operate with a *Neue deutsche Ansiedlungsgesellschaft* founded in May 1839 in Lauenburg, Germany, by a lawyer named Sprewitz. A certain exclusiveness in the management, at least, of the project was shown by the founder members of the Philadelphia Society from the first, and this is a sign of the increasing arrogance that in time created an open breach between the parent organization and the actual settlers on the society's land in Missouri. The society seems not only to have patronised the settlers unduly, but to have attempted a system of remote control that proved to be very irksome.

Very early in the history of the settlement a local board of management had replaced the society's agent residing at Hermann (as the town that had been laid out was called, an interesting manifestation of the *urgermanische* cult brought into being by the historical school, and later to be popularised even more by the nordic hero-worshippers of the later nineteenth and twentieth centuries) and the agent had been recalled in October 1838. Further friction between the colonists and the society resulted in a complete severance of relations and finally the Philadelphia Society was dissolved in January 1840. But it had not lived in vain. Though the settlement planted by it had attracted many fewer Germans than had been expected, and though many of the settlers showed little or no interest in the idea of founding a New Germany, the community was firmly planted before the Society ceased to exist. Though it did not make a "New Germany" of the state of Missouri or even of a group of counties or a single county, the town of Hermann and the countryside around it became popularly known as "Little Germany," and were still known by that name up to 1914 at least. Perhaps the difference between "New Germany" and "Little Germany" sums up best the discrepancy between what was projected and what was achieved by the Philadelphia Society and the colony that it planted.

Many reasons have been advanced to explain the comparative failure of the attempt. The arrogance of the parent society and the attempt at remote control have already been mentioned. Indeed, so exclusive and dictatorial was the policy at Philadelphia that one sometimes suspects the purely philanthropic and patriotic Germanism of some of the founders. The treatment of Dr. Sprewitz and his Lauenburg project points to a possible explanation of the society's attitude. One might surmise that some members of the society were making a good thing out of their land sales and did not wish for any more partnership in their management of the colony. Otherwise the rejection of such potentially valuable co-operation seems inexplicable.

The panic of 1837 undoubtedly played its part in checking the development of the settlement. Not only was the total German emigration to the United States in 1838 less than half that for 1837 (particularly unfortunate for the society, because the settlement was not ready for immigrants until the spring of 1838) but the general effects of the depression, lack of credit, lack of confidence and economic stagnation, all bore down heavily upon the struggling colony. Then the General Agent chosen by the society appeared to be an unfortunate choice, and the location selected for the purchase of land and for the laying out of the town of Hermann, though having many advantages, possessed possibilities for development only along rural and small town lines. Hermann could not become a large city because its growth was inevitably circumscribed by the limited hinterland dependent upon it, nor did it occupy any special position at the crossing place of trade routes or at a point of break of bulk to give it a more than local importance. The Missouri river at Hermann, though providing an excellent means of communication with St. Louis and the

East and South, was a barrier between the settlement and the other German communities to the north of the river. Both wide and swift, it was not bridged at that point until over ninety years after Hermann was founded, and then only with great difficulty. Meanwhile Hermann had become side-tracked by direct lines of communication between St. Louis and Kansas City set further back from the river, and north-south routes developed at more easily bridgeable places on the river.

Though the district was able to develop a prosperous fruit growing and wine producing industry, there was no scope for the growth of any manufacturing activities. Population therefore remained small. By 1860 Hermann had a population of a little over 1500 (a gain of well under a hundred a year since its foundation) and then for forty years its population remained stationary. In 1900 the whole of Gasconade County had only 1453 German-born inhabitants, which shows that Germans had not continued to reach the region in any numbers during the latter part of the nineteenth century. In 1930 Hermann had only just topped the 2000 mark and it is improbable that by its centenary in 1937 it had grown more than very slightly larger.

Nevertheless, Hermann and the eleven thousand acres bought by the society have in their modest way pursued a prosperous existence. Already within a year of the foundation of the colony settlers who were not sent by the society had arrived, and these undoubtedly helped to stir up the feeling of resentment at the continued "colonial" attitude at Philadelphia. The settlement forged ahead more quickly when the tie with the parent society had been severed, and in 1844 the selling of the common and reserved land of the colony to individual settlers made possible the beginning on the hills surrounding Hermann (which had been included in this land) of the culture of the vine, the most characteristic feature of the area between that year and 1920, and possibly destined to be in full swing again by centenary year.

Hermann soon became the recognised centre of life in Gasconade County. It was incorporated in 1839, was made the county seat in 1842 and received a special new charter in 1845. Its first newspaper, the *Lichtfreunde,* was founded by the free-thinking Mühle, who had come from Cincinnati, in 1843. As a counterblast a Lutheran church was built in 1844 and a Roman Catholic church soon after. A second newspaper appeared in 1845; in 1847 the *erste Weinprobe* was made and in 1848 a *Weinfest.* With this and the obtaining of its charter by the bilingual school in 1849 (a schoolhouse had been erected ten years before) the town and community of Hermann may be said to have been more or less firmly planted on its feet. The school charter was perhaps the greatest outward triumph of "Deutschtum" in the whole of Hermann's history, for section fourteen of this charter, duly approved by the legislature of the state of Missouri, stated, "This school shall be and forever remain a German school, in which all branches of science and education shall be taught in the German language." For more than seventy-five years this provision remained unassailed.

For more than seventy-five years too the settlement remained essentially German in appearance, language and culture, though early in the twentieth century some signs of Americanization appeared to disturb the scene, and the events of the World War served to hasten the process of disintegration, though not to complete it by any means.

In 1858 Friedrich Münch paid a visit to Hermann from his own home some miles further down and across the Missouri river and found it with 1400 inhabitants, a main station of the Pacific Railroad, its two churches, its German society, its German newspapers and its wine production, in surroundings very similar to parts of the Rhine and Mosel valleys. He was particularly interested in its two schools "of which one must ever remain German" and concludes his impression with the words: "In Hermann one forgets that one is not actually in Germany itself." In 1878 Gert Goebel, son of one of Münch's fellow Giesseners who had also settled in Missouri, records a very similar impression.

In 1855, Franz Löher, a strong advocate of the idea of a New Germany in America, waxed enthusiastic about Hermann. "One of the most delightful journeys that I ever made in my life was this from St. Louis to the little German town of Hermann," he claims, and his description of Hermann is correspondingly ecstatic. "Joyfully we greeted the German vineyards" on approaching the town, which "Not yet twenty years old . . . is neither a great commercial nor a great trading centre, but a collection of lovely little houses and gardens, of vine-clad hills and neat farms. The surrounding country contains a number of farms, which like the town are almost exclusively inhabited by Germans." "Here," he continues "is to be found a most inviting countryside, in which exists more German sociability than perhaps in anywhere else in America." "Jene grünen Hermanner Hügel geben mit der freundlichen Stadt dazwischen ein liebliches Gesammtbild" is typical of the lyric style of Löher's eclogue.

In addition to admiring the surroundings so effusively Löher notes with interest the disappearance of the earlier American settlers, with their slaves, from the district. "Their Anglo-American neighbours are being bought out, thanks to the Germans, who give them dollars for their improved land, and they then proceed deeper into the backwoods to clear new ground." He comments rather bitterly that "If the Germans were partial to this tree-felling occupation of the American backwoodsman, their detractors would undoubtedly treat it as a taste for prosaic labour and menial tasks, though in the native-born Americans they choose to regard it the sign of a romantic temperament." Löher, it must be remembered was writing after the era of embitterment had commenced. Duden, thirty years earlier, would have been incapable of acidulating his narrative in this way. The preoccupation of Löher with slavery in Missouri is another sign of the times. Duden had conveniently omitted to refer to the complications that might be presented to the German settler, fleeing to the land of freedom, by the existence of this peculiar institution all around him, but Löher notes with satisfaction not only (as had Koerner in 1834) that the Germans in Missouri did not themselves own slaves, but also that wherever Germans settled slavery tended to disappear. "In the neighbourhood of Hermann too" he adds "the land of the slave-owners is being gradually bought up." He does not openly claim this as a calculated policy on the part of the Germans to combat slavery, but he seems to think, or at least to hope that it is.

In the year 1907 W. G. Bek found Hermann very little altered since the time of the visits of Löher and Münch a half a century before. Even its population was about the same. It still had its two schools (the one of them giving all instruction in German) and its two churches, its vineyards and its musical society. The production of beer and spirits had been added to that of wine, and there was also (the connection is obscure and arouses interesting conjectures) a shoe factory. The neighborhood was still known throughout the state as "Little Germany" and "on the streets and in business houses German is still generally spoken."

By 1919 the occasion of the seventy-fifth jubilee of the local Evangelical Union (which had built its first church in 1844, and a larger one on its site in 1907) a retrospective stock-taking of itself revealed Hermann as very considerably changed, though not appreciably larger as compared with twenty years before. The crisis of the war years had greatly hastened matters, but the charmed circle of Hermann's *Deutschtum* had already been broken before Sarajevo. On the occasion of the laying of the foundation stone of the new Lutheran church in 1907 the incumbent pastor had delivered an address in English. When the church was dedicated one of the four visiting ministers invited to participate also used the English tongue, while in 1910, up to which date all services had been held in German, it was decided that one English service per month should be regularly held. It was recognized that the membership of the younger members of the church would not be retained if an exclusive use of the German tongue was still insisted upon.

By 1929 more changes had taken place and Americanization had proceeded much further, but still the older inhabitants of the town naturally spoke German together, and the writer spent a whole day visiting with the local Lutheran pastor without hearing English spoken. The vineyards had disappeared, though their site was still kept clear for "better days." The local distillery had developed in its cellars a mushroom-forcing industry of impressive dimensions, the *Hermanner Pilz* being in great demand and being equivocally said to possess a flavour "all its own." True to their traditions, the stalwart Germans of Hermann continued to show their opinion of Prohibition by leading the visitor to the toolshed or the cellar directly introductions had been made, for a strictly private and illegal *Wein-, Schnapps-* or *Bierprobe,* in some cases all three! Rarely does the sociological investigator have the opportunity of making a "Case-Study" of this nature.

Those members of the Giessen Society who did not accompany Münch and Follen and settle in Missouri, either remained in the city of St. Louis or crossed the Mississippi river to the adjacent counties of Illinois, which had been admitted to the Union in 1816 and which was not a slave state. As in Missouri the Giesseners who settled in Illinois chose a region which had already been favoured by German immigrants and located themselves in St. Clair County, in or near the community of Belleville, some fifteen miles south-east of St. Louis.

There had been early German settlers in Madison County (in Edwardsville) and in Bond County (where a German named Ernst had, with a small group of Hanoverians, laid out the settlement of Vandalia, which for a time was the state capital, in 1819) but St. Clair County (the oldest in the state, first settled in 1789) had always attracted them in greater numbers, being directly across the river from St. Louis. Belleville became the county seat in 1813 and before 1820 possessed two German families, the Maurers and the Bornmanns or Bornemanns. The latter were of Pennsylvania Dutch stock and when they moved to Illinois had already anglicised their name to Borman. Both heads of these families, Conrad Bornmann and Jacob Maurer were still living in 1874 and a son of the former died only in April 1929, aged ninety.

A few other Germans found their way into the county during the twenties, but only in and after 1829 did they start arriving in considerable numbers, attracted it is said by the superiority of the land (a mixture of woodland and prairie), the low price asked for it and the proximity of a large and growing market in nearby St. Louis. These Germans came as individuals and in small groups, but from about 1832 onward they tended to congregate together in a settlement occupying the area of one township (thirty six square miles) situated between five and ten miles east of Belleville. This German settlement has been called one of the most noteworthy and successful in the United States, and though there was no such deliberate planning of a New Germany in this instance as at Hermann, it too became in time and remained for a long period a "Little Germany" and spread its Germanising influence very decisively over the neighbouring town of Belleville, which was all the time increasing its own German population as well.

The earliest settlements in the township had been on the sections of rising ground to the south between 1810 and 1812. The Germans arriving from 1830 onward bought up the farms of the earlier native born settlers, and the brothers Hilgard, arriving in 1832 established at Turkey Hill the nucleus of the famous "Latin Farmer" colony of educated immigrants from Germany. They had themselves been preceded by a few other educated Germans and German-Swiss, and in 1833 a good many more arrived from St. Louis, most of them originating from the Rhenish Palatinate, in groups, in families and as individuals. A Rhenish Bavarian group under Dr. Geiger came at the same time as part of a group from Rhenish Hessen under Sandherr and Wilhelm, while also from Rhenish Bavaria came the Engelmann family and others. It is to Dr. Georg Engelmann that we owe the fullest account of the early days of the township as a place of Germanic concentration, while Gustav Koerner, who himself arrived there the following year has supplemented this account by his own impressions.

Thus, the Giesseners who elected to settle in Illinois, and who reached the township in 1834 under the leadership of Georg Bunsen, found a flourishing German community already in existence and may have thought that here might be developed the New Germany of which they had dreamed. Many of the settlers had been members of the *Burschenschaften* in Germany, some of them (such as Koerner) were political exiles, and the necessary patriotism and loftiness of purpose would have seemed to be present. But the New Germany idea does not seem to have made much headway. Neither Engelmann nor Koerner approved of the Germans forming settlement societies and attempting to preserve their settlements as islands of German culture and interests in America. Koerner advocated emigration by individuals and families, and himself set an example in rapid Americanization, while Engelmann protested against the isolation of the Germans in the settlement, and deplored their clannishness. He pinned his hope on the future, saying, "To the coming generation, which will be at home in both languages, which will be brought up in the ways of its parents, yet will not be unfamiliar too with the predominating English ones, will it first be possible to appear and to behave entirely as natives. Until then the immigrants will live almost entirely for themselves and for each other."

Concentrated as they were, the Germans were not able to keep the township to themselves. Some of the original settlers had remained and other native

Americans had arrived, so that in 1837 of a total population of between four and five hundred, living on between seventy and eighty farms, only 160 people and 30 farms were German.

In 1836 the nearby community of Mechanicsburg was settled by Germans, also from the Rhenish Palatinate for the most part. In 1839 the name was changed to Mascoutah, and by 1874 the town of Mascoutah had a population of over three thousand, most of whom are said to have been Germans. Belleville already had a considerable non-German population before the Germans began to arrive in large numbers in the thirties, but here very soon, with Turkey Hill and Mascoutah nearby, the predominating element was also German. Belleville was incorporated as a city in 1850 and its first mayor, Theodor J. Krafft, was a German. By 1874 it had 12000 inhabitants (with 3000 more in West Belleville), five newspapers, of which three were published in German, fifty miles of macadamised roads, a horse-tramway and considerable industrial importance. St. Clair County had been discovered to contain coal resources, and this coupled with proximity to St. Louis and its location on the direct route between St. Louis and Louisville, Kentucky, had allowed Belleville to flourish and expand in a way quite beyond the reach of a community like Hermann. These factors, tending to attract more settlers and to create a more mixed population, also tended to destroy the German character of the area, but so large and influential had been the German influx of the thirties, and it had subsequently been added to, that right up to the beginning of the twentieth century Belleville is declared to have retained much of its Germanism. A German school and several German churches still adhered to the German language, while even some of the Americans of native stock and the negroes in the district spoke German (as had been the case with the Irish families located in German communities in Wisconsin). This was the situation round 1904 or 1905. Twenty five years later nearly all relics of Germanism had disappeared. No German was spoken in the homes of the descendants of German immigrants any longer, nor was the growing generation even learning German. Not since 1910 (a date which coincides with the beginnings of anglicisation in Hermann religious circles) had German been used in the Sunday school of the leading Lutheran church, while in the church itself only one service in German each month was given in 1929. The German stock of Belleville was said to have no further connections with German culture, and immigrants from Germany arriving in recent years had little or nothing in common with them and did not appear to fit into the community. Americanization, by contrast with Hermann, was all but complete.

As Koerner (who spent only one year on the Engelmann farm near Turkey Hill in 1833 to 1834) and Georg Engelmann had desired, the special German township too, gradually ceased its resistance to assimilation, and followed Belleville's route toward Americanization, descendants of the Giesseners who settled there not apparently putting up any greater resistance than anyone else. Thus the absence of a conscious foundation as a German colony does seem to have left the *Deutschtum* of this area with something lacking as compared with that of the venture of the Philadelphia Society in Missouri. The heading to this chapter makes no mention of the state of Illinois precisely because of this difference, but as some of the Giesseners did go to St. Clair County, and as the concentration of Germans there, numerically considered, was even greater in a comparable period than in Warren and Gasconade counties in Missouri, an extremely interesting and fruitful contrast and comparison is provided by a consideration of both.

The behaviour and development of the German immigrants settled in these Missouri and Illinois communities corresponds very closely to the general characteristics of the German settler in America that were summed up in an earlier chapter.* They were not in the strictest sense pioneers, tending to arrive only after a district had been partially opened up and often buying improved land and existing farms from the Americans in possession. They preferred forest to prairie land, though they often located in the thirties at points where prairie land and forest met, or in the wooded areas beside the rivers in areas that were otherwise prairie. A good proportion of the settlers were skilled farmers and quite a few were highly educated and trained in various professions. They opposed the temperance and prohibition laws as well as the sabbatarian movement, and they founded German schools and churches, attempting in the early days at least to foster and preserve the use of the German language in every possible way. Not only in the New Germanies deliberately founded in Missouri but in the more haphazardly formed areas of German concentration in south-western Illinois, assimilation and Americanization were resisted for many decades, and the German settlers succeeded in creating in their communities a German atmosphere, that outsiders, whether German or American, immediately noticed and usually commented upon. They joined or supported the Democratic party from the first and maintained their allegiance until the middle fifties, many of them later. They disapproved of Slavery, refused to keep slaves and strongly opposed the extension of the institution, but they did not shun states where slavery existed, nor did more than a very small number of them become active abolitionists. In Missouri and south-western Illinois, as elsewhere, they were roused to greater political activity by the Nativist movement, and around the middle fifties their attitude toward America and their position as Germans in it underwent a subtle change.

The effect of the idea of and movement for a New Germany undoubtedly made the German settlements in the Middle-West, founded or developed either directly or indirectly under their influence, rather different from earlier German settlements further East. Oscar Falk, describing in 1855 a typical German settlement in "North-western Missouri," says "The German settlements in the West are remarkable for their completely German appearance and their purely German atmosphere. While the German farmer in Pennsylvania is more accustomed to Anglo-American ways, and has even sacrificed his native language, or half of it at least, on the altar of his new Fatherland, the German settlements in the West have preserved their native colouring pure and unmixed. You think that you are in a village in Germany when you set foot in one of these settlements. The architecture of the houses, owing of course to differences in climate is a little different, but the household furnishings, the family customs, the style and method of plowing, sowing and harvesting all remind one of Germany."

Dr. Engelmann in criticising the deliberate isolation policy of the Germans in his part of Illinois, contrasted as settlers them with their neighbours. He

* Of Hawgood's book.

pointed out that the Americans living in St. Clair County in 1837 (the year in which he wrote) were mostly not recent immigrants, but settlers of the third or fourth American generation; they had come mostly into Illinois from Virginia, Kentucky and Georgia and many were families of standing in the East before they moved Westward. He thought that they did not prosper so well as the German immigrants who came to the same region, because they were not so hard-working, but he advances no explanation of their shiftlessness. More recently it has been suggested that the malarial river bottoms and the ague-provoking swamps and undrained prairies of this part of Illinois had enervated the hardy Southern uplanders who had settled there, reducing their efficiency as settlers. When the Germans arrived, the river-bottom land had nearly all been taken up, or abandoned and given a bad reputation which caused them to avoid it, while their preference for hilly and wooded land perhaps preserved them to some extent from the curse of the ague which had tended to blight and delay the opening-up of the state of Illinois. Though the early German settlers are recorded to have suffered considerably from the cold and the damp in many places Koerner tells how, during the first winter on the Engelmann farm at Turkey Hill, they pulled up part of the wooden fencing of the holding, which had been laboriously put up before winter set in, in order to keep their fires alight so that it would be warm enough to read and—in his case—to study law books. (A pertinent commentary both upon the attitude of these amateur "Latin" farmers toward the land, as well as upon the shortage of wood in the district.) But the Germans do not seem to have been affected by the ills and the physical and mental debility which had attacked some of the American pioneers in southern Illinois. The New Englanders and New Yorkers, who arrived after the southerners, but rather before the Germans, also managed to preserve their health and energies in the new environment, though all complained of its effects.

Engelmann placed the professional and educated German at the bottom of the list as an efficient farmer, rating the German who had been an expert farmer before he emigrated first, and placing the American settler between the two, but he claimed that in time the "Latin Farmer," if he did not give up altogether, became as successful as the American, mainly by perseverence and willingness to learn. His own family is an example. Koerner, on the other hand, deserted the life of a farmer for his original profession of the law after only a few months.

These German settlers of the thirties in both Missouri and Illinois, were joined a decade later by many of the "Forty-Eighters," and here as elsewhere the "Grays" and the "Greens" did not always get along very well together. Between the upper grindstone of the one and the nether grindstone of the other the idea of a New Germany tended to be crushed out of whatever existence it had continued to possess.

The Forty-Eighters were more numerous and consequently more mixed than the earlier arrivals. Somewhat unfairly a Missouri German had stated that "The first period brought us exclusively men of learning and standing, which cannot be said with reference to all the later comers." This is of course doubly incorrect, because not only were a good many peasants and labourers mixed with the "Latin Farmers," but many of the Forty-Eighters were renowned for their culture and learning. In fact the high educational standards and ideals of the Forty-Eighters are today looked back upon with regret by some inhabitants of German communities, who declare that there has been considerable retrogression since the time when the settlers themselves had been trained in German universities and sent their sons to Harvard and Yale.

The Forty-Eighters did undoubtedly take to the cities more readily than to the countryside. In a few cases, such as that of Friedrich Hecker, they bought farms (his was near Belleville) but in most instances they took to journalism or kindred occupations, or continued their old-world professions in the cities. It must be remembered that town and city life was much more developed in the United States by 1850 than it had been in 1830, and also that the era of settlement societies, who bought up land in rural areas, was over. The Forty-Eighters came almost entirely as families, individuals and small informal groups, nor were any of these groups actuated by the idea of forming a New Germany in America. They were, they thought, temporarily flying into exile to escape oppression and adverse conditions in Germany, but many of them hoped soon to return. They were often far too disillusioned by the events of 1848 to 1850 to want to think of a New Germany, though, as will later be seen, they were active in trying to make their fellow Germans who had been settled longer in the United States and who were, in Münch's words "wedded to the New World," more conscious of Germany's plight and of the ability of Germans in America to help the German liberal and national struggle by means of financial encouragement and political agitation. When the possibility of returning to Germany or of liberalising institutions there at last faded for the Forty-Eighters, the more active of them turned to a direct participation in the American politics of the day—the foundation of the Republican party, Abolitionism, participation in the Civil War and in Reconstruction—rather than to a revival of any of the ideals of a New Germany in America which had flourished during the decade before their arrival and still continued to exist during their first few years in the United States. Because of their prominence in journalism the Forty-Eighters tended, from the first, to steal the limelight from the earlier "Grays" and their activity in American politics (in marked contrast to all but a few of the "Grays") kept them there, much to the resentment of those who had preceded them.

In addition, many of the Forty-Eighters were free-thinkers, and came to the aid of such men as editor Mühle in Hermann, and free-thinkers had formed only very small minorities in the God-fearing German settlements of the thirties. It will be seen that the fight against the churches, particularly the Catholic church, in Wisconsin, was particularly bitter after 1848, and in Hermann, Mühle found support among the Forty-Eighters who arrived there for his idea of making the town a free-thinking community, whereas his battle up to then had been almost a lone one. Their anti-religious bias was one of the things that made them less resistant to Americanising influences and less favorable to the idea of a new Germany than were the earlier German settlers, for the churches in their own interests were perhaps the strongest centres of Germanism, and the church schools were the strongest fighters for the retention of the German language in education and in the home. This alienated the free-thinking Forty-Eighters from the type of *Deutschtum* that had flourished up to their time and been championed by the various religious communities. It has yet to be seen how later they were to develop a different type of *Deutschtum* of their own.

Apart from the Forty-Eighters, perhaps the greatest solvent of the remnants of the idea of a New Germany that survived into the fifties in Missouri and south-western Illinois, was the development in the United States, to an acute degree, of a greater sectionalism than the Germans' own. The rivalry of the North and the South, a rivalry which involved above all the future political allegiance and social complexion of the West, tended to cut across other struggles and to side-track them as the fifties progressed. Missouri was in a most delicate position, for by the Compromise of 1820 she had entered the Union as a slave state, but since that date she had received as settlers many thousands of northerners and European immigrants who disapproved of slavery and refused to keep slaves, even though they did not actively oppose the institution as established in Missouri. Between 1820 and 1860 Missouri tended to become in spirit rather less than more of a slave state, and the German settlers in the state undoubtedly played their part in this process. It would be an exaggeration to agree entirely with the claim "That Missouri, a slave and a border state, did remain in the Union instead of joining the Confederacy, was in a great measure due to the firm stand which its German population took at the outbreak of the Civil War," but the fact that slave-holding receded before the advance of the German settler in Missouri from 1830 onward must undoubtedly be reckoned as one of the many factors in the state's adherence to the Union in 1861. Southerners in Illinois also had owned slaves until the constitution of the state forbade it, and the Northern, Irish and German influx into that state undoubtedly influenced its destiny in this respect.

The planting of a new Germany in a border state such as Missouri was in itself an unconscious blow to the institution of slavery in the state and to the balance of power that had existed in favour of the slave-states in the Union, but it was a relatively small force that alone could have had little decisive influence upon the destinies of America. One of the most carefully cherished myths of German America is the belief that the Germans, particularly in the border states, turned the balance of opinion against the South, and this is strengthened by the supposition that a majority of the Germans were abolitionists, which they most emphatically were not. A great fire has been discerned in a very little smoke, but the smoke undoubtedly did exist. The Germans played their part, but it alone was not and could not be decisive.

The idea of a New Germany can hardly be said to have continued to exist in its original form in Missouri after 1848, owing to the complete or comparative failure of the several attempts to found New Germanies in the State in the thirties, and owing to the difference in outlook between the immigrants who arrived from Germany after and those who had arrived before that date, but even if this had not been the case, it is difficult to see how the idea could have continued to progress or even to flourish in the heat of the growing sectional conflict of the fifties and the final conflagration of the Civil War.

Failing in this part of the United States on the grand scale in which it had been planned, the idea nevertheless did succeed to a certain extent in a minor key. The Giesseners were scattered, but their ideas affected others. Hermann is the most tangible result of a partially successful application of the idea. In the region of Illinois nearest to the Missouri experiments, a German concentration, though it was not another attempted New Germany, became much greater than it would otherwise have been by the fact that this idea was in the air. Both in Missouri and in Illinois, districts may therefore be said to have become Germanised either as a direct or as an indirect consequence of the advocacy by the Giesseners and others of the idea of a New Germany being set up on American soil, and to have preserved their essentially German character much longer, with many effects upon the development of the regions concerned, than would have been the case if such an influence had not existed. These New Germanies and their offshoots never acquired a national or even a statewide significance, but their local importance was and has remained considerable.

Irish

OSCAR HANDLIN
The Development of Group Consciousness

The Irish have been the most long-suffering of the European immigrant groups in the United States. The bulk of them arrived in America between 1835 and 1865 too poor to travel inland so they remained in the port cities of Boston and New York. Peasants and ill-educated, they were forced to accept low-paying, unskilled jobs with no prospects for advancement. In Boston Irishmen frequently labored fifteen hours a day, seven days a week. Servant girls rose at 5 A.M. and faced a workday of sixteen to eighteen hours in order to earn $1.50 a week. Massachusetts natives looked down upon the Irish. As Marcus L. Hansen, the late dean of American immmigration historians, wrote about these New England newcomers:

> *Tradition has little that is pleasant to say regarding these Irish immigrants. They were stupid and dirty, superstitious and untrustworthy, diseased and in despair. They were beggars and thieves, the overflow of Irish poorhouses and outcasts from overpopulated estates.*

The condition of their entry, their reception in the new land, and the fears and customs which the Irish brought over with them made it hard to adapt to American society and to form a community. Oscar Handlin's Boston's Immigrants, A Study in Acculturation, 1790–1860 *analyzes the struggles of the Boston Irish to establish themselves in their new surroundings. His study has become the model for all subsequent works on foreign-born groups. Before* Boston's Immigrants *appeared in 1941, with the exception of Marcus Hansen in* The Atlantic Migration *and* The Immigrant in American History, *historians had confined themselves chiefly to detailed descriptions of various phases of immigrant life. Handlin departed from convention by examining the development of Irish communities in Boston. Inevitably this type of investigation involved the merging of historical method with sociological and psychological techniques and concepts. By focusing on cultural adjustment and conflict, impulses toward assimilation or aloofness, and interaction between the Irish subculture and the larger Boston community,* Boston's Immigrants *broke radically with the traditional recounting of facts and anecdotes about movement and settlement. Handlin analyzed social change and the development and modification of institutions and attitudes over seventy years of group organization and interaction. "The Development of Group Consciousness," which is reproduced below, exemplifies the process by which group identity was reformed and reinforced in the New World.*

> Thinking to live by some derivative old country mode in this primitive new country,—to catch perch with shiners. . . . with his horizon all his own, yet he a poor man, born to be poor, with his inherited Irish poverty or poor life . . . not to rise in this world, he nor his posterity, till their wading webbed bogtrotting feet get *talaria* to their heels.[1]

All immigrants to Boston brought with them an awareness of group identity already sharpened by cultural contact with other peoples. Years of conflict with the English had strengthened this feeling among the Irish. The Germans emigrated during a turbulent period of patriotic awakening; and the English, French, and Italians had felt impassioned currents stirred up by the Napoleonic disorganization of Europe. Nationalists to begin with, all retained their ties with the homeland.

As long as it derived from sources external to Boston society, awareness of nationality expressed merely a sentimental attachment. Thus, Englishmen observed the birthdays of the royal family; the Swiss collected funds for the village of Travers, destroyed by fire in 1865; the French celebrated mass at the Cathedral upon the death of Princess Adelaide; while Germans, Polish, and Hungarian emigrés sympathized with, organized for, and assisted the insurrections at home.[2]

Continuous demands from abroad likewise reaffirmed Irish devotion to the "bright gem of the sea."[3] Her needs were so pressing, so apparent, none could refuse assistance. Meager earnings somehow yielded a steady stream of drafts to friends and relatives who remained behind, and great disasters elicited even more remarkable contributions. Stimulated by Bishop Fitzpatrick's pastoral letter, Boston Irishmen remitted more than $200,000 during the scourge of 1847.[4] The less serious famine of 1863 drew £149 from the Montgomery Union Association of Boston alone, while a committee of Irishmen collected $18,000.[5] And Irish parish priests could always rely upon aid from former parishioners when calamity struck their districts.[6]

[1] Henry David Thoreau, *Walden or, Life in the Woods* (*Writings of Henry David Thoreau*, II, Boston, 1894), 325, 326.
[2] Cf., e.g., *Boston Pilot,* November 15, 1862; *Bostoner Zeitung,* November 11, 18, 1865; *Courrier des États-Unis,* March 4, 1848.
[3] "The Irish Emigrant's Lament," *Boston Pilot,* March 2, 1839; T. D. McGee, "A Vow and Prayer," *Poems* . . . (New York, 1869), 123.
[4] Cf. *Boston Catholic Observer,* February 13, March 13, 1847; Robert Bennet Forbes, *Voyage of the Jamestown* . . . (Boston, 1847), xxxix, 8.
[5] Cf. *Cork Examiner,* September 2, 1863; *Boston Pilot,* April 11, May 9, 1863.
[6] Cf., e.g., *Boston Pilot,* June 28, 1862; Thomas D'Arcy McGee, *Catholic History of North America* . . . (Boston, 1855), 148.

Love of Ireland enlisted a host of organizations in the perennial struggle against English oppression. These cropped up sporadically through the twenties and thirties, but until the Repeal Movement of the forties, accomplished little.[7] After 1840, however, agitation against Britain absorbed immigrants' attention for almost a decade, although it proved ultimately only a transitory influence upon Irish life in Boston. "The Friends of Ireland Society," founded October 6, 1840, by J. W. James and John C. Tucker, affiliated in 1841 with O'Connell's Dublin Loyal Association, and established agencies in South Boston, Charlestown, East Boston, Roxbury, and West Cambridge. At regular meetings in each locality it collected large sums of money, and its zeal inspired similar societies throughout the United States, which met in 1842 in convention in Philadelphia. A central directory in New York, formed in 1843, coördinated their activities and established a national fund for Ireland.[8]

Interest waned, however, as Repealers limited their activities to exacting dues. Collections in 1845 were about half those in 1843; and sparsely attended meetings reflected rising dissatisfaction.[9] The Boston Irish had been intensely loyal to O'Connell;[10] but reckless tugging at the lion's tail by Smith O'Brien, Mitchel, and the more active Young Ireland Party, weaned many away, particularly after the old leader's death.[11] Finally, the purge of radicals from the Repeal Society in 1847 alienated many prominent members, and transferred to Young Ireland complete control of Irish opinion in Boston, already inflamed by revolutionary hopes.[12] Implicit approval by the Church in 1848, however, united conservative Repealers and radicals in the Confederation of the United Friends of Ireland, which resumed collections so vigorously as to provoke strenuous protests from the British ambassador at Washington.[13] But failure took the heart out of the movement, and renewed conservative opposition ended it. Nationalist activity thereafter showed life only in sporadic flurries in the radical press, and in momentary excitement over the exile of O'Brien and his followers.[14] In 1857, the last serious hope vanished with the redistribution of the funds collected in 1848 and saved for a new insurrection.[15]

Although residual loyalties rendered immigrants particularly sensitive, appeals from abroad evoked a response from all Bostonians and frequently presented a common denominator for coöperation. Non-Irishmen promptly and

---

[7] Cf. Thomas D'Arcy McGee, *History of the Irish Settlers in North America* . . . (Boston, 1852), 131; *Literary and Catholic Sentinel* (Boston), March 21, 1835, March 26, 1836.

[8] Cf. Grattan to Fox, February 17, 1841, British Consular Correspondence, F.O. 5/360, fol. 59; *Boston Pilot*, January 2, 23, 1841, February 26, 1842, July 15, September 30, December 9, 1843; *Cork Examiner*, March 28, 1842; Dissertation Copy, 282.

[9] Cf. *Boston Pilot*, September 30, 1843, January 3, April 25, May 2, 1846.

[10] *Boston Pilot*, May 28, 1842; *Cork Examiner*, December 24, 1841, July 17, 1844; *Boston Catholic Observer*, July 10, 1847.

[11] *Boston Pilot*, June 26, 1847.

[12] Cf. *Boston Pilot*, July 31, 1847.

[13] *Boston Catholic Observer*, August 23, 1848; *supra*, 137. For English protests, cf. Palmerston to Crampton, July 7, 1848, British Consular Correspondence, F.O. 5/483, no. 37; Palmerston to Crampton, August 4, 1848, *ibid.*, F.O. 5/483, no. 43; Crampton to Palmerston, August 28, 1848, *ibid.*, F.O. 5/486.

[14] Cf. Crampton to Palmerston, October 9, 1848, *ibid.*, F.O. 5/487, no. 122; Bulwer to Palmerston, May 5, 1851, *ibid.*, F.O. 5/528; Crampton to Granville, January 25, 1852, *ibid.*, F.O. 5/544, 112–113; *Cork Examiner*, February 11, 1852.

[15] *Boston Pilot*, November 14, 1857.

generously aided Ireland, loading the *Jamestown* with supplies for the famine stricken land in 1848, and actively participating in relief work in 1863.[16] Political sympathy, although more intense within each group, also existed outside it. Germans, Frenchmen, Italians, and, for a time, the Irish combined for common revolutionary objectives, thinking in terms of a general struggle of western peoples against tyranny—national in form, but liberal in substance.[17]

Thus the recollection of common origin was not a conclusive segregative factor. The group discovered its coherent identity, tested its cohesiveness, and apperceived its distinguishing characteristics only by rubbing against the ineluctable realities of existence in Boston. When experience diluted initial differences, newcomers entered smoothly into the flow of life about them. Otherwise, they remained a discordant element in the closely-knit society; reluctant or unable to participate in the normal associational activities of the community, they strove to reweave on alien looms the sundered fabric of familiar social patterns. Since new soil and new homes called for new forms of behavior, they created a wide range of autonomous organizations to care for their needy, provide economic and political protection for their helpless, and minister spiritual comfort and friendship to those who found it nowhere else.

The yearning for familiar pleasures, for the company of understanding men, and the simple sensation of being not alone among strangers, drew immigrants together in tippling shop and *bierhaus,* and in a wide variety of more formally organized social activities. Of these the most prominent was the Charitable Irish Society. By 1845 it had completely lost its original character and had settled down to the business of commemorating St. Patrick's day with a grand dinner which annually grew more magnificent until it attained the dignity of a Parker House setting in 1856.[18] Few Irishmen could join this venerable association, however. The "bone and sinew" concentrated in the Shamrock Society founded in 1844, and celebrated more modestly, but no less enthusiastically, at Dooley's, the Mansion House, or Jameson's.[19] In addition, informal neighborhood groups sprang up wherever the Irish settled.[20]

Canadians gathered in the British Colonial Society while Scotsmen preserved old customs, sported their kilts, danced to the bagpipe, and played familiar games, either in the ancient Scots Charitable Society, the Boston Scottish Society, or the Caledonian Club (1853).[21] Germans, who felt that Americans lacked *Gemüthlichkeit,* established independent fraternal organizations which

[16] Cf. *Bowen's Boston News-Letter and City Record,* February 25, 1826; McGee, *Catholic History,* 147; Forbes, *op. cit.,* passim; Freeman Hunt, *Lives of American Merchants* (New York, 1858), II, 279; Edward Everett, *Orations and Speeches . . .* (Boston, 1850), II, 533 ff.; *Boston Pilot,* April 11, 1863; *Measures Adopted in Boston, Massachusetts for the Relief of the Suffering Scotch and Irish* Boston, 1847).

[17] Cf., e.g., the annual "democratic banquets" at the International Salon on the anniversary of the February Revolution of 1848 (*Der Pionier,* February 21, 1861). Cf. also Dissertation Copy, 286; McGee, *Irish Settlers,* 133; and Grattan to Fox, February 17, 1841, British Consular Correspondence, F.O. 5/360, f. 59.

[18] Cf. Dissertation Copy, 287; Very Rev. Wm. Byrne et al., *History of the Catholic Church in the New England States* (Boston, 1899), I, II.

[19] Cf. Dissertation Copy, 288.

[20] Cf., e.g., *Boston Pilot,* May 25, 1861.

[21] Cf. *Boston Directory,* 1853, 379 ff.; *Boston City Documents, 1865,* no. 59, p. 74. For the Scots Charitable, cf. George Combe, *Notes on the United States . . .* (Philadelphia, 1841), II, 199; James Bernard Cullen, *Story of the Irish in Boston . . .* (Boston, 1889), 37.

often affiliated with native ones. Thus Herman Lodge was Branch 133 of the Independent Order of Odd Fellows, and Branch 71 of the Independent Order of Redmen was known as the Independent Order of Rothmänner.[22] Jews, however, formed none of their own, at first participating in American and later in German groups.[23]

No society considered its activities complete without a ball, annual, semi-annual, or quarterly. At Hibernian Hall the Irish danced to the familiar music of Gilmore's band, while the Germans waltzed in Spring, Odd Fellow's, Phönix, or Turner halls to the rhythms of the Germania or Mainz's Orchestra.[24] Balls were so successful that Germans organized a *deutschen Ballgesellschaft,* and the Irish, the Erina Association, to sponsor them; and far-sighted entrepreneurs promoted them nightly to bring business to saloons and halls.[25]

Picnics were as popular; everyone arranged them. In Green Mountain Grove, Medford, Highland Grove, Melrose, or Bancroft's Grove, Reading, Germans enjoyed music and dancing, turning and games, absorbed mammoth lunches at ease, and set their children loose to roam in the woods (at half price).[26] For similar amusement, the Irish favored Waverly Grove or Beacon's Grove, Winchester, where even occasional fights and riots did not detract from the pleasure of escape from narrow streets and constricted homes.[27] For other relaxation the Germans turned to indoor gymnastics through the *Turnverein* founded by Heinzen and to shooting, climaxed by the annual *Turkey-schiessen* of the *Schutzenverein Germania.*[28] The Irish preferred rowing and several clubs engaged in vigorous boat-racing, modeled after regattas in Ireland. Run-of-the-mine matches took place in the harbor from Long Wharf to Castle Island, but major contests such as those of the *Maid of Erin* against the *T. F. Meagher,* or the *Superior* of New Brunswick, occurred in the Back Bay while hundreds of Irish spectators watched from along the Mill Dam.[29]

Militia companies were primarily social organizations, less attractive for their martial exploits than for the small bounty, the opportunity to parade in uniform, and the dinner and speeches that followed target practice and parade.[30] Though others joined American companies,[31] the Irish formed their own. Their earliest, the Montgomery Guards, had disbanded in 1839 after a dispute, but

[22] Cf. L. von Baumbach, *Neue Briefe aus den Vereinigten Staaten . . . mit besonderer Rücksicht auf deutsche Auswanderer* (Cassel, 1856), 183; *Der Neu England Demokrat,* December 30, 1857, February 3, 1858; *Bostoner Zeitung,* December 9, 16, 1865.

[23] Moses Hays had been Grand Master of Masons at the turn of the century (cf. Columbian Centinel [Boston], June 4, 1791; Lee M. Friedman, *Early American Jews* [Cambridge, 1934], 18, 19; Carl Wittke, *We Who Built America . . .* [New York, 1939], 41).

[24] Cf. *Literary and Catholic Sentinel,* January 16, October 8, 1836; *Boston Pilot,* March 8, 1862, May 25, 1861; *Bostoner Zeitung,* December 9, 16, 1865.

[25] Cf. *Boston Merkur,* January 16, 1847; Dissertation Copy, 289, 290.

[26] Cf. references to *Der Pionier,* Dissertation Copy, 290, n. 50.

[27] Cf. references to *Boston Pilot* and *Boston Catholic Observer,* Dissertation Copy, 290, ns. 51, 52.

[28] Wittke, *op. cit.,* 217–219; *Bostoner Zeitung,* November 11, 1865; *Der Pionier,* March 11, 1863, September 14, 1864, June 28, 1865.

[29] Cf., e.g., *Cork Examiner,* August 12, 1844; Dissertation Copy, 291.

[30] Cf. L. von Baumbach, *Neue Briefe,* 75; *Boston Pilot,* October 21, 1854; Wittke, *op. cit.,* 174.

[31] Cf., e.g., *Der Pionier,* March 12, 1862; Zacharish G. Whitman, *History of the Ancient and Honorable Artillery Company . . .* (Boston, 1842), 345 ff., 351, 371.

the Columbian Artillery, the Bay State Artillery, and the Sarsfield Guards took its place by 1852. Dissolved by the governor in 1853 as a result of Know-Nothing agitation, they continued their activities in new skins. The Columbian Artillery became the Columbian Literary Association, while the Sarsfield Guards became the Sarsfield Union Association, and their balls, picnics, and lectures suffered no loss in popularity.[32]

Saints' days furnished an annual social climax. The Scots Charitable Society celebrated St. Andrew's Day at a dinner at which "many a 'bannock' and dish of 'haggis' was eaten, and some whiskey punch was drank."[33] But the traditional St. Patrick's Day dinners of the Charitable Irish and the Shamrock Societies soon proved utterly inadequate for the Irish. No banquet room was broad enough to comprehend all the sons of Eire, even had they the price of the dinner. Only a spectacular parade could show their full ranks. Led by music, 2,000 marched in 1841; and thereafter, the number of loyal Irishmen and flamboyant bands grew. Mass usually followed, for the Church stressed the supranational, religious aspect of the holiday. But though German Catholics occasionally participated, St. Patrick remained essentially Irish.[34]

Immigrant fraternal activities often outlived the needs which originally fostered them, becoming ancillary rather than essential to the lives of the newcomers who did not differ basically from their neighbors. Among some, however, economic status, geographical segregation, and alien culture sustained and reinforced the initial feelings of strangeness, and magnified the importance of organizations in absorbing the shock of contact with foreign society. The Irish were almost alone in founding associations for material betterment, for only they were confined to a single economic class by industrial stratification. They unhappily realized their position in the city was distinct from that of any other group—exploited, indispensable, yet lowly and unwanted. Despairing of the prospects around them, persistently questioned,

> In the valleys of New England,
>   Are you happy, we would know?
> Are you welcome, are you trusted?
> Are you not?—then, RISE AND GO![35]

some sought escape to the frontier. But desirous as they were of leaving, few had the funds to carry them to the freedom of cheap lands.[36] And those wealthy enough to subsidize emigration were unwilling to tamper with an adequate, tractable, and inexpensive supply of labor and votes. Bishop Fenwicks plan for a colony in Maine (1833), the New England Land Company's project for one in

---

[32] Cf. *supra*, 203; *Boston Pilot*, July 22, 1854, February 24, April 7, 1855; *Irish-American*, February 24, 1855.

[33] *Boston Pilot*, December 22, 1855; cf. Combe *op. cit.*, II, 199.

[34] Cf. *Boston Pilot*, March 20, 1841, March 6, 1858; *Der Pionier*, March 29, 1865.

[35] McGee, *Poems*, 155; Isabel Skelton, *Life of Thomas D'Arcy McGee* (Gardenvale, Canada, 1925), 261. For interest in the frontier, cf. advertisements of western land agents in *Boston Pilot*, April 24, May 1, 1852, April 2, 1853.

[36] Cf. Sister Mary Gilbert Kelly, *Catholic Immigrant Colonization Projects in the United States, 1815-1860* (New York, 1939), 40.

Iowa (1851), and the Buffalo Convention's day-dream of a new Ireland in Canada, all came to nought.[37]

Necessarily reconciled to remaining within Boston, the Irish turned to sporadic and largely futile efforts to improve their economic position there. In 1855 more than 200 East Cambridge Irishmen contributed $6.00 each and formed the first consumers' coöperative to avoid "the petty domineering of would-be tyrants. . . ."[38] They turned also to their own countrymen for advice on the protection of their savings, consulting first the Bishop and the English consuls, and ultimately establishing banks of their own.[39] After an unsuccessful strike in 1843, the tailors established a producers' cooperative under B. S. Treanor, the Young Irelander. That organization failed, but it evolved by 1853 into the Journeymen Tailors' Trade and Benevolent Association. Stimulated by the panic of 1857, the society reorganized (1858), and affiliated with a similar group in Philadelphia.[40] Another large sector of unskilled Irishmen formed the Boston Laborers Association (1846) in an attempt to control dock and warehouse employment. Though it lost a serious strike in 1856, it reorganized in 1862 and grew in strength and vitality through the Civil War, remaining distinctly Irish, as did similar societies of waiters and granite cutters.[41]

Among all groups, of course, there were those who lived from hand to mouth in the shadow of an involuntary and remorseless improvidence. When illness, fatigue, or unemployment cut short their labor, these turned not to the cold stranger, but each man to his countryman, each to his old neighbor. Resenting

> The organized charity scrimped and iced,
> In the name of a cautious, statistical Christ,

all were reluctant to rely upon Boston social agencies, even those set up for their special benefit.[42] Nor could they fall back upon the organizations of their pre-

[37] Kelly, *op. cit.*, 37–47, 208, 209 223–237, 241; Robert H. Lord, "Organizer of the Church in New England . . . ," *Catholic Historical Review*, XXII (1936), 184; John Gilmary Shea, *History of the Catholic Church within the . . . United States . . .* (New York, 1890), III, 472; *Boston Pilot*, June 22, 1852; Mrs. J. Sadlier, *Biographical Sketch . . .* (in McGee, *Poems*), 28; Skelton, *op. cit.*, 270 ff.

[38] Cf. *Boston Pilot*, September 13, 1856.

[39] Cf. *One Hundred Years of Savings Bank Service . . .* (Boston, 1916), II; British Consular Correspondence, F.O. 5/397, no. 5; the Columbian Mutual in "Fourth Annual Report on Loan Fund Associations . . . ," *Massachusetts Public Documents*, 1859, no. 9, p. II.

[40] *Boston Pilot*, April 24, 1847, July 3, 1858; Norman J. Ware, *Industrial Worker 1840-1860 . . .* (Boston, 1924), 195; John R. Commons et al., eds., *Documentary History of American Industrial Society* (Cleveland, 1910), VIII, 275–285; *Eighth Annual Report of the Bureau of Statistics of Labor . . . 1877, Massachusetts Public Documents*, 1877, no. 31, pp. 85–86; Dissertation Copy, 295. For the strikes, cf. *Third Annual Report of the Commissioner of Labor, 1887 . . .* (Washington, 1888), 1038; John R. Commons, *History of Labour in the United States* (New York, 1918), I, 566, 576; *Irish-American*, July 31, September 4, 1858.

[41] Cf. "Procession," *Boston City Documents, 1865*, no. 59, pp. 71, 72. Cf. also *Third Annual Report of the Commissioner of Labor, 1887 . . .*, 1044; Boston Board of Trade, *Third Annual Report of the Government . . . 1857* (Boston, 1857), 6–13; *Eleventh Annual Report of the Bureau of Statistics of Labor 1880, Massachusetts Public Documents, 1880*, no. 15, p. 15; *Boston Pilot*, October 24, 1863, February 6, October 22, 1864; *Third Annual Report of the Bureau of Statistics of Labor . . . 1872, Massachusetts Senate Documents*, 1872, no. 180, p. 57.

[42] Cf. Dissertation Copy, 297.

cursory compatriots, for both the Scots Charitable Society (1657) and the Charitable Irish Society (1737) had early shed their original functions, becoming primarily wining and dining clubs.[43]

Numerous benevolent enterprises therefore marked the settlement of each new group in the city. But not all flourished. Many societies, hopefully launched, soon met disaster in seas of disinterestedness. The *Società Italiana di Benevolenza,* an early German Charitable Society, a Scandinavian Benevolent Relief Society, and a Swiss group, all failed to survive.[44] A British Charitable Society, founded in 1816, and a German Assistance Society, founded in July, 1847, with sixty members, struggled through the period, but always remained small.[45] The British organization almost disappeared during the Civil War, while apathy kept down the membership of the German Society, which only spent $300 to $400 annually for assistance. Intimate associations with limited functions, like the *Krankenunterstutzungsgesellschaft*—which provided death and illness benefits— were more successful; and religious institutions continued to extend charity. But on the whole the non-Irish immigrants failed to develop autonomous eleemosynary activities.[46]

The Irish, however, segregated in their murky slums, in their lowly occupations, and their dread of losing religion, never ceased to anticipate harsh treatment from strangers or to distrust unknown ways.[47] Centuries of struggles had engendered an acute wariness of Protestants, of Protestant friendship, and of Protestant assistance that too often masked proselytization with the guise of benevolence. "Talk to them of the Poorhouse and they associate with it all the disagreeable features of the prison-like Unions of their native land. Added to which is the horror, if placed there of being exiled, as they fear, from their priests; and *'they will sooner die in the streets'* (such is their language) than go to Deer Island or South Boston. . . ."[48] This misgiving was, of course, not without justification. Despite laws to restrict their influence, Protestant chaplains dominated the spiritual life of public institutions, controlling the inmates' reading material and religious services, while Catholic priests found great difficulty

---

[43] Cf. *supra,* 155 ff.; *Boston Pilot,* April 3, 1841. In 1857, a suggestion that the Scots Charitable Society organize an office to aid immigrant Scots came to nothing (cf. Scots Charitable Society, Records and Minutes . . . [MSS., N.E.H.G.S.], October 15, 1857, 25).

[44] Cf. *Constituzione della società italiana di benevolenza, residente in Boston, Massacciussets, Stati Uniti di America* (Boston, 1842), passim; *Verfassung des deutschen Wohlthätigkeit-Vereins, in Boston* . . . (Cambridge, 1835), passim; Albert B. Faust, *Guide to the Materials for American History in Swiss and Austrian Archives* (Washington, 1916), 27; *Boston City Documents,* 1865, no. 59, p. 74.

[45] *British Charitable Society for the Years 1849 to 1855.* Report . . . (Boston, 1855), 2, 3; *Boston Merkur,* July 10, 24, 31, August 7, 1847; *Der Pionier,* January 16, 1862.

[46] Cf. *British Charitable Society for the Years 1849 to 1855,* 3; *Der Neu England Demokrat,* January 23, 1858; Dissertation Copy, 300; *Boston Merkur,* December 5, 1846, May 9, July 24, 1847; *Constitution, By-Laws and Rules of Order of the Hebrew Congregation Ohabei Shalom* . . . (Boston, 1855), 8; *Der Pionier,* January 5, 1860.

[47] Cf., e.g., *Boston Pilot,* May 15, 1841.

[48] Benevolent Fraternity of Churches, *Annual Report of the Executive Committee* . . . *1851,* no. 17 (Boston, 1851), 21; cf. also *Fifth Annual Report . . . Children's Mission to the Children of the Destitute* . . . (Boston, 1854), 3; "Cross and Beads . . . ," *Boston Catholic Observer,* November 8–15, 1848.

in securing access even after a resolve of the legislature in 1858 admitted them.[49]

The horror of dying in a hospital without the ministrations of a priest was not allayed until 1863 when Andrew Carney gave a South Boston estate to the Sisters of Charity for the institution named after him.[50] Destitute children, in danger of adoption by Protestants or the state, received earlier attention. In 1833, Sister Ann Alexis and the Sisters of Charity founded St. Vincent's Female Orphan Asylum. Accumulating funds from successive fairs and church collections, they finally purchased a building in 1842, and in April, 1858 opened new quarters, donated by Andrew Carney, to house the increasing number of children. The orphanage was exceedingly popular, but at most accommodated only 200.[51] Father Haskins' House of the Angel Guardian, established in 1851 for neglected boys, supplemented the activities of the Asylum.[52] But since the two combined could care for only a small fraction of those who looked to them for aid, the Irish organized a system of adoption by Catholic families.[53] However, when the Home for Destitute Catholic Children opened in 1864, more than one thousand gamins between the ages of eight and twelve were still prosecuted annually for vagrancy.[54]

Financial limitations necessarily relegated the immense problem of pauperism to the government. An early Hibernian Relief Society (c. 1827) was short-lived. The Irish could do little more for the poor than provide much needed clothing through parish societies, and occasional assistance through the Roman Catholic Mutual Relief Society, and, later, through the Society of St. Vincent de Paul.[55] The religious character of these associations drove the small group of Protestant Irish into a separate "Irish Protestant Mutual Relief Society."[56]

Except for the Negroes who in 1860 opened a home for aged women on Myrtle Street, Beacon Hill, the Irish alone established an independent institutional life. Their strength of numbers faciliated but did not cause separation. By 1865, the Germans, more numerous than the Irish in the year St. Vincent's Orphan Asylum opened, had failed to set up a single permanent agency. Social, economic and intellectual development gradually eliminated the necessity for autarchy in non-Irish groups, but ingrained in the Irish the insistence upon independent charities conducted according to Catholic principles.

Beyond the range of material needs, each group organized to preserve a precious cultural heritage, enlisting a wide variety of social instruments—churches, schools, newspapers, and clubs. Each cherished distinctive traditions whose

[49] Cf. *Massachusetts Senate Documents, 1844,* no. 15, 2-4; *ibid.,* no. 79; *Boston Pilot,* December 4, 1858; Bishop John B. Fitzpatrick to J. P. Bigelow, May 29, 1850, Bigelow Papers (MSS., H. C. L.), Box VI.

[50] *Boston Pilot,* March 21, 1863; William H. Mahoney, "Benevolent Hospitals in Metropolitan Boston," *Quarterly Publications of the American Statistical Association,* XIII (1913), 420; Rev. G. C. Treacy, "Andrew Carney . . . ," United States Catholic Historical Society, *Historical Records and Studies,* XIII (1919), 103; Shea *op. cit.,* IV, 516.

[51] Cf. Dissertation Copy, 302, 330, Table XXVI; Lord, *loc. cit.,* 183.

[52] Cf. Shea, *op. cit.,* IV, 511.

[53] Cf., e.g., *Boston Pilot,* June 3, 1855.

[54] Cullen, *op. cit.,* 156; *Boston Pilot,* June 4, 1864.

[55] Cf. T. A. Emmet, *Memoir of Thomas Addis and Robert Emmet . . .* (New York, 1915), I, 501; *Jesuit or Catholic Sentinel,* January 29, 1831; *Boston Catholic Observer,* April 17, 1847, October 4, 1848; *Constitution of the Boston Roman Catholic Mutual Relief Society . . . 1832 . . .* (Boston, 1837); Dissertation Copy, 304.

[56] Cf. *Boston Pilot,* June 25, 1842.

chances of survival varied with the strength of the differences developed by experience in Boston. Language was the weakest barrier. Attempts to preserve German were futile. Pastors preached the necessity of learning English, and despite difficulties English words inevitably crept into German usage.[57] Thrown into continuous contact with neighbors who spoke no German, even purists inevitably "schäkt" hands, referred to "dem feinsten Köntry der Welt" and "unser City," and used "no, sörri" and "ohl wreit" as liberally as any Yankee. Business taught them "aber Käsch daun," "Dammädsches," "engahdschd," and "indiht?."[58] Some used the two languages interchangeably, and all adapted the forms of one to the other.[59] French and German easily became second languages which could be acquired by the immigrants' children in the public schools. Separate organizations, founded on linguistic differences alone, proved superfluous.[60]

Similarly, the urge to maintain familiar forms of worship was most meaningful when it embodied a vital social difference. Thus although the Portuguese Jews had a synagogue as early as 1816, when Abraham Touro requested "that his religious profession might be recorded on the Town's books—& that he belonged to a Synagogue of the Jews," German Jews erected their own building in 1843 which in turn did not satisfy the Polish Jews who dedicated still another in 1849.[61] On the other hand, though German Protestants organized a congregation as early as 1839, constructing Zion Church (Shawmut Street, South End) in 1846–47, and a Methodist Church in Roxbury in 1852, they often accepted the facilities of natives. A number of German families, stopping in Roxbury for a few months in 1833, were content to attend St. James Episcopal Church and to send sixty children regularly to Sunday School, and the Reverend A. Rumpff, pastor of the Lutheran Church, worked as a missionary for the Unitarian Fraternity of Churches.[62]

Within the Catholic Church three nativity groups insisted upon national forms. When the Abbé de la Poterie read his first mass in 1788 to a congregation of between sixty and a hundred communicants, primarily French by na-

[57] Cf. F. W. Bogen, *German in America* . . . (Boston, 1851), 11, 13.
[58] For the use of such words, cf. Karl Heinzen, Luftspiele (*Zweite Auflage, Gesamelte Schriften,* II, Boston, 1872), 172, 176, 177, 179, 181, 195, 212 and passim; A. Douai, "Der Ueberfall," *Meyer's Monatschefte,* April, 1855, V, 241; *Der Pionier,* January 31, 1861.
[59] Thus the Germans adapted the past prefix "Ge" to English words, viz., "hab' ich denn gesuppos't," "gekillt," "getschähnscht" (cf. Heinzen, *Luftspiele,* 170, 191). For English words in American French, cf. references to *Courier des États-Unis,* Dissertation Copy, 306.
[60] Cf. "Annual Report of the Boston School Committee, 1864," *Boston City Documents, 1865,* no. 39, p. 164.
[61] Cf. *Minutes of the Selectmen's Meetings, 1811 to 1817* . . . (*Volume of Records Relating to the Early History of Boston* . . . , XXXVIII), *Boston City Documents,* 1908, no. 60, p. 171; Abraham G. Daniels, *Memories of Ohabei Shalom, 1843 to 1918* . . . (s.l., n.d. [Boston, 1918]); *Constitution, By-Laws and Rules of Order of the Hebrew Congregation Ohabei Shalom* . . . (Boston, 1855); *Boston Pilot,* September 23, 1849.
[62] Cf. Lemuel Shattuck, *Report . . . Census of Boston . . . 1845* . . . (Boston, 1846), 123; *Boston Merkur,* December 19, 1846; Justin Winsor, *Memorial History of Boston* . . . (Boston, 1880), III, 444; cf. *Journal of the Proceedings of the Annual Convention of the Protestant Episcopal Church in . . . Massachusetts . . . 1833* (Boston, 1833), 30; *Journal of the Proceedings . . . 1834* (Boston, 1834), 17; Benevolent Fraternity of Churches, *Twenty-Third Annual Report of the Executive Committee* (Boston, 1857), 3.

tivity, but including some Irishmen, dispute arose as to the language to be used.[63] As soon as the English-speaking Reverend John Thayer appeared in Boston, the Irish seized the church by force, ousting the French priest whom the Bishop had delegated "to provide a Preacher for the most numerous part of the congregation."[64] Bishop Carroll finally ended the rift in the tiny Catholic community by retiring both Thayer and de Rousselet and installing the French Father Matignon.[65] Although the French had once preferred to be buried with Protestants rather than with Irish Catholics, and had felt bitter enough to remove their furniture from the church, the tact and kindly wisdom of Matignon and of the saintly Bishop Cheverus reconciled and reunited the two groups. Small in number, facing no serious problems until the forties, they remained harmonious in sentiment.[66]

But as immigration increased, the Church acquired a thoroughly Irish cast, marked by the accession to the episcopacy of John Bernard Fitzpatrick, the Boston-born son of Irish parents, who replaced the Maryland aristocrat Fenwick in 1846, and by an ever larger proportion of Irish-born clergymen, many from All-Hallows Missionary College near Dublin.[67] In its first four decades, the Church had scarcely grown at all. In 1816, Boston contained not more than 1,500 Catholics of all nativities, and Bishop Cheverus felt it could well be served as part of the New York diocese.[68] By 1830, only little St. Augustine's Chapel, South Boston (1819), had joined Holy Cross Cathedral, Franklin Square (1801–03). The three churches built in the thirties to provide for the inhabitants of the North End, the South End and Roxbury, and Charlestown could not serve those arriving in the forties. For in 1843, the absolute maximum capacity of all Catholic places of worship, including 2,000 seats reserved for Germans, was still less than 14,000—clearly inadequate for the Irish.[69]

Active expansion, however, met the demands. In 1843, the Rev. J. B. M'Mahon opened the indispensable Moon Street Free Church in the heart of the North End slums, the first to accommodate the very poorest. In 1848, the Bishop bought the meeting house of the Purchase Street Unitarian Society for the use of the Irish in Fort Hill, naming it St. Vincent's. Finally, in 1855, the dedication of the Church of St. James, prepared to serve a congregation of 10,000, temporarily settled the problem within peninsular Boston, the Irish population of which did not increase sharply thereafter.[70]

[63] E. Percival Merritt, "Sketches of the Three Earliest Roman Catholic Priests in Boston" (*Publications of the Colonial Society of Massachusetts,* XXV), 173 ff. Cf. also Shea, *op. cit.,* II, 315 ff., 387 ff.
[64] Cf. Merritt, *loc. cit.,* 185, 191 ff., 212 ff.
[65] Cullen, *op. cit.,* 125; *Boston Catholic Observer,* April 3, 1847; Leo F. Ruskowski, *French Emigré Priests in the United States . . .* (Washington, 1940), 11 ff.
[66] Cf. Merritt, *loc. cit.,* 198–201; Shea, *op. cit.,* II, 435 ff., 617, 621, III, 107 ff.; *Boston Catholic Observer,* May 29, 1847; McGee, *Catholic History,* 97 ff.; Ruskowski, *op. cit.,* 121; Frances S. Childs, *French Refugee Life in the United States . . .* (Baltimore, 1940), 40, 41.
[67] Cf., e.g., *Annales de la propagation de la foi . . . 1865,* XXXVII, 485. For Fitzpatrick, cf. Cullen, *op. cit.,* 131, 132. For Fenwick, cf. Lord, *loc. cit.*
[68] Bishop Cheverus to Archbishop Neale, December 19, 1816, quoted in *Boston Pilot,* February 16, 1856.
[69] Cf. *Boston Pilot,* January 28, February 25, 1843; Shattuck, *op. cit.,* 123; *Boston Catholic Observer,* April 17, 1847; *United States Catholic Almanac,* 1833, 46, 47.
[70] Cf. *Boston Catholic Observer,* May 10, 17, 1848; *Boston Pilot,* January 21, 1843, September 29, 1855.

As the Irish spread from the heart of the city, the Church followed, frequently purchasing the empty buildings of displaced Yankees. In 1842, they laid the cornerstone of St. John's Church in East Cambridge, and in 1848, opened St. Peter's, Cambridge. In 1844 the Meeting House of the Maverick Congregational Society in East Boston became the Church of St. Nicholas, joined before long by St. Mary's, the Star of the Sea, and Sacred Heart and Assumption. In 1845 a new church dedicated to SS. Peter and Paul replaced old St. Augustine's Chapel in South Boston, supplemented a few years later by the "Gate of Heaven" Church at City Point (1863). In 1855 a church was built in Brighton and in 1858 one in Brookline.[71]

Thoroughly Irish in character, the Church nevertheless profited by its early quarrels and made special provision for worship by each new national group. By 1840 the French element was thoroughly insignificant, but there were enough German Catholics to require attention. Served at first only by pastors who made occasional trips from New York, and by special masses in the Cathedral, the Germans soon demanded a church of their own. In 1841, they organized Trinity Church and erected a building (completed 1846) on Suffolk Street in the South End, which also served those in Roxbury and East Boston. Disturbed by a quarrel with Bishop Fenwick, however, they built their church slowly and with great difficulty, and remained in debt for many years, for Catholicism did not play the intimate role in German it did in Irish life.[72]

While immigrants might possibly transplant the familiar form of their churches as a matter of habit, they established successful independent educational organizations only in response to needs arising in America. Having no Old-World model—schools at home were either nonexistent or state-controlled—they created new institutions to protect a vital cultural difference. A German school system therefore remained a chimerical hope in the minds of isolated individuals. The ambition of intellectuals to establish a great German university in the New World led to fascinating speculations, but to nothing more. German Catholic priests may have given instruction throughout the period, but their attempt to found a formal academy failed; not until 1863 could they even buy a lot.[73] And the classes maintained by non-Catholic Germans in Roxbury and Boston had no more than ninety students by 1860.[74] Jews provided religious training for their children, but otherwise sent them to the public schools although a six-day teaching week made observance of their Sabbath difficult.

But a separate system was essential to the Irish, for compulsory education drew their children into the common schools, endangering their Catholic souls. Thus challenged, the Church attempted to cope with the problem even before

[71] *Boston Pilot*, May 21, 1842, November 10, December 8, 1855, December 13, 1862, March 28, 1863; *Boston Catholic Observer*, July 5, September 13, 1848; *Cambridge Directory, 1865–6*, 185; Cullen, *op. cit.*, 136; C. Bancroft Gillespie, *Illustrated History of South Boston* . . . (South Boston, 1900), 67, 73.
[72] Cf. Rev. James Fitton, *Sketches of the Establishment of the Church in New England* (Boston, 1872), 146, 147; Shea, *op. cit.*, III, 486, 488, IV, 145; *Boston Pilot*, June 25, 1842, January 14, February 25, 1843, May 30, 1846.
[73] Cf. *Boston Pilot*, October 31, 1863; *Boston Merkur*, June 12, 1847; *Boston Catholic Observer*, June 5, 1847; Richard J. Quinlan, "Growth and Development of Catholic Education in the Archdiocese of Boston," *Catholic Historical Review*, April, 1936, XXII, 32.
[74] Cf. *Bostoner Zeitung*, September 1, 1865; *Der Pionier*, March 5, 1862.

the first Provincial Council of Bishops in 1829 urged the establishment of truly Catholic schools in each community.[75] Sunday Schools, the first line of defense, grew slowly; by 1829 not more than 500 Catholic children received instruction in the whole area. But after 1835 the Young Catholics Friend Society, over-whelmingly Irish by nativity, assumed the burden of these schools in Boston, organized branches in the Irish sections of the city, and educated more than a thousand pupils annually. By 1845 there were 4,100 children in Boston Catholic Sunday Schools. And thereafter societies of the same name exercised similar functions in South Boston and Roxbury.[76]

Parochial schools likewise started slowly, but expanded to meet the influx of Irish. The school Father Matignon is traditionally said to have kept in Holy Cross Church at the beginning of the century, probably offered only occasional haphazard instruction.[77] In 1820, the Ursuline nuns, with the aid of John Thayer and Bishop Cheverus, set up the first school for girls in their convent near the Cathedral. Although almost one hundred pupils attended at one time, it lost contact with the Boston Irish after moving in 1826 to Mt. Benedict, Charles-town.[78] There were classes of some sort in the Cathedral in 1826 and 1829, in Craigie's Point, Charlestown, in 1829, and in connection with St. Vincent's Orphan Asylum after 1830, but another permanent formally organized school was not founded until 1849, when the Sisters of Notre Dame de Namur from Cincinnati established one at St. Mary's, North End. The Sisters extended their activities by 1853 to the Church of SS. Peter and Paul, South Boston, opened academies by 1858 in Roxbury and on Lancaster Street, Boston, a convent on Berkeley Street, Back Bay, in 1864, and, after a quarrel over the use of the Bible in public schools, "Father Wiget's" in the North End in 1859.[79]

Higher education, less important to the mass of Irish laborers, came later. Holy Cross College in Worcester, established in 1843, attracted few Massa-chusetts residents, for its fees—more than $150 a year—were out of the reach of most.[80] But when the Jesuits opened Boston College on Harrison Street in the South End in 1863, the thirty-dollar annual charge and the possibility of living at home enabled more to attend.[81] Bishop Fenwick's hopes of founding a theo-logical seminary were not realized, however, and in this period Boston Irishmen still found it necessary to send their children to France or to Canada for in-struction leading to the priesthood.[82]

On all levels, of course, tuition charges limited attendance to those who could pay. Some, perforce, relied upon common schools. But many failed to attend at all, and the insistence upon parochial education often became a shield

[75] Cf. *Official Catholic Year Book*, 1928, 407.
[76] Cf. Fitton, *op. cit.*, 134, 135; Dissertation Copy, 316; *Boston Catholic Observer*, October 25, 1848; *Boston Pilot*, November 18, 1854, November 24, 1855; Shattuck, *op. cit.*, 124.
[77] Cf. Quinlan, *loc. cit.*, 28.
[78] Cf. *Boston Catholic Observer*, June 5, 1847; Quinlan, *loc. cit.*, 29; Winsor, *op. cit.*, III, 519; [Charles Greely Loring], *Report of the Committee Relating to the Destruction of the Ursuline Convent . . .* (Boston, 1834), 5.
[79] Cf. Quinlan, *loc. cit.*, 30, 34; Gillespie, *op. cit.*, 67; *Boston Pilot*, July 24, 1858; Cullen, *op. cit.*, 134, 136; Moses King, *Back Bay District . . .* (Boston, 1880), 18.
[80] Cf. *Massachusetts House Documents, 1849*, no. 130, p. 2; Lord, *loc. cit.*, 183.
[81] Cullen, *op. cit.*, 135; Shea, *op. cit.*, IV, 515; *Boston Pilot*, December 24, 1864.
[82] For examples, cf. *Boston Pilot*, January 18, 1862, June 4, 1864; Cullen, *op. cit.*, 132. Cf. also [Report on Dioceses Subject to the College of the Propaganda] (MS., B. A. Vat. No. 9565), fol. 132; Quinlan, *loc. cit.*, 30.

for truancy, creating a serious problem of child vagrancy.[83] But though the principle of Catholic instruction for every child remained an ideal rather than a reality, the Irish resisted the temptation of free public schools, and at considerable cost sponsored their own.

Among the Irish, educational efforts took special form in the total abstinence societies. Unable to deal with intemperance as other Bostonians did, they formed groups to provide nonalcoholic relaxation and entertainment. The earliest (1836) had been nonsectarian.[84] But after 1841, these organizations affiliated with the Church, their most active sponsor. Stimulated by the visit of Father Mathew in 1849, these groups grew rapidly. In addition to the Hibernian and Father Mathew Total Abstinence Societies, clubs flourished in each parish and suburb, closely interrelated, but having no contact with non-Catholics. Thus, in 1865, at a procession after the death of President Lincoln, the nineteen non-Irish temperance groups marched together in Division 2, while the Irish paraded in Division 7.[85]

Their distinctive needs also shaped the less formally organized education of the Irish. Though some took advantage of such non-Catholic agencies as the adult evening school and the sewing school of the Benevolent Fraternity of Churches, most turned all their activities into Catholic channels.[86] Thus, the Young Catholics Friend Society early renounced its plan of inviting lecturers without regard to sect; and other groups adopted the same exclusive Catholic policy. The Hibernian Lyceum, the Tom Moore Club, literary institutes, debating societies, and Young Men's Sodalities all applied religious ideas to literature and current events, while the Boston Gregorian Society, formed in 1836 by young Irishmen, applied them to music.[87]

The French and Germans sponsored similar cultural activities. The *Gesangverein Orpheus* and the *Solo-Club* gave popular concerts for many years, and a society founded in 1847 offered numerous lectures and plays. Even earlier, German Jews founded a "Hebrew Literary Society" which met twice weekly for discussions and kept a file of Jewish, German, and English periodicals. In addition, enterprising saloonkeepers found it profitable to keep *Lesezimmer* where nostalgic countrymen could scan the pages of the *Berliner National-Zeitung*, the *Leipziger Illustrierte*, and the good-natured *Kladderadatsch*.[88]

Periodicals from home were not enough. Each group at one time or another attempted to develop newspapers to express its own needs in the new world. However, though the press was the immigrants' most powerful educational instrument, it flourished in Boston only to the degree that it satisfied a significant social need. Since almost all these journals appeared weekly they competed with

[83] Cf. *Boston City Documents, 1864,* no. 30, p. 42; *Massachusetts Senate Documents, 1850,* no. 55, pp. 1 ff. For fees, cf. *Boston Pilot,* August 28, 1858.
[84] Cf. *Literary and Catholic Sentinel,* April 16, 1836.
[85] Cf. "Proceedings at the Memorial to Abraham Lincoln . . . ," *Boston City Documents, 1865,* no. 59, pp. 69, 73; also Dissertation Copy, 320.
[86] Benevolent Fraternity of Churches, *Twenty-second Annual Report of the Executive Committee* . . . (Boston, 1856), 7, 8; Benevolent Fraternity of Churches, *Twenty-third Annual Report* . . . (Boston, 1857), 13; Benevolent Fraternity of Churches, *Twenty-fifth Annual Report* . . . (Boston, 1859), 23.
[87] Cf. Dissertation Copy, 320–321; *Literary and Catholic Sentinel,* November 26, 1836.
[88] Cf. *Boston Directory, 1853,* 382; *Der Neu England Demokrat,* November 21, 1857; *Bostoner Zeitung,* January 6, 1866; *Boston Merkur,* December 12, 1846, April 24, 1847; *Der Pionier,* March 14, 28, 1861.

the superior resources of those in New York and failed unless supported by a group conscious of its identity. Thus, the French, first in the field with Joseph Nancrede's *Courrier de Boston* and de Rousselet's *Courier politique de l'univers* (1792–93), were unable to support one in Boston for any length of time because of competition from the splendid *Courrier des États-Unis* of New York.[89] Edited with great care, displaying an unusual regard for taste and accuracy, the latter was the outstanding immigrant newspaper of the period. In turn weekly, bi-weekly, and tri-weekly, it finally became a daily.[90] Vying with it, *Le Littérateur français* (1836), the *Petit Courrier des familles et des pensions* (1846), *Le Bostonien,* the *Gazette Française,* all of Boston, and the *Phare de New York,* could last only a short time.[91] Newspapers in other groups started hopefully, but faded rapidly. Short-lived Spanish and Italian sheets had little influence.[92] After the quick failure of the first British paper, *Old Countryman,* the English depended upon the *New York Albion* until one of its editors moved to Boston in 1855, and started the *Anglo-Saxon.* In the same year the *European* and in 1857 the *Scottish-American* were established in New York. But none succeeded.[93]

The only non-Irish immigrant paper that flourished in Boston was founded upon the personality of a brilliant editor. The *Boston Merkur* (1846–48), and *Der Neu England Demokrat* (a semi-weekly) had already disappeared when Karl Heinzen transplanted *Der Pionier* from Louisville and New York to Boston. A fiery radical, of deep culture and acute intelligence, extreme on every social issue, Heinzen, exiled from Prussia, had participated in the 1848 revolution in Baden, and had led a stormy career on several German-American papers. His personal organ thrived in Boston's friendly atmosphere, scarcely affected by the founding of the somewhat more popular *Bostoner Zeitung* in 1865, and exercised a deep influence both on Germans and on the Americans like Wendell Phillips and Garrison who read it.[94]

[89] Cf. *Courrier de Boston, affiches, annonces et avis . . . ,* April 23–October 15, 1789; Merritt, *loc. cit.,* 210; Howard Mumford Jones, *America and French Culture* (Chapel Hill, 1927), 136; George Parker Winship, "Two or Three Boston Papers," *Papers of the Bibliographical Society of America,* XIV, 57 ff., 76 ff.; Childs, *op. cit.,* 129.

[90] Cf. *Courrier des États-Unis, journal politique et littéraire,* March 1, 1828, November 14, 1829, November 12, 1839, June 10, April 24, 1851.

[91] Cf. *Literary and Catholic Sentinel,* December 10, 1836; *Courrier des États-Unis,* April 16, 1837; *Boston Almanac,* 1846, 145; *Le Bostonien, journal des salons* (Boston), May 12, 1849 ff.; *Gazette Francaise* (Boston), September 14, 1850–July 19, 1851; *Le Phare de New York, echo . . . des deux mondes,* February 24, 1851 ff.; also Henri Herz, *Mes Voyages en Amérique . . .* (Paris, 1866), 192 ff.

[92] *El Redactor* (New York), March 10, 1828 ff. (apparently founded in 1827); *L'Eco d'Italia, giornale politico populare letterario* (New York), February 8, 1850 ff.; *Il Proscritto, giornale politico, aristoco e litterario* (New York), August 7, 1851 ff. For others, cf. *Courrier des États-Unis,* August 2, 1849.

[93] Cf. *Old Countryman: and English, Irish, . . . Colonial Mirror,* October 10, 1829; *Anglo-Saxon, European and Colonial Gazette* (Boston), December 22, 1855 ff., September 12, 1856; *Boston Pilot,* December 29, 1855; *European* (New York), November 15, 1856 ff.; *Scottish-American Journal,* January 30, 1864.

[94] Cf. *Boston Merkur, ein Volksblatt für Stadt und Land,* November 21, 1846 ff.; *Der Neu England Demokrat,* October 17, 1857; Karl Heinzen, *Erlebtes, zweite Theil: nach meiner Exilirung* (*Gesammelte Schriften,* IV, Boston, 1874); *Gedenkbuch, Erinnerung an Karl Heinzen . . .* (Milwaukee, 1887), 8, 32; *Der Pionier,* April 29, 1863, February 28, 1861; *Bostoner Zeitung, ein Organ für die Neu England Staaten . . . ,* September 1, 1865 ff.

The strongest organs naturally developed among the Irish, who turned to them for news of home, for accounts of their own activities and organizations, and, above all, for sympathetic advice, derived from their own ideas, on the strange issues they faced as residents and citizens of a new world. But until the forties, even the Irish had no stable newspapers in Boston and relied on the New York *Shamrock,* the *Western Star and Harp of Erin,* and their successors.[95] Starting with Bishop Fenwick's short-lived children's paper, the *Expostulator,* a succession of very Catholic papers ingloriously collapsed.[96] The first, edited by the Bishop and Father O'Flaherty, and known variously as the *Jesuit or Catholic Sentinel* (1829–31), and the *United States Catholic Intelligencer* (1831–33), failed completely. Its successor, the *Literary and Catholic Sentinel.* edited by the popular poet, George Pepper, and by Dr. J. S. Bartlett, appeared at the opening of 1835. By the end of the year, to strengthen its appeal to the Irish, it became the *Boston Pilot* "in honor of one of the most popular and patriotic Journals in Dublin."[97] Subsisting from appeals to the generosity of its subscribers, it lasted through a second year, and gave up. Pepper then attempted to issue a secular paper, *The O'Connellite and Irish Representative,* but neither that nor his other ventures survived.[98]

The second *Boston Pilot,* founded after his death in 1838 to express the interests of the Irish-Catholic population of New England, like its less permanent predecessors, did not pay its way; by the end of the year, it had only 600 subscribers. It staggered on, however, although a meeting of its friends to raise funds was only partially successful. At the end of 1839, it was still in serious difficulties. But the immigration of the forties brought security.[99]

Prosperity completely reoriented the *Pilot's* policy. In 1842, Thomas D'Arcy McGee, a green Irishman of seventeen, electrified a Boston audience with a patriotic oration that won him an editorial position on the *Pilot,* and made him editor-in-chief in 1844. Set by him on a radical course, the *Pilot* preached Irish nationalism, even after he returned to Dublin to edit the *Nation.* Once drawn into the Repeal Movement, the paper became dependent less upon the support of the Church than upon that of popular opinion. And with the aid of that support it could outlive occasional rivals such as the *New England Reporter and Catholic Diary.*[100]

Repeal under the respectable auspices of O'Connell was safe, but after 1845, the *Pilot* espoused the program of Young Ireland and became intolerable to the Church. To counteract the *Pilot's* influence, the Bishop, through Brownson, sponsored the *Boston Catholic Observer,* a religious rival. At the same time a political newspaper, the *Boston Vindicator,* appeared and was hailed as an ally

[95] Cf. *Western Star and Harp of Erin* (New York), May 16, 1812–May 1, 1813; Louis Dow Scisco, *Political Nativism in New York State* (New York, 1901), 19.

[96] Lord, *loc. cit.,* 177. Another children's newspaper, *Young Catholics Friend,* edited by H. B. C. Greene, appeared for a short time in March, 1840.

[97] *Literary and Catholic Sentinel,* January 3, December 19, 1835, January 2, 1836. To avoid confusion with a later paper of the same name, it is referred to throughout this work by its original title.

[98] *Ibid.,* June 11, October 22, November 12, 19, 1836; McGee, *History of the Irish Settlers,* 132.

[99] *Boston Pilot,* December 22, 29, 1838, November 16, 1839.

[100] Cf. Mrs. J. Sadlier, *Biographical Sketch,* 17, 18; Robert D. McGibbon, *Thomas D'Arcy McGee . . .* (Montreal, 1884), 7; Skelton, *op. cit.,* 11 ff.; *Boston Pilot,* July 23, 1842, October 11, 1845.

by the *Observer*.[101] Neither the *Vindicator* nor J. R. Fitzgerald's *Nation* which replaced it, lasted long; but for two years the *Observer* and *Pilot* bitterly fought out the issues of Irish conservatism and radicalism.[102] In 1848, however, the *Pilot* acquired still another competitor. In that year, McGee returned from Ireland, established the New York *Nation,* and by the glamor of actual participation in the revolution drew many readers away from the *Pilot.* Weakened further by continued opposition from the clergy, the *Pilot* recanted in 1849 and turned conservative. The cross and dove replaced the red cap of liberty in its masthead, and Father John T. Roddan, an American priest, became its editor. Although many felt that "Donahoe will have a jolly grill in Purgatory for the evil he has done," his paper remained religiously dependable thereafter.[103]

Meanwhile, McGee's radicalism had antagonized Archbishop Hughes of New York, who forced the *Nation* out of business by a vigorous destructive campaign in 1850. Left without a journal, the Massachusetts radicals invited the still unrepentant rebel to come to Boston where he established the *American Celt* in 1850. But McGee failed to prosper. The *Pilot* and the clergy attacked him and he faced the serious competition of Phelim Lynch's *Irish-American,* which had taken his place in New York by 1849. After two years he finally shed his radicalism and made peace with the Church. But since there was no room in Boston for two conservative papers, he left for Buffalo and eventually for Montreal.[104]

No longer strong enough to support a newspaper, the radicals thereafter confined their reading to the New York *Irish-American.* As the former revolutionaries splintered into cliques, each established an organ: John Mitchel's *Citizen,* Doheny's *Honest Truth* and, *Meagher's Irish News.* But neither these nor occasional fugitive papers like William Jackson's *Irish Pictorial Miscellany* or Patrick X. Keating's *Illustrated Irish Nation* menaced the secure hold of the *Pilot* upon the Irish reading public.[105]

Only the Negroes developed a group consciousness comparable to that of the Irish. Although accepted as equals in some sects,[106] sharp color prejudice compelled colored Methodists and Baptists to organize their own churches in the West End.[107] Discrimination kept them out of the common schools and made

---

[101] Cf. Shea, *op. cit.,* IV, 154; *Boston Catholic Observer,* January 23, 1847, June 21, 1848. The break was not open at first, the *Observer* being printed by P. Donahoe, owner of the *Pilot* (*ibid.,* January 16, 1847).

[102] The *Pilot* was at a tremendous disadvantage, since it could not openly attack the priest who edited the *Observer.* Its criticisms were guarded and apologetic. But its rival had no scruples, attacking it as "avowedly anti-Catholic," "guilty of uttering heresy" cf. *Boston Catholic Observer,* June 7, 14, May 24, and especially June 28, 1848).

[103] Cf. Henry F. Brownson, *Orestes A. Brownson's Middle Life* . . . (Detroit, 1899), 441; Skelton, *op. cit.,* 162 ff.; *Boston Pilot,* January 1, 1848, January 4, 1851.

[104] Cf. Sadlier, *loc. cit.,* 22, 23, 27–30; Skelton, *op. cit.,* 163 ff., 183 ff., 194 ff., 199, 281 ff.; *Irish-American,* August 12, 1849, May 30, 1857.

[105] Cf. *Citizen* (New York), January 7, 1854; *Boston Pilot,* March 24, 1855, April 24, March 27, 1858, April 2, 1859; *European,* December 6, 1856.

[106] Cf., e.g., *Memoir of Mrs. Chloe Spear, a Native of Africa . . . by a Lady of Boston* (Boston, 1832), 41, 49, 71 ff.

[107] John Hayward, *Gazetteer of Massachusetts* . . . (Boston, 1849), 88, 90, 97; *Massachusetts House Documents, 1840,* no. 60, p. 22; Winsor, *op. cit.,* III, 424, 425, 441; *Bowen's Picture of Boston* . . . (Boston, 1829), 149, 151, 152; *Boston Directory, 1830,* 31; W. H. Siebert, *Underground Railroad from Slavery to Freedom* (New York, 1898), facing 235.

necessary the organization of a distinct system with the aid of the town and of the Abiel Smith legacy.[108] The refusal of the white Masons to admit Negroes caused the formation of autonomous lodges affiliated not with other Massachusetts lodges, but with the Grand Lodge of England.[109] Similar motives provoked the attempt to organize a Negro military company, while the struggle for equality for themselves and for freedom for their enslaved kinsmen fostered Russworm's *Freedom's Journal* and the New York *Colored American,* and the organization of vigilantes that helped save Shadrach and attempted to rescue Burns.[110] But Negro awareness of race derived not from differences they desired to cherish, but rather from a single difference—color—which they desired to discard. Thus, as soon as a change in law in 1855 admitted Negroes to the common schools, their own closed.[111] Their consciousness was a factor of the prejudice of others, and declined as that subsided. They lacked the cohesiveness and coherence generated in the Irish by their economic, physical, and intellectual development in Boston.

The flourishing growth of Irish institutions was an accurate reflection of their consciousness of group identity. These autonomous activities had no counterpart in the Old World where the community was a unified whole, adequately satisfying all the social desires of its members. Independent societies developed among immigrants only in Boston in response to the inadequacy of the city as it was to fill their needs. Since the non-Irish foreigners felt differences only at occasional particular points, they diverged from native social organizations infrequently, in localized activities of diminishing vitality. But the development of the Irish had broadened original differences so widely that the *Pilot* concluded, "cooperation for any length of time in important matters between *true* Catholics and *real* Protestants is morally impossible."[112] Unable to participate in the normal associational affairs of the community, the Irish felt obliged to erect a society within a society, to act together in their own way. In every contact therefore the group, acting apart from other sections of the community, became intensely aware of its peculiar and exclusive identity.

The degree of intermarriage at once reflected and buttressed the distinction between the Irish and all others. Among the Irish, religious and social considerations reënforced the natural tendency to mate with their own kind. As Catholics, they were repeatedly warned that union with Protestants was

[108] Cf. Dissertation Copy, 333 ff.; George W. Crawford, *Prince Hall and His Followers* . . . (New York, n.d. [1914]), 13 ff.; *Minutes of the Selectmen's Meetings . . . 1818 . . . 1822 (Volume of Records Relating to the Early History of Boston,* XXXIX), *Boston City Documents, 1909,* no. 61, p. 192; *African Repository and Colonial Journal,* May 1830, VI, 89; *ibid.,* November, 1827, III, 271; Helen T. Catterall, *Judicial Cases Concerning American Slavery and the Negro* . . . (Washington, 1936), IV, 512 ff.
[109] Lewis Hayden, *Grand Lodge Jurisdictional Claim* . . . (Boston, 1868), 30 ff., 84; Charles H. Wesley, *Richard Allen* . . . (Washington, n.d. [1935]), 93; *Boston Almanac,* 1866, 166, 167.
[110] Cf. *Boston Pilot,* September 8, 1855, June 12, 1852, October 5, 1850, February 22, 1851; Catterall, *op. cit.,* IV, 502 ff.; *Colored American* (New York), January 7, 1837 ff.; Vernon Loggins, *Negro Author* . . . (New York, 1931), 53 ff.; William S. Robinson, *"Warrington" Pen-Portraits* . . . 1848 to 1876 . . . (Boston, 1877), 71 ff., 191; Siebert, *Underground Railroad,* 72, 251.
[111] "Report of the State Board of Education," *Massachusetts Public Documents, 1860,* no. 2, p. 134; *Boston Pilot,* September 15, 1855.
[112] *Boston Pilot,* July 29, 1854.

tantamount to loss of faith; while the great majority of non-Irish in the city considered marriage with them degrading.[113] As a result, the percentage of Irish intermarriage was lower than that of any other group including the Negroes, 12 per cent of whose marriages were with whites.[114]

Group consciousness in the newcomers provoked a secondary reaction in native Bostonians, almost nonexistent in the eighteenth and early nineteenth centuries, when French Huguenots, Jews, Scots, Scotch-Irish and Irishmen had had no difficulty in assimilating with the older stock.[115] Americans now became more conscious of their own identity. They began to distinguish themselves, the Anglo-Saxons, from the Irish "Kelts."[116] The old society felt a sense of *malaise* because newcomers did not fit into its categories, and resentment, because they threatened its stability. Uneasy, it attempted to avoid contact by withdrawing ever farther into a solid, coherent, and circumscribed group of its own, until in the fifties it evolved the true Brahmin who believed, with Holmes, that a man of family required "four or five generations of gentlemen and gentlewomen" behind him.[117]

[113] Cf., e.g., *Courrier des États-Unis,* May 15, 1851; Edward Dicey, *Six Months in the Federal States* (London, 1863), II, 179.

[114] "Annual Report by the City Registrar . . . 1865," *Boston City Documents, 1866,* no. 88, p. 15; *Der Pionier,* January 26, 1860. Table XXVII gives figures of intermarriages in 1863–65 when the degree of assimilation should have been at its height. Only German women married more closely into their own group than the Irish, and that because they were so far outnumbered by German men. However, German male intermarriages more than counterbalanced this.

[115] Cf., e.g., Winsor, *op. cit.,* II, 553 ff.; Wittke, *op. cit.,* 24 ff.; Cullen, *op. cit.,* 194, 195.

[116] Cf., e.g., "The Anglo-Saxon Race," *North American Review,* July, 1851, LXXIII, 53, 34 ff.; and Emerson's use of the term in "English Traits," *Collected Works* (Boston, 1903), V.

[117] Cf. M. A. DeWolfe Howe, *Holmes of the Breakfast Table* (New York, 1939), 7, 12.

Chinese

RODMAN W. PAUL

The Origin of the Chinese Issue in California

The yellow man presented perplexing problems to a Caucasian society. Most white Protestant immigrants disappeared as distinctive groups but American racist assumptions inhibited the acceptance of Orientals.

The Chinese, who entered California after the Gold Rush of the late 1840s, established settlements in San Francisco and the mining camps of northern California. Grudgingly accepted because they would perform the menial labor that Caucasians shunned, they were accused of having a strange-tongued babble and foul body odors. Typical of many new minorities, the Chinese also fell victim to the laborers' cries of "unfair competition" because they worked for wages that native- or European-born Americans spurned.

In the article below Rodman Paul discusses the origins of the antagonism toward the Chinese which resulted in the passage of the Exclusion Act in 1882. Although this federal law ostensibly barred Chinese immigration for a ten-year period only, it proved the first step in excluding Orientals from American shores. The restrictionist policy prevailed until the Immigration Act of 1965 ended the national origins stipulations concerning those allowed entry to the United States.

In February, 1848, the territory of California received its first Asiatic immigrants when the brig "Eagle" brought from Hong Kong two Chinese men and one woman.[1] The region to which these three pioneers came had witnessed the discovery of gold less than a month before. The stampede to the diggings had already begun. From every quarter of the globe there converged on California a horde too numerous, too polyglot, and too intent on the search for gold to make possible an advance in the maintenance of law and order consistent with the advance in population. Of the many tendencies to disorder displayed by

Reprinted by permission of the Organization of American Historians from the *Mississippi Valley Historical Review,* XXV (1938), 181–96.
[1] San Francisco *Daily Alta California,* May 10, 1852; Harris Newmark, *Sixty Years in Southern California* (Boston, 1930), 123.

this heterogeneous aggregation of expectant millionaires, two were of outstanding importance. One was the general sense of irresponsibility prevalent among the footloose, adventurous frontier population; the other "a diseased local exaggeration of our common national feeling towards foreigners, an exaggeration for which the circumstances of the moment were partly responsible."[2]

The "circumstances of the moment" consisted in the presence in California of an unusually large number of foreign-born newcomers, together with the several variations of Indian and Spanish races which had been established on the Pacific Coast prior to the advent of American settlement. This condition aroused in many Californians of American and North European stock speculation regarding the desirability of permitting so large a proportion of the population to be of "un-American" races.

In dramatic form this hostility toward "foreigners" first expressed itself through the mob action of the "American" miners against the Spanish-American and Latin races.[3] Here much of the agitation probably had its origin in the selfish but natural desire to restrict the number and type of persons benefiting from the mines. Parallel with this motive, however, went a deep and genuine concern for the state's future. Thoughtful Californians who decried the miners' outbreaks nevertheless realized fully the significance of the immigration question. As the San Francisco *Daily Alta California* remarked:

> The character of the immigration daily pouring on to our shores is a subject in which every good citizen feels a deep and intense interest. To those who are permanently settled here, and who have families, the moral worth of foreign arrivals commands more attention than a passing thought. The prosperity of our State, the peace and comfort of our citizens, and the happiness of society generally, are in a great measure affected by those who come from foreign climes to seek their fortunes in this country.[4]

In more sensational terms the California legislature, in its initial session, was warned: "The wonderful gold discovery . . . has excited [abroad] the wildest cupidity, which threatens California with an emigration overwhelming in number and dangerous in character . . . a vast multitude *en route* and preparing to come hither, of the worst population [of Latin America and convict Australia] who seek and possess themselves of the best places for gold digging, whether upon their own or on account of foreign employers, and carry from our country immense treasure."[5]

This alarmist picture was fairly typical of Californian thought and agitation regarding foreign immigrants in general. From it the transition to a definite hostility towards one specific race, the Chinese, was natural and perhaps in-

[2] Josiah Royce, *California from the Conquest in 1846 to the Second Vigilance Committee in San Francisco* (Boston, 1886), 275.

[3] It has been suggested that hatred engendered by the Mexican War was an important contributory cause for the outbursts against Spanish-Americans. Theodore H. Hittell, *History of California* (San Francisco, 1897), III, 263.

[4] *Daily Alta California*, March 5, 1852.

[5] Thomas J. Green, "Report on Mines and Foreign Miners," *California Senate Journal*, 1 Sess., March 15, 1850, *Appendix S*, 493.

evitable. By the spring of 1852 the Chinese had entered the state ii
bers. S. E. Woodworth, their agent and legal representative, claime
11,787 were in California by May 7, 1852,[6] but the state census of 18
basis of incomplete returns, estimated the number at 25,000.[7] Anoι
fornia authority, cited by the superintendent of the United States cer.
that 17,000 was a more reasonable number.[8] The leading secondary work
subject gives a "corrected figure" of approximately 25,000 in 1852.[9]

At this same time California possessed a total population reckoned at
264,435 by the state census but at 255,122 by the superintendent of the United
States census.[10] Thus the Chinese formed somewhat less than one-tenth of the
population at the time when their presence excited unfavorable comment.

Had this tenth been scattered over the entire state, it would hardly have
occasioned serious notice as early as 1852. The Chinese, however, had concentrated in the mining counties in the northern half of California, and in the
city of San Francisco, the port through which they entered the western world.
For example, if the state census may be taken as at least approximating the
truth, Nevada County reported a population of 3,886 Chinese out of a total
population of 21,365, Placer County 3,019 out of a total of 10,784, and Yuba
County 2,100 out of 22,005.[11]

At a time when Los Angeles was yet to receive its first Chinese resident,[12]
the San Franciscans were persistently being made aware of the Asiatics in their
midst. Thus, according to the *Daily Alta California,* in one day two ships from
Hong Kong "brought an addition of five hundred and twenty-five to our already
large Chinese population."[13] A month later, the same journal reported: "So
great has been the influx of Celestials into this city that they have been unable
to stow themselves away in houses, and accordingly have pitched their tents in
Sacramento Street."[14]

Not only by their color, but also by their dress, customs, language, and
clannishness, these Chinese tended to set themselves apart from the general
population.[15] When an educated, English-speaking Chinese was discovered in
San Francisco, the *Daily Alta* considered it a rare enough event to warrant a

[6] *Daily Alta California,* May 10, 1852. He admitted that surreptitious entries
might swell the total to 12,000.
[7] Governor's Message; and Report of the Secretary of State on the Census of
1852 of the State of California, *California Senate Journal,* 4 Sess., January 26, 1853,
no. 14, p. 7.
[8] As cited in James D. B. DeBow, *Statistical View of the United States . . .
being a Compendium of the Seventh Census . . .* (Washington, 1854), 122–123.
[9] Mary R. Coolidge, *Chinese Immigration* (New York, 1909), 498.
[10] Governor's Message; and Report of the Secretary of State, *California Senate
Journal,* no. 14, p. 5; DeBow, *Seventh Census,* 394. DeBow's figure was obtained by
reworking the same statistics used by the California census statistician—a sufficient reflection on the accuracy of the State Census of 1852.
[11] Governor's Message; and Report of the Secretary of State, *California Senate
Journal,* 4 Sess., no. 14, pp. 29–31, 54–55.
[12] Newmark, *Sixty Years,* 123, 657, n. 1
[13] *Daily Alta California,* March 26, 1852.
[14] *Ibid.,* April 26, 1852; reprinted *in toto,* April 27.
[15] Hubert H. Bancroft, *History of California,* VII, *1860–90,* in *The Works of
Hubert Howe Bancroft* (San Francisco, 1890), XXIV, 336; John S. Hittell, *The Resources of California* (San Francisco, 1874), 42. Hittell says that after five or six
years in California, most of the Chinese still could not speak "the most common
English words."

news story.[16] So little was actually known about the speech and customs of the Oriental newcomers that one early writer asserted with complete finality that they bore "a striking resemblance" to the American Indians, "and are known to be able to converse with them, in their respective languages."[17]

To the foreign traveler who viewed San Francisco for the first time in 1851, the crowds of Chinese formed one of the city's most striking features. Their huge basket hats, their flopping clothes and over-size boots, and the jumble of ill-assorted equipment which they carried on bamboo poles were only less noticeable than the eternal "gabbling and chattering" of "their horrid jargon," which produced "a noise like that of a flock of geese."[18] Already a distinct Chinese quarter had arisen, characterized by its stores with their unintelligible signs, an Oriental theater, and "a peculiarly nasty smell" popularly ascribed to the use of rats as table fare.[19] So typical of frontier California had the Chinese become that Chinese shawls and trinkets were considered as essential a souvenir for the departing traveler as a revolver and bowie-knife.[20] The Asiatics' "pagan" religion added an additional distinguishing factor.[21]

Beyond all these social differentiations the Chinese established for themselves a peculiar economic position "by their industry, frugality, and strict attention to business,"[22] quite as much as by their less admired willingness to work at unusually low wages. By exercising these talents in the field of personal service, they had by the opening of the year 1852 gained control first of the restaurant business in San Francisco, and then of the laundry industry throughout the northern part of the state.[23] This brought down upon them the anger of whites who attacked "in terms of great bitterness their elliptical-eyed, long-tailed rivals in business."[24]

In the mining regions they created for themselves an even stronger hostility by their ability to take up supposedly worthless mining claims and make them pay by long hours of toil too hard and unpleasant for the average white man's liking.[25] Very early the white miners' enmity towards them became sufficiently organized to produce a series of district and county enactments forbidding them to work in the mines or own claims.[26] In fact, the only department of life where the Chinese seem not to have made themselves conspicuous was in the courts. It was usually agreed that "they have generally been a peaceable and orderly class of the community."[27]

Only an overt act was lacking to raise to a statewide issue the latent hostility to the Chinese revealed in the local opposition of the launderers and miners. Such an "overt act" was provided on March 6, 1852, when Senator George B. Tingley introduced into the state legislature a bill to legalize and

[16] *Daily Alta California*, April 24, 1852.
[17] Titus F. Cronise, *The Natural Wealth of California* (San Francisco, 1868), 31.
[18] J. D. Borthwick, *Three Years in California* (Edinburgh, 1857), 51.
[19] *Ibid.*, 75.
[20] *Ibid.*, 79.
[21] *Daily Alta California*, March 28, 1852.
[22] *Ibid.*, February 17, 1852.
[23] *Ibid.*
[24] *Ibid.*, March 8, 1852.
[25] Hittell, *History of California*, III, 264.
[26] *Ibid.* Note, however, that as late as 1850 the Chinese in San Francisco were treated as a valued and desirable curiosity. *Ibid.*, IV, 98–99.
[27] *Daily Alta California*, February 17, 1852; see also *ibid.*, March 26, 1852.

make possible the enforcement of contracts by which Chinese laborers could sell their services to employers for periods of ten years or less at fixed wages.[28] In an editorial inspired by this bill, the *Daily Alta* stated that Chinese contract labor had been tried in California from the beginning of Chinese immigration, but had always failed, sometimes at heavy loss to the contract holders, because of "the ease with which all labor contracts could be set aside [in California], the temptation of the mines, and the impossibility of coercion."[29]

The Tingley bill, as the *Daily Alta* indicated, was designed to meet California's great need for low-priced labor. With the mines offering every man a chance to be his own employer and become a potential millionaire, it was exceedingly difficult to induce workingmen to stay in regular employment.[30] Where labor could be secured, it demanded and received as much as five dollars a day outside the mining regions,[31] and wages for workers in the mines themselves were running as high as six dollars on the very day Tingley introduced his bill.[32]

As the *Daily Alta* remarked, in a subsequent editorial, in the past labor in California had held the whip hand over capital, and thereby had undoubtedly discouraged prospective investment. But, the *Alta* cautioned, immigration during the current year was soaring towards a record high figure, which would greatly help to make possible a proper balance between the supply of labor and the demands of capital. For this reason the editorial concluded in measured tones:

> To be frank, we have not much faith in the system [of contract labor]. It undoubtedly has its advantages, and would work exceedingly well for a brief period; but we conceive that its permanent results are not of that estimable character which should highly recommend it as a true system for a country like ours.[33]

This stand was distinctly more moderate than the view which the general populace took of the proposed measure. While Tingley's bill was just emerging from the committee stage in the senate, a similar measure actually passed the assembly. This bill provided for a complete system of contract labor, according to which a Chinese or Pacific Islander could sign away his services for not more than five years—one-half the duration of Tingley's measure—with the California courts serving as umpire and supervisor of the execution of the contract.[34]

The effect on California public opinion proved electric. Immediately on learning of the passage of the bill, the citizens of Sacramento condemned the bill at an indignation meeting in decidedly strong language.[35] "The news-

[28] *California Senate Journal*, 3 Sess., 168.
[29] *Daily Alta California*, March 8, 1852.
[30] Katherine Coman, *Economic Beginnings of the Far West* (New York, 1925), II, 257–260, 269–270.
[31] *Ibid.*, 269–270; Borthwick, *Three Years*, 65–66.
[32] *Daily Alta California*, March 6, 1852.
[33] *Ibid.*, March 10, 1852.
[34] Complete text printed in *Daily Alta California*, March 21, 1852; as an interesting reflection on the slavery issue, Section 1 included: "Provided, that no contract made with any free negro, shall be of binding force."
[35] *Daily Alta California*, March 21, 1852.

papers, too, who have so long been silent as to the doings of the legislature, have finally opened in full cry against this contract labor law," declared the editor of one California paper, "They have now all at once, with a most liberal display of patriotism, made a tremendous onslaught upon this contract law."[36]

The strength and violence of the opposition surprised many, among them this same editor of the *Daily Alta,* who had anticipated popular indifference.[37] Despite his prediction, the editor was forced to admit: "If the expressions of opinion which have been made in different portions of the state be an index to the public sentiment, there can be no doubt that the contract law is generally condemned."[38]

Adding fuel to the now rapidly burning flame was a vigorous minority report submitted in the assembly in opposition to the bill by Philip A. Roach. Roach declared free labor to be the basis of California society and the chief hope for its future. For the first time in any public document, he expounded the doctrine of unfair economic competition with white labor by Orientals possessing an abnormally low standard of living. "We are called upon," he declared, "to enact a law by which the surplus and inferior population of Asia may be brought into competition with the labor of our own people."[39]

To find this doctrine in Roach's report is the more interesting since in that same document he labelled the foreign miners' tax of 1850 "a concession to public clamor,"[40] and freely recognized the need for cheap labor in certain enterprises that demanded more man-power than frontier California could supply.[41] Provided that they be excluded from citizenship, he said, he had "no objection" to the utilization of Chinese contract laborers in such noncompetitive but valuable fields as draining the swamp lands, in order to make possible the cultivation of rice, tea, sugar, cotton, and similar commodities.[42]

In the compromise nature of this attack on Oriental labor, Roach showed clearly that his was the pioneer, or transitional, declaration against the Asiatic. His report and the widespread public outcry against the measure had the desired effect on the senate, with which the issue had thus been deposited. On April 12 a motion to postpone the bill indefinitely was accepted by a vote of 18 to 2, Tingley and one other senator alone standing by it.[43] On the same day Senator Paul K. Hubbs introduced a bill "to prevent coolie labor in the mines, and to prevent involuntary servitude."[44]

In this manner, just four years after the entrance into California of the first Chinese, the Oriental issue had come to a head, had received its initial test, and had gone down in defeat before the first widespread anti-Orientalism to manifest itself in California. It should be remembered, of course, that the particular spark which set off this first blaze was the question of Chinese as con-

[36] *Ibid.*
[37] *Ibid.,* March 10, 1852.
[38] *Ibid.,* March 21, 1852.
[39] Minority Report of Select Committee on Senate Bill No. 63, *California Assembly Journal,* 3 Sess., March 20, 1852, *Appendix,* 669–670.
[40] *Ibid.,* 670–671.
[41] *Ibid.,* 672–673.
[42] *Ibid.;* note that Roach's report also speaks of the dangers of inter-racial breeding and the threat to American institutions inherent in this "pagan" race.
[43] *California Senate Journal,* 3 Sess., 305–307.
[44] *Ibid.,* 303.

tract laborers, and not the wider question of Chinese as immigrants. But as the latter part of Roach's report showed, this distinction was not sharply maintained even during this opening phase of the dispute, and in the later history of the problem there was a general tendency to use the terms "Chinese" and "serf labor" as synonyms.

Four days after the shelving of the assembly measure by the senate, the assembly itself joined the opposition to Orientals, when the seven members of the Committee on Mines and Mining Interests presented a report which blended dislike of the Chinese as a race with opposition to them as "serf" labor, and mixed the whole with similar remarks regarding Mexicans, South Americans, and Pacific Islanders. Prophetically the committee declared concerning the Chinese:

> The time is not far distant when absolute prohibition of entry will be necessary for our own protection. . . . We respectfully recommend that the attention of Congress shall be called to this subject, and that we forward to our own Representatives instructions to seek a remedy at the hands of the Federal Government by proper treaty provisions . . . determining here at home to exercise the right of our State sovereignty, and protect ourselves should necessity demand.[45]

Thus early did talk of outright exclusion of Orientals appear on the California scene. Up to this time, however, the dispute had lacked an effective mouthpiece. No one had yet seized upon the problem and developed its latent possibilities up to the rank of a first-class political issue. To this task Governor John Bigler devoted himself, some ten days after the defeat of the Tingley bill. Bigler is one of those unfortunate figures who have received severe treatment at the hands of every historian who has discussed them. John S. Hittell called him "a man who had neither the capacity, nor the education, nor the manners to grace the position . . . a good fellow with the multitude . . . unscrupulous."[46] Royce named him "a popular and unprincipled politician."[47]

If this be his character, then there would seem to be some reason for speculation regarding the motives that produced the message which he delivered to the legislature on April 23. The governor declared himself to be "deeply impressed" with the need for taking measures "to check this tide of Asiatic immigration, and to prevent the exportation by them of the precious metals which they dig up from our soil without charge, and without assuming any of the obligations imposed upon citizens."[48] He further opposed the Chinese as being mere transient partakers of California's bounty, as possessing questionable morality, and as endangering "the public tranquility."[49] He said nothing regarding assimilability, a contention which later was to be so important a point in the debates over the issue.

[45] Report of Committee on Mines and Mining Interests, *California Assembly Journal*, April 16, 1852, *Appendix*, 831.
[46] John S. Hittell, *A History of San Francisco and Incidentally of the State of California* (San Francisco, 1878), 280–281.
[47] Royce, *California*, 494; *cf.* Theodore H. Hittell, *History of California*, IV, 180.
[49] *Ibid.*, 373–376.
[48] *California Senate Journal*, 3 Sess., 373.

At the time that he made public this message Bigler was a candidate for re-election in the state campaign of 1852. His sudden attack on the Chinese, when viewed in the light of his political career, bears a suspicious resemblance to an attempt to curry favor with the numerically large anti-foreign element among the miners and dissatisfied population of the city. It has been so interpreted by the chief student of the problem.[50] If this is the case, then Bigler deserves the distinction of being the first politician to utilize the issue for his own ends.

In analyzing the effect of Bigler's pronouncement, Mrs. Coolidge has expressed the belief that it "failed to carry public opinion."[51] Yet she has also admitted that "the organized antagonism might have been long postponed"[52] but for Bigler's action. In reaching her first conclusion Mrs. Coolidge has apparently been influenced by the undoubted fact that thinking society in California reacted against Bigler. The reaction found its most notable expression in a series of famous lectures in favor of the Chinese, delivered by the Reverend William Speer, a former missionary to China. These talks stressed California's needs for Orientals as cheap laborers, servants, and miners, and enunciated America's duty to enlighten the heathen.[53] While not disputing the appeal which such arguments would have for the wealthier class, it is difficult to see how the first point could have anything but an unfavorable reception among the laboring and independent mining classes.

Consequently it is necessary to look somewhat further afield. It must be admitted at the start that although Governor Bigler was re-elected, no tenable evidence has survived to show whether or not his immigration stand influenced his victory. On the other hand, the *Daily Alta* felt that Bigler's declaration was symptomatic of a growing sensitiveness by the public to the character of the immigration that was coming to its shores.[54] A week later it reported "a lively interest among our citizens on the subject of Asiatic immigration."[55] According to the *Alta,* the Chinese had been flowing into California in increasing numbers since about the time of the Tingley bill's defeat. So large was this immigration becoming that even a number of men who had supported the contract labor law took alarm and began to agree that some restrictive action might become necessary.[56] In short, there was "an evident strong desire that Chinese laborers" should "not be permitted to come into the country."[57]

For public opinion to develop in this direction does not seem unreasonable. Governor Bigler had given as his excuse for addressing the legislature the reported arrival from China of the ship, "Challenge," with from seven to eight hundred immigrants aboard.[58] As a matter of fact, this was only half the story. Within forty-eight hours of the "Challenge," the "Osceola" arrived with a sufficient contingent to bring the total of incoming Orientals up to 1,019 for two

[50] Coolidge, *Chinese Immigration,* 55–56.
[51] *Ibid.,* 56.
[52] *Ibid.,* 55.
[53] William Speer, *China and California* (pamphlet, San Francisco, 1853), 12–23.
[54] *Daily Alta California,* April 26, 1852.
[55] *Ibid.,* May 4, 1852.
[56] *Ibid.*
[57] *Ibid.*
[58] *California Senate Journal,* 3 Sess., 375.

days alone.[59] Woodworth, the agent for the Chinese, admitted that between January 1 and May 7, 1852, at least 4,434 had arrived, and he estimated that the number for the year 1852 might reach 10,000—a figure less than 200 short of Woodworth's total for the entire number of Asiatic arrivals prior to this time.[60] The California Senate Committee of 1876 later quoted the *Journal of Commerce* to the effect that 20,025 Chinese entered and only 1,768 departed in 1852.[61]

In view of this sudden increase, coming as it did in conjunction with the contract labor dispute and Bigler's declaration, it would be unnatural not to find added antagonism and interest in the subject. The question thus turns to considering how much of this was due to Bigler and how much to the other factors. No final answer can be given, but there is one interesting indication. According to evidence collected in 1853 by the Committee on Mines and Mining Interests of the assembly from the records and agents of the Chinese companies, the numbers of their race had reached the record point of 25,000 sometime in 1852, but had by the time of the investigation fallen back to 21,000 or 22,000. The cause for the decline was said by the Chinese to be Bigler's message, which had aroused such popular hostility to those Orientals already in America that the Chinese merchants of San Francisco had thought it wise to warn their fellow-countrymen at home not to migrate at such an unpropitious time.[62]

The agitation to which the merchants referred was evinced chiefly in the mining districts. It broke out in the spring of 1852, so soon after the contract labor dispute and the governor's message that there is every reason to assign to these legislative and political manoeuverings the immediate inspiration. The more remote bases, of course, lay in the mining camps' four years of general anti-foreign disturbances. There had not, however, been a wide-spread movement specifically against the Chinese until shortly before the first of May, 1852. Beginning with that date, reports were received of a series of mass meetings held by the miners in all parts of the state.[63] The action usually taken by these meetings was to adopt resolutions forbidding Asiatics to work in the mines of that particular locality. Generally a committee was chosen to see that the resolutions were carried out.

A typical example was the action taken at Columbia, in Tuolumne County, on May 8. Here the resolutions showed clearly what had instigated the trouble, for the preamble opened with the charge that, despite its defeat in the Senate, the spirit and aims of the Tingley bill lived on. To avoid a "system of peonage on our social organization" action was necessary, the resolutions asserted.[64] The problem lay in deciding how to act, and the solution adopted fully accorded with the traditions of the American frontier. The meeting dismissed both Congress and the California legislature as incapable of "any efficient action" suf-

[59] *Daily Alta California*, April 24, 1852.
[60] *Ibid.*, May 10, 1852.
[61] Senate Committee of the State of California, *Chinese Immigration* (Sacramento, 1876), 171.
[62] Majority and Minority Reports of Committee on Mines and Mining Interests, *California Assembly Journal*, 4 Sess., no. 28, pp. 7–8.
[63] *Daily Alta California*, May 1, 12, 14, 15, 16, 21, 22, 26, 1852.
[64] *Ibid.*, May 15, 1852.

ficient to meet the need. Instead, it went on record, *"Resolved,* That it is the duty of the miners to take the matter into their own hands."[65] Thereupon it was voted to exclude all Asiatics from the mines and to appoint a Vigilance Committee of twenty to enforce the decision as an integral part of the mining codes.[66]

Similar action was taken at many places in both the northern and southern areas.[67] Usually the scene was a small boom camp like the appropriately named Rough and Ready, in Nevada County, or Wood's Creek, in Tuolumne County, or Foster's Bar, or the Yuba River camp.[68]

The movement seems to have been confined to the mining areas despite the presence in San Francisco of a considerable crew of loafers and hangers-on from whom trouble might well have been expected.[69] It was opposed by such newspapers as the *Daily Alta*[70] and the Shasta *Courier*[71] and by a flood of anonymous letters written to many different journals.[72] These letters usually claimed to be the work of Chinese, but the literary style indicates their authorship to have come from that class of the more well-to-do who had reacted against Bigler's message. As far as the miners were concerned, "these appear to have little effect," as the editor of the *Alta* regretfully concluded.[73] The nature of this opposition to anti-Oriental agitation was realized by the miners themselves. In the Columbia resolutions it was claimed that "certain ship owners, capitalists and merchants" were the ones who were encouraging Asiatic immigration, and that they did so for the selfish purpose of developing the value of their own investments.[74]

Reasons of commerce and trade do indeed seem to have formed the chief ground for supporting the Chinese at this time. Questions of fairness and abstract right were of course an important factor, but material advantage seems to have been a greater determinant. Thus the assembly Committee on Mines and Mining Interests in March, 1853, reversing its extreme stand of a year earlier (April 16, 1852), declared it would be better to encourage rather than discourage the coming of the Orientals. The stated reason for so doing was that the exclusionist talk of the previous year had produced a serious decline in trade with China.[75]

Two years later, when the miners of Shasta County presented a petition asking action to get rid of the Chinese, the committee to which it was referred returned several separate reports. The two minority, or dissenting, ones argued chiefly from economic considerations. Wilson Flint felt that the Chinese could be used to great profit by capitalists in developing the state's latent natural

[65] *Ibid.*
[66] *Ibid.*
[67] *Ibid.,* May 16, 1852.
[68] *Ibid.,* May 14, 21, 22, 26, 1852.
[69] *Ibid.,* May 19, 1852.
[70] Editorial, *ibid.,* May 15, 1852.
[71] Editorial as quoted in *ibid.,* May 26, 1852.
[72] *Ibid.,* May 16, 1852.
[73] *Ibid.*
[74] *Ibid.,* May 15, 1852.
[75] Majority and Minority Reports of Committee on Mines and Mining Interests, *California Assembly Journal,* March 9, 1853, no. 28, pp. 5–6.

resources.[76] The two dissentients who jointly handed in the other document were willing to restrict future Chinese immigration, but felt that at the moment it would be financial suicide to push the matter too far, since both the state and county treasuries relied heavily on the proceeds of the foreign miners' licenses purchased by the Chinese.[77]

Similarly, when the first incumbent of the office of Commissioner of Immigrants refused to enforce a special law against Orientals, and was summarily dismissed for so doing, it was a group of seventy-six San Francisco merchants and importers who upheld his action in 1856. They claimed that the state's revenue would benefit from a population increase of any sort and that their interests required "an unrestricted China trade."[78] To this train of thought the Committee on Mines and Mining Interests tartly replied, on another occasion, "The commercial classes, however, are but too apt to place too high an estimate upon their relative importance."[79]

The law which caused this dispute was the one attempt by the state of California in this early period to restrict Chinese immigration by some means other than foreign miners' taxes. Approved by Governor Bigler on April 30, 1855, it set a head tax of fifty dollars for the importation of all persons "who cannot become citizens."[80] This is the first instance of the use of a descriptive device that was to prove very popular in the next seventy years. For the moment it came to nought, since the California Supreme Court declared it unconstitutional.[81]

In the passage of this law, the elements opposed to the Chinese had been greatly aided by the hard times which struck the Pacific Coast in 1854. Declining yields from a number of the mining areas sent into San Francisco many of the miners who had been instrumental in securing the local anti-Asiatic resolutions of 1852. In the city this group became affiliated with the western equivalent of the Know Nothing movement, and under the urging of demagogues, who were often themselves immigrants, became so restless and lawless that the Vigilance Committee of 1856 was necessitated. The Chinese were a favorite object of persecution, the more so since many of them still had jobs at a time when large numbers of white men were unemployed. Their attacks on the Chinese found that race peculiarly defenceless, since in 1854 the California Supreme Court had declared inadmissible in court the testimony of "Mongolians" against white persons.

Shortly, however, the work of the Vigilance Committees, the rise of the absorbing issues leading to the Civil War, and the discovery of such new mines

[76] Wilson Flint, "Report from the Select Committee to Whom was Referred the Resolutions of the Miners' Convention at Shasta County," *California Senate Journal,* 6 Sess., March 28, 1855, *Appendix.*
[77] Minority Report of Select Committee on Resolutions of the Miners' Convention of Shasta County, *California Senate Journal,* 6 Sess., March 17, 1855, no. 16.
[78] Report of Committee on Mines and Mining Interests on the Memorial of Citizens of San Francisco, *California Assembly Journal,* 7 Sess., *Appendix.*
[79] Report of Committee on Mines and Mining Interests, *California Assembly Journal,* 7 Sess., *Appendix.* N.B.: This is a different report from the one referred to in the previous footnote; neither bears any series notation.
[80] *California Journal of the Legislature,* 6 Sess., 704, 722–723, 755, 772, 779, 786.
[81] Hittell, *History of California,* IV, 167–168.

as the Comstock Lode drained away, for the moment, the worst of this intensified agitation, and provided a slight surcease until the close of the Civil War.[82]

If one surveys this period in review, it is apparent that by the middle fifties the Chinese had passed into the status of a special race that would always receive public and political attention of a particular sort. In the half dozen years since their arrival in California, they had drawn upon themselves political debates and attacks, and had been the cause of a state-wide popular agitation among the mining class. To their support they had attracted chiefly the missionary, mercantile, and propertied groups. In these first few years not only the type but also the arguments of nearly all subsequent opposition to Orientals had their origin. Factors of labor, agriculture, and prices were to provide important new subsequent developments to the issue, especially after the opening of the transcontinental railroad. In general, however, it can be said that the main lines which the Oriental race problem was to follow during the seventy-five years of its active history in America were all laid down in the period which saw the issue originate.

[82] *Ibid.,* 111–229 *passim.;* Hittell, *History of San Francisco,* 215–217, 283–297, 329; Coolidge, *Chinese Immigration,* 58–62.

The Industrial Transformation

Between the end of the Civil War and the Second World War more than twenty million Europeans migrated to the United States. The bulk of these people came from Italy, the Balkans, and eastern Europe between the 1880s and the 1920s. Together with the Chinese and Japanese and the Indians and blacks, they constituted the largest ethnic minorities of this period. The European and Oriental immigrants repeated the experience of earlier newcomers. They toiled in unremunerative, blue-collar occupations for one, two, and sometimes three generations, before moving into the mainstream of middle-class America. The Indians during this era became wards of the American government, confined to a barren existence on isolated reservations. For the blacks, the Civil War meant the end of slavery but after a few false starts and weak efforts during Reconstruction, the federal government abandoned them and the erstwhile slaves found themselves with little or no hope for future progress.

For several decades after the Civil War the bulk of immigrants continued to come from northern and western Europe. But the industrial and agricultural revolution in Europe, which earlier had dislocated millions of Germans, Irish, English, and Scandinavians, moved eastward and southward in the second half of the nineteenth century. East Germany, Italy, the Balkans, and the Austro-Hungarian and Russian empires began to feel the impact of competition from American grain and British manufacturing as advances in rail and sea transport opened markets to the east. Improved transit also enabled dispossessed peasants, victims of agricultural modernization and consolidation, and displaced laborers and artisans, rendered superfluous by industrialization, to seek new lives elsewhere. Millions left for the United States.

The appearance of the new immigrants in the 1880s and '90s coincided with the growth of social unrest in the United States. Strikes, urban crime and poverty, and the emergence of socialist and anarchist movements alarmed America's white middle class, who attributed these trials of industrialism to the newcomers. The Haymarket Affair in 1886, in which the explosion of a bomb at a Chicago labor rally led to a riot and the killing of three policemen, gave rise to a stereotype of the immigrant as a lawless creature. Labor unions also opposed further entry of foreigners because numerous employers used colonies of Italians and Slovakians as scabs. Finally, respectable reformers associated urban

uthern and eastern European immigrants and municipal
lic bosses.

h the foreign born aroused spawned a variety of anti-
roups. The Order of American Mechanics, the American
the Immigration Restriction League, and some ministers
sced to agitate against further infiltration of foreigners. In
Chinese, contract laborers, imbeciles, epileptics, and
rican shores. Restrictionists gathered momentum in the
ssive era and their efforts culminated in the passage of a
literacy test in 1917 and Quota Acts of 1921 and 1924. The Quota Acts, unlike
most of the barriers erected earlier, were intended not to exclude general categories of undesirables but to establish quotas favoring newcomers from England,
Germany, and Scandinavia. Because the Irish had also come to American shores
in the earlier part of the nineteenth century the formula favored them as well.

Nativistic outbursts during World War I and the 1920s alarmed many
members of the minority groups. The compulsive, ungenerous Americanism
manifested itself in Henry Ford's anti-Semitic Dearborn Independent (Henry
Ford was himself the grandson of an Irish immigrant who left in the famine),
in the resurgence of the Ku Klux Klan, and in the bitter anti-Catholicism of
the presidential campaign of 1928 when Herbert Hoover defeated Al Smith.
On the West Coast white Americans persecuted those of Japanese descent. Segregated into ghettos, precluded by racial heritage from even second- or third-
generation integration, and barred from numerous occupations because of
prejudice, the Japanese-Americans shouldered enormous burdens. Restrictive
legislation in California prohibited them from owning land and in the state of
Washington they could not obtain even a fishing permit. The high point of
hostility toward Japanese-Americans occurred during the Second World War
when people of Japanese descent on the West Coast—both native and foreign
born—were removed from their homes and placed behind barbed-wire detention
camps in inland states like Utah and Arkansas.

Despite indications of vast hostility most of the white minority groups
made significant political, social, and economic progress. The public schools
opened a wide variety of opportunities for enterprising individuals and the mass
amusement industries provided another avenue of escape from poverty and the
ghetto. Intellectuals, journalists, public relations men, actors, and athletes, embarked on professional careers in foreign language newspapers, the immigrant
theater, or local sporting clubs. Some of the better known people who advanced
themselves in this fashion include Walter Winchell, Ed Sullivan, Fanny Brice,
Al Jolson, John McCormack, George M. Cohan, Frank Sinatra, Honus Wagner,
Benny Leonard, and Rocky Graziano. Neighborhood ethnic groups vicariously
shared the recognition received by exploits in the theater or the stadium.

As the minorities grew more experienced in American ways they realized
that vital interests concerning employment, protection, and government benefits
could be secured only by political power. Politics also offered a route to respectability, as well as a source of individual power, to sharp young first- or
second-generation Americans. The Irish, the earliest minority group to settle in
American cities, first cracked the Anglo-Saxon political monopoly. By the Civil

War they controlled Tammany Hall in New York and were politically influential in Boston and Chicago. In antebellum Milwaukee and Cincinnati the Germans infiltrated urban machines. After the war the new immigrants, Slavs and Jews, sought careers in urban politics. Italians were relative latecomers to political power, but once started they achieved notable triumphs in the 1930s and '40s in Rhode Island and in the 1940s they seized Tammany from the Irish.

Minority groups also organized voluntary associations to secure mutual benefits. At first the chief function of these organizations was to guarantee a decent burial for their members but soon they acquired other functions. As these organizations solidified their structures and established financial stability, they extended payment of benefits for injuries, illnesses, and insurance for survivors. A few of these groups flourished so splendidly that large surpluses accumulated and they assisted improvident compatriots who were not members. Orphanages, homes for the aged, and other charitable institutions were erected by the wealthy associations to care for the unfortunate with whom they had once shared tribulations. As the organizations grew in magnitude and wealth, informal arrangements gave way to constitutions, bylaws, elected officials, and incorporated bodies. The essential purpose of these groups, however, was not charity but sociability. Members could relax in warm conviviality with those who came from the old culture and more often than not from the same hometown. Typically those ethnic groups, Germans and Jews, for example, with the greatest resources, the highest rate of mobility, and the most efficient organizations formed the most useful societies.

The leaders of the voluntary associations were also the leaders of the various ethnic groups of which migrant society consisted. Prominence among the more accepted ethnic minorities came to those who had made good in their new environment, such as wealthy businessmen, who could contribute handsomely and who knew how to deal with the outside world. Ethnic elites were also recruited from those who had matured or had been born here. They knew both worlds and could interpret one for the other. Governor Alfred E. Smith of New York and Mayors Anton Cermack (Chicago), James Michael Curley (Boston), Abe Ruef (San Francisco), and Fiorello H. La Guardia (New York) are the best-known leaders of this type.

Substantial access to American society came through upward mobility and growing prosperity. Immigrants and their offspring gradually improved their status, but not all ethnic groups moved up at the same rate. Factors such as type and level of skills, amount of capital and nature of cultural values brought from abroad, region of ultimate settlement, era when migration occurred, reception given the incoming group, and the degree of preparation made by those already here determined how quickly each group would move in American society. The Germans, one of the most welcomed newcomers, possessing artisan and agricultural skills, aided by strong immigrant assistance societies, carrying over greater wealth than most other immigrant groups, found relatively free access to middle-class America. Jews, although considered less desirable, came with urban skills and characteristics. Their vocational and material accomplishments in industrial America were also due to a tightly knit, ambitious family structure, and a plentitude of effective benevolent agencies that enabled them to

*achieve great business and professional success in spite of anti-Semitism in the
United States. The Irish and Italians, poorer than any other contemporary immigrant groups, and less educated and having fewer relevant skills than the
Jews and Germans, progressed much more painfully and slowly in America. In
general only a minority of the first generation were able to take that crucial
small step from worker to individual proprietor of a neighborhood retail store.
Many slipped back into blue-collar employment, but enough had risen to lend
a semblance of reality to immigrant dreams that they or their children would
not always be on the outside looking in. Especially for the second generation
improved education and the growing need for experts and professionals in an
increasingly technological society enabled thousands to move up into more desirable social statuses and functions. Many filled places in the burgeoning cor-
porate and civil service bureaucracies. Even those whose mobility was limited
by chance, poverty, skill, prejudice, personality, or lack of education frequently
improved their situation. Growing national wealth and expansion of unions resulted in better working conditions and larger paychecks. Increased prosperity
enabled them to imitate the life styles of middle-class America and provided
better opportunities for their children, thus giving them a greater share in the
American dream.*

*The American dream turned into a nightmare for those ethnic minorities
barred by bigotry from sharing in the prestige and prosperity that came to other
groups. Indians suffered most from the restrictions and prejudices of the dominant culture. For the last time in the 1880s and 1890s the Indians turned to
fight for their remaining land. Penned into the Plains, the Rockies, and the
Southwest by advancing settlement, the Apaches and the Dakota Sioux violently,
but unsuccessfully, resisted imprisonment in reservations. With their defeat
went the last shred of independent territory held by the red men. The 250,000
Indians remaining, a fraction of their earlier population, finally became wards
of the government. Laws enacted in Washington and politics pursued by the Department of Interior's Indian Bureau destroyed the tribal structure and stripped
future generations of their cultural heritage. Within twenty years of the Dawes
Act (1887) the government had disposed of 60 percent of Indian land, three-
quarters to white buyers. The money obtained from the sale was held in a trust
fund to be used for "civilizing" the Indians. The federal government also set up
boarding schools for Indian children outside the reservations. Children from the
age of six and up were taken from their parents—willingly or unwillingly—and
sent thousands of miles away where they were superficially trained for obsolete
manual vocations. Unless the parents could pay their children's fare back to the
reservations during vacations the boys and girls remained away from home for
as long as ten years. Deprived of land, equipped neither for white society nor
permitted to live in peace in their tribal community, robbed of their children,
the Indians' lot was even more tragic after the white men's efforts to "help" the
"Noble Savages" than it had been in an earlier day when red men had simply
been forced to move westward.*

*In 1924 the American government, still committed to a policy of Ameri-
canization, sought to redress long-standing grievances by granting citizenship to
all Indians. A decade later President Franklin D. Roosevelt appointed John*

Collier, the nation's most ardent champion of Indian rights, Commissioner of Indian Affairs. Collier drew attention to the dire results of white paternalism and attempted to encourage community revival through tribal ownership of land and rejuvenation of the Indians' cultural heritage. However, his efforts could not reverse decades of demoralization due to acute poverty and cultural disintegration.

Unlike the Indians, the blacks had hopes for a better life after the Civil War. The Republican Congresses during Reconstruction emancipated the bondsmen, guaranteed them civil and political rights, and financed the Freedman's Bureau, which provided welfare and education for the exslaves. Reconstruction governments in the southern states, frequently containing black judges and legislators, also embarked upon improvement projects. Federal troops protected the black man's rights, and sympathetic northerners contributed money for relief and education. But land ownership was the major vehicle for independence in the agrarian South and the failure of the state and federal governments to provide freedmen with 40 acres and a mule doomed them to generations of agricultural peonage.

The North started removing its troops and withdrawing protection from southern blacks in the early 1870s. By 1900, spurred by conflicts over agricultural reform, the process of eliminating supposedly guaranteed constitutional rights was virtually complete. Poll taxes, literacy tests, and all-white primaries deprived blacks of political rights; terror, debt, segregation, violence, poor education, and the arbitrary use of the law oppressed them almost as severely as had slavery.

In the late nineteenth century sizeable migrations to the North began. Even before the first massive influx during World War I, New York, Philadelphia, and Chicago had significant black enclaves. The desire to escape southern bigotry played a role in these evacuations, but economic factors, such as rural poverty, the ravages of the boll weevil on the cotton crop, and broader occupational opportunities, had a greater influence. Movement to the city accelerated during World War I when northern industry needed vast quantities of labor. This resettlement, combined with normal wartime tensions and anxieties, resulted in race riots and an expanding pattern of residential and social segregation. The fears of working-class whites led to bloody riots in East St. Louis in 1917 and thereafter in Philadelphia, Chicago, and other cities.

In the 1920s the black community made some strides in material self-improvement, cultural achievement, and ethnic pride. Blacks also made more vigorous demands for equal rights. The prosperity of the decade and the growing urbanization of the race enabled a few thousand to emerge from poverty into an expanding middle class. Black literary magazines, jazz spots, and coffee houses provided opportunities to exchange ideas and to publish or perform the work of black musicians, poets, and novelists. And for the first time in America, they were appreciated as serious performers by white audiences. The singer Paul Robeson was the most famous example.

Improvements also occurred for those who remained in the working class. Long-standing exclusion from labor unions had made blacks readily available strikebreakers. While the pattern of exclusion and scab labor did not disappear,

A. Philip Randolph succeeded in organizing railroad employees into the Brotherhood of Sleeping Car Porters, the first black labor union.

The New Deal and World War II also improved the status and the material conditions of many American blacks. For the first time since Reconstruction the federal government gave them the feeling that their interests were of concern to Washington. Prominent New Dealers, particularly Eleanor Roosevelt and Harold Ickes, the Secretary of the Interior, voiced support for equal treatment and an unprecedented number of blacks received federal patronage appointments. The real benefit of the New Deal, however, came not from humanitarian utterances or the official recognition of a few middle-class spokesmen but through the impact of relief programs. Segregation was the dominant practice in federal agencies, and the blacks received the smallest benefits, but for the first time since the Freedmen's Bureau, they shared in government bounties. Similar gains were made in the labor movement. The formation of the CIO, with its integrationist policy, was a tremendous spur toward organizing black workers and consequently to ending the use of black strikebreakers. Appreciative of the party responsible for this policy, large numbers of them switched their allegiance to the Democrats in the 1936 elections.

During World War II the pull of high wages in defense industries drew many blacks out of the rural South into northern, midwestern, and West Coast cities. War created prosperity and scarcity of labor benfited black workers, businessmen, and professionals. But occupational progress and higher incomes were accompanied by race riots in New York and Detroit.

The militancy of black leaders also grew more pronounced during World War II. In the 1940s, with even greater vigor and better results than in the 1930s, the NAACP steadily undermined the legal defense of segregation and white political supremacy. A. Philip Randolph's threat to lead a march on Washington moved President Roosevelt to create the Fair Employment Practices Committee. In 1942 activists established the Congress of Racial Equality (CORE), an organization committed to nonviolent demonstrations for civil rights. At the same time the Reverend Adam Clayton Powell, Jr., led successful boycotts against Harlem chain stores lacking black employees.

Between the 1860s and the end of the Second World War ethnic minorities, except for the Indians and the Mexican-Americans, significantly improved their material conditions and occupational status. Irish teachers and public officials, Italian shopkeepers, Jewish businessmen and professionals, and the black urban bourgeoisie made vast leaps in American society. Some members of white minorities even achieved a social status equal to, or almost equal to, Americans with a longer lineage in the United States. Rarely, however, were blacks accepted in white residential areas; most white-collar jobs were still barred to them; and many hotels, restaurants, and recreation centers in every part of the country still refused their patronage. Economic advancement resulted in much greater social progress for whites than blacks during the major part of the industrial transformation. During the post-World War II period, however, the blacks would begin to make significant progress.

Selected Bibliography

Minority group labor experiences are intelligently discussed in Charlotte Erickson, American Industry and the European Immigrant, 1860–1885 *(Cambridge, Mass.: Harvard University Press, 1957). The problem of peonage received widespread coverage in contemporary periodicals at the turn of the century. Representative items include Dominic T. Ciolli, "The 'Wop' in the Track Gang,"* Immigration in America Review, *July, 1916, pp. 61–64; "Life Story of a Pushcart Peddler" (Greek),* Independent, *60 (1906), 274–379; "The Life Story of a Hungarian Peon," ibid., 63 (1907), 557–64; and Gino C. Speranza, "Forced Labor in West Virginia" (Italian),* Outlook, *74 (1903), 407–10.*

At the end of the nineteenth century numerous Americans agonized over the Indian problem. H. L. Dawes, "Have We Failed With the Indian?" Atlantic Monthly, *84 (1899), 280–85, is typical of the lot. On the life of the Indian see Chauncey Shafter Goodrich, "The Legal Status of the California Indian,"* California Law Review, *14 (1925), 83–100, and 14 (1926), 157–87, and Ferdinand F. Fernandez, "Except a California Indian: A Study in Legal Discrimination,"* Southern California Quarterly, *50 (June, 1968), 161–75. An excellent volume detailing conditions on Indian reservations in the 1920s is Robert Gessner,* Massacre *(New York: J. Cape and H. Smith, 1931).*

For Progressive attitudes toward blacks see Dewey W. Grantham, Jr., "The Progressive Movement and the Negro," South Atlantic Quarterly, *54 (October, 1955), 461–77; Seth M. Scheiner, "President Theodore Roosevelt and the Negro, 1901–1908,"* Journal of Negro History, *47 (1963), 169–83; Henry Blumenthal, "Woodrow Wilson and the Race Question," ibid., 48 (1963), 1–21; and August Meier, "The Rise of Segregation in the Federal Bureaucracy, 1900–1930,"* Phylon, *28 (1967), 178–84. The feelings of white southerners come through clearly in Philip Alexander Bruce, "Evolution of the Negro Problem,"* Sewanee Review, *19 (1911), 385–99, and Carl Holliday, "The Young Southerner and the Negro,"* South Atlantic Quarterly, *8 (1909), 117–31. A very important work on the Caribbean blacks who emigrated to the United States is Ira de A. Reid,* The Negro Immigrant *(New York: Columbia University Press, 1950).*

For the French-Canadians in New England see Jacques Ducharme, The Shadows of the Trees *(New York: Harper & Bros., 1943), Bessie B. Wessel,* An Ethnic Survey of Woonsocket, Rhode Island *(Chicago: University of Chicago Press, 1931), and David Bradstreet Walker,* Politics and Ethnocentrism *(Brunswick, Me.: Bowdoin College, Bureau of Research in Municipal Government, 1961).*

Robert F. Foerster, The Italian Emigration of Our Times *(Cambridge, Mass.: Harvard University Press, 1919), is the standard work. Rudolph Vecoli, "Chicago's Italians Prior to World War I" (Unpublished Ph.D. dissertation, University of Wisconsin, 1963), is outstanding, as are Joan Younger Dickinson, "Aspects of Italian Immigration to Philadelphia,"* Pennsylvania Magazine of History and Biography, *90 (1966), 445–65, and William Foote Whyte,*

"Race Conflicts in the North End of Boston," New England Quarterly, *12 (December, 1939), 623–42. The most recent and impressive scholarship is represented by Andrew F.* Rolle, The Immigrant Upraised *(Norman: University of Oklahoma Press, 1968), which has an outstanding bibliography; Grazia Dore, "Some Social and Historical Aspects of Italian Emigration to America,"* Journal of Social History, *2 (Winter, 1968), 95–122; Rudolph J. Vecoli, "Prelates and Peasants: Italian Immigrants and the Catholic Church,"* ibid., *2 (Spring, 1969), 217–68; two articles by Edwin Fenton, "Italians in the Labor Movement,"* Pennsylvania History, *26 (1959), 133–48, and "Italian Immigrants in the Stonecutters' Union,"* Labor History, *3 (1962), 188–207; and three by Humbert S. Nelli, "The Italian Padrone System in the United States,"* Labor History, *5 (1964), 153–67, "Italians in Urban America: A Study in Ethnic Adjustment,"* The International Migration Review, New Series, *1 (1967), 38–55, and "Italians and Crime in Chicago: The Formative Years, 1890–1920,"* The American Journal of Sociology, *74 (1969), 373–91.*

There are no really scholarly histories of either the Jews or anti-Semitism in the United States. Rufus Learsi, The Jews in America *(New York: World Publishing Co., 1954), is about the best of the histories extant while John Higham, "Social Discrimination Against Jews in America, 1830–1930,"* Publications of the American Jewish Historical Society, *47 (1957-58), 1–33, and Oscar Handlin, "American Views of the Jew at the Opening of the Twentieth Century,"* ibid., *40 (1951), 323–44, are insightful analyses. Charles Herbert Stember, ed.,* Jews in the Mind of America *(New York: Basic Books, 1966), is a useful collection of articles on anti-Semitism and related concerns. The single most violent episode of anti-Semitism in the United States is treated in Leonard Dinnerstein,* The Leo Frank Case *(New York: Columbia University Press, 1968).*

Joseph A. Wytrwal, America's Polish Heritage *(Detroit: Endurance Press, 1961), and Ed Falkowski, "Polonia to America,"* Common Ground, *2 (Autumn, 1941), 28–36, are good as starting points on the Poles.*

The best material on the Japanese include Roger Daniels, The Politics of Prejudice* *(New York: Atheneum, 1968), Morton Grodzins,* Americans Betrayed *(Chicago: University of Chicago Press, 1949), Raymond L. Buell, "The Development of Anti-Japanese Agitation in the United States,"* Political Science Quarterly, *37 (1922), 605–38, and 38 (1923), 57–81; Carey McWilliams, "The Nisei Speak,"* Common Ground, *4 (Summer, 1944), 61–74; and Eugene V. Rostow, "Our Worst Wartime Mistake,"* Harper's, *191 (September, 1945), 193–201. Two recent studies which convey the experiences of Japanese-Americans during World War II are Bill Hosokawa,* Nisei *(New York: William Morrow & Co., 1969), and Audrie Girdner and Anne Loftis,* The Great Betrayal *(New York: The Macmillan Co., 1969).*

Good studies of other groups are Theodore Saloutos, The Greeks in the United States *(Cambridge, Mass.: Harvard University Press, 1964), Emil Lengyel,* Americans From Hungary *(Philadelphia: J. B. Lippincott Co., 1948), and Wasyl Halich, "Ukranian Farmers in the United States,"* Agricultural History, *10 (1936), 25–39.*

Indians

YOUNG JOSEPH

An Indian's View of Indian Affairs

White Americans took whatever lands that they wanted from the Indians. Some-
times the taking was made legal in the white man's eyes because treaties were
signed. On other occasions treaties were ignored because land-hungry frontiers-
men and capitalists bent on expansion found them too constricting. Eventually
Americans possessed virtually all the land that had belonged to Indians. The
few red men who had not been killed were confined to reservations, usually the
most arid and infertile lands where no white man saw immediate value.

One episode in the encroachment of white settlements into Indian land
evoked the following selection, the lament of Chief Joseph. Joseph was chief
of the Nez Percé Indians, a friendly tribe that inhabited the Snake Valley in
western Idaho. In 1877, when settlers began to move into land reserved for his
people, Chief Joseph led the Nez Percés out of their reservation across Idaho
and Montana in a seventy-five-day flight. The fugitives did no damage and
even paid farmers for supplies on the way. The army finally trapped the Nez
Percés and the federal government assigned them to barren lands in Indian
territory in Oklahoma, where the tribe quickly succumbed to malaria and other
diseases.

I wish that I had words at command in which to express adequately the interest with which I have read the extraordinary narrative which follows, and
which I have the privilege of introducing to the readers of this "Review." I feel,
however, that this *apologia* is so boldly marked by the charming *naïveté* and
tender pathos which characterize the red-man, that it needs no introduction,
much less any authentication; while in its smothered fire, in its deep sense of
eternal righteousness and of present evil, and in its hopeful longings for the
coming of a better time, this Indian chief's appeal reminds us of one of the old
Hebrew prophets of the days of the captivity.

I have no special knowledge of the history of the Nez Percés, the Indians
whose tale of sorrow Chief Joseph so pathetically tells—my Indian missions
lying in a part at the West quite distant from their old home—and am not competent to judge their case upon its merits. The chief's narrative is, of course,
ex parte, and many of his statements would no doubt be ardently disputed.

Reprinted from *North American Review*, 128 (1879), 412–33.

General Howard, for instance, can hardly receive justice at his hands, so well known is he for his friendship to the Indian and for his distinguished success in pacifying some of the most desperate.

It should be remembered, too, in justice to the army, that it is rarely called upon to interfere in Indian affairs until the relations between the Indians and the whites have reached a desperate condition, and when the situation of affairs has become so involved and feeling on both sides runs so high that perhaps only more than human forbearance would attempt to solve the difficulty by disentangling the knot and not by cutting it.

Nevertheless, the chief's narrative is marked by so much candor, and so careful is he to qualify his statements, when qualification seems necessary, that every reader will give him credit for speaking his honest, even should they be thought by some to be mistaken, convictions. The chief, in his treatment of his defense, reminds one of those lawyers of whom we have heard that their splendid success was gained, not by disputation, but simply by their lucid and straightforward statement of their case. That he is something of a strategist as well as an advocate appears from this description of an event which occurred shortly after the breaking out of hostilities: "We crossed over Salmon River, hoping General Howard would follow. We were not disappointed. He did follow us, and we got between him and his supplies, and cut him off for three days." Occasionally the reader comes upon touches of those sentiments and feelings which at once establish a sense of kinship between all who possess them. Witness his description of his desperate attempt to rejoin his wife and children when a sudden dash of General Miles's soldiers had cut the Indian camp in two: "About seventy men, myself among them, were cut off. . . . I thought of my wife and children, who were now surrounded by soldiers, and I resolved to go to them. With a prayer in my mouth to the Great Spirit Chief who rules above, I dashed unarmed through the line of solders. . . . My clothes were cut to pieces, my horse was wounded, but I was not hurt." And again, when he speaks of his father's death: "I saw he was dying. I took his hand in mine. He said: 'My son, my body is returning to my mother Earth, and my spirit is going very soon to see the Great Spirit Chief. . . . A few more years and the white men will be all around you. They have their eyes on this land. My son, never forget my dying words. This country holds your father's body—never sell the bones of your father and your mother.' I pressed my father's hand, and told him I would protect his grave with my life. My father smiled, and passed away to the spiritland. I buried him in that beautiful valley of Winding Waters. I love that land more than all the rest of the world. A man who would not love his father's grave is worse than a wild animal."

His appeals to the natural rights of man are surprisingly fine, and, however some may despise them as the utterances of an Indian, they are just those which, in our Declaration of Independence, have been most admired. "We are all sprung from a woman," he says, "although we are unlike in many things. You are as you were made, and, as you were made, you can remain. We are just as we were made by the Great Spirit, and you can not change us: then, why should children of one mother quarrel? Why should one try to cheat another? I do not believe that the Great Spirit Chief gave one kind of men the right to tell another kind of men what they must do."

But I will not detain the readers of the "Review" from the pleasure of perusing for themselves Chief Joseph's statement longer than is necessary to express the hope that those who have time for no more will at least read its closing paragraph, and to remark that the narrative brings clearly out these facts which ought to be regarded as well-recognized principles in dealing with the red-man:

1. The folly of any mode of treatment of the Indian which is not based upon a cordial and operative acknowledgment of his rights as our *fellow man.*

2. The danger of riding rough-shod over a people who are capable of high enthusiasm, who know and value their national rights, and are brave enough to defend them.

3. The liability to want of harmony between different departments and different officials of our complex Government, from which it results that, while many promises are made to the Indians, few of them are kept. It is a home-thrust when Chief Joseph says: "The white people have too many chiefs. They do not understand each other. . . . I can not understand how the Government sends a man out to fight us, as it did General Miles, and then break his word. Such a Government has something wrong about it."

4. The unwisdom, in most cases in dealing with Indians, of what may be termed *military short-cuts,* instead of patient discussion, explanations, persuasion, and reasonable concessions.

5. The absence in an Indian tribe of any truly representative body competent to make a treaty which shall be binding upon all the bands. The failure to recognize this fact has been the source of endless difficulties. Chief Joseph, in this case, did not consider a treaty binding which his band had not agreed to, no matter how many other bands had signed it; and so it has been in many other cases.

6. Indian chiefs, however able and influential, are really without power, and for this reason, as well as others, the Indians, when by the march of events they are brought into intimate relations with the whites, should at the earliest practicable moment be given the support and protection of our Government and of our law; not *local* law, however, which is apt to be the result of *special* legislation, adopted solely in the interest of the stronger race.

WILLIAM H. HARE, *Missionary Bishop of Niobrara.*

My friends, I have been asked to show you my heart. I am glad to have a chance to do so. I want the white people to understand my people. Some of you think an Indian is like a wild animal. This is a great mistake. I will tell you all about our people, and then you can judge whether an Indian is a man or not. I believe much trouble and blood would be saved if we opened our hearts more. I will tell you in my way how the Indian sees things. The white man has more words to tell you how they look to him, but it does not require many words to speak the truth. What I have to say will come from my heart, and I will speak with a straight tongue. Ah-cum-kin-i-ma-me-hut (the Great Spirit) is looking at me, and will hear me.

My name is In-mut-too-yah-lat-lat (Thunder traveling over the Mountains). I am chief of the Wal-lam-wat-kin band of Chute-pa-lu, or Nez Percés (nose-pierced Indians). I was born in eastern Oregon, thirty-eight winters ago. My father was chief before me. When a young man, he was called Joseph by Mr. Spaulding, a missionary. He died a few years ago. There was no stain on his hands of the blood of a white man. He left a good name on the earth. He advised me well for my people.

Our fathers gave us many laws, which they had learned from their fathers. These laws were good. They told us to treat all men as they treated us; that we should never be the first to break a bargain; that it was a disgrace to tell a lie; that we should speak only the truth; that it was a shame for one man to take from another his wife, or his property without paying for it. We were taught to believe that the Great Spirit sees and hears everything, and that he never forgets; that hereafter he will give every man a spirit-home according to his deserts: if he has been a good man, he will have a good home; if he has been a bad man, he will have a bad home. This I believe, and all my people believe the same.

We did not know there were other people besides the Indian until about one hundred winters ago, when some men with white faces came to our country. They brought many things with them to trade for furs and skins. They brought tobacco, which was new to us. They brought guns with flint stones on them, which frightened our women and children. Our people could not talk with these white-faced men, but they used signs which all people understand. These men were Frenchmen, and they called our people "Nez Percés," because they wore rings in their noses for ornaments. Although very few of our people wear them now, we are still called by the same name. These French trappers said a great many things to our fathers, which have been planted in our hearts. Some were good for us, but some were bad. Our people were divided in opinion about these men. Some thought they taught more bad than good. An Indian respects a brave man, but he despises a coward. He loves a straight tongue, but he hates a forked tongue. The French trappers told us some truths and some lies.

The first white men of your people who came to our country were named Lewis and Clarke. They also brought many things that our people had never seen. They talked straight, and our people gave them a great feast, as a proof that their hearts were friendly. These men were very kind. They made presents to our chiefs and our people made presents to them. We had a great many horses, of which we gave them what they needed, and they gave us guns and tobacco in return. All the Nez Percés made friends with Lewis and Clarke, and agreed to let them pass through their country, and never to make war on white men. This promise the Nez Percés have never broken. No white man can accuse them of bad faith, and speak with a straight tongue. It has always been the pride of the Nez Percés that they were the friends of the white men. When my father was a young man there came to our country a white man (Rev. Mr. Spaulding) who talked spirit law. He won the affections of our people because he spoke good things to them. At first he did not say anything about white men wanting to settle on our lands. Nothing was said about that until about twenty winters ago, when a number of white people came into our country and built houses and made farms. At first our people made no complaint. They thought there was room enough for all to live in peace, and they were learning many things from the white men that seemed to be good. But we soon found that the white men were growing rich very fast, and were greedy to possess everything the Indian had. My father was the first to see through the schemes of the white men, and he warned his tribe to be careful about trading with them. He had suspicion of men who seemed so anxious to make money. I was a boy then, but I remember well my father's caution. He had sharper eyes than the rest of our people.

Next there came a white officer (Governor Stevens), who invited all the Nez Percés to a treaty council. After the council was opened he made known his heart. He said there were a great many white people in the country, and many more would come; that he wanted the land marked out so that the Indians and white men could be separated. If they were to live in peace it was necessary, he said, that the Indians should have a country set apart for them, and in that country they must stay. My father, who represented his band, refused to have anything to do with the council, because he wished to be a free man. He claimed that no man owned any part of the earth, and a man could not sell what he did not own.

Mr. Spaulding took hold of my father's arm and said, "Come and sign the treaty." My father pushed him away, and said: "Why do you ask me to sign away my country? It is your business to talk to us about spirit matters, and not to talk to us about parting with our land." Governor Stevens urged my father to sign his treaty, but he refused. "I will not sign your paper," he said; "you go where you please, so do I; you are not a child, I am no child; I can think for myself. No man can think for me. I have no other home than this. I will not give it up to any man. My people would have no home. Take away your paper. I will not touch it with my hand."

My father left the council. Some of the chiefs of the other bands of the Nez Percés signed the treaty, and then Governor Stevens gave them presents of blankets. My father cautioned his people to take no presents, for "after a while," he said, "they will claim that you have accepted pay for your country." Since that time four bands of the Nez Percés have received annuities from the United States. My father was invited to many councils, and they tried hard to make him sign the treaty, but he was firm as the rock, and would not sign away his home. His refusal caused a difference among the Nez Percés.

Eight years later (1863) was the next treaty council. A chief called Lawyer, because he was a great talker, took the lead in this council, and sold nearly all the Nez Percés country. My father was not there. He said to me: "When you go into council with the white man, always remember your country. Do not give it away. The white man will cheat you out of your home. I have taken no pay from the United States. I have never sold our land." In this treaty Lawyer acted without authority from our band. He had no right to sell the Wallowa (*winding water*) country. That had always belonged to my father's own people, and the other bands had never disputed our right to it. No other Indians ever claimed Wallowa.

In order to have all people understand how much land we owned, my father planted poles around it and said:

"Inside is the home of my people—the white man may take the land outside. Inside this boundary all our people were born. It circles around the graves of our fathers, and we will never give up these graves to any man."

The United States claimed they had bought all the Nez Percés country outside of Lapwai Reservation, from Lawyer and other chiefs, but we continued to live on this land in peace until eight years ago, when white men began to come inside the bounds my father had set. We warned them against this great wrong, but they would not leave our land, and some bad blood was raised. The white men represented that we were going upon the war-path. They reported many things that were false.

The United States Government again asked for a treaty council. My father had become blind and feeble. He could no longer speak for his people. It was then that I took my father's place as chief. In this council I made my first speech to white men. I said to the agent who held the council:

"I did not want to come to this council, but I came hoping that we could save blood. The white man has no right to come here and take our country. We have never accepted any presents from the Government. Neither Lawyer nor any other chief had authority to sell this land. It has always belonged to my people. It came unclouded to them from our fathers, and we will defend this land as long as a drop of Indian blood warms the hearts of our men."

The agent said he had orders, from the Great White Chief at Washington, for us to go upon the Lapwai Reservation, and that if we obeyed he would help us in many ways. "You *must* move to the agency," he said. I answered him: "I will not. I do not need your help; we have plenty, and we are contented and happy if the white man will let us alone. The reservation is too small for so many people with all their stock. You can keep your presents; we can go to your towns and pay for all we need; we have plenty of horses and cattle to sell, and we won't have any help from you; we are free now; we can go where we please. Our fathers were born here. Here they lived, here they died, here are their graves. We will never leave them." The agent went away, and we had peace for a little while.

Soon after this my father sent for me. I saw he was dying. I took his hand in mine. He said: "My son, my body is returning to my mother earth, and my spirit is going very soon to see the Great Spirit Chief. When I am gone, think of your country. You are the chief of these people. They look to you to guide them. Always remember that your father never sold his country. You must stop your ears whenever you are asked to sign a treaty selling your home. A few years more, and white men will be all around you. They have their eyes on this land. My son, never forget my dying words. This country holds your father's body. Never sell the bones of your father and your mother." I pressed my father's hand and told him I would protect his grave with my life. My father smiled and passed away to the spirit-land.

I buried him in that beautiful valley of winding waters. I love that land more than all the rest of the world. A man who would not love his father's grave is worse than a wild animal.

For a short time we lived quietly. But this could not last. White men had found gold in the mountains around the land of winding water. They stole a great many horses from us, and we could not get them back because we were Indians. The white men told lies for each other. They drove off a great many of our cattle. Some white men branded our young cattle so they could claim them. We had no friend who would plead our cause before the law councils.

It seemed to me that some of the white men in Wallowa were doing these things on purpose to get up a war. They knew that we were not strong enough to fight them. I labored hard to avoid trouble and bloodshed. We gave up some of our country to the white men, thinking that then we could have peace. We were mistaken. The white man would not let us alone. We could have avenged our wrongs many times, but we did not. Whenever the Government has asked us to help them against other Indians, we have never refused. When the white men were few and we were strong we could have killed them all off, but the Nez Percés wished to live at peace.

If we have not done so, we have not been to blame. I believe that the old treaty has never been correctly reported. If we ever owned the land we own it still, for we never sold it. In the treaty councils the commissioners have claimed that our country had been sold to the Government. Suppose a white man should come to me and say, "Joseph, I like your horses, and I want to buy them." I say to him, "No, my horses suit me, I will not sell them." Then he goes to my neighbor, and says to him: "Joseph has some good horses. I want to buy them, but he refuses to sell." My neighbor answers, "Pay me the money, and I will sell you Joseph's horses." The white man returns to me, and says, "Joseph, I have bought your horses, and you must let me have them." If we sold our lands to the Government, this is the way they were bought.

On account of the treaty made by the other bands of the Nez Percés, the white men claimed my lands. We were troubled greatly by white men crowding over the line. Some of these were good men, and we lived on peaceful terms with them, but they were not all good.

Nearly every year the agent came over from Lapwai and ordered us on to the reservation. We always replied that we were satisfied to live in Wallowa. We were careful to refuse the presents or annuities which he offered.

Through all the years since the white men came to Wallowa we have been threatened and taunted by them and the treaty Nez Percés. They have given us no rest. We have had a few good friends among white men, and they have always advised my people to bear these taunts without fighting. Our young men were quick-tempered, and I have had great trouble in keeping them from doing rash things. I have carried a heavy load on my back ever since I was a boy. I learned then that we were but few, while the white men were many, and that we could not hold our own with them. We were like deer. They were like grizzly bears. We had a small country. Their country was large. We were contented to let things remain as the Great Spirit Chief made them. They were not; and would change the rivers and mountains if they did not suit them.

Year after year we have been threatened, but no war was made upon my people until General Howard came to our country two years ago and told us that he was the white war-chief of all that country. He said: "I have a great many soldiers at my back. I am going to bring them up here, and then I will talk to you again. I will not let white men laugh at me the next time I come. The country belongs to the Government, and I intend to make you go upon the reservation."

I remonstrated with him against bringing more soldiers to the Nez Percés country. He had one house full of troops all the time at Fort Lapwai.

The next spring the agent at Umatilla agency sent an Indian runner to tell me to meet General Howard at Walla Walla. I could not go myself, but I sent my brother and five other head men to meet him, and they had a long talk.

General Howard said: "You have talked straight, and it is all right. You can stay in Wallowa." He insisted that my brother and his company should go with him to Fort Lapwai. When the party arrived there General Howard sent out runners and called all the Indians in to a grand council. I was in that council. I said to General Howard, "We are ready to listen." He answered that he would not talk then, but would hold a council next day, when he would talk plainly. I said to General Howard: "I am ready to talk to-day. I have been in a great many councils, but I am no wiser. We are all sprung from a woman, although we are unlike in many things. We can not be made over again. You are as you were made, and as you were made you can remain. We are just as we were made by the Great Spirit, and you can not change us; then why should children of one mother and one father quarrel—why should one try to cheat the other? I do not believe that the Great Spirit Chief gave one kind of men the right to tell another kind of men what they must do."

General Howard replied: "You deny my authority, do you? You want to dictate to me, do you?"

Then one of my chiefs—Too-hool-hool-suit—rose in the council and said to General Howard: "The Great Spirit Chief made the world as it is, and as he wanted it, and he made a part of it for us to live upon. I do not see where you get authority to say that we shall not live where he placed us."

General Howard lost his temper and said: "Shut up! I don't want to hear any more of such talk. The law says you shall go upon the reservation to live, and I want you to do so, but you persist in disobeying the law" (meaning the treaty). "If you do not move, I will take the matter into my own hand, and make you suffer for your disobedience."

Too-hool-hool-suit answered: "Who are you, that you ask us to talk, and then tell me I sha'n't talk? Are you the Great Spirit? Did you make the world? Did you make the sun? Did you make the rivers to run for us to drink? Did you make the grass to grow? Did you make all these things, that you talk to us as though we were boys? If you did, then you have the right to talk as you do."

General Howard replied, "You are an impudent fellow, and I will put you in the guard-house," and then ordered a soldier to arrest him.

Too-hool-hool-suit made no resistance. He asked General Howard: "Is that your order? I don't care. I have expressed my heart to you. I have nothing to take back. I have spoken for my country. You can arrest me, but you can not change me or make me take back what I have said."

The soldiers came forward and seized my friend and took him to the guard-house. My men whispered among themselves whether they should let this thing be done. I counseled them to submit. I knew if we resisted that all the white men present, including General Howard would be killed in a moment, and we would be blamed. If I had said nothing, General Howard would never have given another unjust order against my men. I saw the danger, and, while they dragged Too-hool-hool-suit to prison, I arose and said: "*I am going to talk now. I don't care whether you arrest me or not.*" I turned to my people and said: "The arrest of Too-hool-hool-suit was wrong, but we will not resent the insult. We were invited to this council to express our hearts, and we have done so."

Too-hool-hool-suit was prisoner for five days before he was released.

The council broke up for that day. On the next morning General Howard came to my lodge, and invited me to go with him and White-Bird and Looking-Glass, to look for land for my people. As we rode along we came to some good land that was already occupied by Indians and white people. General Howard, pointing to this land, said: "If you will come on to the reservation, I will give you these lands and move these people off."

I replied: "No. It would be wrong to disturb these people. I have no right to take their homes. I have never taken what did not belong to me. I will not now."

We rode all day upon the reservation, and found no good land unoccupied. I have been informed by men who do not lie that General Howard sent a letter that night, telling the soldiers at Walla Walla to go to Wallowa Valley, and drive us out upon our return home.

In the council, next day, General Howard informed me, in a haughty spirit, that he would give my people *thirty days* to go back home, collect all their stock, and move on to the reservation, saying, "If you are not here in that time, I shall consider that you want to fight, and will send my soldiers to drive you on."

I said: "War can be avoided, and it ought to be avoided. I want no war. My people have always been the friends of the white man. Why are you in such a hurry? I can not get ready to move in thirty days. Our stock is scattered, and Snake River is very high. Let us wait until fall, then the river will be low. We want time to hunt up our stock and gather supplies for winter."

General Howard replied, "If you let the time run over one day, the soldiers will be there to drive you on to the reservation, and all your cattle and horses outside of the reservation at that time will fall into the hands of the white men."

I knew I had never sold my country, and that I had no land in Lapwai; but I did not want bloodshed. I did not want my people killed. I did not want anybody killed. Some of my people had been murdered by white men, and the white murderers were never punished for it. I told General Howard about this, and again said I wanted no war. I wanted the people who lived upon the lands I was to occupy at Lapwai to have time to gather their harvest.

I said in my heart that, rather than have war, I would give up my country. I would give up my father's grave. I would give up everything rather than have the blood of white men upon the hands of my people.

General Howard refused to allow me more than thirty days to move my people and their stock. I am sure that he began to prepare for war at once.

When I returned to Wallowa I found my people very much excited upon discovering that the soldiers were already in the Wallowa Valley. We held a council, and decided to move immediately, to avoid bloodshed.

Too-hool-hool-suit, who felt outraged by his imprisonment, talked for war, and made many of my young men willing to fight rather than be driven like dogs from the land where they were born. He declared that blood alone would wash out the disgrace General Howard had put upon him. It required a strong heart to stand up against such talk, but I urged my people to be quiet, and not to begin a war.

We gathered all the stock we could find, and made an attempt to move. We left many of our horses and cattle in Wallowa, and we lost several hundred in crossing the river. All of my people succeeded in getting across in safety. Many of the Nez Percés came together in Rocky Cañon to hold a grand council. I went with all my people. This council lasted ten days. There was a great deal of war-talk, and a great deal of excitement. There was one young brave present whose father had been killed by a white man five years before. This man's blood was bad against white men, and he left the council calling for revenge.

Again I counseled peace, and I thought the danger was past. We had not complied with General Howard's order because we could not, but we intended to do so as soon as possible. I was leaving the council to kill beef for my family, when news came that the young man whose father had been killed had gone out with several other hot-blooded younk braves and killed four white men. He rode up to the council and shouted: "Why do you sit here like women? The war has begun already." I was deeply grieved. All the lodges were moved except my brother's and my own. I saw clearly that the war was upon us when I learned that my young men had been secretly buying ammunition. I heard then that Too-hool-hool-suit, who had been imprisoned by General Howard, had succeeded in organizing a war-party. I knew that their acts would involve all my people. I saw that the war could not then be prevented. The time had passed. I counseled peace from the beginning. I knew that we were too weak to fight the United States. We had many grievances, but I knew that war would bring more. We had good white friends, who advised us against taking the war-path. My friend and brother, Mr. Chapman, who has been with us since the surrender, told us just how the war would end. Mr. Chapman took sides against us, and helped General Howard. I do not blame him for doing so. He tried hard to prevent bloodshed. We hoped the white settlers would not join the soldiers. Before the war commenced we had discussed this matter all over, and many of my people were in favor of warning them that if they took no part against us they should not be molested in the event of war being begun by General Howard. This plan was voted down in the war-council.

There were bad men among my people who had quarreled with white men, and they talked of their wrongs until they roused all the bad hearts in the council. Still I could not believe that they would begin the war. I know that my young men did a great wrong, but I ask, Who was first to blame? They had been insulted a thousand times; their fathers and brothers had been killed; their mothers and wives had been disgraced; they had been driven to madness by whisky sold to them by white men; they had been told by General Howard that all their horses and cattle which they had been unable to drive out of Wallowa were to fall into the hands of white men; and, added to all this, they were homeless and desperate.

I would have given my own life if I could have undone the killing of white men by my people. I blame my young men and I blame the white men. I blame General Howard for not giving my people time to get their stock away from Wallowa. I do not acknowledge that he had the right to order me to leave Wallowa at any time. I deny that either my father or myself ever sold that land. It is still our land. It may never again be our home, but my father sleeps there, and I love it as I love my mother. I left there, hoping to avoid bloodshed.

If General Howard had given me plenty of time to gather up my stock, and treated Too-hool-hool-suit as a man should be treated, there *would have been no war.*

My friends among white men have blamed me for the war. I am not to blame. When my young men began the killing, my heart was hurt. Although I did not justify them, I remembered all the insults I had endured, and my blood was on fire. Still I would have taken my people to the buffalo country without fighting, if possible.

I could see no other way to avoid a war. We moved over to White Bird Creek, sixteen miles away, and there encamped, intending to collect our stock before leaving; but the soldiers attacked us, and the first battle was fought. We numbered in that battle sixty men, and the soldiers a hundred. The fight lasted but a few minutes, when the soldiers retreated before us for twelve miles. They lost thirty-three killed, and had seven wounded. When an Indian fights, he only shoots to kill; but soldiers shoot at random. None of the soldiers were scalped. We do not believe in scalping, nor in killing wounded men. Soldiers do not kill many Indians unless they are wounded and left upon the battle-field. Then they kill Indians.

Seven days after the first battle, General Howard arrived in the Nez Percés country, bringing seven hundred more soldiers. It was now war in earnest. We crossed over Salmon River, hoping General Howard would follow. We were not disappointed. He did follow us, and we got back between him and his supplies, and cut him off for three days. He sent out two companies to open the way. We attacked them, killing one officer, two guides, and ten men.

We withdrew, hoping the soldiers would follow, but they had got fighting enough for that day. They intrenched themselves, and next day we attacked them again. The battle lasted all day, and was renewed next morning. We killed four and wounded seven or eight.

About this time General Howard found out that we were in his rear. Five days later he attacked us with three hundred and fifty soldiers and settlers. We had two hundred and fifty warriors. The fight lasted twenty-seven hours. We lost four killed and several wounded. General Howard's loss was twenty-nine men killed and sixty wounded.

The following day the soldiers charged upon us, and we retreated with our families and stock a few miles, leaving eighty lodges to fall into General Howard's hands.

Finding that we were outnumbered, we retreated to Bitter Root Valley. Here another body of soldiers came upon us and demanded our surrender. We refused. They said, "You can not get by us." We answered, "We are going by you without fighting if you will let us, but we are going by you anyhow." We then made a treaty with these soldiers. We agreed not to molest any one, and they agreed that we might pass through the Bitter Root country in peace. We bought provisions and traded stock with white men there.

We understood that there was to be no more war. We intended to go peaceably to the buffalo country, and leave the question of returning to our country to be settled afterward.

With this understanding we traveled on for four days, and, thinking that the trouble was all over, we stopped and prepared tent-poles to take with us.

We started again, and at the end of two days we saw three white men passing our camp. Thinking that peace had been made, we did not molest them. We could have killed or taken them prisoners, but we did not suspect them of being spies, which they were.

That night the soldiers surrounded our camp. About daybreak one of my men went out to look after his horses. The soldiers saw him and shot him down like a coyote. I have since learned that these soldiers were not those we had left behind. They had come upon us from another direction. The new white war-chief's name was Gibbon. He charged upon us while some of my people were still asleep. We had a hard fight. Some of my men crept around and attacked the soldiers from the rear. In this battle we lost nearly all our lodges, but we finally drove General Gibbon back.

Finding that he was not able to capture us, he sent to his camp a few miles away for his big guns (cannons), but my men had captured them and all the ammunition. We damaged the big guns all we could, and carried away the powder and lead. In the fight with General Gibbon we lost fifty women and children and thirty fighting men. We remained long enough to bury our dead. The Nez Percés never make war on women and children; we could have killed a great many women and children while the war lasted, but we would feel ashamed to do so cowardly an act.

We never scalp our enemies, but when General Howard came up and joined General Gibbon, their Indian scouts dug up our dead and scalped them. I have been told that General Howard did not order this great shame to be done.

We retreated as rapidly as we could toward the buffalo country. After six days General Howard came close to us, and we went out and attacked him, and captured nearly all his horses and mules (about two hundred and fifty head). We then marched on to the Yellowstone Basin.

On the way we captured one white man and two white women. We released them at the end of three days. They were treated kindly. The women were not insulted. Can the white soldiers tell me of one time when Indian women were taken prisoners, and held three days and then released without being insulted? Were the Nez Percés women who fell into the hands of General Howard's soldiers treated with as much respect? I deny that a Nez Percé was ever guilty of such a crime.

A few days later we captured two more white men. One of them stole a horse and escaped. We gave the other a poor horse and told him he was free.

Nine days' march brought us to the mouth of Clarke's Fork of the Yellowstone. We did not know what had become of General Howard, but we supposed that he had sent for more horses and mules. He did not come up, but another new war-chief (General Sturgis) attacked us. We held him in check while we moved all our women and children and stock out of danger, leaving a few men to cover our retreat.

Several days passed, and we heard nothing of General Howard, or Gibbon, or Sturgis. We had repulsed each in turn, and began to feel secure, when another army, under General Miles, struck us. This was the fourth army, each of which outnumbered our fighting force, that we had encountered within sixty days.

We had no knowledge of General Miles's army until a short time before he made a charge upon us, cutting our camp in two, and capturing nearly all of our horses. About seventy men, myself among them, were cut off. My little daughter, twelve years of age, was with me. I gave her a rope, and told her to catch a horse and join the others who were cut off from the camp. I have not seen her since, but I have learned that she is alive and well.

I thought of my wife and children, who were now surrounded by soldiers, and I resolved to go to them or die. With a prayer in my mouth to the Great Spirit Chief who rules above, I dashed unarmed through the line of soldiers. It seemed to me that there were guns on every side, before and behind me. My clothes were cut to pieces and my horse was wounded, but I was not hurt. As I reached the door of my lodge, my wife handed me my rifle, saying: "Here's your gun. Fight!"

The soldiers kept up a continuous fire. Six of my men were killed in one spot near me. Ten or twelve soldiers charged into our camp and got possession of two lodges, killing three Nez Percés and losing three of their men, who fell inside our lines. I called my men to drive them back. We fought at close range, not more than twenty steps apart, and drove the soldiers back upon their main line, leaving their dead in our hands. We secured their arms and ammunition. We lost, the first day and night, eighteen men and three women. General Miles lost twenty-six killed and forty wounded. The following day General Miles sent a messenger into my camp under protection of a white flag. I sent my friend Yellow Bull to meet him.

Yellow Bull understood the messenger to say that General Miles wished me to consider the situation; that he did not want to kill my people unnecessarily. Yellow Bull understood this to be a demand for me to surrender and save blood. Upon reporting this message to me, Yellow Bull said he wondered whether General Miles was in earnest. I sent him back with my answer, that I had not made up my mind, but would think about it and send word soon. A little later he sent some Cheyenne scouts with another message. I went out to meet them. They said they believed that General Miles was sincere and really wanted peace. I walked on to General Miles's tent. He met me and we shook hands. He said, "Come, let us sit down by the fire and talk this matter over." I remained with him all night; next morning Yellow Bull came over to see if I was alive, and why I did not return.

General Miles would not let me leave the tent to see my friend alone.

Yellow Bull said to me: "They have got you in their power, and I am afraid they will never let you go again. I have an officer in our camp, and I will hold him until they let you go free."

I said: "I do not know what they mean to do with me, but if they kill me you must not kill the officer. It will do no good to avenge my death by killing him."

Yellow Bull returned to my camp. I did not make any agreement that day with General Miles. The battle was renewed while I was with him. I was very anxious about my people. I knew that we were near Sitting Bull's camp in King George's land, and I thought maybe the Nez Percés who had escaped would return with assistance. No great damage was done to either party during the night.

On the following morning I returned to my camp by agreement, meeting the officer who had been held a prisoner in my camp at the flag of truce. My people were divided about surrendering. We could have escaped from Bear Paw Mountain if we had left our wounded, old women, and children behind. We were unwilling to do this. We had never heard of a wounded Indian recovering while in the hands of white men.

On the evening of the fourth day General Howard came in with a small escort, together with my friend Chapman. We could now talk understandingly. General Miles said to me in plain words, "If you will come out and give up your arms, I will spare your lives and send you to your reservation." I do not know what passed between General Miles and General Howard.

I could not bear to see my wounded men and women suffer any longer; we had lost enough already. General Miles had promised that we might return to our own country with what stock we had left. I thought we could start again. I believed General Miles, or *I never would have surrendered.* I have heard that he has been censured for making the promise to return us to Lapwai. He could not have made any other terms with me at that time. I would have held him in check until my friends came to my assistance, and then neither of the generals nor their soldiers would have ever left Bear Paw Mountain alive.

On the fifth day I went to General Miles and gave up my gun, and said, "From where the sun now stands I will fight no more." My people needed rest— we wanted peace.

I was told we could go with General Miles to Tongue River and stay there until spring, when we would be sent back to our country. Finally it was decided that we were to be taken to Tongue River. We had nothing to say about it. After our arrival at Tongue River, General Miles received orders to take us to Bismarck. The reason given was, that subsistence would be cheaper there.

General Miles was opposed to this order. He said: "You must not blame me. I have endeavored to keep my word, but the chief who is over me has given the order, and I must obey it or resign. That would do you no good. Some other officer would carry out the order."

I believe General Miles would have kept his word if he could have done so. I do not blame him for what we have suffered since the surrender. I do not know who is to blame. We gave up all our horses—over eleven hundred—and all our saddles—over one hundred—and we have not heard from them since. Somebody has got our horses.

General Miles turned my people over to another soldier, and we were taken to Bismarck. Captain Johnson, who now had charge of us, received an order to take us to Fort Leavenworth. At Leavenworth we were placed on a low river bottom, with no water except river-water to drink and cook with. We had always lived in a healthy country, where the mountains were high and the water was cold and clear. Many of my people sickened and died, and we buried them in this strange land. I can not tell how much my heart suffered for my people while at Leavenworth. The Great Spirit Chief who rules above seemed to be looking some other way, and did not see what was being done to my people.

During the hot days (July, 1878) we received notice that we were to be moved farther away from our own country. We were not asked if we were willing to go. We were ordered to get into the railroad-cars. Three of my people died on the way to Baxter Springs. It was worse to die there than to die fighting in the mountains.

We were moved from Baxter Springs (Kansas) to the Indian Territory, and set down without our lodges. We had but little medicine, and we were nearly all sick. Seventy of my people have died since we moved there.

We have had a great many visitors who have talked many ways. Some of the chiefs (General Fish and Colonel Stickney) from Washington came to see us, and selected land for us to live upon. We have not moved to that land, for it is not a good place to live.

The Commissioner Chief (E. A. Hayt) came to see us. I told him, as I told every one, that I expected General Miles's word would be carried out. He said it "could not be done; that white men now lived in my country and all the land was taken up; that, if I returned to Wallowa, I could not live in peace; that law-papers were out against my young men who began the war, and that the Government could not protect my people." This talk fell like a heavy stone upon my heart. I saw that I could not gain anything by talking to him. Other law chiefs (Congressional Committee) came to see me and said they would help me to get a healthy country. I did not know who to believe. The white people have too many chiefs. They do not understand each other. They do not all talk alike.

The Commissioner Chief (Mr. Hayt) invited me to go with him and hunt for a better home than we have now. I like the land we found (west of the Osage reservation) better than any place I have seen in that country; but it is not a healthy land. There are no mountains and rivers. The water is warm. It is not a good country for stock. I do not believe my people can live there. I am afraid they will all die. The Indians who occupy that country are dying off. I promised Chief Hayt to go there, and do the best I could until the Government got ready to make good General Miles's word. I was not satisfied, but I could not help myself.

Then the Inspector Chief (General McNiel) came to my camp and we had a long talk. He said I ought to have a home in the mountain country north, and that he would write a letter to the Great Chief at Washington. Again the hope of seeing the mountains of Idaho and Oregon grew up in my heart.

At last I was granted permission to come to Washington and bring my friend Yellow Bull and our interpreter with me. I am glad we came. I have shaken hands with a great many friends, but there are some things I want to know which no one seems able to explain. I can not understand how the Government sends a man out to fight us, as it did General Miles, and then breaks his word. Such a Government has something wrong about it. I can not understand why so many chiefs are allowed to talk so many different ways, and promise so many different things. I have seen the Great Father Chief (the President), the next Great Chief (Secretary of the Interior), the Commissioner Chief (Hayt), the Law Chief (General Butler), and many other law chiefs (Congressmen), and they all say they are my friends, and that I shall have justice, but while their mouths all talk right I do not understand why nothing is done for my people. I have heard talk and talk, but nothing is done. Good words do not last long unless they amount to something. Words do not pay for my dead people. They do not pay for my country, now overrun by white men. They do not protect my father's grave. They do not pay for all my horses and cattle. Good words will not give me back my children. Good words will not make good the promise of your War Chief General Miles. Good words will not give my people good health and stop them from dying. Good words will not get my people a home where they can live in peace and take care of themselves. I am tired of talk that comes to nothing. It makes my heart sick when I remember all the good words and all the broken promises. There has been too much talking by men who had no right to talk. Too many misrepresentations have been made, too many misunderstandings have come up between the white men about the Indians. If the white man wants to live in peace with the Indian he can live in peace. There need be no trouble. Treat all men alike. Give them all the same law. Give them all an even chance to live and grow. All men were made by the same Great Spirit Chief. They are all brothers. The earth is the mother of all people, and all people should have equal rights upon it. You might as well expect the rivers to run backward as that any man who was born a free man should be contented when penned up and denied liberty to go where he pleases. If you tie a horse to a stake, do you expect he will grow fat? If you pen an Indian up on a small spot of earth, and compel him to stay there, he will not be contented, nor will he grow and prosper. I have asked some of the great white chiefs where they get their authority to say to the Indian that he shall stay in one place, while he sees white men going where they please. They can not tell me.

I only ask of the Government to be treated as all other men are treated. If I can not go to my own home, let me have a home in some country where my people will not die so fast. I would like to go to Bitter Root Valley. There my people would be healthy; where they are now they are dying. Three have died since I left my camp to come to Washington.

When I think of our condition my heart is heavy. I see men of my race treated as outlaws and driven from country to country, or shot down like animals.

I know that my race must change. We can not hold our own with the white men as we are. We only ask an even chance to live as other men live. We ask to be recognized as men. We ask that the same law shall work alike on all men. If the Indian breaks the law, punish him by the law. If the white man breaks the law, punish him also.

Let me be a free man—free to travel, free to stop, free to work, free to trade where I choose, free to choose my own teachers, free to follow the religion of my fathers, free to think and talk and act for myself—and I will obey every law, or submit to the penalty.

Whenever the white man treats the Indian as they treat each other, then we will have no more wars. We shall all be alike—brothers of one father and one mother, with one sky above us and one country around us, and one government for all. Then the Great Spirit Chief who rules above will smile upon this land, and send rain to wash out the bloody spots made by brothers' hands from the face of the earth. For this time the Indian race are waiting and praying. I hope that no more groans of wounded men and women will ever go to the ear of the Great Spirit Chief above, and that all people may be one people.

In-mut-too-yah-lat-lat has spoken for his people.

Blacks

A GEORGIA NEGRO PEON

The New Slavery in the South—An Autobiography

Emancipation did not significantly change racial attitudes in the United States. Although the legal position of the black man had been altered, most white southerners—and northerners, too—intended to keep him subservient. Jim Crow laws ("Jim Crow" was a stereotype black in a nineteenth-century song-and-dance act) relegated blacks to second-class citizenship in most southern states during the last decade of the nineteenth century and more informal arrangements accomplished the same purpose in the North. Black men had few recognized rights in white America and they rarely received justice from the legal establishment.

The peonage system—one example of racial exploitation—existed in every state in the union during the Progressive era with the exception of Oklahoma and Connecticut. It shackled both minority group members and unknowing whites. Blacks would sign contracts for one or more years of agricultural work and at the end of the stipulated period the landlord's records usually showed the tenant in debt for supplies that he had been forced to buy at the landlord's commissary. According to the law the owner had the option of allowing the peon to leave or else insisting that the debt be paid. If the tenant refused to remain and could not pay the landlord's claim the law intervened and usually sentenced him to work out his debt on the same land that he had been tilling. In reality, this meant involuntary servitude for as long as the landowner desired.

In the following selection a former peon describes the life that many black agricultural workers endured in the turn-of-the-century South.

[The following article was secured by a representative of THE INDEPENDENT specially commissioned for this work. It is a reliable story, and, we believe, a typical one. It was dictated to our representative, who took the liberty to correct the narrator's errors of grammar and put it in form suitable for publication. . . .]

I am a negro and was born some time during the war in Elbert County, Ga., and I reckon by this time I must be a little over forty years old. My

Reprinted from *Independent*, 56 (1904), 409–14.

mother was not married when I was born, and I never knew who my father was or anything about him. Shortly after the war my mother died, and I was left to the care of my uncle. All this happened before I was eight years old, and so I can't remember very much about it. When I was about ten years old my uncle hired me out to Captain _____. I had already learned how to plow, and was also a good hand at picking cotton. I was told that the Captain wanted me for his house-boy, and that later on he was going to train me to be his coachman. To be a coachman in those days was considered a post of honor, and, young as I was, I was glad of the chance. But I had not been at the Captain's a month before I was put to work on the farm, with some twenty or thirty other negroes —men, women and children. From the beginning the boys had the same tasks as the men and women. There was no difference. We all worked hard during the week, and would frolic on Saturday nights and often on Sundays. And everybody was happy. The men got $3 a week and the women $2. I don't know what the children got. Every week my uncle collected my money for me, but it was very little of it that I ever saw. My uncle fed and clothed me, gave me a place to sleep, and allowed me ten or fifteen cents a week for "spending change," as he called it. I must have been seventeen or eighteen years old before I got tired of that arrangement, and felt that I was man enough to be working for myself and handling my own wages. The other boys about my age and size were "drawing" their own pay, and they used to laugh at me and call me "Baby" because my old uncle was always on hand to "draw" my pay. Worked up by these things, I made a break for liberty. Unknown to my uncle or the Captain I went off to a neighboring plantation and hired myself out to another man. The new landlord agreed to give me forty cents a day and furnish me one meal. I thought that was doing fine. Bright and early one Monday morning I started for work, still not letting the others know anything about it. But they found it out before sundown. The Captain came over to the new place and brought some kind of officer of the law. The officer pulled out a long piece of paper from his pocket and read it to my new employer. When this was done I heard my new boss say:

"I beg your pardon, Captain. I didn't know this nigger was bound out to you, or I wouldn't have hired him."

"He certainly is bound out to me," said the Captain. "He belongs to me until he is twenty-one, and I'm going to make him know his place."

So I was carried back to the Captain's. That night he made me strip off my clothing down to my waist, had me tied to a tree in his backyard, ordered his foreman to give me thirty lashes with a buggy whip across my bare back, and stood by until it was done. After that experience the Captain made me stay on his place night and day,—but my uncle still continued to "draw" my money.

I was a man nearly grown before I knew how to count from one to one hundred. I was a man nearly grown before I ever saw a colored school teacher. I never went to school a day in my life. To-day I can't write my own name, tho I can read a little. I was a man nearly grown before I ever rode on a railroad train, and then I went on an excursion from Elberton to Athens. What was true of me was true of hundreds of other negroes around me—'way off there in the country, fifteen or twenty miles from the nearest town.

When I reached twenty-one the Captain told me I was a free man, but he urged me to stay with him. He said he would treat me right, and pay me as much as anybody else would. The Captain's son and I were about the same age, and the Captain said that, as he had owned my mother and uncle during slavery, and as his son didn't want me to leave them (since I had been with them so long), he wanted me to stay with the old family. And I stayed. I signed a contract—that is, I made my mark—for one year. The Captain was to give me $3.50 a week, and furnish me a little house on the plantation—a one-room log cabin similar to those used by his other laborers.

During that year I married Mandy. For several years Mandy had been the house-servant for the Captain, his wife, his son and his three daughters, and they all seemed to think a good deal of her. As an evidence of their regard they gave us a suit of furniture, which cost about $25, and we set up house-keeping in one of the Captain's two-room shanties. I thought I was the biggest man in Georgia. Mandy still kept her place in the "Big House" after our marriage. We did so well for the first year that I renewed my contract for the second year, and for the third, fourth and fifth year I did the same thing. Before the end of the fifth year the Captain had died, and his son, who had married some two or three years before, took charge of the plantation. Also, for two or three years, this son had been serving at Atlanta in some big office to which he had been elected. I think it was in the Legislature or something of that sort— anyhow, all the people called him Senator. At the end of the fifth year the Senator suggested that I sign up a contract for ten years; then, he said, we wouldn't have to fix up papers every year. I asked my wife about it: she consented; and so I made a ten-year contract.

Not long afterward, the Senator had a long, low shanty built on his place. A great big chimney, with a wide, open fireplace, was built at one end of it, and on each side of the house, running lengthwise, there was a row of frames or stalls just large enough to hold a single mattress. The places for these mattresses were fixed one above the other; so that there was a double row of these stalls or pens on each side. They looked for all the world like stalls for horses. Since then I have seen cabooses similarly arranged as sleeping quarters for railroad laborers. Nobody seemed to know what the Senator was fixing for. All doubts were put aside one bright day in April when about forty able-bodied negroes, bound in iron chains, and some of them handcuffed, were brought out to the Senator's farm in three big wagons. They were quartered in the long, low shanty, and it was afterward called the stockade. This was the beginning of the Senator's convict camp. These men were prisoners who had been leased by the Senator from the State of Georgia at about $200 each per year, the State agreeing to pay for guards and physicians, for necessary inspection, for inquests, all rewards for escaped convicts, the costs of litigation and all other incidental camp expenses. When I saw these men in shackles, and the guards with their guns, I was scared nearly to death. I felt like running away, but I didn't know where to go. And if there had been any place to go to, I would have had to leave my wife and child behind. We free laborers held a meeting. We all wanted to quit. We sent a man to tell the Senator about it. Word came back that we were all under contract for ten years and that the Senator would hold us to the letter of the contract, or put us in chains and lock us up—the same as the other prisoners. It was made plain to us by some white people we talked to that in the contracts we had signed we had all agreed to be locked up in a stockade at night or at any other time that our employer saw fit; further, we learned that we could not lawfully break our contract for any reason and go and hire ourselves to somebody else without the consent of our employer; and, more than that, if we got mad and ran away, we could be run down by blood-hounds, arrested without process of law, and be returned to our employer, who, according to the contract, might beat us brutally or administer any other kind of punishment that he thought proper. In other words, we had sold our-selves into slavery—and what could we do about it? The white folks had all the courts, all the guns, all the hounds, all the railroads, all the telegraph wires, all the newspapers, all the money, and nearly all the land—and we had only our ignorance, our poverty and our empty hands. We decided that the best thing to do was to shut our mouths, say nothing, and go back to work. And most of us worked side by side with those convicts during the remainder of the ten years.

But this first batch of convicts was only the beginning. Within six months another stockade was built, and twenty or thirty other convicts were brought to the plantation, among them six or eight women! The Senator had bought an additional thousand acres of land, and to his already large cotton plantation he added two great big saw-mills and went into the lumber business. Within two years the Senator had in all nearly 200 negroes working on his plantation—about half of them free laborers, so-called, and about half of them convicts. The only difference between the free laborers and the others was that the free laborers could come and go as they pleased, at night—that is, they were not locked up at night, and were not, as a general thing, whipped for slight offenses. The troubles of the free laborers began at the close of the ten-year period. To a man, they all wanted to quit when the time was up. To a man, they all refused to sign new contracts—even for one year, not to say anything of ten years. And just when we thought that our bondage was at an end we found that it had really just begun. Two or three years before, or about a year and a half after the Senator had started his camp, he had established a large store, which was called the commissary. All of us free laborers were compelled to buy our sup-plies—food, clothing, etc.—from that store. We never used any money in our deal-ings with the commissary, only tickets or orders, and we had a general settle-ment once each year, in October. In this store we were charged all sorts of high prices for goods, because every year we would come out in debt to our employer. If not that, we seldom had more than $5 or $10 coming to us—and that for a whole year's work. Well, at the close of the tenth year, when we kicked and meant to leave the Senator, he said to some of us with a smile (and I never will forget that smile—I can see it now):

"Boys, I'm sorry you're going to leave me. I hope you will do well in your new places—so well that you will be able to pay me the little balances which most of you owe me."

Word was sent out for all of us to meet him at the commissary at 2 o'clock. There he told us that, after we had signed what he called a written acknowl-edgment for our debts, we might go and look for new places. The storekeeper took us one by one and read to us statements of our accounts. According to the books there was no man of us who owed the Senator less than $100; some of us were put down for as much as $200. I owed $165, according to the book-keeper. These debts were not accumulated during one year, but ran back for three and four years, so we were told—in spite of the fact that we understood that we had had a full settlement at the end of each year. But no one of us would have dared to dispute a white man's word—oh, no; not in those days. Besides, we fellows didn't care anything about the amounts—we were after getting away; and we had been told that we might go, if we signed the acknowledgments. We would have signed anything, just to get away. So we stepped up, we did, and made our marks. That same night we were rounded up by a constable and ten or twelve white men, who aided him, and we were locked up, every one of us, in one of the Senator's stockades. The next morning it was explained to us by the two guards appointed to watch us that, in the papers we had signed the day before, we had not only made acknowledgment of our indebtedness, but that we had also agreed to work for the Senator until the debts were paid by hard labor. And from that day forward we were treated just like convicts. Really we had made ourselves lifetime slaves, or peons, as the laws called us. But, call it slavery, peonage, or what not, the truth is we lived in a hell on earth what time we spent in the Senator's peon camp.

I lived in that camp, as a peon, for nearly three years. My wife fared better than I did, as did the wives of some of the other negroes, because the white men about the camp used these unfortunate creatures as their mistresses. When I was first put in the stockade my wife was still kept for a while in the "Big House," but my little boy, who was only nine years old, was given away to a negro family across the river in South Carolina, and I never saw or heard of him after that. When I left the camp my wife had had two children for some of the white bosses, and she was living in fairly good shape in a little house off to herself. But the poor negro women who were not in the class with my wife fared about as bad as the helpless negro men. Most of the time the women who were peons or convicts were compelled to wear men's clothes. Sometimes, when I have seen them dressed like men, and plowing or hoeing or hauling logs or working at the blacksmith's trade, just the same as men, my heart would bleed and my blood would boil, but I was powerless to raise a hand. It would have meant death on the spot to have said a word. Of the first six women brought to the camp, two of them gave birth to children after they had been there more than twelve months—and the babies had white men for their fathers!

The stockades in which we slept were, I believe, the filthiest places in the world. They were cesspools of nastiness. During the thirteen years that I was there I am willing to swear that a mattress was never moved after it had been brought there, except to turn it over once or twice a month. No sheets were used, only dark-colored blankets. Most of the men slept every night in the clothing that they had worked in all day. Some of the worst characters were made to sleep in chains. The doors were locked and barred each night, and tallow candles were the only lights allowed. Really the stockades were but little more than cow lots, horse stables or hog pens. Strange to say, not a great number of these people died while I was there, tho a great many came away maimed and bruised and, in some cases, disabled for life. As far as I remember only about ten died during the last ten years that I was there, two of these being killed outright by the guards for trivial offenses.

It was a hard school that peon camp was, but I learned more there in a few short months by contact with those poor fellows from the outside world than ever I had known before. Most of what I learned was evil, and I now know that I should have been better off without the knowledge, but much of what I learned was helpful to me. Barring two or three severe and brutal whippings which I received, I got along very well, all things considered; but the system is damnable. A favorite way of whipping a man was to strap him down to a log, flat on his back, and spank him fifty or sixty times on his bare feet with a shingle or a huge piece of plank. When the man would get up with sore and blistered feet and an aching body, if he could not then keep up with the other men at work he would be strapped to the log again, this time face downward, and would be lashed with a buggy trace on his bare back. When a woman had to be whipped it was usually done in private, tho they would be compelled to fall down across a barrel or something of the kind and receive the licks on their backsides.

The working day on a peon farm begins with sunrise and ends when the sun goes down; or, in other words, the average peon works from ten to twelve hours each day, with one hour (from 12 o'clock to 1 o'clock) for dinner. Hot or cold, sun or rain, this is the rule. As to their meals, the laborers are divided up into squads or companies, just the same as soldiers in a great military camp would be. Two or three men in each stockade are appointed as cooks. From thirty to forty men report to each cook. In the warm months (or eight or nine months out of the year) the cooking is done on the outside, just behind the stockades; in the cold months the cooking is done inside the stockades. Each peon is provided with a great big tin cup, a flat tin pan and two big tin spoons. No knives or forks are ever seen, except those used by the cooks. At meal time the peons pass in single file before the cooks, and hold out their pans and cups to receive their allowances. Cow peas (red or white, which when boiled turn black), fat bacon and old-fashioned Georgia corn bread, baked in pones from one to two and three inches thick, make up the chief articles of food. Black coffee, black molasses and brown sugar are also used abundantly. Once in a great while, on Sundays, biscuits would be made, but they would always be made from the kind of flour called "shorts." As a rule, breakfast consisted of coffee, fried bacon, corn bread, and sometimes molasses—and one "helping" of each was all that was allowed. Peas, boiled with huge hunks of fat bacon, and a hoe-cake, as big as a man's hand, usually answered for dinner. Sometimes this dinner bill of fare gave place to bacon and greens (collard or turnip) and pot liquor. Tho we raised corn, potatoes and other vegetables, we never got a chance at such things unless we could steal them and cook them secretly. Supper consisted of coffee, fried bacon and molasses. But, altho the food was limited to certain things, I am sure we all got a plenty of the things allowed. As coarse as these things were, we kept, as a rule, fat and sleek and as strong as mules. And that, too, in spite of the fact that we had no special arrangements for taking regular baths, and no very great effort was made to keep us regularly in clean clothes. No tables were used or allowed. In summer we would sit down on the ground and eat our meals, and in winter we would sit around inside the filthy stockades. Each man was his own dish washer—that is to say, each man was responsible for the care of his pan and cup and spoons. My dishes got washed about once a week!

To-day, I am told, there are six or seven of these private camps in Georgia —that is to say, camps where most of the convicts are leased from the State of Georgia. But there are hundreds and hundreds of farms all over the State where negroes, and in some cases poor white folks, are held in bondage on the ground that they are working out debts, or where the contracts which they have made hold them in a kind of perpetual bondage, because, under those contracts, they may not quit one employer and hire out to another, except by and with the knowledge and consent of the former employer. One of the usual ways to se-cure laborers for a large peonage camp is for the proprietor to send out an agent to the little courts in the towns and villages, and where a man charged with some petty offense has no friends or money the agent will urge him to plead guilty, with the understanding that the agent will pay his fine, and in that way save him from the disgrace of being sent to jail or the chain-gang! For this high favor the man must sign beforehand a paper signifying his willingness to go to the farm and work out the amount of the fine imposed. When he reaches the farm he has to be fed and clothed, to be sure, and these things are charged up to his account. By the time he has worked out his first debt another is hanging over his head, and so on and so on, by a sort of endless chain, for an indefinite period, as in every case the indebtedness is arbitrarily arranged by the employer. In many cases it is very evident that the court officials are in collusion with the proprietors or agents, and that they divide the "graft" among themselves. As an example of this dickering among the whites, every year many convicts were brought to the Senator's camp from a certain county in South Georgia, 'way down in the turpentine district. The majority of these men were charged with adultery, which is an offense against the laws of the great and sovereign State of Georgia! Upon inquiry I learned that down in that county a number of negro lewd women were employed by certain white men to entice negro men into their houses; and then, on certain nights, at a given signal, when all was in readiness, raids would be made by the officers upon these houses, and the men would be arrested and charged with living in adultery. Nine out of ten of these men, so arrested and so charged, would find their way ultimately to some convict camp, and, as I said, many of them found their way every year to the Senator's camp while I was there. The low-down women were never punished in any way. On the contrary, I was told that they always seemed to stand in high favor with the sheriffs, constables and other officers. There can be no room to doubt that they assisted very materially in furnishing laborers for the prison pens of Georgia, and the belief was general among the men that they were regularly paid for their work. I could tell more, but I've said enough to make anybody's heart sick. I am glad that the Federal authorities are taking a hand in breaking up this great and terrible iniquity. It is, I know, widespread throughout Georgia and many other Southern States. Since Judge Speer fired into the gang last Novem-ber at Savannah, I notice that arrests have been made of seven men in three different sections of the State—all charged with holding men in peonage. Some-where, somehow, a beginning of the end should be made.

But I didn't tell you how I got out. I didn't get out—they put me out. When I had served as a peon for nearly three years—and you remember that they claimed that I owed them only $165—when I had served for nearly three years, one of the bosses came to me and said that my time was up. He happened to be the one who was said to be living with my wife. He gave me a new suit of over-alls, which cost about seventy-five cents, took me in a buggy and carried me across the Broad River into South Carolina, set me down and told me to "git." I didn't have a cent of money, and I wasn't feeling well, but somehow I managed to get a move on me. I begged my way to Columbia. In two or three days I ran across a man looking for laborers to carry to Birmingham, and I joined his gang. I have been here in the Birmingham district since they released me, and I reckon I'll die either in a coal mine or an iron furnace. It don't make much difference which. Either is better than a Georgia peon camp. And a Georgia peon camp is hell itself!

South Carolina.

French-Canadians

IRIS SAUNDERS PODEA

Quebec to "Little Canada": The Coming of the French Canadians to New England in the Nineteenth Century

Most American minorities came to the United States from the east, the south, or the west. Only the French-Canadians migrated from the north. They emigrated from Quebec in the 1840s because of depressed conditions in the ship-building and lumber industries and because of difficulty in obtaining land, most of which was in the hands of the speculators. Like most other minorities the French-Canadians sought greater economic opportunities. They settled mainly in New England, although some moved to Illinois, Wisconsin, Michigan, and New York and found employment as agricultural laborers, lumbermen, textile operators, and brickyard workers. New England Yankees dubbed them "the Chinese of the Eastern states," an indication, as Marcus Hansen has written, that New Englanders considered the Canadians ignorant, poor, and degraded; an unwelcome influx that would lower wages and raise the proportion of criminals; and an element that showed no disposition to become "American." Many natives also thought that the newcomers really were loyal to another country, or, since they were Catholic, ruled by the priesthood. For these worried New Englanders the French-Canadians constituted a dangerous class in the community.

By 1900 New England had about 275,000 French-Canadians; thereafter immigration declined as economic conditions in Canada improved. Diminished entry and the influx of southern and eastern Europeans at the end of the nineteenth century changed the older image of "the Chinese of the Eastern states." In the 1880s and '90s New Englanders started to describe French-Canadians as industrious, frugal, and quick to learn; the Italians, Greeks, and Syrians had replaced them on the lower rungs of society. Despite partial assimilation and acceptance, the French-Canadians clung to their own language and customs. The refusal to drop their own ways prevented the group from achieving social equality with Yankee New Englanders.

In the following selection Iris Saunders Podea describes the early experiences of French-Canadians in New England.

New England Quarterly, 23 (1950), 365–80. Reprinted by permission.

New Englanders have long been accustomed to hearing the French language spoken in the streets and shops of Lewiston, Manchester, Woonsocket, and other manufacturing towns. This phenomenon may have led to a conjecture whether the "struggle for a continent" still continues, and the presence of the French Canadians in New England is but a phase of Quebec's expansion in North America. The Canadian French invaders who poured into New England in the last three or four decades of the nineteenth century, however, did not come as warriors. They were simply seeking their daily bread, and their peaceful penetration has proved far more successful than the earlier French efforts at military conquest. Leaving Quebec's impoverished farms, they entered the expanding American industrial life at an opportune moment and were quickly transformed into an urban people. A few, of course, remained farmers, especially in Vermont and New Hampshire, but they constitute a rural minority. This essay will be concerned with the ancestors of today's Franco-Americans, the French Canadians who migrated to New England mill towns prior to 1900.

This migration southward from their native province of Quebec was induced by a variety of reasons: geographical proximity, colonial struggles, and seasonal opportunities. Lumber camps and farms, canals and railroads, quarries and brickyards, river and lake steamers: all were clamoring for manpower in the growing Republic and Quebec had more than an ample supply. Political unrest in Canada before Confederation also contributed to the migration, but those who came as refugees after the 1837 Rebellion or as malcontents following the union of Upper and Lower Canada in 1840 were relatively few. Higher wages in the United States were always a magnet, but more important than occupational attractions across the frontier or political forces at home was the economic distress which became increasingly intense in rural Quebec throughout a large part of the nineteenth century.

No real understanding of the French-Canadian migration into New England can be gained without some idea of what the French Canadian left behind. Quebec agriculture presented a dismal outlook, and industry was undeveloped. In his journey through the province in 1819, Benjamin Silliman had commented on the wasteful farming techniques then employed,[1] and this criticism was still valid half a century later. It was the prevailing prejudice that land improvement did not pay.[2] The special committees appointed by the Legislative Assembly in 1849 and 1857 to investigate the extent and causes of emigration from Quebec confirmed the backward state of agricultural affairs.[3] Many French-Canadian youths were landless, while crown lands remained too dear and requirements for settlement too difficult. Little land was available for colonization, and even when it was available, inadequate roads and bridges made it difficult of access and deprived it of markets for its produce. The committees' pleas for better

[1] Benjamin Silliman, *Remarks made on a Short Tour between Hartford and Quebec, in the Autumn of 1819* (New Haven, 1824), 293.

[2] *P. Q. Sessional Papers,* 1874–75, VIII, Doc. No. 4, "Rapport général du commissaire de l'agriculture et des travaux publics de la Province de Québec pour l'année finissant le 30 juin 1874," xlii–xliii.

[3] *Rapport du comité spécial de l'assemblée legislative, nommé pour s'enquérir des causes et de l'importance de l'émigration qui a lieu tous les ans du Bas-Canada vers les Etats-Unis* (Montreal, 1849), *passim; Rapport du comité spécial nommé pour s'enquérir des causes de l'émigration du Canada aux Etats-Unis d'Amérique ou ailleurs* (Toronto, 1957), *passim.*

roads, bridges, and other reforms such as homesteads and the guarantee of wood rights went almost unheeded, except by colonization societies, many of which were ineffective.

Quebec agriculture continued to decline. While the Dominion Government was making every effort to induce European immigrants to settle in the Canadian West, French Canadians continued to leave their farms for the United States, for the West, or for the cities. The *habitants* who remained behind still pursued their old methods of soil depletion and, in addition, the old inheritance system still prevailed. Farms, already small, were repeatedly subdivided among the many children of French Canada's large families, reducing them to strips too narrow to produce an adequate living. It is no wonder that the Seventh Census of Canada stated that it "was not in quest of a higher standard of living but to avoid a lower" that the French Canadian was impelled to migrate.[4] The people of Quebec, rather than risk the shrinking of an already precarious existence, preferred to leave behind the land of their ancestors. It is hard to believe that a people so gregarious and loyal to their province as the French Canadians would have chosen to venture into a formerly hostile New England for the sake of uncertain financial gain, had it not been for these disheartening prospects at home.

In view of the predicament in which French-Canadian youth found itself, the Civil War in the United States was a welcome opportunity to many young men. The inducement of bounties for army recruits was irresistible, and it is estimated that approximately 40,000 French Canadians served in the Union armies, a number of whom undoubtedly were already resident in the United States.[5] The war also coincided with and accelerated an unprecedented industrial development in New England. Labor was at a premium, and improved technology made it possible to employ unskilled workers to an increasing extent, a fact which vastly broadened the opportunities for women, children, and immigrants. With this crying need, it was not surprising that wide-awake mill owners in New England should tap Quebec's overflowing supply, especially when it lay so much nearer than Europe.

New England manufacturers gave French-Canadian workers a ready welcome. Even before the war they had discovered the advantages of importing French-Canadian labor—quick accessibility, low wages, industrious and uncomplaining employes. Factories adopted the practice of sending recruiting agents to Quebec and entire families and parishes were transported to New England. Many are the accounts of desolation in Quebec's deserted villages. Railroads were also instrumental in promoting the migration, first, by facilitating means of travel, and secondly, by stimulating this French-speaking traffic through agents and interpreters. The most effective recruiting agent of all, however, was the *émigré* himself. His letters home spread the *fièvre des Etats-Unis* among relatives and friends, and when he visited his native village dressed in city clothes, wearing the inevitable gold watch and chain, he personified success in the United States.

[4] Dominion Bureau of Statistics, *Seventh Census of Canada, 1931* (Ottawa, 1936), 110.
    [5] John Bartlet Brebner, *North Atlantic Triangle* (New Haven, 1945), 161–162; *Catholic Encyclopedia* (New York, 1913), VI, 272. Other estimates vary from 30–60,000.

No more than mere mention can be made here of the growing alarm felt in Canada at increasing emigration from the province, but it was widespread. It became a subject of legislative investigation, ecclesiastical concern, and propagandistic literature. Discrediting motives were imputed to the departing inhabitants in an effort to stay the tide—misconduct, extravagance, love of luxury, adventure, and so on—but emigration continued to gain in volume until about 1896, a date which marked several significant trends. A period of prosperity in Canada followed close on the heels of its return in the United States, and the advent of the first French-Canadian Prime Minister enhanced Quebec's prestige. In this last decade of the century the Canadian-born French in the United States increased by over 90,000 but in the succeeding ten years they decreased by more than 9,000.[6] French Canadians were apparently beginning to find a more adequate outlet for their talents at home.

In the meantime, what of the thousands of French-speaking workers absorbed in the gigantic maw of the New England mills? By no means the first immigrants to invade the northeastern states, they followed the Irish who had long since achieved the "second colonization" of New England. In many New England towns they were the first sizable group of non-English speaking people and by 1900 they numbered more than half a million in New England alone.[7] Americans looked down upon *habitants* arriving on New England station platforms in rustic garb, followed by broods of children. These large families without financial reserves were obliged to seek work at once, and usually friends from their native village guided them to both jobs and shelter. Mostly farmers, they had no experience in the industrial world. The few who were skilled in various trades were handicapped by language and temporarily had to join the rank and file in the mills.

The cotton textile industry offered the greatest opportunity for unskilled labor and absorbed a large portion of these French Canadians, whose descendants have become "a permanent factor in the labor supply of the cotton mills" of New England.[8] The French Canadians made themselves felt in this industry in the 1870's, when there were over seven thousand Canadian-born engaged in it in New England. Within thirty years this number soared to nearly 60,000.[9] French-Canadian operatives in cotton rose from 20% to nearly 37% of the total number in Massachusetts between 1890 and 1900, and in Maine and New Hampshire they exceeded 60%.[10] In 1888 over 3,000 French-speaking women were employed in the cotton mills of Lewiston, Biddeford, Saco, and Waterville, out of a total of approximately five and a half thousand female employees.[11] Although fewer French-Canadian women workers than those of any

[6] Leon E. Truesdell, *The Canadian Born in the United States* (New Haven, 1943), 77, Table 30. The author is Chief Demographer of the Bureau of the Census, Washington, and figures in this book are from the U.S. Census.
[7] Truesdell, *The Canadian Born in the United States.* French-Canadian stock in the New England states numbered 518,887, according to the U.S. Census of 1900.
[8] Melvin T. Copeland, *The Cotton Manufacturing Industry of the United States* (Cambridge, 1912), 120.
[9] Copeland, *The Cotton Manufacturing Industry . . . ,* 118–121.
[10] *Report of the Immigration Commission, Immigrants in Industries* (Washington, 1911), x, 33, Table 17, and 36, Table 19.
[11] *2nd Annual Report of the Bureau of Industrial and Labor Statistics for the State of Maine* (Augusta, 1889), 131.

other nationality had ever been employed for wages before coming to the United States,[12] over 40% of those in Massachusetts over ten years of age were employed in 1885.[13]

In 1888 the Maine Bureau of Industrial and Labor Statistics appointed Flora Haines as special agent to survey conditions for women textile workers in that state.[14] After more sordid accounts of textile mills, it is refreshing to come upon her description of a clean and cheerful spinning room with open windows, of the mill girls with neat white linen collars and whisk brooms to brush lint from their frocks. She reported defective eyes as a common ailment among the French and the use of tobacco by French-Canadian children. Women took snuff and signs were posted in French and English requesting those using tobacco not to "spit on the floor." Most French-Canadian girls lived at home in very crowded quarters, but those who lived in boarding houses enjoyed a good reputation in the community. In view of the French-Canadian retention of their language in the United States, it is worthy of note that Miss Haines recommended the use of textbooks such as those employed in New Brunswick where both English and French instruction was given. She felt that American children in the public schools could profit by learning a little French.

The charge has often been made that French Canadians, with their large families, had more child operatives in the mills than any other group of workers. Child labor, nevertheless, was prevalent in the textile mills long before the coming of the French Canadians.[15] They simply followed a long-established custom when they sent their children to work, one further reinforced by necessity. Actually a study of cotton mill workers made in 1905 indicated that the French-Canadian children contributed only one-third of the income in the families covered, while Irish children in the same survey contributed 45% of the family income.[16]

More justifiable was the accusation that the French Canadians evaded the school laws, sometimes falsifying the ages of their children. The Massachusetts Bureau of Labor Statistics went so far as to state in its report of 1881 that when the French-Canadian parents were finally "cornered" by the school officers and "there is no other escape, often they scrabble together what few things they have, and move away to some other place where they are unknown, and where they hope by a repetition of the same deceits to escape the schools entirely, and keep the children at work right on in the mills."[17] Although much evidence to the contrary was presented by indignant French Canadians in Massachusetts at a special hearing before the Bureau in 1881 in an effort to disprove this and other equally derogatory statements of the Report, there can be little doubt that very young French-Canadian children were commonly employed and that existing child labor laws were violated. At this time Commissioner Wright, head

[12] *Report of the Immigration Commission*, X, 72.
[13] *20th Annual Report of the Bureau of Statistics of Labor* (Boston, 1889), 577.
[14] *2nd Annual Report of the Bureau of Industrial and Labor Statistics for the State of Maine, passim.*
[15] Samuel Slater had employed children from seven to twelve years of age and then adopted the practice of hiring whole families.
[16] *Report of the Immigration Commission*, X, 114, Table 64.
[17] *12th Annual Report of the Bureau of Statistics of Labor* (Boston, 1881), 469–470.

of the Massachusetts Bureau of Statistics of Labor, while admitting that the re-
marks were not true for Massachusetts, indicated that they were applicable to
French Canadians in Connecticut and New York.[18] This was confirmed by the
Connecticut Bureau of Labor Statistics in its annual report for the year 1885:

> Another element which affects child labor is that of race. The native
> American almost always wants to educate his children. The Irishman
> feels this want even more strongly, and will make great sacrifices for
> the sake of his family. On the other hand, the French Canadian, in a
> great many instances regards his children as a means of adding to the
> earning capacity of the family, and, in making arrangements for work,
> he urges, and even insists upon the employment of the family as a whole,
> down to the very youngest children who can be of any possible service.
>
> It is in places like Baltic, with a large French-Canadian population,
> that these evils have been felt in their severest form. There was a time
> when the Baltic Mills employed a large number of children under ten
> years of age. The worst of these abuses seem to have been done away
> with in that place; but there are many mills, especially among the less
> important ones, where it has been impossible to stop or even to detect
> them.[19]

An overseer in Southbridge reported in 1872 that he used to tell the French
Canadians that the law did not permit employment of children under ten years,
"and the next day they were all ten."[20] Reports of factory accidents of the
1860's and '70's included French-Canadian children under ten. Felix Gatineau,
in his history of the Franco-Americans of Southbridge, observed the tendency
of these first French Canadians to send children from seven to eight years old
to work instead of to school.[21]

It is certain that the school laws were poorly enforced in New England.
Not only were parents and manufacturers hostile; the school authorities themselves did not want the schools flooded with the undisciplined children of the
working class.[22] Sometimes at the beginning of a semester, children were all
turned out of the mills, but within a few weeks most of them were back. Although Massachusetts led in child labor legislation, statistics for 1891 showed a
higher proportion of French-Canadian children at work in the cotton industry
in that state than elsewhere in New England.[23] Rhode Island likewise found
fault with the French Canadians on the score of illiteracy and child labor.[24]
Evidence from a number of sources, therefore, obliges one to conclude that the
French Canadians were conspicuous offenders, even where violations of school
and minimum-age laws were common.

[18] *13th Annual Report, Bureau of Statistics of Labor* (Boston, 1882), 27.
[19] *1st Annual Report, Bureau of Labor Statistics of the State of Connecticut*
(Hartford, 1885), 48–49.
[20] *3rd Annual Report, Bureau of Statistics of Labor* (Boston, 1872), 379.
[21] Felix Gatineau, *Histoire des Franco-Américains de Southbridge, Mass.* (Fra-
mingham, 1919), 46.
[22] Forest C. Ensign, *Compulsory School Attendance and Child Labor* (Iowa City,
1921), 62–63, 96–97.
[23] *7th Annual Report, Commissioner of Labor, 1891* (Washington, 1892), II,
1588–1590, Table XX.
[24] *5th Annual Report, Commission of Industrial Statistics, Rhode Island* (Providence, 1892), 44–52.

As newcomers, they had little choice but to accept the lowest wages. With their large families they were able to get along on less than the native American workers used to a higher standard of living. This and the fact that they were frequently introduced into New England industry as strike-breakers did not endear them to their co-workers. At West Rutland, Vermont, when they were imported into the marble quarries during a turn-out of Irish quarrymen in 1868, bloodshed resulted.[25] In Fall River during a strike in 1879, employers had to build special houses in the mill-yards for French-Canadian "knobstick" spinners, for fear strikers would persuade them to leave town.[26] Many similar instances of strike-breaking occurred. Thanks to this unfortunate role, which immigrants in the United States have often been called upon to play, they won the enmity of organized labor. Nor did they wish to join in strikes and unions. Experience had taught them, they claimed, that when they did participate in strikes they lost their jobs while others went back to work without telling them.[27] The Knights of Labor (condemned in Quebec by Cardinal Taschereau) were not very successful in recruiting French-Canadian members and tried to influence state legislation against them.[28] French-Canadian influence was held partly responsible for the failure of New England cotton mill operatives to build a stronger organization,[29] but rather than do without wages during strikes they preferred a low income regularly.

On the other hand, there were evidences of a dawning labor consciousness among them before the end of the century. A few joined the Knights of St. Crispin and even the Knights of Labor. At the time Chinese were introduced into the Sampson shoe factory at North Adams in 1870, several French Canadians participated in the protest against the Chinese.[30] In 1879 sixty French Canadians at the Douglas Axe Company in Massachusetts struck for a 10% wage increase.[31] Unions, which at first had been indifferent toward immigrants, began to print notices in French.[32] In Worcester, French-Canadian carpenters formed their own union.[33] After being in the United States long enough to understand labor aims and methods, their attitude began to change. In general, however, the language barrier and the influence of their leaders discouraged the early French-Canadian *émigrés* from association with strikes and labor organizations. They prided themselves on refusing to take part and on being law-abiding citizens.[34]

Although general wages and working conditions slowly improved, wages in the textile and paper industries lagged behind, a fact especially significant for

[25] George H. Perkins, "The Marble Industry of Vermont" in *Report of the State Geologist on the Mineral Industries and Geology of Vermont, 1931–1932* (Burlington, 1933), 292.

[26] George E. McNeill, editor, *The Labor Movement: The Problem of To-day* (Boston, 1887), 230.

[27] E. Hamon, *Les Canadiens-français de la Nouvelle Angleterre* (Quebec, 1891), 45–47.

[28] E. Hamon, *Les Canadiens-français . . . ,* 45.

[29] William Z. Ripley, "Race Factors in Labor Unions," *Atlantic Monthly,* XCIII (March, 1904), 302.

[30] *Report of the Bureau of Statistics of Labor, 1870–71* (Boston, 1871), 106.

[31] *11th Annual Report, Bureau of Statistics of Labor* (Boston, 1880), 51.

[32] *29th Annual Report, Bureau of Statistics of Labor* (Boston, 1899), 620; McNeill, editor, *The Labor Movement,* 230.

[33] *30th Annual Report, Bureau of Statistics of Labor* (Boston, 1900), 163, 209.

[34] *13th Annual Report, Bureau of Statistics of Labor* (Boston, 1882), 25–26.

the French Canadians. Statistics showed a definite relationship between length of residence in the United States and wages received. French Canadians were advancing to more skilled positions in industry by the end of the century, and many French-Canadian girls were anxious to leave the cotton mills for something better.[35] Despite the steady upward push toward higher economic, social, and professional levels, distinction was reserved for the few and the majority had to endure the hardships that accompanied their low wage scale. It was the poverty and dirt of their "Little Canadas" in the nineteenth century that gained for them a sorry reputation when they first came to New England.

Nearly every manufacturing town where they settled had its French-Canadian quarter. The usual picture of these squalid "Frenchvilles" dispels at once the Quebec allegation that the *émigrés* departed for love of luxury. Most of them began life in the United States in tenements and were locally referred to as "Canucks." Sanitation and cleanliness were at a minimum and the high death rate in some of the "Little Canadas" was to be expected in these overcrowded and unwholesome lodgings. Fall River and Holyoke were notorious for their "hell holes," and William Bayard Hale described French-Canadian tenements in Fall River in 1894 as not fit "to house a dog." The Slade Mill tenements, he said, were worse than the old-time slave quarters, and in the Globe Mill houses rats had driven out the inhabitants.[36] The first large-scale tenement dwellings in Lowell were built in "Little Canada," and the population density in these structures was claimed to surpass that anywhere in the United States outside the Fourth Ward in New York City.[37] Darkness, foul odors, lack of space and air, shabby surroundings, all these were universal tenement characteristics, to which the French Canadians had no exclusive claim, but their quarters were repeatedly singled out as among the worst or most ill-kept in New England. Mill owners, nevertheless, apparently kept their lodgings in better condition than private exploiters who later purchased them. The Granite Mills in Fall River had the best maintained houses in town and vacancies there were rare. If the French Canadians were provided with good housing, commented a Salem investigator in 1873, they were too proud a people not to keep it that way.[38] This, alas, did not always prove true.

French Canadians, as well as Irish, were a problem to the health authorities. They were frightened by compulsory vaccination and did not understand why wakes were prohibited during a period of epidemic disease. The Lowell Health Department made an earnest effort to reach its "Little Canada." School children there were generally vaccinated free of charge and parental opposition was attributed more to the necessity of caring for the child's sore arm than to prejudice against vaccination.[39] Detailed child-care instructions were printed in French and English and a medical inspector was sent into the district with two boys acting as interpreters. Disease was widespread among French-Canadian

[35] *Report of the Immigration Commission,* X, 177, 289.
[36] William Bayard Hale, "Impotence of Churches in a Manufacturing Town," *Forum* (November, 1894), 298–300.
[37] *Annual Report of the Board of Health of the City of Lowell, 1882* (Lowell, 1883), 18.
[38] *4th Annual Report, Bureau of Statistics of Labor* (Boston, 1873), 378–379.
[39] *Annual Report of the Board of Health of the City of Lowell, 1880* (Lowell, 1881), 5–6.

children and infant mortality high, much of it due to improper feeding and ignorance. The Health Department deplored the laziness and indifference of parents who failed to send for the ward physician when their children were ill.
People who could afford a funeral better than they could preventive measures
were hard to get along with, wrote one health officer despairingly.[40]

These humble and insalubrious beginnings were the common immigrant
lot. There was, happily, a brighter side for the French Canadians. The impression is all too common that the farmer lives an idyllic and healthful life, but
evidence often reveals the simple life as a synonym for mere subsistence. In
moving to the mill towns of New England, the French Canadians enjoyed
better food than in Quebec and many wrote home that they ate meat every day.
"The proud housekeeper," wrote Archambault in his novel, *Mill Village*, "was
the one who would place five pounds of fried pork chops and a half peck of
boiled potatoes before an invited guest."[41] Such a housekeeper was luckier than
most, but the French-Canadian laboring man in Massachusetts consumed about
five pounds of food per day in 1886, a pound and a half more than his confrere
in Quebec. The Massachusetts Bureau of Statistics of Labor compared French-
Canadian family and boarding-house diets in Holyoke, Lawrence, Lowell,
Montreal, Rivière du Loup, and Quebec and found both nutritive value and
quantity considerably in favor of Massachusetts.[42]

Clothing also showed improvement. The French Canadians were quick to
adopt the American mode and sometimes sacrificed food or home comforts for
fashion.[43] Sewing machines were not unknown in homes of French-Canadian
workers and seemed to have a beneficent influence on the aspect of the whole
household.[44] French Canadians were reputedly well dressed, but there were relatively few silks and satins. Necessity at times drove economy to the extreme of
avoiding walking to save shoe leather or wearing outgrown garments when
there were no younger children to inherit them.[45]

Toward the end of the century, the "Little Canadas" were being abandoned
to other immigrants. The coming of the street railway was an important factor
in enabling workers to quit the tenements,[46] and in towns such as Worcester and
Marlboro where textiles were not the predominant industry, French-Canadian
home ownership made progress. Investment in real estate was regarded as an
indication of stability and an excellent way to train the French Canadians in
economy through the habit of saving to pay off mortgages.[47] The property requirement for voting by naturalized citizens in Rhode Island was an added
stimulus there to the purchase of real estate, but general progress toward home
ownership was slow.[48] In view of the French-Canadian reputation for thrift,
this pace is disappointing.

[40] *Annual Report of the Board of Health . . . , 1888* (Lowell, 1889), 37–41.
[41] A. A. Archambault, *Mill Village* (Boston, 1943), 126.
[42] *17th Annual Report, Bureau of Statistics of Labor* (Boston, 1886), 311–312.
[43] William Kirk, *A Modern City* (Chicago, 1909), 114–115.
[44] *6th Annual Report, Bureau of Statistics of Labor* (Boston, 1875), 313.
[45] Camille Lessard, *Canuck* (Lewiston, 1936), 19, 33.
[46] *Report of the Immigration Commission*, X, 342.
[47] Hamon, *Les Canadiens-français de la Nouvelle Angleterre*, 18–19.
[48] French Canadians have not come up to the general average or that of the foreign-born in the U.S. for home ownership and median rental, a situation which prevailed down to the census of 1940.

Frugality was a Quebec trait which on occasion excited the jealousy or envy of others. The first savings of French Canadians usually went to the church, and their fine record for financing church properties is in contrast to their slower private advancement, at the same time demonstrating their willingness to sacrifice for their faith. The amazing feature about their religious, educational and philanthropic institutions is that they were paid for by small contributions, mostly from the working class, with very few large donations.[49] Saving was encouraged by the clergy, and toward the end of the century special savings institutions for French Canadians began to appear in New England. Holyoke's second coöperative bank was founded in 1889 to enable French-Canadian workers to buy homes on a monthly installment plan; it was the first Franco-American financial institution in the United States.[50] Woonsocket's Institution for Savings soon had to employ French-speaking clerks to take care of French-Canadian accounts, and Aram Pothier, later Governor of Rhode Island, served in that capacity. In 1900 the first *caisse populaire,* a form of credit union, was founded in Quebec, and this movement soon spread to the United States. Another Quebec habit which promoted savings was the family system, whereby children turned over their earnings to their parents.

French-Canadian thrift, nevertheless, has probably been overestimated. Early *émigrés* had little confidence in banks or investments, their mistrust justified by such experiences as the fraudulent New England Investment Company and the loss of savings deposits in bank failures. The average annual surplus among French-Canadian families in Massachusetts in 1875 was only $10.59, and they saved less than any other ethnic group in the state at that time.[51] Although saving doubtless increased with improvement in occupation, the estimate made by Father Hamon in 1890 that a French-Canadian worker with a family of four children should have about $80 a month left after deduction of major expenses[52] seems high. One of the great mistakes in estimating ability to save has been simply to multiply daily wages by the number of persons working per family and to deduct the cost of living, without regard to age, occupation, or steadiness of employment. Furthermore, both Father Hamon and Ferdinand Gagnon, father of Franco-American journalism, repeatedly exhorted their compatriots to economy instead of spending money on picnics, carriage rent, circuses, and trips to Canada.

The close of the nineteenth century found the French Canadians a settled people in New England numbering over half a million. By this time they were experienced in industry and, where statistics distinguished the older residents from the new, they had proved themselves able to compete with other workers in New England. It must not be forgotten that the steady influx of new arrivals from Quebec, who yet had to pass through their period of orientation, held back the general average of the group. Instances were even known of French Canadians replacing other French Canadians at lower wages.[53] It required time

[49] Abbé D. M. A. Magnan, *Histoire de la race française aux Etats-Unis* (Paris, 1912), 283–284.
[50] Constance M. Green, *Holyoke, Massachusetts, A Case History of the Industrial Revolution in America* (New Haven, 1939), 171–172.
[51] *6th Annual Report, Bureau of Statistics of Labor* (Boston, 1875), 377.
[52] Hamon, *Les Canadiens-français de la Nouvelle Angleterre,* 16–17.
[53] *Ferdinand Gagnon, Sa Vie et ses oeuvres* (Worcester, 1886), 76.

to learn to demand the same working and living standards as native-born citizens in the United States, but unbeknown to themselves, the French Canadians were conforming to the usual immigrant pattern, starting at the lowest level and surmounting it in the second and third generations. Meanwhile their United-States-born descendants were growing up bilingual, thus better equipped for broader participation in American life.

Their economic situation gradually improved, freeing them from complete preoccupation with earning a livelihood, and they turned their attention to the problem of their own ethnic survival. It became almost the breath of life to the newly forming mutual benefit societies and the Franco-American press. Unlike European immigrants, French Canadians did not sever the bond with the land of their birth, for Quebec adjoined New England and visits, newspapers, and education in the province were easily accessible. Their dual loyalty, so openly avowed, puzzled Americans and often became suspect when reinforced by aloofness from public schools, non-French churches, and organizations. Thus, friction in the new environment was not confined to labor competition.

Within the limits of the century the French-Canadian migration into New England was still in a state of flux. It had, however, transplanted almost in its entirety the French-Canadian parish, with separate French churches, schools, and homes for the needy. Indeed, theirs was a splendid record in caring for their own. It was too soon to foretell the extent of change from their traditional ways until more Franco-Americans had experienced a generation of life in the United States. The old melting-pot theory has been somewhat discredited in recent years, but economic forces have remained a persistent assimilator. The twentieth century ushered in great change for French Canadians in Quebec, now become the most highly industrialized province of Canada, and it may give the Franco-Americans a chance to guide their Canadian cousins along the path of ethnic tenacity in an industrial world.

Italians

RUDOLPH J. VECOLI

Contadini in Chicago:
A Critique of *The Uprooted*

*Almost three million Italians came to the United States between 1880 and 1914.
They came primarily from southern Italy and established colonies in every part
of the country. They could be found as laborers on construction gangs, peons
on farms, in the fisheries, in the mines, in the stockyards. "Little Italies" sprang
up in Boston, New York, Philadelphia, New Orleans, San Francisco, Chicago,
and numerous other American cities. Like almost all of the other minority
groups Italians were victims of vicious stereotyping and accused of being "volatile," "unstable," "undesirable," and "largely composed of the most vicious, ignorant, degraded and filthy paupers, with something more than an admixture of
the criminal element." Because most Italians worked at unskilled, low-paying
jobs, they lived in crowded and unhealthy quarters. At the end of the nineteenth
century 417 Italians in one Chicago district had bathtubs in their apartments
while 13,943 did not; in a Sicilian area in New York City 1,231 people were
squeezed into 120 rooms; one-third of the families in Philadelphia's Italian area
had one-room apartments, only a few had toilets and those were in outdoor
shacks, and almost none had bathtubs.*

*Aside from the miserable living conditions Italians endured, more than
any other white group they suffered greatly from vigilante justice. Between 1891
and 1914 Italian-Americans were lynched in New Orleans, murdered in Colorado, beaten in Mississippi, and shot by mobs in Illinois. Frequently they were
considered criminals by nature. Accordingly, vigilante action was undertaken
for the good of society. Hostility toward them reflected more than the usual
animosity minorities have come to expect in America. At the turn of the century the Italian served, as one Connecticut observer reported, as "the symbol
of all the recent immigrants who spoke no English and blotted the native
landscape."*

*In the following selection Rudolph Vecoli discusses the conditions of Chi-
cago's Italians in the late nineteenth century and criticizes one of the conclusions in Oscar Handlin's 1951 Pulitzer-Prize-winning study,* The Uprooted. *By
depicting the process of migration from its origins in European villages to the
struggles between first- and second-generation Americans, Handlin sought to*

Reprinted from the *Journal of American History*, LIV (1964), 404–17, by permission of the Organization of American Historians.

convey in a generalized way the experience of those ethnic groups involved in the mass transplantation from Europe to America between the 1840s and World War I. Vecoli argues that Handlin's analysis of this movement inadequately distinguishes the varied cultures and adjustments of different foreign-born groups and he specifically disputes Handlin's contention that the immigrants came from harmonious peasant village communities which were disrupted as a consequence of migration, leaving the newcomers lonely and isolated in their new land. Vecoli asserts that, at least in the case of southern Italian peasants who came to Chicago, the origins of the migrants were not idyllic nor was their adjustment to the new environment so great an ordeal.

In *The Uprooted*[1] Oscar Handlin attempted an overarching interpretation of European peasant society and of the adjustment of emigrants from that society to the American environment. This interpretation is open to criticism on the grounds that it fails to respect the unique cultural attributes of the many and varied ethnic groups which sent immigrants to the United States. Through an examination of the south Italians, both in their Old World setting and in Chicago, this article will indicate how Handlin's portrayal of the peasant as immigrant does violence to the character of the *contadini* (peasants) of the Mezzogiorno.[2]

The idealized peasant village which Handlin depicts in *The Uprooted* did not exist in the southern Italy of the late nineteenth century. Handlin's village was an harmonious social entity in which the individual derived his identity and being from the community as a whole; the ethos of his village was one of solidarity, communality, and neighborliness.[3] The typical south Italian peasant, however, did not live in a small village, but in a "rural city" with a population of thousands or even tens of thousands.[4] Seeking refuge from brigands and malaria, the *contadini* huddled together in these hill towns, living in stone dwellings under the most primitive conditions and each day descending the slopes to work in the fields below.

Nor were these towns simple communities of agriculturists, for their social structure included the gentry and middle class as well as the peasants. Feudalism died slowly in southern Italy, and vestiges of this archaic social order were still

[1] Oscar Handlin, *The Uprooted* (Boston, 1951).
[2] The Mezzogiorno of Italy includes the southern part of continental Italy, i.e., the regions of Abruzzi e Molise, Campania, Puglia, Basilicata, Calabria, and the island of Sicily.
[3] *Uprooted*, 7–12.
[4] On south Italian society see Edward C. Banfield, *The Moral Basis of a Backward Society* (Glencoe, Ill., 1958); Robert F. Foerster, *The Italian Emigration of Our Times* (Cambridge, 1919), 51–105; Leopoldo Franchetti and Sidney Sonnino, *La Sicilia nel 1876* (2 vols., Florence, 1925); Carlo Levi, *Christ Stopped at Eboli* (New York, 1947); Leonard W. Moss and Stephen C. Cappannari, "A Sociological and Anthropological Investigation of an Italian Rural Community" (mimeographed, Detroit, 1959); Luigi Villari, *Italian Life in Town and Country* (New York, 1902); Arrigo Serpieri, *La Guerra e le Classi Rurali Italiane* (Storia Economica e Sociale della Guerra Mondiale, Pubblicazioni della Fondazione Carnegie per la Pace Internazionale, Bari, 1930), 1–21; Friedrich Vöchting, *La Questione Meridionale* (Casa per il Mezzogiorno Studi e Testi 1, Naples, 1955); Phyllis H. Williams, *South Italian Folkways in Europe and America* (New Haven, 1938); Rocco Scotellaro, *Contadini del Sud* (Bari, 1955).

visible in the attitudes and customs of the various classes. While the great landowners had taken up residence in the capital cities, the lesser gentry constituted
the social elite of the towns. Beneath it in the social hierarchy were the professional men, officials, merchants, and artisans; at the base were the *contadini*
who comprised almost a distinct caste. The upper classes lorded over and exploited the peasants whom they regarded as less than human. Toward the upper
classes, the *contadini* nourished a hatred which was veiled by the traditional
forms of deference.[5]

This is not to say that the south Italian peasants enjoyed a sense of solidarity either as a community or as a social class. Rather it was the family which
provided the basis of peasant solidarity. Indeed, so exclusive was the demand of
the family for the loyalty of its members that it precluded allegiance to other
social institutions. This explains the paucity of voluntary associations among
the peasantry. Each member of the family was expected to advance its welfare
and to defend its honor, regardless of the consequences for outsiders. This
singleminded attention to the interests of the family led one student of south
Italian society to describe its ethos as one of "amoral familism."[6]

While the strongest ties were within the nuclear unit, there existed among
the members of the extended family a degree of trust, intimacy, and interde-
pendence denied to all others. Only through the ritual kinship of *comparaggio*
(godparenthood) could non-relatives gain admittance to the family circle. The
south Italian family was "father-dominated but mother-centered." The father
as the head of the family enjoyed unquestioned authority over the household,
but the mother provided the emotional focus for family life.

Among the various families of the *paese* (town), there were usually jealousies and feuds which frequently resulted in bloodshed. This atmosphere of
hostility was revealed in the game of *passatella,* which Carlo Levi has described
as "a peasant tournament of oratory, where interminable speeches reveal in
veiled terms a vast amount of repressed rancor, hate, and rivalry."[7] The sexual
code of the Mezzogiorno was also expressive of the family pride of the south
Italians. When violations occurred, family honor required that the seducer be
punished. The south Italian was also bound by the tradition of personal vengeance, as in the Sicilian code of *omertà*. These cultural traits secured for southern Italy the distinction of having the highest rate of homicides in all of Europe
at the turn of the century.[8] Such antisocial behavior, however, has no place in
Handlin's scheme of the peasant community.

[5] The following thought, which Handlin attributes to the immigrant in America,
would hardly have occurred to the oppressed *contadino:* "Could he here, as at home,
expect the relationship of reciprocal goodness between master and men, between just
employer and true employee?" *Uprooted,* 80.
[6] Banfield, *Moral Basis of a Backward Society,* 10. In his study of a town in
Basilicata, Banfield found that both gentry and peasants were unable to act "for any
end transcending the immediate, material interest of the nuclear family." On the south
Italian family see also Leonard W. Moss and Stephen C. Cappannari, "Patterns of
Kinship, Comparaggio and Community in a South Italian Village," *Anthropological
Quarterly,* XXXIII (Jan. 1960), 24–32; Leonard W. Moss and Walter H. Thomson,
"The South Italian Family: Literature and Observations," *Human Organization,* XVIII
(Spring 1959), 35–41.
[7] Levi, *Christ Stopped,* 179.
[8] Napoleone Colajanni, "Homicide and the Italians," *Forum,* XXXI (March
1901), 63–66.

If the south Italian peasant regarded his fellow townsman with less than brotherly feeling, he viewed with even greater suspicion the stranger—which included anyone not native to the town. The peasants knew nothing of patriotism for the Kindom of Italy, or of class solidarity with other tillers of the soil; their sense of affinity did not extend beyond town boundaries. This attachment to their native village was termed *campanilismo,* a figure of speech suggesting that the world of the *contadini* was confined within the shadow cast by his town campanile.[9] While this parochial attitude did not manifest itself in community spirit or activities, the sentiment of *campanilismo* did exert a powerful influence on the emigrants from southern Italy.

During the late nineteenth century, increasing population, agricultural depression, and oppressive taxes, combined with poor land to make life ever more difficult for the peasantry. Still, misery does not provide an adequate explanation of the great emigration which followed. For, while the peasants were equally impoverished, the rate of emigration varied widely from province to province. J. S. McDonald has suggested that the key to these differential rates lies in the differing systems of land tenure and in the contrasting sentiments of "individualism" and "solidarity" which they produced among the peasants.[10] From Apulia and the interior of Sicily where large-scale agriculture prevailed and cultivators' associations were formed, there was little emigration. Elsewhere in the South, where the peasants as small proprietors and tenants competed with one another, emigration soared. Rather than practicing communal agriculture as did Handlin's peasants, these *contadini,* both as cultivators and emigrants, acted on the principle of economic individualism, pursuing family and self-interest.

Handlin's peasants have other characteristics which do not hold true for those of southern Italy. In the Mezzogiorno, manual labor—and especially tilling the soil—was considered degrading. There the peasants did not share the reverence of Handlin's peasants for the land; rather they were "accustomed to look with distrust and hate at the soil."[11] No sentimental ties to the land deterred the south Italian peasants from becoming artisans, shopkeepers, or priests, if the opportunities presented themselves. Contrary to Handlin's peasants who meekly accepted their lowly status, the *contadini* were ambitious to advance the material and social position of their families. Emigration was one way of doing so. For the peasants in *The Uprooted* emigration was a desperate flight from disaster, but the south Italians viewed a sojourn in America as a means to acquire capital with which to purchase land, provide dowries for their daughters, and assist their sons to enter business or the professions.

If the design of peasant society described in *The Uprooted* is not adequate for southern Italy, neither is Handlin's description of the process of immigrant adjustment an accurate rendering of the experience of the *contadini.* For Handlin, "the history of immigration is a history of alienation and its conse-

[9] Richard Bagot, *The Italians of To-day* (Chicago, 1913), 87.

[10] J. S. McDonald, "Italy's Rural Social Structure and Emigration," *Occidente,* XII (Sept.–Oct. 1956), 437–55. McDonald concludes that where the peasantry's "aspirations for material betterment were expressed in broad associative behavior, there was little emigration. Where economic aspirations were integrated only with the welfare of the individual's nuclear family, emigration rates were high." *Ibid.,* 454.

[11] Kate H. Claghorn, "The Agricultural Distribution of Immigrants," in U.S. Industrial Commission, *Reports* (19 vols., Washington, 1900–1902), XV, 496; Banfield, *Moral Basis of a Backward Society,* 37, 50, 69.

quences."[12] In line with this theme, he emphasizes the isolation and loneliness of the immigrant, "the broken homes, interruptions of a familiar life, separation from known surroundings, the becoming a foreigner and ceasing to belong." While there is no desire here to belittle the hardships, fears, and anxieties to which the immigrant was subject, there are good reasons for contending that Handlin overstates the disorganizing effects of emigration and underestimates the tenacity with which the south Italian peasants at least clung to their traditional social forms and values.

Handlin, for example, dramatically pictures the immigrant ceasing to be a member of a solidary community and being cast upon his own resources as an individual.[13] But this description does not apply to the *contadini* who customarily emigrated as a group from a particular town, and, once in America, stuck together "like a swarm of bees from the same hive."[14] After working a while, and having decided to remain in America, they would send for their wives, children, and other relatives. In this fashion, chains of emigration were established between certain towns of southern Italy and Chicago.[15]

From 1880 on, the tide of emigration ran strongly from Italy to this midwestern metropolis where by 1920 the Italian population reached approximately 60,000.[16] Of these, the *contadini* of the Mezzogiorno formed the preponderant element. Because of the sentiment of *campanilismo,* there emerged not one "Little Italy" but some seventeen larger and smaller colonies scattered about the city. Each group of townsmen clustered by itself, seeking, as Jane Addams observed, to fill "an entire tenement house with the people from one village."[17] Within these settlements, the town groups maintained their distinct identities, practiced endogamy, and preserved their traditional folkways. Contrary to Handlin's dictum that the common experience of the immigrants was their inability to transplant the European village,[18] one is struck by the degree to which the *contadini* succeeded in reconstructing their native towns in the heart of industrial Chicago. As an Italian journalist commented:

> Emigrating, the Italian working class brings away with it from the mother country all the little world in which they were accustomed to live; a world of traditions, of beliefs, of customs, of ideals of their own.

[12] *Uprooted,* 4.
[13] *Ibid.,* 38.
[14] Pascal D'Angelo, *Son of Italy* (New York, 1924), 54.
[15] These chains of emigration are traced in Rudolph J. Vecoli, "Chicago's Italians Prior to World War I: A Study of Their Social and Economic Adjustments" (doctoral dissertation, University of Wisconsin, 1963), 71–234.
[16] On the Italians in Chicago see Vecoli, "Chicago's Italians"; U.S. Commissioner of Labor, *Ninth Special Report: The Italians in Chicago* (Washington, 1897); Frank O. Beck, "The Italian in Chicago," *Bulletin of the Chicago Department of Public Welfare,* II (Feb. 1919); Jane Addams, *Twenty Years at Hull-House* (New York, 1910); Giuseppe Giacosa, "Chicago e la sua colonia Italiana," *Nuova Antologia di Scienze, Lettere ed Arti,* Third Series, CXXVIII (March 1, 1893), 15–33; Giovanni E. Schiavo, *The Italians in Chicago* (Chicago, 1928); Alessandro Mastro-Valerio, "Remarks Upon the Italian Colony in Chicago," in *Hull-House Maps and Papers* (New York, 1895), 131–42; Harvey Warren Zorbaugh, *The Gold Coast and the Slum* (Chicago, 1929), 159–81; I. W. Howerth, "Are the Italians a Dangerous Class?" *Charities Review,* IV (Nov. 1894), 17–40.
[17] Jane Addams, *Newer Ideals of Peace* (New York, 1907), 67.
[18] *Uprooted,* 144.

There is no reason to marvel then that in this great center of manufacturing and commercial activity of North America our colonies, though acclimating themselves in certain ways, conserve the customs of their *paesi* of origin.[19]

If the south Italian immigrant retained a sense of belongingness with his fellow townsmen, the family continued to be the focus of his most intense loyalties. Among the male emigrants there were some who abandoned their families in Italy, but the many underwent harsh privations so that they might send money to their parents or wives. Reunited in Chicago the peasant family functioned much as it had at home; there appears to have been little of that confusion of roles depicted in *The Uprooted*. The husband's authority was not diminished, while the wife's subordinate position was not questioned. If dissension arose, it was when the children became somewhat "Americanized"; yet there are good reasons for believing that Handlin exaggerates the estrangement of the second generation from its immigrant parentage. Nor did the extended family disintegrate upon emigration as is contended. An observation made with respect to the Sicilians in Chicago was generally true for the south Italians: "Intense family pride . . . is the outstanding characteristic, and as the family unit not only includes those related by blood, but those related by ritual bonds as well (the *commare* and *compare*), and as intermarriage in the village groups is a common practice, this family pride becomes really a clan pride."[20] The alliance of families of the town through intermarriage and godparenthood perpetuated a social organization based upon large kinship groups.

The south Italian peasant also brought with them to Chicago some of their less attractive customs. Many a new chapter of an ancient vendetta of Calabria or Sicily was written on the streets of this American city. The zealous protection of the family honor was often a cause of bloodshed. Emigration had not abrogated the duty of the south Italian to guard the chastity of his women. Without the mitigating quality of these "crimes of passion" were the depredations of the "Black Hand." After 1900 the practice of extorting money under threat of death became so common as to constitute a reign of terror in the Sicilian settlements. Both the Black Handers and their victims were with few exceptions from the province of Palermo where the criminal element known collectively as the *mafia* had thrived for decades. The propensity for violence of the south Italians was not a symptom of social disorganization caused by emigration but a characteristic of their Old World culture.[21] Here too the generalizations that the immigrant feared to have recourse to the peasant crimes of revenge, and that the immigrant was rarely involved in crime for profit,[22] do not apply to the south Italians.

[19] *L'Italia* (Chicago), Aug. 3, 1901. See also Anna Zaloha, "A Study of the Persistence of Italian Customs Among 143 Families of Italian Descent" (master's thesis, Northwestern University, 1937).
[20] Zorbaugh, Gold Coast, 166–67. *Commare* and *compare* are godmother and godfather. See also Zaloha, "Persistence of Italian Customs," 103–05, 145–48.
[21] *The Italian "White Hand" Society in Chicago Illinois. Studies, Actions and Results* (Chicago, 1906); Illinois Association for Criminal Justice, *Illinois Crime Survey* (Chicago, 1929), 845–62, 935–54; Vecoli, "Chicago's Italians," 393–460.
[22] *Uprooted*, 163.

To speak of alienation as the essence of the immigrant experience is to ignore the persistence of traditional forms of group life. For the *contadino,* his family and his townsmen continued to provide a sense of belonging and to sanction his customary world-view and life-ways. Living "in," but not "of," the sprawling, dynamic city of Chicago, the south Italian was sheltered within his ethnic colony from the confusing complexity of American society.

While the acquisition of land was a significant motive for emigration, the south Italian peasants were not ones to dream, as did Handlin's, of possessing "endless acres" in America.[23] Their goal was a small plot of ground in their native towns. If they failed to reach the American soil, it was not because, as Handlin puts it, "the town had somehow trapped them,"[24] but because they sought work which would pay ready wages. These peasants had no romantic illusions about farming; and despite urgings by railroad and land companies, reformers, and philanthropists to form agricultural colonies, the south Italians preferred to remain in the city.[25]

Although Chicago experienced an extraordinary growth of manufacturing during the period of their emigration, few south Italians found employment in the city's industries. Great numbers of other recent immigrants worked in meat-packing and steelmaking, but it was uncommon to find an Italian name on the payroll of these enterprises.[26] The absence of the *contadini* from these basic industries was due both to their aversion to this type of factory work and to discrimination against them by employers. For the great majority of the south Italian peasants "the stifling, brazen factories and the dark, stony pits" did not supplant "the warm living earth as the source of their daily bread."[27] Diggers in the earth they had been and diggers in the earth they remained; only in America they dug with the pick and shovel rather than the mattock. In Chicago the Italian laborers quickly displaced the Irish in excavation and street work, as they did on railroad construction jobs throughout the West.[28]

The lot of the railroad workers was hard. Arriving at an unknown destination, they were sometimes attacked as "scabs," they found the wages and conditions of labor quite different from those promised, or it happened that they were put to work under armed guard and kept in a state of peonage. For twelve hours a day in all kinds of weather, the laborers dug and picked, lifted ties and rails, swung sledge hammers, under the constant goading of tyrannical foremen. Housed in filthy boxcars, eating wretched food, they endured this miser-

[23] *Ibid.,* 82.

[24] *Ibid.,* 64.

[25] Vecoli, "Chicago's Italians," 184–234; Luigi Villari, *Gli Stati Uniti d'America e l'Emigrazione Italiana* (Milan, 1912), 256. Villari observed that even Italian immigrants who worked as gardeners in the suburbs of Boston preferred to live with their countrymen in the center of the city, commuting to their work in the country. *Ibid.,* 224.

[26] In 1901, for example, of over 6,000 employees at the Illinois Steel works only two were Italian. John M. Gillette, "The Culture Agencies of a Typical Manufacturing Group: South Chicago," *American Journal of Sociology,* VII (July 1901), 93–112. In 1915 the Armour packing company reported that there was not one Italian among its 8,000 workers in Chicago. U.S. Commission on Industrial Relations, *Final Report and Testimony* (11 vols., Washington, 1916), IV, 3530.

[27] *Uprooted,* 73.

[28] Chicago *Tribune,* March 20, 1891; Frank J. Sheridan, "Italian, Slavic and Hungarian Unskilled Laborers in the United States," U.S. Bureau of Labor, *Bulletin* XV (Sept. 1907), 445–68; Vecoli, "Chicago's Italians," 279–337.

able existence for a wage which seldom exceeded $1.50 a day. Usually they suffered in silence, and by the most stern abstinence were able to save the greater part of their meager earnings. Yet it happened that conditions became intolerable, and the *paesani* (gangs were commonly composed of men from the same town) would resist the exactions of the "boss." These uprisings were more in the nature of peasants' revolts than of industrial strikes, and they generally ended badly for the *contadini*.[29]

With the approach of winter the men returned to Chicago. While some continued on to Italy, the majority wintered in the city. Those with families in Chicago had households to return to; the others formed cooperative living groups. Thus they passed the winter months in idleness, much as they had in Italy. Railroad work was cyclical as well as seasonal. In times of depression emigration from Italy declined sharply; many of the Italian workers returned to their native towns to await the return of American prosperity. Those who remained were faced with long periods of unemployment; it was at these times, such as the decade of the 1890s, that the spectre of starvation stalked through the Italian quarters of Chicago.[30]

Because the *contadini* were engaged in gang labor of a seasonal nature there developed an institution which was thought most typical of the Italian immigration: the padrone system.[31] Bewildered by the tumult of the city, the newcomers sought out a townsman who could guide them in the ways of this strange land. Thus was created the padrone who made a business out of the ignorance and necessities of his countrymen. To the laborers, the padrone was banker, saloonkeeper, grocer, steamship agent, lodginghouse keeper, and politician. But his most important function was that of employment agent.

While there were honest padrones, most appeared unable to resist the opportunities for graft. Although Handlin states that "the padrone had the virtue of shielding the laborer against the excesses of employers,"[32] the Italian padrones usually operated in collusion with the contractors. Often the padrones were shrewd, enterprising men who had risen from the ranks of the unskilled; many of them, however, were members of the gentry who sought to make an easy living by exploiting their peasant compatriots in America as they had in Italy. The padrone system should not be interpreted as evidence "that a leader in America was not bound by patterns of obligation that were sacred in the Old World"; rather, it was a logical outcome of the economic individualism and "amoral familism" of south Italian society.

[29] D'Angelo, *Son of Italy*, 85–119; Dominic T. Ciolli, "The 'Wop' in the Track Gang," *Immigrants in America Review*, II (July 1916), 61–64; Gino C. Speranza, "Forced Labor in West Virginia," *Outlook*, LXXIV (June 13, 1903), 407–10.
[30] U.S. Commissioner of Labor, *Italians in Chicago*, 29, 44; Rosa Cassettari, "The Story of an Italian Neighbor (as told to Marie Hall Ets)," 342–50, ms., on loan to the author; Mayor's Commission on Unemployment (Chicago), *Report* (Chicago, 1914); Vecoli, "Chicago's Italians," 279–337.
[31] On the padrone system see Grace Abbott, "The Chicago Employment Agency and the Immigrant Worker," *American Journal of Sociology*, XIV (Nov. 1908), 289–305; John Koren, "The Padrone System and the Padrone Banks," U.S. Bureau of Labor, *Bulletin* II (March 1897), 113–29; S. Merlino, "Italian Immigrants and Their Enslavement," *Forum*, XV (April 1893), 183–90; Gino C. Speranza, "The Italian Foreman as a Social Agent," *Charities*, XI (July 4, 1903), 26–28; Vecoli, "Chicago's Italians," 235–78; Giovanni Ermenegildo Schiavo, *Italian-American History* (2 vols., New York, 1947–1949), I, 538–40.
[32] *Uprooted*, 69–70.

In their associational life the *contadini* also contradicted Handlin's assertion that the social patterns of the Old Country could not survive the ocean
voyage.[33] The marked incapacity of the south Italians for organizational activity
was itself a result of the divisive attitudes which they had brought with them to
America. Almost the only form of association among these immigrants was the
mutual aid society. Since such societies were common in Italy by the 1870s,[34]
they can hardly be regarded as "spontaneously generated" by American conditions. Instead, the mutual aid society was a transplanted institution which was
found to have special utility for the immigrants. An Italian journalist observed:
"If associations have been found useful in the *patria,* how much more they are
in a strange land, where it is so much more necessary for the Italians to gather
together, to fraternize, to help one another."[35] Nowhere, however, was the spirit
of *campanilismo* more in evidence than in these societies. An exasperated Italian
patriot wrote: "Here the majority of the Italian societies are formed of individuals from the same town and more often from the same parish, others are not
admitted. But are you or are you not Italians? And if you are, why do you exclude your brother who is born a few miles from your towns?"[36] As the number of these small societies multiplied (by 1912 there were some 400 of them
in Chicago),[37] various attempts were made to form them into a federation.
Only the Sicilians, however, were able to achieve a degree of unity through two
federations which enrolled several thousand members.

The sentiment of regionalism was also a major obstacle to the organizational unity of the Italians in Chicago. Rather than being allayed by emigration, this regional pride and jealousy was accentuated by the proximity of
Abruzzese, Calabrians, Genoese, Sicilians, and other groups in the city. Each
regional group regarded those from other regions with their strange dialects
and customs not as fellow Italians, but as distinct and inferior ethnic types. Any
proposal for cooperation among the Italians was sure to arouse these regional
antipathies and to end in bitter recriminations.[38] The experience of emigration
did not create a sense of nationality among the Italians strong enough to sub-
merge their parochialism. Unlike Handlin's immigrants who acquired "new
modes of fellowship to replace the old ones destroyed by emigration,"[39] the
South Italians confined themselves largely to the traditional ones of family and
townsmen.

The quality of leadership of the mutual aid societies also prevented them
from becoming agencies for the betterment of the *contadini*. These organizations, it was said, were often controlled by the "very worse [sic] element in the
Italian colony,"[40] arrogant, selfish men, who founded societies not out of a

[33] *Ibid.,* 170–71.
[34] Franchetti and Sonnino, *La Sicilia,* II, 335.
[35] *L'Unione Italiana* (Chicago), March 18, 1868.
[36] *L'Italia,* Oct. 23–24, 1897.
[37] Schiavo, *Italians in Chicago,* 57.
[38] Giacosa, "Chicago," 31–33; Comitato Locale di Chicago, *Primo Congresso
degli Italiani all'estero sotto l'atto patronato di S. M. Vittorio Emanuele III* (Chicago,
1908).
[39] *Uprooted,* 189.
[40] Edmund M. Dunne, *Memoirs of "Zi Pre"* (St. Louis, 1914), 18. Father Dunne
was the first pastor of the Italian Church of the Guardian Angel on Chicago's West
Side.

sense of fraternity but to satisfy their ambition and vanity. The scope of their leadership was restricted to presiding despotically over the meetings, marching in full regalia at the head of the society, and gaining economic and political advantage through their influence over the members. If such a one were frustrated in his attempt to control a society, he would secede with his followers and found a new one. Thus even the townsmen were divided into opposing factions.[41]

The function of the typical mutual aid society was as limited as was its sphere of membership. The member received relief in case of illness, an indemnity for his family in case of death, and a funeral celebrated with pomp and pageantry. The societies also sponsored an annual ball and picnic, and, most important of all, the feast of the local patron saint. This was the extent of society activities; any attempts to enlist support for philanthropic or civic projects was doomed to failure.[42]

Since there was a surplus of doctors, lawyers, teachers, musicians, and classical scholars in southern Italy, an "intellectual proletariat" accompanied the peasants to America in search of fortune.[43] Often, however, these educated immigrants found that America had no use for their talents, and to their chagrin they were reduced to performing manual labor. Their only hope of success was to gain the patronage of their lowly countrymen, but the sphere of colonial enterprise was very restricted. The sharp competition among the Italian bankers, doctors, journalists, and others engendered jealousies and rivalries. Thus this intelligentsia which might have been expected to provide tutelage and leadership to the humbler elements was itself rent by internecine conflict and expended its energies in polemics.

For the most part the upper-class immigrants generally regarded the peasants here as in Italy as boors and either exploited them or remained indifferent to their plight. These "respectable" Italians, however, were concerned with the growing prejudice against their nationality and wished to elevate its prestige among the Americans and other ethnic groups. As one means of doing this, they formed an association to suppress scavenging, organ-grinding, and begging as disgraceful to the Italian reputation. They simultaneously urged the workers to adopt American ways and to become patriotic Italians; but to these exhortations, the *contadino* replied: "It does not give me any bread whether the Italians have a good name in America or not. I am going back soon."[44]

Well-to-do Italians were more liberal with advice than with good works. Compared with other nationalities in Chicago, the Italians were distinguished by their lack of philanthropic institutions. There was a substantial number of men of wealth among them, but as an Italian reformer commented: "It is strange that when a work depends exclusively on the wealth of the colony, one can not hope for success. Evidently philanthropy is not the favored attribute of

[41] Comitato Locale di Chicago, *Primo Congresso; L'Italia*, Feb. 18, 1888, Oct. 21, 1899.
[42] Beck, "The Italian in Chicago," 23; Comitato Locale di Chicago, *Primo Congresso; L'Italia*, Aug. 24, 1889, April 28, 1906.
[43] Amy A. Bernardy, *Italia randagia attraverso gli Stati Uniti* (Turin, 1913), 293; Giacosa, "Chicago," 31; *L'Italia*, Jan. 19, 1889.
[44] Robert E. Park and Herbert A. Miller, *Old World Traits Transplanted* (New York, 1921), 104; Mastro-Valerio, "Remarks Upon the Italian Colony," 131–32; *L'Italia*, Aug. 6, 1887, April 5, 1890.

our rich."[45] Indeed, there was no tradition of philanthropy among the gentry of southern Italy, and the "self-made" men did not recognize any responsibility outside the family. Projects were launched for an Italian hospital, an Italian school, an Italian charity society, an Italian institute to curb the padrone evil, and a White Hand Society to combat the Black Hand, but they all floundered in this morass of discord and disinterest. Clearly Handlin does not have the Italians in mind when he describes a growing spirit of benevolence as a product of immigrant life.[46]

If there is one particular in which the *contadini* most strikingly refute Handlin's conception of the peasant it is in the place of religion in their lives. Handlin emphasizes the influence of Christian doctrine on the psychology of the peasantry,[47] but throughout the Mezzogiorno, Christianity was only a thin veneer.[48] Magic, not religion, pervaded their everyday existence; through the use of rituals, symbols, and charms, they sought to ward off evil spirits and to gain the favor of powerful deities. To the peasants, God was a distant, unapproachable being, like the King, but the local saints and Madonnas were real personages whose power had been attested to by innumerable miracles. But in the devotions to their patron saints, the attitude of the peasants was less one of piety than of bargaining, making vows if certain requests were granted. For the Church, which they had known as an oppressive landlord, they had little reverence; and for the clergy, whom they knew to be immoral and greedy, they had little respect. They knew little of and cared less for the doctrines of the Church.

Nor was the influence of established religion on the south Italian peasants strengthened by emigration as Handlin asserts.[49] American priests were scandalized by the indifference of the Italians to the Church.[50] Even when Italian churches were provided by the Catholic hierarchy, the *contadini* seldom displayed any religious enthusiasm. As one missionary was told upon his arrival in an Italian colony: "We have no need of priests here, it would be better if you returned from whence you came."[51] As in their native towns, the south Italian peasants for the most part went to church "to be christened, married or buried and that is about all."[52]

Because they were said to be drifting into infidelity, the south Italians were also the object of much of the home mission work of the Protestant churches of Chicago. Drawing their ministry from Italian converts and Waldensians, these missions carried the Gospel to the *contadini,* who, however, revealed little in-

[45] *L'Italia,* Aug. 24–25, 1895; Luigi Carnovale, *Il Giornalismo degli Emigrati Italiani nel Nord America* (Chicago, 1909), 67; Comitato Locale di Chicago, *Primo Congresso.*
[46] *Uprooted,* 175–76.
[47] *Ibid.,* 102–03.
[48] Levi, *Christ Stopped,* 116–18; Leonard W. Moss and Stephen C. Cappannari, "Folklore and Medicine in an Italian Village," *Journal of American Folklore,* LXXIII (April 1960), 85–102; Banfield, *Moral Basis of a Backward Society,* 17–18, 129–32.
[49] *Uprooted,* 117.
[50] On the religious condition of the Italian immigrants, see the discussion in *America,* XII (Oct. 17, 31, Nov. 7, 14, 21, 28, Dec. 5, 12, 19, 1914), 6–7, 66, 93, 121, 144–45, 168–69, 193–96, 221, 243–46.
[51] G. Sofia, ed., *Missioni Scalabriniane in America, estratto da "Le Missioni Scalabriniane tra gli Italiani"* (Rome, 1939), 122.
[52] "Church Census of the 17th Ward, 1909," Chicago Commons, 1904–1910, Graham Taylor Papers (Newberry Library).

clination to become "true Christians." After several decades of missionary effort, the half dozen Italian Protestant churches counted their membership in the few hundreds.[53] The suggestion that Italians were especially vulnerable to Protestant proselyting was not borne out in Chicago. For the *contadini,* neither Catholicism nor Protestantism became "paramount as a way of life."[54]

According to Handlin, the immigrants found it "hard to believe that the whole world of spirits and demons had abandoned their familiar homes and come also across the Atlantic,"[55] but the *contadino* in America who carried a *corno* (a goat's horn of coral) to protect him from the evil eye harbored no such doubts. The grip of the supernatural on the minds of the peasants was not diminished by their ocean crossing. In the Italian settlements, sorcerers plied their magical trades on behalf of the ill, the lovelorn, the bewitched. As Alice Hamilton noted: "Without the help of these mysterious and powerful magicians they [the *contadini*] believe that they would be defenseless before terrors that the police and the doctor and even the priest cannot cope with."[56] For this peasant folk, in Chicago as in Campania, the logic of medicine, law, or theology had no meaning; only magic provided an explanation of, and power over, the vagaries of life.

The persistence of Old World customs among the south Italians was perhaps best exemplified by the *feste* which were held in great number in Chicago. The cults of the saints and Madonnas had also survived the crossing, and the fellow townsmen had no doubt that their local divinities could perform miracles in Chicago as well as in the Old Country. Feast day celebrations were inspired not only by devotion to the saints and Madonnas; they were also an expression of nostalgia for the life left behind. The procession, the street fair, the crowds of townsmen, created the illusion of being once more back home; as one writer commented of a *festa:* "There in the midst of these Italians, with almost no Americans, it seemed to be truly a village of southern Italy."[57] Despite efforts by "respectable" Italians and the Catholic clergy to discourage these colorful but unruly celebrations, the *contadini* would have their *feste.* After the prohibition of a *festa* by the Church was defied, a priest explained: "The feast is a custom of Sicily and survives despite denunciations from the altar. Wherever there is a colony of these people they have the festival, remaining deaf to the requests of the clergy."[58] The south Italian peasants remained deaf to the entreaties of reformers and radicals as well as priests, for above all they wished to continue in the ways of their *puesi.*

The *contadini* of the Mezzogiorno thus came to terms with life in Chicago within the framework of their traditional pattern of thought and behavior. The

[53] Palmerio Chessa, "A Survey Study of the Evangelical Work among Italians in Chicago" (bachelor of divinity thesis, Presbyterian Theological Seminary, Chicago, 1934); Jane K. Hackett, "A Survey of Presbyterian Work with Italians in the Presbytery of Chicago" (master's thesis, Presbyterian College of Christian Education, Chicago, 1943).

[54] *Uprooted,* 117, 136.

[55] *Ibid.,* 110.

[56] Alice Hamilton, "Witchcraft in West Polk Street," *American Mercury,* X (Jan. 1927), 71; Chicago *Tribune,* Jan. 19, 1900; *L'Italia,* Oct. 3, 1903. See also Zaloha, "Persistence of Italian Customs," 158–63.

[57] *Italia,* July 28–29, 1894; Cassettari, "Story of an Italian Neighbor," 419. See also Zaloha, "Persistence of Italian Customs," 90–100.

[58] Chicago *Tribune,* Aug. 14, 1903.

social character of the south Italian peasant did not undergo a sea change, and the very nature of their adjustments to American society was dictated by their "Old World traits," which were not so much ballast to be jettisoned once they set foot on American soil. These traits and customs were the very bone and sinew of the south Italian character which proved very resistant to change even under the stress of emigration. Because it overemphasizes the power of environment and underestimates the toughness of cultural heritage, Handlin's thesis does not comprehend the experience of the immigrants from southern Italy. The basic error of this thesis is that it subordinates historical complexity to the symmetrical pattern of a sociological theory. Rather than constructing ideal types of "the peasant" or "the immigrant," the historian of immigration must study the distinctive cultural character of each ethnic group and the manner in which this influenced its adjustments in the New World.

Jews

THE EDITORS OF FORTUNE

Jews in America

Most minority groups in the United States have been accused of degeneracy, laziness, stupidity, criminality, and genetic inferiority. Although the Jews, too, have been characterized as criminal and degenerate they are unique in drawing hostility for their alleged acquisitiveness and for their vocational and material successes and intellectual achievements. Those Jews who have fulfilled themselves according to the American dream and the American promise (poor boy works hard, makes money, and becomes rich) have received the greatest censure. The key to this paradox lies embedded in the traditions of anti-Semitism. Jews have been condemned for inheriting the guilt of Christ's murderers, for failing to accept Christianity, and for remaining an island unto themselves. While these factors contribute to anti-Semitism, none alone, or all together, sufficiently explains the historic hostility directed against Jews.

Jews have been in the United States since 1654. By 1790 they numbered perhaps 1,200 and sixty years later about 15,000. Spread thinly throughout the land, they were not initially regarded as a threatening group. Concentrated in the cities, they had relatively little difficulty in taking advantage of the abundant economic opportunities that awaited the enterprising. Most of the pre-Civil War Jews originally came from either Portugal or Spain via Brazil in the colonial era or later from the German states in Europe. In the 1880s, however, millions fled from Russian pogroms and by the First World War New York contained more Jews than any other city in the world. These newcomers, like other eastern and southern European immigrants, worked in sweatshops, lived in dingy tenements, and barely earned enough to keep alive. Their strange garb and unusual religious customs exacerbated anti-Jewish feelings and led to widespread restrictions in employment, educational and recreational opportunities, and housing accommodations. These barriers (like signs reading "No Jews or Dogs allowed") applied to newcomers as well as those of extended lineage in this country. Despite the roadblocks, though, many became prosperous businessmen and professionals. Some succeeded in achieving great wealth and intellectual or vocational distinction.

Hostility toward Jews intensified during the periodic economic depressions which widened the chasm between the haves and have-nots. The fact that some Jews made money at times when most other Americans suffered acute depriva-

tion caused the half-hidden resentment against them to surface. Organized anti-Semitism (in contrast to personal and individual hostility toward Jews) never made much headway in the United States, but its greatest impact coincided with the Great Depression (1929–41) and the rise of Adolph Hitler in Germany. Anti-Semites perpetrated the falsehood that Jews controlled the economy and the government. Even though Jews suffered from discrimination and deprivation many unemployed Christians believed that the Jews caused their troubles.

The following article, published by Fortune *magazine in 1936, shows that Jews had little control over the major manufacturing and commercial establishments in the nation but predominated in apparel manufacturing and entertainment. (It is probable that Jews still have the same proportionate interests in these industries today.)*

The essay, although crammed full of facts and apparently aiming at accuracy, has dated very quickly. Most intelligent people in America today no longer discuss Jewish "racial" characteristics since the Jews are not a race. Nor are categories like "Nordic," "Alpine," and "Mediterranean" types, remainders from pseudoscientific investigations during the Progressive era, used to describe different groups of Europeans. Finally, the implied query in the last paragraph of the essay: "Can this universal stranger be absorbed in the country which has absorbed every other European stock? Does he wish to be absorbed? Can he live happily and in peace if he is not absorbed?" is strikingly reminiscent of writers like Burton J. Hendrick, who asked of the newly arrived Russian Jew in 1907, "Is he assimilable? Has he in himself the stuff of which Americans are made?" The basic assumption in 1936, as in 1907, and still in evidence today, is that "American" means absorption into white, Anglo-Saxon, Protestant culture. There are large numbers of Jews, now as then, who dispute this dictum. Other Jews who have become superpatriots or have adopted Christian names reveal their eagerness to gain approval from Anglo-Saxon America. The necessity for this behavior contradicts the current national rhetoric which glorifies cultural pluralism and declares that harmony can exist among Americans of divergent cultural backgrounds.

> When the head of Louis XVI fell, all the monarchs of Europe felt their necks; when the blow fell on the head of German Jewry, many of us other Jews began to wonder what the future had in store for various branches of our people.

Professor L. B. Namier, the distinguished professor of modern history at Manchester University, who wrote these words, is not alone in wondering. Misgivings and uneasiness have colored the thinking of American Jews as well. Faced with the unbelievable record of Nazi barbarities, faced now with the proposal of Sir Herbert Samuel that they aid in the enormously costly deportation of all Jews from Germany, leading members of the Jewish community in the United States—men who had previously looked to the future with complete confidence—have been shocked into fear. The apprehensiveness of American Jews has become one of the important influences in the social life of our time.

It is important to non-Jews as well as to Jews. Any nation which permits a minority to live in fear of persecution is a nation which invites disaster. Fearful minorities become suspicious minorities and suspicious minorities, their defensive reactions set on the hair trigger of anxiety, create the animosities they dread. The consequence is a condition dangerous to the State at any time and doubly dangerous at a time like the present when the primitive emotions of men have been deliberately exploited in the interest of Fascism. The connection between Fascism and Jew-hatred is not accidental. Fascism, having nothing for sale but dictatorship and no selling point but the necessity for force, requires civil riots in order to advertise its goods and a civil triumph to complete the sale. Jew-hatred, as the Nazis have proved, does very well as an excuse for the first and the Jew as a victim for the second.

Consequently any man who loathes Fascism will fear anti-Semitism. And fearing anti-Semitism he will fear also the various conditions which encourage it —of which the apprehensiveness of the Jews themselves is one. Aware though he is of the European reasons for Jewish anxiety he will nevertheless be troubled to find his American-Jewish neighbor taking offense where no offense is intended. He will be troubled by the uneasy reticence, the circumlocutions, the sense of strain. He will be troubled by the fact that certain Jews carry their race like an Irishman's fighting shillelagh while others resent, as though it were a deliberate insult, any reference to their blood, avoiding friends who speak of it, boycotting publications which publish it in print. He will wonder whether such an attitude is necessary. He will wonder specifically whether the growing apprehensiveness of American Jews has any justification in fact. The leaders of American Jewry have earnestly asked themselves the same question in the recent past.

It is a question to which an answer can be given. First of all it may be stated authoritatively that there is no reason for anxiety so far as concerns the record to date of the organized forces of anti-Semitism. Attempts have been made to "expose" an anti-Semitic offensive of dangerous proportions. But neither these attempts nor the activities of an efficient Jewish information service have succeeded in turning up anything of serious importance. Shaken down to bare fact and described without the Scotland Yard mystifications dear to the professional exposers, American organized anti-Semitism is a poor thing indeed.

By anti-Semitism is here intended not the latent prejudice against Jews which is a common phenomenon in history and which, as Rabbi Joel Blau put it, "dates back to the beginnings of the Jewish people." Prejudice against Jews is at least as old as 1654 in North America and its negative evidences may be found in the histories of most of the clubs and colleges and residential districts of the country. By anti-Semitism is meant the deliberately incited, affirmative racial phobia which has produced the social and economic and sometimes physical pogroms of modern Germany just as it produced the murderous pogroms of Czarist Russia. Of that disease there is no American clinical record. Not because the history of America has been free of intolerance and persecution, but because the victims of intolerance and persecution were not, down to 1921, Semites. They were Quakers and Baptists in the seventeenth century, Irish Catholics and Negroes in the nineteenth. Jews suffered certain legal civil disabilities in the colonies and in some of the later states and certain extralegal social disabilities in both, but they suffered no persecution until three years after the War. Then, in the atmosphere of post-War nationalism and reaction, with the Ku Klux Klan "riding" again (in Fords) at the instigation of a pair of high-powered publicity panjandrums, Jews came in for a share of the Catholic opprobrium. But even so the persecutions were bloodless and brief. In the early twenties there were up to 2,500,000 "Aryan" citizens parading in sheets. Thirty journals including Henry Ford's *Dearborn Independent* were in full bray. Serious-minded people were telling each other about the Jewish plot to take over the earth. And copies of the forged Protocols of the Elders of Zion were passing solemnly and secretly from hand to hand. But a few years later the New York *World*'s exposure of the racket behind the Klan had had its effect, the Coolidge boom had given the paraders something else to think about, Henry Ford had apologized and retracted, and the Protocols were on their way to the judicial examination which eventually stripped them to the fraudulent skin.

From that collapse not even the depression, traditional ally of all phobias, was able to save the cause. Anti-Semitism languished and still languishes. The great shift from sheets to shirts has failed to save it. Although an estimated half million people may attend occasional anti-Semitic meetings, etc., there are probably no more than 15,000 loyal Jew-hating group members in the whole United States and many of these are loyal only in a negative and receptive manner. The principal anti-Semitic organization is German in name and almost entirely German or German-American in membership. The second in point of fame is bankrupt. And the rest hardly supply material for a half column in the county papers. . . .

The truth of the matter is that the virus has not been acclimated on this continent and that the efforts of the doctors to inoculate the American mind have failed for that reason. Surveys of national opinion indicate either hostility to anti-Semitic dogmas or, what is worse from the agitator's point of view, complete indifference. It was the opinion of 95 per cent of those questioned in October, 1935, by the National Conference of Jews and Christians that there was less anti-Semitism in their communities at that time than there had been at the beginning of the depression. An inquiry made by FORTUNE a month later incidentally to the preparation of this article produced a comparable result. Few of those replying felt that anti-Semitism was a live issue. On the contrary a considerable number felt that it was no issue at all.

More informative than either of these responses, however, is the reply to a question in the most recent FORTUNE Survey (published on page 157 of the January issue). That question avoided the habitual reticences by aiming its inquiry at the much publicized German situation. *"Do you believe that in the long run Germany will be better or worse off if it drives out the Jews?* The answers were as follows:

	Worse	Don't Know	Better
Total	54.6%	31.4%	14.0%
Northeast	52.7	32.2	15.1
Midwest	55.1	28.8	16.1
Southeast	60.0	32.5	7.4
Southwest	52.4	32.9	14.7
West	41.0	49.2	9.8
Pacific Coast	61.1	24.6	14.3

The significant category here is the "Don't know" category. "Don't know" in this connection is almost certainly equivalent to indifference. And indifference, though Jews may think it callous, is the most effective prophylactic against the pestilence of hate: those who don't care either way will smash no windows. It will be observed that anywhere from a quarter to a half of the replies were "Don't know," while from 40 per cent to 60 per cent were explicitly opposed to discrimination against Jews. The result is to suggest that even in the Midwest an anti-Semitic propagandist would have up to 84 per cent of the population actively or passively against him.

The conclusion is inescapable that current American anti-Semitism is feeble. It is German in manufacture and was to be expected in the light of Hitler's career. But Germany is 4,000 miles away. It is not pleasant to have individuals like the Reverend Winrod of the Defenders of the Christian Faith or like Mr. Robert Edward Edmondson who manufactures hate in New York City inviting the country to attack your people. But neither is it important.

All this the intelligent and informed American Jew knows perfectly well. He may occasionally lose his sense of proportion and see Silver Shirts under the bed but in general it is not Silver Shirts that bother him. What keeps him awake at night is the thought that a situation exists in America which may at some future time breed animals much worse than Silver Shirts and much more numerous—animals as nearly like a Nazi Brown Shirt as one species can be like another. That situation may be described as follows: in the year 1800 there were 2,500,000 Jews in the world, half of them in the old Kingdom of Poland and not more than 3,000 of them in the United States. In 1933 there were 16,000,000 Jews in the world of whom more than a fourth were resident in the United States. The Jews, in the phraseology of Doctor Ruppin of the Hebrew University at Jerusalem, having changed in the eighteenth century from an Oriental people to an Eastern European, have in the last few generations changed from an Eastern European people to a Western European and an American.

The apprehensiveness of intelligent Jews springs from this fact. Realizing that Jews have been the scapegoats of all Western history, that they have been made to bear responsibility for everything from the Black Death to the economic ills of the Germans, these observers fear that the enormous increase in Jewish numbers in America will lead to charges that the Jews have monopolized the opportunities for economic advance and that these charges will pave the way for Fascism here as they paved the way for Hitler in Germany. Non-Jews who prefer democratic institutions to dictatorship share that fear.

To determine whether it is a fear deserving of serious attention, it is necessary to inquire, first, what significance the extraordinary numerical increase in American Jewry actually has, and, second, whether there is any factual basis for charges of Jewish monopolization of American economic opportunity.

As to the increase in numbers, a little reflection should persuade even those Jews who, like Professor Namier, think of numbers as dangerous ("to a nation rooted in its own soil . . . they mean strength and security, but for us, outside Palestine, they have always constituted a danger") that the danger here is more apparent than real. Numerical increase is always purely relative. A 1,500-fold U.S. increase since 1800 means nothing without an examination of the figure from which departure is taken. And in any case it is the trend and not the total which is significant. There were only a few thousand Jews in America in 1800 and the reason why there were only a few thousand was that Jews were not permitted to live in England at the time of the first British settlements in America. The reason for the enormous sixfold increase in world Jewry between 1800 and 1933 was the fall in the death rate, chiefly the infant death rate, brought about by medical, sanitary, and economic advance—phenomena from which all populations profited more or less equally, though the Jews, whose high fertility was noticed by Tacitus, increased more than twice as rapidly as the world population. That rate of increase no longer holds. The Jewish birth rate, like other birth rates beginning with the French about 1811, has now fallen to meet the new conditions of survival and longevity. Ruppin remarks that the most striking present feature of Jewish vital statistics is the fall from an eighteenth-century birth rate of forty-five per 1,000 to a rate of eighteen in 1932. This rate moreover declines from East to West in Europe, having been 24.1 in Russia in 1926 and 5.9 in Vienna in 1929. In New York the rule breaks down, the Jewish rate being higher than the non-Jewish. (The Jewish 1932 rate of 17.5 is to be compared with the rate for non-Jews of 16.5.) The Jewish advantage, however, is probably to be explained by the fact that about half the Jews living in America are still first-generation immigrants largely from Eastern Europe with the high Eastern European birth rate.

The fact of the matter is, in other words, that an enormous increase has taken place. But the further facts are, first, that that increase is attributable to a temporary unbalance between Jewish birth rate and Jewish death rate in Eastern Europe in the nineteenth century, second, that that unbalance has largely corrected itself, and, third, that the gates of immigration into the United States are now closed. The three tides, first, of Sephardic Jews from Brazil, Holland, England, and the Spanish Americas in the eighteenth century, second, of German Jews in the first half of the nineteenth, and, third, of Polish and Russian Jews between 1882 (the year of the great Russian pogroms) and 1925 are not likely to be followed by a fourth. There is therefore little reason for apprehensiveness on the ground merely of anti-Semitic propaganda based upon increasing numbers.

The second and fundamental question then presents itself. Are there any facts to support a charge that Jews have monopolized or are monopolizing economic opportunity in the United States? Before this question can be answered it is desirable to see precisely why it presents itself. What difference does it make even if Jews do run away with the system? Why shouldn't they monopolize any profession or branch of industry they are intelligent enough to capture? A man's job should not be determined by his parentage. To this proposition and to the related proposition that any discrimination against Jews in the professions or in industry is unjust there is no answer in logic or morality. Both are unanswerably sound. But there is an historical answer. Which is that a disproportionate Jewish participation in the economic life of a country has been found capable of arousing anti-Semitic feeling.

Why this should be so—why the success of the Jewish minority should be so particularly resented by other peoples—is a complicated question which is rendered more complicated by the fact that anthropologists are now generally agreed that the Jews are not a race in any scientific sense of the term—no more of a race, for example, than the Germans. They were originally a cross between a longheaded, tallish, dark Mediterranean race (the Bedouins) and a short-headed, shortish, dark Alpine race. Those who remained in the Mediterranean basin, working around into the Spanish peninsula, were further modified by additional Mediterranean blood. Those who crossed through Syria into Eastern Europe and on into Germany received additions of Mongol, Alpine, and Nordic characteristics. The result is the distinction of the two types familiar in America —the Sephardim or Spanish Jews on the one hand and the Ashkenazim or German Jews on the other. The first, of whom Justice Cardozo and Bernard Baruch are examples, are characterized by thin features and spare bodies which often take on a typically Yankee look, while the second have quite frequently the heavy features, swarthy complexion, curly hair, and short body of common association. A third type is sometimes distinguished as representative of those Ashkenazim (a great majority of the group) who have lived for centuries among the Slavs of Eastern Europe. This type is physically like the German Jew save that light hair and eyes are common and pug noses are more frequent than hooked.

The three groups, moreover, are distinct not only in appearance. They originally differed also in language, since the first spoke Spanish or Ladino (a fifteenth-century Spanish), the second German, and the third Yiddish (an alloy of Hebrew and German). And they maintain a certain aloofness among themselves. The pride and exclusiveness of the Spanish Jews of ancient settlement in this country are most sharply felt by the Ashkenazim. And the hatred of German Jews which Elma E. Levinger attributes to Polish Jew immigrants was warmly reciprocated by their predecessors of German origin. The word "kike" is not of Gentile but of German-Jewish coinage.

What then is the explanation of anti-Jewish prejudice if the Jews are not a racial unit? The answer would seem to be that anti-Jewish prejudice is the classic example of that dislike and fear of strangers which the Greeks knew as xenophobia and which appears as a familiar phenomenon among primitive peoples and peoples reverting to primitivism. The outstanding fact about the Jewish people is the fact that they have preserved, though scattered among the nations of the earth, their national identity. They are unique among the peoples of the world not because they have bold noses—only a small percentage of Jews have the Jewish nose—but because they alone, of all peoples known to history, have retained in exile and dispersion and over a period of thousands of years their distinction from the peoples among whom they live. The Jew is everywhere and everywhere the Jew is strange. Japanese are strangers in California but not in Japan. Scotsmen are outlanders in Paris but not in Edinburgh. The Jews are outlanders everywhere. The country of the Jew, as Schopenhauer puts it, is other Jews.

And therein is the key to the peculiar destiny of the Jews. The quality which makes them the scapegoats of Western history is the quality which makes them strangers in Western history—their devotion to their own cultural tradition under conditions of almost impossible hardship and the psychological traits which that devotion has established. Jews themselves, but not non-Jews, think of the Jewish religion as the chief cause of the Jew's universal strangeness, and the Christian religion as the chief cause of the prejudice from which he suffers. Non-Jews, on the other hand, cite such complaints as those gathered together in *Catholics, Jews, and Protestants,* a study undertaken at the request of the National Conference of Jews and Christians. These are: "Aggressiveness, 'sharp business practices,' clannishness, and lack of sensitivity to the feelings of Gentile groups," the preservation among the Jews of "the 'haggling' habit which most of the Western world has outgrown," "the use of shoddy or poor materials," the fact that "Jews are considered by certain leading insurance companies as a poor fire risk," etc.

The truth is that neither these ancient chestnuts of racial prejudice nor the equally ancient references to religious history explain the Jew's position. They are merely rationalizations of the underlying feeling of foreignness—instances of difference made to stand for the difference itself. The true difference is cultural. All other immigrant peoples accept the culture of the country into which they come. The Jews for centuries have refused to accept it and are now, in many cases, unable to accept it when they would. The habit of pride, the long, proud stubbornness of their ancestors, is too strong in them. Even many of those who have deserted the traditions of their people and accepted in every detail the dress and speech and life of the non-Jewish majority are still subtly but recognizably different.

That difference alone, with ignorant or parochial minds, is cause for prejudice. When it is combined, as it frequently is, with an equally strong sense of difference and hence of clannishness on the part of the Jews, it may also affect minds to which neither ignorance nor narrowness can be ascribed. Any minority, and particularly any self-conscious minority, will develop centripetal tendencies. Members of the minority will tend to agglomerate. And this the Jews have notoriously done. Though they are very far, as we shall see, from monopolizing American industry, they have nevertheless made fair progress toward monopolizing those subdivisions of industry in which they have established themselves. Indeed the very fact of the existence of discriminatory quotas and barriers and the like in industry and education and the professions is proof, not only of Gentile injustice, but also of the Jewish tendency to inundate a field where other Jews have made entrance. It is a natural trait and an understandable trait but it serves to exaggerate the feeling of strangeness and hence the prejudice which that feeling inspires. Seeing Jews clannishly crowding together in particular businesses and particular localities the non-Jew (who does not think of himself as acting clannishly) is more than ever impressed with the exotic character of this unusual people.

And being impressed with the Jews' difference from himself and hence their foreignness he is all too ready to resent their economic successes as a kind of outside invasion of *his* world. He is all too ready to agree that if the Jews have more than their "share," the Jews must be opposed. It is useless to argue that the conclusion is a *non sequitur:* that there is no reason on earth why a man's blood stream should qualify his economic achievements. The only truly convincing answer and the only real obstacle to anti-Semitic propaganda of this most dangerous sort is the appeal to fact.

And the fact is this: that there is no basis whatever for the suggestion that Jews monopolize U.S. business and industry.

Two points should be made at the outset. First, the number of Jews who can be thought of as threatening non-Jewish control of U.S. industry is not so large as the Jewish population estimate of 1933 would suggest: the great mass of the 4,500,000 American Jews, like the great mass of American non-Jews, is made up of workers, employed or unemployed, to whom the control of U.S. industry is a purely academic matter. Second, the number of Jews who can be thought of as threatening non-Jewish control of U.S. industry is not so large as the *seeming* prevalence of Jews would make it appear. The Jews *seem* to play a disproportionate part for two reasons: the Jews and particularly the Polish Jews with their ghetto background are the most urban, the most city-loving, of all peoples, and the favored occupations of Jews in the cities are those occupations which bring them into most direct contact with the great consuming public. These are matters of common observation. The proclivity of the Jews for finance, trade, and exchange has been frequently noticed by Jewish writers and the concentration of Jews in the cities is a present as well as an historical fact. Over 1,000,000 of the 4,500,000 Jews of the first century lived in Alexandria alone and 95 per cent of present American Jews live in American cities of more than 10,000, while 84 per cent live in cities of more than 100,000. This urban concentration is a circumstance of considerable importance in the present connection. One of the effects of modern industrialism has been to increase the relative importance of the cities. The great metropolis is the true expression of modern life as the country and the castle were the true expressions of medieval life. In consequence any group which is numerous in the cities will seem more important than its actual numerical strength would make it. For example, nearly half the Jews in America live in New York City alone, and the fact that the city of New York is so important to the life of the country taken together with the fact that 30 per cent of the population of that city is Jewish has the effect of throwing its 1,765,000 Jews into very high relief.

Urbanization has also of course certain substantial effects upon Jewish life and hence upon Jewish successes. It is largely responsible, for example, for the Jewish concentration in the learned professions. The Jews share with the Scotch and certain other peoples an almost morbid passion for higher education. But that passion would have been fruitless had the immigrant Jews not remained in the large cities. The American system of education makes it possible for a poor boy living in a great city to carry himself through college and even through certain professional schools free, whereas a similar boy living in a rural community will be stopped after high school by the costs of transportation to the state-college town and by the cost of board and food away from home. The result has been to give the children of certain city-dwelling types of recent immigrant an educational advantage over the children of native American and other stocks living in rural areas. The proposed nationwide scholarships at Harvard are one response to this situation.

But though the urbanization of the Jews is a matter of real importance in some connections its principal effect remains in the field of appearances. If appearances are disregarded and replaced with facts the general impression of Jewish ubiquity and power disappears. Indeed the immediate reaction is that the Jews, who can lay better claims than most non-Jews to credit for the creation of the present economic order, are less well represented in many directions than they should be. The Jews and the English were the chief designers of finance capitalism in the last century but only the English have profited correspondingly. The Jews have seen themselves surpassed in one business or banking province after another by upstarts who were still swinging swords or pushing plows when the Jews were the traders and the bankers of Europe. It is one thing for a non-Jew to say "Oh, the Jews run everything." It is another for an impartial observer to see exactly what they *do* run.

First of all and very definitely, they do not run banking. They play little or no part in the great commercial houses. Of the 420 listed directors of the nineteen members of the New York Clearing House in 1933 only thirty were Jews and about half of these were in the Commercial National Bank & Trust Co. and the Public National Bank & Trust. There were none in the Bank of New York & Trust Co., National City, Guaranty Trust, Central Hanover, First National, Chase, Bankers Trust, or New York Trust. Indeed there are practically no Jewish employees of any kind in the largest commercial banks—and this in spite of the fact that many of their customers are Jews. In the investment field although there are of course Jewish houses, of which Kuhn, Loeb & Co., Speyer & Co., J. & W. Seligman & Co., Ladenburg, Thalmann & Co., and Lehman Bros. are the best known, they do not compare in power with the great houses owned by non-Jews. (Dillon of Dillon, Read & Co. is considered a Jew by other Jews but he is not, as his name suggests, an active member of his race nor is his firm considered Jewish by either Jews or non-Jews.) If these houses are ranked upon the amounts of foreign loans outstanding on March 1, 1935, J. P. Morgan with 19.87 per cent, National City Co. with 11.71, Dillon, Read with 11.44, Chase, Harris, Forbes with 8.45, Guaranty Co. with 6.68 per cent, Bancamerica-Blair with 6.18 per cent, and Lee, Higginson with 4.23 per cent all rank above the highest Jewish house, which is Kuhn, Loeb with 2.88 per cent. Ranked on the basis of domestic activity, Kuhn, Loeb, which has been very active of late in the steel industry and which has a long and honorable record of general activity in American business, would of course stand very near the top, but even in the domestic field non-Jewish interests are still far and away the most influential.

Furthermore these so-called Jewish houses are by no means exclusively Jewish. In Kuhn, Loeb Messrs. Elisha Walker, Bovenizer, Wiseman, and Knowlton, none of them Jews, are extremely active, while control of J. & W. Seligman is now shared with Frederick Strauss by Earle Bailie and Francis Randolph, a member of the proudest family in the Virginia Tidewater.

On the New York Stock Exchange, 148 of the 919 members, or 16 per cent, are Jews, while fifty-five of the 637 firms listed by the Exchange directory are Jewish, twenty-four are half-Jewish, and thirty-nine have dominant Jewish influence. The absence of Jews in the insurance business is noteworthy. Herman A. Behrens, President of Continental Assurance Co., and J. B. Levison, President of the Fireman's Fund Insurance Co. in San Francisco, are two of the few Jewish executives of large insurance companies. In the insurance-agency field, however, about half the business is Jewish in New York. And the New York insurance-brokerage business is predominantly Jewish although the three or four nationwide brokerage houses with New York offices are non-Jewish. Outside New York Jewish representation follows the Jewish population proportion.

If the Jews have a subordinate place in finance, which they are often said to control, they have an even more inconspicuous place in heavy industry. The only outstanding Jews in that field are the Blocks and Max Epstein of Chicago, the Blocks being largely interested in Inland Steel . . . the No. 7 producer, and Mr. Epstein being Chairman of the Board of General American Transportation Corp., which manufactures tank cars. Inland Steel is a successful company well liked and much respected in the trade but its share of the steel business is relatively small. The only exception to the rule that steel is not a Jewish industry is the scrap business. Scrap iron and steel, a half-billion-dollar business in 1929, which provides the steel industry with half its metal requirements, is owned 90 per cent by Jews, being an outgrowth of the junk business, which at the end of the last century was in the hands of Russian Jews. The largest company in the business is Luria Bros. & Co. of Philadelphia owned by Russian Jews. Others are Hyman Michaels Co. of Chicago, founded by Joseph E. Michaels, a Portuguese Jew, Charles Dreifus Co. of Pittsburgh, and Luntz Iron & Steel Co. of Canton, Ohio. It may be added in passing that practically the whole waste-products industry including nonferrous scrap metal (a $300,000,000 a year business in 1929), paper, cotton rag, wool rag, and rubber, is Jewish.

Something the same situation exists in automobiles. There are only three Jews of any prominence in the executive end of manufacturing—Morris Markin, President of Cord-controlled Checker Cab, Meyer L. Prentis, Treasurer of General Motors, and A. E. Barit, First Vice President and General Manager of Hudson. There are only two Jews in positions of importance on the financial end—Jules Bache in Chrysler and John Hertz of Lehman Bros. on the Board of Studebaker. And there are few Jews in the new-car distributing business. No considerable number appears until the second-hand trade is reached.

The coal industry is almost entirely non-Jewish. It is doubtful whether the roster of the leading twenty-five companies would show a single Jew from miner to manager or on up to the board of directors. And they are not numerous in distribution. Conceivably 2 per cent of the wholesale selling and possibly 10 per cent of the retail trade—most of the latter around New York—is in Jewish hands.

Rubber is another non-Jewish industry. Of the tire manufacturers only Kelly-Springfield was ever Jewish and Kelly-Springfield is now in non-Jewish hands. There are Jewish concerns in rubberized fabric and to a lesser extent in the rubber-heel-and-shoe business but they are not dominant. Neither do they control petroleum. On the contrary the Jewish interest is solely in the marketing of petroleum products and even there it is probably no more than 5 per cent, the chief marketer being American Oil of Baltimore, and American Oil, though still managed by the Blausteins, who founded it, is now controlled by a Standard of Indiana subsidiary. The chemical industry is in a comparable position. Neither in Du Pont, Allied Chemical & Dye, U.S. Industrial Alcohol, or Air Reduction is there a single Jew in a managerial position. There are two Jewish directors, Alfred A. Cook of Allied Chemical and Jules Bache of U.S. Industrial Alcohol. Otherwise Jews appear as researchers and laboratory men, in which positions several of them have made considerable reputations.

Shipping and transportation are equally non-Jewish. There are no Jews of any importance in railroading save Jacob Aronson, Vice President in Charge of the Legal Department of the New York Central, and the only notable Jew in shipping is Samuel Zemurray, managing director of United Fruit. There is a corporation of Jewish control named American Foreign Steamship Corp. but it is relatively insignificant. On inland waterways only the Hudson River Navigation Corp. recently bought by subway-tunneling Mr. Samuel Rosoff seems to have Jewish ownership. There are no Jewish shipbuilders of any kind. In passenger bus transportation the Jewish interest is minuscule, being limited to a half dozen little lines like Capitol Coach, Lincoln Transit, and Manhattan Coach in the New York area. In aviation the situation is about the same. There is no Jewish control in the management or ownership end of either transport or manufacture. Jewish financial interest there undoubtedly is, as for example, through Lehman in T.W.A. But Lehman is associated in T.W.A. with Atlas and financial control is non-Jewish throughout.

A vast continent of heavy industry and finance may therefore be staked out in which Jewish participation is incidental or nonexistent. To this may be annexed other important areas into which Jews have rarely penetrated such as light and power and telephone and telegraph and engineering in general and heavy machinery and lumber and dairy products. In brief, Jews are so far from controlling the most characteristic of present-day American activities that they are hardly represented in them at all.

To find Jewish participation in industry it is necessary to turn to the light industries. And even there it is necessary to turn from the manufacturing to the distributing end. There is an entire group of industries like wool, silk, cotton, and rayon weaving where the Jewish interest in production is small, being 5 to 10 per cent in wool (for example, L. Bachmann of Uxbridge Worsted, Austin T. Levy of Stillwater Worsted, and Allen and Bernard Goldfine), 15 per cent in silk (for example, Hess, Goldsmith & Co., David Silks, Inc., Widder Bros.), 5 per cent in cotton (the Cone family of North Carolina, Sigmund Odenheimer of New Orleans, Elias Reiss of New York), and 16 per cent in rayon-yarn production (Industrial Rayon and Celanese Corp.). But in these same industries the Jewish interest in distribution is large, half the wool sales agents and jobbers, three-quarters of the silk converters, and three-quarters of the cotton converters being Jews. In the underwear and dress-cutting trades using rayon 80 to 90 per cent are Jews.

In other industries like meat packing a special Jewish branch of the business brings up the total: the kosher meat pack, for example, amounts to almost 10 per cent of the wholesale meat-packing total. While in furniture making a particular Jewish affinity for the upholstered (as opposed to the "case" or wooden) field gives Jewish manufacturers like Artistic in Detroit, Angelus in Los Angeles, and S. Karpen in Chicago almost half the total. But these victories have their counterbalancing defeats. There are light-industry sectors like boots and shoes where on the manufacturing end the Jews are a 40 per cent minority in numbers and a 29 per cent minority in volume. Only in the traditional Jewish bailiwick of the clothing industry can any claim for a Jewish monopoly be made. There, about 85 per cent of men's clothing and about 95 per cent of women's dresses and about 95 per cent of furs and almost the whole wearing-apparel business are in Jewish hands with the interest of New York Jews predominating.

But the clothing business is the spectacular and outstanding exception to the statement that Jewish industrial interests are generally in the minority. Not even in the liquor business, which was always the prerogative of the Jew in Poland, nor in the tobacco business, in which many a rich Jew made his start, are Jewish interests dominant. Jews have practically blanketed the tobacco-buying business, where Jew and buyer are synonymous words, and control three of the four leading cigar-manufacturing concerns including Fred Hirschhorn's General Cigar, which makes every seventh cigar smoked in America. But their cigarette interest is confined in the Big Four to P. Lorillard and even there they appear only as bankers through J. & W. Seligman. As for the liquor business about half the important distilling concerns are Jewish. The largest U.S. concern, National Distillers (1934 sales: $50,000,000), is under non-Jewish management though Daniel K. Weiskopf, an active Vice President, is a Jew. The second, Schenley (1934 sales: $40,000,000), is controlled by Jews though with Grover A. Whalen as Chairman of the Board. The third, Seagrams (sales figure not published), is owned, controlled, and managed by the Bronfman brothers who are Jews. These three companies do about 50 per cent of the business. Of the next three, Frankfort, Hiram Walker, and Continental, only the last named is under Jewish management. But in the wholesale liquor trade in New York Jews do probably only a quarter of the business. Three of the leading firms are non-Jewish—R. C. Williams, Austin Nichols, and McKesson & Robbins. Outside New York, Jewish participation is even less. In the importing business it is small. In the domestic wine business it is trifling.

With the perspective of a broad review such as this it becomes apparent that Jews are most frequently to be found in those reaches of industry where manufacturer and merchant meet. Consequently their predominance in retailing might be expected. It will not be found. The Jewish interest, though easily dominant in New York and in the northeastern cities in general, is not as great throughout the country as is commonly supposed. Department stores are largely Jewish-owned in New York, where Macy, Gimbel, Saks, Abraham & Straus, Bloomingdale, Hearn, all are Jewish—the chief non-Jewish concerns being Stern, Wanamaker, McCreery, Loeser, Lord & Taylor, and Best. Altman is owned by two foundations created by the late Benjamin Altman and Colonel Friedsam, both Jews. But in Chicago the two leading stores are Marshall Field and Carson, Pirie, Scott & Co., one of Yankee origin and the other of Scotch and both under Scotch management at present. The third in rank, Mandel Bros., is Jewish. And farther west the relative number of Jewish stores of importance further decreases. The department-store chains like May, Allied, Interstate, and Gimbel are Jewish but the Five and Ten, etc., chains like Woolworth and Kress are 95 per cent not. In the food-and-grocery field, where the greatest number of chains operate, 95 to 99 per cent including A & P are non-Jewish. Montgomery Ward in the mail-order field is non-Jewish while Sears, Roebuck has a Jewish history (Julius Rosenwald) but active management of Sears Roebuck now is in the hands of General Robert Wood. Drugstore chains are about 90 per cent non-Jewish and apparel-store chains 90 per cent the other way. Jews in other words are in a definite retailing minority over the country.

By and large, then, the case for Jewish control of American industry falls pretty flat. But the little propagandists of the Shirts have another tune to their whistle. They contend that, whatever the facts about industry, the Jews control opinion in America through their control of newspapers, publishing, radio, the theatre, and above all the movies. Even granted, in the face of the notorious inability of Jews to agree and the wide divergence of their interests, that such a thing as "Jewish opinion" could exist, it would still be difficult to prove that Jewish opinion directs U.S. opinion.

As to the newspapers the facts are strongly the other way round. Save for the prestige of the New York *Times,* which must rank on any basis of real distinction as the leading American newspaper, the interest of Jews is small. There are only four important Jewish chains in the field: the Ochs interests owning the *Times* and the Chattanooga *Times,* J. David Stern owning the New York *Post,* the Philadelphia *Record,* and the Camden (New Jersey) *Courier* and *Post,* Paul Block owning the Newark *Star-Eagle,* the Toledo *Blade* and *Times,* and the Duluth *Herald* and *News-Tribune,* and Emanuel P. Adler of Davenport, Iowa, owning a string of papers in towns such as Davenport and Ottumwa, Iowa; Madison, Wisconsin; Hannibal, Missouri; Lincoln, Nebraska, etc. On the basis of daily circulation these four groups total respectively 489,871, 391,209, 289,126, and 198,610. These figures may be compared with the 5,500-000 daily of Hearst who is not a Jew, Patterson-McCormick's 2,332,156, and Scripps-Howard's 1,794,617. Jewish department-store owners unquestionably influence newspaper policy in cities where they are numerous like New York but the influence is rather negative (against criticism of Jews) than positive (for particular Jews or particular Jewish programs).

The magazine situation is even more striking. Save for the *New Yorker,* in which the largest stockholder is Raoul Fleischman but the directing head Harold Ross, the only important Jewish general magazines are the *American Mercury* and *Esquire.* And *Esquire* is closely related, through its male-fashion department, to the traditionally Jewish clothing business.

Advertising presents something the same picture. The Jewish participation may be put at about 1 to 3 per cent. Of the 200 large agencies six may be Jewish, the most important by all odds being Lord & Thomas of which Albert D. Lasker is President. Of the 1,800 small agencies perhaps 100 or 150 are run by Jews.

So far as book publishing is concerned there were practically no Jews in the business prior to 1915 and today Viking, Simon & Schuster, Knopf, Covici, Friede, and Random House do not rank in size of annual list with such non-Jewish houses as Macmillan, Scribner's, Harpers, Houghton Mifflin, Appleton-Century, Doubleday, Doran, and the like. In job- and trade-printing plants Jews are perhaps dominant in New York, Philadelphia, and Chicago and the two largest bookbinding companies, American Book Bindery and the H. Wolff concern, are run by Jews.

In radio the Jewish interest is extremely important. Of the two great broadcasting chains one, Columbia, is under Jewish control. The other, N.B.C., though non-Jewish in management, is headed by David Sarnoff. Of the local stations the vast majority outside New York, however, are non-Jewish.

As to theatre, the theatre being a New York institution and New York being the largest Jewish city in the world and Jews being drawn to the amusement business and to the dramatic arts, a Jewish monopoly might be expected. In the days of Erlanger and the Shuberts it may have existed. Today, however, a count of active New York producers shows fifty-eight non-Jewish producers and fifty-six Jewish and an estimate of their relative importance shows them pretty much in balance. This count, however, does not include the various groups such as the Theatre Guild, the Group Theatre, and the Theatre Union. The inclusion of these predominantly Jewish organizations would probably serve to restore the Jewish advantage both in prestige and in commercial importance. The commercial importance of the Guild is very high and it still retains a certain prestige. The prestige of the Group is at present probably greater than that of any other producing organization.

The movies however are the chief point of anti-Semitic reliance. And there a persuasive case may be made. Jews were the first exhibitors of movies because the early movie theatres could be operated with little capital: they were commonly empty stores with folding chairs for seats and a derelict piano. Large returns in such ventures tempted them into production. American movies, in consequence, were made for years as Marcus Loew, Adolph Zukor, Sam Goldwyn, Carl Laemmle, Louis Selznick, Louis B. Mayer, Jesse Lasky, and William Fox thought they should be made. That certain of the Jewish producers were men whose influence upon the popular taste was unfortunate no one, and least of all the cultivated Jew, will deny. But neither can the Jew-baiter deny that the greatest artist so far produced by the moving pictures is a man named Chaplin[1] whom all Jews are proud to claim.

Today Jewish control of the great moving-picture companies is less than monopolistic. An examination of the various producing corporations . . . will suggest that three of the eight principal companies are owned and controlled by Jews, two are probably owned and controlled by non-Jews, and in three management and ownership are divided. But though Jews do not monopolize the industry moneywise they do nevertheless exert pretty complete control over the production of pictures. A majority of directors, including such men as Frank Borzage, Howard Hawks, John Ford, W. S. Van Dyke, King Vidor, and Frank Capra are non-Jews. But directors are subordinate in authority to producers. Of eighty-five names engaged in production either as executives in production, producers, or associate producers (including independents) fifty-three are Jews. And the Jewish advantage holds in prestige as well as in numbers. Of non-Jews, Darryl Zanuck, the new luminary at Twentieth Century-Fox, and Alexander Korda at United Artists are among the outstanding producers. On the Jewish side of the roster are such names as Irving Thalberg, Carl Laemmle, Jr., David Selznick, Ernst Lubitsch, B. P. Schulberg, and Jack Warner.

It is difficult on these figures to conclude that American organs and instruments of opinion are predominantly Jewish. Granted the great power of the movies in the influencing of modern society and the great influence of Jews in the movies, it still remains true that the Jewish interest in journalism and advertising is extraordinarily small and that journalism and advertising also have their persuasiveness. With radio and the theatre standing midway between, each about half owned by Jews, it may perhaps be guessed that they more fairly reflect the actual situation. At the very most half the opinion-making and taste-influencing paraphernalia in America is in Jewish hands.

[1] Chaplin himself has denied that he is a Jew. The fact seems to be that one grandfather was Jewish.

The whole picture of industry, business, and amusements, then, may be summed up by repeating that while there are certain industries which Jews dominate and certain industries in which Jewish participation is considerable there are also vast industrial fields, generally reckoned as the most typical of our civilization, in which they play a part so inconsiderable as not to count in the total picture. Perhaps as good a comment as any is that offered by figures published recently in the *American Hebrew*. Of 80,000 individual names listed in *Poor's Register of Directors* 4.7 per cent appear to be Jewish as against a Jewish population percentage of about 4 or a little less. It is admitted by the *American Hebrew* writer that certain Jews are omitted in any such tabulation because of the penchant of certain Jews for adopting non-Jewish names, but it is contended with justice that some non-Jews with Jewish-sounding names will also be included so that the total error will be diminished. And in any case it seems fair to assume that the 4.7 per cent figure is out of line to no considerable extent.

The impression thus given that Jews are very far from controlling American life is increased if the eye is permitted to wander over the agricultural scene. No census of Jews in agriculture has ever been made but even the Jewish Agricultural Society places the total no higher than 80,000 out of a farm population of 30,500,000. Attempts by Jews to move their people out of the urban centers and into colonies on the land have not been successful save in the neighborhood of big cities or in special circumstances. The reason probably is the long legal exclusion of the Jews from landowning in Europe. The total of Jews on the land has increased about 100 per cent since 1900. But the record of the formal settlements is still discouraging. Major Noah's "Ararat" on Grand Island in the Niagara River, a half-agricultural venture, was an unrealized dream in 1818. Then followed "Sholom," which survived from 1837 to 1850 in Ulster County, New York. Third in order were the short-lived colonies established by German Jews already in this country to take care of part of the flood of penniless Russian Jews in the eighties. Subsequently, with the aid of funds supplied by the great Jewish philanthropist, Baron de Hirsch, other and luckier colonies were started. The most famous of these is Woodbine in Cape May County, New Jersey, an agricultural-industrial settlement, with an important Jewish agricultural school. Numerous Jewish farming communities have sprung up in other localities in southern New Jersey. In addition to New Jersey, the states with the largest Jewish farm population are New York, Connecticut, Massachusetts, Michigan, and North Dakota. Well-known individuals are Simon Fishman, a successful wheat farmer who sits in the Kansas Senate, Jacob Karlin, who has a profitable truck farm in Calverton, Long Island, valued at $20,000, Irving Kauder of Ulster County, New York, who is a leading breeder of White Leghorns, and Max D. Cohen, who runs 2,000 to 2,500 head of cattle on 3,600 acres in Idaho.

There remain for consideration the two related fields of politics and the professions—particularly law and medicine. The anti-Semitic contention as to the professions is that the Jews have crowded out the rest of the population and are monopolizing all opportunities. To prove which anti-Semites cite estimates guessing that a third to a half of the lawyers in New York City and at least a third of the doctors are Jews. One obvious rejoinder is that a third of the population of New York is also Jewish and that the percentage of Jewish lawyers and doctors in other cities with smaller Jewish populations is correspondingly smaller.

Another equally obvious reply is that 50 per cent of New York lawyers does not mean 50 per cent of New York's lawyer *power*. The most important office law business in America such as the law business incidental to banking, insurance, trust-company operation, investment work, railroading, patents, admiralty, and large corporation matters in general is in the hands of non-Jewish firms many of which, even though they have numerous Jewish clients, have no Jewish partners. Jewish legal activity will be found most commonly in the bankruptcy courts, real-estate law, negligence, divorce, collections, and litigation in general. In other words, Jews are largely to be found in those branches of law which do not interest non-Jewish lawyers or in those branches of law related to commercial activities like real estate and textiles where Jews are peculiarly active. It is for that reason that the importance of Jews in trial work is significant. Their presence in the courts means not only that Jews are able trial lawyers but also that non-Jewish lawyers tend to prefer the fat fees and regular hours and routine, solicitor-like labors of their offices to the active, combative, professional service of the law courts. Non-Jewish lawyers have themselves to thank if they think the trend of judicial decisions has recently been contrary to the spirit of Anglo-Saxon law.

The medical situation is not unlike the legal. There is no equally clear-cut separation of fields of professional activity but there is the same disparity between numbers of Jewish doctors and extent of Jewish medical influence. New York, for example, has numerous good Jewish doctors and a few very great Jewish doctors. But Jews do not occupy a position of power corresponding to their abilities or their numbers in the profession. Hospital medical boards and the like are apt to be controlled by non-Jewish doctors, though revolving officiates with Jews and non-Jews alternating are sometimes employed. And north, west, and south of New York the conflict lessens.

The chief difference between law and medicine is that the feeling between Jews and non-Jews is much stronger in the latter profession than in the former. The reason for that feeling is this: of approximately 14,000 young men and women attempting annually to enter the seventy-six reputable U.S medical schools 50 per cent are Jews, while of the 6,000 more or less who get in only 17 per cent are Jews. Non-Jewish doctors cite these figures as proof of the danger of Jewish aggressiveness and commercialism in the profession while Jewish doctors cite them as proof of discrimination, arguing that if there are a disproportionate number of Jews in medical schools the reason may be that Jews are brighter than non-Jews. The truth seems to be that medicine is merely the most obvious point of collision between forces set in motion by the peculiar development of Jewish life in America. Given the desire of Jews to see their sons in the learned professions, and given their urbanization and hence their access to free college education, and given the assiduity of Jewish children, a clash was inevitable. There is no occasion to explain it by reference to an alleged Jewish intellectual superiority.

The Jewish advantage in the professions, then, is rather shadow than substance. And so, but much more so, is the Jewish importance in politics. Anti-Semites usually put that importance in two ways for purposes of effect if not for purposes of logic. First, "the New Deal is the Jew Deal." Second, "all Communists are Jews and all Jews are Communists." As to the New Deal, FORTUNE has already pointed out ("The Case Against Roosevelt," December, 1935) that Jewish influence in Mr. Roosevelt's Washington is minor. Attempts to make it seem important rest on misrepresentations and no amount of political whispering can change that fact. As to Communism the finding of the Congressional Committee of 1931 that 70 per cent of the U.S. Communist Party was alien with Jews predominating has been effectively rebutted. The truth is that of the 27,000 U.S. Communists, few of the higher officers and only 3,500 to 4,000 of the members of the party are Jews.

The reason for the general impression of Jewish and Communist identity is simple. First of all, as we have had occasion to observe, the Jews are urban and largely concentrated in New York. The radical movement is also urban and largely centered in New York. Secondly, the Jewish members of the Communist Party are very commonly the intellectual and hence the articulate members of that party. The second-generation Jewish intellectual with his background of Talmudic dialectic is mentally predisposed to Marxism to a degree which he himself rarely appreciates. And Marxism with its internationalism and anti-nationalism is eminently fitted to the emotional needs of a people without a fatherland. The attachment of men of other blood to the earth on which they were born is sometimes incomprehensible to the traditionally earthless Jew. But most important, Jewish intellectuals are attracted to radicalism because the Jewish intellectual very understandably feels that the "system" is against him. Non-Jews wishing to become teachers and scientists and professional men are able to find more or less open opportunities for the exercise of their talents. Such opportunities are frequently closed to the Jew. In consequence the Jewish intellectual is frequently against the existing order. In consequence he is frequently a radical. And since he is able and idealistic and courageous and articulate he becomes the voice of radicalism. He provides, under his own name or under non-Jewish names chosen for tactical reasons, a very great deal of the magazine writing, the propaganda, the general literature, of the movement in New York. In so doing he puts himself very much in the public eye and his 15 per cent membership in the Communist Party looks like 100 per cent. It is not the natural propensity of the Jews for revolution which produces the impression. It is their natural propensity for journalism and excited, persuasive speech.

But because the Jewish intellectual is a formidable member of the Communist Party it does not follow that "the revolution" in America is Jewish. There are two unanswerable reasons why it is not. One reason is that for every revolutionary Jew there are thousands of Jewish capitalists, shopkeepers, traders, and the like who stand to lose everything in a revolution as 90 per cent of the Jews in Russia (who were traders and the like) lost everything—including, in many cases, their lives. The other reason is that the revolution in America is much more likely to come from the native-born Americans of Yankee and Nordic stock in the agricultural regions of the Midwest and Northwest than from the Americans of Jewish stock in New York City.

Examination of Jewish participation in American life might be carried further but the findings would remain the same. Jews do not dominate the American scene. They do not even dominate major sectors of the American scene. They do, however, monopolize certain minor provinces. What is remarkable about the Jews in America, in other words, is not their industrial power but their curious industrial distribution, their tendency to crowd together in particular squares of the checkerboard. The reason for their crowding must be found in their most pronounced psychological trait—their clannishness, their tribal inclination. The reason for their choice of particular squares into which to crowd must be found in historical accident. Jews are in scrap iron because they were once in the junk business and they were once in the junk business because a penniless immigrant could make a start there on a shoestring. Jews are in movies because they were in movie theatres and because a few successful cloak-and-suit manufacturers invested their cloak-and-suit profits usefully in the amusement business. (The connection between the movies and the cloak-and-suit business is still esthetically betrayed from time to time.) Were the four and a half millions of American Jews scattered more or less evenly over the whole industrial acreage, and were they as fond of rural communities and small towns as they are of great cities, their presence as Jews would hardly be noticed by other Americans. The whole point of the whole inquiry is that wherever the Jews may be, industrially or culturally or professionally or merely geographically, they are always present in numbers and they are almost always present as Jews.

And therein too lies the point of the so-called Jewish problem. Granted, as any open-minded man who has read the facts here collected must grant, that the Jews do not come within gunshot of running America and that their numbers are no longer rapidly increasing and that there is no color of reason for expecting successful anti-Semitism here. Granted that the FORTUNE Survey, above quoted, demonstrates the ability of the American people to suffer Klan propaganda and Silver Shirt propaganda and the propaganda of the Nazis and still maintain common sense and basic decency. Granted that there is strong reason therefore for believing that Fascism can be defeated in this country. Granted all this, it still remains true that the future of the Jew in America is puzzling. Can this universal stranger be absorbed in the country which has absorbed every other European stock? Does he wish to be absorbed? Can he live happily and in peace if he is not absorbed? The answers must be guesses. Upper-class Spanish and German Jews *have* been pretty well absorbed. There are, however, numerous Jews who look upon the loss of Jewish identity as a kind of social suicide. If those groups, Jewish and non-Jewish, who wish the identity and distinction of the Jews preserved are able to carry their point then the only hope for the Jews in America is mutual toleration and respect. Since, however, toleration and mutual respect are also the only hope of all who wish to preserve or reestablish democratic institutions in this country the Jews in America will have numerous allies. The first condition of their success will be the quieting of Jewish apprehensiveness and the consequent elimination of the aggressive and occasionally provocative Jewish defensive measures which the country has recently and anxiously observed.

Poles

WILLIAM I. THOMAS and FLORIAN ZNANIECKI
The Polish-American Community

The Poles are one of the most significant of the twentieth-century minorities. Only the Italians and Jews outnumbered the 875,000 Polish immigrants who came to the United States between 1870 and 1924. Most of the newcomers settled in the cities of Buffalo, Chicago, Milwaukee, Pittsburgh, Detroit, and New York and took on available laboring jobs; some migrated to mining areas and farming communities. In what has now become almost a repetitive annotation, it is necessary to indicate that they lived in crowded quarters and worked for barely livable wages. In the Shenandoah coal mines Polish children worked ten hours a day, six days a week, and took home $2.68 for their efforts. Adult wages were not much better.

The following selection is taken from The Polish Peasant in Europe and America, *a pioneering effort in social research and theory. This multi-volume work by William I. Thomas and Florian Znaniecki explores the organization of the Polish peasant society undergoing fundamental social change. Psychological responses, social processes, class, migration, vagabondage, law breaking, tradition, alienation, assimilation, cultural values, patterns of social control, prejudice, efficiency, and happiness are among the subjects treated in Thomas and Znaniecki's analysis. The chapter reprinted below focuses on the roles played by vocation, benevolent societies, religion, and the ethnic press in creating a cohesive ethnic community.*

The tide of Polish immigration grew continually until 1914. The number of returns to Poland was also, indeed, increasing, but these on the average did not exceed 30 per cent. of the arrivals. The population of the old Polish colonies (in Pittsburg, Buffalo, Cleveland, Detroit, Chicago, Milwaukee, etc.) rivalled that of Polish cities in Europe, Chicago with its 360,000 Poles ranking after Warsaw and Łódź as the third largest Polish center in the world. Outside of these, numerous new colonies have developed, for the most part founded by immigrants sufficiently familiar with American conditions to search for work away from the traditional centers, but recruited later chiefly from Europe. Since

William I. Thomas and Florian Znaniecki, *The Polish Peasant in Europe and America* (2 vols., New York: Alfred A. Knopf, Inc., 1927), II, 1511–49. Reprinted from the Dover Publications edition published in 1958.

the beginning of the present century hundreds of new colonies were founded in the East, which originally had only a few old and small Polish settlements. Some of them have developed rapidly. Thus, according to Polish sources, one-third of the population of New Britain, Conn., is Polish and the Polish parish in that city is among the most flourishing and best organized. In the far West the development has been slower, in the South quite insignificant.[1]

The process by which Polish colonies appear and grow can thus be observed in detail during the last 20 or 30 years. It seems to present a uniformity of outline which permits us to construct a general sociological scheme of the development of a Polish-American community applicable with some variations to all such communities except agricultural colonies, which we have not had the opportunity to study, and a few of the oldest and largest groups which originated under different conditions and are now organized around several centers, thus presenting a greater complexity of life than the smaller settlements, each with one main social center.[2]

When a Polish immigrant finds work which pays well and promises to be permanent in a locality where there is no Polish settlement yet, he usually tries at once to attract his friends and relatives from other Polish-American communities. His motives are evident. He has been accustomed to such social response and recognition as only a primary group with old social bonds and uniform attitudes can give, and however well he may be adapted to American economic and political conditions he seldom is at once accepted as a member by an American primary-group (or by a primary-group of some other immigrant people). Even if he were he would miss the directness and warmth of social relations to which he has been accustomed in his own group. Sometimes, indeed, he does not succeed in attracting any one. Then if he does not leave the place driven by loneliness, he becomes gradually absorbed in the American milieu. Usually, however, a small group of Polish workmen is soon formed; and their first attempt, partly for economic, partly for social reasons, is to have a Polish boarding-house. Often some one of them who has some money and a wife in America assumes the initiative, brings his wife as soon as his situation seems settled, rents a large apartment and takes the others as roomers or boarders. It may happen that a bachelor marries some Polish girl he knows, with the understanding that they are going to keep a boarding place. Sometimes under such conditions a wife or a fiancée is even brought from Europe. Frequently, however, the initiative comes not from an individual but from the group; all the workmen put some money into renting and furnishing the apartment and induce one of their number who has a wife or fiancée to bring her. In this case they buy their own food and the woman only cooks it and cleans the house, receiving for these services a small sum from each ($1 to $2 a week)

[1] There are no reliable official statistics of the Polish population in this country. According to the data privately collected by Mr. Stanislaw Osada of Chicago for a work which he is preparing under the title "Polonia Americana," there are about 1,200 Polish parishes with a membership of nearly 2,000,000. The number of Poles not directly connected with parishes may be estimated roughly at about 1,000,000.

[2] The following typical scheme of development of Polish-American colonies was outlined to us in its main features in private conversation by the Rev. Priest Syski of Boston, who has observed Polish American life very closely and intelligently for many years. We are also using materials collected by ourselves. Our explanation of the social process here described is based in a large measure on the results of our preceding volumes.

and by tacit understanding feeding herself and her children on her boarders' superfluous food.

If the locality has a permanent industry the small Polish colony continues to grow, partly by invited, partly by independent arrivals. Almost every individual or small family once settled attracts new members from the outside, however large the colony may already be, provided the economic conditions are favorable. The reason why, even when there is a Polish group formed, its members still invite their friends and relatives to come is once more to be found in the desire for response and the desire for recognition. As long as the Polish immigrant is isolated among Americans or immigrants of different nationalities he welcomes the arrival of any Pole. But even among people of the same nationality and the same class the desires for response and recognition are not satisfied as fully as among relatives or friends. Relatives are on the average more satisfactory than strangers, those who come from the same community in Poland or from the same town in America are next best and tend to keep together more closely than those born or reared in different parts of the country; friends with a long past of common interests are more united than recent acquaintances. Each individual desires the fullest response and the widest recognition possible. He may accept provisionally whatever he finds but very soon begins to desire more. On the one hand he is ready to lavish his social feelings on any one within his reach, if he has only a few possible objects; but, on the other hand, when his social milieu widens and he can select the objects of his social feelings more consciously, he becomes more reserved and discriminating. Thus when a mere acquaintance comes into a colony formed of close friends and relatives, or when a group of immigrants coming from the same community is joined by an individual born in a different part of the country, the newcomer feels like an outsider. He naturally tends to call in his own relatives and his own friends, or people from his neighborhood. It often happens that a Polish colony is divided into several distinct groups which, though more closely connected with one another than with their American milieu, still look at one another with some mistrust and even a slight hostility. As we shall see later this division is soon overcome by cooperation for common purposes and does not exist in the older colonies, except that immigrants who have recently come from the same communities always associate with each other more willingly than with those who lack the same early neighborhood connections and sometimes a colony— or a parish in a large colony like Chicago—is composed principally of immigrants from some one of the provinces of Poland, Posen, Silesia, Galicia, the Congress Kingdom of Lithuania. The fact that the emigration from these provinces started at different periods has probably something to do with this phenomenon.

Dissensions between immigrants are also indirectly a factor in the growth of new colonies, for when relatives, friends or acquaintances have quarreled each party wishes to be independent and to bring more relatives, friends or acquaintances to satisfy the social needs formerly satisfied by the other and to furnish additional support against it. As long as the existence of the new colony is not quite assured, the colony is naturally recruited more from the unsettled part of the population of other Polish-American communities than from the new immigrants, since the former can more easily risk moving temporarily to a new place. There are many instances of new settlements springing up in connection with an increased demand for labor in a given locality and suddenly disappearing after a relatively short time, if the labor conditions grow worse, a factory goes bankrupt, or a mine or lumber field is exhausted, etc. But if a colony lasts for several years, after having attracted chiefly the shifting and unsettled Polish-American elements from other colonies it usually begins to depend more on European immigration, since there are always many members who maintain their connections with Poland. The influx of new immigrants thus often becomes for a time the most important factor in its growth. Later when the community is definitely settled marriages and births—at first relatively insignificant—gradually acquire the predominant importance.

In this respect it must be remembered that from the standpoint of the traditional family system the family group should tend to be as numerous as possible and that this old conception perfectly harmonizes with the view of the Catholic Church according to which many children are to be considered a "blessing of God." Of course the family system loses much of its power through emigration, but it remains still strong enough, at least in the first generation, to prevent any rapid decay of this attitude, which is one of the oldest and most deeply rooted family attitudes. We may add that the immigrant seldom knows any means of preventing childbearing except abortion, which is considered shameful—probably because resorted to mostly by unmarried girls— and sexual abstinence, which the peasant considers hardly worth while merely in order to limit his family. Moreover the economic conditions here favor the growth of large families. For although the children cannot be utilized economically as early as they are on a peasant farm in Poland, still there is seldom any real difficulty in bringing them up, for the average wages of an immigrant are certainly sufficient to support a large family on the scale to which he has been accustomed in the old country, if not on a higher one. When the children grow up they are expected to preserve family solidarity at least to the extent of turning over to the family most of their earnings, so that whatever expenses the family incurs to support them until working age are treated as an investment of the family funds from which a return is expected. Furthermore, a large family is considered normal, for the social and economic status of the second generation will probably be above that of the first here, whereas in the old country a too numerous family often means a division of the property into such small parts that the children are unable to maintain the economic and social level of their parents. And if we realize that the power of the parish is here, as we shall see presently, greater than in Poland and that the parish favors for obvious reasons a rapid growth of the population, it will not be surprising that social opinion maintains the old standard of "propagation" and the prestige of a family group grows with the number of its children. Of course in cases of individual disorganization all these factors may cease to work. Generally, however, they work well enough to make the Polish immigrants at least as prolific as the peasants in the old country. Propagation has been even emphasized recently as a patriotic duty to both Poland and the local colony.[3]

[3] We know an intelligent Pole, a relatively recent immigrant, who has been very successful in business and who openly says he desires to fulfil his national duty by returning to Poland with twelve children and a million dollars for each of them.

Along with the growth of the new colony goes progress in unity and cohesion. In the beginning the group of Polish immigrants is naturally more or less scattered territorially, particularly when the locality has several factories or mines, since every workman tends to live near his working place. There are no interests to keep it together, except the personal ties of relationship and friendship between particular members of marriage groups and the general feeling of racial solidarity. But individuals always appear in every group—usually those who have had some experience in other Polish-American colonies—with whom the feeling of racial solidarity and perhaps also the desire to play a public rôle become motives for starting a closer organization. A "society" is established invariably whenever the colony reaches 100 to 300 members. . . .

The first purpose for which such a "society" is usually established is mutual help in emergencies (sickness, death, and, more seldom, lack of work). For however vague may be originally the bond of racial solidarity between the members of a new colony, it never fails to manifest itself at the death of a member. Usually a severe sickness or disabling accident also provokes sympathetic feelings and the desire to help. Just as in matters concerning the increase of the family, so in cases calling for communal solidarity there are in the conditions surrounding the new Polish-American colony factors that are able to counterbalance in some measure and for a certain time the disorganizing influences of the new milieu. The workman who has no productive property and is hired by the week is evidently more seriously affected by misfortune than the peasant farmer or even the manor-servant hired by the year. Yet during times of prosperity his increased earning power makes him more able to help others in case of need and more willing to do so, since money has less value for him than in the old country, particularly after he has once resigned himself to considering his earnings as a means to live rather than as a means to acquire property. Further, the group of workmen constituting a Polish-American colony is isolated and cut off from all wider social milieux, instead of constituting, like a group of working men in Poland, an integral part of a larger society disposing of some wealth. Private charity from wealthy people, which in the country districts of Poland still remains a valuable source of help in emergencies, is thus necessarily very limited in this country. As to public charity, an appeal to a charitable institution is considered even in Poland a mark of social downfall; it is even more of a disgrace in the eyes of Polish immigrants here because of the feeling of group responsibility which is imposed, or thought to be imposed by the American milieu. The immigrant has been accustomed to see the wider social group hold every narrower social group within its limits responsible for the behavior of every member; the village praises or blames the family as a whole for the activities of an individual, the parish does the same with reference to the village group, the wider community with reference to the parish or village. The American population is supposed to do the same—and, of course, in some measure actually does the same—with reference to the foreign colony in its midst. Every Pole who accepts the help of American institutions is thus considered not only disgraced personally as a pauper, but as disgracing the whole Polish colony. If in spite of this social attitude many relatively self-respecting individuals do not hesitate to claim assistance from American institutions, it is because they misinterpret the meaning of this assistance and consider it as being *due* to them, taking the institution as part of the whole American social and political system on which they place the blame for the evil befalling them. And thus they expect all kinds of relief and benefits as a perfectly normal method of redressing their grievances. But such misinterpretations are found mainly in unfamiliar situations, and help given in ordinary sickness or after a natural death preserves the traditional character of charity, from whatever source it comes. No individual who has preserved some self-respect will accept it from an American institution unless his traditional conceptions have been obliterated owing to the new conditions and to insufficient contact with the Polish-American group.

Originally, during the early stages in the evolution of a Polish-American community mutual help is exercised sporadically, from case to case, by means of collections made for the benefit of the individual or family in distress. Naturally, the more settled and well-to-do members of the community on whom most of the burden falls are eager to substitute for this unregulated voluntary assistance a regular system of mutual death and sickness insurance, and thus favor the establishment of an association which will diminish their risks. The very fact that such a regulation of mutual assistance is necessary shows, of course, that the old naïve and unreflective communal solidarity, where each individual had rightful claims on the help of every other individual in a degree dependent on the closeness of their social connection, has been radically modified. As a matter of fact, most of the individuals who under the old system would be the first to be called to assist a member—his nearest relatives and old neighbors—are not here; their function has to be assumed, at least in part, vicariously by relative strangers who in Poland would never be asked to interfere. In the eyes of these, the help which they have to give appears not as a natural duty to be unreflectively performed but as, we might say, an artificial duty, the result of abnormal conditions. And this attitude communicates itself gradually even to those who under the old system would always be obliged to help, as friends and close relatives. The duty to help cannot be disclaimed entirely, for the member in distress is at least a fellow-countryman; but it is no longer connected with the very foundation of social life. Mutual insurance is a reflective solution of this difficulty. It is the best method of escaping the conflict between the rudiments of the old attitudes of communal solidarity, strengthened by the feeling of group responsibility, and the individualistic unwillingness to endorse claims for assistance which no longer seem rooted in the very nature of things Since communal solidarity was a universal social institution among Polish peasants and the new individualistic attitude develops in all immigrant colonies, it is clear that the institution of mutual insurance, being the effect of this combined cause—pre-existing institution and new social attitude—must be found everywhere in Polish-American society. The individual's own tendency to have a fund assured for himself or his family in case of sickness or death is in the beginning only a secondary matter. It assumes, however, increasing importance as the institutions of mutual insurance in a given community grow in economic power and social opinion begins to appreciate this growth and to require that every individual be adequately insured, while, on the other hand, as we shall see later on, the individual's feeling of responsibility for other members of the colony decreases with the numerical and social progress of the latter. In the older and larger colonies the individual's desire to be insured plays, therefore, perhaps even a greater part in the development of mutual insurance associations than his desire to insure others.

But the "society" founded in a new colony is much more than a mutual insurance institution. Not only does it bring the scattered members of the colony periodically together, thus actively encouraging social intercourse, but it becomes the social organ of the community, the source of all initiative and the instrument for the realization of all plans initiated. This is probably the most important of its functions. In a peasant village there is no need for such an organ, for the territorial concentration and the close social cohesion of the village make direct individual initiative and immediate spontaneous cooperation of the concrete group possible from case to case. For the old country community, the *okolica* which includes a number of villages, the ready institutions of the commune and, in certain matters, the parish are more than sufficient to effect such changes as the community is legally entitled and practically able to introduce into the traditional system. Thus the cooperative organization which in Poland corresponds to the Polish-American "society," though it may exercise a strong influence over the primary community in which it exists and works, seldom acts as the organ of this community in proposing or realizing plans concerning the community as a whole except, of course, in its own special line of interest—establishment of cooperative shops for public use, public artistic performances, etc. The Polish-American community on the contrary, is too loose socially and territorially to do without an organ and has no old, political or religious centers which could play this rôle, while it needs organized initiative much more than the old Polish community whose activities can run for a long time more or less smoothly in the established channels of the traditional system.

Thus in a new Polish-American colony it is the "society" which assumes the care of the hedonistic interests of the group by organizing balls, picnics, etc., of its intellectual interests by giving theatrical representations, inviting lecturers, subscribing to periodicals; of its religious interests by arranging religious services to which some priest from an older Polish colony is invited. It is a center of information for newcomers, visitors, travellers; it sends to the press news about any opportunities which the locality may offer to Poles. It acts as a representative of the colony in its relations with the central institutions of Polish-American society, and eventually also with American institutions which try to reach the Polish community for political or social purposes. Thus all the campaigns for funds for Poland and for American Liberty Loans were waged in small communities by these associations. Finally, the great work of the society, through which it assures the permanence of the social cohesion of the colony, gains extraordinary prestige and security, though at the same time resigning its exclusive leadership, is the foundation of a parish.

When studying this most important Polish-American institution we should again be careful not to ascribe too much significance to its external form and official purpose. Just as the "benefit society" is much more than a mutual insurance company, so the Polish-American parish is much more than a religious association for common worship under the leadership of a priest. The unique power of the parish in Polish-American life, much greater than in even the most conservative peasant communities in Poland, cannot be explained by the

predominance of religious interests which, like all other traditional social attitudes, are weakened by emigration, though they seem to be the last to disappear completely. The parish is, indeed, simply the old primary community, reorganized and concentrated. In its concrete totality it is a substitute for both the
narrower but more coherent village-group and the wider but more diffuse and
vaguely outlined *okolica*. In its institutional organization it performs the functions which in Poland are fulfilled by both the parish and the commune.[4] It
does not control the life of its members as efficiently as did the old community for, first of all, it seldom covers a given territory entirely and is unable
to compel every one living within this territory to belong to it; secondly, its
stock of socially recognized rules and forms of behavior is much poorer; thirdly,
the attitudes of its members evolve too rapidly in the new conditions; finally, it
has no backing for its coercive measures in the wider society of which it is a
part. But its activities are much broader and more complex than those of a parish or of a commune in the old country.

Its religious character is, of course, important in itself since there is a certain minimum of religious ceremonies—christenings, weddings, funerals—which
are considered absolutely indispensable even by the least religious among the
immigrants and which are sufficient to justify the existence of a church and a
priest in the eyes of all of them. The majority consider the Sunday service—at
least the mass—and even more the Easter confession as also essential. But all
these purely religious needs could be satisfied almost as well and at less expense
by joining the local Irish-American church with an occasional visit from a Polish
priest for confession and a sermon. It would even seem to be the wiser course,
since the Irish-American clergy, coming from a better social class, better controlled by its bishops and by American society and having to compete with
the Protestant churches, are on a much higher intellectual and moral level than
the Polish-American clergy, recruited from an uneducated milieu and exercising
their power without any competition and practically uncontrolled except by the
Polish-American society which not only does not have very high standards but is
bound by its own interests to support them even while criticizing them.[5] If the
Poles with few exceptions refuse to join Irish-American parishes it is because
what the Polish colony really wishes in establishing a parish is not merely religious services but a community center of its own.

Of course a church is for many reasons best fitted for this purpose. The
religious activities, even when religious interests are weakened, still constitute
a very good foundation for community organization, first because every member, man, woman or child, can share in them, secondly because among the
Polish peasants, where the mystical current is very low and heterodoxy therefore very rare, religion is less apt to give birth to struggle and competition than
political or economic activities. The church organization is familiar to every

[4] Mr. Bronislaw Kulakowski, of New York, first attracted our attention to the
social rather than religious character of the Polish-American parish. He identifies it
sociologically with the old Slavic commune. We cannot, however, follow this analogy
to the end, since in the preceding volumes we have studied only the modern social
organization of the peasants.

[5] The American Catholic Church does not dare to interfere too much with the
education and morals of Polish priests lest the latter emancipate themselves from the
control of Rome altogether and join the Independent Polish Church.

member of the community, it has firmly established forms and well-trained professional leaders, and it introduces at once a contact between the activities of the community and a world-wide system of activities—all advantages which in any other field of social cooperation could be gained only after long efforts. The church building with its annexes is a traditional object of the æsthetic interest of the community and can easily become a *locus* for all important common activities, to which its more or less marked sacred character imparts a kind of superior sanction and official meaning.

But it is clear that the Irish-American church, though on the religious side its organization is similar, can never become for the Polish community anything more than a religious institution; its framework cannot be successfully utilized by the Poles for other social purposes, since they do not feel "at home" in a parish whose prevalent language and mores are different and with whose other members they have no social connections. The parish is not "their own" product, they have less control over its management than over that of a Polish parish which they have founded by free cooperation, they get little encouragement for the various common activities which they wish to initiate and obtain little prestige by their achievements; they cannot use the parish system to satisfy their desire for personal recognition, and so on. In short, unless they are already Americanized individually they do not get out of the English-speaking Catholic parish any satisfaction of their "social instinct." Of course if they are not numerous enough to establish a parish of their own, many join the nearest Irish-American church, which then becomes an important factor of their Americanization. But in this case a large proportion—all those whose religious interests are not particularly strong—remain outside of all religious life.

It is a mistake to suppose that a "community center" established by American social agencies can in its present form even approximately fulfil the social function of a Polish parish. It is an institution imposed from the outside instead of being freely developed by the initiative and cooperation of the people themselves and this, in addition to its racially unfamiliar character, would be enough to prevent it from exercising any deep social influence. Its managers usually know little or nothing of the traditions, attitudes and native language of the people with whom they have to deal, and therefore could not become genuine social leaders under any conditions. The institution is based on the type of a "club," which is entirely unknown to the Polish peasant. Whatever common activities it tries to develop are almost exclusively "leisure time" activities; and while these undoubtedly do correspond to a real social need, they are not sufficient by themselves to keep a community together and should be treated only as a desirable superstructure to be raised upon a strong foundation of *economic* cooperation. Whatever real assistance the American social center gives to the immigrant community is the result of the "case method," which consists in dealing directly and separately with individuals or families. While this method may bring efficient temporary help to the individual it does not contribute to the social progress of the community nor does it possess much preventive influence in struggling against social disorganization. Both these purposes can be attained only by organizing and encouraging social self-help on the cooperative basis. Finally, in their relations with immigrants the American social workers usually assume, consciously or not, the attitude of a kindly and protective superiority, occasionally, though seldom, verging on despotism. This attitude may be accepted by peasants fresh from the old country where they have been accustomed to it in their relations with the higher classes, but it is apt to provoke indignation in those who, after a longer stay in this country, have acquired a high racial and personal self-consciousness. In either case the result is the same. The immigrant associates his connections with the American institution with humiliation, submitted to willingly or unwillingly, whereas in his own Polish institutions not only his self-consciousness is respected, but he expects and easily obtains personal recognition. Of course his priest has also a strong attitude of superiority, but this is fully justified in the peasant's eyes by his sacral character.

We see that the parish as instrument for the unification and organization of the Polish-American community is thus quite unrivalled. The radical elements among Polish immigrants have sometimes tried to oppose its influence by establishing a lay community center, for instance, a theater.[6] But except in large colonies such as Chicago, Detroit, Milwaukee, Pittsburgh or Buffalo, where community life is too complex to concentrate itself entirely around parishes, these efforts seem to have met but little success, since even the majority of those who are opposed to the control of the clergy—the so-called "national" party—still group their local life around the church and cooperate in parish activities.

However the establishment of a new Polish-American parish meets with many obstacles. The parish has to be recognized and its rector appointed by the bishop. But the bishop, usually an Irish-American, is not inclined to favor the development of foreign-speaking parishes within his diocese. His opposition is further stimulated by the local Irish-American priest who wants the Polish sheep in his sheepstall, and by the Polish priest of the nearest Polish-American parish who expects them to come to his church on important occasions or to build a chapel and invite him or his vicar to come once or twice a month to perform the services. The latter solution is usually accepted provisionally as long as the colony is relatively small and poor. But if the Polish parish is not near enough, or if the colony increases rapidly, or if its "society" is strong and ambitious and has active and independent leaders, the matter is soon taken up again. Sometimes the opposition of the bishop is broken by an appeal to Rome, where the Polish-American clergy has influential connections due to the order of the Redemptionists. . . . Sometimes a different weapon is resorted to, particularly if the colony has many "free-thinkers." (A very moderate degree of heterodoxy is usually enough to earn this name.) These suggest the establishment of an "independent" parish, *i.e.*, a parish which, while preserving most of the traditional Catholic dogmas and ceremonies, does not belong to the Roman Catholic Church and does not recognize the authority of the Pope nor of the Roman Catholic bishops. The proposition may be accepted by the community. In fact there are at this moment nearly 50 "independent" Polish parishes unified into a "Polish National Church," whose head is Bishop Hodur of Scranton, Pa., besides an unknown number of isolated independent parishes which have not joined this church. The establishment of an independent parish is easy if the community agrees, for any member of the Roman Catholic clergy who is willing to emancipate himself from the Roman Catholic Church is ac-

[6] Kulakowski.

ceptable as priest. The Polish National Church requires also the rejection of a few dogmas, the chief of which is belief in Hell and the use of Polish instead of Latin during the mass; but among the young vicars, who are often badly treated by their rectors, many would gladly accept an invitation to become the rector of an independent parish. More frequently, however, the American Catholic bishop, in view of this danger of heresy, yields to the demand of the Polish colony and recognizes the new parish and appoints a priest for it.

When the parish has been organized the mutual help association to which this organization is due ceases to be, of course, the central and only representative institution of the community, for the leadership naturally passes into the hands of the priest. But it does not surrender entirely any of its social functions; it simply shares the initiative in communal matters and the representation of the community with the priest on the one hand, and on the other hand with the other associations which now begin to appear in rapid succession. The establishment of the parish opens new fields of social activity, widens the sphere of interests and calls for more and better social cooperation. For *the ideal of the development of the community,* which did not consciously exist while the community had no organ and was only vaguely conceived and intermittently realized during the period when the local mutual help "society" played the leading rôle, becomes now clearly formulated as the common ideal of the whole group and relentlessly pursued. The existence of a framework for the permanent organization of the community in the form of a parish produces both a tendency to utilize this framework to the full extent of its possibilities and a corresponding desire to see the community grow in numbers, wealth, cohesion and complexity of activities. While individualistic motives—economic reasons with those whose living depends on the Polish colony, desire for wider recognition with those who fulfill public functions, etc.—may give a strong additional incentive to individual activities tending to realize this ideal, the chief foundation of the latter is social. It is the same "community spirit" which makes the individual identify his interests with those of his group in the "we"-feeling, which makes the mass of the population of a state desire its expansion. We shall see the fundamental part which this aspiration to have one's group grow plays in the development of all Polish-American institutions.

The priest, far from limiting the activities of local associations, favors their development and utilizes them consistently as instruments for all purposes connected with the progress of the parish. While in Polish country parishes the chief method of obtaining the cooperation of the community in matters connected with the church is an appeal to the large mass of parishioners directly or through the parish council, in Polish cities the help of religious "fraternities" is largely used for such purposes as special religious celebrations and pilgrimages, æsthetic improvements of the church building, development of church music and song, organization of charities, etc. In America this system of collaboration of organized groups is extended in two ways. First, in addition to religious fraternities, which are for the most part initiated by the priest himself for purely devotional purposes and remain under his complete control, lay associations with economic or cultural purposes, and more or less independent of the priest, are also expected to contribute to the aims of the parish. Secondly, these aims are no longer limited to matters of cult and charity, but embrace all fields of social life.

Immediately after the completion of the church or even before, the parish school is organized. Usually the church is planned as a two-story building, the lower story including class rooms and halls for small meetings. Sometimes a private house is rented or bought for school purposes. Both arrangements prove only provisional usually, for the growth of the parish sooner or later forces it to erect a special school building. There are many parishes—five in Chicago alone—whose school is attended by more than 2,000 children. The teachers are mainly nuns of the various teaching orders, though sometimes priests and lay men-teachers are also found, particularly in the larger colonies. Polish and English are both employed as teaching languages, the proportion varying in different schools.

We cannot study here the much discussed question of the educational inferiority or superiority of parochial schools as compared with public schools. Good or bad, the parochial school is a social product of the immigrant group and satisfies important needs of the latter. The most essential point is neither the religious character of the parochial school, nor even the fact that it serves to preserve in the young generation the language and cultural traditions of the old country; it is the function of the parochial school as a factor of the social unity of the immigrant colony and of its continuity through successive generations. The school is a new, concrete, institutional bond between the immigrants. Its first effect is to bring them territorially together, for it has been noticed that proximity to the school—where the children must go every day—is considered even more desirable than proximity to the church. Further, the education of the children is an interest common to all members, just as the religious interest, and this community is fostered by the participation of the parents in all school celebrations and festivities. But even more important than this unification of the old generation is the bond which the parish school creates between the old and the young generation. Whereas children who go to public school become completely estranged from their parents, if these are immigrants, the parish school, in spite of the fact that its program of studies is in many respects similar to that of the public school, in a large measure prevents this estrangement, not only because it makes the children acquainted with their parents' religion, language and national history but also because it inculcates respect for these traditional values and for the nation from which they came. Moreover the school is not only a common bond between all the members of the old generation but is also considered by the young generation as their own institution thus fostering their interest in the affairs of the Polish-American colony. The parochial school is a necessary expression of the tendency of the immigrant community to self-preservation and self-development.

Some large and wealthy parishes have gone further still and established high schools. One—the parish of St. Stanislaw Kostka in Chicago—has even founded a college which is, however, only a little more than a high school. In these cases some economic help from other parishes is expected and obtained, so that these institutions though located within the territories of certain parishes are already in a measure part of the superterritorial Polish-American system. Quite above the territorial parochial organization are such educational institutions as seminaries for priest and for teachers, and the College of the Polish National Alliance in Cambridge Springs, Pa.

The social attitudes manifested with reference to questions of public charity and social work in general are interesting. It has been noticed that as compared, for instance with the Jewish charitable institutions, the Poles in America have little to show in this line. Care for orphans and care for the old and incurable are practically the only problems which are more or less seriously dealt with; in other fields initiative is rare and realization insufficient. The few charitable institutions belong for the most part to the super-territorial system, and seldom to territorial communities. They are due to the personal efforts of a few leading members of Polish-American society acting through the church and influenced by Christian principles rather than to the recognition of altruistic obligations by the society at large. In a word, no social need to take care of the weak seems to be felt by Polish-American communities. This seems strange in view of the old traditions of social solidarity and of the fact that in the beginning of the development of a new colony, as we saw above, assistance is invariably given to the needy. The more coherent and self-conscious the community becomes, the less is it inclined to bother with the misadapted and the disabled. This is simply a manifestation of the tendency of the group to self-preservation, made possible by the facility of excluding the weak members from, or more exactly, of not including them in the community system. As long as the community is small and loose, scattered among Americans, any "fellow-countryman" belongs to it by the same right as any other, and common national origin connected with the feeling of group responsibility before American society is sufficient to maintain the obligation to help in distress. But when the community has grown large and has more or less concentrated itself territorially and created by social cooperation a system of institutions, it becomes more exclusive. It is no longer sufficient to be a Pole and to live in the given locality in order to be considered a member of the community, the subject of social rights and the object of social responsibility. The individual must voluntarily cooperate in the construction and development of the social system of the community, join the parish and one or more of the local associations, contribute economically to common aims and take part in common activities. Unless he does this he is an outsider with reference to whom the community has no obligations and for whom it does not feel responsible before American social opinion, because it is proud of its positive achievements in social organization and, imagining that American society knows and appreciates its work, does not think that this appreciation can be counterbalanced by any individual cases of despondency or pauperism which may be found among the Poles not actually belonging to the organization.

In a new form we find here the well-known old method of dealing with the undesirable individual—the method of severing all connection between this individual and the group. But in groups whose social unity is chiefly based on ties of kinship or on the exclusive control of a given territory the undesirable individual is primarily the anti-social individual, and the individual who is merely inefficient is seldom explicitly qualified as undesirable and, with rare exceptions, is kept within the group, unless the solidarity of the latter has been weakened as a consequence of social disorganization; whereas in a group whose social unity is the result of conscious efforts the mere inability or unwillingness to participate in these efforts is sufficient to disqualify the individual. Nothing shows more clearly the difference between the old organization which we have found among the peasants in Poland and the Polish-American social system than the fact that the same phenomenon—ignoring or dropping the inefficient and misadapted—which there was a sign of weakness and decay is here a mark of strength and growth. The moral reason by which the Polish-American community justifies its apparent egotism is found in the very basis of its organization. The latter is socially and economically an organization for self-help; its first purpose is to prevent the individual from becoming a burden to the community, and the individual who does not choose to avail himself of the opportunities which this organization offers voluntarily resigns all claims to the help of the group. If the latter still feels obliged to assist in some measure the orphans, the old and the incurables, it is only in so far as it feels that the system of mutual insurance is not yet efficient enough to cover these cases adequately.

Of course since the Polish-American community tends to ignore even the merely inefficient, we cannot expect it to take any care of the demoralized. The contrast is striking between the intense reformatory activities found in Poland . . . and the entire lack of interest in reformatory work in this country. Individual demoralization is either ignored or the demoralized individual is simply dropped at once. No one bothers about the innumerable cases of family decay, juvenile delinquency, alcoholism, vagabondage, crime. Few know the full extent of the demoralization going on among American Poles. We expect that the study of demoralization which constitutes the second part of this volume and is based on American sources will be a painful surprise to most of the constructive elements of Polish-American society. Here again the contrast with peasant communities in Poland is instructive. The latter could not get rid of demoralized individuals unless demoralization had proceeded as far as crime. Thus, they had to make efforts to control their anti-social members. Further, the community was the only social milieu of the individual, and the closeness and complexity of social contacts were such that every action of the individual more or less affected the group, whereas here the Polish-American community can easily cut off a harmful member by excluding him from its organizations or, in radical cases, giving him up to American institutions. The problem is solved as soon as raised. But it seldom has to be raised at all, for the Polish-American community does not claim to absorb the individual completely; it is not necessarily and directly affected by everything he does in his private circle or in his contacts with American society. It needs only a part of his activity for its social purposes, and as long as he remains able to perform this part and does not draw others into conflict with American social opinion and law, it matters little to the parish or the local association what else he does or does not do. In Polish country communities the interest of the group is to know everything about the individual and to control his entire behavior, whereas the interest of the Polish-American community is to leave out of consideration anything in the individual's past and present which has no direct bearing on his positive social obligations so as not to impair the growth of its institutions by scrutinizing too closely the private life of those who can be useful in its public affairs. Of course there is gossip, which represents a degenerate remnant of the social opinion of the primary group. The clergy still, though vaguely and impersonally, preach against sin in private life and continue to exercise some of their old reformatory influence through confession. A few idealists from the old country, imperfectly adapted to local conditions, and some religious or political *revoltés* disclose through the press the private life histories of certain prominent members of Polish-American communities. In general, however, by a tacit understanding individuals enjoy immunity from social control in all except their social activities in Polish-American institutions.

This does not mean, however, that the Polish-American community does not attempt to extend the field of its control. The method reflectively or unreflectively used for this purpose can perhaps never completely subordinate all individuals in all respects to the influence of the group, but is very efficient as far as it goes. We may characterize it as aiming 1) to attract every individual into the sphere of public activities and to open for him the way to social prominence in some field; 2) to institutionalize as many activities as possible. The first tendency is manifested very clearly. By multiplying indefinitely associations and circles, and by a very active propaganda exercised through all possible mediums, nearly all the members of the parish—men, women and young people—even those who for some reason or other have not yet joined the parish or have dropped out, can become in some way connected with the system and thus acquire a minimum of public character. This public character grows whenever an individual is, even if only momentarily, connected as public functionary with some scheme for common action—religious ceremony, entertainment, meeting, bazaar, collection for a social purpose, etc.—and this increased public importance is every year attained by a large proportion of the community. The highest degree of public dignity is, of course, the share of those who are elected officers in associations or become members of permanent committees or directors of institutions; and if we realize that every association has from 6 to 20 officials, that every committee numbers on the average 10 members and that some large parishes have more than 70 associations and committees while even a small parish has at least a dozen of them, we see that every active and fairly intelligent individual of whatever sex and age, is sure of becoming some time a public dignitary; and even if the existing organization does not give him enough opportunities, he can always initiate a new institution and gain recognition as organizer and charter member.

By thus giving the individual favorable attention and inducing him to take voluntarily a place "in the limelight" among the leaders, the community controls him better than by making him a passive object of its "ordering and forbidding" regulations, particularly when the latter cannot be physically enforced. The conscious purpose of the multiplication of public "dignities" is to interest personally as many members as possible in the development of the community and to give everybody a chance to get recognition. But the individual who believes himself elected for his positive qualities, who feels that public opinion is interested in his behavior (and usually exaggerates this interest), and who knows that the community expects him to be and to remain superior to the average, usually tries to adapt his behavior, if not his character, to these expectations. It happens, of course, that an individual placed in a responsible position with opportunities for abuse cannot withstand the temptation, particularly if the position is too far above his intellectual and moral capacities, as is sometimes the case with officials of the great super-territorial institutions which have outgrown the level of their leaders. Such cases are, however, rare in territorial communities and small local institutions, and the often ridiculous vanity and importance of the innumerable "public dignitaries" are more than offset by their positive qualities. This moralizing influence of "public dignities" is, of course, noticeable only with members of the communities who owe their positions to election and are raised above the level by social opinion. Positions which are obtained by appointment and superiorities based not upon the recognition of the community but upon other factors, such as the sacral character of the priest, economic supremacy, "jobs" in American institutions, fail to produce the same effect, for the individual considers himself independent of the community and above social opinion.

The other method of extending social control—institutionalization of activities—is evidently involved in the very organization of the community. The church and church associations institutionalize religious activities, the mutual insurance associations certain economic interests, and the parish school education. This method is further extended to other fields. Thus public entertainments under the auspices of local associations or parochial committees play a large part in the life of a Polish-American colony and are gradually taking the place of private entertainments; and if we remember that a hall, a picnic, a theatrical representation or a concert with a mixed program—song, music, recitals, speeches require much time and energy in its preparation, we see that by this means a large proportion of individual activities are transferred from private to public life and subjected to social control. A custom which has an old origin but has been developed to an unprecedented extent during the war—the custom of making a collection for some public purpose at all weddings, christenings, etc.—gives even to private entertainments some institutional meaning. Among the local associations we find theatrical and literary circles and even circles for sewing and crocheting in common at periodical meetings. Informally and unreflectively, buying and selling have become more or less a public matter, for every Polish-American shop is a meeting-place for the neighborhood, where private and public matters are discussed. It would seem that the best way to institutionalize all leisure-time activities would be to introduce the Anglo-American principle of clubs. Strangely, however, the club does not seem to thrive in Polish-American communities. A few associations (particularly the *sokol*, a gymnastic organization) have, indeed, become clubs by acquiring houses of their own which are continually open to members, establishing reading rooms, dining-rooms, billiard rooms, gymnasiums, etc., but the use made of these club arrangements is still very limited. Attempts have been made to establish clubs for young people, and some have been successful; but the failures are more striking than the successes, for they show that for the Polish immigrant, just as for the Polish peasant in the old country, the institutionalization of leisure time activities is still indissolubly connected with the excitement of public meetings.

The double tendency to draw as many personalities and activities as possible into the sphere of public attention culminates in the press. The wealth of printed material bearing on the local life of Polish-American colonies is surprising, particularly if compared with the limited use which primary communities in Poland make of the press. Whereas the popular press there is mainly an instrument for the unification and centralization of many primary communities into a wider community, here its predominant functions are to express, perpetuate, control and unify the social life of each particular primary community. Of course professional publications and those connected with the super-territorial Polish-American system have other purposes similar to those of the popular press in Poland; but even these, the newspapers in particular, have to serve in some measure the interests of the local communities within which they are published.

The desire of the Polish-American community to give its personalities and activities official publicity and to have them recorded for the future manifests itself at first chiefly, as in Poland, in correspondence addressed to the Polish newspapers which are published in neighboring Polish-American centers or are the organs of super-territorial institutions. But very early it begins to show a tendency to have a press of its own in the form at least of commemorative pamphlets and sheets—statutes and yearly accounts of associations, programs of meetings, records of successive steps in the organization of the parish, etc. Publicity has to remain on this stage until some local newspaper is started which, of course, is possible only when the colony is numerous or is a center of several small colonies scattered in the neighborhood. The local newspaper originates in various ways. Sometimes it is started as a political organ connected with an institution which is strong enough to support it and make it an instrument of propagation; in these cases it usually develops into a super-territorial publication serving the interests of a party of cooperative organization and only secondarily those of the local community. Such has been the history of several newspapers which have come to play an important rôle in Polish-American national life. Sometimes the priest initiates the publication of a paper devoted at first chiefly to religious matters, and then the printing-office may be used also for the publication of religious pamphlets and books. Such a paper, to which the parish or at least its religious associations are usually made to contribute in some form, either becomes slightly secularized and, by paying attention to all local affairs, fulfils the function of a community organ, or continues to serve the more exclusively professional interests of the church in general, and in this case may obtain a country-wide circulation; or it combines both the local and the professional religious functions, as is the case, for instance, with the organ of the Polish National Church, published in Scranton, and with several Roman-Catholic papers. In other cases the newspaper is supported by some business man—banker, real estate agent, owner of a printing-office—and then it is an instrument for advertising his business or helping to raise his standing in American circles. But often, particularly in the larger American cities, where there is the hope of obtaining advertisements from American firms, the foundation of a newspaper is a free personal enterprise, motivated by idealistic reasons or by the desire for recognition, or treated as purely private business. Then the newspaper cannot be anything else than an organ of the community, for its circulation and its very existence depend entirely on the way it expresses the social life of the group.

Through this organ not only the attention of which the public personalities and activities are the object is continually revived (for the paper prints, of course, all the records of public institutions, meetings, etc.) but many individuals and facts which otherwise would remain private and would be at most objects of unregulated gossip are drawn into the circle of official public interest. The newspaper becomes a factor of prime importance in community life, for it partly reorganizes the degenerated and disorganized social opinion which, as we have seen in our first volumes, was the main factor of unity and control of the primary group in the old country. It does this on a new basis which is not perhaps as solid as the old, for social opinion is no longer formed by the community directly in personal contacts but indirectly through the instrumentality of print and through the medium of the editor, whose own personality constitutes an incalculable factor of variation. And yet when the old standards by which the community spontaneously selected and judged phenomena of public importance are no longer strong enough to assure without conscious regulation a unified and consistent social opinion, the concentration of news in a specialized organ which standardizes it before spreading it around is probably the only way of substituting some uniformity, order and public spirit for the chaos of gossip.

An interesting development in the same line is the so-called "album" of the parish, a commemorative publication which in older parishes is issued on important anniversaries by the parish committee presided over by the priest and contains an illustrated history of the parish up to date, with brief records of all the institutions included within its limits, collective photographs of all the associations, portraits and short biographies of the most prominent members and families, etc.—in short, a perfectly standardized synopsis of everything which social opinion considers worth knowing and remembering about the community.

Simultaneously with this process of social organization of the Polish-American group its territorial concentration goes on. There is, of course, a certain minimum of concentration preceding the establishment of the parish and resulting from the tendency of the immigrants to be sufficiently near one another for frequent social intercourse. But this tendency alone cannot completely counterbalance the desire to live near the place of work and results only in drawing together the Poles who work in the same or neighboring factories and shops. In large cities the obstacle of distance is only partially overcome and if the colony grows fast each separate neighborhood tends to become the nucleus of a separate parish. This is, for instance, the case in Chicago, where we find three large Polish neighborhoods, each including several primary parish-communities—located on the north side, around the stockyards, and in South Chicago—and a number of smaller ones, each constituting an independent primary-community. If the colony remains small, relatively to the size of the city, it may not form any territorially concentrated communities even after parishes have been established. This is the case in New York, where no exclusively Polish neighborhoods exist. This situation, however, is rare; usually the majority of the members of a parish gather around their church and school. This process is consciously fostered by the parish committee and the priest who endeavor to select the location for the church as close as possible to the centers where most of the Poles work and also take care to choose a neighborhood where rent is low and real estate cheap. If the choice has been successful the process of territorial concentration begins at once. The original population of the district is slowly but ceaselessly driven away, for an Irish, German or

Italian tenant or houseowner who sees Polish families take the place of his former neighbors and knows that they have come to stay near their parish-center soon moves to a more congenial neighborhood. At the same time a Polish real estate agency or, on a higher stage of social organization, a building association or a cooperative savings and loan bank pursues a campaign among the Poles which leads to a progressive transfer of houses and vacant lots into Polish hands. The campaign favored by the parish leaders from social considerations is evidently also good business, for the same reasons which make the neighborhood of the Polish church less valuable for other national groups raise its value for the Poles. The very growth of concentration produces new factors of further concentration. Polish shops, originally selling everything indispensable for the household and later specializing as various businesses— groceries, liquor, shoes, clothes, photographs, books, banking, undertaking, contracting—attract Polish customers and consciously contribute to the Polonization of the neighborhood. In the older colonies the entire practical business of the immigrants living near their social center is transacted exclusively with Polish firms. Later still, Polish professional men, chiefly lawyers and physicians, settle in the colony or at least have offices there. Curiously, the Jews who in Poland almost monopolize small trade in provincial localities, here relatively seldom settle within a Polish neighborhood; though they try to reach Polish customers also, they evidently, with rare exceptions, do not wish to limit the sphere of their business to one immigrant group.

The evolution of the Polish community in this country is thus in a sense the reverse of the evolution of primary peasant communities in Poland. Whereas territorial vicinity is there the original foundation of community life, and all social organization is built upon this basis, here reflective social organization becomes the main factor of territorial concentration. When, however, the latter has been in a considerable measure achieved the process is reversed again and social organization, just as in Poland, begins to depend on territorial neighborhood.

This is well exemplified by the history of secessionist groups. The latter exist in every community, for the subordination of all social life to the parish system always meets some opposition, particularly because it leads to a supremacy of the clergy. The reason for opposition is more or less a matter of principle, but no doubt personal antagonisms often contribute to its development. The secessionists form an organization independent of the parish system and often attempt to create a territorial center away from the church in the form of a "national home" as locus for common activities. But since religious activities are not included, and the group lacks the means and the framework for establishing a regular school, and the parish is a well-known old country institution, whereas the national home is an entirely new thing, the latter does not exercise the same attraction as the church in the way of territorial grouping, though it may become an important center of social organization. Therefore in older communities the concentration of the Polish-American colony around the church is usually accepted and utilized by the secessionists who by establishing their social centers near the parish center and developing their activities within the territorial community introduce new complications into Polish-American life.

There are two important types of secessionist groups—the "nationalists" and the socialists. We shall study these groups in the next chapter as components of the super-territorial Polish-American organization where they play a very important part, more important, indeed, than those groups which are integral parts of the parish system. But there is no doubt that as elements of the territorial organization of the community they are relatively weak. The only way in which they can obtain predominance in community life is not by opposing another local organization to the parish organization but by becoming a part of the parish organization and controlling it. This is naturally often the case with "independent" parishes; but there are also Roman-Catholic parishes in which "nationalistic" organizations have the upper hand even in the parish activities. These parishes—as, for instance, the Holy Trinity in Chicago—are usually characterized by a more democratic spirit, a greater independence with reference to the theocratic policy of the clergy, and the higher intellectual and moral level of their priests; and of course the parish as a form of community organization is strengthened by the cooperation of its more liberal elements. But the parishes are more numerous in which the "nationalist" associations resign themselves to the rôle of forming a minority opposition *within* the parish, while acknowledging some common interests with the majority, and there remain a large number of communities where nationalist associations stay *outside* of and in permanent opposition to the whole parish system. The institutions initiated or controlled by socialists are still more consistent and active in struggling for a lay community organization. Thus the parish can seldom if ever permanently monopolize all the social life of the community, particularly as its opponents have usually most of the intelligent members of the colony on their side. And even if it succeeds in overcoming active opposition, it cannot prevent the increasingly rapid growth of associations which, while not aiming to supplant it as community center, wish to remain free and separate from the parochial system, and do not care to cooperate in its development. To this class belong, besides some mutual help organizations, many of the gymnastic, educational and professional societies. In every large community there are thus a number of small social circles whose functions are independent of those of the parish. Nevertheless, the latter continues to keep its hold through religion and primary education upon individual members of those circles, with the exception of the socialists and a few free-thinkers.

Japanese

FRED H. MATTHEWS

White Community and "Yellow Peril"

American prejudice against Orientals, initially aimed at Chinese, primarily focused on Japanese immigrants. In 1880, two years before the passage of the Chinese exclusion act, fewer than 200 Japanese lived in the United States. A decade later they immigrated at an annual rate of about 1,000; from 1899 to 1903 60,000 Japanese entered the United States. They came largely because of the acute labor shortage in California—the exclusion of the Chinese had left many menial and unskilled jobs without takers. The appearance of the Japanese generated the same hostility suffered by Chinese who settled on the West Coast. Leagues formed to bar further entry, separate, inferior schools were established to educate their children, and in 1905 the Labor Council of San Francisco resolved to encourage boycotts of Japanese goods as well as those of white merchants and manufacturers who employed Japanese. In 1907 the San Francisco Call, demanding a Japanese exclusion law, editorialized: "California is the white man's country, and not the Caucasian graveyard." Later that year President Theodore Roosevelt concluded the "Gentlemen's Agreement," which halted further entry of Japanese laborers. Nevertheless in 1908 Californians launched an anti-Japanese Laundry League and advertised:

> *Foolish woman!*
> *Spending your man's*
> *Earnings on Japs.*
> *Be Fair, patronize*
> *Your Own.*
> *We support you.*

In 1913 and 1921 the state legislature restricted Japanese occupancy and purchase of agricultural lands. Finally, in 1942, nervous California bigots induced John L. DeWitt, commanding general of the Western Defense Command of the United States army, to recommend relocation of all Japanese and their descendants in the state to detention camps further inland. Eugene Rostow later characterized these places as "little better than concentration camps."

Professor Fred Matthews describes America's hostile attitudes toward the

Reprinted from the *Mississippi Valley Historical Review*, L (March, 1964), 612–33, by permission of the Organization of American Historians.

Japanese in the following essay. He traces their experiences in the West from the 1890s through the Second World War and indicates how prominent scholars adapted scientific theories to rationalize unscientific ideas about "racial pollution."

Until the 1890's Japan had figured in American eyes as a potential market for products, arena for missionary activity, or exotic contrast to the dull routine of the home culture. The literati revelled in this "topsy-turvy" dream world of painted chrysanthemums and exquisite tea ceremonies, a "huge, comical" antithesis of the "main Western stream of development." The art historian Ernest Fenollosa insisted in 1892 that Japan's true destiny was to preserve her artistic sweetness and delight, so as to conquer the materialistic West with "the sword of the spirit."[1]

Events soon outmoded these attitudes as Japanese and Americans came into direct contact on the Pacific Coast of North America. In the decade after 1895, Japan proved her worth by western standards in two major wars and sent an increasing flow of emigrant farm workers to Hawaii and California. On the Pacific Coast these Japanese were received with joy by business and farm employers, but they also inherited much of the hostility visited earlier upon the Chinese. Hatred toward one common enemy after another was a strong social cement in this constantly new society. The state's isolation before the age of commercial aviation, with the nearest comparable centers of population several days' journey by train, intensified the sense of common loneliness on this "White Frontier" against Asia and the new yellow peril.[2] Many Californians were angry that these new heathen were not only as well-organized for mutual protection as were the Chinese, but also demanded equality and assimilation with the support of a proud, sensitive home government. So began a quarter-century cycle of events: discrimination in California, useless anger and helpless apology in Washington, outraged protest but more stringent emigration curbs in Tokyo. The spiral ended in 1924 with the almost total exclusion of Japanese immigrants. Hostility subsided somewhat until the war scares of the 1930's and final explosion during World War II.[3]

[1] Percival Lowell, "The Soul of the Far East," *Atlantic Monthly* (Boston), LX (September, 1887), 405–13; Ernest F. Fenollosa, "Chinese and Japanese Traits," *ibid.,* LXIX (June, 1892), 774.

[2] Carey McWilliams, *California: The Great Exception* (New York, 1949), 185. Indeed, Japanese-baiting was a ticket of admission for men who might otherwise have been targets themselves. Most revealing is the career of Anthony Caminetti—son of an Italian immigrant, tireless opponent of Orientals in the state legislature, and zealous deporter of alien radicals as Commissioner-General of Immigration in the Wilson Administration. See John Higham, *Strangers in the Land* (New Brunswick, 1955), 228n.; Franklin Hichborn, *Story of the Session of the California Legislature of 1913* (San Francisco, 1913), 213–74. See also Arthur Mann, "Gompers and the Irony of Racism," *Antioch Review* (Yellow Springs, Ohio), XIII (June, 1953), 203–14.

[3] For accounts of the anti-Japanese agitation and relevant background material, see Dorothy S. Thomas and Richard S. Nishimoto, *The Spoilage* (Berkeley, 1946); Jacobus tenBroek and others, *Prejudice, War and the Constitution* (Berkeley, 1954); Jesse Steiner, *The Japanese Invasion* (Chicago, 1917); Jean Pajus, *The Real Japanese California* (Berkeley, 1937); Thomas A. Bailey, *Theodore Roosevelt and the Japanese-American Crisis* (Stanford, 1934). Annual Japanese emigration to the United States

Throughout the controversy, scholars and agitators alike worked from common assumptions about the "good society," the ideal community which they nostalgically created out of the past and strove to recreate in the future. The negative response to the Japanese was shaped by memories of earlier ethnic conflicts, growing fear of rapid social change, and the concomitant concern with contrasting values and ways of life in a nation dedicated to homogeneity and perfection. Scholarly theories of race conflict and change were developed in response to perceived threats and were then used as evidence by agitators.

Early agitation centered in San Francisco, a labor center where a Japanese colony received and distributed new arrivals to jobs in the hinterland. This colony soon provoked much of the fear and fascination attached to the city's Chinatown, a tenement ghetto of gambling and opium dens, tong wars, and an army of allegedly exotic prostitutes.[4] By 1896 an astute politician was already campaigning against the new yellow peril. This was James D. Phelan, a young independent businessman of Irish ancestry, who entered politics to "clean out" a rotten city government. Apparently he used the Japanese bugaboo to win support from the violently anti-Oriental Irish-dominated labor unions. During May, 1900, Phelan staged a "monster rally" against Japanese immigration and invited a young sociologist from Stanford University named Edward A. Ross to speak. Ross accepted Phelan's bid and in so doing the new science of society was united with politics to create a sophisticated front for California's anti-Japanese movement.

In his speech, the well-known lecturer expounded the popular Darwinian view of races as basic units in the struggle for control of a static supply of resources. He spoke of the new concern with relative birth rates which accompanied the widespread loss of confidence in the 1890's. In 1893, Frederick Jackson Turner had lamented the profound social changes attending the passing of the frontier in America; a whole chorus of social theorists, gloomy over the future of the expansive Occident in a fixed environment whose limits it had reached, was spotting scapegoats and tuning up for the mournful dirge of alarm and blame. Herbert Spencer had popularized the idea that fecundity declined as intelligence advanced, and this theory was converted into the notion that fertility—the actual birth rate—declined as civilization advanced. So the higher races cowered at the onslaught of inevitably inferior breeds. "I tried to show," wrote Ross, "that, owing to its high, Malthusian birth rate, the Orient is the land of 'cheap men,' and that the coolie, though he cannot outdo the American,

---

was under the 1,000 mark until 1891, had reached 2,844 in 1899, then jumped to 12,635 in 1900, and reached almost 20,000 in 1903. Peak year was 1907 with 30,226 legal immigrants; after the "Gentlemen's Agreement" the number dropped to a few thousand per year, then rose to between 8,000 and 10,000 annually between 1913 and 1924. U.S. Department of Commerce, Bureau of the Census, *Historical Statistics of the United States: Colonial Times to 1957* (Washington, 1960), 58. Yamato Ichihashi stressed that over half of those admitted between 1901 and 1910 went to Hawaii and not to the mainland. However, a considerable number of these did later move from Hawaii to the Pacific coast. See Yamato Ichihashi, *Japanese in the United States* (Stanford, 1932), 29.

[4] See Gladys Waldron, "Antiforeign Movements in California, 1919 to 1929" (Ph.D. dissertation, University of California, Berkeley, 1956), 80; Samuel Gompers and Herman Gutstadt, *Meat vs. Rice: American Manhood against Asiatic Coolieism, Which Shall Survive?* (San Francisco, 1908).

can underlive him." California would be flooded with cheap laborers and their slave-brides, multiplying as rabbits to drive away the frugal, self-limiting white pioneer. "In thus scientifically coordinating the birth-rate with the intensity of the struggle for existence, I struck a new note in the discussion of Oriental immigration. . . ."[5]

Ross at thirty-four was already an established figure in public and scholarly life. Known for his frequent and lively speeches on monetary and business reform, and for his Bryanite heresy in 1896, he was well-launched on the path which in the next decade made him a leading academic muckraker. His research interests had changed while at Stanford from economics to the ways in which society manipulates its members for the good of the whole. *Social Control,* published in 1901, defined this new field, and was followed by a long series of texts and popularizations which helped shape the new discipline. Like so many of his generation in social science, this "Scottish Highlander from Iowa" was a farm boy of "old American" stock determined to understand and fix the blame for the tremendous social changes obliterating his boyhood way of life. And he fixed the pattern of much discussion by picking out two major devils: the power of finance capitalism operating through the great corporations, and, as symbol of national decadence, the swarm of alien immigrants which commercial greed was injecting into the body social.[6]

Ross's characteristic bluntness led to a direct confrontation of his radical view with entrenched conservatism. The text of his anti-Japanese speech, delivered May 7, 1900, was sober enough, but the local press reported an interpolation. According to the news item, Ross exclaimed, "And should the worst come to worst it'd be better for us to turn our guns on every vessel bringing Japanese to our shores rather than permit them to land." Next day this account was read by Jane Lathrop Stanford, the elderly widow of Stanford University's founder. Already suspicious of Ross as a radical and a demagogue, Mrs. Stanford now wrote President David Starr Jordan ordering the professor's dismissal.[7]

The local response to Ross's discharge revealed the attitudes which polarized in the struggle over the Japanese. Ross's Populist position would be taken up in a few years by the Progressive movement of which he became an academic leader. But for a moment, polite middle-class morality was largely content with a social and economic order which had brought prosperity and respected individualistic canons. Christian idealism and class contempt outweighed community solidarity for the ministry, many academics, and the literati who wrote for conservative magazines; they shared Mrs. Stanford's disgust with the rambunctious popular agitation, and gave at least mild approval to the Japanese. The editor of *Overland Monthly* contended that "the laboring ele-

[5] Edward A. Ross, *Seventy Years of It* (New York, 1936), 70. On Spencer and fertility, see David C. Eversley, *Social Theories of Fertility and the Malthusian Debate* (Oxford, 1959), 186–89.

[6] Ross, *Seventy Years of It,* 1–25, 223–26; Barbara M. Solomon, *Ancestors and Immigrants* (Cambridge, 1956), 128, 130, 133–35; Howard W. Odum, *American Sociology* (New York, 1951), 98–102.

[7] San Francisco *Call,* May 8, 1900, quoted in Orrin L. Elliott, *Stanford University: The First Twenty-five Years* (Stanford, 1937), 340–41. For a full account of the Ross case, see *ibid.,* 326–78. See also Richard Hofstadter and Walter P. Metzger, *Development of Academic Freedom in the United States* (New York, 1955), 436–45.

ment has transferred its former fierce hatred for the Chinese race to the Japanese. . . ." In contrast to California's "lazy" white farm laborers—not to mention disreputable "sandlot Irish" agitators—the Japanese were regarded as healthy, patient, cooperative, clean—"and . . . cleanliness is next to Godliness."[8]

A hard-headed defense came from the commercial and farming interests who benefited from Japanese immigration. The very ambition of the Japanese created important allies. Through careful effort, shrewd purchasing, and hard work, they were able to buy or lease farm land for intensive cultivation on the model of their tiny plots in rural Japan. Their desire for land raised prices, and thus supported native property interests which cooperated with Japanese organizations. To such groups the revival of yellow peril talk after the Russo-Japanese War was a threat to trade and prosperity, "screamed by voices that tremble with pious cant," "obstructionists in humanity's highways," who would have muttered darkly of a "steam peril" in earlier years.[9]

The most eloquent spokesman for this group was "Colonel" John P. Irish, an elderly politician from Iowa, longtime editor and Democratic wheelhorse, who, unlike Ross, saw the exclusion campaign as another radical assault on traditional values. Irish believed that individuals found their place in the natural competitive order wholly by their own efforts and ethics; there was no need to restrict the arena of equal competition to a small in-group with similar customs and attitudes. Irish was so firmly rooted in the values of his youth that he never understood the desire of the reformers to recapture the competitive small-unit open society he still took for granted. The axioms of his confident creed of benevolent competition eliminated the need for defensive hostility toward the racial outsider.[10]

The theories about "race" and "culture" current in America until the late 1890's gave some support to Irish's tolerant view. In the terminology of popular Darwinism, every society rested at a certain stage on the evolutionary sequence from simple and homogeneous to complex, heterogeneous, industrial civilization. Daniel Brinton, the dean of American anthropologists, in 1891 ranked Mongolians second to Caucasians in the racial hierarchy, judged by artistic, scientific, and commercial progress. Brinton's faith in moral and industrial progress toward a secular millennium assumed that races and nations were not necessarily permanent units of competition, but would be merged into a higher whole by the evolutionary process.[11] Scholars holding to this Victorian confidence accepted the Japanese as educable equals within a single system of values. Public intolerance and chauvinism disgusted them. William James attacked American imperialism, and his California-born colleague, Josiah Royce,

[8] "The Editor's Philosophy," *Overland Monthly* (San Francisco), LIV (October, 1909), 423–27; Billee Glynn, "Lights Reminiscent: The Orientals and Portola," *ibid.*, LV (February, 1910), 204–10. See also A. Stead, "Race Prejudice against Japanese," *Fortnightly* (London), LXXXVIII (October, 1907), 637–51.

[9] T. B. Wilson, "The Yellow Peril, So-called," *Overland Monthly,* XLV (February, 1905), 133–36.

[10] "Letters Written by John P. Irish to G. F. Parker," *Iowa Journal of History and Politics* (Iowa City), XXXI (July, 1933), 421–512; see especially pp. 426, 451, 467, 478, 492.

[11] Daniel Brinton, *The American Race* (New York, 1891), 39–43; "The 'Nation' as an Element in Anthropology," reprinted from *Memoirs of the International Congress of Anthropology* (Chicago, 1894).

spiritedly denounced community intolerance and the pseudo-science which rationalized it. The race theorist, he wrote in 1908, simply used "his science to support most of his personal prejudices"; racial theories were like yacht races, a field for proving one's superiority to outsiders.[12]

Royce had been born in a Sierra mining town in 1855 and grew up a lonely, scholarly boy, cut off from the compact majority of his peers. He never lost his burning indignation at group persecution of the deviant individual even though his popular social philosophy demanded thorough subordination of individual desires to the community interest.[13] Royce hoped as passionately as any of the racist scholars to recreate the imagined simple idealism of the small community, but he accepted enthusiasm for and loyalty to varying ideals and divergent communities as potentially of equal value and honor. Thus he saw the Japanese neither as copycats nor robots, but as complex, cultured men trying to reconcile contradictory values. When Royce tackled the origins of racial prejudice, his idealism and concern for free will led him to conclusions directly opposed to the contemporary desire to make sociological deductions based upon biological premises. Every child, he argued, possessed "elemental tendencies to be socially sensitive," which responded to random encounters with strangers in terms of the individual's infinitely variable emotional states. The "momentary subjective intensity" of an early experience, reinforced by social customs which gave a "name" to this transient emotion, was the true cause of racial as of other fears and phobias.[14]

The most prolific and tireless defender of the Japanese was Sidney Luther Gulick, scion of an old Pacific missionary family noted for scientific speculation and social uplift, who had seen America only during his college years. Gulick's defense of the Japanese rested on organic social idealism. National character was determined by cultural environment and conscious choice, not by biological type. He insisted that "Japanese and Chinese are just as assimilable as Italians or Russians"—perhaps more so, since the language difficulty cut off American-born Orientals from their heritage more thoroughly than it did Europeans. Analysis of Japanese ethics suggested that even first-generation immigrants would be loyal to the United States, since *giri*—"duty in spite of natural feelings"—obliged one to be utterly loyal to a new group once duty had been transferred.[15]

Such theories as these were considered both outdated and misleading by the opponents of the Japanese; for them, the issue involved nothing less than "the entire structure and character of American society."[16] Interest groups and reformers, anxious to restrain undesirable social change, saw the Japanese not

---

[12] Josiah Royce, *Race Questions, Provincialism and Other American Problems* (New York, 1908), 8–10.

[13] See the autobiographical note in Josiah Royce, *The Hope of the Great Community* (New York, 1916), 126–27; Royce, *The Philosophy of Loyalty* (New York, 1908), 51–98; but see especially Royce, *California* (New York, 1948), 281–90 and *passim*. This volume was first published in 1886.

[14] Royce, *Race Questions*, 10–15, 24–25, 31–47, 48–50.

[15] Sidney L. Gulick, *Evolution of the Japanese* (New York, 1903), 14, 51, 57, 549. See also Gulick, *Hawaii's American-Japanese Problem* (Honolulu, 1915); "Race Betterment and America's Oriental Problem," *Proceedings First National Conference on Race Betterment* (Battle Creek, 1914), 548ff.

[16] San Francisco *Chronicle*, March 6, 1905, cited in Eleanor Tupper and George E. McReynolds, *Japan in American Public Opinion* (New York, 1937), 22.

only as an economic threat but as disruptive to the common consciousness and value consensus which they felt must underlie a democratic society. The very success of the Japanese in American terms made them a threat; many smaller farmers who had hired them as seasonal labor now feared these dangerous competitors, combining in inscrutable groups to force the independent white farm operator off his land. After 1906 the growing anti-Japanese movement coincided with the Progressive revolt against rule by large corporations and their labor dupes. As the Progressives gained statewide power in California they joined the Japanese issue to that of corporations. While no politician dared openly champion the Japanese, the Progressives used the race issue to embarrass corporation politicians. An "old guard" legislature in 1909 was willing to defer to Theodore Roosevelt's pleas for caution; but the Progressives in 1913 ignored a personal visit by Secretary of State William Jennings Bryan, who asked them not to arouse Japan.[17]

George Mowry in *The California Progressives* showed that the leaders of this very successful movement were independent business or professional men determined to break the "impersonal, concentrated" power of the "behemoth corporation" and restore the model of a remembered small-town community, a classless society in which the educated independent was the respected leader in opinion and action.[18] Many of these leaders still lived in the smaller cities of the central valley; all seemed to share this nostalgic dream of a homogeneous community working on the model of free economic competition.

At the turn of the century, there were many sincere men who felt that America already possessed one such unassimilable group, whose presence warned eloquently against the addition of other ethnic groups. As it grew up, the Progressive generation saw the American Negro as this permanent clot in the social bloodstream. Most of the Progressive politicians and sociologists were born in the 1860's, and their maturing years were influenced by the disillusionment resulting from the failure of the Reconstruction period "experiments." Many sociologists saw the Negro as permanently inferior, unable to adapt to the white cultural norm, advancing as far as he did only through the intermixture of white blood. His permanent backwardness, some thought, "must be sought in different body and brain structure."[19] But if one agreed with Ross that "the success of democracy requires that a people be fairly homogeneous and like-minded," then the presence of the Negro struck at the heart of the search for community. Because of the Negro, said William Graham Sum-

[17] Hichborn, *Legislature of 1913*, pp. 213–64. See also Hichborn, *Story of the Session of the California Legislature of 1909* (San Francisco, 1909), 202–16. For the association of Progressives with Democrats against a "Republican-Jap" coalition in 1924, see *Cong. Record*, 68 Cong., 1 Sess., 6314 (April 14, 1924).

[18] George E. Mowry, *The California Progressives* (Berkeley, 1951), 88–89; see also Richard Hofstadter, *The Age of Reform* (New York, 1960), 145, and Ch. 4, *passim*. For a discussion of Progressive racism, see especially Mowry, *The Era of Theodore Roosevelt* (New York, 1958), 92–94. For its relevance in California see Hichborn, *Legislature of 1909*, pp. 202–16; *Legislature of 1913*, pp. 213–64. Higham, *Strangers in the Land*, 174, notes that in the South and Far West "progressivism was for white men only." For racial stereotypes in the Midwest, see William Allen White, *The Old Order Changeth* (New York, 1910), 130, 197ff.

[19] Ulysses G. Weatherley, "Race and Marriage," *American Journal of Sociology* (Chicago), XV (January, 1910), 433–53; Frank H. Hankins, *The Racial Basis of Civilization* (New York, 1926), 307. Almost all students saw a long period of racial hostility lying ahead.

ner, the United States were not a nation. Since the Negro could never be absorbed into the community, a working symbiotic relation must be developed, as the South was doing along caste lines.[20]

An eloquent apostle of equalitarian democracy was Charles H. Cooley, the Michigan sociologist and pioneer student of individual socialization. Cooley preached an open-class society based on a common group consciousness which inculcated similar values and attitudes in the plastic personality of each member. But with the Negro this continuity of consciousness was lacking; the social division had hardened into a caste barrier.[21] While Cooley recognized that the biological rationale for this barrier might well be false, he thought that any biracial society would develop it. The problem then became one of accommodating to the caste division, securing just and friendly relations across it. And national policy should discourage the creation of a new race problem on the Pacific Coast. Even the sympathetic sociologist, Robert E. Park, wrote in 1913: "The Japanese, like the Negro, is condemned to remain among us an abstraction, a symbol . . . of that vague ill-defined menace we sometimes refer to as the 'yellow peril'."[22] The leading scholar in politics, Woodrow Wilson, invoked the race argument during the presidential campaign of 1912. "We cannot make a homogeneous population out of a people who do not blend with the Caucasian race," he warned. "Democracy rests on the equality of the citizen. Oriental coolieism will give us another race problem to solve and surely we have learned our lesson."[23]

Supporting this rather vague, sometimes environmentally-based theory were more specific racial ideas imported from Europe. The passion for scientific precision coincided with the popular need for a simple explanation of social change to produce a rigid, respectable racism based in biology. The publicist most frequently invoked in this regard was Gustave Le Bon, a French "social embryologist" who equated race with nationality. Races had been formed in prehistory; they must be kept stable so that their members would possess common adaptive traits for strength and survival. Henry Cabot Lodge on the Senate floor in 1896 cited Le Bon as "a disinterested witness of another race" to prove his contention that the "new immigration" would breed out "America's fixed, inherited national character."[24] Other students went beyond Le Bon to attempt a close correlation of physical type with cultural and linguistic data. Structure and function were after all two faces of the same biological coin, constantly affecting each other in a reciprocal relation, and man must be treated as another unit in the animal kingdom. Enthusiasm for the

[20] Edward A. Ross, *Principles of Sociology* (first revision, New York, 1930), 201; William G. Sumner, cited in Henry P. Fairchild, *Immigration* (New York, 1913), 413.

[21] Charles H. Cooley, *Social Process* (New York, 1922), 268–80. For the "progressive" and meliorist bent of Cooley's social psychology, see Donald Fleming, "Social Darwinism," in Arthur M. Schlesinger, Jr. and Morton White, eds., *Paths of American Thought* (Boston, 1963), pp. 141–42.

[22] Robert E. Park, "Racial Assimilation in Secondary Groups," *Publications of the American Sociological Society* (Chicago), VIII (1913), 71.

[23] Hichborn, *Legislature of 1913*, p. 213n.

[24] Gustave Le Bon, "Influence of Race on History," *Popular Science Monthly* (New York), XXXV (August, 1889), 495–503; George E. Fellows, "Anthropology and History," *American Journal of Sociology*, I (July, 1895), 41–49; *Cong. Record*, 54 Cong., 1 Sess., 2817–20 (March 16, 1896); Higham, *Strangers in the Land*, 142.

new study of genetics, which at last seemed to offer the key to physical change in animals and plants, reinforced the emphasis on determined biological causation.[25]

Tolerance and even acceptance of the theories such as those of Le Bon revealed a desire on the part of American social scientists to discover a precise association of physical and cultural traits. In short, the social scientists sought to establish the study of humanity on a truly scientific basis and thereby give their discipline validity and prestige equal to those of the older sciences. Two interrelated tendencies dominated. One of these was the quest for a generalized body of theory which could both describe and predict social behavior —ideally in mathematical terms on the model of physics. Abstract, unverifiable concepts were to be eliminated. There was a strong urge to explain as much of behavior as possible by fixed presocial instincts. Physiology did not merely set limits or determine predispositions; it supplied the actual content of daily behavior.[26] There was, in addition, a strong desire to quantify, to make precise statistical statements on the model of the "exact sciences." Quantification of data was just as essential as biological causation, and easier with cephalic indexes than with marriage customs or systems of social control. The statistician Karl Pearson in 1920 scorned cultural anthropology as "purely descriptive and verbal" like sociology, but he predicted the coming millennium when exact science and higher mathematics would replace verbalizing and arithmetic.[27]

The desire for scientific precision joined with the moral dilemma posed by imperial exploitation to force a sharp split between two currents of evolutionary thought: idealistic meliorism and "tooth-and-claw" scientific determinism. As one sad member of the former camp, William B. Smith of Tulane, wrote in 1903, the biological justification of imperialism and race hatred sprang from "the post-Darwinian, more especially the post-Weismannian . . . perception, whether real or imagined, of the lordship of heredity in history and in life." "Modern science," Smith wrote, "proclaims 'Blood will tell'." Hope for man's future called for "perfecting the strong, not strengthening the weak."[28]

Ross's generation of American social scientists applied these tools to the problems facing their culture. The labor economist John R. Commons warned of "dissident elements" whose coming threatened American democracy, since "race differences are established in the very blood and physical constitution."[29] Initially, Ross attacked pseudo-scientific lumping of culture and breed, but by 1901 he had written "Causes of Race Superiority," which read like a nostalgic glorification of his own old stock—their energy, self-reliance, foresight, "progressiveness . . . spirit of adventure, migrancy and the disposition to flock to cities." Ross's fascination with the city, that center of diversity where old social controls seemed suspended, led him back to pseudo-ethnology; he accepted a

[25] For Karl Pearson's theories on this question, see Pitirim A. Sorokin, *Contemporary Sociological Theories* (New York, 1928), 235, 252–61.
[26] See, for example, Henry P. Fairchild, *The Melting Pot Mistake* (Boston, 1926), 74.
[27] Karl Pearson, "The Problem of Anthropology," *Scientific Monthly* (New York), XI (November, 1920), 451–58; Sorokin, *Contemporary Sociological Theories,* 260.
[28] *The Nation* (New York), LXXVI (March 5, 1903), 191.
[29] John R. Commons, "Race and Democracy," *Chautauquan* (Meadville, N.Y.), XXXVIII (September, 1903), 33–42.

theory of the French anthropologist Vacher de Lapouge that the city was "a magnet" for long-headed Teutonics. Ross had trouble with these Teutonics: they were not really urban, but wanted adventure and excitement. At any rate, they would not stay on Iowa farms: the Teutonic "betakes himself to the Far West or the Klondike, whereas the Jew betakes himself to the Board of Trade or the Bourse. . . . Since the higher culture should be kept pure as well as the higher blood, that race is stronger which, down to the cultivator or the artisan, has *a strong sense of its own superiority*. When peoples and races meet, there is a silent struggle to determine which shall do the assimilating." Here the higher race is in danger; success saps native drive: the cultured fail to reproduce; the spectre of "race suicide" is on the horizon. Ross was proud of coining this phrase, which Theodore Roosevelt took up. The proper race policy was clear: "The Spaniard absorbed the Indians, the English exterminated them by fair means or foul . . . the net result is that North America from the Bering Sea to the Rio Grande is dedicated to the highest type of civilization; while for centuries the rest of our hemisphere will drag the ball and chain of hybridism."[30]

This bogey of miscegenation was the most powerful of the evolutionary arguments in stampeding sentiment against the Japanese. If culture was biologically determined, then only intermarriage could merge the Japanese into the white community. But this would degrade the original stock. Californians here could support their distaste by quoting the sage Herbert Spencer, who had once warned a Japanese statesman that racial intermarriage would produce a type of man "not fitted for any set of conditions whatever." Writing in 1892, Spencer had applied his classic rule to California's Orientals: "they must either, if they remain unmixed, form a subject race standing in the position . . . of a class approaching slaves; or if they mix they must form a bad hybrid."[31] Senator Francis Newlands of Nevada summed up the case for the West: it was race war or race amalgamation. Either was fatal. Racial mixture, said a journalist, was violation of natural law—which, as all good laws should, brought "inevitable retribution" in the form of inferior offspring.[32] Politicians quickly exploited this fear. Demanding segregated schools, a California assemblyman viewed with alarm the "matured Japs, with their base minds, their lascivious thoughts . . . sitting in the seats next to the pure maids of California. I shuddered then and I shudder now, the same as any other parent will shudder."[33]

The miscegenation argument was reinforced by a more rigorous environ-

[30] Edward A. Ross, "Causes of Race Superiority," *Annals of the American Academy of Political and Social Science* (Philadelphia), XVIII (July, 1901), 67–68, 85–86.
[31] Quoted in John B. Trevor, *Japanese Exclusion*, in *House Docs.*, 68 Cong., 2 Sess., No. 600 (Serial 8427), 4. This is also found in varying form in Wallace A. Irwin, *Seed of the Sun* (New York, 1921), 333; James G. Phelan, "The False Pride of Japan," *Atlantic Monthly*, CXXVII (March, 1921), 401–402; Madison Grant, *Conquest of a Continent* (New York, 1933), 9. See also Charles W. Eliot in *Chautauquan*, LXX (May, 1913), 257–59.
[32] Francis G. Newlands, "A Western View of the Race Question," *Annals of the American Academy of Political and Social Science*, XXXIV (September, 1909), 270; John L. Cowan, "The Japanese Question," *Overland Monthly*, XLIX (January, 1907), 87–89.
[33] Grove L. Johnson (father of Hiram Johnson), quoted in Hichborn, *Legislature of 1909*, p. 207n.

mentalist justification of exclusion, based on William Graham Sumner's *Folk-ways*, published in 1906. Folkways, said Sumner, were human habits which became fixed when a satisfactory adaptation to environment in the struggle for existence was repeated so often that it became automatic, invariable, subject to change only in the same slow, blind, partly adaptive manner. Mores were folkways given an ethical coloring, made into standards of conduct hallowed by tradition. The mores of each community were unique, not comparable or controllable. Each community's point of view was ethnocentric, judging all other groups by its own mores. But there was no basis for trying to impose one's own mores on an unwilling group.[34]

Sumner's cultural relativism would later be used by liberals to defend persecuted minorities, but by emancipating group norms from any universal standard of justice it served as a powerful conservative tool in his own society. Here was a perfect weapon for attacking the optimistic notion of "assimilation." In the common "melting pot" image the alien was dissolved culturally and recreated anew in the true American mold. Assimilation was complete "only when the individuals or ethnic groups are emotionally dead to all their varied past."[35] The argument that racial fixity prevented assimilation was under indirect attack from anthropologists like Franz Boas, but those glacial mores shifted the argument away from physical types.

This argument was developed by another grass-roots midwesterner, Henry Pratt Fairchild, a student of Sumner at Yale who later achieved the presidency of the American Sociological Society and gloried in the reputation of being the leading academic advocate of immigration restriction. Fairchild grew up in a Nebraska town named Crete, surrounded by Germans and Bohemians. He very early was worried by the problems of immigration and population which became his life's work. "At the tender age of nine or ten I remember asking myself over and over, 'What is going to happen when the world gets full?' "[36] The adult Fairchild treated racial prejudice as a fixed element of the group's mores, invulnerable to demands for change. He stressed the necessity and virtue of an intolerant, homogeneous community. Americanism meant the surrender of any ideas of politics, status, or morals alien to the classless liberal society where all differences were due to merit. Groups with visible differences were blocked by community prejudice and their own inevitable reaction to it. Racial hatred prevented Orientals from being assimilated; this hatred could change only very slowly if at all; therefore, for a long period the Orientals would be an active threat to national unity.[37] What Fairchild had expounded academically about ethnic isolation, Ross expressed more explicitly by advocating an ideal America—the city on a hill. Others should emulate this source of "high standards of living, institutions, and ideals" while keeping a respectful distance.[38]

[34] William G. Sumner, *Folkways* (Boston, 1911), 2ff., 37, 78.
[35] Albert E. Jenks, "Assimilation in the Philippines as Interpreted in Terms of Assimilation in America," *American Journal of Sociology,* XIX (May, 1914), 773.
[36] Fairchild's autobiographical note in Odum, *American Sociology,* 178–79.
[37] Fairchild, *Immigration,* 100–103, 361–62. He also used the biological argument as additional ammunition. Fairchild, *Melting Pot Mistake,* 74.
[38] Edward A. Ross, *The Old World in the New* (New York, 1913), ii. For an example of a Californian exploiting these arguments against the Japanese, with citations from Ross, Sumner, and his students Fairchild and Albert G. Keller, see Montaville Flowers, *The Japanese Conquest of American Public Opinion* (New York, 1917), especially 70n., 75, 180, 194, 202–19.

Trying to reconcile the same broad goals with the aggressive demands of local entrepreneurs, Chester H. Rowell, the state's leading Progressive publicist, gave a Sumnerian defense of regional custom and prejudice. Rowell contended that the state needed peasant labor of some sort, though it must be rigidly segregated from community participation. Rowell looked back nostalgically on the Chinese coolie, "that perfect human ox . . . that biped domestic animal in the white man's service. . . . He will transform less food into more work, with less administrative friction, than any other creature." Docile, confined to his ghetto, "Western" only in faithfully fulfilling his contracts, the Chinese served without disturbing. Rowell was quite willing to allow such semislavery, but these new Japanese serfs were ambitious. Their values were upside down: since business failure was a personal humiliation, honor led them to break rather than keep contracts in an emergency. Worst of all, they expected to rise to social equality through work, thrift, and education. They did not "confine themselves to 'Japtown'," but paid premium prices for decent homes, threatening middle class residential uniformity. "Right or wrong our people will not live with those of a physically different race except on the basis of that race's inferiority. Since the Japanese are . . . in some respects superior, there is friction"[39]

Anti-Japanese sentiment in California continued to mount; in the 1913 state legislature racial sentiment triumphed over selfish commercialism. In the eyes of many Central Valley farmers, California's racial problem could assume such proportions that it would "make the black problem of the South look white." Agitation among the lawmakers was intense for an act prohibiting Oriental aliens from purchasing land. The Panama-Pacific exposition interests —eager not to disturb the racial status quo until the conclusion of their enterprise—attempted unsuccessfully to kill the bill. However much the Exposition would mean for the state's trade, the decision was trumpeted with the words: "We will not jeopardize our race."[40]

Passage of alien land legislation did not end anti-Japanese agitation, either locally or nationally. Indeed, in the postwar excitement after 1918 the campaign reached a new peak of intensity. The progressive urge to restore equalitarian democracy tended to harden in "100%" native Americanism—a suspicion of aliens, of radicals, of personal emancipation—of everything which had broken the past idyll. Imperial Wizard Hiram Wesley Evans of the Ku Klux Klan warned that white Protestant natives were in a death struggle with the city, center of cosmopolitanism and foreign influences.[41] In California the American Legion assumed the Klan's mantle and produced a motion picture modeled on David L. W. Griffith's "Birth of a Nation," showing Legionnaires rescuing white womanhood from Oriental wiles.[42]

Nativists saw the mere presence of difference, the awareness of cultural choice, as sealing the fate of their community. And, for a Californian, what

[39] Chester H. Rowell, "Chinese and Japanese Immigrants: A Comparison," *Annals of the American Academy of Political and Social Science*, XXXIV (September, 1909), 223-30; 'California and the Japanese Problem," *New Republic* (New York), XXIV (September 15, 1920), 64–65; Hichborn, *Legislature of 1913*, p. 215n.
[40] Hichborn, *Legislature of 1913*, p. 230.
[41] Hiram W. Evans, "The Klan: Defender of Americanism," *Forum* (New York), LXXIV (December, 1925), 801–14.
[42] TenBroek and others, *Prejudice, War and the Constitution*, 45.

better symbol than the Oriental for the whole process of introspection and alienation, of submersion of old values? In the 1921 *Overland Monthly* a local poetess praised California, the alert Athens of America, for defending the in-different nation against "incoming Orientals." The implacable Japanese were enticing American women away from Christianity—there were "temples to strange gods going up all over the land—while our own churches are hardly able to survive." The white woman was

> the weakest link in our chain of civilization, and easily succumbs to the fascination and hypnotic spells of the clever Japanese man. . . . Already the wearing of the Japanese garment, called the kimona [sic] by our white women . . . , has entered in as a sinister influence to break down our traditions of Christian modesty. The women parading the streets bareheaded at night and boldly eyeing the men as they pass is an unlovely sight not known to us when our Pioneer Fathers ruled the land.

The Japanese were "subtle and cunning and sinister," always "wearing a mask to cover up what is beneath the surface"; California could survive only if she encouraged immigration from southern Europe to replenish her stock of "in-genuous, . . . primal farmer men and women."[43]

Ethnic diversity became the nativist scapegoat for the changing values of urban America. "Alien minds," said an NAM spokesman, brought alien ideas.[44] Alfred L. Kroeber, in describing objectively for *American Mercury* readers the "Anthropological Attitude," defined precisely the new outlook which na-tivists feared as a product of foreigners. Kroeber explained cultural relativism, the "attitude of detachment from the culture we are in," as arising "because our culture happens to have finally reached the abnormal—and possibly patho-logical—point where it is beginning to be culturally introspective, and lay itself on the dissecting table alongside a foreign or dead culture."[45] Alienation was endemic in at least the first generation of the new, urban, sophisticated soci-ety, but to nativists it remained literally foreign. The migrant radicals of the IWW, most of them native Americans, were described by the ironic Thorstein Veblen as "homebred aliens," rightly hounded by the forces of justice.[46]

The Japanese were another convenient hook on which to drape fears of radicalism. Senator Morris Sheppard of Texas warned that Japanese farmers used "socialistic practices subversive of American tradition."[47] Fairchild, elab-orating his earlier argument, saw the nation as a tree, and aliens as "minute hostile organisms," particles too tough to be transformed into food. Since aliens were ignorant of American institutions, they must not be allowed to criticize them. Citizens should still be allowed freedom to criticize, "as long as they are

[43] Ella S. Mighels, "Dangerous Tendencies of the Day," *Overland Monthly*, LXXVIII (August, 1921), 39–41. The "yellow peril" led Californians, like Aus-tralians, to welcome from Europe the peoples rejected as inferior by many other Americans. In the face of the greater "peril," the lesser seemed a blessing.
[44] John E. Edgerton, in Madison Grant and Charles S. Davison (eds.), *The Alien in Our Midst* (New York, 1930), 7.
[45] Alfred L. Kroeber, "The Anthropological Attitude," *American Mercury* (New York), XIII (April, 1928), 490–96.
[46] Joseph Dorfman, *Thorstein Veblen and His America* (New York, 1935), 470.
[47] *Cong. Record,* 68 Cong., 1 Sess., 6310 (March 14, 1924).

honest and candid," but there was a danger of pro-immigrant natives over-re-acting against ethnocentrism into disloyalty.[48]

Intransigent orators sought to assuage expressed fears of national deca-dence with uncompromising, assertive nationalism. Japan's threatening polit-ical position merged with the internal menace; the multiplying local Japanese were seen as agents of the Mikado. Any attempt at slight concessions to Japan or the Japanese was a threat to national safety and pride. Valentine S. Mc-Clatchy, the leader of the post-World War I exclusion movement, warned against a delay in stopping immigration: all the single Japanese in California might choose to import mates from Japan, even though they already enjoyed an even sex balance. The "Gentlemen's Agreement," through which Theodore Roosevelt had avoided formal exclusion by allowing Japan to restrict her own emigration, was now seen as an insult to American sovereignty; it must be abrogated, not by negotiation but by unilateral congressional action. Japan's demand for a racial equality clause in the League Covenant was a focus of patriotic fears. Ex-Senator Phelan, the pioneer of the movement, warned that not "Japanese susceptibilities" but the "American right of self-preservation" was at stake.[49] In Peter B. Kyne's serialized novel of 1921, *Pride of Palomar,* the hero was a masculine, race-baiting ranchero who symbolized for white-collar readers the old independence, the control over one's destiny for which they still yearned. But the *nation's* destiny was still free and unfettered; God willing, it would remain so if alien minds and ideas could be excluded. If not, says the hero—perhaps with a twinge of guilt for those Indians—the yellow tide will rise to drown the white: "They will dominate us, because they are a dom-inant people; they will shoulder us aside, control us, dictate to us, and we shall disappear from this beautiful land as surely and as swiftly as did the Mission Indian."[50]

The fate of Sidney Gulick's long campaign for justice showed the strength of this desire to assert absolute national power. Gulick had returned to America in 1913 to lead the Federal Council of Churches' crusade for racial brother-hood, world disarmament, and similar causes which aroused the ire of suspi-cious chauvinists in a land as alien to him as Japan. To head off complete exclusion of the Japanese, he suggested an immigration quota system for all na-tionalities. Congress picked up the idea and adopted it for Europeans, but at the risk of humiliating Nippon, Congress proceeded to vote the dreaded ex-clusion of the Japanese.[51]

[48] Fairchild, *Melting Pot Mistake,* 254–56. Simeon Strunsky, New York *Times* book review (February 21, 1926), 4, gave the book a long, laudatory review, re-marking that "we want very few aliens of any sort." See also *Saturday Review of Literature* (New York), II (March 27, 1926), 661. An attack by a cultural relativist is in *New Republic,* XLVII (June 2, 1926), 67.

[49] *Hearings . . . Immigration . . . Senate . . .* on S.2576, 68 Cong., 1 Sess., 1–34 (March 11–15, 1924); *Hearings . . . Immigration and Naturalization, House . . . , on H. R. 6544,* 69 Cong., 1 Sess., 34–35 (February 16, 1926); *Hearings . . . Immigration and Naturalization, House . . . ,* 66 Cong., 2 Sess., 25 (July, 1920). See also Waldron, "Antiforeign Movements in California, 1919 to 1929," 180–86; *Cong. Record,* 68 Cong., 1 Sess., 6208 (April 12, 1924), 6310 (April 14, 1924), 6613 (April 18, 1924), 8086 (May 8, 1924).

[50] Peter B. Kyne, *Pride of Palomar* (New York, 1921), 12-13, 42.

[51] Carey McWilliams, *Prejudice* (Boston, 1944), 54–56; Bertram J. O. Schrieke, *Alien Americans* (New York, 1936), 32; LeRoy F. Smith and E. B. Johns, *Pastors, Politicians, Pacifists* (Chicago, 1926), 49, 59, 92.

The Immigration Act of 1924 was an occasion for rejoicing, but it provided no sound reason for relaxing the guard. Fairchild celebrated Japanese exclusion on the ground that it merely corrected an old imbalance. All other "colored" races had been excluded; Japanese power and pride had not blocked a return to the true racial ideal of the Founding Fathers. Some misguided liberals wished to end discrimination, but "nothing could be more unsound, unscientific, or dangerous. Racial discrimination is inherent in biological fact and in human nature . . . American nationality is inseparably bound up with white race feeling." In modern industrial society the nation was the only viable carrier of cultural health and personal identity—therefore its internal homogeneity and external sovereignty must be put above all else.[52]

So the situation remained frozen by prejudice. By 1927 a pioneer field study of California race relations had suggested that in fact the Nisei, the rising native generation of Japanese descent, had actively assimilated to American values. At whatever cost in parental misery and personal loneliness, the urban Nisei spurned Japanese nationalism for the values of the American public school and movie house. But opportunities to lose oneself in the white community were rare. Indeed, by the nativist's test the Nisei were not assimilated after all, since many whites were reluctant to employ or associate with them. As Madison Grant remarked, the second-generation Oriental was a man without a country: he had rejected Japan; America rejected him. The common consciousness, the complete mutual acceptance, were blocked by prejudice. "Thus," concluded the tireless agitator McClatchy in 1930, "the racial barrier, through no apparent fault on either side . . . ," remained.[53]

The popular stereotype was carried to its logical conclusion by General John L. DeWitt of the Western Defense Command when he wrote in 1942, to justify his exclusion of Nisei from the war zone, "The Japanese race is an enemy race . . . the racial strains are undiluted . . . along the vital Pacific Coast over 112,000 potential enemies, of Japanese extraction, are at large today." As the Los Angeles *Times* later paraphrased the General for a larger audience, "A Jap's a Jap . . . it makes no difference whether he is an American citizen or not. . . ."[54]

Yet long before the tragic evacuation of 1942, scholars had transformed their approach to the study of ethnic conflict into one which laid a basis for reconciliation. The path followed by earlier defenders of the Japanese like Royce and Gulick was endless not only because their "clerical" backgrounds and altruistic arguments offended popular prejudice, but because they lacked the scientific credentials now prerequisite in the scholarly world. Royce had closed his plea for tolerance with an invocation of "human justice" and the unity of humanity.[55] Such expressions were anathema both to the prejudiced

[52] Fairchild, *Melting Pot Mistake,* 239–43; *Race and Nationality as Factors in American Life* (New York, 1947), 200ff. A unanimous Supreme Court in 1922 had agreed with the Solicitor General that the Naturalization Act of 1790 referred to Northern Europeans, "men of their own kind." *Ozawa v. United States,* 260 U.S. 187 (1922).
[53] Grant, *Conquest of a Continent,* 266; Grant and Davison (eds.), *The Alien in Our Midst,* 190. On the Nisei, see William C. Smith, "Changing Personality Traits in Second-generation Orientals in America," *American Journal of Sociology,* XXXIII (May, 1928), 922–27.
[54] Thomas and Nishimoto, *The Spoilage,* 19–20, 20n.
[55] Royce, *Race Questions,* 53.

and the believers in objective science. It would take a change of norms and focus of attention within the science of society itself to break down the scholarly rationale for prejudice.

As C. Wright Mills pointed out, all the great sociological theories responded to the change from "personal" rural to "impersonal" urban society.[56] Thus, many American scholars of the early twentieth century rationalized their recoil from the brute society of *Sister Carrie* and *The Jungle*. But this same generation began the study of the processes by which society inculcated values and assured conformity sufficient for survival. As this school developed its theories of socialization through personal interaction, a pedagogy searching for the answer to its new mass tasks took them up gratefully to orient youth toward "adjustment" to an overwhelmingly complex and rapidly changing society. The process of manipulation itself was emphasized: the individual became self-conscious of his relations, his functioning—the "formal" aspects of his life —and attached less importance to the fixed values and attitudes which the first generation of sociologists still held firmly. Observation changes the observed reality; the knowledge that observation and manipulation are routine may change the individual's attitudes and values. The sociologists studying California's racial conflict in the 1920's reflect this reorientation of outlook.

Even as the exclusion agitation triumphed in 1924, a new and contrary viewpoint was leading scholars to examine the corpse of hatred and fear itself. Stanford University played host to one of the first large-scale field studies, The Survey of Race Relations, sponsored by the Institute of Social and Religious Research in New York City. Colleges along the coast cooperated in turning loose a swarm of graduate students on the defenseless communal corpse.[57] Directing the survey was Robert E. Park, the nation's leading analyst of race and culture contacts.

Park was a member of the "Chicago School" which, under the leadership of the tireless organizer Albion W. Small, focused on the interplay of groups, the "social process" as the unit of social change.[58] With the resulting shift in attention away from pre-social causes of behavior came a more relaxed attitude toward the possibility of successful change, of the merging of diverse groups into a viable if complex society. Robert Park, a former newspaperman and muckraker, was fascinated with the role of "news," of the increasing mass of information directed at the average man during a day's existence, in increasing the tempo of social change. His observation of a changing America led Park to a dynamic model of historical change, the image of an expanding industrial society, slowly embracing the entire world and homogenizing its distinctive, antagonistic cultures. From this process of conflict and accommodation emerged the "marginal man," the racial and cultural hybrid, who lived with an uneasy sense of half-belonging and intellectual sensitivity.[59] Ap-

[56] C. Wright Mills, *The Sociological Imagination* (New York, 1959), 152.
[57] *Tentative Findings of the Survey on Race Relations* (Stanford, 1925), 5.
[58] Albion W. Small, "Fifty Years of Sociology in the United States (1865–1915)," *American Journal of Sociology*, XXI (May, 1916), 721–864; Harry E. Barnes, "Albion Woodbury Small," in Harry E. Barnes (ed.), *An Introduction to the History of Sociology* (Chicago, 1948), 766–92.
[59] Robert E. Park, *Race and Culture* (Glencoe, Ill., 1950), v–ix, xi–xiv; Park, "Introduction" to Steiner, *Japanese Invasion*, reprinted in *Race and Culture*, 223–29; Park, "Human Migration and the Marginal Man," *American Journal of Sociology*, XXXIII (May, 1928), 881–93.

plying his theory to the American scene, Park in 1921 concurred with William I. Thomas in the common argument that our democracy required an acceptance of personal responsibility, honest face-to-face dealings among men, active civic participation. But they now contracted the sphere of this core culture just far enough to transform the conclusion: all ethnic groups would in time be able to assimilate to essential democratic values while retaining many traits from their old cultures.[60]

Discussing the problem of ethnic conflict after his California survey, Park in 1928 distinguished between specific racial prejudice and antipathy, which were culturally acquired, and the underlying emotions involved, which were founded in "fundamental human nature."[61] And the two influential books which came out of the California survey were studies of attitudes—their early development in children, their changes and reversals with time and circumstance.[62] Rejecting any one-to-one relation of physiology to prejudice, race to mentality, or even of parental values to lifetime beliefs, students now assumed that attitudes had a dynamic life which might be traced—and influenced. As the goals of scholars changed, the descriptive model became a desirable normative progression. And where the previous generation had rationalized popular prejudice, scholars now fought to reverse sentiment with data and shame.

It was all very hard for the old school to take; Fairchild in 1947 was still attacking the attitude surveyors in California for their failure to define "race."[63] But now his was a lonely voice proclaiming the primary role of the "stimulus object"; the majority of his peers had accepted racial hatred as an internal process in groups and in individual psyches. Thus, one postwar study of California's racial clash said, "the problem of prejudice is to an important degree the problem of the prejudiced."[64] A UNESCO study remarked, "race itself, in the biological sense, is irrelevant to racial attitudes and thinking."[65] The reaction which had angered Fairchild was now routine among students of racism: "anything that the people thought of as a race, we called a race."[66] The "objective" world of economic competition and visible racial differences was now seen as a stage for the acting-out of deeper frustrations lurking within individuals shaped by a fluid, competitive social order.[67] California's Japanese were no longer pictured as independent causes of conflict, but as catalysts precipitating impulses held latent in American national character.

[60] Robert E. Park and Herbert A. Miller, *Old World Traits Transplanted* (New York, 1921), 260–65. (Apparently, this book was written primarily by William I. Thomas with Park's assistance but appeared without Thomas' name. Helen MacGill Hughes, "Robert E. Park," unpublished manuscript in Mrs. Hughes' possession.)

[61] Park, *Race and Culture*, 237. See also E. Franklin Frazier, "Sociological Theory and Race Relations," *American Sociological Review* (Menasha), XII (June, 1947), 265–67.

[62] Emory S. Bogardus, *Immigration and Race Attitudes* (Boston, 1928); Bogardus, "A Race Relations Cycle," *American Journal of Sociology*, XXXV (January, 1930), 612–17. See also Bruno Lasker, *Race Attitudes in Children* (New York, 1929).

[63] Fairchild, *Race and Nationality*, 70.

[64] Floyd Matson, in tenBroek and others, *Prejudice, War and the Constitution*, 22.

[65] Kenneth L. Little, *The Race Question in Modern Science: Race and Society* (New York, 1961), 58.

[66] Quoted in Fairchild, *Race and Nationality*, 70.

[67] See for example Oscar Handlin's essay, "The Horror," in Handlin, *Race and Nationality in American Life* (Boston, 1957), 111–32.

Ethnic Minorities
in Contemporary America

Today the descendants of those who came in the great migrations from Europe and Asia are relatively free of persecution. With the passage of time they have fled the slums, acquired political power, and dropped their foreign ways. First-, second-, and third-generation Americans enter college, move to the suburbs, and occupy remunerative positions. Discrimination against these groups in country clubs, trade unions, and universities has diminished and in some places has disappeared. Unfortunately the latest entrants from Latin America, the West Indies, and Puerto Rico and at least two indigenous ethnic groups, the Indians and blacks, have not made similar gains.

Within the past decade there has been renewed interest in the miserable existence of the 750,000 surviving Indians. Sympathetic national figures like the late Robert Kennedy and his brother Edward have critically reexamined reservation life and the Department of Interior's Indian Bureau policies. The chief of the Bureau of Indian Affairs himself acknowledge that agency programs had yielded few significant results. In 1964 he stated that unemployment on the reservations averaged 40 to 50 percent, that nine out of ten Indians lived in housing "far below minimum standards of comfort, safety, and decency," and that the average age at death on the reservation was 42 years. Fortunately for the Indians, however, a younger generation of militants has tried to unite their beleaguered minority with other downtrodden groups in an effort to improve conditions. In 1968 some of them joined the Christian Leadership Conference's Poor People's March on Washington, a radical break with the red man's traditional isolation, and in 1969 some took over Alcatraz, the federal prison in San Francisco Bay, because, they claimed, the land had belonged to their ancestors.

The plight of the Spanish-speaking Americans, the most recent migrants to the United States, is less severe than the problems of the Indians but it represents another chapter in the long history of injustice toward minority groups in America. Uninhibited by the quota system established by Congress in 1921 and 1924, Western Hemisphere and nonmainland American citizens, Mexicans, Puerto Ricans, West Indians, and Cubans, have constituted the bulk of new minorities in the past four decades.

Mexicans began to enter the United States in large numbers at the turn of the century when railroad and agricultural expansion in the Southwest and Far West created a demand for cheap, unskilled labor. The low wages paid for seasonal agricultural and construction labor appealed to the dismally poor Mexicans. Depression in the 1930s stemmed immigration for a decade but manpower shortages after World War II revivified the inflow from Mexico. By 1945 approximately 2,500,000 Mexicans lived in the United States. Completion of the railroad system and mechanization of agriculture constricted older forms of employment and forced many migrants to search for work outside the region of their original entry. Sizeable colonies of Mexican-American agricultural and industrial laborers now exist in the midwestern and Rocky Mountain states.

The Mexicans had a more difficult life in the United States than most immigrant groups. Most of the entrants were poor and illiterate refugees from a traditional rural culture. Their mixed Spanish, Indian, and sometimes Negro ancestry subjected them to the American caste system and narrowed their opportunities for economic and social advancement. White Protestants in Texas, California, Arizona, and other states of settlement disdained the Mexicans' Roman Catholicism and dark complexions. Unaccustomed to such prejudice in their home country, the newcomers confronted a raw and ugly situation of racial and religious bigotry. The jobs for which they were hired added to these burdens. Most Mexican immigrants worked as seasonal agricultural laborers; many were smuggled in by American labor contractors. Temporary residence and migratory, seasonal, and isolated work facilitated exploitation. Unorganized and frequently unaware of their rights, restricted by bigotry and illiteracy, they remain very much at the mercy of their employers. Recently the Mexican laborers who have remained on the farms and ranches of the Southwest and the Far West have tried to improve their working conditions by unionization and striking under the leadership of César Chavez, himself a grape picker. Although they have been aided in these efforts by Walter Reuther of the United Auto Workers and have acquired a political spokesman in Democratic Senator Ralph Yarborough of Texas, the outcome at this point is still undecided, though promising.

After World War II large numbers of Puerto Ricans began moving to the mainland. In 1940 there were fewer than 70,000 Puerto Ricans on the East Coast, but overpopulation and poverty in Puerto Rico, postwar prosperity in the States, and quick, low-cost air travel induced hundreds of thousands to emigrate. By 1957 the chief port of entry, New York City, housed 550,000 Puerto Ricans. The new arrivals grouped in Brooklyn, the South Bronx, and East Harlem. They took jobs in light industry, in the garment factories along Seventh Avenue in Manhattan, and in hotels and restaurants. Color, culture, and language held back their progress toward wealth and higher status in much the same manner as it did the Mexicans. The problem of bigotry was even worse for the Puerto Rican because of friction between the Spanish-speaking and black communities in New York City. Puerto Ricans, never before subject to racial prejudices, quickly learned the ethnic pecking order and attempted to distinguish themselves from the blacks. Nonetheless, white Americans rejected them on racial grounds and blacks resented them for adopting conventional prejudices and feared their competition for jobs and living quarters.

The Cubans who arrived in the United States are unique among American minority groups. Unlike most other immigrants many were among the political, social, and economic leaders in their homeland until shortly before they left. But their privileged position abruptly disappeared when Fidel Castro seized power. Unable or unwilling to adjust to the reorganized society, about 5 percent of the population—or those who had something to lose by the revolutionary character of the new Cuba—fled to other nations. Most came to the United States and the majority of these remained in and around Miami, Florida. Once in this country they encountered conditions similar to those that other minorities had experienced but because they had been educated and had marketable skills—and the federal government made efforts to assist them—adjustment proved less difficult than it had for so many other groups.

The contemporary era has witnessed the greatest upheaval in black-white relations since the Civil War. Whites have felt increasingly guilty for society's ill-treatment of the black man and have gradually altered established policies (too gradually from the black man's point of view). President Harry S. Truman desegregated the armed forces and public facilities (schools, transportation, recreational areas, etc.) in Washington, D.C. In the 1950s the United States Supreme Court reversed a sixty-year-old policy by declaring segregation in public facilities unconstitutional. In 1957 Congress passed its first civil rights act since 1870. Subsequently Presidents John F. Kennedy and Lyndon B. Johnson expressed their concern for the plight of all minority groups and prodded Congress to pass additional legislation supposedly guaranteeing voting rights, access to public schools and housing facilities financed with federal funds, and job training. Despite these endeavors, many blacks saw little change or material progress in their own lives. They grew even more uneasy after the promise of federal assistance turned out to be insignificant. False hopes and unfulfilled promises spawned the growth of radical black leaders like Malcolm X, H. Rap Brown, and Eldridge Cleaver, who demanded immediate and full equality. Failure of the whites to respond to what they considered hasty and costly reforms led to urban riots, especially in the blistering summer days when affluent whites retreated to their air-conditioned homes or seashore resorts while blacks simmered in the heat of closely packed urban ghettoes.

President Johnson's National Advisory Commission on Civil Disorders reported in 1968 that the United States was a racist society. It recommended a massive infusion of federal funds to be spent for decent housing, improved educational and recreational facilities, and job training. The billions of dollars necessary to implement these proposals staggered the vast majority of the white public and members of Congress. Instead of grappling with the basic causes of discontent, members of both federal and state legislatures advocated harsher law enforcement. The slogan "Law and Order" had the appeal of immediate action at a cheap price and inspired enthusiasm in Americans still shackled to a heritage of racist repression.

The slow pace toward material and social equality is a fundamental but not total explanation for racial conflict today. Statistical studies in The Negro American *(Talcott Parsons and Kenneth Clark, eds., New York: The Daedalus Library, 1965), the most complete study of black society in the United States, indicated that blacks were improving their incomes and occupational status* (*i.e., increasingly more blacks were moving into white-collar jobs and middle-class status*), *but at a slower rate than whites. More recent figures released by the Department of Labor indicate that between 1959 and 1967 blacks living in cities were slowly closing the family income gap between white and black families. No gains were registered in increasing the proportion of males in white-collar occupations, but substantial advances (a 12-percent increase) occurred in the proportion of female white-collar workers. These figures disclose the root of the American blacks' grievance against white society. Until the 1960s they were making agonizingly slow gains in status and wealth while many lower-class whites were striding rapidly into a comfortable middle-class existence. By the late 1960s they seemed to have begun to close the income and status gap, mostly because of a considerable upgrading of the status and income of females. These types of advances have convinced blacks that they are relatively worse off, even though their income is higher, than at any time since World War II. Mass movement to the city and the advances made by black women, amidst the comparative stagnation of income and vocational improvements among black men, have intensified the disintegration of the black urban family. In 1959 23 percent of such families were headed by women. Eight years later the total was 30 percent. In 1959 71 percent of black children in the city lived with both parents; in 1967 61 percent lived with both parents. Leaving aside issues of justice or humanity, the simple necessity for social stability demands that these trends be reversed. The nation will not have domestic peace until the most volatile element in the black community, the young males, are confident of their vocational and familial future.*

Selected Bibliography

For the contemporary period there are a number of good comparative studies. Oscar Handlin's The Newcomers: Negroes and Puerto Ricans in a Changing Metropolis (*Cambridge, Mass.: Harvard University Press, 1959*) is excellent. Nathan Glazer and Patrick Moynihan have analyzed five groups (Irish, Italians, Jews, blacks, and Puerto Ricans) in New York City in Beyond the Melting Pot* (*Cambridge, Mass.: M.I.T. Press, 1964*). Alphonso Pinkney, "Prejudice Toward Mexican and Negro Americans: A Comparison," Phylon, 24 (1963), 353–59, is also recommended.

Good introductions to Indians in contemporary America are found in David A. Baerreis, ed., The Indian in Modern America (*State Historical Society of Wisconsin, 1956*), and the Fall, 1965, issue of Mid-Continent American Studies Journal, which is devoted exclusively to "The Indian Today." Stan Steiner's The New Indians* (*New York: Harper & Row, 1968*) is both sympathetic and insightful. Must reading for those interested in an Indian's point of view is Vine Deloria, Jr., Custer Died for Your Sins: An Indian Manifesto (*New York: Macmillan, 1969*).

On what it is like to be black in the United States see five outstanding books: Claude Brown, Manchild in the Promised Land* (*New York: New American Library, 1965*), H. Rap Brown, Die Nigger Die!* (*New York: Dial Press, 1969*), Eldridge Cleaver, Soul On Ice* (*New York: Dell Publishing Co.,*

1968), The Autobiography of Malcolm X* *(New York: Grove Press, 1965), and Julius Lester,* Look Out Whitey, Black Power Gonna Get Your Mama!* *(New York: Dial Press, 1968). Two superb essays on black power are Hugh Davis Graham, "The Storm Over Black Power," Virginia Quarterly Review, 43 (1967), 545–65, and Martin Duberman, "Black Power in America," Partisan Review, 35 (1968), 34–48. Another article that should not be missed by anyone interested in contemporary problems is Allen J. Matusow, "From Civil Rights to Black Power: The Case of SNCC, 1960–66," in Barton J. Bernstein and Allen J. Matusow, eds.,* Twentieth-Century America: Recent Interpretations* *(New York: Harcourt, Brace & World, Inc., 1969).*

On the Mexican-Americans there are three worthwhile articles of comparatively recent vintage: Leo Grebler et al.,* The Mexican-American People *(New York: The Free Press, 1970); Ozzie G. Simmons, "The Mutual Images and Expectations of Anglo-Americans and Mexican Americans," Daedalus, 90 (Spring, 1961), 286–99; and Manuel P. Servín, "The Pre-World War II Mexican-American: An Interpretation," California Historical Society Quarterly, 45 (1966), 325–38. Books of recent origin include Peter Nabokov,* Tijerina and the Courthouse Raid *(Albuquerque: University of New Mexico Press, 1969), and Stan Steiner,* La Raza *(New York: Harper & Row, 1970). Still worth consulting are older studies like Carey McWilliams,* North From Mexico *(Philadelphia: J. B. Lippincott Co., 1948), and Paul S. Taylor,* An American-Mexican Frontier *(Chapel Hill: University of North Carolina Press, 1934). McWilliams' article, "Mexicans in Michigan,"* Common Ground, 2 (Autumn, 1941), 5–18, details their midwestern experience.*

There is a great deal of informative material on the Puerto Ricans in the 1950s. The best books are by journalists: Dan Wakefield,* Island in the City* *(New York: Corinth Books, 1959), and Christopher Rand,* The Puerto Ricans* *(New York: Oxford University Press, 1958). Three good articles are M. R. Werner, "The Puerto Ricans in New York,"* The Reporter, September 12, 1950, 20–23, and September 26, 1950, 20–23; Bill Breisky, "Looking For the Promised Land,"* Saturday Evening Post, 231 (April 11, 1959), 18, 40–44; and Joseph P. Fitzpatrick, "The Integration of Puerto Ricans,"* Thought, 30 (1955), 402–20. For some inexplicable reason much less of value has been written on the Puerto Ricans recently. For the 1960s see Oscar Lewis,* La Vida* *(New York: Random House, 1966), and the much less sophisticated article by Pete Hamill, "Coming of Age in Nueva York,"* New York Magazine, 2 (November 24, 1969), 33–47. The Spring, 1968, issue of* International Migration Review *is devoted to a study of the Puerto Ricans.*

Aside from newspaper and magazine commentary, we have seen no informative analyses of the Cubans in the United States. One brief survey of interest is C. K. Yearley, "Cubans in Miami,"* Commonweal, 83 (November, 1965), 210–211.*

Indians

CALVIN KENTFIELD

Dispatch from Wounded Knee

A convention of the National Congress of American Indians met at the University of Chicago in 1961 and issued a Declaration of Purpose which read in part, "What we ask of America is not charity, not paternalism, even when benevolent. We ask only that the nature of our situation be recognized and made the basis of policy and action." Uprooted from traditional ways of life, the Indians have not yet found a suitable alternative to their former ways. Government and private assistance has been insufficiently considered and funded. Within weeks after its establishment in 1965 the Office of Economic Opportunity in Washington declared all Indian reservations as "pockets of poverty" entitled to assistance. Yet the following year a New York Times *reporter wrote that the 380,000 Indians on reservations remained the poorest people in the country. The reporter also noted that the Chippewas at the Turtle Mountain, North Dakota, reservation, lived in hovels "unfit for pigs."*

The plight of the Indians, suspended between a vanished past and a bleak future, is indeed tragic. No amount of education, medical care, or job training can restore self-respect and self-confidence to a people shorn of its traditions. In a recent comment an Indian student reflected bitterly: "It is funny to hear the isolated white man advocating integration for the Indians. . . . It is dishonest to use the word integration. You never wanted us to integrate but conform. Why is it that any cultural difference—not only Indian but anywhere in the world—is an aggravation to white people?"

In the following essay Calvin Kentfield captures the Indian's pathetic present-day existence.

Wounded Knee, S.D.

From time to time over the years, since long before the frigid Plains winter of 1890 when United States forces armed with Hotchkiss machine guns mowed down men, women, children and some of their own soldiers in the final slaughter at Wounded Knee, the Congress of the United States has become guiltily concerned about the condition and fate of the native American Indian. The most recent manifestation of that concern is the House of Representatives Bill 10560, also known as the Indian Resources Development Act of 1967, sponsored by Representative James Haley, a Florida Democrat, and a fellow Democrat, Representative Wayne N. Aspinall of Colorado, chairman of the Committee on Interior and Inuslar Affairs with which the bill now resides.

If enacted, the bill would allow the Indians greater freedom in selling, mortgaging, and developing what lands they still possess, encourage them through Government loans to bring industry to the reservations, and enable them with the approval of the Interior Department's Bureau of Indian Affairs to obtain loans from private sources. Indians in general, after years of bitter experience with Congressional maneuvers and of watching the depletion of their lands despite Federal largesse, are wary of the bill's benevolence, but most of their tribal councils have chosen to go along with it, chiefly because they hope that this time around the economic provisions will really work and because they figure that this is as good a bill as they can get at this time.

Out where the battle of Wounded Knee took place, however, the tribal elders are decidedly unenthusiastic about the bill and its Government backers. "We know they mean well," says Johnson Holy Rock, the chairman of the Tribal Council of the Oglala Sioux at Pine Ridge Reservation in South Dakota. "Their intentions in putting forth this bill are undoubtedly of the best, but they don't understand the Indian mind, and we here at Pine Ridge have simply said we won't accept it, we want to be left out, we're not ready for it, we know we'd lose more than we'd gain and we've lost too much already."

And Brice Lay, the chief of the Pine Ridge Agency of the Bureau of Indian Affairs to which an Indian must apply in order to sell or lease his land, says, "We here at the bureau know, and the council knows, that if a piece of land comes up for bids, a non-Indian's going to get it." He pointed to a chart of the reservation that showed 42 percent of the land already in white hands. "The Indians have first choice," he went on, "but very few of them can afford it, not even the council acting for the tribe as a whole. It's simply going to go out of Indian hands, and there's nothing on earth we can do about it."

The ever-diminishing land is almost the sole source of subsistence for the inhabitants of the Pine Ridge Reservation—or, more colorfully, the Land of Red Cloud—which is the seventh largest of the 300-odd reservations in the United States. It stretches for 90 miles east from the Black Hills and about 50 miles from the northern Badlands south to the Nebraska line.

In the eastern part some of the land is fertile enough to bear wheat, oats, safflower and the like, but 99 per cent of this farm land is now and forever in the hands of the white man. The rest of the reservation consists of rolling short-grass prairie land, an enormous landscape divided into four parts: endless green grass, tall blue sky, low ridges of ponderosa pine, and a constant rustling, sighing wind. Through these great plains wander cottonwood-shaded creeks such as Bear In the Lodge, Potato, Wounded Knee, and the twisted White and Cheyenne Rivers. In the summer, thunderclouds build up towers on the far horizons and the uninhibited sun may produce temperatures of 120 degrees; in the winter, the creeks become ice and blizzard winds such as those that froze the bodies at the massacre of Wounded Knee into such baroque and unusual shapes can bring the thermometer down to 40 below.

U.S. Highway 18 passes east-west through the southern edge of the reservation. There are miles and miles of good black-top kept in repair by Indians working for the Interior Department road service; and there are miles and miles of roads that are no good at all. There are modern boarding schools exclusively for Indian children as well as local public schools and a Catholic mission school, outlying clinics and a good free hospital with doctors, surgeons, dentists and a psychiatrist. There are churches of all kinds (40 per cent of the Indians profess to be Catholics and more to be Protestants, but the old beliefs still lie heavily in their souls). There is an American Legion Post, a Lions Club, a Ladies' Aid, a P.T.A. and a Boy Scout troop. Nearly all of the Sioux (or Dakotas, their own pre-reservation name for themselves) speak English as well as their native Lakota dialect, and there are still a few medicine men around, like old Frank Fools Crow who usually presides over the annual Sun Dance. The center of nearly everything—government, society, law and order, education—is Pine Ridge, a town of 1,256 people close enough to the state line to have a "suburb" in Nebraska, Whiteclay, center of shopping (three supermarkets) and entertainment (bars and dance halls).

On this reservation live, in one fashion or another, nearly 10,000 Teton Sioux of the Oglala tribe. They are not the poorest nor the richest of the country's Indians. The Hopis and some of the Apaches of the Southwest are poorer, and the inhabitants of the Aguacaliente reservation in Southern California, who more or less own Palm Springs, are richer, to say nothing of those few tribes that have oil wells. But the Oglalas range from a state of imminent starvation to fair affluence.

On the reservation itself, unemployment is 43 per cent, so some of the younger people go elsewhere for summer work. There is a new factory at Pine Ridge that employs about a hundred people to make "handmade" moccasins. A fishhook factory near Wounded Knee employs nearly 200 more, and a few more work for the Bureau of Indian Affairs. Most of the businesses—filling stations, grocery stores—are owned by whites, and the rest of the Indians work for white ranchers or live off the land which they work themselves or lease to white ranchers. The land, though it belongs to the Indians, is held in trust by the Department of the Interior, which takes care of all the leasing arrangements and issues checks to the owners each month from a computer in Aberdeen.

Aside from Interior Department employes and a few Indian ranchers, the average annual income per family is less than $900. The 34 members of the Tribal Council, however, have voted themselves a yearly salary of $7,500, paid out of proceeds from tribal lands under grazing leases. "Those earnings are supposed to be divided up amongst us all," one man told me, "but we ain't none of us seen a pinny of it for years." Most of the money, of course, goes into the operation of the tribal government, which has charge of all municipal services—police, fire and courts—as well as the maintenance of lawyers in Rapid City and Washington to represent the tribe in all higher dealings with the Government, such as House Bill 10560. Though technically wards of the Federal Government under the guiding thumb of the Bureau of Indian Affairs, the Indians, since 1924, have enjoyed the rights and privileges of full American citizenship, including the right to fight in Vietnam and the privilege of paying income taxes. They enjoy some extra privileges as well, such as untaxed land.

"We try to help them," said Brice Lay in his office in the new air-conditioned bureau headquarters in Pine Ridge, "to make the best possible use of the land they have, but it's very hard." Like most of the non-Indian (the bureau does not use the term "white man") employes of the bureau, he is intensely sincere in his desire to help the Indian become a white man. "Here in Pine Ridge most of the people live fairly well, but you go out on the reservation—the way some of those people live!" He made a gesture of despair. "No one should have to live that way."

And, indeed, out on the windy treeless tracts of the reservation, at the end of two dirt ruts across the prairie, will be a one-room shack, possibly a log cabin, possibly a frame house walled in tarpaper, for a family of six, eight, ten people and surrounded by a circle of old car bodies that, like the bodies of U.S. soldiers killed in a battle of olden times, have been striped and mutilated and left to rot where they lay. An outhouse nearby. No electricity, no running water. A monthly ration of rice, flour, powdered milk, peanut butter, margarine, lard, raisins, oatmeal, cornmeal, potted meat, dried beans, dried peas, bulgar and rolled wheat, plus $50 in cash from Welfare. This kind of poverty engenders horror, pity and disgust in the Anglo-Saxon breast, but all the Oglalas are not that badly off, and many of them simply don't want some of the amenities that the Great White Father insists they must have, if possible, for their own good.

"We had one old woman out on the reservation," Brice Lay said, "that was all by herself and living in a tent, so we found a house for her, but she wouldn't move in. She said she'd die if she lived in a house, that the air in a house was bad air. Oh, she was stubborn. But finally," he concluded with a tone of great satisfaction, "we got her in there."

Out at Wounded Knee about two miles from the general store and post office lives a man in his late 50's, his wife, two married sons, six grandchildren, three dogs, two cats, some hens and a rooster. He is a full blood, very dark, though his wife is not. He owns a section of land (640 acres) through which runs Wounded Knee Creek and on which graze about 200 head of cattle and 60 or 70 horses. He has a field of alfalfa which, this year, because of the late rains, is exceptionally rich and high and, when I visited him, was ready for cutting. There are tall shade trees along the creek, plenty of water, and a small field of sweet corn nearby.

He and his wife and one orphaned grandchild live in a very old, one-room log cabin with a shade, or "squaw cooler" (though "squaw" is an insulting word these days), a kind of summer house made of poles and pine boughs that keep off the sun but let the breeze come through, making it a comfortable outdoor kitchen and sleeping place during the hot months. His sons and their families live in small asphalt-shingled houses on either side of the parental house. One son is a cowboy and works the section, the other works at the fishhook factory over the hill. Standing to one side at the edge of the alfalfa is a two-hole outhouse.

They carry their water from the creek, build their fire with wood and light their lamps with kerosene. They walk to the store and back, as they have no car. They are well and presumably happy. They are members of the Native American Church who use peyote, the hallucinatory cactus, in their services, during which, under the spell of the drug, they chant and sing and pray to God that the day will come when all men will be at peace and all men will be brothers. Not half a mile from this man's house reside the bones in a mass hilltop grave of the victims of the massacre of Wounded Knee.

Though a Peace Sacrifice was the climax of this year's Sun Dance—"Richard 'Buddy' Red Bow," the posters read, "17 years old, member of the Oglala Sioux tribe, will pray for worldwide peace by performing the traditional Sun Dance worship. Red Bow will pierce his flesh and offer his blood, praying for the safety of American Servicemen and a peaceful speedy end to war in Vietnam"—the Sioux were not always a peaceable people.

"Sioux" is short for "Nadowessioux," which is French for "Nadowessi," which is Chippewa meaning "little snakes" or, in other words, treacherous enemies. The Sioux fought everybody—the Chippewa, the Crow, the Cheyenne, the Kiowa and the white man after he came pushing onto the plains, stealing, pushing, lying, slaughtering the buffalo, always pushing. In 1866, Red Cloud, "the first and only Indian leader in the West to win a war with the United States," said to a Colonel Carrington, come to open a road to the Montana goldfields, "You are the White Eagle who has come to steal the road! The Great Father sends us presents and wants us to sell him the road, but the White Chief comes with soldiers to steal it before the Indian says yes or no! I will talk with you no more. As long as I live I will fight you for the last hunting grounds of my people."

Red Cloud and Crazy Horse, Custer's Last Stand, Sitting Bull and Big Foot, and the final slaughter at Wounded Knee! After all that misery, bravery, and bloodshed, the Sioux, romanticized by the white man, became the Ideal Indian, the Mounted Warrior in War Bonnet, the End of the Trail, the Indian at the Medicine Show, the All-American Buffalo-Nickel Indian.

The last treaty the Sioux made with the United States Government (1868–69) set aside nearly half of South Dakota, including the sacred Black Hills, and part of North Dakota as the "Great Sioux Reserve." But white men discovered gold in the Black Hills (as Johnson Holy Rock said to me, "The Indians still don't understand gold, it's a white man's concept and the white man just can't understand that"), so an Act of Congress in 1877 removed the Black Hills from the Indians' reserve. Later, another act divided what was left of the "Great Sioux Reserve" into five reservations with still more loss of land, settling the Oglalas at Pine Ridge. It is no wonder, indeed, that the Indian leaders look twice and twice again at Acts of Congress.

The Indian Bureau demands at least one-quarter Indian blood as a prerequisite for donating its paternalistic blessings—but the Pine Ridge Tribal Council has *never* been able to decide upon who is and who is not an Indian.

"The Tribal Council is ridiculous," said a man I shall call Edgar Running Bear because he has asked me not to use his real name. "Two of them are stupid women who have not even had a sixth-grade education, one of them is a hopeless alcoholic, and they're all prejudiced."

We were sitting in Edgar Running Bear's house in one of the several new Pine Ridge subdivisions financed by the Public Housing Authority and built by Indian labor against the fierce objections of half-a-dozen union leaders. It is a two-bedroom house, pink and white, with a carport and a front lawn like millions of others all over America. In the living room were two modernistic armchairs, a huge radio-phonograph-television combination set in the corner. On top of the TV stood a vase of plastic flowers and on the wall opposite the picture window hung a small imitation tapestry of a roaring tiger printed in lurid colors on black velvet.

It was a hot day and through the open windows we could hear the drumming and amplified chanting of one of the bands, the Oglala Juniors or the Sioux Travelers, who had gathered at the nearby campground for the four-day Sun Dance celebration, a kind of county fair, carnival and tribal get-together combined with ancient ritual which was just then beginning. The celebration is an annual rite that Edgar at one point in our conversation, referred to scornfully as a reversion to primitivism, though he later took his children over to the campground to ride the Space-Mobile.

"Why do you say they're prejudiced?" I asked. "Against whom?"

"Against the mixed bloods."

Both Edgar and his wife, and indeed most of the population of the reservation, are mixed bloods. The classic face of Red Cloud is seldom seen. Johnson Holy Rock himself is three-quarter Oglala and one-quarter Scotch-Irish. I mentioned this fact and elicited only a shrug from Edgar.

"Do you find," I asked, "that white people on the reservation or off it show prejudice toward you because you're Indians?"

"Oh, yes," Edgar's wife said quickly. "They move onto our land, look down their noses at us, and complain about our laws and our dogs and—"

"When I go off the reservation," Edgar broke in, "I expect to abide by the ways of the people there. It doesn't bother me, if we don't get served one place, we'll go someplace else, but *you* could go staggering drunk down the main street of Rushville [Rushville, Neb., the nearest town of any size] and nobody'd look at you, but if *I* did—well, not me because being a policeman they know me—but if an ordinary Innun did the same thing he'd be in jail so fast. . . ."

I related an incident I had witnessed in a restaurant-bar in Rushville. The television had been giving news of the aftermath of the Negro riots in Detroit and the waitress had said, "I know it's a funny attitude to take, but if one of them come in here, I just couldn't serve him. I don't know what it is, but—" Then she had given a little laugh and said, "But nobody kin accuse me of racial prejudice because I feel the same damn way about the dirty Indians."

There was a moment of silence while the drums beat at the Sun Dance grounds.

"Well," Edgar said, "that's the kind of thing you run into."

"Well, us Innuns aren't prejudiced against the niggers," Edgar's wife said. "Of course, I wouldn't want my daughter to marry one any more than I'd want her to marry a full blood."

Edgar, slouching deeply in his armchair, gave the living room wall a kick with the side of his foot. "Look at this damn house," he said. "It's coming apart already."

"That's why we send our kids to public school instead of the B.I.A. Innun school," his wife went on, "because we don't want them to grow up with nothing but Innuns."

"To live here, to live this life we live here," Edgar said, shaking his head, "you have to be half-drunk all the time."

Until 1953, it was, as a Klamath Indian friend of mine once explained, "against the law to feed liquor to Indians." It's still against the law on Pine Ridge because the members of the tribe voted for a dry reservation, though in the "suburb" of Whiteclay there are bars and dance halls that get quite lively on a Saturday night or just after the computer has issued the Mother's Aid or Welfare check.

In those resorts, there is, as well as drunkenness, a great deal of laughter and joking and horseplay; the Oglala is a friendly and, at times, very witty creature. He loves athletic games and plays them well, and his manual deftness makes him an excellent carpenter, machinist or technician if he takes the trouble to develop his talents and possesses the courage to go into the outside world and exercise his skills. One of the commonest reasons, of course, for Indian apathy toward Government training programs is that once an Indian learns a white man's trade there is no place on the reservation where he can exercise it. He has to leave his home and relatives and work in some foreign place, and he doesn't want to. The sponsors of H.R. 10560 eagerly point out that the bill will help relieve that condition.

In one Whiteclay bar, I met a fat jolly Oglala lady who, although she has an excellent secretarial job with the bureau, also creates fine tomahawks for the ever so slightly increasing tourist trade. She has three daughters who are or are becoming registered nurses, one son who has a Ph.D. in sociology and is working with other Indians in Nebraska, and a young son who is a good-for-nothing drunk. She knows Edgar Running Bear very well.

"Pooh! You can't believe a word Ed says," she said, although she allowed that the council was, in fact, incompetent and overpaid and that Johnson Holy Rock was unfair in his recommendations for loans. In general, she felt, the Innuns on the reservation were a passably contented lot and pretty much satisfied with the way the Bureau was handling their affairs.

"This is our place," she said. "Some of us go away, but an awful lot of us come back. See those two boys over there in the ball caps? They've been in Oakland, California, making good money, but they've come back."

I asked them why they had come back. One of them laughed and said, "Hell, *I* don't know. I guess to play baseball."

Johnson Holy Rock told me he had been to Washington and explained to the Interior Department people that the chief complaints they have against the Government were that the Government treated them like digits instead of human beings, that it didn't understand the Indians' attachment to their people and their land, and that the Indians themselves didn't yet understand the white man's notion of business and money and private property. "We're not ready to be let out on our own," he had told them, "but treat us like people instead of numbers."

I remarked that all of us, not just the Indians, were victims of the official digital computer, that we were all cards full of little holes. *"We've* given up," I said, but this time he didn't understand, because he means to go right on trying to keep his people what they are, more so than any other Americans I know —human beings. But I'm sure that one day he, too, will give up just as Red Cloud, in spite of his vow to fight for his lands forever, gave up, finally telling his people in tones of scornful irony:

"You must begin anew and put away the wisdom of your fathers. You must lay up food and forget the hungry. When your house is built, your storeroom filled, then look around for a neighbor whom you can take advantage of and seize all he has."

That was the way, he said, to get rich like a white man.

Blacks

ELDRIDGE CLEAVER
Sorties in Mad Babylon

The hopeful years of the late 1950s and early 1960s augured success for leaders such as Roy Wilkins of the National Association for the Advancement of Colored People (NAACP) and Martin Luther King, Jr., of the Southern Christian Leadership Conference (SCLC). Congress passed its first civil rights bill since Reconstruction in 1957 and in the next decade followed through with additional legislation designed to protect political rights and advance residential, educational, and vocational integration. Municipal and state legislatures and commissions apparently guaranteed blacks long-withheld citizenship rights and laid the groundwork for integration in housing and schools. By the mid-1960s, however, the promise of these years had already become a bitter memory. Tempers rose as expectations went unfulfilled. Voting rights were not transformed into political power; black ghettos deteriorated; and segregated schools spread despite legislation to the contrary. Lack of progress discredited older leaders and more moderate civil rights organizations. Accumulated grievances and prejudices led to riots in black ghettos which resulted in killing, looting, and millions of dollars' worth of property damage. The civil rights movement and the black community itself split between older groups like the NAACP and the Urban League, which advocated integration and working through the legal and political process, and radicalized organizations of younger blacks like the Congress of Racial Equality (CORE) and the Student Nonviolent Coordinating Committee (SNCC).

On May 2, 1967, a recently formed black militant organization from Oakland, California, the Black Panthers, drew public attention by marching into the state legislature with loaded weapons to protest a gun control bill. (The group regarded its possession of firearms as a symbol of black manhood and as necessary protection against attacks by whites.) Black Panthers continue to make headlines as their clashes with the authorities have resulted in the liquidation or imprisonment of their top leaders. The organization asserts that twenty-eight Panthers have been killed by the police since 1968. The F.B.I. and police in New York, Chicago, and Oakland charge that the group is conspiring to overthrow the American government and that the Panthers initiated all the gun battles. The Panthers claim that the police provoked incidents in order to murder members of the organization. Evidence from a 1969 shoot-out in Chicago

Eldridge Cleaver, "Letters from Prison," *Ramparts,* August, 1966, pp. 16–26.

throws considerable suspicion on the validity of police justifications. Bullet holes in this episode were concentrated near the bed where a Panther leader was shot, rather than scattered throughout the area of the alleged firefight. If the police explanation of a general gun battle begun by Panthers had been correct, a more general pattern of bulletholes should have appeared.

Eldridge Cleaver, Minister of Information in the organization, as well as the Peace and Freedom Party candidate for President of the United States in 1968, wrote the letters reproduced below. Cleaver, born in 1935, has been imprisoned several times for narcotics possession and assault. While in prison for the latter offense he became a follower of Malcolm X and a proselytizer for the Black Muslins. During these years, as did Malcolm X before him, he discovered the integrity of his black identity. After release from prison Cleaver had his parole revoked because of alleged participation in a gun battle against the police and he fled the country to escape reincarceration. These letters, written to his lawyers while in prison, describe the ordeal and triumph of Cleaver's coming to terms with himself and his race.

[On Becoming]

Folsom Prison, June 25, 1965

Nineteen fifty four, when I was 18 years old, is held to be a crucial turning point in the history of the Afro-American—for the USA as a whole—the year segregation was outlawed by the U.S. Supreme Court. It was also a crucial year for me because on June 18, 1954, I began serving a sentence in state prison for possession of marijuana.

The Supreme Court decision was only one month old when I entered prison, and I do not believe that I had even the vaguest idea of its importance or historical significance. But later, the acrimonious controversy ignited by the end of the separate but equal doctrine was to have a profound effect on me, for this controversy awakened me to my position in America and I began to form a concept of what it meant to be black in white America. Of course I'd always known that I was black, but I'd never really stopped to take stock of what I was involved in. I met life as an individual and took my chances. Prior to 1954, we lived in an atmosphere of novocain. Negroes found it necessary, in order to maintain whatever sanity they could, to remain somewhat aloof and detached from "the problem." We accepted indignities and the mechanics of the apparatus of oppression without reacting by sitting-in or holding mass demonstrations. Nurtured by the fires of controversy over segregation, I was soon aflame with indignation over my newly discovered social status, and inwardly I turned away from America with horror, disgust, and outrage.

In Soledad state prison, I fell in with a group of young blacks who, like myself, were in vociferous rebellion against what we perceived as a continuation of slavery on a higher plane. We cursed everything American—including baseball and hotdogs. All respect we may have had for politicians, preachers, lawyers, governors, Presidents, senators, congressmen was utterly destroyed as we watched them temporizing and compromising over right and wrong, over legal-

ity and illegality, over constitutionality and unconstitutionality. We knew that
in the end what they were clashing over was us, what to do with the blacks,
and whether or not to start treating them as human beings. I despised all of
them. I had gotten caught with a shopping bag full of marijuana, a shopping
bag full of love—I was in love with the weed and I did not for one minute think
that anything was wrong with getting high; I had been getting high for four or
five years and was convinced, with the zeal of a crusader, that marijuana was
superior to lush—yet the rulers of the land seemed all to be lushes.

While all this was going on, our group was espousing blatant atheism. Unsophisticated and not based on any philosophical rationale, our atheism was
pragmatic and only confirmed what I had more or less come to believe: there
is no God; if there is, men do not know anything about him. Therefore, all
religions were phony—which made all preachers and priests, in our eyes, fakers,
including the ones scurrying around the prison who, curiously, could put in a
good word for you with the Almighty Creator of the universe, but couldn't get
anything down with the warden or parole board—they could usher you through
the Pearly Gates *after you were dead*, but not through the prison gate *while you
were still alive and kicking*. Besides, men of the cloth who work in prisons have
an ineradicable stigma attached to them in the eyes of convicts because they
are instrumental in escorting condemned men into the gas chamber. Such men
of God are powerful arguments in favor of atheism. Our atheism was a source
of enormous pride to me.

Through reading I was amazed to discover how confused people were. I
had thought that out there, beyond the horizon of my own ignorance, unanimity
existed, that even though I myself didn't know what was happening in the universe, other people certainly did. Yet here I was discovering that the whole USA
was in a chaos of disagreement over segregation/integration. In these circumstances I decided that the only safe thing for me to do was go for myself. It
became clear that it was possible for me to take the initiative: instead of simply
reacting I could *act*. I could unilaterally—whether anyone agreed with me or not
—repudiate all allegiances, morals, values—even while continuing to exist within
this society. My mind would be free and no power in the universe could force
me to accept something if I didn't want to. But I would take my own sweet time.
That, too, was a part of my new freedom. I would accept nothing until it was
proved that it was good—for me. I became an extreme iconoclast. Any affirmative assertain made by anyone around me became a target for tirades of criticism and denunciation.

I attacked all forms of piety, loyalty and sentiment. As I pranced about,
club in hand, seeking new idols to smash, I encountered really for the first time
in my life, with any seriousness, The Ogre, rising up before me in a mist. I discovered, with alarm, that The Ogre possessed a tremendous and dreadful power
over me, and I didn't understand this power or why I was at its mercy. I tried
to repudiate The Ogre, root it out of my heart as I had done to God, Constitution, principles, morals and values—but The Ogre had its claws buried in the
core of my being and refused to let go. I fought frantically to be free, but The
Ogre only mocked me and sank its claws deeper into my soul. I knew then
that I had found an important key, that if I conquered The Ogre and broke its
power over me I would be free. But I also knew that it was a race against time

and that if I did not win I would certainly be broken and destroyed. I, a black man, confronted The Ogre—the white woman.

It is understandable that in prison those things withheld from and denied to the prisoner become precisely what he wants most of all. Because we were locked up in our cells before darkness fell, I used to lie awake at night racked by painful craving to take a leisurely stroll under the stars, or to go to the beach, to drive a car on a freeway, to grow a beard, or to make love to a woman.

In the process of enduring my confinement, I decided to get myself a "pin-up" girl to paste on the wall of my cell. I would fall in love with her and lavish my affection upon her. She, a symbolic representative of the forbidden tribe of women, would sustain me until I was free. Out of the center of Esquire, I married a voluptuous bride. Our marriage went along swell for a time: no quarrels, no complaints. And then, one evening when I came in from school, I was shocked and enraged to find that the guard had entered my cell, ripped my Sugar from the wall, torn her into little pieces, and left the pieces floating in the commode: it was like seeing a dead body floating in a lake. Giving her a proper burial, I flushed the commode. As the saying goes, I sent her to Long Beach. But I was genuinely beside myself with anger: almost every cell, excepting those of the homosexuals, had a "pin-up" girl on the wall and the guards didn't bother them. Why, I asked the guard the next day, had he singled me out for special treatment?

"Don't you know we have a rule against pasting up pictures on the walls?" he asked me.

"Later for the rules," I said. "You know as well as I do that that rule is not enforced."

"Tell you what," he said, smiling at me (the smile put me on my guard), "I'll compromise with you: get yourself a colored girl for a pin-up—no white women—and I'll let it stay up. Is that a deal?"

I was more embarrassed than shocked. He was laughing in my face. I called him two or three dirty names and walked away. I can still vividly recall his big, moon-face, grinning at me over yellow teeth. The disturbing part about the whole incident was that a terrible feeling of guilt came over me as I realized that I had chosen the picture of the white girl over the available pictures of black girls. I tried to rationalize it away, but I was fascinated by the truth involved. Why hadn't I thought about it in this light before? So I took hold of the question and began to inquire into my feelings. Was it true, did I really prefer white girls over black? The conclusion was clear and inescapable: I did. I decided to check out my friends on this point and it was easy to determine, from listening to their general conversation, that the white woman indeed occupied a peculiarly prominent place in all of our frames of reference.

One afternoon, when there was a large group of Negroes on the prison yard shooting the breeze, I grabbed the floor and posed the question: which did they prefer, white women or black? Some said Japanese women were their favorite, others said Chinese, some said European women, others said Mexican women—they all stated a preference, and they generally freely admitted their dislike for black women.

"I don't want nothing black but a Cadillac," said one.

"If money was black I wouldn't want none of it," put in another.

A short little stud, who was a very good lightweight boxer with a little man's complex that made him love to box heavyweights, jumped to his feet. He had a yellowish complexion and we called him Butterfly.

"All you niggers are sick!" Butterfly spat out. "I don't like no stinking white woman. My grandma is a white woman and I don't even like her!"

But it just so happened that Butterfly's crime partner was in the crowd, and after Butterfly had his say, his crime partner said, "Aw sit down and quit that lying, lil ol chump. What about that grey girl in San Jose who had your nose wide open? Did you like her, or were you just running after her with your tongue hanging out of your head because you hated her?"

From our discussion, which began that evening and has never yet ended, we went on to notice how thoroughly, as a matter of course, a black growing up in America is indoctrinated with the white race's standard of beauty. Not that the whites made a calculated effort to do this, we thought, but since they constituted the majority, the whites brainwashed the blacks by the very processes the whites employed to indoctrinate themselves with their own group standards. It intensified my frustrations to know that I was indoctrinated to see the white woman as more desirable than my own black woman. It drove me into books seeking light on the subject. In Richard Wright's *Native Son,* I found Bigger Thomas and a keen insight into the problem.

My interest in this area persisted undiminished and then, in 1955, an event took place in Mississippi which turned me inside out: Emmett Till, a young Negro down from Chicago on a visit, was murdered, allegedly for flirting with a white woman. He had been shot, his head crushed from repeated blows with a blunt instrument, and his badly decomposed body was recovered from the river with a heavy weight secured on it. I was, of course, duly angry over the whole bit, but one day I saw in a magazine a picture of the white woman with whom Emmett Till was said to have flirted. While looking at the picture, I felt that little tension in the center of my chest which I experience when a woman appeals to me. I was disgusted and angry with myself. Here was a woman who had caused the death of a black, possibly because, when he looked at her, he also felt the same tensions of lust and desire in his chest—and probably for the same general reasons that I felt them. It was all utterly unacceptable to me. I looked at the picture again and again, and in spite of everything and against my will and the hate I felt for the woman and all that she represented, she appealed to me. I flew into a rage at myself, at America, at white women, at the history that had placed those tensions of lust and desire in my chest.

During this period, I was concentrating my reading in the field of economics. Having previously dabbled in the theories and writings of Rousseau, Thomas Paine, and Voltaire, I had added a little polish to my iconoclastic stance. In economics, because everybody seemed to find it necessary to attack and condemn Karl Marx, I sought out his books, and although he kept me with a headache, I took him for my authority. I was not prepared to understand him, but I was able to see in him a thoroughgoing critique and condemnation of capitalism. It was like taking medicine for me to find that, indeed, American capitalism was deserving of all the hatred and contempt that I felt for it in my heart. This had a positive, stabilizing effect upon me, to an extent—because I was not about to become stable—and it diverted me from my previous preoccupation: morbid broodings on the black man and the white woman. Pursuing my readings into the history of socialism, I read, with very little understanding, some of the passionate, exhortatory writings of Lenin; and I fell in love with Bakunin and Nechayev's Catechism of the Revolutionist—the principles of which, along with some of Machiavelli's advice, I sought to incorporate into my own behavior. I took the "Catechism" for my bible and, standing on a one-man platform that had nothing to do with the reconstruction of society, I began consciously incorporating these principles into my daily life, to employ tactics of ruthlessness in my dealings with everyone with whom I came into contact. And I began to look at white America through these new eyes.

Somehow I arrived at the conclusion that, as a matter of principle, it was of paramount importance for me to have an antagonistic, ruthless attitude toward white women. The term "outlaw" appealed to me and at the time my parole date was drawing near, I considered myself to be mentally free—I was an "outlaw." I had stepped outside of the white man's law, which I repudiated with scorn and self-satisfaction. I became a law unto myself—my own legislature, my own supreme court, my own executive. At the moment I walked out of the prison gate, my feelings toward white women in general could be summed up in the following lines:

TO A WHITE GIRL

I love you
Because you're white,
Not because you're charming
Or bright.
Your brightness
Is a silky thread
Snaking through my thoughts
In redhot patterns
Of lust and desire.

I hate you
Because you're white.
Your white meat
Is nightmare food.
White is
The skin of Evil.
You're my Moby Dick,
White Witch,
Symbol of the rope and hanging tree,
Of the burning cross.

Loving you thus
And hating you so,
My heart is torn in two.
Crucified.

I became a rapist. To refine my technique and *modus operandi,* I started out by practicing on black girls in the ghetto—in the black ghetto where dark and vicious deeds appear not as aberrations or deviations from the norm, but as part of the sufficiency of the Evil of a day—and when I considered myself smooth enough, I crossed the tracks and sought out white prey. I did this consciously, deliberately, willfully, and methodically—though looking back I see that I was in a frantic, wild and completely abandoned frame of mind. It seemed to me that the act of rape was an insurrectionary act. It delighted me that I was defying and trampling upon the white man's law, upon his system of values, and that I was defiling his women—and this point, I believe, was the most satisfying to me because I was very resentful over the historical fact of how the white man has used the black woman. I felt I was getting revenge. From the site of the act of rape, consternation spreads outwardly in concentric circles. I wanted to send waves of consternation throughout the white race. Recently, I came upon a quotation from one of LeRoi Jones' poems, taken from his book, *The Dead Lecturer:*

> A cult of death,
> need of the simple striking arm under
> the street lamp. The cutters from under
> their rented earth. Come up, black dada
> nihilismus. Rape the white girls. Rape
> their fathers. Cut the mothers' throats.

I have lived those lines and I know that if I had not been apprehended I would have slit some white throats. There are, of course, many young blacks out there right now who are slitting white throats and raping the white girl. They are not doing this because they read LeRoi Jones' poetry, as some of his critics seem to believe. Rather, LeRoi is expressing the funky facts of life.

After I returned to prison, I took a long look at myself and for the first time in my life I admitted that I was wrong, that I had gone astray—astray not so much from the white man's law as from being human, civilized—for I could not approve the act of rape. Even though I had some insight into my own motivations, I did not feel justified and I lost my self-respect. My pride as a man dissolved and my whole fragile moral structure seemed to collapse, completely shattered.

And that is why I started to write. To save myself.

I had to seek out the truth and unravel the tangled web of my motivations. I had to find out who I am and what I wanted to be, what type of man I should be, and what I could do to become the best of which I was capable. I understood that what had happened to me had also happened to countless other blacks and it would happen to many, many more. I believe that a true understanding of this problem is a must for our nation—yes, I am concerned with this nation—about what is happening to us.

I learned that I had been taking the easy way out, running away from problems. I also learned that it is easier to do evil than it is to do good. And I have been terribly impressed by the youth of America, black and white. I am proud of them because they have reaffirmed my faith in humanity. I have come to feel what must be love for the young people of America and I want to be part of the good and greatness that they want for all people. From my prison cell, I have watched America slowly coming awake. It is not fully awake yet, but there is soul in the air and everywhere I see beauty. I have watched the sit-ins, the freedom rides, the Mississippi Blood Summers, demonstrations all over the country, the FSM [Free Speech Movement] movement, the teach-ins and the mounting protest over Lyndon Strangelove's foreign policy—all of this, the thousands of little details, show me it is time to straighten up and fly right. That is why I decided to concentrate on my writings and efforts in this area. We are a very sick country—I perhaps am sicker than most.

What must be done, I believe, is that all these problems—particularly the sickness between the white woman and the black man—must be brought out into the open, dealt with and resolved. I know that the black man's sick attitude toward the white woman is a revolutionary sickness: it keeps him perpetually out of harmony with the system that is oppressing him. Many whites flatter themselves that the Negro male's lust for the white dream girl is purely an esthetic attraction, but nothing could be further from the truth. His motivation is often of such a bloody, hateful, bitter and malignant nature that whites would really be hard pressed to find it flattering.

I have discussed these points with prisoners who were convicted of rape, and their motivations are very plain. But they are reluctant to discuss these things with the white men who, by and large, make up the prison staffs. I believe that in the experience of these men lies the knowledge and wisdom that must be utilized to help other youngsters who are heading in the same direction. I think all of us, the entire nation, will be better off if we bring it all up front. A lot of people's feelings will be hurt, but that is the price that must be paid.

[On Watts]

Folsom Prison, August 16, 1965

As we left the mess hall Sunday morning and milled around in the prison yard, after four days of abortive uprising in Watts, a group of low riders[1] from Watts assembled on the basketball court. They were wearing jubilant, triumphant smiles, animated by a vicarious spirit by which they, too, were in the thick of the uprising taking place hundreds of miles away to the south in the Watts ghetto.

"Man," said one, "what they doing out there? Break it down for me baby."

They slapped each other's outstretched palms in a cool salute and burst out laughing with joy.

---

[1] *Low Rider.* A Los Angeles nickname for ghetto youth. Originally, the term was coined to describe the youth who had lowered the bodies of their cars so that they rode low, close to the ground; also implied was the style of driving that these youngsters perfected. Sitting behind the steering wheel and slumped low down in the seat, all that could be seen of them was from their eyes up, which used to be the cool way of driving. When these youthful hipsters alighted from their vehicles, the term low rider stuck with them, evolving to the point where all black ghetto youth—but *never* the soft offspring of the black bourgeoisie—are referred to as low riders.

"Home boy, them Brothers is taking care of Business!" shrieked another ecstatically.

Then one low rider, stepping into the center of the circle formed by the others, rared back on his legs and swaggered, hunching his belt up with his forearms as he'd seen James Cagney and George Raft do in too many gangster movies. I joined the circle. Sensing a creative moment in the offing, we all got very quiet, very still, and others passing by joined the circle and did likewise.

'Baby," he said, "They walked in fours and kicking in doors; dropping Reds[2] and busting heads; drinking wine and committing crime; shooting and looting; high-siding[3] and low-riding; setting fires and slashing tires; turning over cars and burning down bars; making Parker mad and making me glad; putting an end to that 'go slow' crap and putting sweet Watts on the map—my black ass is in Folsom this morning but my black heart is in Watts!" Tears of joy were rolling from his eyes.

It was a cleansing, revolutionary laugh we all shared, something we have not often had occasion for.

Watts was a place of shame. We used to use Watts as an epithet in much the same way as city boys used "country" as a term of derision. To deride one as a "lame," who did not know what was happening (a rustic bumpkin), the "in-crowd" of the time from L.A. would bring a cat down by saying that he had just left Watts, that he ought to go back to Watts until he had learned what was happening, or that he had just stolen enough money to move out of Watts and was already trying to play a cool part. But now, blacks are seen in Folsom saying, "I'm from Watts, Baby!"—whether true or no, but I think their meaning is clear. Confession: I, too, have participated in this game, saying, I'm from Watts. In fact, I did live there for a time, and I'm *proud* of it, the tired lamentations of Whitney Young, Roy Wilkins and The Preacher notwithstanding.

[Beautiful, Beautiful Brown Eyes]

Folsom Prison, October 28, 1965

Once I was walking down Main Street in L.A. around noon on a Saturday and it was a beautiful sunny day. I was just a young stud about 16, I guess, and I had one of those I-think-I'm-cute type walks, prancing and rolling on my toes. Before me and adjacent to the sidewalk was a shoeshine stand facing in my direction. A jukebox was blaring a tune of the times and I got caught up in the music as I walked along. I was kind of walking in time to the music. Sitting up on the customer's seat was a big fine sister who was popping her fingers and wiggling to the music and smiling at me because our eyes had met. There was no one else in the shinestand and just as I came up even with the stand the record ended and I stopped in my tracks, staring at the girl in a fascinated stupor. Then, without warning, she sang: *"Beautiful, beautiful brown eyes."*

Wow. That did me in, cleaned me out, and I realized that I was standing

[2] *Reds.* A barbiturate, called Red Devils; so called because of the color of the capsule and because they are reputed to possess a vicious kick.
  [3] *High-siding.* Cutting up. Having fun at the expense of another.

there gaping at her like a country fool. I was really confused and embarrassed and I cut out, completely blowing my cool. And as I split, I saw her cracking up with kicks. It really made me feel good though, and I've always treasured that memory because the incident was so penetrating.

I had quite a different experience during a factional power struggle among the Muslims in San Quentin. A right-wing brother tried to undercut me with a smear tactic: "Brothers," he said to all of us one day, "Brother Eldridge should not be allowed to hold any position until he's been a Muslim for 7 years. He's got the Mark of the Beast on him. Look at his eyes—he's got the devil's eyes."

That startled me and touched a sore spot. A lot of other brothers were also confused. But one of my friends saved the day by pointing out that "many so-called Negroes have funny beast eyes. The devils have mixed us all up. Even the Honorable Elijah Muhammad has light-colored eyes. Brother Malcolm has light-colored eyes. So don't be going around here talking like that because you're only spreading *dis*unity. The Honorable Elijah Muhammad teaches *Unity*. If you call yourself a Muslim, brother, you're going to have to start thinking Positive and put down all that Negative."

The cat had to beat a hasty retreat, but I was bleeding inside.

[Soul on Ice]

Folsom Prison, October 9, 1965

I'm perfectly aware that I'm in prison, that I'm a Negro, that I've been a rapist, and that I have a Higher Uneducation. I never know what significance I'm supposed to attach to these factors. But I have a suspicion that, because of these aspects of my character, "free-normal-educated" people rather expect me to be more reserved, penitent, remorseful, and not too quick to shoot off my mouth on certain subjects. But I let them down, disappoint them, cause them to gape at me in a sort of stupor, as if they're thinking: "You've got your nerve! Don't you realize that you owe a debt to society?" My answer to all such thoughts lurking in their split-level heads, crouching behind their squinting bombardier eyes, is that the blood of Vietnamese peasants has paid off all my debts; that the Vietnamese people, afflicted with a rampant disease called Yankees, through their suffering—as opposed to the "frustration" of fat-assed American geeks safe at home worrying over whether to have bacon, ham, or sausage with their grade-A eggs in the morning, while Vietnamese worry each morning whether the Yankees will gas them, burn them up or blow away their humble pads in a hail of bombs—have cancelled all my I.O.U.'s.

In beginning this, I could just as easily have mentioned other facets; I could have said: I'm perfectly aware that I'm tall, that I'm skinny, that I need a shave, and that I'm hard-up enough to suck my grandmother's old withered tits, and that I would dig (deeper than deeply) getting *clean* once more—not only in the steambath sense, but in getting sharp as an Esquire square with a Harlem touch—or that I would like to put on a pair of bib overalls and become a Snicker, or that I'd like to leap the whole last mile and grow a beard and don whatever threads the local nationalism might require and comrade with Che Guevara, and share his fate, blazing a new pathfinder's trail through the stymied upbeat brain of the New Left, or how I'd just love to be in Berkeley right now, to roll in that mud, frolic in that sty of funky revolution, to breathe in its heady fumes, and look with roving eyes for a new John Brown, Eugene Debs, a blacker-meaner-keener Malcolm X, a Robert Franklin Williams with less rabbit in his hot blood, an American Lenin, Fidel, a Mao-Mao, A MAO MAO, A MAO MAO . . . All of which is true.

But what matters is that I have fallen in love with my lawyer! Is that surprising? A convict is expected to have a high regard for *anyone* who comes to his aid, who tries to help him and who expends time, energy, and money in an effort to set him free. But can a convict really love a lawyer? It goes against the grain. Convicts hate lawyers. To walk around a prison yard and speak well of a lawyer is to raise the downcast eyebrows of felons who've been bitten by members of the Bar and Grill. Convicts are convinced that lawyers must have a secret little black book which no one else is ever allowed to see, and which schools lawyers in an esoteric morality in which the Highest Good is Treachery, and that to cross one's dumb and trusting client is the noblest of deeds. It was learned by the convicts that I'd gotten busted with some magazines given to me by my lawyer and that I was thrown in the Hole. Convicts smiled knowingly and told me that I had gone for the greasy pig, that my lawyer had set me up, and that if I couldn't see through the plot I was so stupid that I would buy not only the Golden Gate Bridge but some fried ice cream.

It was my turn to smile knowingly. A convict's paranoia is as thick as the prison wall—and just as necessary. Why should we have faith in anyone? Even our wives and lovers whose beds we shared, with whom we shared the tenderest moments and most delicate relations, leave us after a while, put us down, cut us clean aloose and treat us like they hate us, won't even write us a letter, send us a Christmas card every other year, or a quarter for a pack of cigarettes or a tube of toothpaste now and then. All society shows the convict its ass and expects him to kiss it: the convict feels like kicking it or putting a bullet in it. A convict sees man's fangs and claws and learns quickly to bare and unsheath his own, for real and final. To maintain a hold on the ideals and sentiments of Civilization in such circumstances is probably impossible. How much more incredible is it, then, while rooted in this pit, to fall in love, and with a lawyer! Use a lawyer, yes: use anybody. Even tell the lawyer that you're in love. But you will always know when you are lying and even if you could manage to fool the lawyer you could never manage to fool yourself.

And why does it make you sad to see how everything hangs by such thin and whimsical threads? Because you're a dreamer, an incredible dreamer, with a tiny spark hidden somewhere inside you which cannot die, which even you cannot kill or quench and which tortures you horribly because all the odds are against its continual burning; and in the midst of the foulest decay and putrid savagery, this spark speaks to you of beauty, of human warmth and kindness, of goodness, of greatness, of heroism, of martyrdom, and it speaks to you of love.

So I love my lawyer. My lawyer is not an ordinary person. My lawyer is a rebel, a revolutionary, who is alienated fundamentally from the status quo, probably with as great an intensity, conviction and irretrievability as I am alienated from it—and probably with more intelligence, compassion, and humanity. If you read the papers, you are no doubt aware of my lawyer's incessant involvement in agitation against all manifestations of the monstrous evil of our system, such as our intervention in the internal affairs of the Vietnamese people, the invasion of the Dominican Republic by U.S. Marines. And my lawyer defends civil rights demonstrators, sit-iners and the Free Speech students who rebelled against the Kerr-Strong machine at U.C. [University of California at Berkeley]. My love for my lawyer is due, in part, to these activities and involvements, because we are always on the same side of the issues. And I love all my allies. But this, which may be the beginning of an explanation, does not nearly explain what goes on between my lawyer and me.

I suppose that I should be honest and, before going any further, admit that my lawyer is a woman—or maybe I should have held back with that piece of puzzle—a very excellent, unusual and beautiful woman. I know that *she* believes that I do not really love her and that I am confusing a combination of lust and gratitude for love. Lust and gratitude I feel abundantly, but I also love this woman. And I fear that, believing that I do not love her, she will act according to that belief.

At night, I talk with her in my sleep, long dialogues in which she answers back. We alternate in speaking, like the script of a play. And let me say that I don't believe a word she says. While we are talking, I participate and believe everything, taking her word as her bond. But when I awake, I repudiate the conversation and disbelieve her. I awake refreshed, and though my sleep has been restless, I am not tired. Except for a few lost hours in which she slips away and I fall into a deep sleep, I hover on a level between consciousnesss and peace, and the dialogue ensues. It does not bother me now. I have often gone through this when something seizes my mind.

If a man is free, with the usual multiplicity of social relations with individuals of both sexes, it may be that he is incapable of experiencing the total impact of another individual upon himself. The competing influences and conflicting forces of other personalities may dilute one's psychic and emotional perception, to the extent that one does not and cannot receive all that the other person is capable of sending. Our relations with each other in such circumstances are apt to lack depth and substantiality.

Yet I may believe that a man whose soul of emotional apparatus had lain dormant in a deadening limbo of desuetude, is capable of responding from some great sunken well of his being, as though a potent catalyst had been tossed into a critical mass, when an exciting, lovely, and lovable woman enters the range of his feelings. What a deep, slow, torturous, reluctant, frightened stirring! He feels a certain part of himself in a state of flux, as if a bodiless stranger has stolen inside his body, startling him by doing calisthenics, and he feels himself coming slowly back to life. His body chemistry changes and he is flushed with new strength.

When she first comes to him his heart is empty, a desolate place, a dehydrated oasis, unsolaced, and he's craving womanfood, without which sustenance the tension of his manhood has unwound and relaxed. He has imperative need of the kindness, sympathy, understanding, and conversation of a woman, to hear a woman's laughter at his words, to answer her questions and to be answered by her, to look into her eyes, to sniff her primeval fragrance, to hear—with slaughtered ears—the sensuous rustling of frivolous garments as legs are crossed and uncrossed beneath a table, to feel the delicate, shy weight of her hand in his—how painfully and totally aware is he of her presence, her every movement! It is as if one had been left to die beneath a bush on a lonely trail. The sun is hot and the shade of the bush, if not offering an extension of life, offers at least a slowing down of death. And just when one feels the next breath will surely be the last, a rare and rainbow-colored bird alights upon a delicate twig of the bush, and with the magic of melodious trillings and beauty of plumage, charms the dying one back to life. The dying man feels the strength flowing into and through the conduits of his body from the charged atmosphere created by the presence of the bird, and he knows intuitively in his clinging to life that if the bird remains he will regain his strength and health—and live.

[On Malcolm X]

Folsom Prison, June 19, 1965
Sunday is movie day at Folsom Prison and I was sitting in the darkened hulk of Mess Hall No. One, watching Victor Buono in a movie named "The Strangler," when a convict known as Silly Willie came over to where I was sitting and whispered in my ear:

"Brother J sent me in to tell you it just came over the TV that Malcolm X was shot as he addressed a rally in New York."

For a moment the earth seemed to reel in orbit. The skin all over my body tightened up as I gave voice to my immediate thought, "How bad?" I asked.

"The TV didn't say," answered Silly Willie. The distress was obvious in his voice. "We was around in Pipe Alley checking TV when a special bulletin came on. All they said was Malcolm X was shot and they were rushing him to the hospital."

"Thanks," I said to Silly Willie. I felt his hand on my shoulder in a reassuring gesture as he faded away in the darkness. On the screen before me Victor Buono had a woman by the throat and was frantically choking the last gasping twitches of life out of her slumping body. I was thinking that if Malcolm's wounds were not too serious, that if he recovered, the shooting might prove to be a blessing in disguise. It would focus more intensified attention on him and create a windfall of sympathy and support for him throughout America's black ghettos, and so put more power into his hands. The possibility that the wounds may have been fatal, that as I sat there Malcolm was already dead, was excluded from my mind.

After the movie ended, as I filed outside in the long line of convicts and saw the shocked, wild expression on Brother J's face, I still could not believe that Malcolm X was dead. He's dead, their faces said, although not one of them spoke a word. As we stood there in silence, two Negro inmates walked by and one of them said to us, "That's a goddamn shame how they killed that man! Of all people, why'd they kill Malcolm? Whyn't they kill some of them Uncle Tomming M.F.'s? I wish I could get my hands on whoever did it." And he walked away, talking and cursing animatedly to his buddy.

Malcolm X had a special meaning for black convicts. A former prisoner himself, he had risen from the lowest depths to great heights. For this reason he was a symbol of hope, a model for thousands of black convicts who found themselves trapped in the vicious PPP cycle: prison-parole-prison. One thing that judges, policemen, and prison administrators never seem to have understood, and for which they certainly do not make any allowances, is that Negro convicts, rather than see themselves as criminals and perpetrators of misdeeds, look upon themselves as prisoners of war, the victims of a vicious, dog-eat-dog social system that is so heinous by its very nature as to cancel out their own malefactions: in the jungle there is no right or wrong.

Rather than owing and paying a debt to society, Negro prisoners feel that they are being abused, that their imprisonment is simply another form of the oppression they have known all their lives.

America's penology does not take this into account. Malcolm X did, and black convicts know that the ascension to power of Malcolm X or a man like him would eventually have revolutionized penology in America. Malcolm delivered a merciless and damning indictment of prevailing penology. It is only a matter of time until the question of the prisoner's debt to society versus society's debt to the prisoner is injected forcefully into national and state politics, into the civil and human rights struggle, and into the consciousness of the body politic. It is an explosive issue that goes to the very root of America's system of justice.

The Black Muslim movement was destroyed the moment Elijah cracked the whip over Malcolm's head, because it was not the Black Muslim movement itself that was so irresistibly appealing to true believers. It was the awakening into self-consciousness of 20,000,000 Negroes which was so compelling. Malcolm X articulated their aspirations better than any other man of our time. When he spoke under the banner of Elijah Muhammad he was irresistible. When he spoke under his own banner he was still irresistible. If he had become a Quaker, a Catholic, or a Seventh Day Adventist, or a Sammy Davis-style Jew, and if he had continued to give voice to the mute ambitions in the black man's soul, his message would still have been triumphant: because what was great was not Malcolm X but the truth he uttered.

The truth which Malcolm uttered had vanquished the whole passel of so-called Negro leaders and spokesmen who trifle and compromise with truth in order to curry favor with the white power structure. He was stopped, in the only way such a man can be stopped, in the same way that the enemies of the Congolese people had to stop Lumumba, by the same method that exploiters, tyrants, and parasitical oppressors have always crushed the legitimate strivings of peoples for freedom, justice, and equality—by murder, assassination and mad dog butchery.

So now Malcolm is no more. The bootlickers, Uncle Toms, lackeys and stooges of the white power structure have done their best to denigrate Malcolm, to root him out of his people's heart, to tarnish his memory. But their million-worded lies fall on deaf ears. As Ossie Davis so eloquently expressed it in his immortal eulogy of Malcolm: "If you knew him you would know why we must honor him: Malcolm was our manhood, our living, black manhood! This was his meaning to his people. And in honoring him, we honor the best in ourselves."

We shall have our manhood. We shall have it or the earth will be leveled by our attempts to gain it.

Sincerely, Eldridge Cleaver

Mexican-Americans

MARJORIE FALLOWS

The Mexican-American Laborers: A Different Drummer?

An advertisement in The New Yorker *magazine in the summer of 1968 began boldly, "WE SAW A MAN. NOT A MEXICAN-AMERICAN. The day we saw Ray Baldenegro we saw a man with a good brain and capable hands." The caption, along with a picture of the smiling subject, said that he and his brother-in-law had enrolled in a Western Electric training school for machinists. Both men are now successful lathe operators. "Any company would be lucky to find them," the message concluded.*

It is indeed noteworthy to see American manufacturers making sincere efforts to encourage members of this minority group to utilize their skills in industry. Just a decade ago Ozzie G. Simmons ("The Mutual Images and Expectations of Anglo-Americans and Mexican-Americans," Daedalus, Spring, 1961) wrote that Anglo-Americans in the Southwest labelled Mexican-Americans "improvident, irresponsible, childlike, and indolent." Mexican-Americans are not yet considered the equals of whites in the region but attempts are being made to alter the plight of "one of America's most overlooked, neglected and poverty-stricken minorities."

In the following essay Marjorie Fallows explores the nuances of Mexican-American culture and the special difficulties this minority has in American society.

Since Mexican-Americans have seldom inspired public interest outside the Southwest, it was an occasion for wonder when, in the spring of 1966, major reports appeared in news media ranging from *The Wall Street Journal* to *Life Magazine,* describing this group as one of America's most overlooked, neglected and poverty-stricken minorities, now finally on the move. The image that triggered public sympathy was of a straggling band of Mexican-American grape pickers making the dogged two hundred and fifty mile march on foot from Delano, California to the state capitol in Sacramento, climaxing an eight month strike to protest their right to organize and bargain for better wages. The "grape

s movement," started from within the ranks of the Mexican-American
nt laborers by their own Cesar Chavez, not only caught the sympathy of
l church, student, and civil rights groups in California but made its impact
he national consciousness when Schenley, the leading grape grower in the
region, finally recognized the right of the predominantly Mexican-American
farm workers to bargain through their new National Farm Workers Association.

That this breakthrough in organizing and establishing the right to bargain
among the depressed migratory farm workers should have occurred at all was
remarkable enough, for these have been workers generally characterized as both
unorganized and unorganizable. That the impetus should have come from
within the Mexican-American group itself has seemed doubly unexpected, for
by tradition and inclination these have been people more willing to accept fate
than to challenge it. Yet it is not as unintelligible as we might suppose if we
investigate the framework within which Mexican-American acculturation is taking place in the Southwest, and if we place the "grape picker's movement" in
the context of the larger society to which it has appealed and to which it re-
sponds. Ultimately the Mexican-Americans face the need to find a place within
this larger society—highly organized, predominantly urban and industrial—for
which they have been grossly unprepared by anything in their past experience.
The success of the "grape picker's movement" may offer some clues to how such
a place may be found.

If we recall the characteristics of the rural folk society from which these
people were thrust by gradual loss of the means to support themselves, and picture then the *colonias* and *pueblitas* of the Southwest where they gathered for
psychological support, or the migratory labor camps where they worked in predominantly ethnic gangs, it is not hard to see why the nearly four million Mexican-Americans in the Southwest have clung to their Spanish language so long,
have retained their Mexican cultural values so long, have failed to make what
we have come to regard as normal steps toward acculturation. They have never
really emerged from isolation. If they have not rejected the past to the extent
that other immigrant groups have, it has been largely because they have not
come into significant contact with an intelligible and accessible substitute. The
psychological costs of culture abandonment may be heavy, even when one sees
an adequate substitute. When one does not, the costs may be so great that life
no longer has dignity and purpose. Yet a reality of the Mexican peasant heritage
least understood by Americans is that life may have dignity and purpose, that
prestige may be won and the good life lived, in terms quite different from ours.

Our assumption has usually been that our terms must be accepted by the
incoming immigrant before he could begin to share the fruits of American affluence. It was the price immigrants paid, and the majority have seemed content
with the bargain. But the Mexican-American has been more wary, and until ten
years ago it was logical to predict that, because of this wariness, he would suffer
semi-permanent exclusion from American society. Has it really been he who
has changed so much in a decade that we can alter this prediction? Probably
not. It may be instead the climate of opinion, the level of self-awareness, the
sense of direction in the United States that have been changing. There are at
least enough tentative signs of change to suggest that the Mexican-American
may emerge from his ethnic isolation into a climate more understanding of his
own values.

The lowest social and economic levels, of which this group is clearly a part, are suddenly of considerable concern to Americans at large. They are being "understood" as never before, and in this surge of "understanding" the Mexican-Americans emerge from anonymity with a rather favorable image—unobtrusively hugging the Mexican border, caught by the rhythm of a different drummer. That they have been out of step they have sensed, and we have reminded them. But as we take stock of ourselves in a flush of self-consciousness we are reminded by those like William Madsen who know them well that we could learn much from our Mexican-American citizens about family solidarity, child rearing, respect patterns and religious values. These words touch the quick of our own fears, for in precisely these areas we feel ourselves most insecure. The question we put to ourselves in candid moments is whether we can have the best of a material abundance and still retain the spiritual values to give it meaning. And if so, how? This is precisely the dilemma many Mexican-Americans have been facing, and for want of an answer they have moved slowly and have accepted the second-class citizenship that was the price. It is only recently that national concern has discovered them and begun to ask questions about their future.

Just what have we been expecting of immigrant groups as they move toward assimilation? The loss of any identifying ethnic differences that might set them apart from the "average" American? If so, the Mexican-American has little to hope for, since he is marked off from the dominant American pattern by his own unique blend of Spanish and Indian in racial type as well as in culture, religion and language. He cannot easily merge into the white, Protestant, English-speaking group of Anglo-Americans with whom he comes in contact in the Southwest. Yet should merging even be the goal? Are we perhaps ready to recognize that the "melting pot" described an assumption rather than a reality in American social life? That there are immigrant groups of long residence in this country who have neither melted nor merged in the areas of their personal and private social lives, yet have still found a secure place in the economic and political sphere? And is this not a legitimate alternative to our earlier assumption that there is something wrong with any group that does not merge on all levels? It is the rigidity of the demand for either total assimilation or subordination that the Mexican-American questions when he says "This country should be big enough to allow us the freedom to be different without being oppressed."

But just how different can a minority group be without inviting oppression? Can its value system be diametrically opposed to that of the host culture, a mirror-image of it? Observers of Mexican-American life in the Southwest point out that the demands of an urban industrial economy will require significant shifts in traditional values for these people, if they would make even nominal headway in America, for the Mexican-American characteristically values the present in contrast to planning for a better future; he values "being," with its spontaneous expression of impulses, in contrast to "doing" for the sake of accomplishing something; he values a dignified acceptance of life rather than efforts to change and control it; he looks for guidance and support from someone in authority in contrast to coveting individualistic independence. Even where individuals may have adopted American values, the group as a whole has clung to the security offered by traditional ways—ways which have seemed hopelessly backward to the majority of Americans in the Southwest.

typing comes easily in response to such stark contrasts in outlook. he Anglo been the only one to criticize those undesirable "foreign" which he believes to be virtually bred in and unalterable. If he sees the Mexican-American as lazy, dirty, unpredictable and childishly willing himself when there is little to enjoy, the Mexican-American in turn has viewed the typical Anglo as exploitive, willing to sacrifice his family and his honesty for money, and as having little regard for spiritual values. The stereotypes sound surprisingly familiar, for they reflect the images the successful middle classes and the unsuccessful lower classes often have of each other. In the Southwest, where the majority in the lower class are indeed Mexican-American, it has been easy to equate the culture of the poor with the culture of Mexico, and to regard the defense mechanisms of the group as part of their unalterable racial and cultural inheritance. Yet even supposing we are willing to recognize that poverty develops its own rationale which undergirds and makes bearable the life of the poor wherever they may be, is there any reason to suppose that the culture of poverty could be assimilated more easily than the culture of Mexico? Perhaps there is. The Mexican-American may not have changed from the person he was, but our viewpoint about him is altered when we see him as a product of more or less permanent poverty, rather than as a product of racial or cultural inadequacy.

Inchoate and lacking in focus as our current war on poverty may be in many areas, it has provided for many the first awareness that the poor are not necessarily poor because they deserve to be poor. For a group like the Mexican-American is may also have provided a first awareness that poverty is not inevitable. But if not inevitable, what alternative do we offer? Money and influence through which to acquire the social status he is now denied? He would quickly admit the desirability of enough money to share in the fallout of American technological progress, for in this area he clearly sees America as superior, but his own definition of wealth is something to use and enjoy, not something to invest or convert into prestige or make an end in itself. As for power and influence, these are to be distrusted in one's self as much as in others. One does not seek power; one is occasionally awarded it or entrusted with it as a mark of high esteem, but it is a byproduct. As for social status—status in whose terms? The Mexican-American sees status in the Anglo world as something to be bought or seized. In his own world it is something to be won through adherence to the ideals of the group: loyalty to one's own, devotion to the family, a dignified acceptance and appreciation of things as they are because this is the way God has planned it. He who achieves status and respect in his own group virtually cuts himself off from achieving it in Anglo terms.

Yet there are some who have wanted it in Anglo terms and who have achieved enough wealth, or power, or prestige to illustrate to the rest that they too can dream a different dream. The reaction toward this mobile group may be to reject them as having gone *inglisado,* but evidence of success does not go unnoticed, even when it is denigrated. There are even some, like Cesar Chavez with his "grape picker's movement," who have managed to achieve power and status in both Mexican-American and Anglo terms at the same time.

It becomes a matter of significance, then, to ask why so few leaders of Chavez' stature have emerged within the Mexican-American group. Here we find, throughout the Southwest, that those who have advanced themselves have tended to forsake their identity with the Mexican-American goup. Some have dispersed to Midwestern industrial centers like St. Paul, Chicago and Detroit, where relatively small clusters of Mexican-Americans suffer little of the special discrimination produced by their denser concentration in the Southwest. Still others have moved out of the group socially, rather than spatially, a movement made possible by the existence of an old established upper class, dating back to the days of Spanish conquest, which identifies itself as Spanish-American, and which has traditionally remained aloof from both the Mexican peasantry and the Anglo upper class. A Mexican-American whose racial characteristics are Castilian enough and whose educational level is high enough, can identify with this respected group, whether or not he actually joins it socially. Of importance to the Mexican-American community is the fact that both these forms of movement away from the group represent serious losses, both in potential leadership and in models for successful adaptation to American life. As for an emerging middle class which may have improved its lot while remaining within the Mexican-American group, we find little evidence that such a class has reached significant numbers or status to assume effective leadership.

Indeed, since leadership is difficult to assume in a group which is traditionally resistant to, and suspicious of, any attempts at organization, it has been lack of leaders which has consistently been the greatest obstacle to effective improvement of the Mexican-American's lot. The form of leadership the Mexican peon best understood was lost with the breakdown of the patrón-peon relationship, familiar throughout rural Mexico and in those northern reaches of the colonial empire which later became the American Southwest. The land-owning patrón had been expected to take responsibility for the entire well-being of the peons and their families, providing employment, social and economic security, and leadership for those who did the manual work. The peons, in return, had been expected to give complete loyalty and cooperation, often to get necessary communal tasks done. Stripped of this secure and dependent position, the Mexican-American still often reflects the values and attitudes appropriate to the lost relationship, for he prefers to leave major decisions to those with the prominence or wealth or political power equivalent to a patrón's, feeling that such a person is best equipped to take the responsibility involved. He still prefers friendly person-to-person relationships in a stable hierarchical social system, where mutual obligations and statuses are clearly spelled out. He resists those social and cultural changes which require personal initiative in a competitive world.

In terms of these values and attitudes, Cesar Chavez' success in organizing the grape pickers in Delano, California becomes intelligible and significant, for where other leaders and organizers, working within the American value system, failed to inspire interest or action among the clearly exploited migratory group, he achieved unexpected success by operating within their value system and providing a form of leadership they understood. It was no easy task, given both the militant resistance of the large growers in Southern California to any efforts to organize the farm workers and the suspicion with which the workers themselves viewed such efforts. Nor was there any guarantee of success, even as the group staged its last-ditch march to Sacramento. Father Vizzard, Chairman of the National Council on Agricultural Life and Labor, who had been in close touch with Chavez and the work he was doing, told a group of students on April 1st that the strikers were near the end of their resources then, and if the march failed to bring results he didn't know what they would do. Chavez had been slowly developing the National Farm Workers Association since 1962, leading to this cooperative action, but much of the success of the eight month strike stemmed from the quality of his leadership. Father Vizzard described him as "one of only two really charismatic leaders I have ever met," suggesting that the devotion of the workers was so great that even though Chavez had been developing leadership among others in the group and had several potential leaders who might replace him, "if anything happened to Cesar, I'm not sure the men would give their loyalty to anyone else. The whole thing might collapse." As it turned out the strikers won their significant victory nine days later when Schenley recognized their union's right to bargain.

What, if anything, did this strike actually accomplish for the Mexican-Americans in the Southwest? At the very least, it illustrated that these people are not unorganizable and that they are capable of enormous massed strength if they find leadership they can trust and to which they can give their loyalty. Of primary importance, perhaps, in understanding the conditions that led to the organization of this "unorganizable" group is the fact that the grape pickers had established a home base in Delano, where they put down tenuous roots. Their social organization was not one of the migratory camps but one of the town and valley. Cesar Chavez had a relatively stable group with that same potential for cooperative community action that would have existed in the Mexican village under the leadership of a patrón. He operated, in fact, within the patrón-peon pattern, but in a way curiously adapted to the American environment. The patrón, it must be understood, does not win the loyalty of the group simply because he is well-liked. He fills an institutionalized role, and the success of the patrón-peon relationship depends on how well each fulfills the reciprocal obligations involved. Yet Chavez was not an established patrón, nor could he personally provide any of the social or economic securities attendant on this role. He could only help to build the organization which would do it in his place. Such was the character of the National Farm Workers Association which he founded. We need hardly be reminded that he could not initially have won the respect of the migrants had he not shown those qualities by which status is measured in Mexican-American eyes and for which loyalty is given: unwillingness to seek self-aggrandizement, and devotion to the group. His personal charisma and his training under Saul Alinsky were vital assets too, but his National Farm Workers Association won the support of the migrants because he was the "right" kind of leader and it was the "right" kind of organization.

To understand what kind of patrón the migrants of Delano needed requires a glimpse of the conditions under which they worked. For the 500,000 agricultural workers in California's largest industry, the average yearly income has been one sixth that of other industrial workers. They have had no minimum wage, no holidays, paid vacations, sick leave, unemployment insurance or pension plan. The large growers who hired them frequently violated child labor laws and consistently denied them the right to collective bargaining. They have been the only industry in America exempt from the Taft-Hartley Act and from the jurisdiction of the National Labor Relations Board. It was no mere literary fancy that dubbed this "the 'grapes of wrath' strike," for the massive social legislation passed since the Depression had never touched this group.

The National Farm Workers Association, in response to the migrants' desperate need, operated more as a welfare cooperative than as a labor union. It provided a credit union, cooperative food store, drug store and service station; ran a newspaper; provided legal help, a burial insurance program and a grievance committee to investigate job misrepresentation. The Association itself, as far as it could, provided social and economic security within the social and economic insecurity of the occupation, filling the institutionalized role of the patrón. But to Cesar Chavez as its symbol went the loyalty due the patrón as a man, for here was no outside organizer but one of the group. It was not, then, so much that the Mexican-American migrants were unorganizable as that the right vehicle for cooperative action had not been offered under the right leadership.

Still another, if seemingly less spectacular, gain emerged from the events that led to the march on Sacramento. The cooperation required to put the National Farm Workers Association on its feet and to survive an eight month strike brought an awareness that social and economic gains need not be solely in terms of mobility out of and away from the group. We have seen that both spatial and social distance have tended to separate those who "succeeded" from those who did not, but the National Farm Workers Association represented a group effort requiring minimal change of established patterns. The members, far from having to strike out on their own with all the attendant personal risks, made their bid for the right to bargain within the security of the group. Once this right was won, other gains might follow.

That this sequence of events—from group effort to collective gains which would have expanding and beneficial repercussions for the group—did not seem self-evident to the Mexican-Americans shows clearly in the reluctance with which they entered the strike. The Mexican peasant has had little personal experience with the successful operation of any revolutionary action. He has lived under one authoritarian rule after another, and even the gains in the Revolution of 1910-20 left many of the peasants untouched. The large landowners of California, enjoying much the same monopolistic control as the wealthy landowners with whom the Mexicans had been familiar, represented a formidable adversary. Like other agriculturists in the Southwest, they had for years employed *braceros* brought up from Mexico under government auspices to work for less than the resident Mexican-Americans. The official ending of the *bracero* program in the fall of 1964 had given the local workers that first leverage which was a prerequisite for action, but the National Farm Workers Association still might not have made the decision to strike had it not been pushed. On September 8, 1965, the AFL-CIO farm labor organizers called a strike in Delano for the predominantly Filipino agricultural workers they had been able to organize, and rather than let this strike fail, as it seemed almost certain to do, Chavez formed a joint committee with the AFL-CIO leadership and joined the strike. From that time on, the character of the strike was molded almost entirely by Cesar Chavez.

Father Vizzard described the reluctance with which this decision was reached: "He didn't want the strike then. He didn't think they were ready to risk it. It was a forced choice." It is not hard to understand the hesitancy, if we recall the Mexican-American's desire for stability and his dislike of aggressive competition, if we recall the strength of his opponent and the loss of morale that might follow a failure. For such modest demands as a minimum wage of $1.40 an hour, as opposed to the old average of $1.20, "standard" working conditions, and the right to negotiate, the risks were great. There was danger of losing what small security the National Farm Workers Association had been able to provide.

In recognition of these risks, a frank appeal went out to the wider community for support of the strikers. This is vital for understanding what the strike accomplished, for the accomplishment would have been significant for the Mexican-Americans whether their immediate demands had been met by the growers or not. Had the growers provided the economic and social security needed by the migrants they could have counted on the loyalty of their workers, for the dependent position is not onerous for the Mexican-American provided the reciprocal obligations are met by both parties. But clearly the growers neither understood nor took any interest in this type of relationship. It was to others in California that the strikers appealed for support: church and Civil Rights groups, students at Berkeley, labor unions, SNCC. From these groups came picketers, funds, speakers, cooperation in establishing an effective boycott of the growers' products, and ultimately those volunteers who swelled the ranks of the Mexican-Americans as they marched on Sacramento.

Protestant, Catholic, and Jewish clergymen joined to issue a strong statement calling for the same kind of "active support that . . . Christians and Jews have given to the basic demands for justice for Negroes in the South." The Mexican-Americans had finally tied into the growing public awareness that the South does not have a monopoly on discrimination! In the support of those liberal forces already mobilized in defense of Civil Rights, they found a more effective patrón than the growers could ever have been. The big growers like Schenley and DiGiorgio, cast in the role of villains, found themselves facing more than a pitiful group of protesting Mexican-American migrant workers, for their land monopolies came under fire in the press and in Congress.

Now, along with the growers, it may be that others of us in America face a need to answer some questions about ourselves. We have seen ourselves described as having values that are diametrically opposed to those of the Mexican-Americans. We take the initiative in planning for a better future, we are told. Yet we have a Social Security program that has ironically covered almost everyone in the nation *except* groups like the migrant workers. We value "doing" for the sake of accomplishing something, we are told. Yet we are facing the economic necessity of entering the job market late and retiring from it early in order to make the available jobs go around. (How well equipped are we to appreciate "being"—to use our increasing leisure?) We value efforts to change and control life, we are told. Yet we are now in the process of relinquishing control to the federal government in such areas as health, education and welfare. We value individualism and independence, we are told. Yet our economic affairs have become so massive and complex that businessmen are more than ever dependent on the federal government to manipulate the economy for continued prosperity.

The burden of this comparison is not to suggest that our self-image has been wrong, but merely to suggest that these values which we have held up to the Mexican-American as characteristic may be values we are moving away from. David Riesman has spoken of the Mexican-Americans as examples of those vanishing remnants of tradition-directed peoples whose resentment and resistance to the demands of the host culture often drain them of emotional energy and make them appear lazy or apathetic. Since the official culture of schools, businesses, and public agencies is still inner-directed, the contrast in values appears to them extreme, and the requirements of such radical adjustment produce strain and confusion. In a society which has always valued individual initiative and autonomy, hard work and thrift, as well as freedom from government interference, the growing need to adjust to a more leisure-oriented consumption economy produces strain and confusion for the very people Mexican-Americans are urged to emulate. The big growers may well fall in this category.

It is those whom Riesman describes as other-directed who have taken up the cause of the poor, for they have shed much of the scarcity psychology of the inner-directed group. Being themselves in search of values consistent with what they feel to be a new time, they may think they have found in the culture of poverty some attitudes and values with which they can be in sympathy. For in the poor's defense against the desolation of never winning, they may feel they have found a defense against the desolation of having won. Having heard a different drummer themselves, they may be more in sympathy with the right of others to step to the music which they hear.

Today, in spite of recent publicity, the Mexican-Americans in the Southwest still remain a group little known in the United States, and still without champions of the stature of those who have spoken out for the Negro. Yet it may well be that they will never need champions in quite the same way, for we have begun to recognize the injustice in the kinds of demands we have made of these remnant groups that are largely unacculturated and chronically poor. We have demanded proof of their ability to succeed in our terms, without having provided them with the economic and social supports with which to achieve success—supports on which the rest of the nation has come to depend. The "grape picker's movement" reminded us that the Mexican-Americans sense this injustice and are ready to band together to ask that something be done. The response to the strike indicates that we within the nation sense that such injustice must be dealt with—not just because we see the Mexican-Americans as a group in need of special protection, but because we see them as citizens in need of equal protection.

Puerto Ricans

OSCAR LEWIS

I'm Proud to Be Poor

There are 1½ million Puerto Ricans in the United States and two-thirds of them live in New York City and environs. They are the Jews and the Italians and the Irish and the Poles of yesteryear. They live, for the most part, in squalid tenements or institution-like housing developments, work in sweatshops and factories or as hospital orderlies or restaurant menials, and send their children to public schools where both students and teachers have difficulty in crossing the cultural barriers. Like the earlier immigrants a number of first generation Americans are "making it" and the expectation is that with the passage of time the white Puerto Ricans will assimilate as have other groups. Although color prejudice was not a significant factor in Puerto Rico, it is crucial on the mainland. As a result, lighter skinned Puerto Ricans have an easier time adjusting to the dominant culture than their darker brothers. (Piri Thomas, in his autobiographical tale, Down These Mean Streets, *poignantly reveals how his dark complexion plagued him during youth and adolescence.) Some white Puerto Ricans have left their ghettos and have succeeded as politicians, writers, athletes, lawyers, and college teachers. Herman Badillo is perhaps the best known member of the group in New York City but baseball players like Roberto Clemente and Orlando Cepeda have national reputations.*

Since most Puerto Ricans are New Yorkers it is apt for us to include here a chapter from anthropologist Oscar Lewis' classic La Vida (The Life), *which describes the life of one family that migrated from San Juan to the mainland. In a study based on tape-recorded interviews Lewis conveys the family's values, conflicts, hopes, and disappointments. "Simplicio, I'm Proud to be Poor," the selection reproduced below, is the story of one member.*

Well, here I am in New York and I'm doing fine. I earn sixty-five dollars a week in a *finishing* factory where they do all sorts of work—buttons, belts, everything except *coats.* I do many kinds of jobs. I sew with machines, make ladies' *scarfs,* big silk buttons, well, everything. I work very hard there, it's true, but I do it because they are considerate of me.

At first my job was *el delivery,* walking all over everywhere with a big suitcase, eight hours a day, for forty-five dollars a week. Soledad showed me how to take *el subway* to Manhattan where the factory is, and after that they just turned me loose. It's lucky that the streets in New York are numbered and easy to find. So I learned as I walked around, making my deliveries. I often got lost. But when I did, I just wandered around until I found my way back. It took me about a month to learn to go places on *el subway.* I got lost there, too, but that was plain stupidity. In my hurry I often caught the wrong train. But early rising has never hastened the dawn.

That's all I did when I started working there, *el delivery.* But I didn't mind because I know that if you don't have schooling you go down instead of up when you first come here. That's what many Puerto Ricans won't do and that's why they give themselves up to a life of vice. Because you feel lower than other people when you have to take a job as a delivery boy. And that might make you turn to stealing or to taking drugs, it might lead you to quit your job and become a tramp. And then you'd be a failure for sure. Because here in New York if you don't work, you don't eat. This isn't Puerto Rico, where if the neighbor sits down to a meal he'll send a plate of food over to you. Here people, even the Puerto Ricans, throw out food rather than give it away. That's because people change when they came here, on account of always having to think about working. That makes you use your mind, think of tomorrow, you know. If I have twenty dollars to last me all week, I can't go out and spend ten now. Because I wouldn't be spending only today's money but also tomorrow's and the next day's. And when the money's gone, there's nobody you can turn to for more. So we become used to that and lose our own customs little by little.

My *bosso* is a Jew, like most factory owners in New York. Those people expect you to work hard. But if you do a good job they're swell, because after a time they'll do any favor you ask them for. They never say no to you. Whenever I tell my *boss,* "I need this," he gives it to me. Right now, they often give me buttons for my wife and sister to cover. The pay is a nickel per button. Last week they covered fourteen hundred buttons. That's about eighty dollars, I think. My *boss* has even told me, of his own free will, that if I get myself a bigger apartment he'll help me. I want to do it but Flora doesn't. And after all, why should I pay more than seventeen dollars a week I'm paying now for a place for Flora, Gabi and me? But that just shows you how good the *boss* is to me. He trusts me, too. He leaves me the keys and I am the one who closes the factory and opens it in the morning.

I've never been absent once in the year I've worked there. And I've never been late, either, in spite of the cold and the distance. This isn't Puerto Rico, where every place is near; it takes me at least half an hour to get from my home to the factory. I always get there an hour ahead of time. That's why I can read *El Imparcial* and chat with my friends awhile before starting work. At seven forty-five I start working, and I'm happy to do so. Sweeping the place isn't part of my job but I like to have everything clean before I start. After that, I change my shirt and settle down to sew *scarfs* on the sewing machine. I stick to that until *el bosso* sends me out to deliver packages.

The only thing I don't like about my job is the way *el bosso's* father comes around to hurry us. But I know him well enough to speak frankly. So I say to him, in English, *"I'm not coming to work to kill myself."* El bosso doesn't say a word. He's the old man's son but they're Jews and have their own customs. It doesn't seem strange to them that a son should order his own father around. And fathers treat their children like strangers.

They also have the custom of saving money. They won't eat a lollipop so as not to waste the stick! And they spit on coins for good luck so they'll get more money. For them, work is the thing. They kill themselves working, week in and week out. When they go out, they go alone. They never make love to women or anything like that.

For that reason, most of them are rich and able to send their children to school to get a good education. When the kids graduate and grow up, their father says to them, "We have such and such an amount of money. This is my share and this is yours, to work with or enjoy now, as you wish. Only remember, if you go broke you'll have to take a job with me like any other employee." It's as if they weren't very close to each other as a family. As if they don't feel they have a duty to help a relative who's badly off. That's the way they are; I don't know why. Maybe it's because they suffered so much because Hitler didn't like them. Hitler killed twenty million Jews, including newborn babies, for having killed God. Hitler was bad. He took no pity on anybody.

Look here, they say a lot of things about the Jews. That they killed God and spat on him and nailed him on the cross. But that's not their fault. Because the ones who killed God all died ages ago. There's not a single one of them left. All that's over and done with and it isn't important now.

They say that God died for us. Everywhere you go they tell you that. But how could he have died for us when we're Puerto Ricans and Christ never went to Puerto Rico? God didn't die in Puerto Rico, so it couldn't have been for us.

It isn't true that the Jews are bad. The trouble is that they have been labeled by history. But they are really good. Of course it's true they don't believe in God but they do have a religion. They believe in Moses, who saved them from a land where they were held as slaves. And they have churches of their own where they pray and sing. They don't have saints but they have everything else. And those people have been good to me. They have given me the chance to earn a lot of money. The only reason I don't earn even more is because I don't want to. I don't like to work *overtime*. Sometimes *el bosso* asks me to go to work Saturday and Sunday but I don't want to do that. I don't like to drive myself too hard.

Sometimes I get to thinking and I say, "Hell, it's a good thing I wasn't born rich." I wouldn't have enjoyed it. Because those people have everything, they have nothing to do with their time. Hey, I'm proud to be poor! We poor people may gossip about each other, but we're good-hearted. And after all, the rich depend on the poor and the poor on the rich. We're all flesh and blood, and when we die we're all stuck into a hole.

I would rather my wife didn't work outside the house, but Flora is ambitious that way. She leaves for work at seven in the morning and gets home at five-thirty every evening. I don't like that, because if I have a woman, it's so she can take care of my needs. Now my pants are all unpressed. Before, when she stayed at home, Flora kept my things nice, and the house was always clean and neat. Her working is no advantage to me in any way; I never see a cent of her wages. In fact, I never have asked how much she earns. When I get paid I give her the money to pay the bills, fifty dollars a week for rent, electricity and food. So Flora's money doesn't do anybody any good. We're going to have a big fight about that someday. I don't spy on her or anything, but I like to keep my woman at home.

With what I earn, I'm sure of a home, food, clothes, and everything. I mean, I feel more settled here because I have a home where I rule. That's something I never managed to have in Puerto Rico. There I was like a waif. Nothing in the house was my own. Here, everything I have is my own, so I think of the future. I have responsibilities, see? I live with Flora, who is a good woman and satisfies me. So I have to make sure I have a decent life and that my woman doesn't ever have to go hungry.

It's true we have our arguments and all that, because when I buy a gift for her she never likes it. I always like the things she gives me, at least I never let her know any different. We quarrel, too, because she doesn't like me to go out with my own relatives. But I do as I please, no matter what she says.

What really drives her wild is my going out with other women. When she finds out she slaps my face. I control myself so as not to hit back too hard. She's suffered a lot, you see, because her first husband was a drunk. Fontánez gave her money, but he left the house on Thursday afternoon and never showed up until the following Tuesday. I mean, he never gave her love or anything of the kind. I have given her a little love and she has been good to me. With her advice and by controlling me, she has made a man of me. When I met her I was a street urchin. I didn't even wear underclothes. She made me wear them, instructed me, taught me how to dress. And then I'd go out with my girl friends and come back two days later, with lipstick on my clothes and kiss marks all over!

In spite of all that Flora has done for me, I won't marry her. If you marry a woman legally you have to stay with her even if it doesn't work out. You can't remarry. If you fall in love with another woman, you can't have her because you're married to the one before and she's the one who gives the orders. Of course, it's true that if you marry under the law the woman belongs more to you. But there's something forced about it. A man and a woman who marry legally have to put up with each other, no matter what. Suppose I wanted to divorce a woman and she didn't love me either, but refused, out of spite, to let me go. I couldn't do a thing about it. And one couldn't kill her or anything like that. I'd have to stay with her simply because she was my *missus*. And she couldn't leave me because I'd be her husband.

Flora and I stay together for love, because we do love each other. We can both be sure of that because we are under no obligation to stay together. If we weren't in love, each would go his own way. When I get to be thirty-five and, God willing, I have children, then I'll marry. By then I can be perfectly sure of what I want. But not now. I'm only twenty-one and I don't know what life may have in store for me.

Flora's family likes me and is good to me. There's not a two-faced one in the bunch except for that brother of hers. I tell him my secrets and he runs to repeat them to my wife. I spoke to him about it once. "You know how Flora is. Don't play that game of making my wife jealous. I don't go stirring up trouble at your house. I always show you the same face, I'm not changeable or a hypocrite. As I treat you today, I will always treat you." I haven't spoken to him since. I know myself and I don't want to risk getting mad at him. I'm not what you would call a violent man. I think before I act. But if I'm pushed beyond a certain point, I lose control of myself and don't know what I do.

I don't like to fight. Not me. I like to treat other people with respect and have them respect me too. But sometimes people like to make fools of others and lots of people have tried to make a fool of me. I won't stand for that. There's only one way anybody can make a fool of me—by being nice and getting around me that way. I'll do anything for someone who's good to me but you can't get anything out of me by force. And if anyone tries it, I'll get even. That's why I try not to get into a spot where I'll lose my temper, and I'm trying to break away from my old life. That's another thing I owe to Flora. She has helped me make a decent life for myself. Just think, all my old friends are in jail now, Pipo, Benito, Geño, Johnny, El Indio, the whole bunch except me. I'm the only one who's come up to New York.

Up here in New York the family doesn't mean the same as it does in Puerto Rico. No. Here you go to stay at the house of a relative and they're fond as can be of you, for the first few days. After that they kick you. You can't do like you do in Puerto Rico, go into a relative's house and say, "Let me have a clean shirt, this one's dirty," and put on the shirt and go your way. Not here. I have gone to my sister and said, "Soledad, lend me one of your husband's coats." And she has answered, "No, I won't. Why should I go around lending things?"

Like when I first came to New York, I went to stay with Felícita. I was only sixteen then and I had left my woman behind in San Juan. Felícita threw her arms around me when I came; she was happy to see me. After a few days I got work and I always gave Fela fifteen dollars on payday. But she got real nasty about it; she thought I ought to turn over my whole pay check to her. She'd curse me and she never gave me anything to eat. If I happened to open the refrigerator she got mad. She's always been that way. When I got home, tired, at five o'clock, she never said, "Here's your dinner." So I went out again and came back about seven after eating a good meal at a restaurant. Sometimes I spent as much as ten dollars a week on food. And I had to pay to send all my clothes to *el laundry* too.

One week I sent Flora some money and Felícita got angry. She refused to take the money I gave her and she told me to get the hell out of her house. Then Edmundo, my brother-in-law, said I had to leave, and Felícita, my own sister, didn't speak up for me.

To show you how Felícita is: one night when I was in her house in La Esmeralda she was saying nasty things about all the Negroes around, especially her own brother-in-law, Crucita's husband, who was there. She went on and on, spoiling for a fight. Finally he couldn't stand it any more and knocked her down. Then I hit him and we started to fight. I really got into *trouble* that time. He picked up a handful of stones and I dared him to throw them. He did. I threw them back and hit his neck. He flung a bottle at me, but I stooped and it didn't hit me. I picked up a piece of the broken glass and drove it into his arm. They had to take him to the hospital.

After that I always went to see Crucita when he was out of the house.

Crucita cooked my meals, washed and ironed my clothes, and gave me money. She was so good to me. If I wanted to do anything, she told me to go ahead and do it. She let me eat all I wanted and she never asked for anything in return.

But I have fought with that husband of hers. One time he asked me what was wrong, were we two going to fight? I said, "Fight with you? I should say so! Wait for me here." I went to my house to get a big knife and a baseball bat, but when I came back he was gone. I went looking for him but couldn't find him. Since then I've always been stand-offish with him, polite but distant.

One day he hit Crucita on the mouth. She came to me, bleeding. "Simplicio, my husband hit me."

"He did? But tell me, *chica,* how did that happen?" I asked her about it but I didn't go saying anything disagreeable to him on that account. I know how women are. Never have I interfered in his quarrels but when I was in New York I did send word to Crucita that if I were to go back to Puerto Rico and meet him, and if he were to say something to me, I'd shoot him. The next time we get into a fight, it's him or me. One of us is going to wind up in the graveyard.

Right now Soledad has Benedicto. You can see he's a real man, because he took her out of a bar and set her up in a place of her own. And he loves her children and everything. I say this even though I know he went around saying I was boastful and a queer. But he's good to my sister. Well, one day I was visiting them and they got into a fight. You see, she's been to Puerto Rico on a visit and Benedicto found out she'd slept with an American there. And her a married woman. But that time Benedicto did something I don't like. He waited until I went home and then he beat her. I don't like that. I never mentioned it to him, though. One shouldn't butt into the affairs of a married couple.

I did talk to Soledad about it later. I told her she'd done wrong and if she didn't change her ways I'd stop going to see her. I said it was wrong to quarrel in front of me. When married people want to quarrel, they should wait until they're alone.

The truth is, I don't think much of my family, except for Crucita and my *mamá.* Because *mamá* is a woman and she has been a good mother, too. She used to beat me. Well do I remember how hard, but she was right. This two-inch scar on my arm is from a blow she gave me. I even have a scar on my back, too, from that time. But that wasn't her fault, she can't help it if she's hot-tempered. That happened once when I got drunk and met Flora's brother. We both went to Fernanda's house and smashed everything we could lay our hands on. That made her mad and she struck at my face with a stick. I warded off the blow with my arm and the stick broke. But she herself took me to the hospital and everything.

Another time Catín went and told Fernanda that I was with a woman in a bar. Flora rushed over and I socked her. Cruz butted in and I fell on her too. Then Fernanda grabbed a bottle of Pepsi-Cola and hit me with that. I had a black eye for about a month. You can still see the scar where she split open my upper lid. And God help anyone who butted in! It make no difference to her that I was already a grown man with a woman of my own.

I don't give a damn about the rest of my family. I don't care for my sisters. None of them has ever been satisfied with only one man. They like to lead the gay life. I think that's wrong and I tell them so. I don't bother to explain that I say it for their own good or anything like that. No word recommending any special man ever passes my lips. I never say, "Look, this boy is my friend." I simply don't introduce my friends to them. And I don't say, "This or that would be good for you." They never pay any attention to me anyway.

But in spite of everything, I do love my sisters. And I won't let anyone speak badly of them in my hearing. Sometimes they even appear in my dreams. Now and then I dream that I'm in a wonderful, beautiful place full of dancing, singing people. I sit by the shore fishing when suddenly fish, or sometimes it's snakes, come and bite off my arm. And there I stand, with one arm missing, when Soledad appears and gets in besides the snakes, into a sort of puddle. And suddenly there are about a thousand snakes all over her. Seeing her in that fix, I fight and struggle with the snakes until finally I get her out of the puddle, out of the water, see?

Of course, I treat all my sisters as a brother should. I help them out with food and everything. I won't deny them my help simply because I disapprove of the life they lead. Because the truth is that whatever is going to happen when you grow up is predestined from the day you're born. Many are born to steal, others to be whores and some to loaf their lives away. Just like some are born to go to jail, and they do. But destiny isn't all. You yourself have a part in deciding what you are, and what you do. Before you can do that, you have to know yourself. And it's up to each one of us to know himself.

We Puerto Ricans here in New York turn to each other for friendship. We go out on Fridays because that's the beginning of the *weekend*. A whole bunch of us Puerto Ricans go out together. Because as far as having friends of other races goes, the only one I have now is an American Negro who owns *un bar*.

Lots of people here have relatives in New Jersey, Pennsylvania, well, all over. So they often spend the *weekends* out of town. Others go to dances or to the beach. That's what we mostly do for entertainment in summer, have picnics at Coney Island. A big group of us Latins go together. Coney Island is full of people—all sorts mixed together. There you find white and black Americans. But many other beaches are different; they don't want Negroes or Puerto Ricans.

We have our own clubs here too. There's one that holds a meeting every Sunday over the radio. They talk about the governors, what they're like and what they have done. That club is now trying to get rid of that law of Rockefeller's, the one that says a cop can go into your house at five o'clock in the morning or any hour he pleases and open your door for no reason at all. Rockefeller is a Republican, see? And he's in power in New York, but that law is bad.

The club wants to end racial discrimination like for example in that *World's Fair* where they didn't hire Negroes or Latins. The people at the club said Negroes should work there. But the whites wouldn't allow that and neither would the governor, that Republican, Rockefeller. The land where the Fair was belonged to the government but the *buildings* were private property. They belonged to companies, see? And if a private company doesn't want to hire black people, it's within its rights, isn't it? Like supposing a Latin wanted someone to work in his house. He'd look for another Latin, one of his own people. He has a right to. Well, the companies have that same right. Although it's bad because we all need to work and we're all equal.

I would like to work for the equality of Negroes and whites although I can't say that racial prejudice has really screwed me up much. But I don't agree with this business of the Negroes fighting. Many of them do it as a blind. They steal and shield themselves behind the race problem. I wouldn't get mixed up in those fights; they are Americans and understand each other. I'd let myself be drawn into something like that only if it was the Puerto Ricans who were in it. We have nothing to do with this business, so there's no need to get involved in fights.

If it were in my power to help the Puerto Ricans any way I chose, I would choose a good education for them, for the little ones who are growing up now. I would like them to have good schools where they would be taught English, yes, but Spanish too. That's what's wrong with the system up here— they don't teach Spanish to our children. That's bad, because if a child of yours is born and brought up here and then goes back to Puerto Rico, he can't get a job. How can he, when he knows no Spanish? It's good to know English. But Spanish is for speaking to your own people. That's the problem the children of Puerto Ricans have up here. They understand Spanish but they can't speak or write it.

A good education would help them to get jobs. Because sometimes Puerto Ricans come here to get a job and they can't find one. They want to work and earn money but don't have any schooling at all. They find themselves in a tight spot and maybe they have school children to support, so they'll accept any job that comes their way, usually the worst ones. That's one cause for the delinquency there is among us.

Another thing I would like to work for is better housing. Puerto Ricans can't get good apartments here because the landlords begin raising the rent. They don't want us because they say we're dirty and messy. All pay for what a few of us do. What happens is that when a Puerto Rican rents a place he cracks the plaster on the walls by driving in nails to hang pictures. And then he paints the different rooms different colors. Americans don't like that. So if a Puerto Rican goes to look for an apartment in a pretty part of the city, he finds they charge a hundred and fifty or two hundred dollars' rent. How can we pay that? A Puerto Rican here barely earns enough to pay for rent and food.

It's easy enough for married couples without children to get apartments, but a family with three or four children has trouble. Nobody wants to rent to them. And we Puerto Ricans usually do have children. So we have to look for months and then settle for the worst, for apartments full of rats and crawling with cockroaches. The more you clean, the more they come. There are more rats than people in New York, where we Latins live, I mean.

Not me, I live well. But there are many Puerto Ricans who are much worse off than I am. Just take a look around El Barrio, the section where so many Puerto Ricans live. I went there once with my brother-in-law and Sole-dad, and I haven't been back since. There's too much vice in that place; children fifteen or sixteen years old smoking marijuana right out in public, streets full of people at all hours of the day and night, garbage cans all over the place! People throw bottles, tin cans, all sorts of rubbish onto the street. That place is a calamity.

When they see the way we live here, many Americans get the idea that we came over like the Italians and the Jews did. They have to come with a passport, see? They think we are the same. That and their racial prejudice are the things that make me dislike Americans. Whites here are full of prejudice against Latins and Negroes. In Puerto Rico it isn't like that. You can go any place a white man can, as long as you can pay your way. And a white man can sit down to eat at the same table as a Negro. But not here. That's why the United States is having so many troubles. That's why I say I don't like Americans. What I like is their country. The life here, the way, the manner of living.

Here one lives without gossip, see? You do your work and nobody interferes with anybody else. I also like the atmosphere here. You earn enough money so that you can go and see pretty things. You don't get bored, because you can afford to go to the movies or to the prize fights. When you're broke you can always go to Forty-second Street and look at all the pretty lights. Or you can go to Rockaway. It looks like La Esmeralda, like the Point at Stop 10, except that the people in Rockaway are rich.

Maybe if Puerto Rico became a state it would be like this country, but I don't think so. It's too small to have the things they have here. Why, Puerto Rico would fit into New York City, it's so small! Yet, I'd like to have Puerto Rico become State Fifty-One, just to see what would happen. Although when I left Puerto Rico, the governor was building roads, new hotels, new houses. Well, the people of Puerto Rico are progressing and I know that Muñoz Marín and the Popular Party have done good work. It's a pity that he doesn't want to be governor again next year.

But did you know that his party wants to do away with the slums? That's bad. It means they want to get rid of everything in La Esmeralda and in the slums at Stop 21. Now, if Ferré, the Statehood candidate, wins, he has promised to build new houses in La Esmeralda and let the people stay there. Ferré says that he's going to make a better Puerto Rico, with more work, a better life, more rights. That's what he promises but I don't know if he'll keep his word. His Republican Party was in power once and it fell because it didn't keep its promises.

Not that it makes any difference in the way I feel. I belong to that party because I believe in its ideals. And Nanda does too. Nanda worked in the registration of new voters for the Party. Afterward we would go to the meetings. She'd put on a dress made from a Republican flag and pin a sign on it saying she wanted Ferré to win. We used to go to different places on the island like that, talking the whole night through.

What Republicans want is to have the United States take Puerto Rico over completely, once and for all. Because right now Puerto Rico is half Puerto Rican and half United States. It flies both the Puerto Rican and the American flags. All they have to do to make us into a state is to add one more star to the American flag.

There's another party too, the *Pipiolos.*[1] They want Puerto Rico to be

[1] Partido Independentista Puertorriqueño (PIP).

free like Mexico, Santo Domingo, Jamaica, Venezuela, and such places. That's bad. If that happened, we would need a passport to get out of Puerto Rico. What they want is a republic, which means that if you're a bad governor they'll get you out without an election or anything, with bullets.

The trouble with republics is that they have to defend themselves because they don't have another country to help them. Cuba used to be a republic, right? And what did it have to do? Call on the Russians for help. Now it's Communist. But Castro isn't bad. When he was in the Sierra Maestra with his guerrillas, he asked the Americans for help and the American refused because they were on Batista's side. That's why he had to go to the Russians. If we became a republic now, Fidel Castro could take us over whenever he wanted to. All he'd have to do is send over a couple of Communist war planes.

If only Communism now were as it used to be! I don't know whether this is true or not, but I have read that Communism used to mean that if you had a plate of rice you shared it with everybody. If a man had a thousand dollars in the bank he had to share them with everybody else, and all were equal. That's what Communism used to be but it isn't like that any more. Now under Communism, what's mine is mine and what's yours belongs to you. The man who owns the most is the most respected one. If you have nothing, you're worth nothing. I don't like that kind of Communism. Why, besides all the things I've just told you, I also heard over the radio that in Russia they make children study from the time they are four months old! Besides, Russia is a military country. Do you know what that means? It means that at the age of fifteen a boy is already serving in the *Army* or the *Navy*. That's what's happening in Cuba today, people are forced to do things. You can't say no, because the government gives all the orders. And you can't change the government because there's only one party, the Communists. You can't say, "I don't like this country." You *have* to like it. It's not like here, where you're free. If you don't like one thing, you can go around the corner and get another.

If Puerto Rico were a republic we would starve to death. We have to buy everything from outside. Even our ships we have to buy outside. So if we were free, we would have to call on other republics for help. Naturally, the United States would help us if we were a republic, but it would be only the kind of help they give Mexico, Venezuela, and all those places. We'd have to submit to a lot of regulations.

Lately I have heard that the priests in Puerto Rico have formed a party of their own. It is called the Christian PAC.[2] It belongs to Rome, to Catholic people. If they win, who is going to govern Puerto Rico? The Catholics? I'm Catholic myself so I would be allowed to live, but what about all the people who are not? Religion has nothing to do with politics. President Kennedy was a member of the Catholic Church but that did not keep him from also being a member of the Democratic Party. Tell me now, suppose PAC wins the elections, what will become of Puerto Rico? Who's going to feed us? We would have to wait until ships came from Rome bringing us food. And when Rome falls, who will support us? We'll have to live on bread and wine, I guess.

Well, I live in New York and I don't meddle with what goes on here. I do see that Kennedy, the President who was killed, was pure gold. He was a Democrat and that's the same as being a *Popular* in Puerto Rico. But even so,

[2] Partido Acción Cristiana.

he was good. Do you know what he fought for? For equality between Negroes and whites. For civil rights, which are the rights that belong to us, like not allowing a cop to come into your house and search it without your leave. The privacy of the home is a right that every one of us has. And he was also for your right not to be stopped and searched by a cop for no reason at all as you walk quietly down a street, minding your own business. And for Negroes' rights to get a job as well as white men. All those are civil rights. President Kennedy was in favor of all that.

Imagine, he knew Cuba was Communist but he was willing to help them in spite of that. They were the ones who said no. And then, some of Kennedy's people were jailed over in Cuba and he exchanged them for a shipful of medicines. And that's when they killed him.

Now Johnson has succeeded Kennedy. Johnson is from Texas, where they killed Washington—I mean, Abraham Lincoln. There's a lot of racial prejudice in that state. Although it's so rich in oil wells and such, people have gotten scared of that place. Presidents won't dare to travel through Texas any more. Those people down there are too brutal. The way things are, Texas is having the same trouble as the Jews, one Texan killed Kennedy and now they're all paying for it.

Johnson doesn't seem to be like Kennedy, who was always talking about the Latins and looking out for them. But this one isn't like that. He's not talkative. And when he does talk it's only about politics for himself and his people. What's more, I don't think he writes his own speeches. Somebody else writes them and they give them to Johnson to read. He doesn't put ideas out of his own mind into them.

I have never voted, because I wasn't old enough. I was twenty-one this year and I'd like to vote, now that I'm of age. But I won't have the chance because I didn't register. I didn't know where to go or anything. I asked around but everybody said it was somewhere in Brooklyn, they didn't know exactly where. It isn't like Puerto Rico, where someone comes to your house and asks you which party you plan to vote for and then they send you a little card.

If I could, I'd like to vote for the Republicans because my *mamá* is a Republican. But not for Rockefeller. I'd vote for some other candidate, like Kennedy's brother, for instance. Rockefeller doesn't stand up for the Latins or the Negroes. And yet, if you stop to think, you'll realize that in New York there are more Latins and Negroes than whites. But when two men apply for the same job, a white man and a Negro, they hire the white man and push us aside. They treat us like they treat the Negroes, you see. And that in spite of the fact that the Puerto Rican works hard. If he sees a box that's meant to be carried by two men, he heaves it up and carries it by himself, even if it weighs a hundred pounds. We like the toughest kind of work.

Cubans

TOM ALEXANDER

Those Amazing Cuban Emigres

The political and social revolution created by Fidel Castro in Cuba at the end of the 1950s resulted in a large-scale wave of emigration. Over 300,000 Cubans, including many members of the professional and ruling classes, came to the United States through Miami and settled in places as far away as New York and California. More than 225,000 crowded into Miami and environs. For the first time in the twentieth century a southern city became the major point of entry for an immigrant group. The federal government showed special concern for the welfare of the new minority and even made arrangements to transport the Cubans from Havana to Miami. The government also helped finance shelters, schools, and relocation centers. Of course, this was not a wholly disinterested effort, for both Presidents Dwight D. Eisenhower and John F. Kennedy were dedicated to showing the advantages of American capitalism over Caribbean communism. Nevertheless, government interest, combined with American sympathy for the refugees from communism and the skills of many of the immigrants, has eased Cuban adjustment in this country.

Today the Cuban minority constitutes almost 25 percent of Miami's population. There are three radio stations broadcasting exclusively in Spanish; eight tabloids printed primarily for Cubans; and the sounds of "buenos noches" and "gracias" echo through the city's hotel lobbies and restaurants.

Although they often are employed at a lower level than their skills would warrant, many Cubans have made a successful adjustment in the United States. For a time anti-Cuban sentiment ran high; some members of the NAACP and Urban League expressed concern that Cubans might take jobs that would otherwise go to American blacks; newspapers received letters and phone calls urging them to help prevent further migrations; the superintendent of schools in Dade County (Miami) temporarily suspended the admission of Cuban children until additional financial assistance came from the federal government; and the then governor of Florida, Haydon Burns, warned of the possibility of "economic chaos" with so many Cubans flooding the economy. Monsignor John Fitzpatrick, chancellor of the Roman Catholic diocese of Miami, evidenced little patience with nativists when he said, in 1965, "How unbecoming it is that these foolish, un-American statements are often made by the descendants of the Irish, the Italian, the Polish and the English immigrants who came here since the

Reprinted from *Fortune Magazine*, October, 1966, pp. 144–49, by special permission; © 1966 Time, Inc.

early 1600s seeking refuge from oppression and hunger." As it turned out the Cubans added about $350 million a year to the nation's economy and provided a pool of skilled labor that a number of analysts feel accounted for the major upswing in Florida's industrial development.

The Cubans who have been pouring into the U.S. in recent years—some 300,000 have come since 1959—constitute an extraordinary immigration. Most other waves of immigration have been made up largely of the poor and uneducated, and their early struggles in this country have revolved around changing that condition. Not so with most of the Cubans. Although there are some farmers and blue-collar workers among them, the exodus has been heavily weighted with those from the upper layers of the old Cuban society. Of those who are in their working years, nearly 50 percent have professional, semiprofessional, or managerial backgrounds; more than a third have been clerical, sales, or skilled blue-collar workers. The fact that most of the immigrants actually arrived penniless, and with only a change or two of clothing, has not prevented them from moving rapidly into many different areas of the economy—and in many different areas of the U.S.

Their ready absorption into the economy can be attributed, not only to their own considerable skills and energy, and to the enormous American manpower requirements of the past few years, but to an enlightened U.S. Government policy. Washington has worked hard to get the refugees established in homes and jobs all around the U.S. During his last months in office President Eisenhower set aside a million dollars from his contingency funds to aid refugees. One of President Kennedy's first official acts was to put an expanded refugee-aid program under the Department of Health, Education, and Welfare, and to get the program a special $4-million allocation from foreign-aid funds. Since 1962 the program has had its own budget, providing for a headquarters office in Washington as well as the Cuban Refugee Center in Miami; the center has facilities for processing new arrivals and a 400-bed "Freedom House," where refugees in transit can stay for a few days. The resettlement program is now under the over-all direction of John Thomas, fifty-nine, a hardheaded bureaucrat of mixed Negro-Indian and Swedish descent, who has twenty years of refugee resettlement experience, most of it with displaced persons in Europe after World War II.

The current inflow from Cuba is the most recent of five fairly distinct waves since Fidel Castro seized power in 1959, overthrowing the dictatorship of Fulgencio Batista. Hundreds of Batista's officials and supporters fled to the U.S. as it became clear that Castro would be taking over. They were followed by many top business leaders in 1959 and 1960, after Castro's seizure of oil refineries, factories, and plantations. As the government became overtly Communist, in 1960 and 1961, there was a third wave: the upper-middle class, predominantly business and professional men and technicians. Most of these refugees were disaffected Castro sympathizers. People in lower social groups—small farmers, fishermen, industrial workers—came in from mid-1961 until the missile crisis of October, 1962, when Castro stopped airline flights to the U.S. Many in this fourth wave escaped from Cuba in small boats.

Some are still coming in small boats. But a distinctive fifth wave of migration began nearly a year ago, after Castro astonished the world by offering to let out thousands of Cubans who wanted to leave. Subsequently, he approved arrangements for an airlift to help them along. According to a Memorandum of Understanding drawn up between the U.S. and Cuba (the Swiss Embassy in Havana was the intermediary), first priority was to be given to the immediate relatives of refugees already here—to parents, children, and spouses. (For example, some 13,000 unaccompanied children had earlier been sent out under various pretexts by parents who, unable to leave themselves, nevertheless wanted to be sure that their children were not brought up under Communism. Parents have now joined all but about 1,000 of these.) Later, more distant relatives will be permitted to come and ultimately, it appears, so will many other Cubans. The U.S. has compiled a list of over 800,000 Cubans whose airlifting has been requested by relatives and friends already here. This list is continually matched against one received from the Cuban Government of those whom it will permit to leave—and *that* list carries only about 80,000 names. Much of the discrepancy arises from the fact that Castro still forbids draft-eligible Cubans and those in certain critical occupations to leave, and from the additional poignant fact that many Cubans are reluctant to apply because once listed they usually lose their jobs, and may remain out of work for months, or even years, before they can get out. These delays seem to reflect mainly Cuban Government difficulties in processing more than 4,000 per month—the current level of immigration. When a Cuban finally does leave the country, he must hand over all his money and property to the Cuban Government.

A Plus for Miami

Virtually all the Cubans who come directly to the U.S., rather than by way of some other country, come first to Miami for processing. There they are screened by immigration and naturalization authorities who, among other things, investigate the possibility that Cuban Government agents are included among the arrivals. Once cleared, however, the immigrants are technically free to do what they please. What would please most of them would be to settle in Miami, where the climate is agreeable and where previous immigrants have virtually created a little bit of old Havana. Something over a quarter of the 300,000 refugees are now living in Miami.

For some time this concentration was viewed as a social problem that might get out of control. Ripples of dread have passed through Miami as each of the successive waves of refugees hit town. In the early 1960's there was, indeed, a plausible case for being worried about the immigrants. Miami's was a depressed economy. Nearly 100,000 Cubans had recently been dumped into the metropolitan area, raising its total population by over 10 percent. Over two-thirds of the refugees were then on public assistance. The area's total unemployment rate hung around the 10 percent mark, and loud, anguished cries came from the Negro community and some labor unions because Cubans were going to work for half the prevailing wages. Miami schools had trouble accommodating the 18,000 refugee children, most of whom spoke only Spanish. Furthermore, preoccupied with overthrowing Castro and returning to their homeland, many of the refugees were devoting a lot of their energies and spare capital to roiling agitation and sometimes even to harassing raids on the Cuban mainland.

Most of the refugees have long since given up any ideas about freeing Cuba by their own efforts and are now devoting their talents to getting along in their adopted home. Miami unemployment is down to about 4 percent. Cubans on welfare have declined from nearly 70,000 to about 12,000, with most of these being elderly, juvenile, sick, or otherwise unemployable.

Though some ill-feeling still persists in Miami, by and large the city has come to count its new Cuban community as its own good fortune. "There is no doubt in my mind that the Cubans boosted Miami immeasurably," says William Pallot, president of Miami's fast-growing Inter National Bank. Pallot believes, and others agree with him, that thousands of Miami's houses, apartments, and stores would be vacant had the Cubans not come. There is even something of a real-estate boom in Miami—one of the few cities in the U.S. where housing markets are strong—and an estimated 30 percent of the new FHA commitments there are to Cubans. Enterprising Cubans have been credited with bringing a new commercial vigor to much of the downtown area, especially the former commercial center of Flagler Street, which had been rapidly running down. Many of the former Havana cigar manufacturers and their employees have set up nearly a dozen companies in Miami, helping the city to displace Tampa as the hand-rolled-cigar capital of the U.S. At least one cigarette company, Dosal & Mendes, is thriving; there are also sizable and prosperous Cuban-owned garment companies, shoe manufacturers, import houses, shopping centers, restaurants, and nightclubs. To the northwest of Miami, Cuban entrepreneurs have set up sugar plantations and mills.

Though Miami still has by far the largest Cuban community, several other cities—notably New York, Chicago, and Los Angeles—have each received thousands of refugees. Large colonies of Cubans are now to be found in the northern New Jersey area that encompasses Newark, Elizabeth, Union City, and West New York: the total in the area is estimated to be over 30,000. In part the recent immigrants have congregated there because the area already had a Cuban community dating back as far as 1850. Some estimate that Union City itself has 20,000 Cubans in a total population of 40,000—the highest proportion of any city in the U.S. Just as in Miami, Cubans are credited with having done much to spruce up some of the city's run-down areas, notably the neighborhood around Bergenline Avenue and Forty-eighth Street.

"Send Us a Thousand More"

Most Cubans would almost certainly still be in Miami but for some pressures exerted on them by the Cuban Refugee Center, which has charge of financing and coordinating most of the government and voluntary agencies' aid to refugees. Registration with the center is voluntary, but anyone who fails to register forgoes a wide range of benefits: temporary financial assistance (up to $100 a month per family), medical care, food, hospitalization, and education loans for

Cuban college students, plus a variety of adult-education programs that include English and vocational courses, teacher training, and refresher courses for physicians. At the same time, it is made clear to the refugees that those who register must agree to resettlement as soon as suitable jobs are found for them.

Most of the resettlement work is handled through the center's contracts with four voluntary agencies: the National Catholic Welfare Conference, the Church World Service (a Protestant agency), United HIAS (Hebrew Immigrant Aid Society), and the nonsectarian International Rescue Committee. The refugee is free to choose any one of these agencies and it then helps him find a job outside Miami. Within twenty-four to forty-eight hours of their arrival in the city, most Cubans are on their way to somewhere else. John Thomas, who directs the program from Washington, is convinced that the worst thing that can happen to refugees is to be detained for long periods while they are being "processed." Says Thomas: "Only two weeks in a refugee camp is enough to destroy a person."

Wherever Cubans have settled, they have elicited remarkably consistent praise for their energy, ability, and exemplary conduct. Many of the firms that have employed a few send back to Miami for more. And one company in Texas, which had taken on a lot of Cuban construction workers, later sent a wire to the refugee center, "Send us a thousand more."

Like Miami, most other cities have found that some widespread fears and prejudices about the Cubans are groundless. In Miami, where Cubans make up between 10 percent and 15 percent of the population, they account for only 2.9 percent of the arrests, with most of these being for traffic violations—Cubans seem not to be very good drivers for some reason. In most communities where Cubans have settled, welfare officials have noted with astonishment their powerful urge to stay off relief rolls whenever jobs are available—and, with even more astonishment, have noted the effort that some Cubans make to pay back any welfare money they may have received. Of New York's 30,000-odd Cubans, only about 500 are on relief. Robert Frutkoff, a management expert with the New York State Employment Service, testified in Senate hearings on refugee problems this past spring that the Cubans are "a highly motivated group. We found, for example, that they would prefer to take any type of job than apply for welfare."

A Kind of Limbo

Despite the over-all success of the Cuban immigration, however, it seems clear that from 80 to 90 percent of Cuban refugees are "underemployed"—i.e., working at jobs that are beneath their real qualifications. One reason for this is their difficulty with the English language. Another reason is the peculiar legal status of the refugees. Because most entered after the U.S. had severed diplomatic relations with Cuba, the usual visa requirements have been waived; this leaves the refugees in a "parolee" status, a kind of limbo that does not permit them even to apply for citizenship without first going to another country and then re-entering under a permanent-resident visa—an expensive and uncertain business. Citizenship or declaration of intent, however, is a precondition for licensing in virtually all the professions in most states. It is also a precondition for civil-service qualification, for jobs requiring bonding or travel abroad, and for many others—such as selling real estate—that require licensing. Special legislation that would adjust the Cubans' parolee status to that of immigrants is now being pushed in Congress, and its passage is expected shortly.

Of all the professional men, the Cuban lawyers have the hardest time obtaining employment that uses their talents, since they were trained in the Napoleonic Code rather than the common law practice in the U.S. To help the lawyers, the refugee program has sponsored a special series of training programs aimed at turning lawyers into Spanish teachers, and by now several hundred of them are teaching in U.S. schools and colleges.

There is also a special problem about nearly 2,000 Cuban physicians, in some ways the most valuable single human resource of all to be received from Cuba. The problem is that most states require doctors to be citizens and to serve as interns before they can be licensed for private practice. To get around these barriers, most of the refugee doctors are placed in clinics and hospitals, where they can practice so long as they do so under the direction of an American citizen. Recently, a team of six Cuban physicians went to South Vietnam to aid war refugees—and thereby to get in their licks against Communism.

Coda

JOHN J. APPEL

American Negro and Immigrant Experience: Similarities and Differences

It is fitting that this volume should close with John J. Appel's 1966 "American Negro and Immigrant Experience" because for "American Negro" one may read "all Americans who are not white." Too many white Americans, whose ancestors were victimized by prejudice and exploitation, have shown little understanding of the difficulties that nonwhites have endured and still endure today. Unlike minorities of different national or religious backgrounds, the children of black, brown, Indian, and Oriental Americans could not assimilate with the dominant group in society simply by changing their names. Yet whites who can recall the hardships suffered and surmounted by their parents or grandparents simply cannot—or will not—understand why members of minority groups with different skin colors should have been less successful than their own forebears. "We made it, why can't they?" is the question so often asked. But few whites who have "made it" pause to search for the answer.

The December 1965 issue of the *Journal of American History* carried an article by Rudolph J. Vecoli entitled "Contadini in Chicago: A Critique of *The Uprooted*"* which reminded historians of immigration that constructing ideal-type figures to stand for historical group experience means subordinating "historical complexity to the symmetrical pattern of sociological theory."**

Reprinted from *American Quarterly*, 18 (1966), 95–103 by permission of the publishers and the author. Copyright, 1966, Trustees of the University of Pennsylvania.
    * See p. 216.
    ** An earlier version of this paper was read at the 58th annual meeting of the Organization of American Historians in Kansas City, April 1965, during a session chaired by Mr. Carl Degler, devoted to historical parallels between the Negro rights movement and other social movements. Summaries of the papers presented and the remarks of the commentators, Mr. Herbert Aptheker, Mr. Benjamin Quarles and Mr. Lawrence Levine, appear in *The Journal of American History*, LII (September 1965), pp. 336–7.
    The surge of books, articles and speeches dealing with the history and experiences of Negro Americans has made it impractical for me to acknowledge in footnotes my indebtedness to the writings on Negro and immigrant history from which I have borrowed and profited. My generalizations concerning immigrant history are largely based on work by Oscar Handlin, Carl Wittke, John Higham, Nathan Glazer and Daniel Patrick Moynihan. My association with Jewish Centers during the 1950s alerted me to the growing tension arising from the kind of sub-community life created

I mention this warning in order to say that considerations of space here compel me largely to disregard it. For the same reason, I do not compare the Negro's and the immigrant's religion and education, or show how the two groups have been dealt with by historians, novelists and dramatists. Also, I sometimes use the term immigrant somewhat imprecisely to mean a second- or third-generation person rather than one just off the boat. Finally, while I recognize that inspection of various subgroups would doubtless reveal differences which should qualify my generalizations about Negroes-in-general and immigrants-in-general, I have nevertheless generalized. Challenging each others' generalizations is our chief professional exercise, and paying vigorous heed to Mr. Vecoli's warning would, I fear, lead to slothful ease.

Crucial in any comparison of American Negro and immigrant experience is race. Being a Negro has meant caste status in this country, North and South, through most of its history. Even after "emancipation" it still meant curtailed access to public facilities and unequal treatment in such matters as housing, education and employment. While the immigrant faced difficult obstacles to assimilation and consequent progress to middle-class status, they were not insurmountable.

Even for first-generation immigrants, the strange language, new customs and frequent rebuffs were less formidable than the color barrier and could generally be overcome by their descendants, if not by them. To be sure, immigrants knew anxiety and alienation, but no white immigrant group experienced prolonged pariah status, poverty, frustration, disorganization of family life, and all the rest which has been the Negro's lot and, to some extent, that of other "colored" Americans: Puerto Ricans, Mexicans, Indians. The immigrant advanced in an expanding economy while the Negro remained in a permanent subproletariat, a position today perhaps worsened by automation. Few men who have studied the Negro's history now doubt that his full emancipation depends on either a stable economy with full employment for all or some sort of socially acceptable alternatives for full employment.

Beyond the significant and often visible differences of skin color and social caste position, American Negroes and immigrants are set apart by their cultural memories, however attenuated: forcible capture and enslavement versus self-willed search for opportunity and flight from hardship. And while the Negro,

and envisioned by American Protestants, Catholics and Jews and challenged, *at that time,* by some Negro leaders' critical views of a pluralistic conception of American society. In the meantime, the spread of Black Power ideology has apparently moved my predictions in the concluding paragraphs of this article (drafted in early 1963) closer to actuality.

After I proposed the subject of my paper to the Society of American Historians but before I had completed its final draft, Mr. Nathan Glazer published his study of the clash between Negro and Jewish social goals—"Negroes and Jews: The New Challenge to Pluralism," *Commentary,* XXXVIII (Dec. 1964), on which I have freely drawn here.

I also want to record my indebtedness to suggestions and criticisms by colleagues and friends specializing in immigrant and Negro history, to Mr. H. Aptheker for his detailed comments on the paper, and to Mr. Ben Strandness of Michigan State University for editorial assistance. A Michigan State All University Research Grant helped to defray expenses incurred in the preparation of the essay.

John J. Appel
James Madison College,
Michigan State University,
June 1968 .

like the immigrant, has seldom lost faith in the promises of American dreams and ideals, little in American history vis-à-vis the Negro has been in accordance with American values, however these are defined.

Historians, sociologists and anthropologists have not been able to settle the question of whether the Negro American's break with African culture was complete. Yet whether the break was complete or not, the dominant white outlook, until quite recently, at any rate, regarded this African culture as inferior, even barbaric. The immigrant, on the other hand, usually had a complex cultural heritage of his own which he not only knew but was frequently proud of. True, many immigrants were poorly educated, but they had leaders, both in "the old country" and here, whom they could emulate and in whose achievements they felt pride. Most important, the promise of America remained open for their children.

In short, the story of Negro and immigrant experience in this country contains few significant analogies and many significant differences. Still, if Negro Americans are allowed to progress with reasonable speed toward first-class citizenship, comparative study of the two groups should indicate where progress will be relatively easy and where it will not. Obviously no analogy should be taken literally. All comparisons are inexact. Furthermore, what interests historians may not interest political activists. Consider, for example, the marked contrast between conceptions of American society as described in studies of its immigrant groups and those described or at least implied by Negro civil rights spokesmen. Louis Lomax's excellent account in *The Negro Revolt* candidly notes the inferiority of segregated Negro institutions—inferior *because* segregated—in order to prod Negro leaders to shift from ethnic to general institutions, dismissing the possibility of a viable Negro community because the Negro is the "only American who . . . must reach beyond his own group for absolute identification." Students of immigrant history know that beyond the assertions of brotherhood and equality lies the reality of surviving group loyalties and economic self-interest, or combinations of these factors, which are not likely to give way, in the foreseeable future, to a pure democracy, homogeneous, color-blind, without ethnic churches, associations, newspapers, schools and politicians.

Historians of American immigration and spokesmen for a pluralistic American society have not always agreed on the definition of what is, or should be, the degree of assimilation desired of newcomers. But both groups seem to have discarded the melting pot metaphor at the very time when Negro leaders, except for Black Muslim nationalists, vigorously espouse it.* Historians and sociologists report that distinctions between ethnic groups and religious groups are fading, but few predict their early disappearance, and some see them becoming "new social forms" indigenous to American life.[1] They describe the *white* urban community as a conglomerate of coexisting groups divided on ethnic, religious, occupational and class lines. No white American, to be sure, moves exclusively in any one of these, but his allegiances are generally clear. Movement

---

* Since the publication of this article, there has been a rapid growth in black self-awareness; many black groups and individuals prefer to search for ethnic identity rather than to assimilate. For these blacks, separateness seems the only way to achieve equality and dignity in America today (Eds.).

[1] Nathan Glazer and Daniel P. Moynihan, *Beyond the Melting Pot: The Negroes, Puerto Ricans, Jews, Italians and Irish of New York City* (Cambridge, 1963).

from group to group, especially from "out" to "in" groups, means partial assimilation, with elements of former identities being retained. Negroes, it would appear, cannot expect to be completely assimilated into any one of these groups, i.e. cease to be regarded as Negroes as the door to assimilation is opened for more of them. Whether such assimilation is desired by the Negro American or desirable for society itself is not the issue. The assimilation process itself, immigrant experience shows, spans several generations, continuing even after newcomers achieve economic and social equality. Furthermore, the inevitable sense of separateness created by discrimination heightens ethnic identity. Will the highly visible Negro American, his sense of solidarity developed by separateness and the struggle to achieve first-class citizenship, somehow avoid this paradoxical development?

Immigrants and Negroes have long lived in adjoining urban enclaves, frequently with tension and hostility. Most immigrants eventually leave their areas of first settlement while most Negroes stay. The same holds true for areas of second settlement, districts where the immigrants or their children move during the process of improving their social and economic status. Anti-Negro demonstrations, in fact, generally occur in this "racial middle border" of Negro penetration into former white ethnic enclaves. The kind of ethnic group which adjoined a Negro section has therefore strongly influenced both the direction and rate of urban Negro population movement.

Immigrants tended to fear Negroes, seeing in them a threat to job security and status. The nineteenth-century Irish, for example, having competed with Negroes for the worst jobs in the early days of immigration, were most unfriendly. In the twentieth century Poles and Slavs have been highly resistant to racial change, with riots often traceable to their areas of urban concentration. Though friendships between individual Negroes and Puerto Ricans do occur, fights in New York City between Puerto Rican and Negro gangs are also common. Despite the fact that Puerto Rico itself has little racial prejudice, on the mainland Puerto Ricans generally reject the Negro as one who attracts the discrimination they desperately wish to avoid—while yet maintaining their ethnic identity.

Other examples of friction between immigrant groups and Negroes are not hard to find, though it should be kept in mind that I do not see these as "natural" or inevitable or ineradicable conflicts. Italian immigrants frequently skilled in the building trades, tend to improve the older neighborhoods—"little Italys"—in which many have settled. The arrival of lower-class Negroes often appears as a threat to neighborhood stability, with resultant animosities.

When Jews leave an ethnic enclave Negroes usually take their places. For reasons related to Jewish economic mobility, tradition and custom, Jews have not generally resorted to physical force to discourage the colored newcomers. Another reason for their less stubborn opposition to yielding residential quarters to Negro tenants may be related to their already mentioned high rate of social mobility, higher than that of other comparable ethnic groups, which allows Jews to leave an ethnic neighborhood for better quarters while making the old housing available to Negroes at profitable rental and sale prices.

A determined search of the historical record would probably reveal instances of amicable, neighborly coexistence of colored and immigrant populations in mixed or at least abutting residential areas. Immigrant memoirs and American social history in general do, unfortunately, suggest that the proximity of Negroes and the foreign-born was often a cause of racial strife. Since concentration in ethnic enclaves was and is at least partly voluntary for white ethnic groups and since such affinities, though undoubtedly weakening, still persist, Negro segregation is in part at least a concomitant of continuing ethnic attachments as well as of vested economic interests and racial animosities.

These facts are not cited here as arguments for the status quo: anything that can be done to break up the colored ghetto—school redistricting, open enrollment for school children, even the desertion of the principle of neighborhood schooling and the bussing of school children all over town—ought to be tried. But those who look to completely integrated urban housing should also keep in mind that immigration of rural poor is in Western, highly industrialized nations usually accompanied by a move to the suburbs of newly affluent groups. It is relevant to note that in England and Denmark, for example, the arrival of "out-group" populations in the cities produced results similar to those which have turned the centers of some American cities virtually all Negro sections.

The Negro's attitude toward the immigrant is naturally conditioned by the fact that while the latter may not be a citizen, he yet is white and so enjoys special opportunities. Furthermore, after refusing to live in a racially integrated neighborhood, the immigrant frequently either sells his deteriorating property to a Negro at a tidy profit before moving away or assumes the role of landlord. Similarly, his fraternal organizations exclude the Negro but often control the savings and loan association through which he finances the mortgage of his home. This sort of thing, particularly with respect to Jews, has produced a body of writing by both Jews and Negroes quite predictable in its tensions and ambiguities. For many years Negro leaders met with Jewish leaders in a climate of cordial, though not always tension-free, cooperation—cooperation which coexisted with strong anti-Jewish feelings among the Negro masses and a generally slight but significant anti-Negro feeling among the Jews. Kenneth Clark and James Baldwin, describing Negro anti-Semitism, remark that it permits the Negro to express anti-White feelings at the same time that he identifies with the white majority's prejudice. Jewish leaders have recently blamed some Black Muslim leaders for the anti-Semitism in Harlem. On the other hand, shortly before his murder, Malcolm X, pointing to the progress of American Jews and their ties with Israel, urged American Negroes to become similarly identified with African nations in order to strengthen their sense of group identity.

Both the "diploma society" of advancement by merit and the "democracy of money" under which white immigrants thrived, tend to exclude Negroes because of their defective background and general lack of experience with middle-class skills and behavior. Militant Negro leaders therefore want preferential treatment for their people while Jews and other ethnic groups ascribe their own gains to recognition of merit and the breakdown of preferential quotas in employment. Grandchildren of immigrants in particular mutter that their grandparents got no special help and yet worked their way up to "where we are," so why can't *they?* meaning the Negroes. To condemn such reasoning as imperceptive of the Negro's long history of enforced segregation, poverty and second-class status does not remove the real threat which the arrival of an urban Negro

344   *Contemporary America*

proletariat presents to a stable, middle-class oriented, ethnic neighborhood. Fear of deteriorating schools, poor housing and increased competition for jobs does not invariably stem from racial animosity but can certainly cause it when populations separated by *class* as well as *race* meet. Rhetoric is no remedy. Only massive federal aid promises mitigation of basic causes.

Lastly, it should not be forgotten that the immigrant-created subcommunity itself protects privileges and creates conditions which tend to stand in the way of complete assimilation for Negroes. While no historian can say to what extent color prejudice enters into the resistance to acceptance of Negroes in a given white group, it is clear that in some groups at least complete assimilation would endanger or weaken deeply held values and beliefs. (See, for instance, the articulation of this point of view in a speech by a Los Angeles Jewish Center official, "The Jewish Community Center and the Great Society," in the "house organ" of the Jewish Welfare Board, *JWB Circle,* Sept. 1965, pp. 1-2.)

Is there historical precedent as well as a moral imperative for special aid to Negroes in their struggle for full citizenship? Those familiar with immigrant history might say here that while most nineteenth-century American immigrants received little special aid, other American social groups, ex-soldiers, farmers, industrialists, ship and railroad promoters and builders, and victims of natural disaster, have often been the recipients of special aid. Furthermore, aid-to-migrants has been an accepted feature of British, government-sponsored emigration to Canada, New Zealand and Australia.

Immigrants to the United States depended mainly on mutual help, group solidarity, and hard work, but assistance of various kinds was not uncommon. It is estimated, for example, that more than half the seventeenth-century white immigrants to North America were indentured servants whose passages were prepaid. Later, various national, religious and labor organizations raised money to help people emigrate. Federal and state agencies in 1965 come to the help of Cubans arriving in Florida nearly destitute and requiring extensive financial, social, educational and vocational assistance.

Those who landed on American shores without assistance of some sort were most likely to fill the urban slums, city relief rolls and metropolitan police blotters. "New" immigrants from Southern and Eastern Europe, in many ways comparable to Negro migrants from the South, got help from settlement houses and church missions. Despite the fact that they were regarded as inferior to Anglo-Saxons, they were given this help at a time when the free Negro's shortcomings were felt to condemn him to permanent second-class status. Those who prided themselves on "scientific objectivity" usually concluded that

> if criminality and poverty are simply the result of poor surroundings, there is a possibility that improved economic conditions and higher social positions may remove the tendency and change the immigrant into a virtuous, law-abiding and self-supporting citizen.[2]

And, a fact all too forgotten in accounts of American settlement, some immigrants returned to their home countries broken in health as well as spirit, while others died aboard ship or were turned back at this country's gates. Aid

---

[2] Richmond Mayo-Smith, *Emigration and Immigration* (New York, 1890), p. 15.

and salvage operations for native migrants, on the other hand, have generally been undertaken in full view of society, with failures, successes and costs assessable.

The history of aid-to-immigrants shows that short term and badly planned assistance was usually ineffective and sometimes harmful. Whereas immigrant history offers many instances of unsuccessful settlement schemes, it also provides some examples of successful, planned resettlement activities which took advantage of job opportunities and lack of native resistance in selected geographical areas. Whether the Federal government ought to return to a policy of more purposeful resettlement of entire populations is a question not easily answered by those who remember American efforts involving our Indians and Americans of Japanese ancestry. But a better system of reporting opportunities and apprising migrants of problems awaiting the settlers in their new communities, perhaps administered by special agencies created for this purpose, or at least supplementing existing governmental bureaus like the U.S. Employment Service, would doubtless prove useful, continuing a pattern started when Captain John Smith described for his fellow English opportunities awaiting them in the New World.

Immigrant history shows that the principle of resettlement aid, whether for Jews, Moravians, Hungarians, Southern Whites, Negroes, Puerto Ricans, Mexicans or Cubans, represents a long-standing tradition in American private philanthrophy and, to a lesser but not negligible extent, our public policy.

Immigrants left home when they could see the promise of improved social and economic status; so does the Negro. Barring a miracle in human relations, this means that elimination of de facto segregation awaits elimination of the urban poor. Without a solution of this *social* problem, measures to reduce its racial or ethnic dimensions—preferential treatment of Negroes, enforcement of anti-discrimination laws, better home financing, improved urban planning—will be important but probably less than decisive.

Immigrant experience suggests further that Negro leaders must eventually strengthen already existing Negro communal institutions and perhaps build new or additional facilities which create a sense of individual worth, dignity, identity and responsibility. It will not be easy. The Negro middle class, as Franklin Frazier has pointed out, have contributed little toward helping the Negro masses. Activists capable of organizing protest demonstrations are generally not well qualified for the slow, unspectacular work of building community structures and services. Here again immigrant experience suggests useful patterns.

For the immigrant, ethnic enclaves offered much that was good. His language was spoken there, his customs understood. Churches and newspapers catered to his needs. So did such self-help institutions as hospitals, service clubs, community centers, burial societies, credit unions, child-care centers, old-age homes, and so on. Institution and arrangements which the larger public sometimes saw as threats to "the American way" served in the long run as bridges to it.[3]

[3] The following example should show what I have in mind. In 1960, the question whether to improve the sadly neglected, overcrowded, outmoded facilities of Baltimore's all-Negro Provident Hospital arose. Mr. Gerald W. Johnson, by no means a segregationist, wrote the following letter to the editor of the Baltimore *Sun* (Feb. 21, 1961), from which these excerpts are quoted:

Ethnic bloc voting, for example, advanced minority interests, and "socialistic" arrangements facilitated "free enterprise." Negro politicians may, like Irish politicians before them, solicit political support by agitating ethnic issues. Only those who have never studied the behavior of the American voter in the past will be upset by the notion that he often votes according to ethnic, religious, sectional and class allegiances.

The Negro's cultural heritage, however attenuated, can be made a source of legitimate pride and consequently a prop for a people denied full acceptance. Welfare solicitations can be made to serve status aspirations, and *voluntary* segregation aimed at specific goals can be recognized as not always incompatible with self-respect. After the most urgent demands are met, energies must be channeled into institutions, political and collective bargains struck, realistic plans and priorities decided upon.[4]

The first organized efforts of immigrants aimed to secure basic goals the Negro is still campaigning for: a job, money, decent housing, equal treatment. After these goals were substantially achieved, the immigrant began his quest for status. This was, of course, a more elusive endeavor because status is granted by others and does not depend solely on money. The literature of immigrant life in the United States is filled with subtle and manifold frustrations, real and imagined, which immigrants and their descendants have experienced.

It is too early to assess the Negro community's response to the need for social services and self-help activities. Reports from both North and South already show, however, that Negro leadership is becoming aware of the gaps in their Negro community structure and is developing programs to fill them. As this is done, we may see a pattern of life and organization resembling the pattern of the American immigrant communities which developed in the days of

---

". . . it is undeniable that . . . Provident Hospital . . . originated as a segregated Negro hospital. . . . I venture to suggest, though, that its racial affiliation is a contingent handicap. That is to say, it is a liability that, with skillful handling, might be converted into an asset. We have in this city Catholic hospitals, Jewish hospitals, Lutheran hospitals, Presbyterian hospitals, but no one thinks of them as segregated. The most that the affiliation amounts to is that certain classes of the affiliated—clergy, for example—may be allowed special concessions in rates, and so on.

"But Jewish friends have told me that another reason for building Jewish hospitals is to provide institutions in which a brilliant young Jewish doctor wishing to specialize can be assured that his religion will be no handicap upon his securing a choice appointment. . . .

"Well, now, if a Jew is handicapped, what earthly chance has a young Negro doctor to secure the sort of training needed for high specialization? . . . But this is more than a local proposition. A first-rate Negro medical center would be a national institution, drawing both graduate students and patients from the whole country. . . . If anti-Semitism has been made indirectly the means of opening the door of opportunity to young Jewish doctors, why shouldn't Jim Crowism be made indirectly to assist young Negro doctors? . . ."

4 Since this was written, the trend toward subordinating demonstrations to political organization has already become apparent. See, for instance, Paul Good's "Beyond the Voting Rights Act," in *Reporter,* Oct. 7, 1965, pp. 25-28, for the shift from leadership by zealous young civil rights demonstrators to local Negro political organization in some Georgia counties. Mr. H. Aptheker, commenting upon my paper, has noted that voluntary segregation for the attainment of specific goals, including that of *ending* enforced segregation, is nothing new for American Negroes. There are Negro Masons, Negro Elks, Negro dental and medical associations, a Negro bar association, the Negro press, and other groups which have enabled Negro Americans to cooperate for the attainment of social, economic and professional goals.

mass migration and which, with modifications, still exists for some groups. For as Ralph Ellison said in his *Invisible Man:*

> America is woven of many strands: I would recognize them and let it so remain. Our fate is to become one, and yet many—this is not prophecy but description.